FANNING THE SACRED FLAME

Mesoamerican Worlds: From the Olmecs to the Danzantes

GENERAL EDITORS: Davíd Carrasco and Eduardo Matos Moctezuma
EDITORIAL BOARD: Alfredo López Austin, Anthony Aveni, Elizabeth Boone, William Fash, Charles H. Long, Leonardo López Luján, and Eleanor Wake

After Monte Albán, Jeffrey P. Blomster, editor
The Apotheosis of Janaab' Pakal, Gerardo Aldana
Carrying the Word, Susanna Rostas
Commoner Ritual and Ideology in Ancient Mesoamerica, Nancy Gonlin and Jon C. Lohse, editors
Conquered Conquistadors, Florine Asselbergs
Empires of Time, Anthony Aveni
Encounter with the Plumed Serpent, Maarten Jansen and Gabina Aurora Pérez Jiménez
Fanning the Sacred Flame, Matthew A. Boxt and Brian Dervin Dillon, editors
In the Realm of Nachan Kan, Marilyn A. Masson
Invasion and Transformation, Rebecca P. Brienen and Margaret A. Jackson, editors
The Kowoj, Prudence M. Rice and Don S. Rice, editors
Life and Death in the Templo Mayor, Eduardo Matos Moctezuma
The Lords of Lambityeco, Michael Lind and Javier Urcid
The Madrid Codex, Gabrielle Vail and Anthony Aveni, editors
Maya Creation Myths, Timothy W. Knowlton
Maya Daykeeping, John M. Weeks, Frauke Sachse, and Christian M. Prager
Maya Worldviews at Conquest, Leslie G. Cecil and Timothy W. Pugh, editors
Mesoamerican Ritual Economy, E. Christian Wells and Karla L. Davis-Salazar, editors
Mesoamerica's Classic Heritage, Davíd Carrasco, Lindsay Jones, and Scott Sessions, editors
Mexico's Indigenous Communities, Ethelia Ruiz Medrano, translated by Russ Davidson
Mockeries and Metamorphoses of an Aztec God, Guilhem Olivier, translated by Michel Besson
Negotiation within Domination, Ethelia Ruiz Medrano and Susan Kellogg, editors; translated by Russ Davidson
Networks of Power, Edward Schortman and Patricia Urban
Rabinal Achi, Alain Breton, editor; translated by Teresa Lavender Fagan and Robert Schneider
Representing Aztec Ritual, Eloise Quiñones Keber, editor
Ruins of the Past, Travis W. Stanton and Aline Magnoni, editors
Skywatching in the Ancient World, Clive Ruggles and Gary Urton, editors
Social Change and the Evolution of Ceramic Production and Distribution in a Maya Community, Dean E. Arnold
The Social Experience of Childhood in Mesoamerica, Traci Ardren and Scott R. Hutson, editors
Stone Houses and Earth Lords, Keith M. Prufer and James E. Brady, editors
The Sun God and the Savior, Guy Stresser-Péan
Sweeping the Way, Catherine DiCesare
Tamoanchan, Tlalocan, Alfredo López Austin
Thunder Doesn't Live Here Anymore, Anath Ariel de Vidas; translated by Teresa Lavender Fagan
Topiltzin Quetzalcoatl, H. B. Nicholson
The World Below, Jacques Galinier

Fanning the Sacred Flame

MESOAMERICAN STUDIES
IN HONOR OF
H. B. NICHOLSON

EDITED BY
MATTHEW A. BOXT
AND BRIAN DERVIN DILLON

WITH A FOREWORD BY
DAVÍD CARRASCO AND
EDUARDO MATOS MOCTEZUMA

UNIVERSITY PRESS OF COLORADO

© 2012 by University Press of Colorado

Published by University Press of Colorado
245 Century Circle, Suite 202
Louisville, Colorado 80027

All rights reserved
First paperback edition 2020

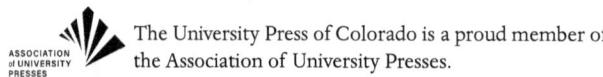 The University Press of Colorado is a proud member of the Association of University Presses.

The University Press of Colorado is a cooperative publishing enterprise supported, in part, by Adams State University, Colorado State University, Fort Lewis College, Metropolitan State University of Denver, Regis University, University of Colorado, University of Northern Colorado, University of Wyoming, Utah State University, and Western Colorado University.

Library of Congress Cataloging-in-Publication Data

Fanning the sacred flame : Mesoamerican studies in honor of H. B. Nicholson / Matthew A. Boxt and Brian Dervin Dillon, editors.
  p. cm. — (Mesoamerican worlds)
 Includes bibliographical references and index.
 ISBN 978-1-60732-160-6 (cloth) — ISBN 978-1-64642-080-3 (pbk) — ISBN 978-1-60732-161-3 (e-book)
 1. Aztecs—History. 2. Olmecs—History. 3. Mayas—History. 4. Indians of Mexico—History. 5. Indians of Central America—History. 6. Nicholson, H. B. (Henry B.) I. Boxt, Matthew A., 1951– II. Dillon, Brian D.
 F1219.73.F36 2012
 972'.01—dc23

                    2012006132

CONTENTS

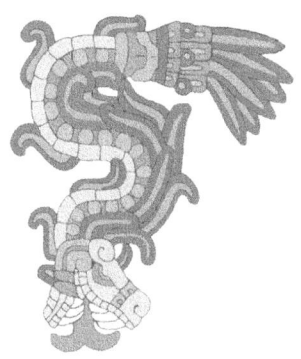

FOREWORD AND REMINISCENCE ix
   David Carrasco and Eduardo Matos Moctezuma

INTRODUCTION 1
   Matthew A. Boxt and Brian Dervin Dillon

1. H. B. Nicholson and the Archaeological Bug 11
   Eloise Quiñones Keber

PART I: THE OLMEC AND THEIR NEIGHBORS

2. The Middle Formative Period Stelae of Chalcatzingo 33
   David C. Grove

3. Isla Alor: Olmec to Contact in the La Venta Hinterland 55
   Matthew A. Boxt, L. Mark Raab, and Rebecca B. González Lauck

4. *Aquí Nació el Mundo*: Takalik Abaj and Early Mesoamerican Civilization 93
   Brian Dervin Dillon

v

Contents

PART II: THE MAYA AND THEIR NEIGHBORS

5. Kingship in the Cradle of Maya Civilization: The Mirador Basin   **139**
   Richard D. Hansen

6. Yaxchilán Structure 23: The House of Ix K'ab'al Xok   **173**
   Sandra L. Orellana

7. Santa Rosa, Chiapas: Human Sacrifice and the Mesoamerican Ballgame   **211**
   Alejandro Martínez Muriel and Emilie Carreón Blaine

8. Pipil Archaeology of Pacific Guatemala   **231**
   Frederick J. Bove, José Vicente Genovez, and Carlos A. Batres

9. Under Ground in Ancient Mesoamerica   **269**
   James E. Brady

PART III: CENTRAL MEXICO

10. The Mixteca-Puebla Tradition and H. B. Nicholson   **293**
    Pablo Escalante Gonzalbo

11. Obsidian Butterfly and Flowery Tree: An Effigy Vessel from Coxcatlán   **309**
    Edward B. Sisson

12. Nick at Night: Cosmic Aspects of Topiltzin-Quetzalcoatl   **327**
    Anthony F. Aveni

13. The Xipe Tótec Cult and Mexica Military Promotion   **333**
    Carlos Javier González González

PART IV: ETHNOHISTORY

14. Prehispanic K'iche-Maya Historiography   **355**
    Robert M. Carmack

15. Connecting Nahua and Mixtec Histories   **389**
    Kevin Terraciano

PART V: THE COLONIAL PERIOD

16. The Final Tribute of Tenochtitlan   **419**
    Lawrence H. Feldman

17. Feathered Serpents, Pulquerías, and Indian Sedition in Colonial Cholula   **425**
    Geoffrey G. McCafferty

18. The Posthumous History of the Tizoc Stone   **439**
    Alfredo López Austin and Leonardo López Luján

19. The *Real Expedición Anticuaria* Collection   **461**
    Marie-France Fauvet-Berthelot, Leonardo López Luján, and Susana Guimarâes

PART VI: ETHNOGRAPHY

20. Yucatec Maya Agricultural Ritual Survivals   **489**
    Ruth Gubler

21. Mesoamerican Indian Clothing: Survivals, Acculturation, and Beyond   **519**
    Patricia R. Anawalt

LIST OF CONTRIBUTORS   **539**

INDEX   **541**

FOREWORD AND REMINISCENCE

Fanning the Sacred Flame: Mesoamerican Studies in Honor of H. B. Nicholson, edited by Matthew A. Boxt and Brian Dervin Dillon, is a superb addition to our Mesoamerican Worlds series. Its twenty-one essays shine the light on the expansive ways Henry Nicholson organized his writing, teaching, and thinking during his lifelong involvement in deciphering Mesoamerican societies. Readers will find insightful essays on Olmec, Maya, Mixtec, and Aztec cultures, as well as on ethnography, ethnohistory, and Mexico's colonial past. As though retracing Nicholson's scholarly footsteps, this book takes us to such places as La Venta, Yaxchilán, Takalik Abaj, Tenochtitlan, and Cholula and touches such topics as the invention of writing, kingship, human sacrifice, caves, the Mixteca-Puebla tradition, flowery trees, Xipe Tótec, K'iche Maya, and Nahua histories, feathered serpents, the Tizoc Stone, and Indian clothing. It is also significant that the range of methodological approaches found in this book parallels the sweep of the approaches that animated our series "Mesoamerican Worlds: From the Olmecs to the Danzantes" over its seventeen years of work and thirty-five publications. Boxt and Dillon worked persistently to produce this outstanding volume, and the results are innovative and expansive. It is very fitting that this book, dedicated to the work and memory of H. B. Nicholson, will be the final publication in the series that has attempted to deepen and broaden our understanding of Mesoamerican worlds.

David Carrasco and Eduardo Matos Moctezuma

When the two of us joined Luther Wilson, then director of the University Press of Colorado, to launch this series, we had several goals in mind. First, we designed the series as an interdisciplinary exercise guided in particular by the approaches of archaeology and the history of religions. Animated by the profound and rich discoveries coming out of the Proyecto Templo Mayor in Mexico City, it was clear that the organization of new knowledge about Mesoamerica had to take more fully into account the dynamic relationship between materiality and the religious imagination, social thought and ritual places, the stones of Mesoamerica and the intellectual and artistic abilities of its peoples. Over the years we have published works by historians of religions, archaeologists, social anthropologists, archaeoastronomers, art historians, and iconographers. Second, while interested in manuscripts by all comers to the series, we also wanted to provide a venue for young scholars whose work showed exceptional promise. Third, we were committed to publishing works by scholars from Mexico as well as from other nations. The first book in the series, Leonardo López Luján's award-winning *The Offerings of the Templo Mayor of Tenochtitlan*, published in 1994, fit these three goals perfectly.

When Luther Wilson moved on to become director of the University of Mexico Press, we were fortunate to have Darrin Pratt step in as director of the University Press of Colorado. Pratt worked diligently to help it become the leading series in Mesoamerican studies in the United States, if not the world. Readers perusing our list of publications at the beginning of this book can evaluate to what extent our series continued to meet these goals. As general editors of the series, we express our deep gratitude to the University Press of Colorado for its skillful support of our work. We also want to share this short reminiscence of our valued colleague H. B. Nicholson because it represents the collaborative working style of both the Moses Mesoamerican Archive and the Mesoamerican Worlds series.

A REMINISCENCE OF H. B. NICHOLSON

Henry B. (Nick) Nicholson is an outstanding symbol of the goals enumerated above because he, in particular, was dedicated to understanding the archaeological, ethnohistorical, iconographical, and religious dimensions of Mesoamerican life. He was an outstanding teacher and supported scores of younger scholars in their efforts to find new pathways to fresh understandings of Mesoamerican lifeways. Nick was also at ease in Mexico and delighted in his collaboration with Mexican scholars. Eduardo Matos Moctezuma wrote, following years of interaction with Nicholson, "Henry B. Nicholson's investigations opened up new ideas and profound knowledge about a variety of themes including Quetzalcoatl, the iconography of numerous deities and their various attributes, and the overall structure of Prehispanic religions. With his death comes an emptiness very difficult to fill but his many writings will stand the test of time."*

Carrasco first met H. B. Nicholson in 1974 at a session on the "Magic Books of Mexico" during the Forty-First International Congress of Americanists in Mexico City. Nicholson and Wigberto Jiménez Moreno were chairing the session, and it was thrilling to observe these two knowledgeable scholars working together. When Nicholson heard that Carrasco was completing his dissertation on Quetzalcoatl at the University of Chicago, he offered to send *his* unpublished thesis as an aid. Soon afterward a photocopy of his 1957 Harvard dissertation, "Topiltzin Quetzalcoatl of Tollan: A Problem in Mesoamerican Ethnohistory," arrived at Carrasco's house. This was the first of many encounters with Nicholson's intellectual generosity.

The clarity, pinpoint research, overall organization, and reconstruction of the Topiltzin Quetzalcoatl "tale" read like a tour de force legal argument making the case that the Aztecs had inherited and internalized a sacred history about the Toltec priest-king that shaped their priestly practices, their religious worldview, *and* their interpretation of the encounter with the Spaniards. The thesis convinced Carrasco that he had to become, albeit from a geographical distance, one of H. B. Nicholson's many students, and he set about the task of starting a lifelong conversation with him.

In 1979, when we were planning the first scholarly conference at the University of Colorado–Boulder on the Templo Mayor excavations, Matos proclaimed: "We must include Nicholson. I want us to collaborate with Nicholson because he knows so much about the Aztecs." From that day until Nick's passing twenty-nine years later, Nick was a crucial and productive part of the Moses Mesoamerican Archive and Research Project at Colorado, Princeton, and Harvard. One of our academic gatherings in Boulder included a special dinner honoring Nicholson. It was a hearty celebration, with food and wine, and during our toasts and reminiscence of Nick's career Elizabeth Boone fondly awarded Nick the "Nitpicker Award." Elizabeth enjoyed ribbing him for the ways he always found some small, often minute problem in the ways the rest of us presented the Mesoamerican sources and our research. Nick, rising to the occasion after a two-hour-long celebration of his career, announced, "I want to thank you all for that summary of my work but I *have a nit to pick* about a few of the historical details." We roared in delight!

As time went on, we became determined to persuade him to publish his famous dissertation in the Mesoamerican Worlds series so that scholars and especially a new generation of students could benefit from his research and

---

* Those interested in reviewing the full range of Nicholson's work will appreciate Matos's compilation in "Henry B. Nicholson, obituario," *Estudios de cultural nahuatl* 38 (2007): 477–507.

interpretations. With the urging of Alfredo López Austin we finally persuaded Nick to publish the dissertation, but it took several years and the editorial work of Scott Sessions to transform it into a book. Sessions, who understood Nicholson's eye for detail, puzzled over how to quickly turn the 1957 dissertation into an electronic text. The uneven condition of the blurry old Harvard Xerox copy made scanning nearly impossible. The original, which Nick's wife, Margaret, had typed out in the Utah desert during his first season of fieldwork, had many typos, "white-out" patches, and other issues. Sessions scanned what he could, re-keyed large portions to clean up the text, and then edited the entire manuscript for style and content—standardizing the orthography, verifying all the quotations and citations, updating the bibliography, and performing similar tasks—to move the process along. After about two weeks, working day and night, Sessions finished the work. He sent it to Nick along with a long letter explaining exactly everything he had done and then waited with some trepidation for Nick's reply to his nitpicking of the great nitpicker! A few weeks later Nick wrote back, graciously thanked him, and said, "I can see that you've saved me an enormous amount of grief from editors at the press!" The book was published in our series in 2001 under the title *Topiltzin Quetzalcoatl: The Once and Future Lord of the Toltecs*, to international appreciation and critical acclaim.

Later, when the Moses Mesoamerican Archive moved with Carrasco to Harvard, we decided to set up the H. B. Nicholson Award for Excellence in Mesoamerican Studies. Nick was thrilled and when I told him that we decided to cast a medal in his honor as part of the award, he immediately had a design in mind: the motif on the "Hackmack Box" that depicted his beloved Quetzalcoatl in dynamic movement. To draw the image for the medal we turned to the artistic talents of Barbara Fash, who did a superb job of creating the H. B. Nicholson Medal, a version of which appears on the cover of this publication and at the beginning of each of its chapters. As though to close a magic circle, the first recipient of the Nicholson medal was none other than Eduardo Matos Moctezuma, who traveled to Harvard University in 2002 to receive the award at a dinner in his and Nick's honor at the Peabody Museum. Subsequent awardees have included Anthony Aveni and Alfredo López Austin, both of whom have published important books in this series.

H. B. Nicholson was, in our view, the greatest Aztec scholar in the United States, not only of his own generation but also of the entire twentieth century. He knew the sources far better than anyone else and understood the interrelationships between material culture and symbolism, and he shared his enormous knowledge in generous and unique ways. All these reasons make the present publication by two of his California colleagues a major addition to Mesoamerican scholarship. We can do no better than quote the volume's editors, Matthew A. Boxt and Brian Dervin Dillon, when they say, "H. B. Nicholson had the unique gift of bringing the dead back to life through his lectures and his writing. The high priest of the Quetzalcoatl cult has now gone to his reward, but his many acolytes continue to spread his message. Nicholson was a time traveler, and those of us he took along with him on his journeys back through the centuries will be forever grateful."

We believe that, in a significant way, this book brings Nick's words and thoughts work back to life. Like our Mesoamerican Worlds series, it will nurture and point the way to new understandings for future generations.

DAVÍD CARRASCO, CAMBRIDGE, MA
EDUARDO MATOS MOCTEZUMA, MEXICO CITY
Series General Editors, Mesoamerican Worlds

FANNING THE SACRED FLAME

INTRODUCTION

Matthew A. Boxt and Brian Dervin Dillon

Five hundred years ago Europe invaded Mesoamerica, and the Old and New Worlds collided with consequences unimaginable for all involved. The resulting mingling of ideas and technologies was beneficial to the Old World, but the collision was catastrophic for the New, for the Spanish Conquest sparked the most rapid and complete depopulation in human history. This depopulation was followed by an equally tragic loss: the destruction and subsequent disappearance of native civilizations.

Over the generations and then the centuries after the Conquest, these great civilizations, owing nothing to Old World sources, were gradually forgotten. The ancient cities were covered by Spanish Colonial towns or overgrown by tropical rainforests, awaiting rediscovery by future archaeologists. Early written accounts of Mesoamerican culture, language, and religion were also forgotten in dusty archives in both the Old World and the New, likewise awaiting rediscovery by future historians.

One of the most influential and important scholars of the Mesoamerican past was H. B. Nicholson, an amazingly prodigious thinker, writer, and teacher. For a half-century he inspired hundreds of students and thousands of readers to embark upon voyages of discovery back into Mesoamerican history and archaeology. He recognized early in his career that archaeology and ethnohistory were much more than just collections of artifacts, sculptures, or documents and

0.1. *Fanning the Sacred Flame. Montezuma [sic] offering incense to Quetzalcoatl [in his guise as Black Ehecatl]. By Keith Henderson, from* The Conquest of Mexico *by W. H. Prescott (1922: I: 185). This was one of the illustrations that sparked H. B. Nicholson's imagination at a young age. Courtesy, Royal Watercolour Society, London.*

that, in their totality, they reflected the traditions, ideology, and aspirations of the peoples who created them. For more than fifty years Nicholson caught the embers of Mesoamerican knowledge wherever and whenever he found them. He then fanned them, with the help of his students and colleagues, back into full flame.

Fanning the Sacred Flame: Mesoamerican Studies in Honor of H. B. Nicholson is a collection of original papers on current and future trends in the rediscovery of Mesoamerican civilizations. The intellectual legacy of H. B. (Nick) Nicholson is honored and enhanced in these pages by Mesoamerican archaeologists, art historians, ethnohistorians, and ethnographers. Our volume, inspired by Nicholson's passing in March 2007, showcases interdisciplinary studies by his students, colleagues, and friends. All of its authors derived inspiration and encouragement from him. Each chapter pays tribute to H. B. Nicholson the teacher, writer, lecturer, friend, and mentor, to the man who became a legend in his own lifetime.

The words of William Duncan Strong (Lowie 1936: 367), in a brilliant paper entitled "Anthropological Theory and Archaeological Fact," helped set H. B. Nicholson down his academic path: "In most of the world . . . scientific archaeology has not as yet scratched the surface. In this regard, Middle America, the cradle of New World civilization, is at present a dark jungle of ignorance lit up at long intervals by tiny match-flares of scientific knowledge."

Once H. B. Nicholson got down to work in Mesoamerican studies, his remarkable accomplishments turned many of these tiny points of light into blazing flame. As with the New Fire Ceremony that meant so much to the ancients, Nick passed his torch of illumination to many others in many different places down through a great many years. Our volume's title connotes this ongoing search for understanding to which each contributor is committed. The chapters that follow span all Mesoamerican regions and time periods, just as Nicholson's own interests did. These works continue to fan the Mesoamerican intellectual flame Nicholson nurtured throughout an inspirational lifetime of scholarship.

But how to organize such a geographically and chronologically diverse corpus of writing? The answer is found in H. B. Nicholson's own approach to scholarship. As archaeologists, we must start at the beginnings of Mesoamerican civilization and work our way forward in time. The six subdivisions in this volume are the same ones Nick used to organize his teaching, writing, and thinking. Woven throughout this chronological and geographical framework recur such common themes as how early subsistence and settlement patterns, even ancient industries, took form; the emergence of Mesoamerican civilization; where and when urban communities first appeared; the interconnection of archaeological and ethnohistoric peoples; the invention of that most unique of all Mesoamerican achievements—writing; the role of art and iconography in ancient society and the development of great art styles; warfare and human sacrifice; the interplay of the natural and supernatural worlds; and the predominant position of religion within the Mesoamerican Culture Area.

We begin with a heartfelt paean by Eloise Quiñones Keber. She paints a vivid picture of Nick's younger years, which accounts for his lifelong dedication to the ancient past. Truly, when the archaeological bug bit Nick, it bit him very hard. In his case, no vaccine was ever developed or even desired to reverse the lifelong culture-historical infection all of us ultimately also caught.

The Olmec and Their Neighbors, our first culture-historical subdivision, contains three chapters. David C. Grove's paper is on the remarkable Chalcatzingo site in Highland Central Mexico, emphasizing its Olmec sculpture. Matthew A. Boxt, L. Mark Raab, and Rebecca B. González Lauck's study of the Isla Alor site calls attention to a small satellite of La Venta, the great, perhaps even the greatest of all the Olmec capital cities. Brian Dervin Dillon writes about the pivotal site of Takalik Abaj, which remains the only major ancient Mesoamerican city where both Olmec and Early Maya sculptures have been found side by side in abundance.

The most pervasive themes unifying the contributions in this section are the birth and growth of Mesoamerican civilization, the genesis of its great art styles, and its most remarkable achievement: writing (Nicholson 1976). Mesoamerica followed a unique path toward civilization, with a flavor all its own from the earliest times onward. Key to this dialogue is our perception of urbanism, which itself encouraged social complexity. How and when can we recognize the earliest cities? What precipitated the invention of the Mesoamerican city? Why did Mesoamerican cities develop where they did and when they did and why not elsewhere? These are questions Nick himself found endlessly fascinating and which will have currency for many decades to come.

As in many other parts of the world, ancient Mesoamerica saw the emergence of simple societies—probably organized on the family-household level—which eventually became small villages. Some of these ultimately became early cities. For every great Mesoamerican city studied, there were hundreds if not thousands of smaller communities that never became cities. In some cases, such small communities continued alongside major urban centers for hundreds and perhaps even thousands of years.

The Maya and Their Neighbors, the book's second section, contains five chapters on the Maya and nearby non-Maya peoples. Richard D. Hansen's international research team, working in the Mirador Basin of the northernmost Petén, has produced an immense body of evidence bearing on the origins of civilization, and the notion of Maya kingship, in the tropical rainforests of the Southern Maya Lowlands. Sandra Orellana takes us more than a millennium back in time to visit the great site of Yaxchilán and the power and influence of Lady Xoc, or Ix K'ab'al Xok, through a fine-tuned epigraphic and art historical study. Her chapter examines that unique Mesoamerican intellectual achievement, literacy, and the way it functioned within the role of women in ancient Maya society. Alejandro Martínez Muriel and Emilie Carreón Blaine's chapter has profound ramifications for culture-historical interpretations of human sacrifice, decapitation, and the Mesoamerican ballgame. Their research reminds us that any interpretation based on iconographic sources must be substantiated through dirt archaeology. During the final stages of editing this volume, we were saddened to learn of Alejandro Martínez M.'s death after a valiant struggle with cancer. This tragedy makes the publication of this, his final paper, all the more poignant.

Next, we "go to the dogs," specifically to the Escuintla region, with Frederick J. Bove, José Vicente Genovez, and Carlos A. Batres. The modern coastal Guatemalan city of Escuintla derives its name from the Mexican word *itzcuintli* (dog) and, in effect, means *Dogtown* in vernacular translation. This chapter on Pipil archaeology explores one of the least known yet most promising research regions of Mesoamerica. Enclaves of Nahuatl speakers on the Guatemalan south coast have been a source of controversy for decades. How can we explain their presence? Military conquest? Migration? Displacement? Could this part of Mesoamerica have been cosmopolitan for millennia? Was it a crossroads of cultures and languages? James Brady examines the connection between natural caves and Maya architecture and city planning, then explores Central Mexican parallels. Brady's work reminds us of the old field archaeology adage that if you don't look for something, you generally won't ever find it. His work shows that in many cases the ancient Mesoamerican worldview unified underground, terrestrial, and heavenly landscapes.

The chapters in this section raise a question uppermost in the minds of all archaeologists, who, unlike historians, must deal with anonymous people and cultures. What was the ethnic identity of the people responsible for the many Mesoamerican civilizations? Most are known today only by names bequeathed them by chronologically distant neighbors, and most are now known primarily by artifacts, art styles, and architecture—all, by definition, mute. Will we ever be able to learn the names by which those peoples discovered through archaeology actually called themselves? This, perhaps, is the most challenging of all culture-historical goals. Possibly, it is also the most rewarding. A logical extension of this research concern with ethnic identity is the ongoing debate over whether Mesoamerica was one civilization or many. We believe, as did Nicholson, that Mesoamerica was a collection of many different civilizations, most of which had different life spans; of them all, Maya civilization was the longest-lived.

Central Mexico, our third culture-historical section, brings us to the places and later time periods Nick knew and loved best. Recurring throughout the writings in this section is the quest of understanding the ancient Mesoamerican mind. Ancient intellectual life is, of course, best accessed through the modern study of writing systems and iconography. In Mesoamerica the stimulus for both was more often than not religious. Religion was a motivating force in Mesoamerican culture and civilization from the earliest times onward. It permeated all forms of thought and action: artistic expression, politics, and even warfare. Religion might even help us understand the organization of farmsteads, villages, and cities. The natural and cultural worlds can be seen as a reflection of an ancient supernatural component largely invisible to present-day scholars. Sacred and secular landscapes can and continue to be discovered by archaeologists and archival researchers in Mesoamerica. Iconography was a particular interest of H. B. Nicholson, and it remains one of the most important means by which contemporary scholars can penetrate the minds of ancient peoples. Many of the following pages are devoted to this avenue of art historical inquiry.

Pablo Escalante Gonzalbo treats us to a thoughtful review of the Mixteca-Puebla artistic tradition, one of Nicholson's favorite subjects and one he returned to time and time again. Edward B. Sisson and Carlos Javier González González address Postclassic themes of warfare and human sacrifice—Sisson from the Tehuacán Valley, González G. from Tenochtitlan. Anthony F. Aveni, the inventor of archaeoastronomy, treats us to a short but sweet exploration of celestial events with a particularly Nicholsonian flavor. In 2004 Aveni received the H. B. Nicholson Award for Excellence in Mesoamerican Studies from the Peabody Museum and the Moses Mesoamerican Archive at Harvard University.

Ethnohistory, the book's fourth section, includes two chapters—one on the Highland Maya, the other on the Mixtec—of Late Postclassic/Early Colonial Mesoamerica. Robert M. Carmack, the dean of Highland Maya ethnohistorians, was one of the first and truest apostles of Nicholson's documents-based approach to scholarship. Kevin Terraciano, one of Nicholson's last students, compares Late Postclassic and Early Colonial Period Mixtec history with that of their Nahuatl neighbors. Such ethnohistoric work provides models for the interpretation of earlier Mesoamerican periods. Acculturation, culture change, and cultural continuity are ongoing processes; they are easy to recognize in historical hindsight, but their detection is difficult through strictly archaeological methods. We are fortunate that, through the work of such prominent researchers, we can begin to hear the muted voices of the long-dead Highland Maya, Zapotec, and Nahuatl speakers that would otherwise be silent.

The Colonial Period is the volume's fifth section and presents four Conquest or Postconquest period studies. Lawrence H. Feldman, one of the unsung heroes of Mesoamerican research, shares a spectacular documentary find with us. In doing so, he reminds us that many of the most important archives containing critical historical information on Mesoamerica still await complete investigation by researchers. Geoffrey G. McCafferty, through careful dirt archaeology followed by rigorous ceramic and faunal analyses, makes the case for an indigenous travelers' drinking establishment on the outskirts of the old Cholula pilgrimage center. This work reminds us of Nick's admonition that the study of Colonial Period Mesoamerican documents cannot be done without constant reference to historical archaeology. The father-son team of Alfredo López Austin and Leonardo López Luján revisits one of the best-known and most familiar Mexica sculptures, the Stone of Tizoc. The Tizoc sculpture presently resides in the National Museum of Anthropology at Chapultepec. It is familiar to millions of foreign visitors, as well as every Mexican who has ever made the pilgrimage to this modern shrine to his or her *antepasados*. Marie-France Fauvet-Berthelot, Leonardo López Luján, and Susana Guimarâes write of a bygone era when interest in Mesoamerica's rich heritage was of concern primarily to a select group of early scientists, travelers, and antiquarians.

INTRODUCTION

Beginning with the Spanish Conquest, much of Mexico's patrimony has been stolen, reappearing in museums and private collections throughout the world. Many of the artifacts taken across the water during the earliest years have vanished forever; others remain, far from home, as powerful symbols of Mexican national identity, now more valuable than ever before because of their rarity and unique condition of preservation. The scourge of looting continues in Mexico, Guatemala, and throughout the rest of Mesoamerica today. The despoliation now is not of native civilizations but instead of their archaeological remnants. More than ever before, the hunger for ancient Mesoamerican treasures stimulates nefarious dealings by dishonest art collectors and museum personnel, revealing that little has changed since the eighteenth century or even since the Conquest.

Ethnography, our sixth division, concludes the volume by bringing us into the present with two ongoing studies. Traces of some of the most unique Mesoamerican achievements still exist today among living peoples, providing cases of cultural continuity going back at least 2,000 years. Ruth Gubler reveals just how resilient traditional Maya religious practices are. All patriotic Mesoamericanists love to read about the persistence of Indian lifeways, despite nearly 500 years of acculturative pressures. Patricia R. Anawalt calls our attention to how rapidly traditional Mesoamerican Indian culture is being lost or changed from its Preconquest antecedents. This notwithstanding, many of the Tepehua-, Sierra Otomí-, Sierra Totonac-, and Nahuatl-speaking peoples of Mexico's Sierra Norte de Puebla, where Anawalt has worked for more than a quarter-century, have managed to retain their cultural identity.

Returning to our motivation for beginning this volume, we conclude this introduction with some final thoughts about the man who inspired us to compile it. H. B. Nicholson was inordinately proud of the two universities he attended. He considered Berkeley and Harvard shrines to the sacred pursuit of knowledge. Nicholson venerated the scholarly traditions, researchers, writers, libraries, archives, and research ideas concentrated in the two institutions that both motivated and encouraged him. The research questions Nicholson took to heart at these two schools back in the 1940s and 1950s remain centered at the core of modern Mesoamerican research.

If Nicholson's anthropological training was deeply rooted in historical and cultural particularism, he nevertheless championed the interdisciplinary approach to Mesoamerican studies. This approach continues in the selection and organization of the chapters in this volume. Nick was concerned with research topics of substance, eschewing the fleeting intellectual fads that come and go as often as the seasons, then as now. In the Berkeley tradition of interdisciplinary study, Nicholson came to be conversant with archaeology, art history, ethnography, geography, and history, never seeing them as separate fields but rather as essentially interrelated. He was one of very few people who could move seamlessly through many different academic disciplines, much like the anthropological giants Kroeber and Tozzer he so admired at Berkeley and Harvard. Nicholson stressed original research, whether in the field, archive, or museum. He believed in the importance of controlling all the evidence bearing on a given research question before engaging in interpretation and tried to instill a similar scholarly rigor in his students. The depth and breadth of Nick's influence in Mesoamerican studies are reflected by the diverse contributions to archaeology, art history, epigraphy, ethnography, ethnohistory, history, iconography, and museology incorporated within this book.

All present and future Mesoamericanists owe and will continue to owe a debt to H. B. Nicholson. Our book is offered in the spirit of two of Nicholson's favorite compendium volumes, which came from the two universities he loved so much and was so proud of having attended. *Essays in Anthropology* was presented to A. L. Kroeber at UC Berkeley on his sixtieth birthday (Lowie 1936), while *The Maya and Their Neighbors* (Hay et al. 1940) celebrated Harvard University's Alfred Marston Tozzer's contribution to what, only a short time later, would come to be called Mesoamerican studies. We have borrowed the Tozzer book's title as a means of organizing our volume. We believe Nick would approve.

H. B. Nicholson had a lifelong fascination with Mesoamerican civilization. Nick was a pioneer in the development of Mesoamerican ethnohistory, and his name will forever be synonymous with Aztec studies. While his original research focused on Postclassic Central Mexico, he nevertheless inspired scores of scholars to study all Mesoamerican time periods, regions, and cultures. Many of us can remember a time when relations between those countries involved in Mesoamerican studies were strained and personal relationships sometimes tainted by suspicion and even outright hostility. Possibly more than any other North American scholar, Nick Nicholson worked to achieve an international meeting of the minds, convincing the present generation that we had much more to gain by working together than by working apart. Nick built bridges not just between departments and disciplines but between entire countries. Just as we are proud and gratified to present contributions from Mesoamericanists from both sides of the border and both sides of the Atlantic, we are also very pleased to offer writings by multiple generations of Nicholsonians. All who survive him feel very fortunate that Nick shared his remarkable vision of the past with us and opened so many doors of Mesoamerican scholarship that we now walk freely through.

Nick is gone and his friends, students, and admirers—much in the role of orphaned children—must soldier on without him. With his passing, the international community of Mesoamericanists lost a brilliant and much-loved teacher, researcher, and friend. We can still see him in our mind's eye, wearing his (slightly spotted) trademark seersucker sport coat and clan tartan tie and staring off into the stratosphere over your shoulder as he boomed out a lecture, a greeting, or his half of a conversation. Nick lives on in the hearts of all who knew him personally; his legacy of research survives in the minds of all who have read him or the works of those he inspired. We are privileged to honor him in these pages. His voice may be stilled, but the research that fascinated him throughout his lifetime lives on in the following pages.

H. B. Nicholson had the unique gift of bringing the dead back to life through his lectures and his writing. The high priest of the Quetzalcoatl cult has now gone to his reward, but his many acolytes continue to spread his message. Nicholson was a time traveler, and those of us he took along with him on his journeys back through the centuries will be forever grateful. *Fanning the Sacred Flame* is our way of thanking you, Nick, for giving us so much for so many years.

Acknowledgments. *Fanning the Sacred Flame* would never have been completed were it not for several sources of constant inspiration and encouragement. All three of Nick and Margaret Nicholson's children—Eric, Bruce, and Alice—were enthusiastic about the project from start to finish. Eloise Quiñones Keber was a driving force who kept us dedicated to the effort. Nancy Troike and the Patterson Foundation of Austin, Texas, supported us in every way possible. Nancy's unbridled optimism was inspirational. Our thanks to Scott Sessions and Debra Nagao for their thoughtful and accurate translation work. We are grateful to Rusty van Rossmann for his superlative maps and for many illustrations, which have greatly enhanced this volume's appearance.

Davíd Carrasco, Eduardo Matos Moctezuma, Darrin Pratt, and the editorial staff of the University Press of Colorado made this book possible. We are indebted to them for their refreshingly positive and energetic approach to archaeological publication. The University Press of Colorado is coming to represent the Alpha and Omega of H. B. Nicholson's professional corpus. It is entirely appropriate that *Fanning the Sacred Flame* appears in its Mesoamerican Worlds series. Here, alongside Nicholson's (2001) own *Topiltzin Quetzalcoatl: The Once and Future Lord of the Toltecs*, it also stands among offerings by Nick's students, close friends, and colleagues.

REFERENCES CITED

Hay, Clarence L., Ralph L. Linton, Samuel K. Lothrop, Harry L. Shapiro, and George C. Vaillant, eds.
    1940   *The Maya and Their Neighbors: Essays on Middle American Anthropology and Archaeology*. D. Appleton-Century, New York.

Lowie, Robert H., ed.
    1936   *Essays in Anthropology, Presented to A. L. Kroeber in Celebration of His Sixtieth Birthday, June 11, 1936*. University of California Press, Berkeley.

Nicholson, H. B.
    1976   *Origins of Religious Art and Iconography in Preclassic Mesoamerica*. UCLA Latin American Center Publications/Ethnic Arts Council of Los Angeles.
    2001   *Topiltzin Quetzalcoatl: The Once and Future Lord of the Toltecs*. University Press of Colorado, Boulder.

Prescott, W. H.
    1922   *The Conquest of Mexico*. 2 volumes, with an introduction by T. A. Joyce, illustrations by Keith Henderson. Chatto and Windus, London.

1

H. B. NICHOLSON AND THE ARCHAEOLOGICAL BUG

Eloise Quiñones Keber

In an earlier tribute to the scholarly life and accomplishments of H. B. Nicholson (1925–2007), emeritus professor of anthropology at UCLA, I surveyed his major contributions to the various Mesoamerican subfields of anthropology, archaeology, ethnohistory, art, and iconography (Quiñones Keber 2007). The present chapter offers another appraisal of Nicholson's scholarship in Mesoamerican, especially Aztec, studies. It highlights the seminal influence of archaeology in propelling his scholarly trajectory, in several cases recalling his own words as expressed in publications and conversations over the years.

Dr. Nicholson was especially renowned for his comprehensive knowledge of the Aztecs (Mexica, Nahua) of Central Mexico, who dominated this area of the late Precolumbian world in the fifteenth and sixteenth centuries. A thorough researcher and archivist; a prolific writer, moderator, and presenter of scholarly papers at numerous conferences in the United States, Mexico, and Europe; and a popular guest speaker, Nicholson was widely acknowledged as the most accomplished Aztec scholar of his time.

A professor at UCLA for thirty-five years, Nicholson trained over two dozen doctoral students in various areas of anthropology; beyond his own department he also served as a teacher and committee member for students specializing in Latin American history and art history. The esteem in which Nick (as he preferred to be called) was held by colleagues, students, and friends alike was evident in

1.1. *The archaeological "bug." Caricature by Nicholson, 1936. Courtesy, Eloise Quiñones Keber.*

a symposium at UCLA in November 2004. The evening's dinner and spirited "roast" brought back memories, hearty laughs, and an overall feeling of appreciation for having had the opportunity to share so many memorable times with the guest of honor.

Nicholson's expertise was not confined to the Aztecs. It reached back three millennia in Mesoamerica to the earliest Formative Period and extended across eons and oceans to the Old World civilizations as well. As he stated in a short introduction to the Mesoamerican section of the Land catalog of Precolumbian art (Nicholson 1979f), Nick was convinced that "Mesoamerica, taken as a whole, deserves to be ranked as one of the great early civilizations of mankind, fully comparable in its overall cultural achievement to Old World civilizations such as those in Mesopotamia, Egypt, the Anatolian-Aegean area, India, and China."

His travels to several of these distant centers of civilizations, particularly in the Middle East, reflected his broad view of human history. He was thus able to assess the accomplishments of the Aztecs of Mexico within a broad comparative framework. Nicholson was blessed with a near-photographic memory of everything he had read or seen, his knowledge of things Mexican and Aztec was encyclopedic, and his astonishing erudition made him a captivating lecturer. His daunting intellectual energy and dogged attention to detail resulted in a lengthy list of publications, commendable not only for their breadth and depth but also for their meticulous research.

IT HELPS TO GET AN EARLY START

H. B. Nicholson had many strengths as a scholar, but underlying them all was a fascination with Mexico itself, its history, archaeology, and art. He was born in La Jolla, California, but his parents soon relocated to the historic city of San Diego, Alta California's first Spanish settlement. Founded in 1769, it prospered as a Mexican pueblo, mission, and presidio until becoming part of the United States. Early on, Nick was familiar with San Diego's rich Spanish and Mexican heritage, and as a boy he enjoyed crossing the nearby border into Mexico with his family for short visits. He loved his hometown and relished hiking in the rugged San Diego back country and swimming in the Pacific Ocean, especially at his favorite spot, La Jolla Cove. Nicholson had the good fortune to attend schools within biking and sometimes walking distance of Balboa Park, the city's cultural center. He recalled that the yard of his elementary school pushed up against San Diego's world-famous zoo, through which he and his pals sometimes took unauthorized shortcuts on their way home.

Balboa Park also housed the Museum of Man, then called the San Diego Museum. The edifice was built in a revival Spanish Colonial style for the Panama-Pacific Exposition of 1915, which was organized to commemorate the opening of the Panama Canal. Originally intended as a temporary construction to house exhibitions, the museum was one of a group of lavishly decorated buildings that went on to have second lives as cultural institutions. In "Reminiscences: The San Diego Museum of Man and Balboa Park in the 1930s and 1940s" (Nicholson 1993), included in a volume of essays on Aztec studies dedicated to him, Nick looked back at the decisive impact these local surroundings had on him as a child. Here "to a large extent is where it all began, where my interest in the culture history of the area now called Mesoamerica was first ignited" (ibid.: 111). As he further recalled in this autobiographical essay, what first attracted his attention on early visits to the museum were the life-size casts of monumental stelae, zoomorphs, and altars from the Maya center of Quiriguá, Guatemala—left over from the 1915 exhibition—as well as impressive painted views of six Maya sites by the artist Carlos Vierra. He was also captivated by full-scale replicas of feathered serpent columns from the stepped pyramid at Chichén Itzá (the "Castillo"), scale models of this structure and of the House of the Governor at Uxmal, and replicas of other Maya hieroglyphs and relief carvings.

Then, in 1935–1936, during another international exposition held at Balboa Park, the California-Pacific International Exposition, two other pivotal events further determined the direction of his life: a compelling lantern-slide lecture on the "fair god" Quetzalcoatl delivered by a young speaker and a dramatic musical staged in an ancient Maya setting. Thus, by about age eleven, the young Nicholson had acquired what would become an abiding fascination with Mexico, Mesoamerican archaeology, and Quetzalcoatl—subjects that would fuel his scholarship for a lifetime. Nick had indeed been "bitten by the archaeological bug." The bespectacled, trowel-carrying self-caricature of himself as a future archaeologist that he drew around this time remained tacked to the door of S-14, his subterranean office in Haines Hall, until he retired in 1991 (figure 1.1).

Young Nicholson's interest in the ancient Aztecs and Maya was also heightened by the evocative black-and-white Keith Henderson drawings embellishing the 1934 edition of William Prescott's *Conquest of Mexico* (Boxt and Dillon, this volume). In San Diego's public libraries he tracked down well-illustrated articles on Maya archaeology from the *National Geographic* written by well-known Mayanists, as well as editions of the various proceedings of the International Congress of Americanists; he was especially fond of two popular publications by Lewis Spence: *Myths of Mexico and Peru* (1913) and *The Gods of Mexico* (1923). He recalled that he took out the 1923 Spence volume on so many occasions that by the time he graduated from high school he could quote it almost verbatim. He later credited the beginning of his lifelong interest in Aztec religion and iconography to this little book. As his interests progressively coalesced around Aztec culture, beginning at age sixteen (figure 1.2) Nicholson began a correspondence with George Vaillant, whose *Aztecs of Mexico* appeared in 1941.

BERKELEY AND HARVARD: AN ARCHAEOLOGICAL EDUCATION

After graduating early from high school, Nicholson attended UC Berkeley for a semester before volunteering for the US Army in 1943. After a year and a half of training, he saw combat in Germany and was sent to the Philippines after V.E. Day. He was discharged in 1946 and in the summer of that year made his first momentous trip to Mexico City. His first destination was the Salón de los Monolítos in Mexico's old National Museum of Anthropology (then housed off the Zócalo on Moneda Street), today the Museo Nacional de las Culturas. Profoundly moved by this long-awaited opportunity to view firsthand the museum's outstanding collection of Aztec sculpture, Nicholson spent days photographing the pieces and taking copious notes. He also met again with ethnohistorian Wigberto Jiménez Moreno, whom he had encountered earlier at Berkeley and who introduced him to Alfonso Caso, Mexico's premier archaeologist and scholar. Nick was familiar with their work and admired their accomplishments, as well as those of Robert Barlow, then doing both archaeological excavations at Tlatelolco and intensive studies of Aztec history with an emphasis on documentary sources.

1.2. *H. B. Nicholson in high school, San Diego. Courtesy, Nicholson family.*

In the fall of 1946 Nicholson returned to UC Berkeley. He had many outstanding teachers there, but none impressed him more than the Andeanist John H. Rowe, whom he recalled as a model of thorough and exemplary archaeological and historical scholarship. Nick obtained his BA in anthropology in 1949, then took an academic detour, spending three years at Boalt Hall, Berkeley's School of Law. While he completed his legal studies, they lacked the appeal of the Aztecs, and Nick claimed to have kept his sanity during those dry years by spending most of his time in the library reading his way through the voluminous publications of Eduard Seler in the original German. This turn-of-the-century polymath provided another early model of dauntingly comprehensive and critical scholarship. Nick came to recognize the limitations of the Spence books, some of whose data and interpretations were derived from Seler's work. Although he granted the usefulness of such books in translating and popularizing publications in foreign languages, he became acutely aware of their diluted and uncritical nature, along with their errors of fact. It may have been such a realization that led him to begin to dig deep into all the documentation available in an effort to seek out for himself the primary sources on the Aztecs in their original languages. As he later stated in a letter, "Moving beyond Seler, I went on to deal directly with the primary sources in Spanish and Nahuatl, my own research culminating in various articles in scholarly journals, beginning in 1954" (personal communication, 1983).

After completing his law degree in 1952, Nick made a career-altering decision to return to anthropology and enrolled in doctoral study at Harvard University. While there, he was able to interact with an outstanding group of fellow students as well as with Maya scholars such as Eric Thompson and Tania Proskouriakoff, who were attached to the Carnegie Institution of Washington next door to Harvard's Peabody Museum. Guided by his mentor, Gordon R. Willey, he also undertook his first archaeological excavations at Point Barrow, Alaska, in 1953 (figure 1.3) and in Puerto Rico in 1954.

In 1955, having chosen a dissertation topic probing the historicity of Topiltzin Quetzalcoatl, the legendary lord of the Toltecs of Tollan, Nicholson spent nearly a year of doctoral research in Mexico. He traveled widely throughout the country, visiting numerous archaeological sites and museums and extensively documenting what he saw with black-and-white photographic prints and later with color slides as well. Having exhausted the Berkeley and Harvard libraries' holdings on the Aztecs and Toltecs, he next turned his sights on Mexican repositories. Even at this early stage of his career, he began to make his mark as a formidable researcher. He conducted extensive archival work in museums and libraries, immersing himself not only in primary documents but also in the full range of secondary scholarship then available, taking voluminous notes and obtaining microfilms and copies wherever possible. Throughout his life, Nick greatly enjoyed the give and take of scholarly exchange. In Mexico he interacted widely with Mexican and other visiting scholars, attending discussion groups and conferences and forming many lifelong friendships.

H. B. NICHOLSON AND THE ARCHAEOLOGICAL BUG

1.3. *H. B. Nicholson excavating at Point Barrow, Alaska, in 1953 while a Harvard graduate student. Courtesy, Nicholson family.*

UCLA: DIGGING DEEPER

While still pursuing his dissertation research in Mexico, in 1956 Nick was interviewed by Clement W. Meighan for a position in UCLA's Anthropology and Sociology Department. This opportunity had resulted from the unexpected death of archaeologist George Brainerd. Nicholson was eventually offered the appointment contingent on his completing his dissertation within the year (figure 1.4). Nick managed to do this despite an exceedingly busy year, with a heavy teaching load and a summer field school to run in Utah.

Upon accepting the UCLA position, Nick also agreed to take over Brainerd's archaeological project at Cerro Portezuelo in Central Mexico, begun in 1954–1955. Located near the now-vanished shoreline of Lake Texcoco, the site had a long history, spanning the Classic and Postclassic Periods from approximately AD 350 to 1500. Beginning as a town within the orbit of the mighty Classic city of Teotihuacan, Cerro Portezuelo survived into the Aztec era. Eight boxes of information, now stored in the Fowler Museum at UCLA, contain records from several years of work at the site, beginning in 1957 under Nick's direction as principal investigator. He was assisted by various UCLA graduate students, some of whom completed dissertations based on research within this project. Among the

HARVARD UNIVERSITY
THE GRADUATE SCHOOL OF ARTS AND SCIENCES

THESIS ACCEPTANCE CERTIFICATE
(*To be placed in Original Copy*)

The undersigned, appointed by the ~~Division~~ Department ~~Committee~~ * of Anthropology

have examined a thesis entitled Topiltzin Quetzalcoatl of Tollan: A Problem in Mesoamerican Ethnohistory

presented by   Henry Bigger Nicholson

candidate for the degree of   Doctor of Philosophy   ~~Doctor of Science~~,* and hereby certify that it is worthy of acceptance.

* Cross out inappropriate words.

Signature *(signed)*
Typed name   Gordon R. Willey

Signature *(signed)* H. E. D. Pollock / per G. R. W.
Typed name   H. E. Pollock

Signature
Typed name

F-54-IV-51-2000

1.4. *Signature page for H. B. Nicholson's doctoral dissertation at Harvard, completed in 1957. Note that Gordon Willey signed both for himself and in proxy for Harry E.D. Pollock. Courtesy, Harvard University.*

holdings are "documentation, inventories, maps, photographs, artifact descriptions and analysis, field notes, correspondence, progress reports" (UCLA Fowler Museum of Cultural History Cerro Portezuelo Archives 1954–1962). Analysis of some of the excavated materials was made possible in 1961 by a National Science Foundation Fellowship. In 1962 Clement Meighan conducted a brief surface survey of Cerro Portezuelo and the surrounding areas, and a second excavation in the area followed at the site of Chimalhuacán. Nick and Frederick Hicks coauthored a paper, "The Transition from Classic to Postclassic at Cerro Portezuelo, Valley of Mexico," interpreting some of this original research, for the International Congress of Americanists held in Mexico City in 1962 (Nicholson and Hicks 1964).

At UCLA Nick also collaborated with Meighan on an archaeological project in West Mexico. In his words:

> The most important archaeological field project on which we collaborated, as Principal Investigators, was The Interrelationship of New World Cultures, A Coordinated Research Program of the Institute of Andean Research, Project A: Central Pacific Coast of Mexico, 1960–1962, financed by the National Science Foundation. A number of New World archaeologists, representing eight US and Latin American institutions, participated in a series of surveys and excavations along the Pacific Coast from Mexico to Ecuador to test the hypothesis of a series of significant maritime/coastal cultural movements on an early or Formative temporal horizon . . .
>
> In three field seasons, we directed graduate student teams in a series of reconnaissances and excavations in this archaeologically little-known region, a logical follow-up to Clem's earlier excavations in 1956 and 1959 at sites near Peñitas and Amapa, Nayarit. A number of reports, papers, and monographs by both of us and our students resulted from this project. (Nicholson 1997: 4)

With his archaeological background and extensive knowledge of Meso-american art, Nick was in demand as a writer of authoritative catalogs for private collections of Precolumbian art. In 1970 the Los Angeles County Museum of Art (LACMA) organized an exhibition of the Precolumbian collection of Proctor Stafford. In collaboration with Michael Kan and his colleague Clem Meighan, Nick wrote the exhibition's catalog, *Sculpture of Ancient West Mexico: Nayarit, Jalisco, Colima* (Kan, Meighan, and Nicholson 1970). In it, Nick and Clem coauthored an introductory article, "The Ceramic Mortuary Offerings of Prehistoric West Mexico: An Archaeological Perspective" (Kan, Meighan, and Nicholson 1970). After the Stafford collection was donated to LACMA in 1987, a revised version of the catalog appeared in 1989. Kan's essay remained virtually unchanged, but Nick revised the coauthored article and updated all the entries.

In conjunction with the exhibition of the Precolumbian collection of Lewis K. Land, held at the California Academy of Sciences in 1977, another catalog, *Pre-Columbian Art from the Land Collection,* appeared in 1979 (Nicholson, Cordy-

Collins, and Land 1979). For this work, Nick wrote a preface (1979i), introduction (1979f), and entries for pieces from Far West Mexico (1979c), N. Michoacan/S. Guanajuato (1979h), Guerrero (1979d), Central Mexico (1979a), the Gulf Coast (1979e), and the Maya region (1979g), while Alana Cordy-Collins (1979a, 1979b) contributed introductions and entries for objects from the Intermediate and Andean areas.

ETHNOHISTORY: AN ARCHAEOLOGY OF WRITTEN SOURCES

In his 1997 tribute to his friend and archaeological collaborator Clem Meighan, Nick confessed that "although I have undertaken archaeological excavations in various places [Alaska, Puerto Rico, Utah, Mexico], my strongest interest has always been in what is usually today termed ethnohistory, the reconstruction of socio-cultural systems derived from written and pictorial sources—above all, in my case, those from Mesoamerica" (Nicholson 1997: 4).

So despite Nick's strong academic training in anthropology at Berkeley and Harvard, a keen parallel interest in ethnohistory drove his choice of a dissertation topic—an exploration of the legendary lord of the Toltecs, Topiltzin Quetzalcoatl, whose tale was entangled with that of the multifaceted deity Quetzalcoatl, the Feathered Serpent. This enigmatic personage had played a pervasive role in the formation of Aztec ideology and become the subject of some of the most striking sculptures in the Aztec artistic canon. Essentially, Nick had to devise his own methodology to carry out his ethnohistorical study.

A number of events were pivotal in Nick's attraction to ethnohistory. They include his early epistolary conversations with George Vaillant, his exposure to the Berkeley style of humanistic studies and especially to John H. Rowe, an impressive Harvard course on Colonial Mexico offered by the visiting Mexican scholar Silvio Závala, and an admiration for the multidisciplinary studies of scholars such as Alfonso Caso and Robert Barlow. Nick also valued early and deep friendships with the multitalented scholars Ignacio Bernal and Wigberto Jiménez Moreno, whose work emphasized a profound knowledge of documentary and other sources. These various personal and intellectual influences contributed to Nick's growing appreciation for a research method that emphasized a broadly interdisciplinary utilization of data—historical, archaeological, documentary, artifactual, and artistic—in the study of ancient cultures. Nick's approach was in effect a creative application of archaeological techniques to other fields of Mesoamerican study. Certainly, no scholar since Eduard Seler had delved so deeply to acquire such an extraordinary command of Central Mexican documentary sources as H. B. Nicholson.

At the same time that Nick was active in teaching and directing archaeological projects at UCLA, he also became a key figure in the decision to devote several volumes of the Handbook of Middle American Indians (Wauchope

1964–1976) to ethnohistory. These four volumes, 12–15 (1972–1975), had their own subtitle, Guide to Ethnohistorical Sources. Calling on the expertise of an international array of outstanding scholars, the volumes attempted to summarize the state of knowledge of the various fields of Mesoamerican studies up to that time. Like an earlier precedent, the Handbook of South American Indians (Steward 1946–1959), the Mesoamerican series was recognized as a landmark project. But the set of volumes on ethnohistory, under the editorship of Howard F. Cline, with Charles Gibson, John B. Glass, and H. B. Nicholson as associate volume editors, was unique to it.

For volume 13 of the Handbook, Nicholson (1973b: 207–217) contributed a study of Bernardino de Sahagún's *Primeros Memoriales*. This section of the sixteenth-century Franciscan missionary's massive ethnographic and linguistic study of the Aztecs, which he called the *Historia General de las Cosas de Nueva España*, was the result of research carried out around 1559–1561 in Tepepulco, Hidalgo, with the indispensable assistance of an indigenous, multilingual team of missionary-trained interviewers, translators, and artists. Nick provided a historiographical study of the manuscript, following Francisco del Paso y Troncoso's initial identification in 1905 of the Tepepulco folios, and went on to analyze their contents and various translations. After comparing the manuscript's folios (as well as subsequent translations and commentaries) against the final stage of Sahagún's *Historia* project of about 1580, today called the *Florentine Codex*, Nick concluded that most of the Tepepulco material had not been utilized in the later manuscript. He thus emphasized that this early part of Sahagún's opus, the *Primeros Memoriales*, stood as a separate document rather than a first version of the later *Florentine Codex*.

Nick also contributed an essay, "Eduard Georg Seler, 1849–1922," to volume 13 of the Handbook (1973a). Although Seler's prodigious scholarship covered a number of fields, Nick focused on his methodology—essentially a more rigorous critical approach to what became known as Mesoamerican ethnohistory—including his penetrating investigations into the documentary and pictorial sources of the area's indigenous cultures. Nick was always cognizant of the historiography of Mesoamerican studies and of the often-forgotten work of its pioneers, especially those publishing in languages other than English and Spanish. He examined Seler's writings, which he divided into translations and commentaries on native-language texts, commentaries on pictorial manuscripts, Maya research, and ethnographic and culture historical syntheses derived from ethnohistorical sources. His appraisal emphasized the monumental scope of Seler's accomplishments while also pointing out the limitations of some of his approaches and interpretations.

Nick was also instrumental in the seven-volume publication of English translations of Seler's articles, *Collected Works in North- and South-American Linguistics and Archaeology* (1990–2002), produced under the direction of General Editor

Frank E. Comparato. In addition to revising earlier English translations done under the supervision of Charles P. Bowditch, Comparato added new translations and also republished Nick's still valuable original review of the five-volume German original of Seler's collected articles, *Gesammelte Abhandlungen zur Amerikanischen Sprach-und Alterthumskunde* (Seler 1990–2002).

Nick's involvement with the Sahaguntine materials took another turn in 1981 with the untimely death of Thelma Sullivan, who had been in the process of translating the *Primeros Memoriales* from Nahuatl to English. Currently divided between the Library of the Palacio Real and the Real Academia de la Historia, both in Madrid, the original document is therefore not available to scholars in cohesive form or in a single location. Because of the importance of the project, Nick, despite his many professional obligations, offered to take it over and see it to completion as editor. It was Nicholson's decision to expand Sullivan's projected translation, initially funded by a National Endowment for the Humanities translation grant, to one that would include a color facsimile and introductory studies of the texts and images. The first volume, *Primeros Memoriales by Fray Bernardino de Sahagún* (1993), reproduced in color facsimile the folios of the original manuscript. The second volume, *Primeros Memoriales: Paleography of Nahuatl Text and English Translation* (1997), featured Thelma Sullivan's translation, completed by Arthur Anderson and Charles Dibble, both earlier translators from Nahuatl to English of Sahagún's *Florentine Codex* (1950–1982). Aside from some of Thelma's notations, Anderson and Dibble wrote most of the linguistic notes. Nick also contributed to these notes and produced most of the other notes and a study of the text. He added an introduction to the manuscript's painted images provided by myself.

Nick's profound knowledge of the Sahaguntine corpus also came to fruition in another volume he edited with J. Jorge Klor de Alva and Eloise Quiñones Keber, *The Work of Bernardino de Sahagún: Pioneer Ethnographer of Sixteenth-Century Aztec Mexico* (1988). In another demonstration of his bibliographic expertise, Nick's introduction to this volume supplied an updating and appraisal of Sahaguntine scholarship published since the Handbook of Middle American Indians (Nicholson 1973b) and the volume edited by Munro Edmonson, *Sixteenth-Century Mexico: The Work of Sahagún* (1974). A second article, "The Iconography of the Deity Representations in Fray Bernardino de Sahagún's *Primeros Memoriales*: Huitzilopochtli and Chalchiuhtlicue," displayed his mastery of Aztec art. In this article he analyzed the thirty-seven (including one set of five) named Aztec deities, their costumes, accoutrements, and roles in Aztec culture. He called attention to the significance of this early set of painted deities, who are uniquely accompanied by a listing in Nahuatl of the diagnostic insignia of the Aztec gods represented.

IDEOLOGY, ART, AND ICONOGRAPHY

Awakened to the subject by his early reading of the Spence books, Nick was intensely interested in the religious and ritual aspects of Mesoamerican culture, and the features of Aztec religion were a frequent focus of his articles. In pursuit of information about these specialized facets of Aztec and other contemporaneous cultures, he became an expert on the style and iconography of Mesoamerican painted manuscripts. In their present-day repositories he studied Prehispanic originals, such as those of the Codex Borgia Group, as well as those copied in the Early Colonial Period, since many of them dealt with religion and ritual. His widely cited article on the religious-ritual system of late Prehispanic Central Mexico in volume 10 of the Handbook of Middle American Indians, titled "Religion in Pre-Hispanic Central Mexico" (Nicholson 1971b), is still recognized as a tour de force of synthesis for the complex and intertwined supernaturals within the teeming Aztec pantheon. Facing a plethora of incomplete and often conflicting information about these personages, he grouped them into three principal cult themes: celestial creative-divine paternalism, rain-moisture-agricultural fertility, and war-sacrifice-sanguinary nourishment of the sun and earth. He then broke these categories down into various subthemes he called deity complexes. Aware of the artificiality of such an organizing construct, which the Aztecs of the sixteenth century certainly would not have recognized, he nevertheless considered his categorization a useful tool for modern-day researchers living long past the time of, and without the resources of, the most knowledgeable Aztec priests and artist-scribes.

Nick was remarkably open to new considerations and new data. This was especially true of the findings of the Templo Mayor Project, which have expanded our understanding about the Aztecs in many new and often surprising directions. He was especially cognizant of the tremendous impact the Templo Mayor excavations, begun in 1978, had on insights into Aztec religion and ritual. It was no surprise that his discussion of the 1983 Dumbarton Oaks symposium on the Aztec Templo Mayor (Nicholson 1987) focused on "the sequence of the successive building stages of the Templo Mayor as known from ethnohistorical references and archaeological evidence" (ibid.: 464). He went on to explain that this interest stemmed from "one of my longest standing preoccupations in Mesoamerican research . . . the problem of correlating archaeological sequences with historical data contained in primary ethnohistorical sources" (ibid.) (figure 1.5). In this connection, he cited two of his early articles, "Native Historical Traditions of Nuclear America and the Problem of Their Archaeological Correlation" (Nicholson 1955) and "Correlating Mesoamerican Historical Traditions with Archaeological Sequences: Some Methodological Considerations" (Nicholson 1979b). Both of these articles, the first of which was written when he was still a graduate student and the second of which was his latest published article at that time, reveal how seriously Nick took these issues and how tenaciously he

1.5. *Nick revisiting the Chapultepec rock carvings in 1983. Photo by Eloise Quiñones Keber.*

pursued them. Even though he researched his articles exhaustively, he was too well aware of the limited information on sixteenth-century Mexico that had come down to the present to consider any subject closed or any interpretation definitive. This awareness also resulted in his insistence on looking at all sides of an issue, his avoidance of dogmatic statements, and his hesitation about claiming to have resolved contentious questions.

Nick's avid interest in religion and ritual themes and the manuscripts in which these themes were so brilliantly painted by indigenous artists was partnered with an equally intense concern with Aztec art and iconography. Since the enormous corpus of Aztec sculpture in particular often depicts a preoccupation with cosmic concepts, religious ideology, sacred time, and supernatural beings, this might seem just a part of his overall fascination with all things Aztec. But Nick brought to the study of Aztec art and iconography not only an unusually perceptive eye and astonishing visual memory but also his encyclopedic Aztec databank, all of which provided singular insights into this aspect of Aztec culture.

These qualities are evident in his other synthesizing article in volume 10 of the Handbook of Middle American Indians, "Major Sculpture in Pre-Hispanic Central Mexico" (Nicholson 1971a). Although he stated that he valued the objects as "indispensable primary sources" (ibid.: 93), he also recognized their independent artistic merit, for he considered Mesoamerica's overall tradition of monumental stone sculpture "a striking aesthetic achievement" (ibid.: 92). Ranging from Formative Olmec-related works to the enormous corpus of Aztec art of the Postclassic Period, Nicholson noted continuities of types and themes over time, as well as innovations devised by the various distinctive cultures. The fact that he had seen and photographed most of this sculptural corpus in situ or in public and private collections throughout Mexico, Europe, and the United States allowed him to identify the main diagnostic features of each major style and the types of objects produced within each one. Over half of the article was devoted to the many striking types of Aztec sculpture, on which Nick was then the world's expert. In a sweeping and laudatory final statement, he concluded:

> In these battered but still powerfully expressive stones, which are all that remain after the passage of centuries of destruction and neglect, the essential cultural spirit of a vigorous, creative people stands revealed. Cut off sharply at the very moment of its apogee, the Aztec sculptural tradition, in the short span which the inexorable march of human political events allowed it, achieved greatness. It left behind one of man's most impressive artistic legacies, which, aside from its enduring aesthetic impact, yields upon analysis a wealth of precious ideological information concerning one of Mesoamerica's most important and interesting cultures. It constitutes a remarkable creative achievement, comparing favorably with any other major sculptural tradition of the past in either hemisphere. (Nicholson 1971a: 133)

Art of Aztec Mexico: Treasures of Tenochtitlan, held at the National Gallery of Art in 1983, was the first comprehensive exhibition of Aztec art to be mounted in the United States. It offered Nick the opportunity to devote his full attention to writing a catalog describing eighty-one choice pieces produced by skilled Aztec and Mixtec artists (Nicholson with Quiñones Keber 1983). In the catalog's introduction, Nick chose to preface the entries with a historiographic overview of the eclipse of this great artistic tradition that came with the fall of Mexico Tenochtitlan in 1521, its subsequent rediscovery beginning in the late eighteenth century, and finally the slowly growing awareness in the modern period of its artistic and iconographic significance. He then discussed the origins of Aztec art and its remarkable flowering in the fifteenth and sixteenth centuries, much of which has not survived. He ended his opening remarks with an elegiac reflection that expresses his deeply felt attachment to the stones of Mexico: "The war drums of the Aztec are stilled forever. The towering temples dedicated to their awesome gods were demolished long ago. But many of the artistic creations placed in and around them to express their faith in these deities have somehow survived. These battered stones, despised and neglected for so long, have begun to speak to us again" (Nicholson 1983: 26).

CONCLUSION

Throughout his life and career, Nick never stopped bringing the past into the present, never stopped sharing his scholarly enthusiasms and knowledge with the greatest generosity. Through his publications and lectures and sometimes through his very presence and everyday eloquence, he had the ability to awaken the sensibilities of contemporary students, colleagues, and lay audiences to the marvels of an earlier time. His was a life dedicated to the study of the past, not in a sterile, disconnected manner but rather in a way that managed to bridge the long-ago preoccupations of ancient people with perennial human concerns and aspirations.

When at the dawn of a new millennium, at the instigation of numerous colleagues, Nick finally returned to his unpublished doctoral dissertation to at last prepare it for publication, he was in effect digging into his own past and bringing it up to date with the more advanced state of knowledge of his present. Perhaps not surprisingly, Nick's return to the transcendent figure of Topiltzin Quetzalcoatl, who himself bridged the Toltec and Aztec periods as he did legend and history, was carried out with the fervor of a new fascination. *Topiltzin Quetzalcoatl: The Once and Future Lord of the Toltecs* (Nicholson 2001), Nick's first and final book, is testimony to a lifelong passion, reborn yet again, for Mexico, the Aztecs, and Quetzalcoatl.

REFERENCES CITED

Cordy-Collins, Alana
    1979a   Introduction: Andean Area. In *Pre-Columbian Art from the Land Collection* by H. B. Nicholson, Alana Cordy-Collins, and Lewis K. Land, pp. 221–224. California Academy of Sciences, San Francisco.
    1979b   Introduction: Intermediate Area. In *Pre-Columbian Art from the Land Collection* by H. B. Nicholson, Alana Cordy-Collins, and Lewis K. Land, pp. 181–211. California Academy of Sciences, San Francisco.

Edmonson, Munro S.
    1974   *Sixteenth-Century Mexico: The Work of Sahagún*. University of New Mexico Press, Albuquerque.

Kan, Michael, Clement W. Meighan, and H. B. Nicholson
    1970   *Sculpture of Ancient West Mexico: Nayarit, Jalisco, Colima*. Los Angeles County Museum of Art, Los Angeles, CA.
    1989   *Sculpture of Ancient West Mexico: Nayarit, Jalisco, Colima: A Catalogue of the Proctor Stafford Collection at the Los Angeles County Museum of Art*. Los Angeles County Museum of Art in association with University of New Mexico Press, Albuquerque.

Klor de Alva, J. Jorge, H. B. Nicholson, and Eloise Quiñones Keber, eds.
    1988   *The Work of Bernardino de Sahagún: Pioneer Ethnographer of Sixteenth-Century Aztec Mexico*. Institute for Mesoamerican Studies, State University of New York at Albany, Albany.

Meighan, Clement W., and H. B. Nicholson
    1989   The Ceramic Mortuary Offerings of Prehistoric West Mexico: An Archaeological Perspective. In *Sculpture of Ancient West Mexico: Nayarit, Jalisco, Co-*

lima: A Catalogue of the Proctor Stafford Collection at the Los Angeles County Museum of Art, pp. 29–67. Los Angeles County Museum of Art in association with University of New Mexico Press, Albuquerque.

Nicholson, H. B.
- 1955 Native Historical Traditions of Nuclear America and the Problem of Their Archaeological Correlation. *American Anthropologist* 56 (3): 594–613.
- 1971a Major Sculpture in Pre-Hispanic Central Mexico. In *Archaeology of Northern Mesoamerica*, Part 1, ed. Gordon F. Ekholm and Ignacio Bernal, pp. 92–134. Handbook of Middle American Indians, vol. 10, Robert Wauchope, ed. University of Texas Press, Austin.
- 1971b Religion in Pre-Hispanic Central Mexico. In *Archaeology of Northern Mesoamerica*, Part 1, ed. Gordon F. Ekholm and Ignacio Bernal, pp. 395–446. Handbook of Middle American Indians, vol. 10, Robert Wauchope, ed. University of Texas Press, Austin.
- 1973a Eduard Georg Seler, 1849–1922. In *Guide to Ethnohistorical Sources*, Part 2, vol. ed. Howard F. Cline, assoc. vol. ed. John B. Glass, pp. 348–369. Handbook of Middle American Indians, vol. 13, Robert Wauchope, gen. ed. University of Texas Press, Austin.
- 1973b Sahagún's "Primeros memoriales," Tepepulco, 1559–1561. In *Guide to Ethnohistorical Sources*, Part 2, vol. ed. Howard F. Cline, assoc. vol. ed. John B. Glass, pp. 207–217. Handbook of Middle American Indians, vol. 13, Robert Wauchope, gen. ed. University of Texas Press, Austin.
- 1979a Central Mexico. In *Pre-Columbian Art from the Land Collection* by H. B. Nicholson, Alana Cordy-Collins, and Lewis K. Land, pp. 105–112. California Academy of Sciences, San Francisco.
- 1979b Correlating Mesoamerican Historical Traditions with Archaeological Sequences: Some Methodological Considerations. *Actes du XLIIe Congrès International des Américanistes*, Paris, September 2–9, 1976, 9-B: 187–198.
- 1979c Far West Mexico. In *Pre-Columbian Art from the Land Collection* by H. B. Nicholson, Alana Cordy-Collins, and Lewis K. Land, pp. 35–90. California Academy of Sciences, San Francisco.
- 1979d Guerrero. In *Pre-Columbian Art from the Land Collection* by H. B. Nicholson, Alana Cordy-Collins, and Lewis K. Land, pp. 99–104. California Academy of Sciences, San Francisco.
- 1979e Gulf Coast. In *Pre-Columbian Art from the Land Collection* by H. B. Nicholson, Alana Cordy-Collins, and Lewis K. Land, pp. 113–128. California Academy of Sciences, San Francisco.
- 1979f Introduction. In *Pre-Columbian Art from the Land Collection* by H. B. Nicholson, Alana Cordy-Collins, and Lewis K. Land, pp. 27–28. California Academy of Sciences, San Francisco.
- 1979g Maya Region. In *Pre-Columbian Art from the Land Collection* by H. B. Nicholson, Alana Cordy-Collins, and Lewis K. Land, pp. 129–156. California Academy of Sciences, San Francisco.
- 1979h N. Michoacan/S. Guanajuato. In *Pre-Columbian Art from the Land Collection* by H. B. Nicholson, Alana Cordy-Collins, and Lewis K. Land, pp. 91–98. California Academy of Sciences, San Francisco.

1979i Preface. In *Pre-Columbian Art from the Land Collection* by H. B. Nicholson, Alana Cordy-Collins, and Lewis K. Land, pp. 3–4. California Academy of Sciences, San Francisco.

1983 Introduction: The Discovery of Aztec Art. In *Art of Aztec Mexico: Treasures of Tenochtitlan* by H. B. Nicholson, with Eloise Quiñones Keber, pp. 17–27. National Gallery of Art, Washington, DC.

1987 Symposium on the Aztec Templo Mayor: Discussion. In *The Aztec Templo Mayor: A Symposium at Dumbarton Oaks, 8th and 9th October, 1983*, ed. Elizabeth Hill Boone, pp. 463–484. Dumbarton Oaks Research Library and Collection, Washington, DC.

1993 Reminiscences: The San Diego Museum of Man and Balboa Park in the 1930s and 1940s. In *Current Topics in Aztec Studies: Essays in Honor of Dr. H. B. Nicholson*, ed. Alana Cordy-Collins and Douglas Sharon, pp. 111–118. San Diego Museum of Man, San Diego.

1997 In Memory of Clem. *Backdirt: Newsletter of the Institute of Archaeology, University of California, Los Angeles* (Fall–Winter): 4.

2001 *Topiltzin Quetzalcoatl: The Once and Future Lord of the Toltecs.* University Press of Colorado, Boulder.

Nicholson, H. B., Alana Cordy-Collins, and Lewis K. Land
  1979 *Pre-Columbian Art from the Land Collection.* California Academy of Sciences, San Francisco.

Nicholson, H. B., and Frederick Hicks
  1964 The Transition from Classic to Postclassic at Cerro Portezuelo, Valley of Mexico. *XXXV Congreso Internacional de Americanistas, México, 1962, Actas y Memorias* 1: 493–506.

Nicholson, H. B., with Eloise Quiñones Keber
  1983 *Art of Aztec Mexico: Treasures of Tenochtitlan.* National Gallery of Art, Washington, DC.

Paso y Troncoso , Francisco del, ed.
  1905 *Historia general de las cosas de Nueva España*, vol. 6. Hauser y Menet, Madrid.

Prescott, William H.
  1934 *The Conquest of Mexico.* Book League of America, New York.

Quiñones Keber, Eloise
  2007 Gifts of the Feathered Serpent: The Life and Career of H. B. Nicholson (1925–2007). *Ancient Mesoamerica* 18 (Spring): 3–10.

Sahagún, Fray Bernardino de
  1950–1982 *Florentine Codex: General History of the Things of New Spain.* Trans. by Charles E. Dibble and Arthur J.O. Anderson. University of Utah Press, Salt Lake City.
  1993 *Primeros Memoriales by Fray Bernardino de Sahagún.* Facsimile edition. University of Oklahoma Press, Norman, in cooperation with the Patrimonio Nacional and the Real Academia de la Historia, Madrid.

1997   *Primeros Memoriales by Fray Bernardino de Sahagún: Paleography of Nahuatl Text and English Translation* by Thelma D. Sullivan; completed and revised, with additions by H. B. Nicholson, Arthur J.O. Anderson, Charles E. Dibble, Eloise Quiñones Keber, and Wayne Ruwet. University of Oklahoma Press, Norman, in cooperation with the Patrimonio Nacional and the Real Academia de la Historia, Madrid.

Seler, Eduard
   1990–2002   *Collected Works in North- and South-American Linguistics and Archaeology: English translations of German papers from Gesammelte Abhandlungen zur amerikanischen Sprach- und Alterthumskunde.* 7 vols. Frank E. Comparato, gen. ed. Labyrinthos, Lancaster, CA.

Spence, Lewis
   1913   *Myths of Mexico and Peru.* Harrap, London.
   1923   *The Gods of Mexico.* T. Fisher Unwin Ltd., London.

Steward, Julian H., ed.
   1946–1959   Handbook of South American Indians. 7 vols. United States Government Printing Office, Washington, DC.

UCLA Fowler Museum of Cultural History Cerro Portezuelo Archives
   1954–1962   http://content.cdlib.org/view?docId=kt50001959&chunk.id=scopecontent1.8.3; accessed March 25, 2009.

Vaillant, George C.
   1941   *Aztecs of Mexico: Origin, Rise and Fall of the Aztec Nation.* Doubleday: Garden City, NY.

Wauchope, Robert, gen. ed.
   1964–1976   Handbook of Middle American Indians. 16 vols. University of Texas Press, Austin.

PART I
THE OLMEC AND THEIR NEIGHBORS

2

THE MIDDLE FORMATIVE PERIOD STELAE OF CHALCATZINGO

David C. Grove

I spent the summer of 1955 traveling throughout Mexico and returned from that trip enamored with the country, its people, and its prehistory. At that time I was an undergraduate geology major at UCLA. Wanting to learn more about Mexico, I enrolled in an anthropology course on Mesoamerican archaeology being offered by a newly hired assistant professor, H. B. Nicholson. I was captivated by his lectures. A friendship developed between us, we kept in contact, and in 1958 Nick invited me to serve as the cartographer for a project he was conducting in Mexico. That field experience, together with Nick's infectious love of everything Mesoamerican, was the stimulus that ultimately convinced me to change careers and enter the world of Mexican archaeology.

In 1962 I enrolled in the anthropology graduate program at UCLA and spent the next four years studying with Nick and working with him in Mexico. Although he was an internationally recognized Aztec scholar, Nick nevertheless always encouraged me to pursue my interest in Formative Period Mesoamerica. My 1966–1967 doctoral research in the State of Morelos included some initial investigations at Chalcatzingo, a site noted at that time for its nine Olmec-style rock carvings. I fell in love with Chalcatzingo, just as Nick might have predicted, and the site has been the major focus of my archaeological research for nearly four decades.

David C. Grove

2.1. *Chalcatzingo, showing the Cerro Chalcatzingo (right) and Cerro Delgado (left). Photograph by David C. Grove.*

CHALCATZINGO AND ITS STONE MONUMENTS

The Highland Central Mexican site of Chalcatzingo is famous for its Middle Formative Period Olmec-style stone monuments. Over thirty such carvings are known there today, the largest concentration for that time period at any site outside the Gulf Coast Olmec region and a quantity surpassed only by the Gulf Coast Olmec sites of San Lorenzo and La Venta.

In the Formative Period, the settlement at Chalcatzingo was situated on the terraced hill slopes at the base of two massive stone hills—the Cerro Chalcatzingo and the Cerro Delgado (figure 2.1). Those mountains dominate both the site and the flat landscape of the surrounding Amatzinac Valley, and there is substantial evidence that during the Formative Period (and probably later periods as well) the peoples of that region esteemed the Cerro Chalcatzingo (or perhaps both hills) as a sacred mountain (for example, Angulo V. 1987: 140; Cook de Leonard 1967: 63–64; Grove 1987b: 430–432).

When Eulalia Guzmán first explored and reported on Chalcatzingo in 1934, she recorded four bas-relief carvings (now registered as Monuments 1, 2, 6, and 8) and a decapitated statue of a seated personage (Monument 16; Guzmán 1934; Grove and Angulo V. 1987: 125, figure 9.18). Although Guzmán realized that the site had great antiquity, it was not until somewhat later that its carvings were

THE MIDDLE FORMATIVE PERIOD STELAE OF CHALCATZINGO

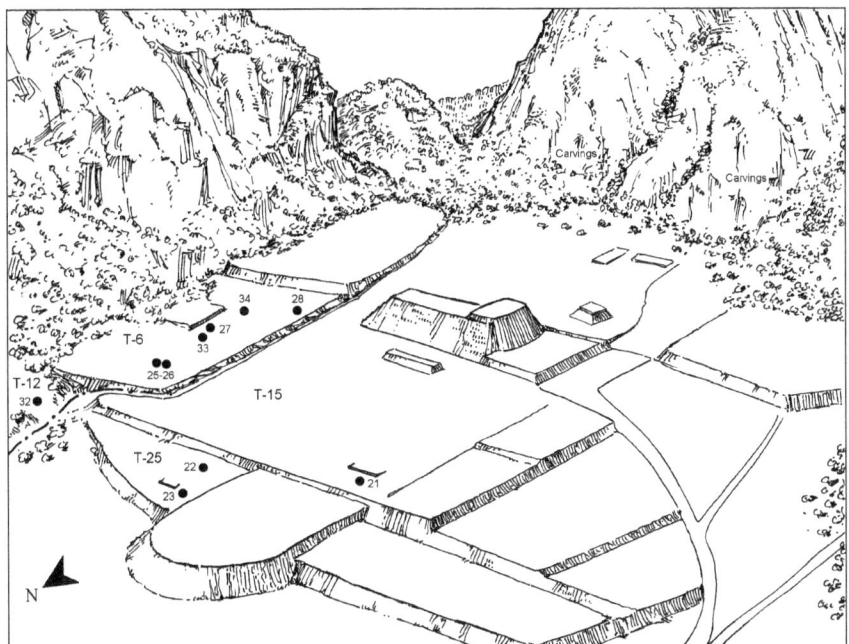

2.2. *Schematic view of Chalcatzingo, Morelos, Mexico, showing Terraces 6, 12, 15, and 25 and the monuments mentioned in the text. Drawing by David C. Grove and Rusty van Rossmann.*

recognized as perhaps contemporaneous with those of the Olmec site of La Venta (for example, Covarrubias 1946). Excavations at Chalcatzingo in 1953 by Román Piña Chan (1955) yielded a good stratified sample of ceramics similar to those found at Zacatenco and Tlatilco in the Valley of Mexico, thereby affirming a Formative Period occupation at the site. Small Classic and Postclassic Period archaeological components are also present there (Arana 1987).

In 1972 the Chalcatzingo Archaeological Project (CAP), under the co-direction of Jorge Angulo V., Raúl Arana, and me, began extensive excavations of the Formative village site in an effort to understand the lifeways of the peoples who had created the site's monuments. The research was carried out from 1972 to 1974 and again briefly in 1976 (Grove 1984; Grove, ed. 1987) and revealed that the hillside at Chalcatzingo had been inhabited and farmed as early as 1500 BC. During the earliest period of occupation, the Amate Phase (1500–1100 BC), the settlement occurred on the natural unmodified hillside at the base of the two hills. About 1100 BC, the beginning of the Barranca Phase (1100–700 BC), the people living at Chalcatzingo modified the hillside into a series of long terraces, the landform still present there today (figure 2.2). The Formative Period village reached its maximum size and importance in the subsequent Cantera Phase (700–500 BC); most of the archaeological data obtained by the CAP is of that phase.

David C. Grove

Archaeological and stylistic evidence indicates that the site's magnificent stone carvings were created during the Cantera Phase, making them contemporaneous with many of the monuments at the Olmec center of La Venta, Tabasco. In fact, a few specific iconographic motifs occur only on monuments at Chalcatzingo and La Venta, providing evidence that some significant form of interaction between the two centers took place (Grove 1987b: 426–430, 1989: 132–142). At the same time, however, Chalcatzingo also shares equally distinctive yet different iconographic symbols with centers in Guerrero and the Pacific Coast of Guatemala, indicating that its interregional interactions were not unidimensional but quite complex (Grove 1987a, 1989).

At the time the CAP was initiated, twelve Formative Period carvings had been recorded at Chalcatzingo (Monuments 1–11, 16; Grove 1968; Gay 1972: 37–71). With only two exceptions (Monuments 9 and 16), all of those carvings occur on the Cerro Chalcatzingo, above and away from the ancient settlement area. During the CAP investigations, an additional sixteen Formative Period stone carvings came to light (Monuments 12–15, 17–28), and another was discovered by the site caretakers in the early 1990s (Monument 31).[1] Significantly, the majority of those newly discovered carvings were unearthed in a very different area of the site, the Formative Period village area on the terraced fields below the Cerro Chalcatzingo.

The carvings on the Cerro Chalcatzingo occur in two spatially separate groupings, each different in thematic content and symbolism from the monuments of the terraced village area. Among the group of reliefs high on the Cerro is the famed "El Rey" (Monument 1), a depiction of a personage seated within a large U-shaped niche—a cave, an entrance to the otherworld. Rain clouds with falling exclamation point–shaped raindrops (!) hang over the cave, and scrolls of mist emanate from the mouth of the cave (Grove 1968: figure 1, 1989: figure 7.6, 1999: figure 2; Guzmán 1934: figure 3). The five adjacent smaller carvings depict small lizard-like creatures crouched atop scroll motifs and peering upward at rain clouds with falling !-shaped raindrops. Squash plants are carved below three of the creatures (Grove and Angulo V. 1987: figures 9.4–9.8). The symbolism of rain and agricultural fertility is very clear in all of the reliefs. The second group of carvings on the Cerro is executed in bas-relief on boulders on the hill's talus slopes. They depict mythical scenes of humans being dominated by supernatural animals (Monuments 3, 4, 5, and recently discovered 31) and one related ritual scene (Monument 2).

Both sets of carvings on the Cerro Chalcatzingo can be described as mythico-supernatural in content (Grove 1984: 109–122, 1999: 258–262; Angulo V. 1987: 132–148; Grove and Angulo V. 1987: 115–122). Importantly, each of those two groups forms a coherent series or sequence, yet within each of them the individual carvings are spaced apart to the extent that the entire group cannot be viewed as a whole. To see the carvings, a viewer must walk from one

THE MIDDLE FORMATIVE PERIOD STELAE OF CHALCATZINGO

to another, a fact that has led me to describe them as laid out or presented in a "processional arrangement" (Grove 1999: 260). That layout will be mentioned again later.

The Cantera Phase village at the base of the Cerro Chalcatzingo was a dispersed settlement, and nearly every one of the site's numerous terraces was characterized by the presence of a single large domestic structure (Prindiville and Grove 1987: 66), while the remaining terrace area was presumably utilized for agricultural activities. However, Terraces 6, 15, and 25 (figure 2.2) were special and different. Instead of domestic terraces, each was the location of a large Cantera Phase stone-faced rectangular platform structure, a rare architectural form for any Middle Formative site; in addition, carved stone monuments were associated with each platform structure (Grove 1984: 57–65; Prindiville and Grove 1987: 64–65). The stone-faced platforms range in size from 15 to 20 m in length and 0.5 to 1.3 m in height. Unfortunately, the upper surfaces of all three platforms occur within the modern plow zone and have long since been destroyed, so the exact function served by the platforms remains uncertain.

Had they been built for ritual purposes or as ancestor shrines, or were they the raised platform foundations for elite domestic architecture? Significantly, the majority of the monuments associated with the platforms are stelae bearing bas-relief carvings of personages. The symbolism of the monuments on those terraces within the Formative Period village can be described as "political" and related to rulership (Grove 1984: 49–68, 109–122, 1987b: 431–432, 1999: 262–263).

To date we have recorded seven stelae or stelae bases from those three terraces (Monuments 21, 23, 26, 27, 28, 33, 34; see Grove and Angulo V. 1987). Six of the seven stelae are broken ("mutilated") in some manner, but I have long argued that such "mutilation" was actually a benign internal social or ritual act rather than evidence of violence or iconoclasm (Grove 1981, 1984: 158–159). Three additional stelae have been discovered in other site areas (Monuments 24, 31, and 32), bringing the total number of stelae at the site to ten. In addition to the known stelae, as I have walked the fields at the site for the past three decades I have noted and recorded the location of several other probable stela bases that merit future exploration. Nevertheless, even without the latter, Chalcatzingo's ten stelae represent the largest quantity of stelae known so far at any Early or Middle Formative site in Mesoamerica, including San Lorenzo and La Venta.

In the next section I discuss the seven stelae from Terraces 6, 15, and 25, as well as a recent stela section discovered on Terrace 12. The discussion begins with the stelae of Terraces 25 and 15 and then turns to those of Terraces 12 and 6. Terrace 6 is particularly important for it is the location of five stelae, two of which are recent discoveries by the Proyecto la Arqueología del Preclásico Temprano en Chalcatzingo (PAPTC) carried out in 1995 and 1998.

David C. Grove

CHALCATZINGO ARCHAEOLOGICAL PROJECT: DISCOVERIES, 1972–1976
One of the PAPTC's most significant discoveries was unearthed on Terrace 25—the only tabletop altar-throne ever found outside the Gulf Coast Olmec region (Monument 22; Grove 1984: 65–68, 1989: 137–139; Fash 1987). The importance and impressiveness of the tabletop altar-throne have completely overshadowed another nearby discovery on the same terrace, a 21-m-long, 6-m-wide stone-faced platform with an in situ stela base (Monument 23; Fash 1987: 92). The upper section of the stela has yet to be found (figure 2.3). The stone-faced platform and the Monument 23 stela are Cantera Phase but stratigraphically post-date the Cantera Phase Monument 22 tabletop altar-throne.

Approximately 60 m southwest of the Terrace 25 platform is a similar Cantera Phase platform on Terrace 15. The latter is ca. 19.5 m in length and poorly preserved (Prindiville and Grove 1987: 65). Importantly, we uncovered a nearly complete stela, Monument 21, shallowly buried immediately in front of that platform. The stela is extremely significant for it depicts a standing woman in right profile (figure 2.4). The gender of this personage is not in doubt because her breast is shown, and she is thus the earliest known unquestionable depiction of a woman in Mesoamerican stone monumental art (see also Monument 32, figure 2.10). She stands facing and touching a large vertical pillar-like object decorated with undulating oval motifs. Similar oval motifs occur on Monuments 22 and 27, and their context in the former may relate that motif and Monument 21's "pillar" to the earth (Grove 1987b: 429–430). It is noteworthy that the woman touches the "pillar" in the same position as the humans in the Postclassic Codex Fejérváry-Mayer touch the world trees. She also stands atop an "earth face" with large incurved fangs (Cyphers Guillén 1984; Angulo V. 1987: 150–151; Grove 1987b: 430, 1989: 136–137, 144, figures 7.5, 7.14, 2000: 281).

The largest stone-faced platform mound and the greatest quantity of monuments in the settlement area at Chalcatzingo occur on Terrace 6 on the east side of the site near the foot of the Cerro Delgado (see figure 2.2). Of course, we did not know that at the time the CAP began, and because our project's emphasis was on excavating Cantera Phase domestic structures and Terrace 6 lacked any surface evidence of such a structure (evidence common on most other terraces; for example, see Prindiville and Grove 1987: 66), no major Terrace 6 excavations were planned. Nevertheless, in 1973 we inspected a large flat stone visible in the plow zone in the north-central section of Terrace 6 and discovered traces of carving on it. Excavations were undertaken and revealed the stone to be a circular "altar" with low relief carving around its circumference; it was registered as Monument 25. Immediately adjacent to the circular altar's west side was the base of a large stela, Monument 26 (figure 2.5). The upper portion of the stela was not discovered, but a few probable engraved lines are visible on the basal section (Grove and Angulo V. 1987: 128–129, figures 9.23, 9.24). Monuments 25 and 26 are particularly significant for while circular altar-stela combinations are com-

2.3. *The Monument 23 stela base, east side, in association with a section of a stone-faced platform (right). The stone's vertical height is 100 cm. Terrace 25. Photo by David C. Grove.*

2.4. Monument 21, a stela, 240 cm in length. The carving depicts a woman touching a vertical pillar-like object. Terrace 15. Photo by David C. Grove.

THE MIDDLE FORMATIVE PERIOD STELAE OF CHALCATZINGO

2.5. *Monuments 25 and 26, a circular altar (right) and stela base (left), as they occur today. The altar is 130 cm in diameter, and the stela base is 100 cm tall. Terrace 6. Photo by David C. Grove.*

mon in southern Mesoamerica at Classic Maya sites and at Late Formative Izapa in Chiapas, the two Chalcatzingo monuments presently represent the earliest known example of that pairing in Mesoamerica (Grove 1984: 62–64, 1987a: 436, 1989: 141). For their protection, the two monuments were moved a few meters away to the north edge of the terrace and placed onto a cement pavement that we built for them. They remain there today.

In 1974 the villager who often farmed on Terrace 6 led the CAP directors to the center of the terrace, showed them a small stone that protruded only a few centimeters above the surface, and pointed out a barely visible carved line on the stone. Excavations were soon begun and revealed that the small stone section exposed on the surface was actually the upper tip of a 2.8-m-tall stela with a bas-relief depiction of a personage in left profile (Monument 27; figure 2.6). The personage appears to be carrying an animal or wearing an animal skin, the hind legs of which hang downward and extend forward. Oval motifs on the animal's skin are similar to the ovals on the Monument 21 pillar and on the upper ledge of the site's tabletop altar-throne (Monument 22; Grove 1987b: figure 27.6). The personage's left arm is bent to hold a thick bundle or "scepter," an object not uncommon in Middle Formative monumental art outside of the Gulf Coast.[2]

Although the Monument 27 stela was broken in half and missing its upper left quarter (the section containing the personage's face), the stela and its base

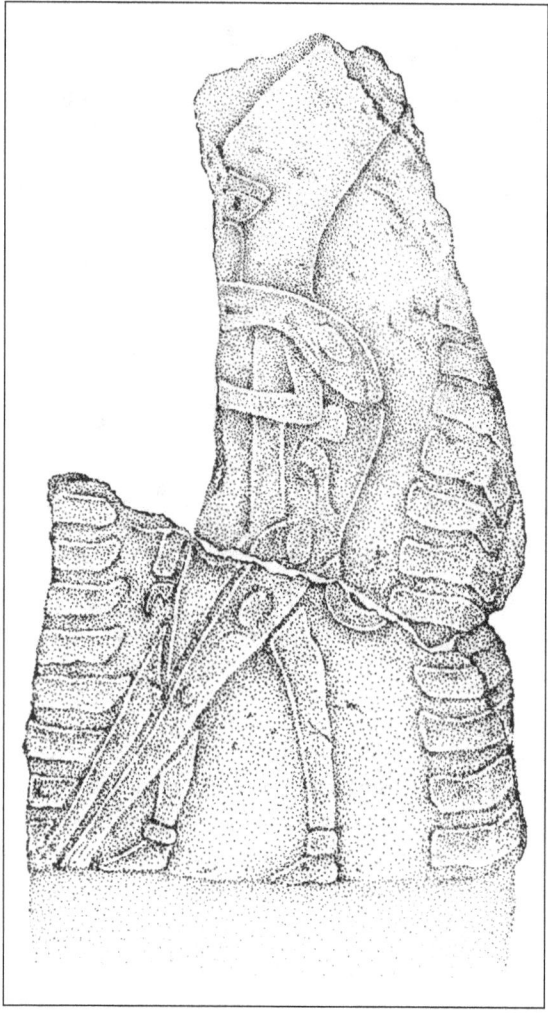

2.6. *Monument 27, a stela, 280 cm in height. The west-facing carving depicts a walking personage. Terrace 6. Drawing by Barbara Fash.*

were still in place and standing in front of Chalcatzingo's third Cantera Phase rectangular stone-faced platform mound (figure 2.7). The platform is 15.7 m in length and rises in two stages, a lower stage 85 cm tall and the 50-cm-tall upper stage. Excavations also revealed an earlier construction stage to the platform (Grove and Cyphers Guillén 1987: 35–36, figure 4.16; Prindiville and Grove 1987: 65, figure 6.4).

Soon after the discovery of Monument 27, the CAP co-director Raúl Arana inspected a large stone exposed by erosion on the western edge of the same terrace. It was another stela, Monument 28, nearly 4 m in length. From its location we infer that Monument 28 had probably once been erected on Terrace 6

THE MIDDLE FORMATIVE PERIOD STELAE OF CHALCATZINGO

2.7. *The 1974 excavation of Structure 1, Terrace 6, a Cantera Phase stone-faced platform with Monument 27 in situ. View is looking north. The wall in the background was built by the project to protect the platform and monument. Photo by David C. Grove.*

(perhaps associated with an early construction stage of the Terrace 6 platform) but had later been removed and buried facedown about 30 m west of the platform. Although the stela's bas-relief carving is highly eroded and difficult to see, it again represents a standing personage in left profile (figure 2.8; Grove 1984: figure 13; see also Angulo V. 1987: figures 10.23, 10.24). The personage appears to hold a bundle or "scepter" in the crook of his left arm and is surrounded by faint background motifs that may represent plumes. After study, the monument was reburied for its protection.

THE 1995 AND 1998 DISCOVERIES

The majority of the data recovered by the CAP's investigations pertain to Chalcatzingo's Cantera Phase, 700–500 BC. However, excavation units on some terraces did encounter earlier Barranca and Amate Phase strata, and one such site area with undisturbed Amate Phase strata is Terrace 6. Because our excavations from 1972 to 1974 had recovered very little information on the Amate Phase, we briefly returned to Chalcatzingo in 1976 and carried out limited stratigraphic excavations on Terrace 6 to obtain additional Amate Phase data. To our surprise, one of the excavation units uncovered a section of a stone-faced Amate

David C. Grove

2.8. *Monument 28, a stela, ca. 400 cm in length. Terrace 6. Drawing by David C. Grove.*

Phase platform (Grove and Cyphers Guillén 1987: 36, figures 4.16, 4.18). Such stone architecture is rare anywhere in Early Formative Period Mesoamerica. Unfortunately, the find was made in the final days of our Terrace 6 research, so we reluctantly covered the new discovery with plastic tarps and reburied it. We would not be able to revisit it for nearly two decades.

In 1995 University of Illinois archaeology doctoral candidate María R. Avilés initiated the PAPTC to investigate the Terrace 6 Amate Phase platform. The Amate Phase research will not be addressed here, but several Cantera Phase discoveries made during that research are discussed later in this chapter.[3] On one of our first mornings of work at the site in 1995, while we were still reestablishing the grid system and uncovering the long-buried Amate Phase platform, we were approached by two young boys who were tending a herd of goats grazing on the hillside. They asked if we would be interested in seeing "a painted rock" (*una piedra pintada*) nearby. Because we knew that a number of boulders in the vicinity of Terrace 6 bear painted red motifs (see Apostolides 1987: 180–183), we were not immediately excited. Nevertheless, we had spare time and went with the boys to see their painted rock. They led us down the hill to the small terrace (Terrace 12) that lies just north of Terrace 6 and brushed the dirt from a large stone lying just below the surface there. The stone was not actually "painted" but rather was lightly carved in bas-relief. They had shown us the upper section of a stela (Monument 32; figure 2.9).

The stela section is 1.92 m in length and broken in three pieces. While its bas-relief is eroded, the primary image is clear. The carving is basically a mirror image of Monument 21 on Terrace 15, that is, a personage (but in left profile) facing and touching a pillar-like object (figure 2.10). No breast is obvious on

2.9. *Monument 32, the upper section of a stela, 192 cm in length. View looking north. Terrace 12. Photo by David C. Grove.*

the eroded image, but the personage wears a long head covering such as also worn by the woman on Monument 21. That style of head covering is probably a gendered clothing trait; if that is the case, then the Monument 32 personage is a woman, too. In addition to the head covering, the Monument 32 woman also wears a tall headdress of a style seen in some Gulf Coast Olmec monuments

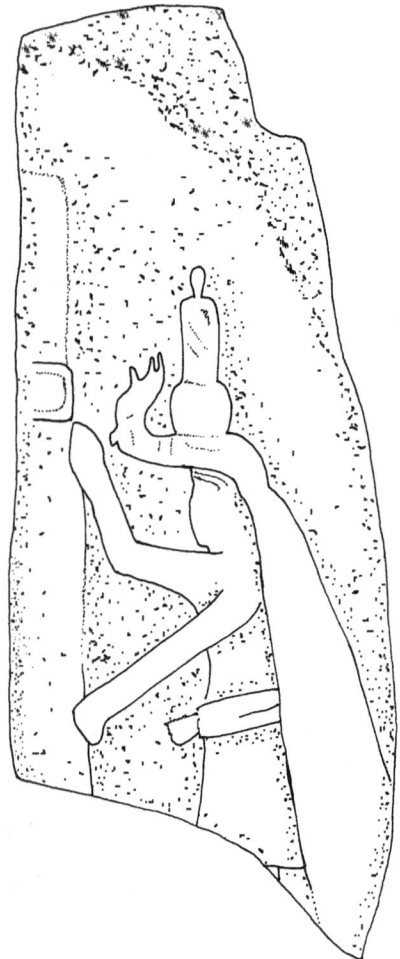

2.10. Carved scene on Monument 32, a person, probably a woman, touching a vertical pillar-like object. Drawing by David C. Grove and Susan Gillespie.

(Grove and Avilés 1997: 157–169).[4] Finally, while Monument 32's heaviness, carving style, and context all suggest to me that it probably predates its Monument 21 counterpart, the comparative age of the two monuments cannot presently be determined. After studying, drawing, and photographing Monument 32, we covered it with plastic and reburied it under a layer of soil for its protection.

Avilés continued her excavations of the Terrace 6 Amate Phase platform in 1998. Of course, to reach Amate Phase levels, over a meter's depth of the overlying Cantera and Barranca Phase strata had to first be excavated and recorded. As the overall excavation area was being expanded eastward in the direction of the terrace's Cantera Phase platform mound, an unusual Cantera Phase feature was unearthed: a long row of large well-faced rectangular stone blocks laid end to end in a horizontal north-south line (figure 2.11). About 7 m of that linear feature were exposed by the excavations. Significantly, the stone alignment occurs at the same elevation as the base of the nearby Cantera Phase stone-faced platform mound and parallels the front face of that structure, indicating that they are related.

To everyone's surprise, as the stones in the alignment were being carefully excavated and cleaned, the upper surface of one of the horizontal stones was found to be carved in bas-relief. That stone turned out to be the upper section of a stela (Monument 33) that measures 1.4 m in length, 56 cm in width, and with a thickness of 35 cm. Although incorporated as one of the linearly arranged faced stones, the upper section of the stela lies beside its still in situ basal section. The upper portion contains nearly the complete bas-relief carving of a personage

THE MIDDLE FORMATIVE PERIOD STELAE OF CHALCATZINGO

2.11. *Stone alignment, Terrace 6, view looking south. The archaeologist in the picture is drawing Monument 33. Photo by David C. Grove.*

in left profile, holding five long plume-like objects (figure 2.12). The personage appears to wear a waist-long cape and a headdress with a "chin strap." Headdress chin straps are also depicted in some Olmec carvings at La Venta. In addition,

2.12. *Monument 33, 140-cm-long stela section next to its in situ base (lower right), at time of their discovery. View is looking north. Terrace 6. Photo by David C. Grove.*

the personage's left wristlet (and perhaps the right wristlet as well) is decorated with a crossed band motif.

Because the basal section of Monument 33 was in situ, we quickly realized that the stela had been erected 4 m in front of the northwest corner of the Cantera Phase platform structure. The decision was therefore made to place an excavation unit at the same distance in front of the platform's southwest corner. That excavation brought to light Monument 34, a 1-m-tall basal section of a large stela (1 m wide, 75 cm thick; figure 2.13). Although the east (platform) side of

2.13. *Monument 34, 100-cm-tall stela base, at time of its discovery. View is of the west side. Terrace 6. Photo by David C. Grove.*

the stela base is heavily damaged, it is clear that the stela had been carved in bas-relief motifs that wrapped around its entire circumference. Large scroll motifs cover the undamaged areas on the front and back of the stela, while a vertical band with a "mat" design occurs on each side (figure 2.13). The area between the two stelae remains unexcavated, so we are uncertain if the stone alignment containing Monument 33 extends to near Monument 34.

It is important to comment that large faced stones such as occur in the alignment mentioned here are a rarity at Chalcatzingo. However, there are two exceptions. The site's tabletop altar-throne (Monument 22) on Terrace 25 was not created from a monolithic block of stone in the manner of Gulf Coast Olmec altar-thrones but instead was constructed from about two dozen large well-faced stones similar in form and size to those of the Terrace 6 alignment (Fash 1987: 82, figure 7.2; Grove 1987b: figure 27.6). Large faced stones were also found in the CAP's excavations on and around Chalcatzingo's impressive 70-m-long Cantera Phase earthen platform mound (Grove 1987c: figures 11.12–11.14; Prindiville and Grove 1987: figure 6.3), but they are much thicker than the Terrace 6 stones. With those examples in mind, it is my opinion that the stones utilized to create the Terrace 6 alignment were not originally created for that

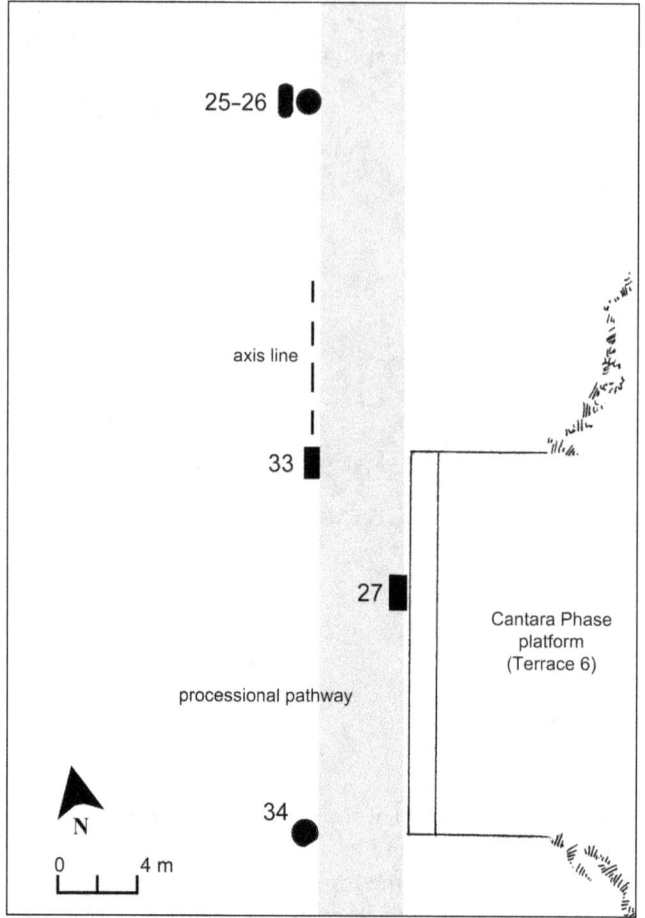

2.14. Layout of Terrace 6 monuments in relation to the platform mound. The shaded area delineates the 4-m-wide "processional pathway." Monument locations indicated by numbers. Drawing by David C. Grove and Rusty van Rossmann.

purpose but instead had probably been components of another constructed feature that at some time had been dismantled, enabling their reuse.

CONCLUSION: EVIDENCE FOR A POSSIBLE PROCESSIONAL ARRANGEMENT OF THE TERRACE 6 MONUMENTS

Monument 27 is erected adjacent to the front face of Terrace 6's Cantara Phase platform, while Monuments 33 and 34 are erected in line with the front corners of the platform but at a distance of ca. 4 m from it. In addition, Monument 33 is associated with a linear arrangement of faced stones that continues the

THE MIDDLE FORMATIVE PERIOD STELAE OF CHALCATZINGO

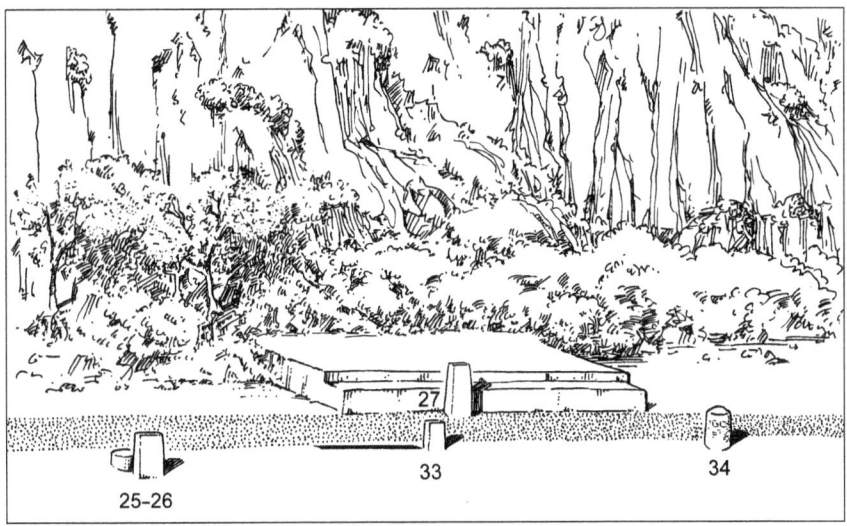

2.15. *Schematic view of Terrace 6 showing monument locations and the platform mound. The shaded area shows the "processional pathway"; north is at left. Drawing by David C. Grove and Rusty van Rossmann.*

Monument 34–33 axis line northward. When that axis is projected another 16 m beyond Monument 33, it reaches to Monuments 25 and 26 (figure 2.14). The four stelae are separated to the extent that the entire group cannot be viewed as a whole but a viewer must walk from one to another. Thus, like the two groups of carvings on the Cerro Chalcatzingo, the Terrace 6 monuments are also laid out in a processional arrangement.[5]

However, they may also have been positioned along a "processional pathway" that ran in front of the platform mound. The evidence for the possible processional pathway lies in the orientation of Monuments 33, 34, and 25–26. Monument 27 stands immediately in front of the platform mound and faces westward toward Monuments 33 and 34 and the site as a whole. However, as Monuments 33 and 34 were being excavated, it was my impression that they had each probably faced eastward, that is, toward the platform mound and Monument 27. That orientation would have made their carved images visible only to people within the 4-m-wide area separating the monuments from the platform mound. Further to the north, the circular altar was positioned on the east side of its companion stela, meaning they faced eastward. Those orientations, if correct, suggest that the 4-m-wide area had been a north-south–oriented "processional pathway" that led viewers past the platform and the associated stelae erected along its extent (figure 2.15).

A second general pattern is also apparent on Terrace 6. It is a pattern that first came to our attention during the CAP's research in the 1970s (Prindiville and Grove 1987: 78), and it is worth reiterating and slightly expanding upon here. The site's Cantera Phase platform mounds were apparently constructed utilizing a measurement module of approximately 3.9 m or its multiples. For example, the Cantera Phase platform of Terrace 15 is 19.5 m long (five modules), and the platform of Terrace 6 is 15.7 m long (four modules). What is new, thanks to the PAPTC's discovery of Monuments 33 and 34, is that those stelae were erected at a distance of 3.9 m (one module) in front of the platform's corners and the recognition that Monuments 25 and 26 seem to have been positioned on Terrace 6 at a distance of four modules north of Monument 33 (figures 2.14, 2.15). We have hopes of carrying out additional excavations on Terrace 6 to further explore the pathway and its associated features.

NOTES

1. The carvings labeled as Monuments 29 and 30 are not Formative Period (Grove and Angulo V. 1987: 130–131).

2. Examples include the carvings at San Miguel Amuco, Guerrero (Grove and Paradis 1971); Xoc, Chiapas (Ekholm 1973); and Chalchuapa, El Salvador's Monument 12 (personages B, C, and D; Anderson 1978: figures 8, 9, 10b).

3. Although circumstances now delegate the responsibility of reporting on Monuments 32, 33, and 34 to me, Avilés very ably directed the 1995 and 1998 excavations and deserves complete credit for the discoveries made during that research. The research was carried out under permits from the Consejo de Arqueología, INAH, Mexico, issued to me, and was made possible by grants to Avilés from the National Science Foundation (G2555 and 9628804), the Wenner-Gren Foundation (Gr. 6346), and the Foundation for the Advancement of Mesoamerican Studies; we are grateful to them for their support. Interpretations presented in this chapter are mine, as is the responsibility for any errors or inaccuracies that might be present.

4. Because the extreme top section of Monument 21 on Terrace 15 is missing, it cannot be ascertained if the woman shown in that carving had worn any additional ornamentation atop her head.

5. Processional arrangements can also be seen in the placement of certain monument categories at La Venta and San Lorenzo (Grove 1999).

REFERENCES CITED

Anderson, Dana
    1978   Monuments. In *The Prehistory of Chalchuapa, El Salvador*, vol. 1, ed. Robert J. Sharer, pp. 155–180. University of Pennsylvania Press, Philadelphia.

Angulo V., Jorge
    1987   The Chalcatzingo Reliefs: An Iconographic Analysis. In *Ancient Chalcatzingo*, ed. David C. Grove, pp. 132–158. University of Texas Press, Austin.

Apostolides, Alex
    1987   Chalcatzingo Painted Art. In *Ancient Chalcatzingo*, ed. David C. Grove, pp. 171–199. University of Texas Press, Austin.

Arana, Raúl Martín
    1987   Classic and Postclassic Chalcatzingo. In *Ancient Chalcatzingo*, ed. David C. Grove, pp. 387–399. University of Texas Press, Austin.

Cook de Leonard, Carmen
    1967   Sculptures and Rock Carvings at Chalcatzingo, Morelos. *Contributions of the University of California Archaeological Research Facility* 3: 57–84. Berkeley.

Covarrubias, Miguel
    1946   El arte "Olmeca" o de La Venta. *Cuadernos Americanos* 5: 153–179. México, D.F.

Cyphers Guillén, Ann
    1984   The Possible Role of a Woman in Formative Exchange. In *Trade and Exchange in Early Mesoamerica*, ed. Kenneth G. Hirth, pp. 115–123. University of New Mexico Press, Albuquerque.

Ekholm, Susanna M.
    1973   *The Olmec Rock Carving at Xoc, Chiapas*. Papers of the New World Archaeological Foundation 32. Brigham Young University, Provo, UT.

Fash, William L., Jr.
    1987   The Altar and Associated Features. In *Ancient Chalcatzingo*, ed. David C. Grove, pp. 82–94. University of Texas Press, Austin.

Gay, Carlo T.E.
    1972   *Chalcacingo*. International Scholarly Book Service, Portland, OR.

Grove, David C.
    1968   Chalcatzingo, Morelos, Mexico: A Re-appraisal of the Olmec Rock Carvings. *American Antiquity* 33: 468–491.
    1981   Olmec Monuments: Mutilation as a Clue to Meaning. In *The Olmec and Their Neighbors*, ed. Elizabeth P. Benson, pp. 49–68. Dumbarton Oaks, Washington, DC.
    1984   *Chalcatzingo: Excavations on the Olmec Frontier*. Thames and Hudson, London.
    1987a   Chalcatzingo in a Broader Perspective. In *Ancient Chalcatzingo*, ed. David C. Grove, pp. 434–442. University of Texas Press, Austin.
    1987b   Comments on the Site and Its Organization. In *Ancient Chalcatzingo*, ed. David C. Grove, pp. 420–433. University of Texas Press, Austin.
    1987c   Miscellaneous Bedrock and Boulder Carvings. In *Ancient Chalcatzingo*, ed. David C. Grove, pp. 159–170. University of Texas Press, Austin.
    1989   Chalcatzingo and Its Olmec Connection. In *Regional Perspectives on the Olmec*, ed. Robert J. Sharer and David C. Grove, pp. 122–147. Cambridge University Press, Cambridge, MA.
    1999   Public Monuments and Sacred Mountains: Observations on Three Formative Period Sacred Landscapes. In *Social Patterns in Preclassic Mesoamerica*, ed. David C. Grove and Rosemary Joyce, pp. 255–299. Dumbarton Oaks, Washington, DC.
    2000   Faces of the Earth at Chalcatzingo: Serpents, Caves, and Mountains in Middle Formative Period Iconography. In *Olmec Art and Archaeology in Mesoamerica*, ed.

John Clark and Mary Pye, pp. 277–295. Center for Advanced Study, National Gallery of Art, Washington, DC.

Grove, David C., ed.
1987   *Ancient Chalcatzingo*. University of Texas Press, Austin.

Grove, David C., and Jorge Angulo V.
1987   A Catalog and Description of Chalcatzingo's Monuments. In *Ancient Chalcatzingo*, ed. David C. Grove, pp. 114–131. University of Texas Press, Austin.

Grove, David C., and María R. Avilés
1997   Informe Provisional del Proyecto La Arqueología del Preclásico Temprano en Chalcatzingo, Morelos, 1995. Manuscript on file, INAH, México, D.F.

Grove, David C., and Ann Cyphers Guillén
1987   The Excavations. In *Ancient Chalcatzingo*, ed. David C. Grove, pp. 21–55. University of Texas Press, Austin.

Grove, David C., and Louise I. Paradis
1971   An Olmec Stela from San Miguel Amuco, Guerrero. *American Antiquity* 36: 95–102.

Guzmán, Eulalia
1934   Los relieves de las rocas del Cerro de la Cantera, Jonacatepec, Morelos. *Anales del Museo Nacional de Arqueología, Historia, y Etnografía*, Epoca 5, 1 (2): 237–251. México, D.F.

Piña Chan, Roman
1955   *Chalcatzingo, Morelos*. Informes 4, INAH, México, D.F.

Prindiville, Mary, and David C. Grove
1987   The Settlement and Its Architecture. In *Ancient Chalcatzingo*, ed. David C. Grove, pp. 63–81. University of Texas Press, Austin.

3

ISLA ALOR: OLMEC TO CONTACT IN THE LA VENTA HINTERLAND

Matthew A. Boxt, L. Mark Raab, and Rebecca B. González Lauck

For the past half-century, the Olmec have taken center stage in Mexican Gulf Coast archaeology, overshadowing other groups and time periods. The great Olmec site of La Venta may have emerged by 1200 BC, focusing archaeological attention on both the Gulf Coast and the birth of Mesoamerican civilization (figure 3.1). Significantly, however, the Gulf Coast, including the region around La Venta, also hosted large, culturally complex native societies at the other end of the pre-European time scale. By all historical accounts, these Postclassic populations were linked by trade, tribute, and political alliances to most other Mesoamerican regions. While Olmec research remains a topic of central importance, much remains to be learned about the course of cultural development on the southern Gulf Coast during post-Olmec times.

Understanding prehistoric cultural development in the La Venta region has long been a formidable challenge. Much of the region is low-lying, swampy terrain that, until recently, was inaccessible. The region's hot, humid climate is hostile to the preservation of organic materials. Large archaeological centers, such as the site of La Venta, were the scene of massive construction projects during antiquity, frequently disturbing earlier archaeological deposits. As a result, it has been difficult to identify intact cultural strata spanning long periods of time. Even more scarce is information about outlying farming communities, whose labor and agricultural productivity were key variables to sustaining the

Matthew A. Boxt, L. Mark Raab, and Rebecca B. González Lauck

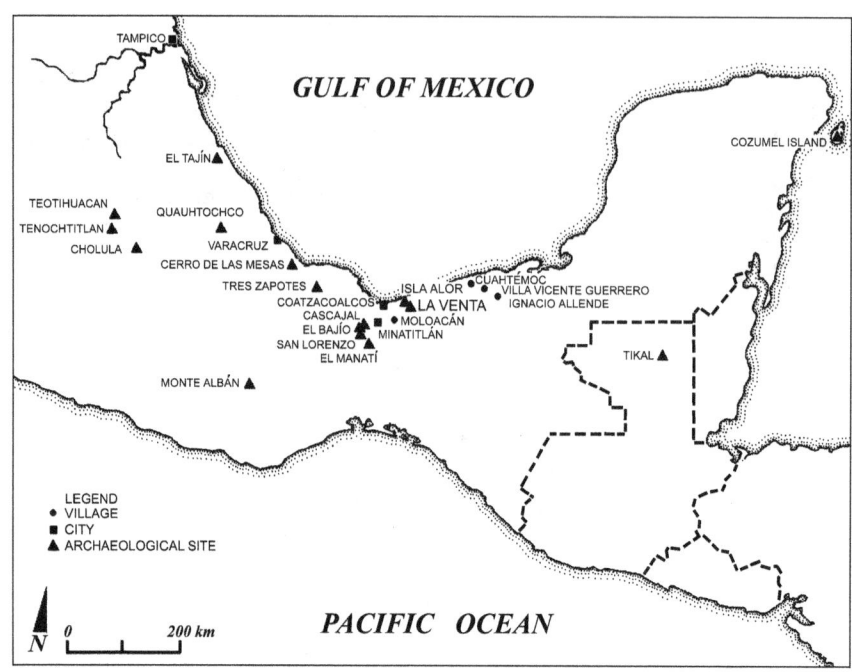

3.1. Locations of archaeological sites, cities, and villages mentioned in the text. Map by Rusty van Rossmann.

development and growth of large ceremonial and population centers, such as La Venta.

Recent investigations suggest that these information gaps can be closed. Archaeological research at Isla Alor, located in the hinterland of La Venta, has revealed a multi-component site with cultural strata spanning at least three millennia. The site's earliest cultural manifestation, dating to around 1000 BC, contains evidence of Olmec occupation, while the most recent strata reveal a Postclassic settlement contemporaneous with Spanish contact. Despite the region's rich ethnohistorical record, which captures some of the initial contacts between Europeans and Mesoamericans, excavated archaeological sites with such great time depth are rare in the archaeological literature.

RESEARCH BACKGROUND

The archaeological site of Isla Alor is located in the municipality of Huimanguillo, Tabasco, Mexico, a short distance to the east of the lower reaches of the Tonalá River at the western margin of the larger Mezcalapa River delta system (figure 3.2). The site lies approximately 3.3 km northwest of the famous Olmec

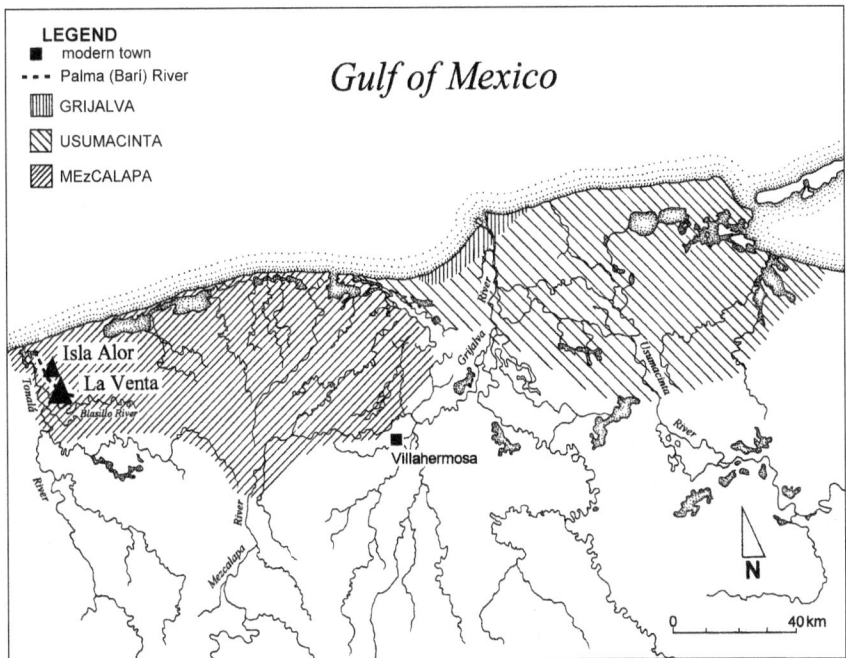

3.2. *Isla Alor and the three major deltaic systems of Tabasco and western Campeche. Redrawn by Rusty van Rossmann from West, Psuty, and Thom 1969: 38.*

city of La Venta. Roughly 400 m by 150 m, Isla Alor occupies a natural levee of the Palma River (also called the Barí in recent archaeological reports). The site's cultural deposits are buried within the sediments of this levee. Deposited by over-bank flooding episodes spanning at least 3,000 years, this levee rises to about 3 m above the seasonally inundated marshlands around it, creating an "isla" (island) that has attracted human settlement for millennia—most recently its current tenant, the Alor González family.[1] Isla Alor is but one location of many dispersed across the low-lying coastal floodplain of the Tonalá River, extending for many kilometers around La Venta. Isla Alor is not marked by mounds or other recognizable Prehispanic architectural constructions but rather contains well-preserved, stratified evidence of domestic activities, including the remains of houses, floors, post molds, storage pits, hearths, and deposits of ceramics and other cultural materials. Features of this kind were found in Olmec and Postclassic strata, hinting at a long sequence of human occupation.

In 1986 and 1987 the Instituto Nacional de Antropología e Historia (INAH)–sponsored Proyecto Arqueológico La Venta (PALV), under the direction of Rebecca B. González Lauck, reconnoitered the La Venta hinterlands, locating dozens of hitherto unknown sites and test excavating a selection of them (Rust and Sharer 1988). Some of these sites, such as Isla Alor, were located on the levee of the ancient Palma River, first reported by Matthew Stirling (1943b: 50). Stirling speculated that this once-active tributary had potential as a means of transport for the enormous boulders destined for sculpture at La Venta:

> The most probable hypothesis would seem to be that the stones were secured near the seacoast, and placed on large rafts, whence they were floated along the coast to the mouth of the Tonalá River, which was then ascended to La Venta Island. At the present time, the river is a considerable distance from the island, but aerial photographs show clearly an old channel which touched the north end of the island. It is quite probable that this marked the course of the river at the time the site was occupied. (1943b: 50)

Until recently, it seemed almost incomprehensible that the Tabascan lowlands could have supported the flourishing native civilizations they did. Tabasco receives one of the heaviest annual rainfalls in all of Mexico and is subject to regular catastrophic flooding; it is characterized by numerous active and inactive tributaries, extensive quagmires, and lakes. Nevertheless, from about 1200 BC to 400 BC, this seemingly hostile and waterlogged deltaic plain supported one of the earliest complex societies in the New World, which has come to be called "Olmec" (Drucker 1947: 1). The perception that Tabasco "declined to a disease-ridden, isolated cultural backwater during the Spanish colonial and early independence period" (West, Psuty, and Thom 1969: 1) may have colored our thinking about the preceding Postclassic Period.

The relationship between prehistoric settlement and landscape dynamics is now considered key to understanding the core-periphery relationship between La Venta and its satellite communities. Tabasco's environmental mosaic of flora, fauna, varied soil types, and myriad hydrographic features afforded nutrient-rich soils for complex agricultural systems, high biomass values for edible plant and animal species, and easy movement of people, food, manufactured products, raw materials, and information through its intricate network of navigable inland and coastal waters. Michael D. Coe (1965: 679) recognized the region's research potential: "This . . . is certainly one of the richest archaeological zones of the world, probably having the highest density of Precolumbian sites per square kilometer in Mesoamerica." Scores of Late Classic and Postclassic Period sites in this and neighboring regions confirm Coe's assertion (Berlin 1953, 1956; Drucker and Contreras 1953; Stirling 1957; García Payón 1971; Sanders 1971; Daneels 1997; Symonds and Lunagómez 1997). Unfortunately, the environmental-cultural relationships of the Classic and Postclassic Periods remain unclear. Most scholarship, past and present, at Olmec La Venta has relegated recent prehistoric cultural manifestations to an undeserved obscurity. Our own research, if nothing else, has revealed that all roads need not, and in all likelihood did not, lead to La Venta, particularly during the Postclassic epoch.

By the sixteenth century AD, La Venta had lost the position of political preeminence it had acquired long before in the Formative. Robert Squier (1957) and Drucker, Heizer, and Squier (1959: 237–246) document a post-Olmec occupation at La Venta, indicating that this ancient city was never completely abandoned—a pattern observable at other Mesoamerican metropoli. Evidence from Tikal (Adams and Trik 1961), Monte Albán (Caso 1969), Teotihuacan (Cabrera Castro 1988: 68), and other Postclassic communities indicates reuse by people who were "obviously ignorant of the old cults" (Thompson 1970: 51). In the case of La Venta, distinctive polychrome sherds were recovered from excavations at the Cerro del Encanto mound group and the Torres site (Drucker, Heizer, and Squier 1959: 237–246). *Olmequistas* noted parallels between La Venta polychromes and the Mixteca-Puebla Codex–style pottery that was highly prized and widely exchanged during the Late Postclassic. Drucker, Heizer, and Squier (1959: 241–242) observed that La Venta polychromes were similar to Complicated Polychrome wares from the Upper 1 horizon of Cerro de las Mesas (Drucker 1943b: 45–56) and that Cerro del Encanto sherds resembled Upper Tres Zapotes Polychrome wares (Drucker 1943a: 36–47).

Notwithstanding sixty years of archaeological inquiry and the identification of distinctive temporal indicators, such as Fine Orange, Fine Gray, Aztec, and Mixteca-Puebla–style pottery, the Postclassic era in western Tabasco remains poorly defined (Brainerd 1941; Drucker 1943a, 1943b, 1952; Weiant 1943: figure 53; Berlin 1953, 1956; Drucker, Heizer, and Squier 1959; Piña Chan and Navarrete 1967; Sisson 1976; von Nagy 2003). In general, scholarly knowledge of the full range of lifeways on every level of the Postclassic social hierarchy, including patterns of settlement, subsistence, and exchange, has remained virtually unchanged for decades.

REGIONAL ETHNOHISTORY

If western Tabasco is archaeologically terra incognita during the Postclassic Period, a rich ethnohistory nevertheless exists for it. Primary accounts by Bernal Díaz del Castillo, Hernán Cortés, and Bernardino de Sahagún of the first contacts between Europeans and Mesoamerican peoples are striking. Later, Colonial Period writers such as William Dampier (Masefield 1906), Manuel Gil y Sáenz (1979), Antonio de Remesal (1932), José Antonio de Villa-Señor y Sánchez (1952), and Francisco Ximénez (1929: 318–327) add descriptions of Indian cultural practices and the locations of many native communities and place names (figure 3.3). Modern syntheses, including Ralph Roys (1972), France Scholes and Roys (1968), and J. Eric Thompson (1970), describe the initial collision of Spanish and Indian civilizations.

Western Tabasco was among the first territories reconnoitered by Spanish expeditionary forces. As early as 1518, Juan de Grijalva and his men sojourned

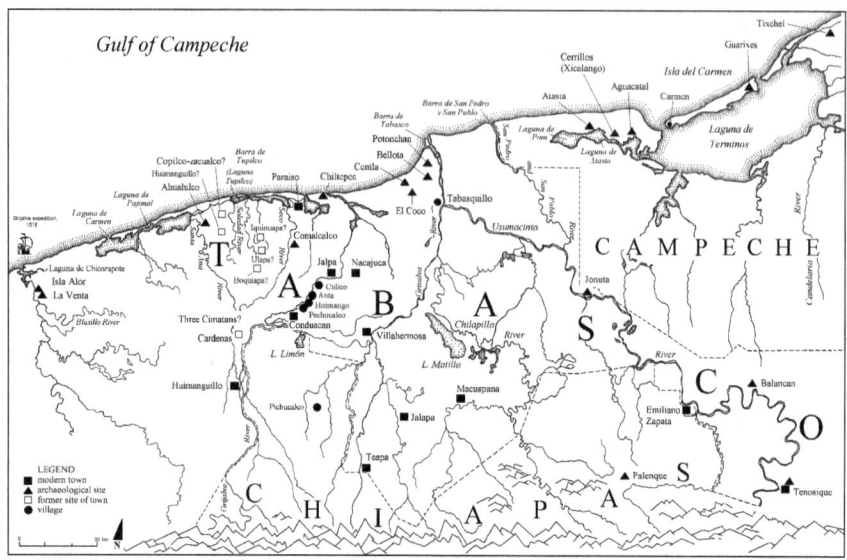

3.3. *The Province of Tabasco. Redrawn by Rusty van Rossmann from Roys 1972: map 2.*

for three days near the mouth of the Tonalá River, no more than 12 to 15 km from Isla Alor and La Venta. This expedition resulted in one of the first and most detailed descriptions of the study area. No less an expert eyewitness than Díaz del Castillo, who participated in that event, provides an account of the 1518 Grijalva penetration of the La Venta area:

> So we turned round and set sail before the wind and in a few days, with the help of the currents, reached the mouth of the great Río de Coatzacoalcos. But we could not enter it on account of unfavorable weather. So, hugging the shore, we entered the Río de Tonalá, which we had named San Antonio. There we careened one of the ships, which was making water fast, for as we came in it had struck the bar, where the sea was shallow.
>
> While we were repairing the ship many Indians came quite peaceably from the town of Tonalá, which is about three miles away, bringing us maize-cakes, fish and fruit, which they gave us freely. The Captain treated them most kindly and ordered that they should be given green beads and "diamonds." He asked them by signs to bring gold for barter and we offered them goods in exchange. So they brought jewels of inferior gold, which they exchanged for beads. Some Indians came also from Coatzacoalcos and other neighboring towns bringing their jewelry, but this was of no value.
>
> Besides these objects for barter, most of the Indians were in the habit of carrying brightly polished copper axes with painted wooden handles, apparently for show, or as a sign of rank; and we began to barter for these in the belief that they were made of low-quality gold. In three days we had collected more than six hundred of them, and were very well pleased. But the Indians

were even more pleased with the beads. There was no profit for either party, however, since the axes were made of copper and the beads were of no value. One soldier bought seven and was quite delighted with them.

I remember that a soldier named Bartólome Pardo went to one of their temples, which stood on a hill—I have already said that these were called *cues*, which means Houses of the Gods. Here he found many idols and some copal, which is a kind of resin that they burn as incense; also some flint knives used for sacrifices and circumcision, and in a wooden chest he discovered a number of gold objects such as diadems and necklaces, and two idols and some hollow beads . . . As there were so many mosquitoes near the river, ten of us soldiers slept in a temple on a hill.

We left the Indians of that province very happy when we re-embarked for Cuba. (Díaz del Castillo 1963: 41–42)

This passage, parenthetically, played a significant role in the discovery of La Venta. The mention of temples, along with previously published references to stone sculptures in the area, led Frans Blom and Oliver La Farge (1926: 79–90) to La Venta, one of the most important discoveries in the annals of American archaeology. Although modern archaeologists have generally turned to on-the-ground surveys as a vehicle of discovery, this case illustrates an early instance of the "direct historical approach."

Cortés (MacNutt 1908: 2: 159–160) and Bernal Díaz del Castillo (1963: 267–268) recount two additional expeditions to the region. In 1520 Cortés sent Diego de Ordáz to the Gulf Coast province of Coatzacoalcos, looking for a port more favorable than anchorage off the coast at Veracruz (Blom and La Farge 1926: 68). Diego de Ordáz (MacNutt 1908: 2: 159–160) passed through thickly populated towns, reporting cordial reception by Indians in a region well-suited for Spanish settlement, lying 30 km to the west of Isla Alor. This report may have influenced a decision by Cortés in 1524 to return to the same area, avoiding the types of problems he experienced in 1519 with Maya groups to the east. After encountering Chontal Maya resistance at Potonchan, Cortés and his forces were driven southwest when, on March 25, 1519, they engaged hostile natives in combat on the fields of Centla—the first engagement on the American continent in which horses and superior metal weapons inflicted a crushing defeat on enemy forces (Brinton 1896; Scholes and Roys 1968: 90). In the aftermath of hostilities and in the spirit of reconciliation, Indian elites swore obedience to the Spanish king; at that time, various Indians converted to Catholicism, and Cortés obtained the Indian woman, Doña Marina, who figured prominently in the historical events that followed (Scholes and Roys 1968: 90). From Centla, Cortés went on to the "Veracruz district, where he eventually dismantled his ships and initiated the remarkable series of campaigns which culminated two years later in the destruction of the Aztec power" (Scholes and Roys 1968: 91).

Unlike their initial contacts with the Maya, who had effectively rebuffed the European intruders, the Spaniards found it comparatively easy to enter the region around the mouth of the Tonalá River and La Venta. Contacts with native groups in this area in 1524 are described in Cortés's fifth letter to Charles V:

> My road being far inland . . . I set out and marched along the coast until I reached a province called Copilco, some thirty-five leagues distant from Espíritu Santo; besides several large swamps and streams, over all of which temporary bridges were built, I had to cross, on this journey, three very large rivers, one near a village, called Tumalo, some nine leagues from the town of Espíritu Santo, the other at Agualulco, nine leagues further on. (MacNutt 1908: 2: 234–235)

Around forty years later, Bernal Díaz del Castillo (1963: 41–42), recounting the same event, substituted the designation of *Guacasualco* for Espíritu Santo (modern-day Coatzacoalcos) and *Tonalá* for Tumalo. Despite possible confusion arising from differing place names, there is no doubt that both Cortés and Díaz del Castillo visited the region of La Venta. This pattern of contact was to have fateful consequences. If Hispaniola was the main staging area for the conquest of New Spain, then Tabasco became the beachhead for a campaign against the Aztec capital at Tenochtitlan.

These early contact reports indicate an important and distinctive native cultural province, one of the most prolific food-growing areas of Mesoamerica—producing tomatoes, chili peppers, sweet potatoes, squashes, corn, and many other products. Tree crops such as mamey, avocado, guava, red zapote, and sapodilla were also important (Roys 1972: 104–105). Turkeys and dogs were raised for food, but terrestrial game animals included peccaries, deer, rabbits, armadillos, coatimundis, iguanas, wild turkeys, and curassows. Aquatic resources included turtles, manatees, fish, ducks, crabs, freshwater shrimps, amphibians, and shellfish.

At the time of early European contact, western Tabasco appears to have flourished between an Aztec sphere of influence to the west and the Maya area to the east. As such, western Tabasco was something of a "no-man's land" situated between the Aztec and Maya frontiers, serving as a buffer between these two cultural-political entities. This zone was clearly engaged in an energetic flow of foods and exotic products between these cultural provinces. Products from this region were part of a vigorous export trade and were offered as tribute to the Aztec (Barlow 1949; Dillon 1975). Prized crops, raw materials, and commodities such as salt, plumage, greenstone, feline pelts, large red seashells, turquoise mosaic shields, dyes, medicinal plants, cakes of liquidambar, cacao beans, vanilla, tobacco, and rubber balls were traded out of the Gulf Coast in exchange for necessities, such as ground and chipped stone materials, or prestigious items, like "the precious capes, precious skirts, precious shifts, the property of Auitzotzin" (Sahagún 1959: 18). Sahagún's (1961: 187–188) informants characterized this territory as a land of riches, a land of flowers, a land of wealth, a land of abundance. There was all manner of food; there grew the cacao bean, and the "divine ear" spice, and wild cacao, and liquid rubber. There the magnolia and all different kinds of flowers grew. And there were the beautiful feathers, the precious feathers, [the feathers of] the troupial, the red spoon-bill, the blue cotinga, the white-fronted parrot, the Mexican parrotlets; the resplendent trogonorus was also there. Also green stones, fine turquoise were found there . . . It was a good, a beautiful place.

Tabasco was also along the route taken by those making their way to the shrines at Cholula or Cozumel Island, two of ancient Mesoamerica's great pilgrimage destinations.

Isla Alor is about 100 km west of the Conquest period "Province of Tabasco," which extended roughly from what is now Laguna Tupilco (east of Laguna Carmen) to Tenosique on the Usumacinta River, lying between the Gulf of Mexico and the base of the Chiapas mountain range (Roys 1972: 98). The Province of Tabasco figured prominently in the writings of Díaz del Castillo (1963) and Cortés (MacNutt 1908), whose accounts contain facts of interest concerning the nature of the land and the native people during the initial stages of conquest.

Early historic records reveal a complex but poorly understood mosaic of polities and linguistic communities on the central and eastern Gulf Coast. From Coatzacoalcos on the west eastward to Campeche, this region's Protohistoric cultural patterns remain largely out of focus (Ochoa 1992, 1999; Izquierdo 1997). The Province of Tabasco was inhabited principally by Maya speakers, particularly in its eastern portion. Yet communities of Mixe, Popoluca, and Nahuatl speakers were also present. According to Roys (1972: 57), the Aztecs referred to this general territory as the Province of Anahuac Xicalango, which included the Nahuatl-speaking commercial centers of Xicalango, Cimatan, and Coatzacoalcos. Cortés identified the territory as the Province of Copilco, for the town of Copilco-zacualco (MacNutt 1908: 2: 235; López de Gómora 1964: 346). Sahagún (1961: 187–188) referred to the inhabitants of this region as the Olmeca ("the rubber people"), Uixtoti ("the saltwater people"), and Mixteca—terms that aptly characterized the ancient inhabitants of southern Veracruz and western Tabasco (Scholes and Warren 1965: 776).

Scholes and Roys (1968: 95) maintain that "little is known about the ethnography of western Tabasco at the time of the Spanish conquest or even in colonial times." Seventeenth- and eighteenth-century writers identify Nahuatl- and Popoluca-speaking settlements in the territory that extended from the Coatzacoalcos River to Ahualulco (Gil y Sáenz 1979: 59; Villa-Señor y Sánchez 1952: 366–369). Apparently, Nahuatl was spoken at La Venta until fairly recently. Shortly after his fifth research expedition to La Venta, Stirling (1943a: 321) cited "Don Sebastian Torres, 86-year-old patriarch of a small clan speaking Aztec among themselves and Spanish to us." However, Blom and La Farge (1926: 86–87) concluded that Nahuatl speakers at La Venta were recent immigrants.

The relationship of the "Historic Olmec" area to the Aztec Empire remains unclear. To the northwest lay the Province of Tochtepec, which occupied the coast of Veracruz from the Alvarado River to Tuxtlas and Coatzacualco (Carrasco 1999: 339). According to Pedro Carrasco (ibid.: 350), "Coatzacualco . . . was on the communication route from Tochtepec towards Xicallanco and Xoconochco. In the reign of Ahuitzotl, Coatzacualco was one of the towns, such as Xicallanco and Cimatlan, that traded with Tenochtitlan." According to Scholes and Roys (1968: 91), "Montezuma explained that his dominion did not extend as far as the Coatzacoalcos River, but he kept garrisons of warriors on his frontier, who would give assistance, if needed."

By all ethnohistoric accounts, then, the region of La Venta and Isla Alor was vibrant at the time of Spanish contact (Garibay K. 1961; Scholes and Warren 1965; Scholes and Roys 1968; Thompson 1970; Lee 1978; Carrasco 1999). This throws the lack of archaeological research on this time period into sharp relief. Given the very high Postcontact native mortality resulting from European-introduced diseases, along with the concomitant rapid disintegration of native communities, archaeology may offer our only chance to understand the final Preconquest centuries within this remarkable region and the contributions its inhabitants made to Mesoamerican civilization.

ARCHAEOLOGY AT ISLA ALOR

The archaeological site encompasses approximately 60,000 m^2 or < 0.06 km^2; its boundaries conform to the isla itself. Results of excavation sampling have been used to calculate the total volume of the cultural deposit at Isla Alor. We estimate the depth of the cultural deposit at 1.8 m. The overall site volume, therefore, we estimate to be about 108,000 m^3. To date, the combined efforts of the Rust and Raab and Boxt excavation teams have sampled < 1 percent of the archaeological site. Isla Alor may represent a cluster of small houses along the edge of a once active river channel. We know that during the Formative, the occupants of Isla Alor shared cultural traditions with their contemporaries at La Venta. In the succeeding Postclassic Period, Isla Alor remains a hamlet-like cluster of houses that may have been related to post-Olmec inhabitants of La Venta. The picture of Isla Alor is that of a rural farming community throughout its entire sequence of occupation.

Work at the archaeological site of Isla Alor has focused on domestic contexts spanning roughly 3,000 years. Excavated data comprise vegetal and animal dietary elements; architectural elements indicating houses of thatch, wattle, and daub; and industrial materials such as *chapopote* or asphaltum, ceramics, and stone tools, including obsidian blades (Raab et al. 2000). Settlement at Isla Alor

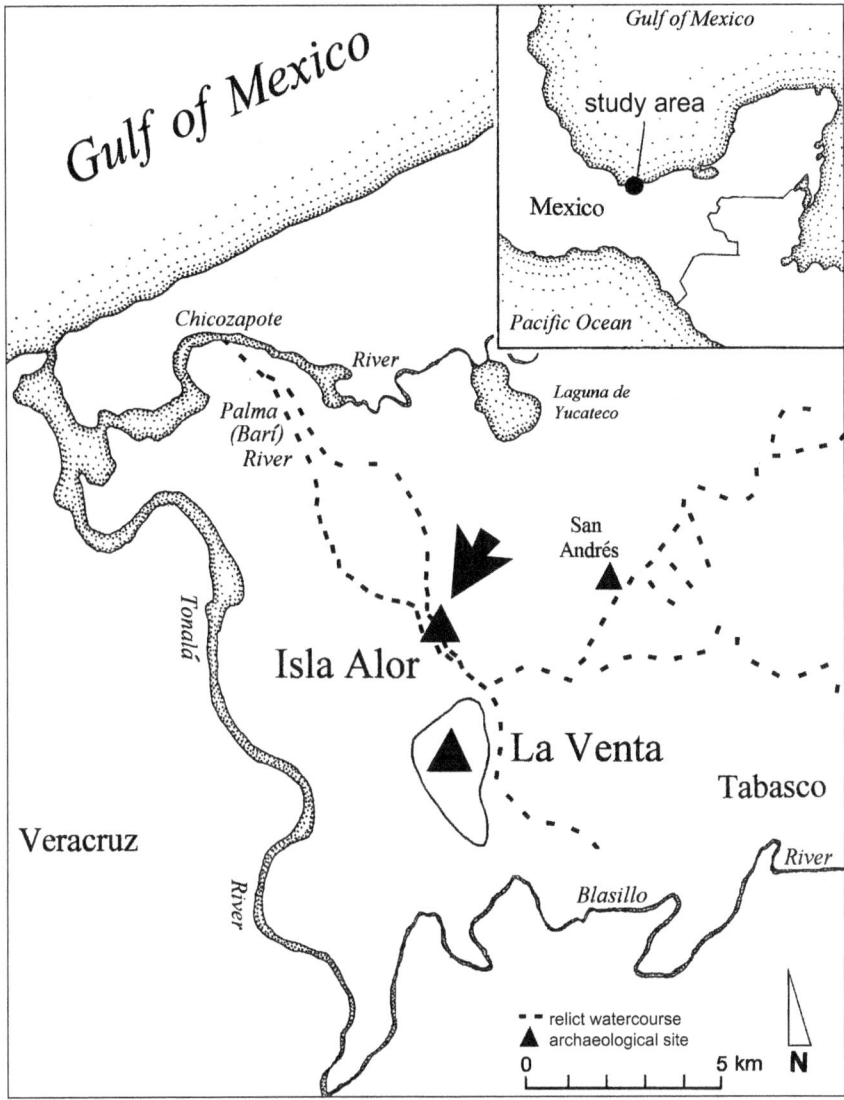

3.4. Map of the archaeological study area, by Rusty van Rossmann.

coincided with the rise of Formative La Venta around 1000 BC and the much later Postclassic Period. Isla Alor offers a relatively rare glimpse into the organization of domestic life during both time periods (figure 3.4).

In 1987, three test excavation units at Isla Alor confirmed the presence of primary cultural deposits interstratified with river levee sediments (Rust 1988: 17–24). Preliminary observations indicated a multi-component site containing

Early (1400 to 1150 BC) to Middle Formative (1150–500 BC), Late or Terminal Classic (AD 600–900), and Late Postclassic (AD 1250–1520) pottery (Rust 2008). At that time, the principal occupation of the site was thought to have occurred during the Middle Formative period, underlying sparse Classic and Postclassic Period deposits. The Formative artifact assemblage incorporated "high proportions of undecorated coarse pottery vessels, few figurines or ceremonial items, utilitarian obsidian and basalt tools and remains of local, easily accessible marine foods" (Rust and Sharer 1988: 104). The architectural data constituted intact house floors, postholes, and *bajareque* (*barro quemado* [burned clay] or architectural daub). The ancient occupants of Isla Alor and other Barí River sites without mounds were identified as "primary subsistence workers, such as fishers and farmers" (Rust 1992: 126).

In 1993 Boxt and Raab visited Isla Alor at the request of González Lauck, at which time plans were made to conduct further inquiry in the La Venta support area. The objective of our initial season's work at Isla Alor was to develop through excavation a detailed site chronology and to determine as far as possible the potential significance of this site in the development of La Venta. Later, comparative and expanded analyses of Isla Alor and La Venta household activities would facilitate regional studies of settlement patterns and social hierarchy. It was our aim from the start of the Isla Alor project to focus on the structure of Olmec life. However, the discovery of intact Postclassic cultural deposits forced the focus of our research to shift to accommodate these unexpected finds.

THE 1994 AND 1995 FIELD SEASONS

Two contiguous excavation units have thus far been completed at Isla Alor (figure 3.5). Each unit measured 2 m^2, reaching culturally sterile sediments at about 1.8 m below surface. Unit 1 was excavated in 20-cm levels using shovels and trowels, with all sediments passed through 6.2-mm (0.25-inch) mesh. Unit 2 followed the strata observable in the sidewall profile of Unit 1. The total volume of scientifically excavated deposit at Isla Alor is roughly 17 m^3.

Both units revealed well-defined cultural strata, including floor features (figure 3.6a, d, f), a pit (figure 3.6e), hearths (figure 3.6b, h), and postholes (figure 3.6c, g).[2] There are currently four radiocarbon dates available from Isla Alor. The youngest of these dates is from the Postclassic/Contact Period, with a calibrated charcoal date of AD 1570. Three radiocarbon assays are available from the Olmec cultural strata, with dates ranging from 1130 BC to 1034 BC to 970 BC (figure 3.6i, f, h).

Several cultural features were identified in both excavation units. In Stratum 2, the Postclassic component, an occupation surface was identified—including a hearth, a posthole, potsherd scatters, a jadeite bead fragment, a greenstone adze, charred vegetal material (beans, maize, and palm nuts), and faunal remains

3.5. *Map of the Isla Alor archaeological site, showing excavation units (arrow) and other landmarks, by Rusty van Rossmann.*

(turtle carapace, fish bone, and small to medium-sized mammal bone). This same stratum yielded 2 kg of bajareque, remnants perhaps of a burned house. Artifacts indicative of domestic activities were also relatively abundant. These included 148 chapopote pebbles (222 gm), chapopote-painted spindle whorls

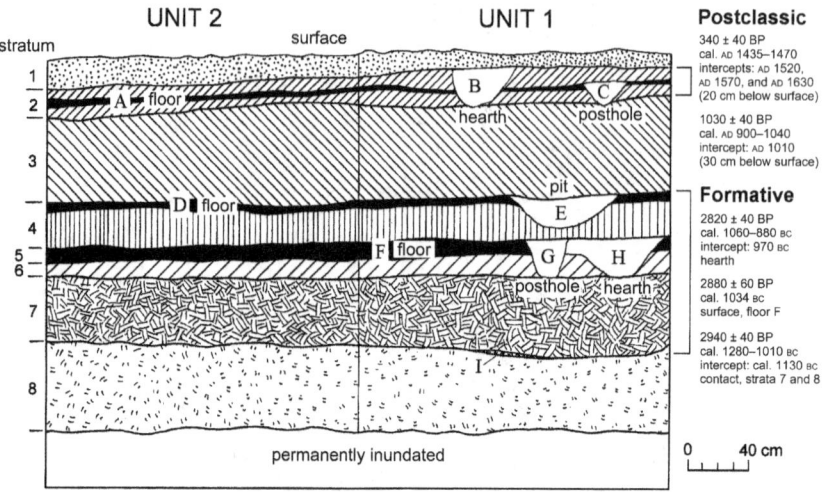

3.6. *The north sidewall profile of excavation Units 1 and 2 at Isla Alor, by Rusty van Rossmann.*

(figure 3.7), green and gray obsidian prismatic blades, ground and chipped stone tools, and 4 kg of potsherds. Among the latter were 1.2 kg of Fine Orange and Fine Gray pottery (figure 3.8), markers of the Postclassic Period.

An Olmec deposit (Strata 4–7) was identified between 90 and 125 cm below surface in both excavation units. A well-defined occupation surface consisting of a yellowish-colored prepared sand and clay floor, similar to the color-washed water-sorted floors noted at La Venta (Drucker, Heizer, and Squier 1959: 44–45), was encountered 95 cm below surface. This level was marked not only by abundant lithic artifacts and pottery fragments but also by the charred remnants of what appears to be a domestic structure constructed of thatch, mud daub, and palm wood. This structure appears to have burned, producing large amounts of carbonized wood, vegetal material, and 2.8 kg of bajareque. Strata 4–7 produced 1.3 kg of chapopote, demonstrating the importance of this material in household contexts across many millennia (figure 3.8). A flotation sample hearth associated with this cultural component produced carbonized vegetal and faunal remains. A total of 9.6 kg of ceramic material was recovered from the Olmec component of Units 1 and 2, including diverse vessel forms, spindle whorls, notched potsherds, potsherd disks, and the lower leg and foot fragment of a hollow-body figurine. Stone artifacts included obsidian blades, ground stone tools, and greenstone jewelry. Three radiocarbon dates, including samples of charred palm wood, bracket this occupation at close to 1000 BC.

Domestic settings of this kind created environments that were both conducive and hostile to the preservation of artifacts, such as ceramics. An example of the former was the recovery of a sample of exceptionally well-preserved pot-

3.7. *Postclassic spindle whorl with chapopote design. Photo by L. Mark Raab.*

sherds from a small pit feature associated with the domestic structure described earlier (Raab et al. 2000: 260–262). Potsherds were deposited in a pit soon after they were discarded, preserving their surface treatment in a way that stands in sharp contrast to potsherds deposited on the surface of the site. Deposits of the latter type were subject to trampling, mixing with other refuse, and degradation resulting from long exposure to the elements. It appears that many of the potsherds recovered from archaeological contexts in and around La Venta in past decades are of this type.

Cultural materials found between 20 cm and 45 cm below surface within our Isla Alor excavations are unambiguously of Postclassic age on both chronometric and stylistic grounds. Cultural materials between 90 and 125 cm date to the Olmec or Formative Period. Stratigraphic deposits between the Postclassic and Olmec occupations were by no means devoid of archaeological evidence. For the sake of brevity, however, we have excluded these segments of the cultural sequence at Isla Alor (described elsewhere, González Lauck et al. 1995; Raab, Boxt, and Bradford 1997) from the present discussion.

CERAMICS

A neutron activation analysis (NAA) of clay sources from the La Venta vicinity and a sample of Formative ceramics from Isla Alor point to local production of

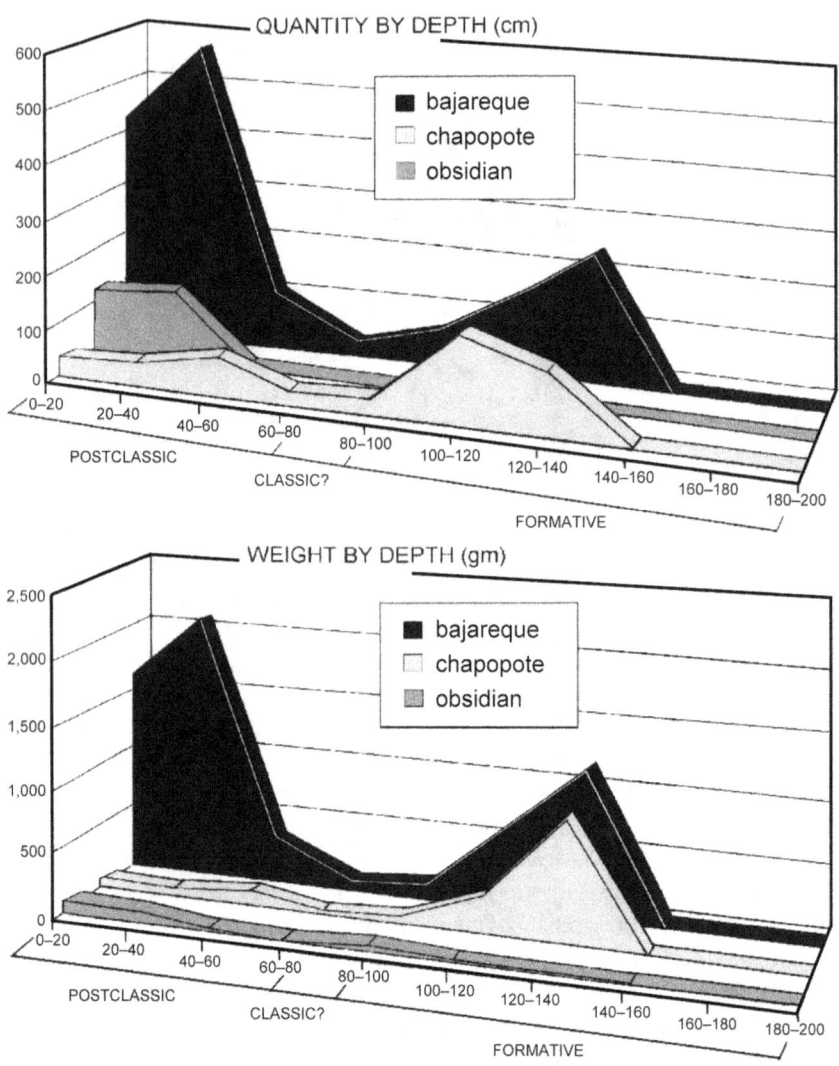

3.8. *Comparison of three categories of evidence (obsidian, bajareque, and chapopote) by quantity (left) and weight (right) from Isla Alor excavations, from Formative to Postclassic contexts. Note the almost complete absence of any Classic Period evidence. Graphs by Matthew A. Boxt and Rusty van Rossman.*

pottery rather than import (Methner 1997). While this study does not rule out the possibility that ceramics made their way to the La Venta area from other regions of Mesoamerica, the available data suggest that it was Formative design elements that were shared widely and not the ceramic vessels themselves. Although no intact vessels were recovered, our excavations at Isla Alor produced

3.9. *Postclassic Fine Orange rim sherds from Isla Alor. Photo by L. Mark Raab.*

appreciable quantities of well-preserved rim and body pottery sherds, permitting the recognition of many Formative and Postclassic vessel forms, including dishes, basins, jars, bowls, and plates. Decorative techniques, paste and temper variables, have also been studied. The Isla Alor pottery is similar to that of La Venta, San Andrés, and other neighboring sites, which facilitates comparisons and identifications (Berlin 1956: 135–136; Sisson 1976: 139, 452–463; von Nagy 2003: 159, 733–739, 742–744, 877–878).

The Isla Alor Olmec ceramic tradition is predominated by differentially fired black-and-white wares (Sisson 1976: 126–137, 256–272; von Nagy 2003: 786–803), La Venta Coarse Buff wares (Drucker 1952: figure 25e), tecomates with zoned rocker-stamping and punctation, bowls with rim ticking and excising, and vessels that were painted with chapopote. Many of the Isla Alor Formative ceramics are stylistically equivalent to Magallanes Incised (Sisson 1976: 193–203), San Isidro Brushed (ibid.: 208), Bronce Unslipped (ibid.: 204), Manantiero Scored (ibid.: 214–219), and Tonalá Incised (ibid.: 360–361). In addition, Isla Alor Olmec

Table 3.1. Subsistence remains identified by flotation analysis at Isla Alor, Tabasco, Mexico

Stratum	Beans	Maize	Palm Nuts	Fish	Turtle	Mollusca	Mammal
1 Recent			X	X		X	X
2 Postclassic	X	X	X	X	X		
3 Sterile[1]							
4 Olmec	X	X	X	X		X	
5 Olmec	X					X	
6 Olmec	X	X					
7 Olmec			X				

Note: 1. Overbank deposit with minor midden component.

specimens show similarities in surface treatment and vessel morphology to San Lorenzo Phase Limón Carved-Incised pottery (Coe and Diehl 1980b: 171–174), Cuadros Phase pottery from Chiapas (Clark 1994: 197–201), and La Florida Blanco y Negro, Agua Fria Anaranjada Sobre Gris, Manzana Incised, and Pajaral Incised specimens from the La Venta type collection.

Isla Alor's Postclassic ceramic assemblage is comparable to the Late Cintla pottery described by Heinrich Berlin (1953, 1956) and the La Venta Cintla and Late Ahualulcos Cintla complexes (ca. AD 1350–1520) discussed by Christopher von Nagy (2003: 877–878). Fine Orange pottery at Isla Alor coincides chronologically with the fine paste U variant from the coastal Tabasco-Campeche region that Berlin (1956) placed in the final part of the Protohistoric Period, possibly AD 1400 to 1530 (Smith 1958: 157). The Fine Gray specimens collected at Isla Alor are reduced in firing yet otherwise identical to Fine Orange. Other identifiable Postclassic ceramics from Isla Alor include Actope Coarse bowls, ollas, and jars (von Nagy 2003: 219), Caoba Plain ollas, and Gogal Plain ollas with interior brushing (ibid.: 883). Brett Methner's (1997) NAA study of Formative ceramic technology suggests that Postclassic potters mined local clays—if not on the "isla" itself, then nearby—for the production of the Fine Orange and Fine Gray vessels that comprise the Isla Alor assemblage (figure 3.9).

To date, no Aztec or Mixteca-Puebla style pottery has been unearthed at Isla Alor. This may simply be the result of limited testing, and future excavation may reverse this situation. For example, Complicated Polychrome, absent at Isla Alor, is nevertheless reported at nearby La Venta. Aztec and Mixteca-Puebla pottery has been identified at several sites in Tabasco and neighboring Veracruz, including Cascajal (Blom and La Farge 1926: 78) and Quauhtochco (Medellín Zenil 1960: 138–146). No Colonial ceramics (for example, Majolica) or modern ceramic complexes, such as Chontalpa Bichrome Glazed or Chontalpa Orange Glazed (von Nagy 2003: 250–251), have been unearthed at Isla Alor.

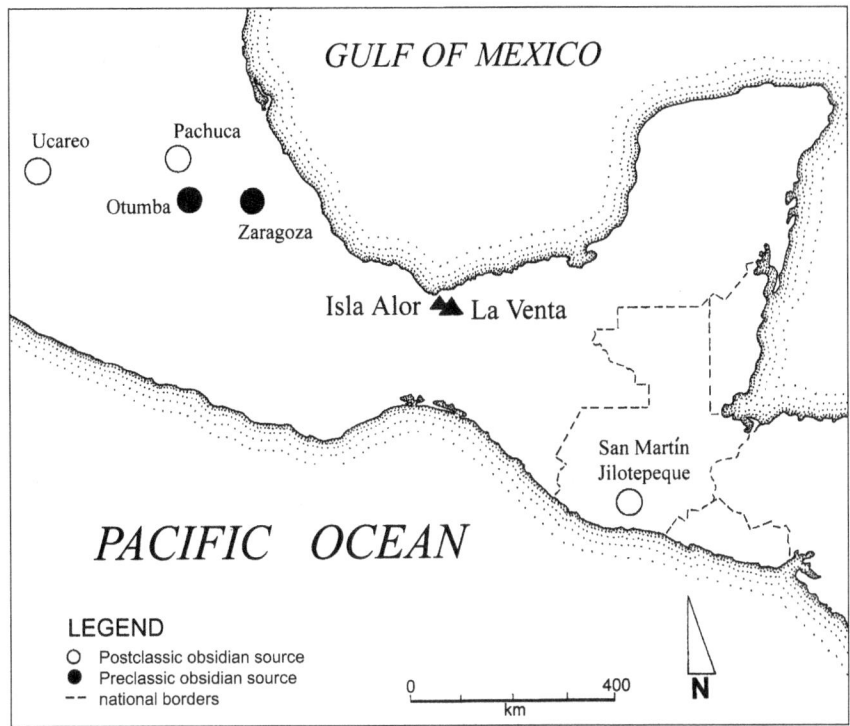

3.10. *Source locations for the obsidian excavated at Isla Alor. Map by Rusty van Rossmann.*

SUBSISTENCE

About 50 liters of soil were recovered from the northeast quadrant of each cultural level of excavation Unit 1, as well as from Formative and Postclassic Period hearths. These soil samples were taken to the La Venta laboratory for flotation analysis; specimens were passed through 1.0- and 0.5-mm mesh screens. Recovery of carbonized plant remains was the primary objective of the flotation procedure, yet other materials were obtained in the process, including fish bone, mollusca, turtle carapace, small- to medium-sized mammal bone, and obsidian microdebitage. A preliminary analysis of the materials from Unit 1 suggests that maize, beans, palm nuts, fish, and shellfish constituted the subsistence base of the site's Formative and Postclassic Period inhabitants (table 3.1). These data corroborate subsistence data from other sites in the La Venta hinterland, suggesting a mixed diet (Rust and Leyden 1994; Pope et al. 2001). In all probability, foods from garden plots producing corn, manihot, squash, and sunflower were complemented by fishing, hunting game, and collecting crustaceans and estuarine shellfish—including crayfish, marsh clams, and oysters (Stross 1992; Pope et al. 2001: 1372–1373).

While the inhabitants of Isla Alor appear to have been farmers engaged in the production of corn, beans, squash, and other crops produced in the more arid highland regions of Mexico, Isla Alor likely reflects a distinctive horticultural pattern, combining typical Mesoamerican cultigens with tree and root cropping, fishing, hunting, and collecting a wide range of other food species. Historical analogy suggests high levels of productivity for such practices (Wilken 1971; Coe and Diehl 1980e, 1980c; Killion 1992; Santley 1992).

OBSIDIAN

Our excavations at Isla Alor produced 280 obsidian artifacts weighing 160 gm. The collection includes 238 proximal, distal, and medial prismatic blade fragments, 41 pieces of debitage, and 1 exhausted core. As well, obsidian debitage was identified in Strata 2 and 4–6 of the flotation samples. The debitage and exhausted core indicate that obsidian tools were produced on-site. A small sample of the Isla Alor obsidian collection was submitted for source analysis, showing preliminary temporal trends (Raab et al. 2000). An interesting separation between the two major chronological periods has been found. Postclassic specimens derive from Ucareo, Michoacan; Pachuca, Hidalgo; and San Martín Jilotepeque, Guatemala. The Otumba, Estado de México, and Zaragoza, Puebla, sources are associated exclusively with the Olmec cultural strata at Isla Alor (figure 3.10).

Obsidian was essential to domestic life, associated with hunting, agriculture, and many other everyday activities. Examples of potential obsidian use at Isla Alor include cutting tools to clear fields, prismatic blades to work wood, and knives to skin and butcher game animals. Insufficient data prevent us from corroborating the Late Postclassic patterns of exchange identified for the Gulf Coast by Geoffrey Braswell (2003). However, the complete absence of local stone in this alluvial plain, combined with the inherent value of obsidian in domestic life, helps explain its value as an import at prehistoric agricultural homesteads such as Isla Alor.

The change in obsidian procurement patterns between the Formative Olmec and Postclassic Periods is striking. Our preliminary interpretation, based on very limited evidence, is that, for whatever reason, the site's Olmec inhabitants were accustomed to an obsidian importation tradition tied to two Central Mexican sources. Conversely, the Postclassic Alor people no longer utilized the two Formative sources but procured obsidian not only from much greater distances than before but also from three completely different culture areas: West Mexico, Central Mexico, and the Maya Highlands. The obsidian data possibly mirror other, larger contemporary economic and political patterns, which at the present time can only be speculated upon.

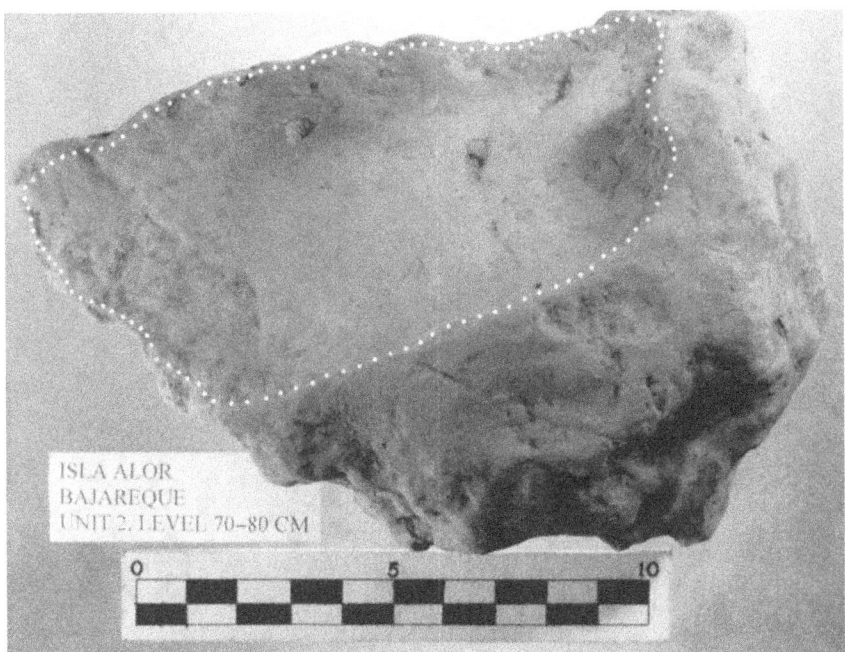

3.11. *Bajareque fragment from Olmec house floor with possible pole impression (white dotted line); scale in cm. Photo by Matthew A. Boxt and L. Mark Raab.*

BAJAREQUE AND CHAPOPOTE

Both the Olmec and Postclassic cultural components at Isla Alor produced bajareque and chapopote. Neither material falls neatly into artifact classifications, yet both are excellent indicators of domestic life. Bajareque connotes house construction, while chapopote suggests a wide range of household activities in both its liquid (asphaltum) and solid forms. Isla Alor bajareque appears to be the same as the "daub and cleft brick" fragments identified by Coe and Diehl (1980a: 284) at San Lorenzo and "briquette" materials Gordon Willey (1965: 511–516) found at Maya sites in the Belize Valley. Willey states:

> "Briquette materials" refers to the fired clay which appears to have been created by the burning of house or other structures. Insofar as we can say, most of the material is of incidental result. That is, buildings were destroyed by fire, either accidentally or purposefully, and the clay plaster which covered pole or wattle walls was hardened in the event. The briquettes are of irregular shapes and sizes. (1965: 511)

Isla Alor bajareque is reddish- and yellowish-brown colored with blackish fire-exposed surfaces. The specimens are amorphous and range in thickness from 2 cm to 12 cm. One rather large chunk from the Olmec component, weighing

3.12. *Formative pottery vessel fragments with chapopote (dark surfaces) adhering; scale in cm. Photo by Matthew A. Boxt and L. Mark Raab.*

586 gm, may represent the squared or finished edge or corner of a wall of a wattle-and-daub structure (figure 3.11). No significant variations in color, size, or weight were noted between Formative and Postclassic examples. Isla Alor residents obviously relied heavily on clay and mud to plaster their dwellings. The absence of alternative building materials in the region, particularly stone, was noted in the late sixteenth century on Melchor Alfaro de Santa Cruz's map of Tabasco: "In all this province, except in the sierras, there is no stone. The houses are made of cane" (Scholes and Roys 1968: map 2).

Most of the chapopote recovered at Isla Alor occurs in small, pebble-sized pieces. We collected roughly 1 kg in Postclassic Strata 1 and 2. The Olmec strata produced roughly 3 kg of the substance, including a broken ceramic vessel with a 1–3-cm-thick crust of chapopote on its interior walls, suggesting a storage function (figure 3.12). Given the proclivity of the indigenous populace of Isla Alor to use this material, it may be worthwhile to consider the uses chapopote had in the ancient households of Gulf Coast Mesoamerica and beyond. This neglected topic can yield potentially interesting inferences about a broad spectrum of prehistoric behaviors, ranging from the mundane to the supernatural. Not only do we find chapopote samples in archaeological contexts across Mexico, but there are also ethnohistoric and contemporary accounts that may help us interpret the applications of this substance in prehistory.

Data collected by Fray Diego de Landa (1941: 75) and Sahagún, who spent his entire adult life in missionary activities around Mexico City, indicate that the Aztec used chapopote (*chapuputli*) for two primary purposes:

> The first [purpose] for which it is used is to be mixed with tobacco, so that the pulverized tobacco may be made pleasing. The pleasing scent of the tobacco spreads over the whole land. As its second use, it is used by women; they chew the bitumen. And what they chew [is] named chicle . . . For this reason the women chew chicle: because thereby they cause their saliva to flow and thereby the mouths are scented. With it they dispel the bad odor of their mouths, or the bad smell of their teeth . . . The men also chew chicle to cause their saliva to flow and to clean the teeth, but this very secretly—never in public. (Sahagún 1961: 89)

Chapopote had numerous domestic, religious, industrial, and craft-related applications (Carreón Blaine 2006). According to Sahagún (Noguera 1971: 260) and the conquistador Andrés de Tápia (1971: 582–583), Toltec and Aztec sculptors attached pieces of amber, amethyst, pearl, and shell to wooden statues with a chapopote-based adhesive; lapidaries created elaborate inlaid mosaic designs with chapopote. Based on these observations and the comments of Sahagún (1961: 77), we infer that ample quantities of chapopote were available in the Tlaltelolco and other regional markets, satisfying the broad consumptive needs of Central Mexican peoples. As well, there must have been a high demand among priests and religious practitioners for chapopote in its solid and liquid forms. When burned, chapopote incense produced clouds of pleasantly scented smoke; in terms of ceremony and spectacle, Aztec priests used asphaltum for face and body painting (Engelhardt 1992: 99–100; Sahagún 1961: 89).

As to the origin of chapopote, Sahagún states:

> Bitumen [is] black, very black, black; [it is] that which flakes, crumbles, breaks up. It comes from the ocean, from the sea; it is produced within the ocean. When it comes forth, [it is] according to the time count. The waves cast it forth. It comes forth, it drops out according to the phase of the moon. When it comes forth, [it is] like a mat, wide, thick. Those of the seashore, those of the coast lands gather it there. They gather it, they pick it up from the sand (Sahagún 1961: 88).

Sixteenth-century descriptions of chapopote are not limited to written accounts. Illustration 138 in the *Florentine Codex* (Sahagún 1961) depicts an individual collecting solid lumps of chapopote. Judging from the waves in the foreground and the large piece of bitumen in that individual's hands, one infers a sixteenth-century Gulf Coast resident scavenging congealed chapopote flotsam washing ashore. This drawing implicates the Gulf Coast as an important, perhaps the principal, source of chapopote for large expanses of Mesoamerica.

Our second historical reference to chapopote is the 1579 map drafted and annotated by Melchor Alfaro de Santa Cruz, a Spaniard who traveled extensively in the Tabasco region. This document clearly describes "springs of a kind of water which coagulates in the sun and forms a dark resin which can be used as pitch. It also occurs in other parts of this province" (Scholes and Roys 1968: map 2). This map describes a *chapopotera*, or pond, near Cimatan, a Postclassic commercial center mentioned in ethnohistorical accounts (ibid.: 31–33), bringing a chapopote source within no more than 45 km of Isla Alor.

European and North American explorers and researchers have recognized the importance of asphaltum for centuries. In 1676, for example, the British explorer and sea captain William Dampier observed lumps of asphaltum, some of which ranged in weight from 3 to 30 pounds, washing up along the shoreline of the Gulf Coast (Masefield 1906: 224). Dampier called this substance *munjack*, tempered it with sand to enhance its elasticity, and employed it as pitch to caulk ships. An early mention of chapopote comes from Blom and La Farge (1926: 76), who noted that oil seeps were frequent throughout the region of Moloacán, Veracruz, 40 km southwest of Isla Alor. In the same region, Coe and Diehl (1980d: 17) identified chapopote sources in the vicinity of San Lorenzo; the presence of seeps near or along watercourses may explain the occurrence of chapopote along coastal beaches. Coe and Diehl (ibid.) noted that modern villagers purchase chapopote in cakes at the Minatitlán market, using it to waterproof dugout canoes. West, Psuty, and Thom (1969: 122) indicated that residents of Tabasco's Macuspana district, ca. 150 km southeast of Isla Alor, collect pitch from chapopoteras to make torches.

According to current beliefs held by Chontal Maya inhabitants in the communities of Villa Vicente Guerrero, Cuauhtémoc, and Ignacio Allende in northeastern Tabasco, *duendes* (spirits) still inhabit specific aquatic and terrestrial regions. One of these supernatural beings, known interchangeably as Doña Bolom Tepe Tepe, la Bolón—la Dueña de los Mares, Doña Bolom—la Reyna del Mar, Doña Bolón, or simply la Bolón, has resided since time immemorial underwater in her house of chapopote. Chontal Maya informants believe "La Bolón is human; people say, it's human. La Bolón is like a genie . . . that lives on the bottom of the sea . . . in a house of bitumen. And then, when—it is said—when the wind blows violently from the north, it breaks up La Bolón's house. And then all the bitumen breaks loose" (Incháustegui 1987: 318, translated by the authors).

The persistence in contemporary Chontal memory of la Bolón, an unseen maritime-dwelling anthropomorphic spirit, may reflect faintly audible echoes of ancient Maya religion that reverberate into the twenty-first century. This myth perhaps recalls the comment of the sixteenth-century priest Sahagún (1963: 61), who said of chapopote what Maya and other people undoubtedly knew for millennia: "It falls out on the ocean floor; it falls out like mud." These data hint at a linkage between chapopote and ancient religious or other ideological systems.

The Gulf Coast Mexican archaeological record reveals a longstanding tradition of chapopote use, hardly surprising since in ancient times the region was the major source of chapopote for all of southeastern Mesoamerica. Natural chapopote seeps proliferate from the Huasteca south to Maya territory. Chapopote was abundant, easily procured, and simple to transport, and its storage was uncomplicated. Chapopote references in the archaeological literature are common from many regions of Mexico, especially the Gulf Coast (Muir 1926: 233; Ekholm 1944: 500; Aguilera 1963; García 1988; Wendt and Lu 2006; Wendt 2008b) and at other archaeological sites within our study region, including La Venta, San Lorenzo, El Bajío, and El Manatí.

At La Venta (Drucker 1952: 56–59), traces of asphalt were found beneath the serpentine blocks of Pavement 1, and chapopote may also have functioned as a joint sealer for abutting trough stones in the site's elaborate hydraulic system (Heizer, Graham, and Napton 1968: 145). Coe and Diehl (1980d: 17) noted abundant chapopote in Olmec deposits at San Lorenzo, including a Chicharras Phase (1250–1150 BC) lump of molded or shaped chapopotle (Coe and Diehl 1980a: 292). At El Bajío in the San Lorenzo hinterland, Carl Wendt (2000, 2005a, 2005b, 2008a; Wendt and Cyphers 2008) detected chapopote on the interior surfaces of Formative tecomate vessels; researchers at El Manatí (Rodríguez and Ortíz Ceballos 1997: 78) unearthed a pottery vessel mended with chapopotle. Asphaltum-painted spindle whorls have been identified throughout Mesoamerica, including the Gulf Coast region, the most likely source of this substance (Blom and La Farge 1926: 16; Drucker 1943a: 87, plate 65; 1943b: plate 55; Parsons 1972: 57; McCafferty and McCafferty 2000: 47).

The reports outlined here make it clear that chapopote was widely utilized throughout ancient Mesoamerica, demonstrating countless medicinal, practical, and ritual applications. In light of these data, the cultural value of chapopote, hiding in plain sight, may be masked by its ubiquity and often mundane applications. Chapopote, as exemplified by Isla Alor, was an integral component of domestic life, rivaling obsidian and pottery as an essential, versatile, and archaeologically visible commodity. Once we add possible links to ritual and ideology, it seems clear that the degree to which this material has thus far been ignored by archaeologists is equaled only by its potential for future research.

CONCLUSIONS

Our 1994–1995 fieldwork at Isla Alor warrants five conclusions. First, the site contains two well-defined cultural deposits, representing the Postclassic and the much earlier Formative Periods. Both natural (periodic inundation) and cultural (refuse discard/loss around domestic living areas) site formation processes resulted in the rapid burial of living surfaces at Isla Alor. This circumstance offers a significant advantage over some larger sites, including La Venta, where frequent large-scale earth-moving activities (including architectural construction and monument resetting) obscured and often destroyed the systemic context and association required for reaching valid archaeological conclusions based on reliable stratigraphic relationships.

Second, conditions of artifact preservation at Isla Alor were better than anticipated. Contrary to the pessimistic assessments of earlier researchers (cf. Drucker 1947: 3; Clewlow 1974: 3) in the La Venta area, based on presumptions about the preservation potential of the region's tropical environment and acidic soils, we found ceramics and other materials from Isla Alor to be both abundant and suitable for productive analyses. Carbonized bone, floral macro-fossils, chapopote, and bajareque evidence offer insights into prehistoric diet, economy, and domestic activities. Preliminary macrobotanical data suggest that the Formative and much later Postclassic economies at Isla Alor were mixed, based on cultivation, tree cropping, hunting, fishing, and collecting. Spindle whorls substantiate the notion that cotton textiles were produced on-site. Side-notched sherds, probably used as net-spacers, strongly suggest cast-net fishing in the local rivers and lagoons. Imported obsidian and greenstone indicates the participation of Isla Alor in long-distance exchange systems.

Third, Isla Alor offers evidence of a vibrant Postclassic population. More than fifty years ago, Berlin (1956: 135) cautioned that "an attempt to identify a protohistoric horizon covering some two hundred years prior to the arrival of the Spaniards, in a region where little or nothing is known about earlier pottery manifestations, is a dangerous undertaking." Our work at Isla Alor reveals that because of the abundant Fine Orange pottery, the premier Postclassic ceramic type fossil, this task is less daunting than previously thought.

Fourth, the Isla Alor research compels further studies on the prehistoric use of chapopote. At Isla Alor we recovered chapopote from well-defined Postclassic and Formative contexts. More chapopote was associated with Formative deposits; however, the present distributional data indicate that chapopote formed an essential part of the economy of both occupations. It seems likely that chapopote seeps existed near La Venta and Isla Alor, yet ancient chapopoteras may be hard to pinpoint because of the growth of Villa La Venta and land modifications resulting from intensive petroleum exploration and production. Many questions about the prehistoric chapopote trade remain unanswered. How extensive were petroleum seeps beyond the Gulf Coast? To the best of our knowledge, there are no surface petroleum sources in the Central Mexican highlands. If such is the case, then chapopote must have been imported, likely from the Gulf Coast, either through tribute or trade. Curiously, chapopote is not listed as tribute in the *Codex Mendoza* (Berdan and Anawalt 1997), nor is its medicinal value discussed in the *Florentine Codex* (Sahagún 1961) or in the *Badianus Manuscript* (de la Cruz 1940). Based on the presumably substantial quantities of chapopote used by the Aztec Empire, we wonder why tribute lists and other ethnohistoric accounts, including discussions of native medicine, fail to mention this material. Is it possible that chapopote was available from so many different Gulf Coast sources that it was not a commodity easily controlled by Aztec state-sponsored trade networks? Future investigation might focus on the question of whether the chapopote trade was comparable to obsidian, greenstone, and other commodities presumably under elite control. Beneficial to this task would be studies aimed at sourcing archaeological chapopote samples.

Fifth, and finally, the Isla Alor data provide a means of evaluating similarities and differences in the settlement-subsistence patterns of Gulf Coast Formative and Postclassic peoples, separated by almost three millennia. Just as studies at large sites such as La Venta have contributed major insights into aspects of urban life and elite behavior, studies at small, rural habitation communities like Isla Alor complement these data by focusing on the mundane aspects of the lowest tier of the settlement hierarchy. Judging from available survey data, Isla Alor is but one of hundreds, perhaps thousands, of Olmec hamlets, farmsteads, or residence units that once sustained the ancient urban center of La Venta (Rust 1987, 1988). Its location alongside a riverbank provided a potable water supply and allowed the river to serve as a highway, facilitating the movement of people and commodities to La Venta itself.

To date, we have not detected a well-defined Classic Period component, yet pottery and obsidian from roughly 65 cm below surface in Stratum 3 suggest limited site use between 1000 BC and the middle fifteenth century. A hitherto undetected Classic Period occupation may be unearthed at Isla Alor. We know that the Formative peoples at Isla Alor were closely related in their cultural traditions to the inhabitants of La Venta, yet Postclassic Isla Alor was likely occupied by completely different peoples living a basically similar way of life. Based on the initial discoveries of Stirling (1943b: 56) and later by Drucker, Heizer, and Squier (1959: 237) in the Cerro Encantado or Cerro del Encanto mound group about a mile northwest of the main La Venta site, it appears that La Venta, or at least a part of La Venta, was reoccupied well after the Olmec capital reached its Middle Formative apogee (ca. 800–500 BC). In all likelihood, the Postclassic Isla Alor farmstead was linked to this community.[3]

Our data indicate that Postclassic Isla Alor was no less vibrant than its Formative era counterpart. We are confident that small, well-preserved agricultural hamlets such as Isla Alor, studied with suitably focused research strategies, can yield valuable new information on the Postclassic Period. Despite western Tabasco's abundant Postclassic occupation and its wealth of early ethnohistoric source material, the region's Precontact social structure, settlement patterns, and other cultural characteristics remain among the least known in Mexico, waiting to be systematically investigated by archaeologists. A future objective is to connect the ethnohistoric Olmeca-Xuixtotin peoples of the study area with the Postclassic archaeological record. Isla Alor's well-preserved Postclassic cultural deposit provides an excellent place to pursue this goal.

Acknowledgments. Our work at Isla Alor is part of the research program of the Instituto Nacional de Antropología e Historia's (INAH) Proyecto Arqueológico La Venta. It was supported by the Convenio Interinstitucional para el Rescate Integral de Zonas Arqueológicas en Tabasco, the California State University at Northridge–Center for Public Archaeology, and the University of California Rammler Grant for La Venta Research. Without these funds, this work would not have been possible. We gratefully acknowledge the logistical support of the Centro INAH Tabasco and permits issued by INAH's Consejo de Arqueología. Don Vicente Alor González, owner of the Isla Alor site, generously permitted the work reported. To him we are deeply grateful. Our thanks to Brian Dervin Dillon, who read the manuscript through many different drafts, providing good advice and extremely useful comments. We are grateful to Rusty van Rossmann for his outstanding illustrations.

NOTES

1. Because it seems unlikely that alluvial deposition could form a 2.8-meter-tall rise, "Isla" Alor may actually be partially anthropegenic. Ancient farmers and their families, not wanting to see their cropland melt away every time the river flooded, may have stabilized the easily erodible alluvial deposits that came and went with seasonal changes in local river flow. Any artificial bank stabilization done in the interests of erosion control would have, over time, created living surfaces at slightly higher elevations than the surrounding floodplain (Dillon, personal communication). The ancients could have easily collected quantities of rich organic marsh muck from the surrounding region, combining it with rotting vegetation, human waste, and silt to either level or enrich agricultural plots—which themselves would have been ideal for the production of corn, squash, beans, cotton, palms, or cacao.

2. Data are insufficient for ancient architectural reconstruction at Isla Alor. The size, shape, floor space, and number of houses comprising the farmstead can only be guessed at. Assuredly, dwellings were humble and construction methods uncomplicated. Isla Alor structures were simple pole-and-mud houses with prepared earthen floors and thatched roofs. Walls were made of a lattice of wooden poles daubed with a mixture of clay and grass, called bajareque today throughout lower Central America. The discovery of a wide variety of tools (e.g., manos, metates, chert and obsidian blades, a chert biface, a greenstone adze, a nutting stone, notched sherds, spindle whorls, and pottery vessels [bowls, plates, dishes, jars, and tecomates]) provides vital information about household activities of all kinds. The residential hearth contained wood charcoal, charred seeds, and small animal remains. The location of the hearth, inside or outside the dwelling, is uncertain.

3. Olmec La Venta flourished from the Early through Middle Formative Periods, yet many centuries after its Formative abandonment, the great site was reoccupied. Matthew Stirling was among the first to detect evidence of non-Olmec peoples there. In 1940 Stirling (1943b: 56) noted that stone sculptures at the Cerro Encantado mound group were "related in concept to the altars from the main La Venta site, but were conspicuously different, the carving being angular and relatively crude." Roughly fifteen years later, Drucker, Heizer, and Squier (1959: 240) observed that Cerro del Encanto potsherds were unlike those unearthed in the site core, instead demonstrating stylistic similarities with late Prehistoric pottery from Matacapan and the Veracruz coast. These data suggest a resurgence of population at La Venta and its hinterland in the late Prehistoric era. Known alternatively as the Cerro Encantando or Cerro del Encanto, this mound group was renamed Complex F by González Lauck in 1985, at which time she noted a significant difference between the architectural layout of Complex F and the rest of La Venta (González Lauck 1995: 39). While the Formative Olmec builders of La Venta oriented the site along a north-south "centerline" 8 degrees west of true north and bisecting the Ceremonial Court (Drucker, Heizer, and Squier 1959: 15), Complex F does not conform to this alignment but is inclined at a much greater angle west of north. This has led González Lauck to propose that the construction of Complex F postdates the Olmec occupation at La Venta.

REFERENCES CITED

Adams, Richard E.W., and Aubrey S. Trik
    1961   Report No. 7. Temple 1 (Str. 5D-1): Post-Constructional Activities. In *Tikal Reports Numbers 5–10*, pp. 113–148. University Museum, University of Pennsylvania, Philadelphia.

Aguilera, Carmen
    1963   Algunos datos sobre el chapopote en las fuentes documentales del siglo XVI. *Estudios de Cultural Nahuatl* 14: 335–343.

Barlow, Robert H.
    1949   *The Extent of the Empire of the Culhua Mexico*. Ibero-Americana 28. University of California Press, Berkeley.

Berdan, Frances F., and Patricia Rieff Anawalt
    1997   *The Essential Codex Mendoza*. University of California Press, Berkeley.

Berlin, Heinrich
    1953   Archaeological Reconnaissance in Tabasco. *Current Reports Carnegie Institution of Washington* 1 (7): 102–135. Carnegie Institution of Washington, Washington, DC.
    1956   Late Pottery Horizons of Tabasco, Mexico. *Contributions to American Anthropology and History* 12 (59): 95–154. Publication 606. Carnegie Institution of Washington, Washington, DC.

Blom, Frans, and Oliver La Farge
    1926   *Tribes and Temples*, vol. 1. Middle American Research Institute, New Orleans, LA.

Brainerd, George W.
  1941 Fine Orange Pottery in Yucatan. *Revista Mexicana de Estudios Antropológicos* 5 (2–3): 163–183.

Braswell, Geoffrey E.
  2003 Obsidian Exchange Spheres. In *The Postclassic Mesoamerican World*, ed. Michael E. Smith and Francis F. Berdan, pp. 131–158. University of Utah Press, Salt Lake City.

Brinton, Daniel G.
  1896 The Battle and the Ruins of Cintla. *American Antiquarian* 18: 259–268.

Cabrera Castro, Rubén
  1988 Horno cerámico posteotihuacano en el palacio de Atetelco. *Arqueología* 4: 47–76.

Carrasco, Pedro
  1999 *The Tenochca Empire of Ancient Mexico: The Triple Alliance of Tenochtitlan, Tetzcoco, and Tlacopan.* University of Oklahoma Press, Norman.

Carreón Blaine, Emilie
  2006 *El Olli en la Plástica Mexica: El Uso de Hule en el Siglo XVI.* Instituto de Investigaciones Estéticas, UNAM, México, DF.

Caso, Alfonso
  1969 *El Tesoro de Monte Albán.* INAH Memorias 3, México, DF.

Clark, John, ed.
  1994 *Los Olmecas en Mesoamérica.* Citibank, México, DF.

Clewlow, C. William, Jr.
  1974 A Stylistic and Chronological Study of Olmec Monumental Sculpture. *Contributions of the University of California Archaeological Research Facility* 19. Berkeley.

Coe, Michael D.
  1965 Archaeological Synthesis of Southern Veracruz and Tabasco. In *Archaeology of Southern Mesoamerica*, Part 2, ed. Gordon R. Willey, pp. 679–715. Handbook of Middle American Indians, vol. 3, Robert Wauchope, gen. ed. University of Texas Press, Austin.

Coe, Michael D., and Richard A. Diehl
  1980a Artifacts. In *In the Land of the Olmec*, vol. 1: *The Archaeology of San Lorenzo Tenochtitlán*, ed. Michael D. Coe and Richard A. Diehl, pp. 223–292. University of Texas Press, Austin.
  1980b Ceramics. In *In the Land of the Olmec*, vol. 1, *The Archaeology of San Lorenzo Tenochtitlán*, ed. Michael D. Coe and Richard A. Diehl, pp. 131–222. University of Texas Press, Austin.
  1980c Human-Animal Relationships. In *In the Land of the Olmec*, vol. 2: *The People of the River*, ed. Michael D. Coe and Richard A. Diehl, pp. 97–123. University of Texas Press, Austin.

1980d The Olmec Landscape. In *In the Land of the Olmec*, vol. 1: *The Archaeology of San Lorenzo Tenochtitlán*, ed. Michael D. Coe and Richard A. Diehl, pp. 11–22. University of Texas Press, Austin.

1980e People, Plants, and Land. In *In the Land of the Olmec*, vol. 2: *The People of the River*, ed. Michael D. Coe and Richard A. Diehl, pp. 69–96. University of Texas Press, Austin.

Daneels, Annick
    1997 Settlement History in the Lower Cotaxtla Basin. In *Olmec to Aztec: Settlement Patterns in the Ancient Gulf Lowlands*, ed. Barbara L. Stark and Philip J. Arnold III, pp. 206–252. University of Arizona Press, Tucson.

de la Cruz, Martín
    1940 *The Badianus Manuscript (Codex Barbarini, Latin 241) Vatican Library: An Aztec Herbal of 1552*, ed. Emily Walcott Emmart, with a foreword by Henry E. Sigerist. Johns Hopkins Press, Baltimore, MD.

Díaz del Castillo, Bernal
    1963 *The Conquest of New Spain*. Translated with an introduction by J. M. Cohen. Penguin Books, Baltimore, MD.

Dillon, Brian Dervin
    1975 Notes on Trade in Ancient Mesoamerica. *Contributions of the University of California Archaeological Research Facility* 24: 79–135. Berkeley.

Drucker, Philip
    1943a *Ceramic Sequences at Tres Zapotes, Veracruz, Mexico*. Smithsonian Institution Bureau of American Ethnology Bulletin 140. Government Printing Office, Washington, DC.

    1943b *Ceramic Stratigraphy at Cerro de las Mesas, Veracruz, Mexico*. Smithsonian Institution Bureau of American Ethnology Bulletin 141. Government Printing Office, Washington, DC.

    1947 Some Implications of the Ceramic Complex of La Venta. *Smithsonian Miscellaneous Collections* 107 (8): 1–9, with six plates. Smithsonian Institution Bureau of American Ethnology. Government Printing Office, Washington, DC.

    1952 *La Venta, Tabasco: A Study of Olmec Ceramics and Art*. With a Chapter on Structural Investigations in 1943 by Waldo R. Wedel and Appendix on Technological Analyses by Anna O. Shepard. Smithsonian Institution Bureau of American Ethnology Bulletin 153. Government Printing Office, Washington, DC.

Drucker, Philip, and Eduardo Contreras
    1953 Site Patterns in the Eastern Part of Olmec Territory. *Journal of the Washington Academy of Sciences* 43 (12): 389–396.

Drucker, Philip, Robert F. Heizer, and Robert J. Squier
    1959 *Excavations at La Venta Tabasco, 1955*. With Appendices by Jonas E. Gullberg, Garniss H. Curtis, and A. Starker Leopold. Smithsonian Institution Bureau of American Ethnology Bulletin 170. Government Printing Office, Washington, DC.

Ekholm, Gordon F.
  1944 Excavations at Tampico and Panuco in the Huasteca, Mexico. *Anthropological Papers of the American Museum of Natural History* 38, Part 5. Museum of Natural History, New York.

Engelhardt, Mayra L.
  1992 Chapopote: Evidence of Shamanism on Pre-Columbian Veracruz Ceramic Figurines. *Journal of Latin American Lore* 18: 95–124.

García, María Teresa García
  1988 El uso de chapopote en la época prehispánica. In *XI Jornadas de Historia de Occidente: Recurso Naturales y Soberanía Nacional*, pp. 29–41. Centro de Estudios de la Revolución Mexicana Lázaro Cárdenas, Jiquilpan de Juárez, Michoacán.

García Payón, José
  1971 Archaeology of Central Veracruz. In *Archaeology of Northern Mesoamerica*, Part 2, ed. Gordon F. Ekholm and Ignacio Bernal, pp. 505–542. Handbook of Middle American Indians, vol. 11, Robert Wauchope, gen. ed. University of Texas Press, Austin.

Garibay K., Ángel María, ed. and trans.
  1961 *Vida económica de Tenochtitlan. 1. Pochtecayotl (Arte de traficar) por Bernardino de Sahagún*. Fuentes indígenas de la cultura Náhuatl, informantes de Sahagún 3. UNAM, México, DF.

Gil y Sáenz, Manuel
  1979 *Compendio histórico, geográfico y estadístico del estado de Tabasco*. 2nd facsimile ed. Consejo Editorial del Gobierno del Estado de Tabasco, Villahermosa, México.

González Lauck, Rebecca B.
  1995 La Venta: Una Gran Ciudad Olmeca. *Arqueología Mexicana* 2 (12): 38–42.

González Lauck, Rebecca B., L. Mark Raab, Matthew A. Boxt, and Katherine Bradford
  1995 Informe técnico parcial. Proyecto Arqueológico La Venta. Temporada 1994. Investigaciones arqueológicas en el área de apoyo de La Venta, Tabasco, Huimanguillo. Manuscript on file, Archivo Técnico de la Coordinación Nacional de Arqueología. INAH, México, DF.

Heizer, Robert F., John A. Graham, and Lewis K. Napton
  1968 The 1968 Investigations at La Venta. *Contributions of the University of California Archaeological Research Facility* 5: 127–154. Berkeley.

Incháustegui, Carlos
  1987 *Las márgenes de Tabasco Chontal*. Gobierno del Estado de Tabasco e Instituto de Cultura de Tabasco, Villahermosa, Tabasco, México.

Izquierdo, Ana Luisa
  1997 *Acalán y La Chontalpa en el siglo XVI: Su geografía política*. UNAM, México, DF.

Killion, Thomas W.
  1992 Residential Ethnoarchaeology and Ancient Site Structure: Contemporary Farming and Prehistoric Settlement Agriculture at Matacapan, Veracruz,

Mexico. In *Gardens of Prehistory: The Archaeology of Settlement Agriculture in Greater Mesoamerica*, ed. Thomas W. Killion, pp. 119–149. University of Alabama Press, Tuscaloosa.

Landa, Fray Diego de
    1941   *Landa's Relación de las Cosas de Yucatán*. Translated and edited by Alfred M. Tozzer. Papers of the Peabody Museum of American Archaeology and Ethnology 18. Harvard University, Cambridge, MA.

Lee, Thomas A., Jr.
    1978   The Historical Routes of Tabasco and Northern Chiapas and Their Relationship to Early Cultural Developments in Central Chiapas. In *Mesoamerican Communication Routes and Cultural Contacts*, ed. T. A. Lee Jr. and Carlos Navarrete, pp. 49–66. Papers of the New World Archaeological Foundation 40. Brigham Young University, Provo, UT.

López de Gómara, Francisco
    1964   *Cortés: The Life of the Conqueror by His Secretary*. Translated and edited by Lesley Byrd Simpson. University of California Press, Berkeley.

MacNutt, Francis A., ed.
    1908   *Fernando Cortes: His Five Letters of Relation to the Emperor Charles V*. 2 vols. Edited by Francis A. MacNutt. Arthur H. Clark, Cleveland, OH.

Masefield, John, ed.
    1906   *Dampier's Voyages Consisting of a New Voyage Round the World, a Supplement to the Voyage Round the World, Two Voyages to Campeachy, a Discourse of Winds, a Voyage to New Holland, and a Vindication, in Answer to the Chemerical Relation of William Funnell by Captain William Dampier*, vol. 2. E. Grant Richards, London.

McCafferty, Sharisse D., and Geoffrey McCafferty
    2000   Textile Production in Postclassic Cholula, Mexico. *Ancient Mesoamerica* 11: 39–54.

Medellín Zenil, Alfonso
    1960   *Cerámicas del Totonacapan: Exploraciones arqueológicas en el centro de Veracruz*. Universidad Veracruzana Instituto de Antropología, Xalapa, Veracruz, México.

Methner, Brett
    1997   Neutron Activation Analysis on Olmec Pottery: A View from La Venta. Report submitted to the Foundation for the Advancement of Mesoamerican Studies, Inc. (FAMSI). Electronic document, http://www.famsi.org; accessed March 28, 2009.

Muir, John M.
    1926   Data on the Structure of Pre-Columbian Huastec Mounds in the Tampico Region, Mexico [with Plates XXVII–XXX]. *Journal of the Royal Anthropological Institute* 56: 231–238.

Noguera, Eduardo
    1971   Minor Arts in the Central Valleys. In *Archaeology of Northern Mesoamerica*, Part 1, ed. Gordon F. Ekholm and Ignacio Bernal, pp. 258–269. Handbook of Middle American Indians, vol. 10, Robert Wauchope, gen. ed. University of Texas Press, Austin.

Ochoa, Lorenzo
    1992   Hilos Nuevos en la Urdimbre de Vieja Historia. La Arqueología en Tabasco. *Estudios de Cultura Maya* 9: 113–132. UNAM, México, DF.
    1999   *Frente al espejo de la memoria: La costa del golfo al momento del contacto*. Editorial Ponciano Arriaga, San Luis Potosí, México, and CONACULTA: Instituto de Cultura, México, DF.

Parsons, Mary Hrones
    1972   Spindle Whorls from the Teotihuacán Valley. Anthropological Papers of the Museum of Anthropology 45: *Miscellaneous Studies in Mexican Prehistory*, pp. 45–80. University of Michigan, Ann Arbor.

Piña Chan, Roman, and Carlos Navarrete
    1967   *Archaeological Research in the Lower Grijalva River Region, Tabasco and Chiapas*. Papers of the New World Archaeological Foundation 22. Brigham Young University, Provo, UT.

Pope, Kevin O., Mary E.D. Pohl, John G. Jones, David L. Lentz, Christopher R. von Nagy, Francisco J. Vega, and Irvy R. Quitmeyer
    2001   Origin and Environmental Setting of Ancient Agriculture in the Lowlands of Mesoamerica. *Science* 292: 1370–1373.

Raab, L. Mark, Matthew A. Boxt, and Katherine Bradford
    1997   Informe técnico parcial. Proyecto Arqueológico La Venta. Temporada Excavaciones en Isla Alor. Manuscript on file, Archivo Técnico de la Coordinación Nacional de Arqueología. INAH, México, DF.

Raab, L. Mark, Matthew A. Boxt, Katherine Bradford, Brian A. Stokes, and Rebecca B. González Lauck
    2000   Testing at Isla Alor in the La Venta Olmec Hinterland. *Journal of Field Archaeology* 27: 257–270.

Remesal, Antonio de
    1932   *Historia general de las indias occidentales y particular de la gobernación de Chiapa y Guatemala*. 2 vols. Ediciones Atlas, Madrid.

Rodríguez, María del Carmen, and Ponciano Ortíz Ceballos
    1997   Olmec Ritual and Sacred Geography at Manatí. In *Olmec to Aztec: Settlement Patterns in the Ancient Gulf Lowlands*, ed. Barbara L. Stark and Philip J. Arnold III, pp. 68–95. University of Arizona Press, Tucson.

Roys, Ralph L.
    1972   *The Indian Background of Colonial Yucatán*. University of Oklahoma Press, Norman.

Rust III, William F.
- 1987 Informe técnico parcial. Proyecto Arqueológico La Venta. Temporada 1986. Prospección arqueológica en el área de apoyo de La Venta. Manuscript on file, Archivo Técnico de la Coordinación Nacional de Arqueología. INAH, México, DF.
- 1988 Informe técnico parcial. Proyecto Arqueológico La Venta. Temporada 1987. Prospección arqueológica en el área de apoyo de La Venta. Manuscript on file, Archivo Técnico de la Coordinación Nacional de Arqueología. INAH, México, DF.
- 1992 New Ceremonial and Settlement Evidence at La Venta and Its Relation to Formative Maya Culture. In *New Theories on the Ancient Maya*, ed. Elin Danien and Robert J. Sharer, pp. 123–129. University Museum, University of Pennsylvania, Philadelphia.
- 2008 A Settlement Survey of La Venta, Tabasco, Mexico. PhD dissertation, Department of Anthropology, University of Pennsylvania, Philadelphia.

Rust III, William F., and Barbara Leyden
- 1994 Evidence of Maize Use at Early and Middle Formative La Venta Olmec Sites. In *Corn and Culture in the Prehistoric New World*, ed. Sissel Johannesen and Christine A. Hastorf, pp. 181–201. Westview, Boulder, CO.

Rust III, William F., and Robert J. Sharer
- 1988 Olmec Settlement Data from La Venta, Tabasco, México. *Science* 242: 102–104.

Sahagún, Fray Bernardino de
- 1959 *Florentine Codex. Book 9, the Merchants*. Translated by Charles E. Dibble and Arthur J.O. Anderson. School of American Research and the University of Utah, Santa Fe, NM.
- 1961 *Florentine Codex. Book 10, the People*. Translated by Charles E. Dibble and Arthur J.O. Anderson. School of American Research and the University of Utah, Santa Fe, NM.
- 1963 *Florentine Codex. Book 11, Earthly Things*. Translated by Charles E. Dibble and Arthur J.O. Anderson. School of American Research and the University of Utah, Santa Fe, NM.

Sanders, William T.
- 1971 Cultural Ecology and Settlement Patterns of the Gulf Coast. In *Archaeology of Northern Mesoamerica*, Part 2, ed. Gordon F. Ekholm and Ignacio Bernal, pp. 543–557. Handbook of Middle American Indians, vol. 11, Robert Wauchope, gen. ed. University of Texas Press, Austin.

Santley, Robert S.
- 1992 A Consideration of the Olmec Phenomenon in the Tuxtlas: Early Formative Settlement Pattern, Land Use, and Refuse Disposal at Matacapan, Veracruz, Mexico. In *Gardens of Prehistory: The Archaeology of Settlement Agriculture in Greater Mesoamerica*, ed. Thomas W. Killion, pp. 150–183. University of Alabama Press, Tuscaloosa.

Scholes, France V., and Ralph L. Roys
　1968　　The Maya Indians of Acalán-Tixchel. University of Oklahoma Press, Norman.

Scholes, France V., and Dave Warren
　1965　　The Olmec Region at Spanish Contact. In *Archaeology of Southern Mesoamerica*, Part 2, ed. Gordon R. Willey, pp. 776–787. Handbook of Middle American Indians, vol. 3, Robert Wauchope, gen. ed. University of Texas Press, Austin.

Sisson, Edward B.
　1976　　Survey and Excavation in the Northwestern Chontalpa, Tabasco, Mexico. PhD dissertation, Department of Anthropology, Harvard University, Cambridge, MA.

Smith, Robert E.
　1958　　The Place of Fine Orange Pottery in Mesoamerican Archaeology. *American Antiquity* 24 (2): 151–160.

Squier, Robert
　1957　　Post-Olmec Occupations at La Venta, Tabasco. *Bulletin of the Texas Archaeological Society* 28: 111–121.

Stirling, Matthew W.
　1943a　La Venta's Green Stone Tigers. *National Geographic Magazine* 84 (3): 321–332.
　1943b　*Stone Monuments of Southern Mexico*. Bureau of American Ethnology Bulletin 138. Smithsonian Institution, Washington, DC.
　1957　　*An Archaeological Reconnaissance in Southeastern Mexico*. Bureau of American Ethnology Bulletin 164: 213–240. Smithsonian Institution, Washington, DC.

Stross, Brian
　1992　　Olmec Crayfish Farming. *Estudios de Cultura Maya* 9: 133–186. UNAM, México, DF.

Symonds, Stacey C., and Roberto Lunagómez
　1997　　Settlement System and Population Development at San Lorenzo. In *Olmec to Aztec: Settlement Patterns in the Ancient Gulf Lowlands*, ed. Barbara L. Stark and Philip J. Arnold III, pp. 206–252. University of Arizona Press, Tucson.

Tápia, Andrés de
　1971　　Relación hecha por el señor Andrés de Tápia, sobre la conquista de México. In *Colección de documentos para la historia de México, Joaquin Garcia Icazbalceta*, vol. 1, pp. 554–594. Editorial Porrua, S.A., México, DF.

Thompson, J. Eric
　1970　　*Maya History and Religion*. University of Oklahoma Press, Norman.

Villa-Señor y Sánchez, José Antoniode
　1952　　*Teatro americano: Descripción general de los reynos y provincias de la Nueva España, y sus jurisdicciones, parte 1*. Editora Nacional, México, DF.

von Nagy, Christopher Lynn
    2003   Of Meandering Streams and Shifting Towns: Landscape Evolution and Community within the Grijalva Delta. Unpublished PhD dissertation, Department of Anthropology, Tulane University, New Orleans, LA.

Weiant, C. W.
    1943   *An Introduction to the Ceramics of Tres Zapotes Veracruz, Mexico.* Smithsonian Institution Bureau of American Ethnology Bulletin 139. Government Printing Office, Washington, DC.

Wendt, Carl J.
    2000   Investigations at an Olmec Community. Report submitted to FAMSI. Electronic document, http://www.famsi.org; accessed March 15, 2005.
    2005a   Excavations at El Remolino: Household Archaeology in the San Lorenzo Olmec Region. *Journal of Field Archaeology* 30: 163–180.
    2005b   Using Refuse Disposal Patterns to Infer Olmec Site Structure in the San Lorenzo Region, Veracruz, Mexico. *Latin American Antiquity* 16 (4): 449–466.
    2008a   El Antiguo Procesamiento y Uso de Chapopote en las Tierras Bajas de San Lorenzo, Veracruz, Mexico. In *Ideología Política y Sociedad en el Periodo Formativo: Ensayos en Homenaje al Doctor David C. Grove*, ed. Ann Cyphers and Kenneth G. Hirth, pp. 55–92. UNAM, Instituto de Investigaciones Antropológicas, México, DF.
    2008b   Los Olmecas: Los Primeros Petroleros. *Arqueología Mexicana* 15 (87): 56–59.

Wendt, Carl J., and Ann Cyphers
    2008   How the Olmec Used Bitumen in Ancient Mesoamerica. *Journal of Anthropological Archaeology* 27: 175–191.

Wendt, Carl J., and Shan-Tan Lu
    2006   Sourcing Archaeological Bitumen in the Olmec Region. *Journal of Archaeological Science* 33 (1): 89–97.

West, Robert C., Norbert P. Psuty, and Bruce G. Thom
    1969   *The Tabasco Lowlands of Southeastern Mexico.* Coastal Studies Series 27. Louisiana State University Press, Baton Rouge.

Wilken, Gene C.
    1971   Food-Producing Systems Available to the Ancient Maya. *American Antiquity* 36: 432–448.

Willey, Gordon R.
    1965   Artifacts. In *Prehistoric Maya Settlements in the Belize Valley*, ed. Gordon R. Willey, William R. Bullard Jr., John B. Glass, and James C. Gifford, pp. 391–522. Papers of the Peabody Museum of Archaeology and Ethnology 54. Harvard University, Cambridge, MA.

Ximénez, Francisco
    1929   *Historia de la provincia de San Vicente de Chiapa y Guatemala de la orden depredicadores*, vol. 1. Biblioteca Goathemala de la Sociedad de Geografía e Historia, Guatemala.

4

AQUÍ NACIÓ EL MUNDO: TAKALIK ABAJ AND EARLY MESOAMERICAN CIVILIZATION

Brian Dervin Dillon

Dón Beto Sinto (figure 4.1) was an honored elder, a *Chimán*, or native priest, and *curandero*. He was older than the twentieth century when we first met in February 1976. Dón Beto kept the old ways and was the only person at Takalik Abaj who could tell you what day it was in the ancient Maya calendar. All the local Indians knew and revered him as a very wise man. He spoke four languages: his native Mam Maya, some Spanish, and, because two of his wives were from other Highland Maya groups, two additional Maya tongues. Too old to work on the finca, he nevertheless considered it his duty to walk around every day—visiting his friends, offering advice, explaining the past, divining the future, curing the sick, and reassuring the faint-hearted.

Dón Beto told us stories of the *Mazacuat*, the giant snake that could climb trees and fly from one side of the *barranca* to the other. He had been doing *costumbre* at various Takalik Abaj sculptures for years, as candle wax drippings and buried offerings of *aguardiente octavos* at their bases testified.[1] Dón Beto guided us to those few sculptures that remained partially exposed above the thick layer of volcanic ash from the 1902 Santa María Volcano eruption.[2] One of these was what he called the *conejo* stone, a low-relief carving of an animal thought to be a rabbit (figure 4.2).

Once we began excavating at Takalik Abaj, nobody was more interested in, and excited about, what we were doing than Dón Beto.[3] Our Mam Maya workmen

Brian Dervin Dillon

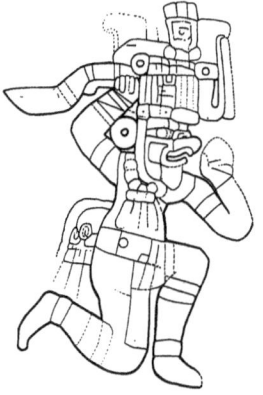

4.1. *Takalik Abaj Monument 1, the Middle Preclassic Olmec petroglyph 1.56 m tall, originally published by Eric Thompson in 1943. (Left): Los 4 ancianos; (left to right): Dón Beto Sinto, Edwin M. Shook, and Robert F. Heizer. Photo by John A. Graham, 1976. (Right): Monument 1. Drawing by James Porter.*

urged us to ask him what he thought about our finds, so we were happy to show him his conejo stone after exposure. This had been named Takalik Abaj Monument 14, the first obviously Olmec sculpture newly encountered that initial season. Dón Beto sat down on Monument 14 and serenely announced, for our benefit: *Aquí Nació El Mundo* (Here the World Was Born).

By the end of that first field season we had found dozens of monumental sculptures at Takalik Abaj. Some were Olmec, others Early Maya, and others still were hard to assign to any established cultural tradition. Overnight, the archaeological site became world-famous, and conventional theories about the birthplace of Mesoamerican civilization and how its earliest civilizations were interconnected were turned upside-down.

TAKALIK ABAJ

Abaj Takalik, literally "stones standing" in Quiché Maya, was the name bequeathed to the archaeological site by Susanna Miles (1965: 246) despite the absence of any historic Quiché presence. Adding one letter to the name in a minor spoonerism results in an obscenity guaranteed to produce chuckles among any Maya within earshot. Miles's name was offered as a means of avoiding the confusion generated by at least three different prior names applied to the same archaeological site. San Isidro Piedra Parada combined "standing stones" with the name of one of many modern fincas presently atop the site. Santa Margarita took the name of the largest of these fincas, immediately south of San Isidro. Colomba made reference to the small settlement 10 km up the

4.2. *Middle Preclassic Takalik Abaj Monument 14. (Above): the "conejo" as found in the Santa Margarita cafetal, with burned mortar used by Dón Beto Sinto for costumbre. Photo by Brian Dervin Dillon, 1976. (Below): Monument 14, 1.25 m tall, after its excavation atop Mound 7. Drawing by James Porter. This is not a "conejo" but instead a squatting Olmec personage holding a feline (left) and an unidentified quadruped (right).*

road, in actuality beyond the site's northern boundary. In 1976 the University of California, Berkeley's program of excavation began work at the site, using Miles's geographically neutral term for it. In 2004 Miguel Orrego Corzo changed the site's name to Takalik Abaj to better fit modern Quiché usage ("standing stones") than did Miles's original word order. I understand Miguel's reasoning for this change; he persuaded me to embrace it myself, as is reflected in these pages. It is hoped that the archaeological site's name has been changed for the final time.

The 1976 Berkeley archaeological team inherited terminological conventions used at Takalik Abaj by earlier researchers, who had divided the small sculptural corpus known until then into three separate categories: stelae, altars, and monuments. This same system had also been used by Robert F. Heizer and John A. Graham during their earlier fieldwork at La Venta. The "monuments" category is something of a catch-all and subsumes more specific sculptural types at Takalik Abaj, including petroglyphic rock art, boulder sculptures, potbellies, and, of course, colossal heads.[4]

WHY IS TAKALIK ABAJ LOCATED WHERE IT IS?

The Pacific Slope of Guatemala (figure 4.3) is normally divided into three climatic zones based on elevation above mean sea level: the Volcanic Highlands (*tierra fría*) above 1,000 m, the Piedmont (La Boca Costa) down to 200 m, and the Coastal Lowlands (Tierra Caliente), the gently sloping alluvial coastal plain running down to the Pacific shoreline. The Piedmont contains a "hot strip" in its lower elevations and a mild zone at its upper limit. Its soil is extremely fertile because of the constant replenishment of nutrients by ongoing volcanic ashfall and vegetational regeneration, abundant precipitation, and excellent drainage. Multicropping is common, and *milperos* obtain two annual crops (McBryde 1947; Shook 1965; Parsons 1967a: 22–23; Dillon 1977: 3). The Piedmont presently offers the most productive farmland in Guatemala, if not in Central America as a whole: this agricultural advantage is probably a very ancient one.

Today, rubber, coffee, and bananas are grown on the Takalik Abaj archaeological site; nearby are commercial crops as diverse as macadamia nuts and citronella grass. The coffee, introduced into the Takalik Abaj area in the 1860s; the rubber, introduced in the 1930s and 1940s; and the macadamia nuts, in the 1960s—tree crops all—do spectacularly well. Early historical accounts (Orellana 1995) relate that both Soconusco and Suchitepéquez were productive cacao-growing areas at European contact. Cacao could have been grown in abundance throughout the entire history of human occupation at Takalik Abaj, perhaps as early as the Middle Preclassic Period. Long ago (Dillon 1975: 113–120) I reviewed the archaeological, ethnohistoric, and ethnographic literature bearing upon cacao production and use in Mesoamerica without suggesting that an eco-

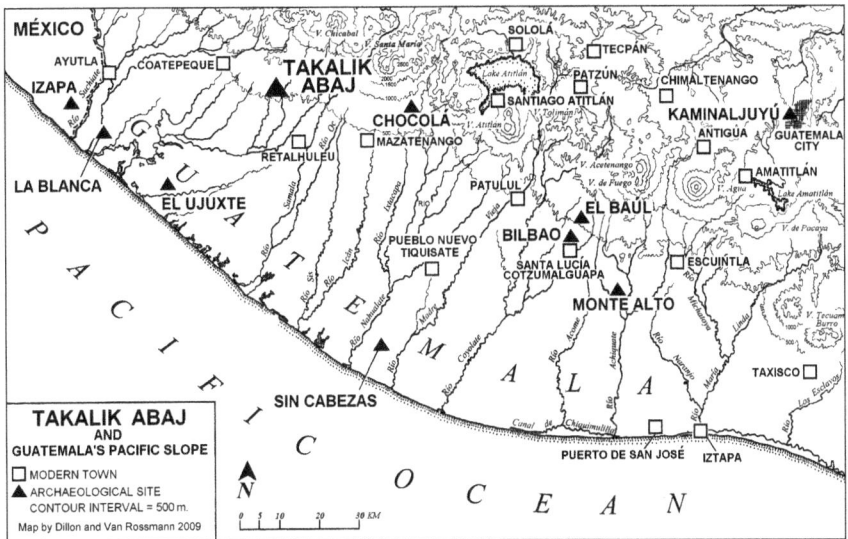

4.3. *Southwestern Guatemala, showing the Coastal Plain, Piedmont, Volcanic Highlands, and selected archaeological sites. Modified from Shook 1965 by Brian Dervin Dillon and Rusty van Rossmann.*

nomic impetus for Olmec presence was control of major cacao-producing areas; Philip Drucker (1981: 36) kindly did this for me a few years later. Cacao grows well on the archaeological site today; it is not difficult to envision vast groves of cacao at ancient Takalik Abaj and the slopes below it where coffee and rubber presently abound.

The Guatemalan Piedmont's remarkable agricultural potential at present almost certainly mirrors the ancient situation. Control of this elevational band in ancient times would have ensured access to three radically different growing zones within a comparatively short distance. Early agricultural Piedmont populations could have "hedged their bets" with different kinds of crops with varying growth cycles in areas with growing seasons of different lengths.[5] Takalik Abaj, placed precisely between two ecotones, dominates all three climatic zones simultaneously. The gently sloping tierra caliente coastal plain is only a few kilometers and a two-hour walk downhill from the site, while the tierra fría of the Volcanic Highlands is a similar time and distance uphill. An energetic farmer could tend *guixquíl* (chayote) in the tierra fría a short distance north of Takalik Abaj, then walk through his *milpas* in the tierra templada to work with New World taro in the tierra caliente a short distance south of the city, all on the same day.

If the Piedmont was the premier location for an ancient city to grow to local predominance, then why this specific part of the Piedmont? Possibly, it was Takalik Abaj's proximity to the Santa María Volcano or to the Volcán Chicabal

Table 4.1. Takalik Abaj radiocarbon age determinations

Laboratory Number	Provenience	Conventional Age	Conventional Date	2 Sigma Calibrated
UCLA 2174A	T60a Cache 41	925 ± 100	AD 1025	AD 950–1276
UCLA 2300C	T11C-j	1,350 ± 60	AD 600	AD 569–782
UCLA 2174C	T73h 1.6 m	1,640 ± 80	AD 310	AD 235–594
UCLA 1996	Stela 2	2,100 ± 170	150 BC	542 BC–AD 259
UCLA 2300A	T103 8.5 m	2,200 ± 60	250 BC	393–107 BC
UCLA 2174B	T20dS1 Mound 12	2,200 ± 150	300 BC	390–158 BC
UCLA 2192C	T103 6.6-.8 m	2,520 ± 60	570 BC	800–485 BC
UCLA 2192B	T88G Feature 3	2,535 ± 70	585 BC	807–483 BC
UCLA 2300B	T96F-I	2,570 ±60	620 BC	838–508 BC
UCLA 2192A	T87A Stela 2	2,900 ± 60	950 BC	1269–919 BC
UCR 808	T63e-2	3,030 ± 100	1080 BC	1497–1002 BC
UCLA 2134A	T30A Mound 7	3,175 ± 60	1225 BC	1541–1312 BC
UCR 807	T33K Mound 7	3,350 ± 100	1400 BC	1886–1433 BC
UCR 909	T63f Pit 1	3,460 ± 100	1510 BC	2026–1526 BC
UCLA 2134B	T25C Mound 7	4,130 ± 80	2100 BC	2891–2558 BC

(Graham and Benson 2005: 359). Mountain worship was an idea proposed by Robert F. Heizer as an explanation for the construction of the great Complex C pyramid at La Venta more than forty years ago; the idea continues to enjoy popularity (Grove 1999, 2007). Santa María Volcano is one of the most spectacular natural landmarks from coastal Chiapas to El Salvador, while Chicabal, with its internal crater lake, remains a powerful center of supernatural activity even today. The tradition of visiting Volcán Chicabal to obtain divinatory power is possibly a very old one, as old as Olmec times.

WHEN WAS TAKALIK ABAJ OCCUPIED?

Fifteen radiocarbon age determinations (table 4.1) were run on charcoal samples obtained during the 1976–1980 seasons, twelve at the University of California–Los Angeles 14^c laboratory by Rainer Berger (Berger and Terry 1979a, 1979b) and three at the University of California–Riverside lab by R. E. Taylor. These dates suggest that the Takalik Abaj site has been occupied for at least 2,000 years. A provisional chronological reconstruction for Takalik Abaj (table 4.2) is based on the UC Berkeley and subsequent Guatemalan National Project excavations (Dillon 1977; Graham 1977, 1979; Graham, Heizer, and Shook 1978; Hatch 1976, 1991; Neff 1987; Castillo 1991; Orrego Corzo 1990; Schieber de Lavarreda 1994,

Table 4.2. Takalik Abaj chronology

Mesoamerican Chronology		Takalik Abaj Periods	Cultural Interpretation
Early Preclassic Period	2000–800 BC	???	Initial period
Early Middle Preclassic Period	800–600 BC	Ixchiya	Early Olmec period
Late Middle Preclassic Period	600–400 BC	Nil	Late Olmec period
Late Preclassic Period	400 BC–AD 100	Rocio	First Early Maya period
Terminal Preclassic Period	AD 100–250	Ruth	Final Early Maya period
Early Classic Period	AD 250–400	Alejos	Disruption and abandonment
	AD 400–600	Castillo	Weak local culture period
Late Classic Period	AD 600–700	Guzmán	Weak local culture period
	AD 600–900	Ralda	Strong local culture period
Early Postclassic Period	AD 900–1200	Sibana	Mam (??) period
Late Postclassic Period	AD 1200–Conquest	Xab	Quiché (??) period

1998; Schieber de Lavarreda and Orrego Corzo 2001a, 2001b, 2002; Orrego Corzo, personal communication, 2010).

The earliest Takalik Abaj periods are poorly known. John Graham (1981, 1982, 1989; Graham and Benson 2005; Graham, personal communication, 2009) believes some of the Takalik Abaj potbellies may be pre-Olmec. If so, they are probably the oldest sculptures at the site. By the end of the Middle Preclassic Period at Takalik Abaj, Olmec sculptures were being positioned at what was becoming a city (Schieber de Lavarreda 1994). The large corpus of Olmec sculpture at Takalik Abaj (figures 4.1, 4.2, 4.5, and 4.6; table 4.3) has direct stylistic similarities with Middle Preclassic Olmec sculpture from La Venta, conventionally dated no later than 400 BC (Clewlow 1974; Graham 1982, 2005). Late Preclassic Period Early Maya sculptures with the oldest hieroglyphic inscriptions yet known were carved at Takalik Abaj (figure 4.8), possibly as early as the end of the 6th Cycle but certainly by the very beginning of the 7th.

The Early Maya occupation continued throughout the entire Late Preclassic Period (tables 4.1, 4.2, 4.4) while the city grew to immense size, rivaled perhaps only by Kaminaljuyú to the east and Izapa to the west. Stela 5 (figures 4.11–4.13) at Takalik Abaj (Dillon 1977; Graham, Heizer, and Shook 1978) is the latest dated Early Maya sculpture at the site. It bears two Long Count dates side by side, the earlier converting to AD 80, the later to AD 126. It is tempting to interpret these two dates as a ruler's birth or accession and death dates. More important than such subjective considerations, however, is an objective one: Takalik Abaj Stela

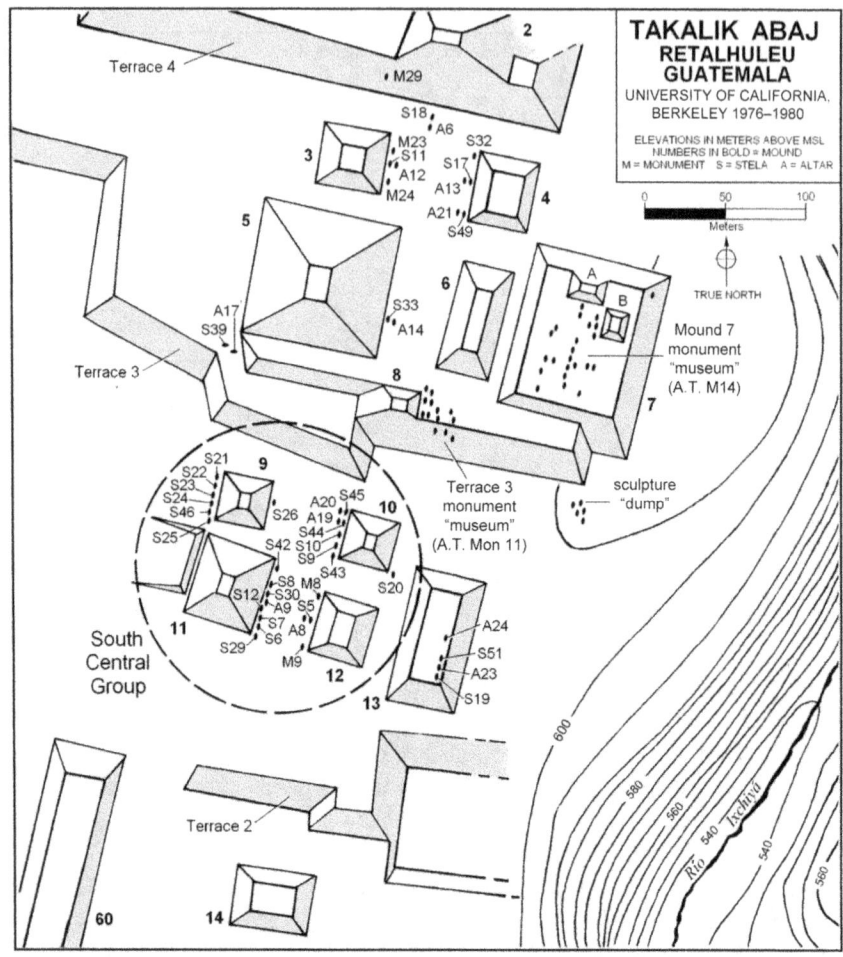

4.4. *A small portion of the Takalik Abaj site map, emphasizing the South Central Group and Dillon's 1976–1977 excavations, with stela, altar, and monument locations numbered. Drafted by Mark Johnson and Kevin Pope, 1983. Additions by Brian Dervin Dillon, 1986 and 2009.*

5 remains 166 years older than the oldest long count inscription from the Petén, Tikal Stela 29, dated to AD 292 (Shook 1960). Stylistic elements shared by Olmec and Maya sculpture and also found at the site of Izapa that are often termed "Izapan" are found at Takalik Abaj (figure 4.9) and Kaminaljuyú, as well as at the site of the same name. Such elements, if they grew out of Olmec art, were more likely conferred upon Izapa from Takalik Abaj, with its strong, antecedent Olmec sculptural presence, than the reverse.

As Protoclassic Maya civilization accelerated in the Petén, the Early Maya city of Takalik Abaj went into decline. How these two events were intercon-

4.5. *Antonio Guzmán and Takalik Abaj Monument 8, 1.10 m tall, at the time of its discovery in 1976. Photo by Brian Dervin Dillon. (Right): rollout drawing of Monument 8 by James Porter. Monument 8, at the northwest corner of Mound 12, was one of two Middle Preclassic Olmec monuments flanking Early Maya Stela 5 on the west side of Late Preclassic Takalik Abaj Mound 12.*

nected remains an exciting subject for future research. Many early sculptures at Takalik Abaj were intentionally defaced or buried at this time. The site enjoyed a resurgence of population and building during the Late Classic Period, without any obvious sculptural or architectural connections with the Southern Maya Lowlands. Simultaneously, the Cotzumalhuapa civilization at cities such as Bilbao, El Baúl, and Palo Gordo came to dominate the Pacific Slope, but a Cotzumalhuapa sculptural presence at Takalik Abaj is absent. Takalik Abaj's presumed Early Classic decline in population and prestige may have created a vacuum, thereby stimulating the Cotzumalhuapa culture to the east. Most Cotzumalhuapa sites (Bilbao, El Baúl, El Castillo, Palo Gordo) are also in the Piedmont. After Takalik Abaj's Middle-Late Preclassic-Protoclassic dominance, power may have shifted eastward, with the Cotzumalhuapa culture flowering in the Late Classic. Takalik Abaj's Terminal Classic resurgence may then, in turn, have eclipsed Cotzumalhuapa.

The Late Classic Period, however, was a time during which many Middle and Late Preclassic Period sculptures were repositioned or buried and probably when many of the dozens of plain stelae were erected. A robust Early Postclassic occupation at Takalik Abaj is denoted by abundant Tohil Plumbate, ladle *incensarios*, and flat and walled *comales* (Hatch 1976; Neff 1987, 2002). The latest rebuilding of most of the cobble-faced structures at Takalik Abaj probably took place during the Terminal Classic and Early Postclassic Periods. The entire Late Postclassic Period is interpreted by Christa Schieber de Lavarrada and Miguel Orrego Corzo (2002) as a time of Quiché occupation. Evidence presented by Sandra L. Orellana (1995) suggests, alternatively, that the Mam

Maya may have preceded them as the latest Prehispanic occupants of Takalik Abaj.

MOVING MOUNTAINS

Takalik Abaj is a huge site, more than 5 km long north-south by 0.5 to 1.5 km wide east-west, stepping up in elevation from around 550 to 700 m above mean sea level. Estimates of Takalik Abaj's size continue to grow as more cartographic work is completed: the initial estimate of 3 km^2 was expanded to 5 km^2 and then again to 9 km^2 (Dillon 1977: 3; Busby and Johnson 1978; Johnson and Pope 1985; Scheiber de Lavarreda 1994: 77). Miguel Orrego's team has been mapping the site continually for more than twenty years; the final estimate of the site's overall size must await completion of this monumental task.

By the Middle Preclassic Period, Takalik Abaj was already a gigantic adobe and taxcal city, but it probably reached its greatest size during the Late Preclassic Period (Schieber de Lavarreda and Orrego Corzo 2001a, 2001b, 2002). By comparison, the famous Gulf Coast Olmec sites of La Venta at 2 km^2 (González Lauck 1995: 39) and San Lorenzo at 1.5 km^2 (Coe and Diehl 1980) in size are much smaller. Other well-known sites are smaller still: Chalcatzingo covers only around 0.6 km^2 (Grove, personal communication, 2009), while Bilbao (Parsons 1967a, 1969) is tiny at 0.25 km^2. Takalik Abaj could swallow up all the aforementioned archaeological sites with plenty of room left over. Takalik Abaj is bounded on its east and west by steep barrancas forming its nominal boundaries in both directions: the eastern, Rio Ixchiyá, barranca contains important archaeological features, including at least one undeniably Olmec petroglyph (Takalik Abaj Monument 1) and at least one possibly Olmec niche figure (Takalik Abaj Monument 25). Takalik Abaj incorporates over seventy major structures—all of earthen fill, most with cobble facings, congregated in architectural groups, and surrounded by hundreds of smaller structures. The tallest structure is Mound 5, a Middle Preclassic earthen pyramid 17 m in height. To its east lies a low and massive platform of similar age, Mound 7; the relationship between these two structures is reminiscent of that between La Venta's great pyramid and Stirling Acropolis.

The mounds and architectural groups at Takalik Abaj rest atop eleven man-made terraces, artificially leveled platforms many thousands of square meters in extent. These artificial terraces were built atop a huge alluvial fan sweeping down from the Volcanic Highlands toward the Coastal Plain. This fan is composed of bouldery volcanic laharic debris transported by the seasonally torrential floods descending from the geologically young Santa María, Siete Orejas, and Chicabal Volcanos (Williams 1960, 1977). The terraces, massive earth-moving efforts of immense scale (figure 4.4), are the single most impressive aspect of the Takalik Abaj site (Graham and Benson 2005: 360). Their dating is problematic; assuredly, at least some are later than others or have been expanded outward, if not upward, over time. Certainly, the earliest terraces at the site predate the earliest structures built atop them, and very early structures were likely "swallowed up" as later terraces were built around and over them. Despite recognition of the Takalik Abaj terraces at the outset of our investigations (Graham, Heizer, and Shook 1978: 88), we spent two seasons mapping Takalik Abaj before we realized that at least five modern fincas and most of the cropland they contained sat atop land leveled for the construction of the ancient city. The tallest and most massive of the Takalik Abaj terraces rise to just under 11 m in height. All were made of millions of cubic meters of artificial fill, moved one basket-load at a time; all level land on or around the archaeological site is anciently leveled land.

Massive earth-moving operations are a hallmark of Olmec civilization. At San Lorenzo six ridges, the largest 6.5 m tall, finger off the main ridge at the site. Originally claimed as artificial (Coe and Diehl 1980; Diehl 1981: 74–75), most of their volume is now seen as natural, albeit with substantial artificial terracing (Cyphers 1997). The largest of the eleven Takalik Abaj terraces is almost twice as tall as any ridge or terrace at San Lorenzo, incorporating many times the volume of the largest San Lorenzo example. At La Venta, the Complex C great pyramid rises more than 30 m above the surrounding terrain and has been estimated (Heizer 1968; Heizer and Drucker 1968; Graham and Johnson 1979) to contain well over 100,000 m^3 of fill: Takalik Abaj Mound 5 is just over half the height and mass of the La Venta great mound. Chalcatzingo (Grove 1987, this volume) is a site built atop at least thirty-seven separate terraces of all different sizes but nothing similar in size or scale to the large Takalik Abaj examples.

Earth moving at both San Lorenzo and La Venta involved heavy lifting, building upward and outward. At Takalik Abaj the work was comparatively easier, involving cutting and filling, the transformation of steep-sloping land into a series of leveled, ascending flats. If the earliest people at Takalik Abaj—long before it became a city—were Early Preclassic rustic farmers, then the earliest terracing efforts were probably done to facilitate agriculture, control runoff, and inhibit erosion of the barranca margins. What may have started small on a family-by-family basis grew to a gigantic effort by thousands of people by the Middle Preclassic Period, creating a city rising on a series of ascending terraces. The ancient Takalik Abaj terrace fronts and tops were probably surfaced with taxcal, a multicolored clay quarried locally today primarily for use as road fill. Anciently, it was used extensively at Takalik Abaj for architectural embellishment. Taxcal is milky white in a varicolored matrix of pale brown and green, shading to orange, pink, and red. Watering or polishing brings out the colors with enhanced brightness, so taxcal floors may have been highly polished during their archaeological use. Howel Williams's (1977) geological analysis reveals that it is partially decomposed, rotten, soft, andesitic lava from the uppermost layer of bouldery deposits overlain by brownish, weathered ash. The use of bright-colored clays and sands is a hallmark of Olmec cities (Drucker, Heizer, and Squier 1959). Viewing such multicolored surfaces at La Venta has been likened to "a truly psychedelic experience" (Diehl 1981: 78); south-facing Takalik Abaj, on its ascending taxcal-faced terraces—which on clear days would have caught sunlight all day long—would have been no less spectacular.

MONUMENT MUSEUMS AND SCULPTURE DUMPS

Few, if any, other Mesoamerican sites are as rich in monumental sculpture as Takalik Abaj. By the end of the fifth UC Berkeley season, 51 stelae, 25 altars, and 61 monuments, not counting small portable sculptures (such as silhouettes, stone dogs, and carved stone lidded boxes)—for a total of 137 sculptures—had been discovered at the site, whereas fewer than a dozen had been known previously. All of this work involved making small excavations in the *cafetal*, removing one coffee bush at a time (see figure 4.5 left; figure 4.11). The ongoing work of Miguel Orrego Corzo, Christa Schieber de Lavarreda, Marion Hatch, and their research team—for the first time doing large area exposures to completely reveal architecture—has greatly expanded the count of sculptures now known from Takalik Abaj. The number of sculptures found at the ancient city—approximately half carved and half plain—now stands at 367, more than from any other early Mesoamerican archaeological site (Orrego Corzo 1998; Schieber de Lavarreda and Orrego Corzo 2002: 26; Orrego Corzo, personal communication, 2010).[6] With less than 5 percent of the total site area systematically searched for stone monuments through large area exposures, the final sculptural tally at Takalik Abaj will not be known until and unless the entire site can be investigated.

At various times in the city's history, its inhabitants collected sculptures and put them on display without strict adherence to either age or stylistic sorting. At least three "monument museums" exist at Takalik Abaj. Sculptural arrays or ancient "monument museums" are also known from San Lorenzo (Diehl 1981; Grove 1999: figure 13) and La Venta (Heizer, Graham, and Napton 1968: map 1). Grove (this volume) suggests that at least part of the Chalcatzingo site was set up to present a series of Olmec stelae on a "processional way." Much later in time but much closer geographically, most Bilbao sculptures were set around a sunken court in yet another monument museum (Parsons 1967a, 1969).

Atop Takalik Abaj Mound 7 in Postclassic contexts were found alignments of stelae, altars, and monuments in both Olmec (see figures 4.2, 4.7) and Early Maya style, side by side with uncarved monuments. Similar arrangements were found along the plaza margins at the feet of most mounds at the site, especially the Mound 12 plaza, where the Protoclassic Stela 5 (see figures 4.11–4.13), bearing two Initial Series dates, was flanked to the north and south by two smaller Olmec monuments (see figure 4.5). Nearly twenty sculptures faced into this plaza (see figure 4.4). A final kind of monument museum or collection of sculptures was made at the edge of Terrace 3, where Monument 11 (see figure 4.8)

4.6. *Middle Preclassic Olmec sculpture from Takalik Abaj. Monument 55, a fragmentary head and upper torso, 0.40 m tall, discovered in the sculpture dump southeast of Mound 7 and Terrace 3. Drawing by James Porter.*

takes pride of place. The sculptures in such monument museums, in some cases 2,000 years older than their final context of display, had probably been repeatedly reset or repositioned, with their original associations obviously compromised in ancient times.

At Takalik Abaj—as at La Venta, Chalcatzingo, Chocolá, Kaminaljuyú, and other early sites—after their original positioning, monumental sculptures were constantly in movement. Three main patterns took place: resetting, repositioning, and burial. Resetting (cf. Graham and Porter 1989: 47), typically upward and outward from the original position, was done as architectural structures were enlarged over time and the sculptures standing at their feet had to be either moved or obscured. Early Maya Takalik Abaj Stela 5 (see figures 4.11–4.13), for example, was reset twice as Mound 12 behind it was expanded. Mound 12 itself, beginning in the Late Preclassic, was rebuilt at least five times (Orrego Corzo 1990; Schieber de Lavarreda and Orrego Corzo 2002). Repositioning involved

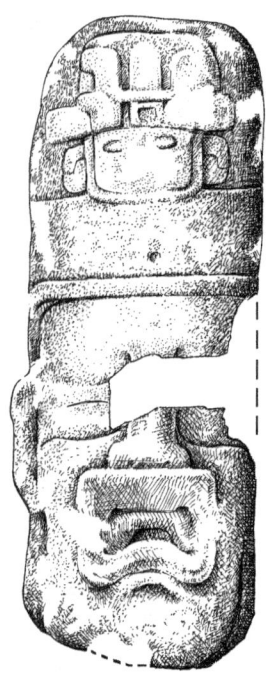

4.7. *Monuments 16 and 17, a columnar head with elaborate headdress snapped in half, 1.9 m tall, found erected as two separate sculptures in the monument museum atop Mound 7. Drawing by James Porter and Rusty van Rossmann.*

collecting sculptures from earlier positions, possibly repeatedly, so as to group them together in alignments either atop later structures or along the fronts of buildings facing into plazas. Takalik Abaj Olmec Monument 14 (see figure 4.2) was moved from its original position to the top of Mound 7, where it formed part of a Postclassic monument museum. Finally, many monuments were intentionally buried, usually after being broken or defaced. Such burial occurred with single sculptures, such as Early Maya Stela 12 (figure 4.10), and multiple ones, including Olmec Monuments 54 and 55 (see figure 4.6), unassigned Monuments 56 and 57, and Altar 25 in what can only be described as a sculpture dump. Sculpture dumps are not unique to Takalik Abaj; others are known from La Venta, San Lorenzo, Kaminaljuyú, and many other, much smaller sites. The single largest example yet found may be at Bilbao, which includes over thirty Cotzumalhuapa Style stone sculpture fragments (Parsons 1969: 90–91).

Why was this done? If you are going to move mountains and you value for whatever reason (e.g., genealogical, political, religious) existing monumental sculptures already hundreds of years old, you can certainly move them, too. Were they simply moved short distances horizontally from other areas within the ancient city as it grew over time, or were they moved upward from their original positions as mounds and terraces were expanded? Or were sculptures collected from other conquered or abandoned sites nearby, "captured" from other sites, and brought to Takalik Abaj to be "held hostage," symbolizing the growing city's dominion over the surrounding area—which extended even to religious or genealogical markers of conquered peoples? This is hardly a new or original idea, for the Conquest period Aztec in Mesoamerica, no less than their Inca counterparts in South America, routinely held the idols of conquered peoples "hostage" in their capital city. Evidence for this practice on the Guatemalan Pacific Slope is tentative at best. Michael Love (1999: 142) has commented on the curious lack of sculptures at El Ujuxte, suggesting that they may have been looted, presumably in ancient times. If so, some may have ended up at Takalik Abaj. While there is no absolute guarantee that all of the Takalik Abaj sculptures were actually carved at that site, they nevertheless were surely of reasonably local

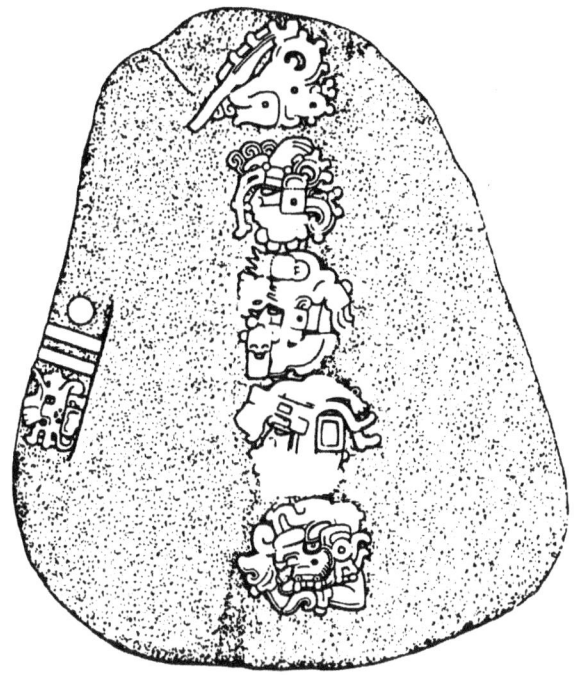

4.8. *Takalik Abaj Monument 11, an Early Maya boulder sculpture, 1.35 m tall, on the edge of Terrace 3 with some of the earliest (late 6th or early 7th Cycle?) Maya hieroglyphs ever found. Day sign (?) bar and dot numeral at left; personified glyphs at center. Drawing by James Porter.*

provenience. Williams (1977), after geological testing, concluded that all of the Takalik Abaj andesite sculptures—whether Olmec, Maya, or in other styles—are of the same local stone from the lower slopes of Santa María Volcano.

Many Takalik Abaj Olmec sculptures show various kinds of intentional recarving similar to that described by Clewlow (1974), Coe and Diehl (1980: 297–298), and Grove (1981) at other Olmec sites such as La Venta, San Lorenzo, Laguna de los Cerros, and Chalcatzingo. At Takalik Abaj, ancient sculptural alteration ranges from facial abrasion (to the point of obliteration) all the way to decapitation. Decapitating Olmec sculptures is also familiar from other Pacific Piedmont sites such as Sin Cabezas. The most extreme form of alteration at Takalik Abaj is that of Monument 23, which began as a colossal head, then had its face removed and converted to a niche figure. Not just Olmec sculptures but Early Maya altars and stelae at Takalik Abaj were also altered. Sometimes this defacement was limited only to the removal of glyphic passages through abrasion or even spalling through fire application, as if angry illiterates were erasing the evidence of earlier literate peoples. In other cases, the entire sculpture was demolished.

A remarkable case of Early Maya intentional stela breaking is found in three almost identical examples: Takalik Abaj Stelae 3 and 12 (see figure 4.10), in combination with the sole Early Maya stela from Bilbao (Monument 42). All three stelae remain as basal portions only; all are similar in size, shape, and thematic content; and all three are broken in essentially the same way, as if snapped by lateral force while still positioned. The upper portions of all three stelae have never been found, possibly because the "stela snapping" was done so as to remove their upper portions for complete obliteration or recarving.

THE BIRTH OF MESOAMERICAN CIVILIZATION

Determining when and where Mesoamerican civilization began remains the most compelling research problem in New World archaeology. Coupled with this is a question of even greater global significance: the birthplace of writing in Mesoamerica. For the past half-century the earliest true cities in Mesoamerica have been identified as the great Olmec sites of La Venta and San Lorenzo on the southern Gulf Coast of Mexico. Recent research in the northern Petén and on the Pacific Slope of Guatemala, however, has revealed sites potentially as early and sophisticated as the better-known Gulf Coast Olmec ones. Consequently, the question now becomes how to recognize civilization archaeologically and how to differentiate it from simpler forms of ancient culture.

A simple definition of civilization that does not employ checklists of archaeologically invisible criteria is *urban culture*. Ignacio Bernal (1969: 49) put it succinctly when he wrote "civilization and urbanism are synonymous." If you have cities, you have civilization. All ancient cities throughout the world have a few basic things in common: permanence, large size, dense population, and monumental architecture. But cities, which are *always* archaeologically visible, usually grow out of something smaller, simpler, and earlier that are not cities. These are towns, which grew out of villages, which grew out of hamlets, and so forth. The smaller and earlier the settlement, the less its archaeological visibility. Differences between these ancient settlement categories are of size and complexity, both of which can be objectively measured and compared by any competent field archaeologist. Evidence for the long, slow progression from simple farming or fishing hamlets to villages, from villages to towns, and from towns to cities has been demonstrated from the Southern Maya Lowlands of Belize (Hammond 2005), from the Petén (Hansen 1998, this volume), and from the Guatemalan Pacific Slope (Coe 1961; Shook 1965; Coe and Flannery 1967; Love 1999, 2002, 2007), where the beginnings appear even earlier. There is consequently no reason to assume that civilization within the Maya area had to have been an "Olmec" idea imported from outside the region (cf. Proskouriakoff 1968: 119; Hammond 1988).

The earliest Mesoamerican cities were probably, in every case, accidental inventions. Beatriz De la Fuente (1995) and Rebecca Gonzaléz Lauck (1996a,

1996b) identify La Venta as an Olmec "capital" and arguably the most important Olmec city of them all. Using the term *capital* automatically invokes the city-state concept. Hansen (this volume) believes he has evidence for an Early Maya Kingdom, in other words, a royal city-state, in the Mirador Basin of the Southern Maya Lowlands by 300 BC or even earlier. These two examples, one Olmec and the other Maya, bracket Takalik Abaj both geographically and chronologically. The large and complex Pacific Guatemalan site was also an early city of great importance, if not a city-state in its own right. The early Mesoamerican city of Takalik Abaj was the capital of its own economic support region and the center of its own ancient intellectual, artistic, and cultural universe.

A larger question bears upon the nature of Mesoamerican civilization itself: was it one civilization or many? Did it have single or multiple antecedents? Was it the product of unilineal succession or of the interplay of many simultaneous exemplars? We need look no farther than Takalik Abaj for the answer.

COSMOPOLITAN MESOAMERICAN CITIES

For several decades, people driving past the modern "metropolis" of Retalhuleu could not fail to remark upon the black-and-white cast cement (proof against the constant tropical decay) sign near the city limits bidding them *"Bienvenidos a Retalhuleu, Capital del Mundo."*[7] Considered risible by the less pretentious citizens of neighboring towns such as Coatepeque (hill of the snake), Mazatenango (place of the deer), and Escuintla (town of the dogs), the modern Retalteco's prideful cosmopolitan pretenses may find roots deep in the distant past but not far away, upslope to the northwest at the great abandoned city of Takalik Abaj. Just as our Mam Maya workmen—newcomers to the Takalik Abaj site—were fascinated with the great achievements of their *antepasados* who had built the city and raised the sculptures, so must earlier peoples have built upon the works of their own distantly remembered or perhaps even unknown antecedents.

Tables 4.3 and 4.4 facilitate the comparison of Olmec and Early Maya cities, sites, and cultural diagnostics; Takalik Abaj takes pride of place within both cultural contexts. Figure 4.14, keyed to both tables, reveals that the supposed geographic separation between Olmec and Maya archaeological sites is hardly as distinct as once thought. Where do the two great early civilizations of Mesoamerica, Olmec and Maya, overlap? They merged and commingled on the Pacific Slope of Guatemala, where both are strongly represented at the region's most prominent ancient city, Takalik Abaj.[8] Takalik Abaj is not remarkable as just another Olmec site far from the so-called Olmec heartland of the Gulf Coast or as an Early Maya site far to the south of the Petén climax area but rather as a fully developed Early Maya city sitting atop an even earlier fully developed Olmec one. Even after the Protoclassic Maya torch was passed from Takalik Abaj to the Petén, the site continued to be occupied for more than another 1,000 years.

Brian Dervin Dillon

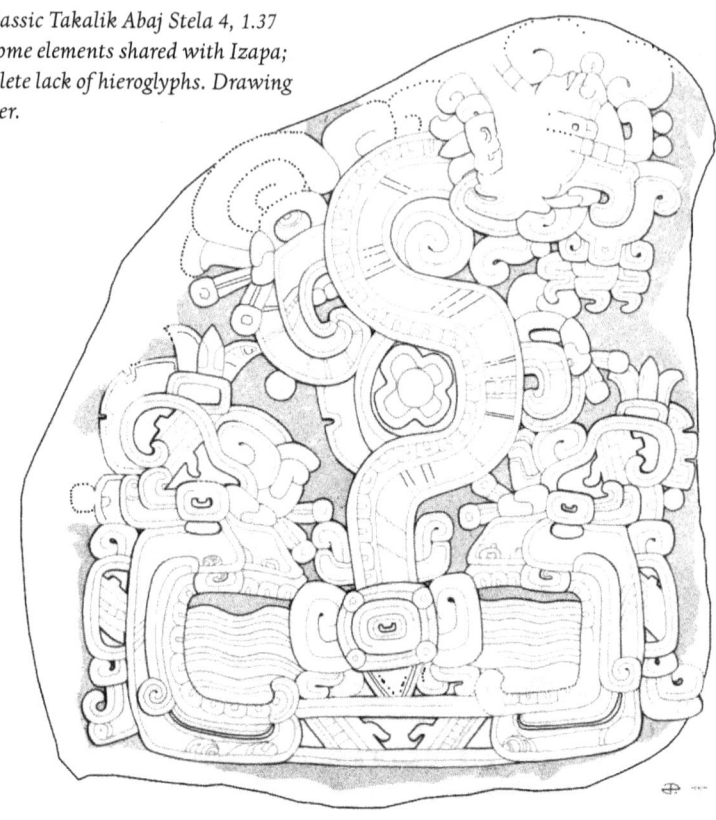

4.9. *Late Preclassic Takalik Abaj Stela 4, 1.37 m tall, with some elements shared with Izapa; note the complete lack of hieroglyphs. Drawing by James Porter.*

Takalik Abaj remains the premier Mesoamerican site that contains both Olmec and Maya sculptures, but it is by no means the only one. Nor are these the only two sculptural styles present at a handful of sites both large and small (Cerro de las Mesas and Tres Zapotes on the Mexican Gulf Coast and Kaminaljuyú, Izapa, Chocolá, El Baúl, and Bilbao on the Guatemalan Pacific Slope) that seem best identified as cosmopolitan cities. Multiple sculptural styles at single archaeological sites probably represent different cultural, ethnic, or linguistic groups, either in succession or contemporaneously. A single great idea, such as writing, may have been the creation of a single human genius but was more likely the outgrowth of cultural give and take between different peoples of different tongues struggling to make themselves understood to each other. Different peoples in close proximity to each other typically create a ferment of new ideas and experimentation; cities are their incubators. Each ancient Mesoamerican city was probably quite different from every other in terms of religion, economy, and politics. The uniquely different variants of early Mesoamerican civilization were probably invented at only a few such cosmopolitan cities, then copied and elaborated upon by other, later peoples who opted to try their own experiments with urbanism and literacy.

GREAT ART STYLES OF THE PACIFIC SLOPE

This chapter's emphasis is primarily on monumental sculpture rather than architecture, jade, chipped stone artifacts, ecofacts, or pottery. Nearly every Mesoamerican site of Preclassic and later age, no matter how tiny, has pottery, but comparatively few of the tens of thousands of sites known contain monumental sculptures. Fewer still are sites where monumental sculptures are numerous. Only a handful of these have large numbers of monumental sculptures in radically different styles, which might indicate either a succession of different cultures over time or the contemporaneity of different peoples. Paramount within this final, exclusive archaeological category is the ancient city of Takalik Abaj.

The Pacific Piedmont of Guatemala and adjacent Chiapas was home to at least four great Mesoamerican sculptural styles: Olmec, Early Maya, Izapan, and Cotzumalhuapa. No other area of similar size in Central America can claim such a long, varied, and rich sculptural expression in such abundance. Two of these sculptural styles, Olmec and Early Maya, are best termed "horizon" or "international" styles, as they were in no way limited to the Piedmont, while the other two, Izapan and Cotzumalhuapa, are best understood as "local" or "national" styles (Schieber de Lavarreda and Orrego Corzo 2002). These four sculptural traditions spanned more than a millennium on the Pacific Slope, from the Middle Preclassic Period through the Late Classic Period.

Olmec is a remarkable Middle Preclassic Sculptural Horizon Style, dating perhaps as early as 1200 BC and as late as 400 BC. Olmec sculptural art perhaps became most widespread throughout Mesoamerica from about 700 to 500 BC, when the great city of La Venta was at its peak. This sculptural style has been associated with an early, if not the earliest, Mesoamerican civilization (Heizer 1976), whose antecedents are firmly in the Early Preclassic Period. Grove (1993: 84–86) laments the frequent confusion between "Olmec" as an art style and archaeological Olmec culture and offers the most precise subdivision of sequential Olmec Horizons from Early to Late. Hallmarks of the Olmec sculptural style are sculpture in the round, low-relief sculpture, and a distinctive iconography often incorporating feline symbolism. Olmec monumental sculpture focuses on the human figure, frequently in action, often in portraiture (Drucker 1952; Proskouriakoff 1968; De la Fuente 1981, 1995, 2000). The most spectacular and unique Olmec portraits are the colossal heads. Other Olmec hallmarks are cities incorporating massive earth-moving projects and earthen architecture.

The best-known Olmec cities of the southern Gulf Coast of Veracruz and Tabasco lay outside the limits of partially contemporaneous Maya civilization.

Table 4.3. Selected Olmec sites and diagnostics

	Earth Moving	Colossal Heads	Stelae	Altars	In the Round	L. R. Carving	Rock Art
1 Takalik Abaj, Retalhuleu, Guatemala	X	X	X		X	X	X
2 La Venta, Tabasco, Mexico	X	X	X	X	X	X	
3 San Lorenzo, Veracruz, Mexico	X	X	X	X	X	X	
4 Tres Zapotes, Veracruz, Mexico		X	X		X	X	
5 Laguna de los Cerros, Veracruz, Mexico		X		X	X		
6 Chalcatzingo, Morelos, Mexico			X	X	X	X	X
7 Chocolá, Suchitepéquez, Guatemala					X		
8 La Blanca, San Marcos, Guatemala					X		
9 Sin Cabezas, Escuintla, Guatemala					X		
10 Padre Piedra, Chiapas, Mexico			X			X	
11 San Miguel Amuco, Guerrero, Mexico			X			X	
12 Teopantecuanitlán, Guerrero, Mexico						X	
13 Tiltepec, Chiapas, Mexico						X	
14 Tzutzuculi, Chiapas, Mexico						X	
15 La Union, Chiapas, Mexico						X	
16 San Antonio Suchitepéquez, Guatemala						X	
17 Xoc, Chiapas, Mexico						X	X
18 Las Victorias, Sta Ana, El Salvador						X	X
19 Pijijiapan, Chiapas, Mexico						X	X
20 Eje Quemado, Amatitlan, Guatemala							Picto
21 Juxtlahuaca, Guerrero, Mexico							Picto
22 Oxtotitlán, Guerrero, Mexico							Picto

Yet Olmec cities and smaller sites have also been found as far south as El Salvador, as far north as Morelos, and as far west as Central Guererro (see table 4.3). Coe and Diehl (1980) and Diehl (2004) term the Mexican southern Gulf Coast the "Olmec heartland." But calling this region the "heartland" presupposes that the Olmec originally developed there and subsequently diffused to all other locations where Olmec sites and traces have been found. This interpretation can be considered correct only if all other Olmec sites known to exist outside this putative "heartland" have been conclusively proven to be later in date, which is still not the case. Takalik Abaj, the most important Olmec city on the Chiapas-Guatemalan Pacific Slope, was occupied at least as early as La Venta and San

4.10. *Takalik Abaj Stela 12, an intentionally shattered Late Preclassic Maya low-relief sculpture buried at the eastern foot of Mound 11. Note remnant glyph at lower left. 1.93 m tall. Drawing by James Porter.*

Lorenzo. When Takalik Abaj became "Olmec" and when it reached the status of a true city are questions still being investigated. When and if they are resolved, a new "Olmec heartland" may need to be proposed on the Guatemalan Pacific Slope.

Early Maya (see table 4.4), as opposed to the more familiar, much later, and more geographically restricted Classic Maya, was a Late Preclassic Period Horizon or International Style incorporating low-relief sculpture, a distinctive iconographic repertoire (Proskouriakoff 1950, 1968), and—most important— glyphs, glyphic passages, and Long Count dates. Early Maya architecture features massive earth-moving projects and elaborate masonry structures. The Early Maya art style of the Late Preclassic and Protoclassic Guatemalan Pacific Slope and adjacent highlands has been called the Miraflores Style by Miles (1965), Proto-Maya by Parsons (1967a), and Early Southern Maya by Sharer (1994). The oldest sculptures in the Early Maya Style are presently known from Takalik Abaj and Kaminaljuyú; these are directly ancestral to the only slightly later ones from the Petén. Maya civilization was in full flower at a few sites by the beginning of the Late Preclassic Period; its antecedents are deeply rooted in the Middle Preclassic. Maya civilization was therefore partially contemporaneous with Olmec yet outlasted it by at least two millennia. If the two great traditions overlapped each other chronologically, then they must have also coexisted, at least for several centuries, at cities such as Takalik Abaj. The same site, centuries later than its time of primacy as an Olmec capital, was also the most important Early Maya city on the Chiapas-Guatemalan Pacific Slope.

Izapan is a Protoclassic narrative local sculptural style that made use of many Olmec and Early Maya artistic conventions (Norman 1973, 1976; Quirarte 1973, 1976). At Izapa, as at nearby Takalik Abaj, Protoclassic sculptures remained in use as late as Postclassic times. Izapa is presently better-known than its contemporary, Takalik Abaj, only through the accident of its chronological primacy of excavation and publication. The relative status of the two sites is slowly being reversed as more work at the ancient Guatemalan city results in more publication. Most Izapan sculpture is in low relief, but some approaching sculpture in the round is also known. A single sculpture (Miscellaneous Monument 2), possibly the earliest at the site, is very similar to Takalik Abaj Monument 23 and may be Olmec. Some Izapan artistic conventions are present at contemporaneous sites such as Kaminaljuyú and Takalik Abaj (Quirarte 1977; Graham 1979), where they tend to be incorporated into sculptures better identified as Early Maya. Much that has been claimed to be "Izapan" is actually not; limiting the definition of the style to the Izapa site itself clears up most confusion on this point.

Izapan is perhaps the most misunderstood and misrepresented artistic tradition in southern Mesoamerica. V. Garth Norman (1973: 1) calls it "post-Olmec and pre-Maya" and "Olmec derived" (ibid.: 2), believing it to be a "link" between Olmec and Maya and also essential to the development of hieroglyphic writing. Michael Coe (1965: 772–773, 1977: 185–186) argues for a ±700-year gap between the collapse of La Venta Olmec and the birth of Classic Maya civilization and invokes a "widespread proto-Maya civilization"—Izapan—to fill that gap. Lee Parsons (1973, 1978, 1981, 1986) believes Izapan was an essential intercalation in a unilineal progression from Olmec to Maya. These scholars are clearly in error, for the Early Maya style was completely contemporaneous with the Izapan Sculptural Style yet also, at Takalik Abaj, earlier. Since the Izapan style is now known to be simultaneous with, and to postdate, Maya culture and the Early Maya art style, it therefore cannot be ancestral to it.

Cotzumalhuapa is a distinctive Late Classic Period local style found at a handful of sites on the Pacific Slope of Guatemala and western El Salvador (Thompson 1948; Parsons 1967a, 1969; Hatch 1989a; Chinchilla Mazariegos 2002). Spot glyphs are known, but no lengthy hieroglyphic passages exist on Cotzumalhuapan monuments. Often claimed as "Mexican" in origin, the low-relief Cotzumalhuapa sculptural tradition owes much to Early Maya local antecedents and is much more sophisticated than anything found in contemporary Highland Central Mexico. Chinchilla Mazariegos (2002: 177) believes the style was of local, not Mexican, derivation. At least two of the Cotzumalhuapa sites, El Baúl and Bilbao, famous for Late Classic sculptures, also contain much earlier Late Preclassic or Protoclassic Early Maya ones as well. This quasi-literate civi-

4.11. *Takalik Abaj Protoclassic Maya Stela 5 on the day of its discovery, February 1976. Note bar and dot numerals visible, lichen growth on previously exposed area. Photo by Brian Dervin Dillon.*

lization probably adapted earlier Maya ideas about writing to its own needs and traditions.

THE INVENTION OF WRITING

Mesoamerica was one of only three areas in the ancient world, the others being Mesopotamia and China, where writing was independently invented. The fundamental question of where writing originally developed in Mesoamerica, which some years ago seemed to have been settled, has become an issue once again. Few would argue that literacy had anything other than a strictly urban genesis; in other words, cities came first, writing second. Apart from very early experimentation in the Valley of Oaxaca, four cultural candidates have been offered as the inventors of Mesoamerican writing: Olmec, Isthmian, Izapan, and Maya.

Olmec, however, was a non-literate civilization. Claims for Olmec writing arise, are refuted and forgotten, then arise anew every decade or so (cf. Pohl, Pope, and von Nagy 2002; Bruhns and Kelker 2007). More than forty years ago Bernal (1968: 140) reluctantly concluded that for writing, the calendar, even the stela-altar complex, "the Olmec world was not the inventor, but . . . the idea originated somewhere else—perhaps in the Guatemalan Highlands or the Pacific Coast." Michael Coe, often identified as a champion of Olmec primacy in most Mesoamerican intellectual developments, has stated: "Nor is there any firm evidence that the Olmec were the originators of Maya writing" (1976: 121).

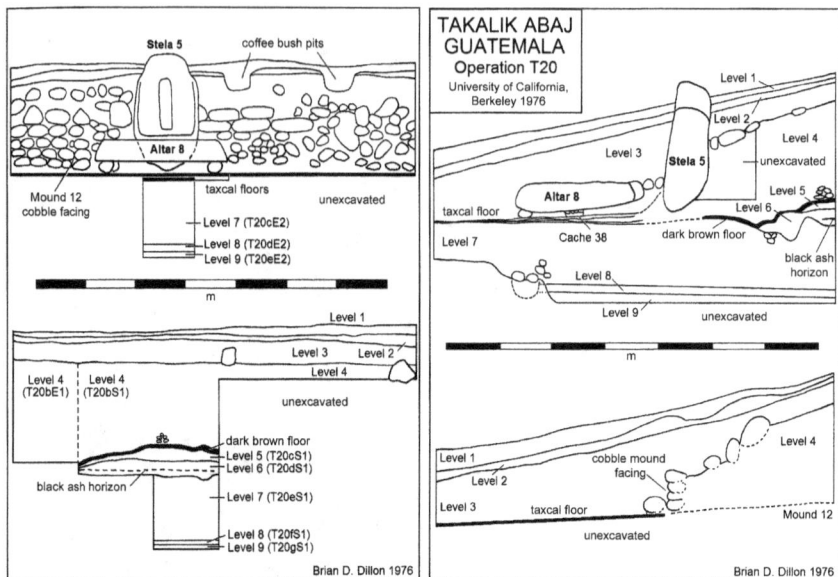

4.12. *Elevation and stratigraphic profiles of Takalik Abaj Operation T20 at the western margin of Mound 12, showing Stela 5, Altar 8, and their associations.* (Top left): *composite elevation, looking east.* (Bottom left): *stratigraphic profile of eastern sidewall.* (Top right): *stratigraphic profile through stela/altar centerline, facing north. Note two earlier sockets for Stela 5.* (Bottom right): *North sidewall. From Dillon 1977, figures 5 and 6.*

Sensing the futility of arguing for Olmec literacy, other students have argued for the primacy of what has recently come to be called "Isthmian Script" as the ancestral Mesoamerican writing system. Unfortunately, instead of using a neutral term like "Isthmian," some writers (Justeson and Kaufman 1993, 1997, 2008; Kaufman and Justeson 2008) term such writing "Epi-Olmec," as if an unbroken line of hieroglyphic development existed from the Middle Preclassic Period Gulf Coast Olmec right up to the end of the Early Classic Period, completely bypassing the contemporaneous—and literate—Maya. But no such unbroken tradition of early hieroglyphic writing linking the Olmec with later peoples exists on the Gulf Coast: arguments for it are forced, misleading, and unsupported by the evidence. The best examples of "Epi-Olmec" writing are in every case later than the earliest Early Maya writing at Takalik Abaj (see table 4.4) and were probably, in the ultimate assessment, Maya-inspired.

La Mojarra Stela 1 features the best example of Isthmian Script. Unfortunately, the sculpture was not discovered in situ and remains unassociated with any large archaeological site. Its text obviously postdates a human figure portrayed in equally obvious Maya style to its left. Terrence Kaufman and John Justeson (2008; also Justeson and Kaufman 2008) have invented a "pre-proto-

4.13. *The Protoclassic Estela Ralda, 2.11 m tall, with associated 2.42-m-diameter Altar 8 in Operation T20 a few days after their discovery. Takalik Abaj Stela 5, at 8.4.5.17.11 or AD 126, is the latest dated Maya monument so far discovered at the site. Stela 5 was reset several times as Late Preclassic Mound 12 behind it was enlarged. (Left): Brian Dervin Dillon; (right): Miguel Simaj. Photo by Edgar Luis Torres, 1976.*

Sokean" language through dubious glotto-chronological methods to account for their putatively phonetic "Epi-Olmec" script. Justeson and Kaufman date La Mojarra Stela 1 at 8.5.17.14.0 (AD 157). They consider the three well-known stelae with hieroglyphic passages from Cerro de las Mesas to be other exemplars of their "Epi-Olmec" writing system. Justeson and Kaufman date Cerro de las Mesas Stela 6 at 9.1.12.14.10 (AD 468), Stela 5 at 9.4.14.1.4 (AD 528), and Stela 8 at 9.4.16.18.8 (AD 533). All four of these "Epi-Olmec" sculptures are obviously later than the latest dated Maya sculpture yet found at Takalik Abaj and centuries later than the half-dozen 7th Cycle Maya sculptures from the Guatemalan site. The "Epi-Olmec" hieroglyphic "corpus" is rounded out by the addition of a single potsherd, a non-provenienced artifact, and the Tuxtla statuette. The Tuxtla statuette, generally accepted as dating to AD 162, once again dates later than the latest Early Maya sculptures at Takalik Abaj. The La Mojarra and Cerro de las Mesas stelae provide convincing evidence for a tradition of Isthmian writing during the Protoclassic and Early Classic Periods, but extending this writing system backward in time for another 500 years on the strength of a single potsherd is not warranted.

Isthmian script can be likened to Sequoyah's Cherokee alphabet, inspired by someone else's preexisting written language but developed for very specific and different cultural purposes. La Mojarra Stela 1, sometimes represented as the tip of an Isthmian hieroglyphic iceberg, is best understood as an early example of a local dead-end effort, inspired by much earlier mainstream Maya developments to the east. Its comparatively late date argues not for primacy in the development of hieroglyphic writing but rather for a non-Maya people, hicks from the sticks, if you will, aping their more sophisticated neighbors, eager to embrace hallmarks of Protoclassic Maya civilization—including writing, costume, and similar developments—already many hundreds of years old (cf. Graham 2005).

Nor can the Izapan tradition, all too often erroneously represented as the "missing link" between Olmec and Maya, be considered a candidate for the development of Maya culture or Mesoamerican writing. A single sculpture (Miscellaneous Monument 60) bears the only complete hieroglyph yet found at Izapa; the example is obviously Maya-inspired. Only one other sculpture at Izapa (Stela 27) appears to have a single cartouche with twin bar numerals superimposed. If this was indeed a glyph, it is presently illegible; a "devil's advocate" interpretation would be that it was an attempt by an illiterate artist to copy something he did not understand. Careful review of the evidence (more accurately, the lack thereof) for glyphs at the site of Izapa itself forces the conclusion that Mesoamerican hieroglyphic writing grew out of literate Early Maya culture, not out of non-literate Izapan culture.

Most of the arguments for a non-Maya genesis of writing raise the question of when artistic motifs and elements, either singly or in regular combination, can be recognized as glyphs; in my opinion, all claims for Olmec and Izapan "writing" refer to iconographic elements that fall short of true glyphs or glyphic writing. Most archaeologists would agree that all art, including iconography, is communication (Proskouriakoff 1971: 147) and that art can have important commemorative, genealogical, religious, or ostentatious functions. Nevertheless, graphic communication is not writing.

Iconographic elements have symbolic meaning but are not hieroglyphs. More simply put, if you don't have hieroglyphs, you don't have hieroglyphic writing. We therefore conclude that Izapa, as with Olmec, was a non-literate civilization bordering on its literate Maya neighbors.

All of the archaeological evidence suggests that Mesoamerican writing was invented within the cultural tradition that made the best and most widespread use of it: the Maya. The Guatemalan Pacific Slope remains the best candidate for its birthplace, based on the sculptural and epigraphic evidence, which is stronger than that for any other part of the Maya area (see table 4.4; figure 4.14). Could Maya writing have been invented at the ancient city of Takalik Abaj when the aged Olmec and infant Maya sculptural styles were undergoing experimentation literally side by side? Graham and Porter (1989) see Maya hieroglyphic writing

Table 4.4. Selected Maya sites, initial series dates, and sculptures in Early Maya style

	I.S. Date	Equivalent
1 Takalik Abaj, Retalhuleu, Guatemala (Mon. 11)	6.?.?.?.?	3rd century BC
Takalik Abaj, Retalhuleu, Guatemala (Altar 12)	7.?.?.?.?	3rd century BC
Takalik Abaj, Retalhuleu, Guatemala (Stela 3)	7.?.?.?.?	2nd century BC
Takalik Abaj, Retalhuleu, Guatemala (Stela 12)	7.?.?.?.?	2nd century BC
Takalik Abaj, Retalhuleu, Guatemala (Stela 50)	7.2.10.2.17	2nd century BC
Takalik Abaj, Retalhuleu, Guatemala (Stela 2)	7.16.?.?.?	1st century BC
Takalik Abaj, Retalhuleu, Guatemala (Stela 5)	8.4.5.17.11	AD 126
2 Tres Zapotes, Veracruz, Mexico (Stela C)	7.15.6.16.18	31 BC
3 Chiapa de Corzo, Chiapas, Mexico (Stela 2)	7.16.3.2.13	36 BC
4 El Baúl, Escuintla, Guatemala (Stela 1)	7.19.15.7.12	AD 36
5 Chocolá, Suchitepéquez, Guatemala (Mon. 1)	7.?.?.?.?	
6 Bilbao, Escuintla, Guatemala (Mon. 42)	7.?.?.?.?	
7 Kaminaljuyú, Guatemala (Stelae 10, 11)	7.?.?.?.?	
8 El Portón, Baja Verapaz, Guatemala (Mon. 1)	7.?.?.?.?	
9 El Mirador, El Petén, Guatemala (Stela 2)	7.?.?.?.?	
10 San Bartolo, El Petén, Guatemala (Painted inscription)	7.?.?.?.?	
11 Polol, El Petén, Guatemala (Altar 1)	7.?.?.?.?	
12 Loltun Cave, Yucatán, Mexico (Petroglyph)	7.?.?.?.?	
13 Nakbe, El Petén, Guatemala (Stela 1)	8.?.?.?.?	
14 El Chiquero, El Petén, Guatemala (Stela 1)	8.?.?.?.?	
15 Casa Blanca, Santa Ana, El Salvador (Mon. 1)	8.?.?.?.?	
16 Tikal, El Petén, Guatemala (Stela 29)	8.12.14.8.15	AD 292
17 Uaxactún, El Petén, Guatemala (Stela 9)	8.14.10.13.15	AD 328

as "intrusive" at Takalik Abaj, yet any investigation of the origins of Maya hieroglyphic writing must consider Takalik Abaj—with the largest concentration of 7th Cycle sculptures of any Maya site—as one of the best potential locations for its place of origin.

WHO BUILT AND LIVED AT TAKALIK ABAJ?

At Takalik Abaj, both Olmec and Early Maya sculptures exist in some abundance, enough to warrant the conclusion that they were not simply souvenirs brought in from somewhere else but instead were in situ products of these two great civilizations. But not all sculpture at Takalik Abaj can be assigned to these two great International Horizon Styles, for various local styles are also present. It is logical to assume that different cultures, perhaps even different ethnic groups, are responsible for the different sculptural styles at the site.

The Mam Maya of present-day Takalik Abaj are recent arrivals, brought down from the Guatemalan Highlands beginning in the 1860s to provide labor on the coffee fincas that began to burgeon throughout the region at that time. Mam expansions southward from the Highlands to the Piedmont and Coastal Lowlands took place much earlier, during the Late Postclassic Period. Early Colonial Retalhuleu was a bilingual town where both Mam and Quiché were spoken (Orellana 1995: 34). Ancestors of this ethnohistoric Mam Maya group may have been present at Early Postclassic Period Takalik Abaj, but there is no way to positively demonstrate a connection at that time and even less so more than a millennium before, during the Early Maya and even earlier Olmec occupations of the site. We therefore have no certain idea as to the language or languages spoken by the first inhabitants of the archaeological site, their point or points of origin, or by what name or names the ancient city was called.

Orellana (1995: 108) summarizes the Conquest period linguistic situation on the Pacific Slope. Six different languages were spoken; Mam became predominant three centuries later. In the Late Postclassic Guatemalan Highlands to the north, independent kingdoms (Quiché, Cakchiquel, Tzutujil, Mam, and Pokomam) centered around capital cities (Utatlán, Iximché, Chuitinamit/Chiya, Zaculeu, Mixco Viejo) squabbled incessantly with each other over territory, boundaries, and prestige (Carmack 1973, 1981, this volume; Orellana 1984). Sometimes allied with each other and sometimes alone, each kingdom had a separate ethnic and linguistic identity, yet all were Maya, albeit the first three highly Mexicanized. The Late Postclassic Guatemalan Highland Maya city-states (Berdan, Kepecs, and Smith 2003) controlled large areas of the Piedmont and the coastal flatlands to the south (Carmack 1973; Orellana 1995). The Mam Maya, today principally known as a Highland group, had extensive holdings on the Piedmont and the coastal strip as well, encroached upon by the later Quiché. This ebb and flow of ethnic groups down from the Highlands to and through the Piedmont and onto the Coastal Plain, and vice versa, is well documented for the Late Postclassic Period; it is tempting to see it as a much older regional tradition, applicable to the great city of Takalik Abaj, possibly even throughout its entire history of occupation.

All of the Late Postclassic Guatemalan Highland capitals were small potatoes compared with the gigantic Classic Lowland Maya cities, such as Tikal and El Mirador, of a thousand years before. They were also dwarfed by the very large and even earlier Preclassic cities of the Highlands and Pacific Slope, such as Kaminaljuyú and Takalik Abaj. Late Postclassic Utatlán, Iximché, and Mixco Viejo could fit together inside Late Preclassic Takalik Abaj's site boundaries with plenty of room left over. Were the earlier Classic and Preclassic cities the seats of independent kingdoms similar to the much smaller Postclassic examples?

AQUÍ NACIÓ EL MUNDO

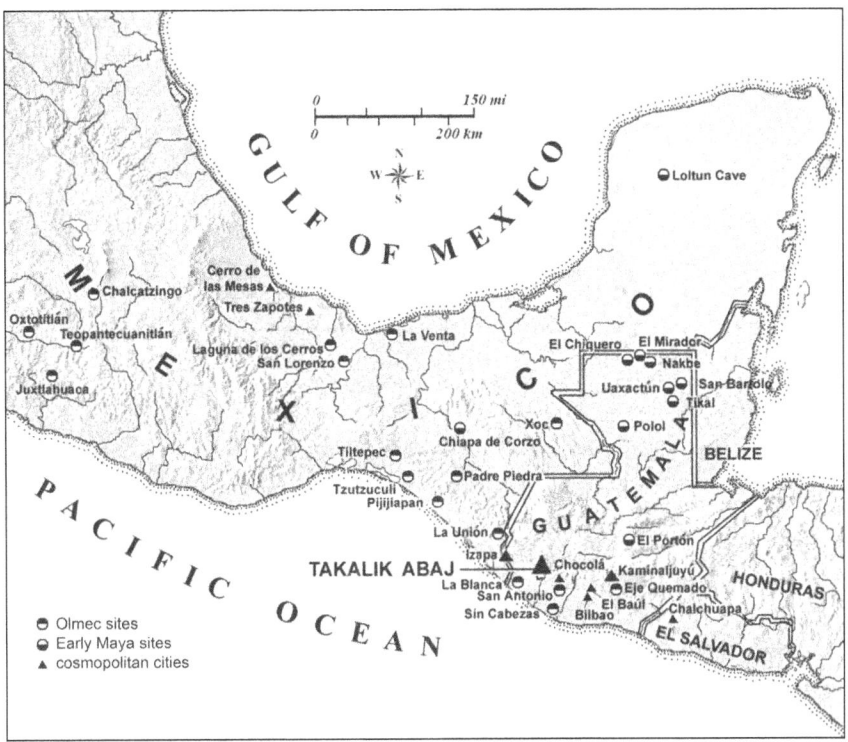

4.14. *Olmec and Early Maya sites in southern Mesoamerica, and selected cosmopolitan cities with occupations of long duration and multiple sculptural styles. Map by Brian Dervin Dillon and Rusty van Rossmann.*

Hundreds of Classic Maya cities throughout the Petén, Yucatán, Chiapas, and the southeastern periphery are coming to be understood as city-states, each with its own developmental history—some independent, some allies, some perhaps even younger colonies or satellites of older parent cities.

Maya is the longest sustained cultural tradition in Mesoamerica, easily over 3,000 years in duration. With literally hundreds of major, independent Classic Period cities, it was also the most successful and diverse Mesoamerican civilization. Different Maya languages were assuredly spoken at different cities throughout the length and breadth of the Classic Maya world, and many cities were undoubtedly bilingual or even polylingual. More than a dozen modern Maya languages survive from the people we presume to have been full participants in Classic and Postclassic Maya civilization; we may never know how many others have become extinct. Guatemala is polyglot now and has been so far back into the past. Depending on how one assigns individual groups, between twelve and fifteen different Indian languages are still spoken in Guatemala as a whole, surely many fewer than must have been the case during the Classic and Preclassic

121

Periods. In my opinion, it is a mistake to limit candidates for ancient occupants of archaeological sites to extant linguistic groups, but it is equally pointless to make up fictional languages accounting for unknown and unknowable people.

I believe Postclassic Takalik Abaj was a bilingual city, with both Mam and Quiché spoken there. I also believe it was a multilingual Maya city during the Classic and Protoclassic Periods and that even earlier, during the Middle and Late Preclassic Periods, it was multiethnic Maya and Olmec. Who were the Takalik Abaj Olmec, and which of the many strains of Maya culture was or were present there? Which Maya people carved hieroglyphs on stone, and which Maya or non-Maya people later defaced both Olmec and Maya sculptures alike? We will probably never know.

CONCLUSION

Takalik Abaj was a great Olmec city, yet it was also an important Early Maya capital. How it could have been both is only conceivable once we abandon the simplistic, moribund theory of Mesoamerican civilizational succession that still exerts a stranglehold on too many imaginations. This simpleminded interpretive approach can be analogized to a stadium in which civilizations enter one after another, each one leaving before the next arrives, only imperfectly remembered once replaced. The Olmecs perform, then depart; the Izapans do the same, followed by the Maya, the Teotihuacanos, Toltec, Aztec, and finally the Spaniards, whereupon the stadium is closed for good. Such a facile theory for the development of Mesoamerican civilization can only be defended if Takalik Abaj is omitted, for this site, with its simultaneity of civilizations, renders all of the old assumptions obsolete.

If Takalik Abaj was indeed occupied for more than 2,000 years, then it is unlikely that a single people lived there from beginning to end. All of the archaeological evidence from the Pacific Slope of Guatemala suggests that Mesoamerican civilization was instead cosmopolitan, the product of cultural interchange, amalgamation, acculturation, and many different lines of development. Many unique civilizations—each originating within its own cities, each city with fluid, ever-changing boundaries—probably interacted with each other. But what form did such interaction (one of H. B. Nicholson's favorite words) take?

Warfare as a means of cultural interaction continues to interest Mesoamericanists (cf. Webster 1977; Dillon 1982; Fahsen 2002; Dillon and Christensen 2005). Much has been made of the supposed Central Mexican domination of the Maya area during the Classic Period. Kaminaljuyú, on the strength of a couple of buildings out of the hundreds known, for a brief period of time out of its many hundreds of years of occupation, is sometimes dismissed as simply a minor colony of Teotihuacan. Tikal is likewise, at a later time, described as a vassal of Teotihuacan on the strength of a single small and obscure building amid the hundreds of much more impressive structures there. Similarly, in my opinion, theories about the supposed "Toltec" domination of Chichén Itzá in the Early Postclassic Period have it backward. You could lose several Tulas within the boundaries of Chichén and have plenty of room left over, and Chichén is a much more spectacular site in every way than the small, dusty "Toltec" town far to the northwest. All three examples are very much the case of the Central Mexican flea referring to his Maya host as "my dog" and more illustrative of Maya willingness to tolerate a foreign minority among themselves than of Central Mexican domination.[9]

Acculturation, not subjugation, is the best means by which one people learns things such as art, religion, and science from another people or peoples. Throughout human history acculturation has best been effected within cosmopolitan urban contexts rather than by one group of warriors destroying the old and supplanting it with the new. The tremendous variety of monumental stone sculpture spanning many centuries at Takalik Abaj suggests most strongly several partly contemporaneous lines of cultural development (Graham 1979; Orrego Corzo 1998). Takalik Abaj was not the only cosmopolitan Mesoamerican city with sculptures in multiple art styles, both international and local. Early local contemporaries were Chocolá, Casa Blanca, and Izapa, with Tres Zapotes a distant one. Later nearby contemporaries were Bilbao and El Baúl, while Cerro de las Mesas was much father afield.

Cosmopolitan urbanism may be as old as civilization itself in Mesoamerica. Must the "Olmec" have been but a single people? Why should we assume that the Olmec of La Venta, Chalchuapa, and Takalik Abaj—separated from each other by time and space—all had the same language, the same history, or considered themselves the same people? Different ethnicities would not make any of them any less "Olmec." The notion that the cities of the so-called Olmec heartland were of mixed ethnicity or hosted "foreign" (aka non-Olmec) populations within them, neither as conquerors nor as conquered, has been floating around for more than half a century (Covarrubias 1957: 77; Proskouriakoff 1968: 122–123; Bernal 1968, 1969; Drucker 1981: 44). Even Michael Coe (1977: 195) has written of "Maya speaking Olmec." Ignacio Bernal (1968: 136–137) suggests that intercultural interaction was indispensable and necessary for the creation of Olmec civilization, which was formed "not by an isolated group, but by a combination of more or less neighboring or related groups." Bernal argues convincingly that as far back as the Middle Preclassic Period, Olmec cities were populated by a "mixture of peoples so necessary to the development of civilization . . . Diverse languages were surely spoken" (ibid.: 138–139). Similarly, Robert J. Sharer and David W. Sedat (1973: 186), in writing of El Portón, Baja Verapaz, and Marion Hatch (2002), considering the great city of Kaminaljuyú, feel that Mesoamerican civilization developed through a series of contemporaneous interacting populations. If this was true of sites such as La Venta and

Kaminaljuyú, then why not Takalik Abaj as well? Its sculptures in different styles are a testimonial to the ebb and flow of different cultures over a very long period of time.

Dón Beto Sinto's mastery of four different languages and his ability to live in three separate worlds—Indian, European, and supernatural—is a modern metaphor for what I believe to have been the ancient situation at Takalik Abaj. Most modern Maya priests, be they Chimánes or *Chuj Ka'jaus*, are bilingual or multilingual; it is logical to assume that the tradition of scholarly or religious polylingualism has very deep roots on the Guatemalan Pacific Slope. Many of the modern Maya craftsmen and traders who "make the rounds" between the markets held on different days in different Indian towns in the Guatemalan Highlands and on the Pacific Slope are also bi-, tri-, or quadrilingual. If Takalik Abaj was a center of learning and literacy, artistic creation, commerce, and religious practice for many centuries, as seems undeniable, then it would have attracted many different people from many different places. Just as Dón Beto was a remarkable man of many years, many accomplishments, and many cultures, Takalik Abaj was probably for a very long time a city of different peoples, different cultures, and different tongues. *Aquí nació el mundo* indeed.

Acknowledgments. Thanks to John A. Graham and the late Robert F. Heizer for inviting me onto the first two seasons of the UC Berkeley Abaj Takalik Project. The Ralda family of Retalhuleu, in an act of extreme generosity, donated the area of my 1976–1977 excavations for the creation of Central America's newest, yet oldest, archaeological park. Thanks to the many members of this outstanding clan, particularly the late Dón Manuel Ralda Ochoa, Doña Estela Ralda de Schaeffer, and Dón José Luis Ralda González. Miguel Orrego Corzo and I spent many productive days together in both California and Guatemala, most recently in June 2010. The future of the Takalik Abaj site could not be in better hands. I am grateful to Matthew A. Boxt for three decades of friendship and for inviting my collaboration on the present volume, our second (Dillon and Boxt 2005). Matthew A. Boxt, Karen O. Bruhns, C. William Clewlow Jr., John A. Graham, David Grove, Marion Hatch, Sandra Orellana, Miguel Orrego Corzo, and Christa Schieber de Lavarreda all read earlier drafts of this chapter; I am grateful for their suggestions and corrections. Finally, the friendship and pride of accomplishment shared with the modern Maya of Takalik Abaj was one of the greatest gifts of my life. Many thanks to all of *mis cuates*, especially Dón Miguel Simaj, and to the late Dón Antonio Guzmán and Dón Beto Sinto.

NOTES

1. *Costumbre* is the modern term for ritual prayers and offerings to local spirits, Preconquest deities, and Catholic saints. Dón Beto was a Chimán with a shrine at Laguna

Chicabal, the crater lake inside the volcano only 20 km northeast of Takalik Abaj yet 2,100 m higher in elevation. Chicabal is where the famous annual "brujo's conference" was held, at least until the late 1970s. The last human sacrifice in the Maya area, if not in all of Mesoamerica, took place on the Santa María Volcano in 1917 when an innocent party of German hikers was murdered in response to earlier desecration of a native shrine. Dón Beto was a teenager when this event took place. Since the creation of the Takalik Abaj National Park, Quiché native priests, in addition to Mam ones, have begun performing costumbre at the site in increasing numbers (cf. Schieber de Lavarreda and Orrego Corzo 2002: 75). I would like to think that Dón Beto Sinto, wherever he may be, both knows of this and approves.

2. Santa María Volcano stands over 12,000 feet in elevation. In 1902 its south side blew out in a massive nineteen-day eruption. Crops were destroyed and cattle died of thirst as ash choked all the streams. The eruption led to the abandonment of the entire South Coast and Piedmont, as far west as the Mexican border, for at least six months; places closer to the volcano were abandoned for over a year. Yet after everyone returned and resumed farming, bumper crops resulted from the enrichment of the soils by the new blanket of volcanic ash. Twenty years later a new cone, Santiaguito, developed within the 1902 crater and has been growing ever since. Santiaguito constantly puffs out fine, white volcanic ash, and Takalik Abaj gets a daily dusting that continues to enrich the soils of the fincas on the site. In 1976–1977 a light coat of very fine ash covered the coffee leaves from each night's ashfall. We pushed our way through the coffee and were soon coated with ash the color and consistency of bleached wheat flour. The first time Robert F. Heizer followed us down our exploratory trails through the *cafetal*, he suddenly began "freaking out"—tearing at his clothes, mouthing expletives, and acting as if a hornet's nest had dropped down his shirt. Heizer thought the coffee had been dusted with DDT and was convinced he was absorbing the poison through his skin.

3. I worked at Abaj Takalik during the first two Berkeley seasons (1976–1977), then made short revisits in 1978, 1981, and 1983. I spent a third full season at the site in 1987 as the leader of a UCLA Extension team doing laboratory work. At this time I also served as an outside mediator in negotiations between the Ralda family and the Guatemalan government for the creation of the Parque Arqueológico Nacional de Abaj Takalik and facilitated archaeologist Miguel Orrego Corzo's assumption of the Abaj Takalik Project as a Guatemalan national effort. I revisited the site in 1990 and again in 2010, honored to be the guest of Orrego Corzo, Christa Schieber de Lavarreda, and the Takalik Abaj National Archaeological Project.

4. Boulder sculptures, including potbellies, are possibly the most confusing category of sculpture on the Guatemalan Pacific Slope. Potbellies had a wide geographic distribution, were executed in different styles, and had great chronological longevity. They are well represented at Takalik Abaj, with at least eight examples, and are also present in some numbers at Chocolá, Kaminaljuyú, Bilbao, El Baúl, Monte Alto, and Santa Leticia on the Pacific Slope; singly at Tikal and Copán; and as far north as Oxkintok. Bruhns (personal communication, 2009) notes an abundance of Late Preclassic/Early Classic potbellies in El Salvador. Miles (1965) and Graham (1989) believe potbellies predate Olmec sculpture in the round, while Parsons (1981) and Demarest (1989) feel they are post-Olmec, perhaps only moderately successful attempts by unskilled sculptors to ape

past glories. If Potbelly as a sculptural category has as long a life span as I suspect, both points of view, which seem implacably opposed, may be equally correct.

5. The only direct evidence for any cultivated crop recovered by the UC Berkeley research effort was a fortuitous find of preserved maize remains by Steven Wegner in 1979 (Dillon et al. 1986).

6. As of 2010 the Takalik Abaj sculptural count stood at 367: 239 monuments, 79 stelae, and 49 altars. By means of comparison, discovered at San Lorenzo are 65 monuments (Coe 1968; Clewlow 1974; Coe and Diehl 1980), subsequently expanded to 89 by Cyphers (2004). La Venta had 87 stone sculptures—3 stelae, 7 altars, and 77 monuments (Clewlow 1974)—subsequently reduced to 73 by González Lauck (2004: 81). Laguna de los Cerros has produced 2 altars and 32 monuments (Clewlow 1974; Gillespie 2000). Chalcatzingo offers 38 monuments, including petroglyph panels, stelae, three-dimensional sculptures, and altars (Grove, personal communication, 2009; this volume). Kaminaljuyú boasts 127 stone sculptures—28 stelae, 14 altars, and 85 monuments, all of them carved (Parsons 1986: table 4). Izapa has 244 stone sculptures, most of them uncarved: 87 stelae, 89 altars, and 68 monuments (Norman 1973: 1). Monte Alto has 15 plain stelae, 3 altars, and 11 carved and 68 uncarved monuments, all boulder sculptures (Shook 1971: 72, 75). Palo Gordo has 26 monuments (Chinchilla Mazariegos 2002).

7. San Antonio Retalhuleu (Arriola 1973; Orellana 1995: 116) was an early Spanish Colonial town in western Suchitepéquez near Soconusco. Its name in literal translation from the Quiché is "hole in the ground" or "boundary marker." As any modern Retalteco will tell you, according to local legend Retalhuleu is where, in 1524, Pedro de Alvarado stabbed his sword in the ground and claimed the land for Spain. One of my favorite articles of clothing is a T-shirt with a globe on its front, Guatemala prominently featured somewhat larger than natural scale, and a giant red arrow pointing to Retalhuleu containing the script *"Capital del Mundo."*

8. Only actual archaeological sites incorporating permanent features are listed in tables 4.3 and 4.4 and incorporated onto figure 4.14. Using portable artifacts to map the extent of ancient civilizations is a fool's errand, so all such "evidence" is omitted. Only stationary features, such as architecture, sculptures, or rock art, are absolute proof of a specific human group's physical presence at any discovery location. Stolen Olmec jades or Maya polychrome pottery vessels on modern mantelpieces in Paris, Tokyo, New York, or Beverly Hills do not indicate that the ancient Olmec or Maya established colonies in Europe, Asia, or North America; only that much later and completely different people still appreciate their artworks. As a naive undergraduate I once asked Robert F. Heizer (1915–1979) what he thought about an Olmec jade without provenience in an archaeological publication. He responded, "Oh yeah, it's a fake." I then asked how one could differentiate between bona fide specimens and fakes through photographs. Heizer said that the only legitimate Olmec jades he knew of were the ones he had personally excavated and that all the others lacking provenience should be dismissed from consideration as fraudulent. Now, as then, these are archaeological words to live by.

9. Demarest and Foias (1993) incisively refute the supposed Teotihuacano domination over the so-called Middle Classic Maya. Escalante Gonzalbo (this volume) accounts for the Early Postclassic Central Mexican Mixteca-Puebla artistic tradition at least in part through Late Classic Maya polychrome mural painting at Cacaxtla. Braswell (2003) has edited a volume containing a wide spectrum of opinions about Maya-Teotihuacan interaction.

REFERENCES CITED

Arriola, Jorge Luis
    1973   *El libro de las Geonimias de Guatemala*. Seminario de Integración Social Guatemalteca, Publicación 31. Editorial José de Pineda Ibarra, Guatemala.

Berdan, Frances F., Susan Kepecs, and Michael E. Smith
    2003   A Perspective on Late Postclassic Mesoamerica. In *The Postclassic Mesoamerican World*, ed. Michael E. Smith and Frances F. Berdan, pp. 313–317. University of Utah Press, Salt Lake City.

Berger, Rainer, and Melissa A. Terry
    1979a   Radiocarbon Dates from Abaj Takalik I: 1979 Season. Typescript manuscript in Dillon's possession.
    1979b   Radiocarbon Dates from Abaj Takalik II: 1979 Season. Typescript manuscript in Dillon's possession.

Bernal, Ignacio
    1968   Views of Olmec Culture. In *Dumbarton Oaks Conference on the Olmec: October 28th and 29th, 1967*, ed. Elizabeth P. Benson, pp. 135–142. Dumbarton Oaks Research Library and Collection, Washington, DC.
    1969   *The Olmec World*. University of California Press, Berkeley.

Braswell, Geoffrey E., ed.
    2003   *The Maya and Teotihuacan: Reinterpreting Early Classic Interaction*. University of Texas Press, Austin.

Bruhns, Karen O., and Nancy L. Kelker
    2007   Did the Olmec Know How to Write? *Science* 315 (5817): 1365–1366.

Busby, Colin I., and Mark C. Johnson
    1978   The Abaj Takalik Site Map. *Contributions of the University of California Archaeological Research Facility* 36: 111–114. Berkeley.

Carmack, Robert M.
    1973   *Quichean Civilization: The Ethnohistoric, Ethnographic, and Archaeological Sources*. University of California Press, Berkeley.
    1981   *The Quiché Mayas of Utatlán: The Evolution of a Highland Guatemala Kingdom*. University of Oklahoma Press, Norman.

Castillo, Donaldo
    1991   La cerámica de Takalik Abaj (antes Abaj Takalik): Un estudio preliminar. In *II Simposio de Investigaciones Arqueológicas en Guatemala, 1988*, ed. Juan Pedro Laporte, Sandra Villagrán, Héctor Escobedo, Dora de González, and Juan Antonio Valdés, pp. 14–15. Museo Nacional de Guatemala.

Chinchilla Mazariegos, Oswaldo
    2002   Palo Gordo, Guatemala, y el estilo artistico Cotzumalguapa. In *Incidents of Archaeology in Central America and Yucatán: Essays in Honor of Edwin M. Shook*, ed. Michael Love, Marion Popenoe de Hatch, and Héctor L. Escobedo, pp. 147–178. University Press of America, Lanham, MD.

Clark, John E., and Mary E. Pye
2000 The Pacific Coast and the Olmec Question. In *Olmec Art and Archaeology in Mesoamerica*, ed. John E. Clark and Mary E. Pye, pp. 217–251. Studies in the History of Art 58, Center for Advanced Study in the Visual Arts, Symposium Papers 35. National Gallery of Art, Washington, DC, and Yale University Press, New Haven, CT.

Clark, John E., and Mary E. Pye, eds.
2000 *Olmec Art and Archaeology in Mesoamerica*. Studies in the History of Art 58, Center for Advanced Study in the Visual Arts, Symposium Papers 35. National Gallery of Art, Washington, DC, and Yale University Press, New Haven, CT.

Clewlow, C. William, Jr.
1974 A Stylistic and Chronological Study of Olmec Monumental Sculpture. *Contributions of the University of California Archaeological Research Facility* 18. Berkeley.

Coe, Michael D.
1961 *La Victoria, an Early Site on the Pacific Coast of Guatemala*. Papers of the Peabody Museum of Archaeology and Ethnology 53. Harvard University, Cambridge, MA.
1965 *The Olmec Style and Its Distribution*. University of Texas Press, Austin.
1968 San Lorenzo and the Olmec Civilization. In *Dumbarton Oaks Conference on the Olmec: October 28th and 29th, 1967*, ed. Elizabeth P. Benson, pp. 41–71. Dumbarton Oaks Research Library and Collection, Washington, DC.
1976 Early Steps in the Evolution of Maya Writing. In *Origins of Religious Art and Iconography in Preclassic Mesoamerica*, ed. H. B. Nicholson, pp. 107–122. UCLA Latin American Center Publications and the Ethnic Arts Council of Los Angeles, Los Angeles, CA.
1977 Olmec and Maya: A Study in Relationships. In *The Origins of Maya Civilization*, ed. Richard E.W. Adams, pp. 183–195. School of American Research, University of New Mexico Press, Albuquerque.

Coe, Michael D., and Richard A. Diehl
1980 *In the Land of the Olmec: The Archaeology of San Lorenzo Tenochtitlan*, 2 vols. University of Texas Press, Austin.

Coe, Michael D., and Kent Flannery
1967 *Early Cultures and Human Ecology in South Coastal Guatemala*. Smithsonian Contributions to Anthropology 3. Smithsonian Institution, Washington, DC.

Covarrubias, Miguel
1957 *Indian Art of Mexico and Central America*. Alfred A. Knopf, New York.

Cyphers, Ann
1997 Olmec Architecture at San Lorenzo. In *Olmec to Aztec: Settlement Patterns in the Ancient Gulf Lowlands*, ed. B. L. Stark and P. J. Arnold, pp. 96–114. University of Arizona Press, Tucson.

2004   Escultura monumental olmeca: Temas y contextos. In *Acercarse y mirar: Homenaje a Beatriz de la Fuente*, pp. 51–73. UNAM, Instituto de Investigaciones Estéticas, México, DF.

De la Fuente, Beatriz
   1981   Toward a Conception of Monumental Olmec Art. In *The Olmec and Their Neighbors: Essays in Memory of Matthew W. Stirling*, ed. Elizabeth P. Benson, pp. 83–94. Dumbarton Oaks Research Library and Collection, Washington, DC.
   1995   El arte olmeca. *Arqueología Mexicana* 2 (12): 18–37.
   2000   Olmec Sculpture: The First Mesoamerican Art. In *Olmec Art and Archaeology in Mesoamerica*, ed. John E. Clark and Mary E. Pye, pp. 253–264. Studies in the History of Art 58, Center for Advanced Study in the Visual Arts, Symposium Papers 35. National Gallery of Art, Washington, DC, and Yale University Press, New Haven, CT.

Demarest, Arthur A.
   1989   The Olmec and the Rise of Civilization in Eastern Mesoamerica. In *Regional Perspectives on the Olmec*, ed. Robert J. Sharer and David C. Grove, pp. 303–344. School of American Research, Cambridge University Press, Cambridge, MA.

Demarest, Arthur A., and Antonia E. Foias
   1993   Mesoamerican Horizons and the Cultural Transformations of Maya Civilization. In *Latin American Horizons*, ed. Don S. Rice, pp. 147–191. Dumbarton Oaks, Washington, DC.

Diehl, Richard H.
   1981   Olmec Architecture: A Comparison of San Lorenzo and La Venta. In *The Olmec and Their Neighbors: Essays in Memory of Matthew W. Stirling*, ed. Elizabeth P. Benson, pp. 69–81. Dumbarton Oaks Research Library and Collection, Washington, DC.
   2004   *The Olmecs: America's First Civilization*. Thames and Hudson, London.

Dillon, Brian Dervin
   1975   Notes on Trade in Ancient Mesoamerica. *Contributions of the University of California Archaeological Research Facility* 24: 80–135. University of California, Berkeley.
   1977   Excavations at Abaj Takalik, Retalhuleu, Guatemala: The South-Central Group, 1976–1977. Typescript manuscript in Dillon's possession, December 30, 1977, revised January 24, 1986.
   1982   Bound Prisoners in Maya Art. *Journal of New World Archaeology* 5 (1): 24–45.

Dillon, Brian Dervin, and Matthew A. Boxt, eds.
   2005   *Archaeology without Limits: Papers in Honor of C. W. Meighan*. Labyrinthos, Lancaster, CA.

Dillon, Brian Dervin, and Wes Christensen
   2005   The Maya Jade Skull Bead: 700 Years as a Military Insignia? In *Archaeology without Limits: Papers in Honor of C. W. Meighan*, ed. Brian Dervin Dillon and Matthew A. Boxt, pp. 369–388. Labyrinthos, Lancaster, CA.

Dillon, Brian Dervin, Walton C. Galinat, Steven A. Wegner, Mark C. Johnson, John A. Graham, and Rainer Berger
    1986   Ancient Maize Remains from Abaj Takalik, Guatemala. Manuscript in Dillon's possession.

Drucker, Philip
    1952   *La Venta Tabasco: A Study of Olmec Ceramics and Art.* Bureau of American Ethnology Bulletin 153. Smithsonian Institution, Washington, DC.
    1981   On the Nature of Olmec Polity. In *The Olmec and Their Neighbors: Essays in Memory of Matthew W. Stirling*, ed. Elizabeth P. Benson, pp. 29–47. Dumbarton Oaks Research Library and Collection, Washington, DC.

Drucker, Philip, Robert F. Heizer, and Robert J. Squier
    1959   *Excavations at La Venta, Tabasco, 1955.* Bureau of American Ethnology Bulletin 170. Smithsonian Institution, Washington, DC.

Fahsen, Federico
    2002   Who Are the Prisoners in Kaminaljuyú Monuments? In *Incidents of Archaeology in Central America and Yucatán: Essays in Honor of Edwin M. Shook*, ed. Michael Love, Marion Popenoe de Hatch, and Héctor L. Escobedo, pp. 359–374. University Press of America, Lanham, MD.

Gillespie, Susan D.
    2000   The Monuments of Laguna de los Cerros and Its Hinterland. In *Olmec Art and Archaeology in Mesoamerica*, ed. John E. Clark and Mary E. Pye, pp. 94–115. Studies in the History of Art 58, Center for Advanced Study in the Visual Arts, Symposium Papers 35. National Gallery of Art, Washington, DC, and Yale University Press, New Haven, CT.

González Lauck, Rebecca B.
    1995   La Venta: Una grán ciudad Olmeca. *Arqueología Mexicana* 2 (12): 38–42.
    1996a   La Venta: A Great Olmec City. *Arqueologia Mexicana, Olmecs* (special edition): 42–47.
    1996b   La Venta: An Olmec Capital. In *Olmec Art of Ancient Mexico*, ed. Elizabeth P. Benson and Beatriz de la Fuente, pp. 73–81. National Gallery of Art, Washington, DC.
    2004   Observaciones en torno a los contextos de la escultura olmeca en La Venta, Tabasco. In *Acercarse y mirar: Homenaje a Beatriz de la Fuente*, pp. 75–106. UNAM, Instituto de Investigaciones Estéticas, México, DF.
    2007   El Complejo A, La Venta, Tabasco. *Arqueología Mexicana* 15 (87): 49–54.

Graham, John A.
    1977   Discoveries at Abaj Takalik, Guatemala. *Archaeology* 30 (3): 196–197.
    1979   Olmec, Maya and Izapans at Abaj Takalik. In *Actes du XLII Congrès de Américanistes, 1976*, vol. 8, pp. 179–188. Paris.
    1981   Abaj Takalik: The Olmec Style and Its Antecedents in Pacific Guatemala. In *Ancient Mesoamerica, Selected Readings*, ed. John A. Graham, pp. 163–176. Peek Publications, Palo Alto, CA.
    1982   Antecedents of Olmec Sculpture at Abaj Takalik. In *Pre-Columbian Art History*, ed. Alana Cordy-Collins, pp. 7–22. Peek Publications, Palo Alto, CA.

> 1989   Olmec Diffusion: A Sculptural View from Pacific Guatemala. In *Regional Perspectives on the Olmec*, ed. Robert J. Sharer and David C. Grove, pp. 227–246. Cambridge University Press, Cambridge, England.
> 2005   Reading the Past: Olmec Archaeology and the Curious Case of Tres Zapotes Stela C. Paper prepared for the Mesa Redonda Olmeca, April. Draft in English.

Graham, John A., and Larry Benson
> 2005   Maya and Olmec Boulder Sculpture at Abaj Takalik: Its Development and Portent. In *Archaeology without Limits: Papers in Honor of C. W. Meighan*, ed. Brian Dervin Dillon and Matthew A. Boxt, pp. 345–367. Labyrinthos, Lancaster, CA.

Graham, John A., Robert F. Heizer, and Edwin M. Shook
> 1978   Abaj Takalik 1976: Exploratory Investigations. *Contributions of the University of California Archaeological Research Facility* 36: 85–109. Berkeley.

Graham, John A., and Mark Johnson
> 1979   The Great Mound at La Venta. *Contributions of the University of California Archaeological Research Facility* 41: 1–5. Berkeley.

Graham, John A., and James Porter
> 1989   A Cycle 6 Initial Series? A Maya Boulder Inscription of the First Millennium B.C. from Abaj Takalik. *Mexicon* 11 (3): 46–49.

Grove, David C.
> 1981   Olmec Monuments: Mutilation as a Clue to Meaning. In *The Olmec and Their Neighbors: Essays in Memory of Matthew W. Stirling*, ed. Elizabeth P. Benson, pp. 48–68. Dumbarton Oaks Research Library and Collection, Washington, DC.
> 1987   *Ancient Chalcatzingo*. University of Texas Press, Austin.
> 1993   "Olmec" Horizons in Formative Period Mesoamerica. In *Latin American Horizons*, ed. Don S. Rice, pp. 83–111. Dumbarton Oaks, Washington, DC.
> 1999   Public Monuments and Sacred Mountains: Observations on Three Formative Period Sacred Landscapes. In *Social Patterns in Pre-Classic Mesoamerica: A Symposium at Dumbarton Oaks, 9 and 10 October, 1993*, ed. David C. Grove and Rosemary A. Joyce, pp. 255–299. Dumbarton Oaks Research Library and Collection, Washington, DC.
> 2007   Cerros sagrados olmecas: Montañas en la cosmovisión mesoamericana. *Arqueología Mexicana* 15 (87): 30–35.

Hammond, Norman
> 1988   Cultura Hermana: Reappraising the Olmec. *Quarterly Review of Archaeology* 9 (4): 1–4.
> 2005   The Dawn and the Dusk: Beginning and Ending a Long-Term Research Program at the Preclassic Maya Site of Cuello, Belize. *Anthropological Notebooks* 11: 45–60.

Hansen, Richard D.
　1998　Continuity and Disjunction: The Pre-Classic Antecedents of Classic Maya Architecture. In *Function and Meaning in Classic Maya Architecture*, vol. 2, ed. Stephen D. Houston, pp. 49–122. Dumbarton Oaks Research Library and Collection, Washington, DC.

Hatch, Marion Popenoe de
　1976　The Ceramics at Abaj Takalik. Typescript manuscript in Dillon's possession.
　1987　Un análisis de las esculturas de Santa Lucía Cotzumalguapa. *Mesoamérica* 14: 467–510.
　1989a　An Analysis of the Santa Lucia Cotzumalguapa Sculptures. In *New Frontiers in the Archaeology of the Pacific Coast of Southern Mesoamerica*, ed. Frederick J. Bove and Lynette Heller, pp. 167–194. Anthroplogical Papers 39. Arizona State University, Tempe.
　1991　Comentarios sobre la cerámica de Tak'alik Ab'aj (antes Abaj Takalik). En *II Simposio de Investigaciones Arqueológicas en Guatemala, 1988* (editado por Juan Pablo Laporte, Sandra Villagrán de Brady, Héctor L. Escobedo, Dora Guerra de González y Juan Antonio Valdés), pp. 16–18. Museo Nacional de Arqueología y Etnología, Guatemala.
　1998　Propuesta Para el Análisis de los Estilos Escultóricos de la Costa Sur de Guatemala. In *Taller Arqueología de la Región de la Costa Sur de Guatemala*, ed. Christa Schieber de Lavarreda, pp. 71–72. Proyecto Nacional Abaj Takalik, INAH, Retalhuleu, Guatemala.
　2002　New Perspectives on Kaminaljuyú, Guatemala: Regional Interaction during the Preclassic and Classic Periods. In *Incidents of Archaeology in Central America and Yucatán: Essays in Honor of Edwin M. Shook*, ed. Michael Love, Marion Popenoe de Hatch, and Héctor L. Escobedo, pp. 277–296. University Press of America, Lanham, MD.

Heizer, Robert F.
　1968　New Observations on La Venta. In *Dumbarton Oaks Conference on the Olmec: October 28th and 29th, 1967*, ed. Elizabeth P. Benson, pp. 9–36. Dumbarton Oaks Research Library and Collection, Washington, DC.
　1976　La Venta: A Cradle of Mesoamerican Civilization. *Texas Archaeological Society Bulletin* 47: 1–24.

Heizer, Robert F., and Philip Drucker
　1968　The La Venta Fluted Pyramid. *Antiquity* 42: 52–56.

Heizer, Robert F., John A. Graham, and Lewis K. Napton
　1968　The 1968 Investigations at La Venta. *Contributions of the University of California Archaeological Research Facility* 5: 127–154. Berkeley.

Johnson, Mark C., and Kevin O. Pope
　1985　The Abaj Takalik Map: Cartographic Recording of Topography and Architecture, 1976–1980. Typescript manuscript in Dillon's possession.

Justeson, John S., and Terrence Kaufman
　1993　A Decipherment of Epi-Olmec Hieroglyphic Writing. *Science* 259 (5102): 1703–1711.

1997   A Newly Discovered Column in the Hieroglyphic Text on La Mojarra Stela 1: A Test of the Epi-Olmec Decipherment. *Science* 277 (5323): 207–210.
2008   The Epi-Olmec Tradition at Cerro de las Mesas in the Classic Period. In *Classic Period Cultural Currents in Southern and Central Veracruz*, ed. Philip J. Arnold III and Christopher A. Pool, pp. 160–194. Dumbarton Oaks, Washington, DC.

Kaufman, Terrence, and John Justeson
2008   The Epi-Olmec Language and Its Neighbors. In *Classic Period Cultural Currents in Southern and Central Veracruz*, ed. Philip J. Arnold III and Christopher A. Pool, pp. 55–83. Dumbarton Oaks, Washington, DC.

Love, Michael
1999   Ideology, Material Culture, and Daily Practice in Pre-Classic Mesoamerica: A Pacific Coast Perspective. In *Social Patterns in Pre-Classic Mesoamerica: A Symposium at Dumbarton Oaks, 9 and 10 October, 1993*, ed. David C. Grove and Rosemary A. Joyce, pp. 127–153. Dumbarton Oaks Research Library and Collection, Washington, DC.
2002   Ceramic Chronology of Preclassic Period Western Pacific Guatemala and Its Relationship to Other Regions. In *Incidents of Archaeology in Central America and Yucatán: Essays in Honor of Edwin M. Shook*, ed. Michael Love, Marion Popenoe de Hatch, and Héctor L. Escobedo, pp. 51–74. University Press of America, Lanham, MD.
2007   Recent Research in the Southern Highlands and Pacific Coast of Mesoamerica. *Journal of Archaeological Research* 15: 275–328.

McBryde, Felix Webster
1947   *Cultural and Historical Geography of Southwest Guatemala*. Smithsonian Institution, Institute of Social Anthropology Publication 4. Washington, DC.

Miles, Susanna W.
1965   Sculpture of the Guatemala-Chiapas Highlands and Pacific Slopes, and Associated Hieroglyphs. In *Archaeology of Southern Mesoamerica*, Part 1, ed. Gordon R. Willey, pp. 237–275. Handbook of Middle American Indians, vol. 2, Robert Wauchope, gen. ed. University of Texas Press, Austin.

Neff, Hector
1987   Plumbate Pottery at Abaj Takalik. Typescript manuscript in Dillon's possession.
2002   Sources of Raw Material Used in Plumbate Pottery. In *Incidents of Archaeology in Central America and Yucatán: Essays in Honor of Edwin M. Shook*, ed. Michael Love, Marion Popenoe de Hatch, and Héctor L. Escobedo, pp. 217–231. University Press of America, Lanham, MD.

Norman, V. Garth
1973   *Izapa Sculpture, Part 1: Album*. New World Archaeological Foundation Papers 30. Brigham Young University, Provo, UT.
1976   *Izapa Sculpture, Part 2: Text*. New World Archaeological Foundation Papers 30. Brigham Young University, Provo, UT.

Orellana, Sandra L.
  1984 *The Tzutujil Mayas: Continuity and Change, 1250–1630.* University of Oklahoma Press, Norman.
  1995 *Ethnohistory of the Pacific Coast.* Labyrinthos, Lancaster, CA.

Orrego Corzo, Miguel
  1990 *Investigaciones arqueológicas en Abaj Takalik, El Asintal, Retalhuleu, Año 1988. Reporte 1, Proyecto Nacional Abaj Takalik.* INAH de Guatemala.
  1998 Problemática de Multiplicidad de Estilos y Patrones Culturales en Abaj Takalik: Preclásico Medio y Tardío (800 AC–250 DC). In *Taller Arqueología de la Región de la Costa Sur de Guatemala,* ed. Christa Schieber de Lavarreda, pp. 53–70. Proyecto Nacional Abaj Takalik, INAH, Retalhuleu, Guatemala.

Parsons, Lee A.
  1957 The Nature of Horizon Markers in Middle American Archaeology. *Anthropology Tomorrow* 5 (2): 98–121. Chicago.
  1967a Bilbao, Guatemala: An Archaeological Study of the Pacific Coast Cotzumalhuapa Region, vol. 1. *Publications in Anthropology* 11. Milwaukee Public Museum, Milwaukee, WI.
  1967b An Early Maya Stela on the Pacific Coast of Guatemala. *Estudios de Cultura Maya* 6: 171–198. Seminario de Cultura Maya, UNAM, México, DF.
  1969 Bilbao, Guatemala: An Archaeological Study of the Pacific Coast Cotzumalhuapa Region, vol. 2. *Publications in Anthropology* 12. Milwaukee Public Museum, Milwaukee, WI.
  1973 Iconographic Notes on a New Izapan Stela from Abaj Takalik, Guatemala. *The 40th Congresso Internazionale Degli Americanisti* 1: 203–212. Rome-Genova.
  1978 The Peripheral Coastal Lowlands and the Middle Classic Period. In *Middle Classic Mesoamerica: A.D. 400–700,* ed. Esther Pasztory, pp. 25–34. Columbia University Press, New York.
  1981 Post-Olmec Stone Sculpture: The Olmec-Izapan Transition on the Southern Pacific Coast and Highlands. In *The Olmec and Their Neighbors: Essays in Memory of Matthew W. Stirling,* ed. Elizabeth P. Benson, pp. 257–288. Dumbarton Oaks Research Library and Collection, Washington, DC.
  1986 *The Origins of Maya Art: Monumental Stone Sculpture of Kaminaljuyú, Guatemala, and the Southern Pacific Coast.* Dumbarton Oaks Studies in Pre-Columbian Art and Archaeology 28. Washington, DC.

Pohl, Mary E.D., Kevin O. Pope, and Christopher von Nagy
  2002 Olmec Origins of Mesoamerican Writing. *Science, New Series* 298 (5600): 1984–1987.

Proskouriakoff, Tatiana
  1950 *A Study of Classic Maya Sculpture.* Publication 593. Carnegie Institution of Washington, Washington, DC.
  1968 Olmec and Maya Art: Problems of Their Stylistic Relation. In *Dumbarton Oaks Conference on the Olmec: October 28th and 29th, 1967,* ed. Elizabeth P. Benson, pp. 119–130. Dumbarton Oaks Research Library and Collection, Washington, DC.

1971   Early Architecture and Sculpture in Mesoamerica. In *Observations on the Emergence of Civilization in Mesoamerica*, ed. Robert F. Heizer, John A. Graham, and C. William Clewlow, pp. 141–156. Contributions of the University of California Archaeological Research Facility 11. Berkeley.

Quirarte, Jacinto
1973   Izapan-Style Art: A Study of Its Form and Meaning. *Studies in Pre-Columbian Art and Archaeology* 10. Dumbarton Oaks, Washington, DC.
1976   The Relationship of Izapan Style Art to Olmec and Maya Art. In *Origins of Religious Art and Iconography in Preclassic Mesoamerica*, ed. H. B. Nicholson, pp. 73–86. UCLA Latin American Center Publications and the Ethnic Arts Council of Los Angeles, Los Angeles, CA.
1977   Early Art Styles of Mesoamerica and Early Classic Maya Art. In *The Origins of Maya Civilization*, ed. Richard E.W. Adams, pp. 249–283. School of American Research, University of New Mexico Press, Albuquerque.

Schieber de Lavarreda, Christa
1994   A Middle Preclassic Clay Ball Court at Abaj Takalik, Guatemala. *Mexicon* 16 (4): 77–84.

Schieber de Lavarreda, Christa, ed.
1998   *Taller Arqueología de la Región de la Costa Sur de Guatemala.* Proyecto Nacional Abaj Takalik, INAH, Retalhuleu, Guatemala.

Schieber de Lavarreda, Christa, and Miguel Orrego Corzo
2001a   *Los Senderos Milenarios de Abaj Takalik.* IDEAH, Guatemala.
2001b   Mil Anos de Historia en Abaj Takalik. *Utz'ib* 3 (1): 1–31.
2002   *Abaj Takalik* [guidebook]. IDEAH, Guatemala.

Sharer, Robert J.
1994   *The Ancient Maya*, 5th ed. Stanford University Press, Stanford, CA.

Sharer, Robert J., and David W. Sedat
1973   Monument 1, El Portón, Guatemala, and the Development of Maya Calendrical and Writing Systems. *Contributions of the University of California Archaeological Research Facility* 18: 177–194. Berkeley.

Shook, Edwin M.
1960   Tikal Stela 29. *Expedition* 2 (2): 28–35. University of Pennsylvania, Philadelphia.
1965   Archaeological Survey of the Pacific Coast of Guatemala. In *Archaeology of Southern Mesoamerica*, Part 1, ed. Gordon R. Willey, pp. 180–194. Handbook of Middle American Indians, vol. 2, Robert Wauchope, gen. ed. University of Texas Press, Austin.
1971   Inventory of Some Preclassic Traits in the Highlands and Pacific Guatemala and Adjacent Areas. In *Observations on the Emergence of Civilization in Mesoamerica*, ed. Robert F. Heizer, John A. Graham, and C. William Clewlow, pp. 70–77. Contributions of the University of California Archaeological Research Facility 11, Berkeley.

Thompson, J. Eric S.
- 1943 Some Sculptures from Southeastern Quetzaltenango, Guatemala. *Carnegie Institution Notes on Middle American Archaeology and Ethnology* 1 (17): 100–112.
- 1948 *An Archaeological Reconnaissance in the Cotzumalhuapa Region, Escuintla, Guatemala.* Publication 574. Carnegie Institution of Washington, Washington, DC.

Webster, David L.
- 1977 Warfare and the Evolution of Maya Civilization. In *The Origins of Maya Civilization*, ed. Richard E.W. Adams, pp. 335–372. School of American Research, University of New Mexico Press, Albuquerque.

Williams, Howel
- 1960 Volcanic History of the Guatemalan Highlands. *Publications in Geological Sciences* 38: 1–88. University of California, Berkeley.
- 1977 Geological Notes on the Abaj Takalik Site. Typescript manuscript in Dillon's possession.

PART II
THE MAYA AND THEIR NEIGHBORS

5

KINGSHIP IN THE CRADLE OF MAYA CIVILIZATION: THE MIRADOR BASIN

Richard D. Hansen

More than two decades of research in the Mirador Basin have led me (Hansen 1982, 1984, 2005; Hansen, Howell, and Guenter 2008) and others (Matheny 1986, 1987a, 1987b), based on specific criteria presented in this chapter and elsewhere (Stutz-Landeen 1986; Howell and Copeland 1989; Hansen 1990, 1991, 1992a, 1992b, 1998, 2000, 2001, n.d.a), to suggest that a true state-level society came to an apogee there during the Late Preclassic Period between 300 BC and AD 150. Earlier excavations at Maya Lowland sites such as Cerros, Cuello, and Colha (Freidel 1981, 1985, 1986; Matheny 1986, 1987a, 1987b; Freidel and Schele 1988a, 1988b; Reese-Taylor 1996; Hansen and Guenter 2005) suggested that the origins of Maya kingship and related cultural sophistication began in the Late Preclassic Period.

However, more recent archaeological evidence suggests that the formation of kingdoms in the Maya Lowlands began much earlier, in the Middle Preclassic Period, temporally comparable to cultural developments in the Gulf Coast and Oaxaca areas (Hansen 1992a, 1992b, 1998, 2001, 2005; Reilly 1994; Marcus and Flannery 1996; Clark and Hansen 2001; Garber, Hartman, and Brown 2002; Hansen and Guenter 2005). Similarly, early developments have been observed at the site of Cival in the eastern Petén (Estrada-Belli 2006) and at Blackman Eddy and Pacbitun in Belize (Hohmann and Powis 1996; Garber, Hartman, and Brown 2002). The dynamic formation of kingly and state-level hierarchies can best be understood through observation of the earlier, incipient stages of development (Fields 1989; Clark 1991; Clark and Blake 1994; Clark and Hansen 2001).

The socio-political dynamics and evolution of kingly authority can be identified and evaluated within the Maya Lowlands. Archaeological evidence from excavations in the Mirador Basin of Northern Guatemala is particularly relevant to questions about the origins of Maya hierarchical structure or "kingship." Specific evidence for the earliest manifestations of status, logistics, and production systems has been documented elsewhere (Hansen 2001, 2005, n.d.a, n.d.b; Hansen and Guenter 2005) and is mentioned only briefly in this chapter. The ideological manifestations of power, which H. B. Nicholson particularly studied, are examined in light of ongoing research within the Mirador Basin and elsewhere in the Maya Lowlands.

Nicholson was justifiably concerned about scholarly inattention to the ideological components of Mesoamerican society. In keeping with his orientation, this chapter explores the ideological foundations and underpinnings of incipient Maya kingship as interpreted from recent archaeological investigations in the Maya Lowlands. I believe that initially, Early Maya Lowland rulers acquired status through production systems, wealth accrual, and logistics control; they maintained their status by incorporating and perpetuating a religious ideology to form an organic solidarity (Hansen 1992a). Display of resultant economic, social, and political disparity was first manifested in residence constructions, but that status was facilitated and perpetuated by ideological display on stone monuments supplanted by human portraiture. Stone monuments, however, became subservient to ritually charged architectural formats, architectural art and iconography, and specialized causeway systems—all symptomatic of a deeply ingrained religious ideology but implemented through control of labor, construction, and artistic resources.

Others have noted the connection between authority and architectural construction programs: "Historically, we can trace the origins of kings as actual or nominal builders to the lineage of headmen, master artisans, and religious specialists who direct the construction of community dwellings, men's houses, initiation quarters, or communal ceremonial-political centers in tribal and chiefdom societies" (Helms 1993: 78).

Privileged individuals most likely attained rank or status originally on the basis of skills, talents, and accrued personal wealth. Their position encouraged them to reduce societal resistance to their accumulation of personal power and the expansion of wealth and prestige (Clark and Blake 1994). As this process evolved, personal qualifiers became less significant than selected lineages, and leadership acquired by achievement became subordinate to ascribed or inherited status sanctioned and recognized by those ruled. The display of power was manifested in stone monuments and monumental architecture imbued with religious, cosmological, and ritual symbolism that displayed true regal and religious authority. The commission of other public works, however—such as water collection systems, agricultural terrace systems, and causeways—demonstrated that the governance was also concerned for the governed; this reciprocity both fueled and maintained kingly power and wealth.

The earliest monuments found thus far in the Mirador Basin do not display human protagonists, although this situation may change as more monuments are identified. Admittedly, the corpus of early sculpture is restricted as of yet, and some of our present interpretations can and will be improved as our database expands. However, based on available information, the subject matter of early monuments is that of ideological and cosmological creatures. La Isla Stela 1 and Nakbé Monument 8 are depictions of saurian monsters rather than portraits of rulers (Hansen n.d.a, n.d.b). The strategic placement of monuments in centerline axis formats, such as Nakbé Altar 4, is consistent with antecedent and contemporary behavior in other areas of Mesoamerica.

Ideological power is first consistently manifested in the construction of specialized Middle Preclassic Period architectural groups of ritual and cosmological importance termed "E-Groups." In addition, the first intra- and inter-site causeways were constructed by at least the later part of the Middle Preclassic Period (ca. 500–400 BC). The ability to marshal such labor forces for the construction of large, labor-intensive, and ritually significant architecture indicates that centralized authority had been established by the Middle Preclassic Period, early in the developmental sequence of the Maya.

By the time of the Late Preclassic apogee of Early Maya kingship, rulers were using a highly specialized and ubiquitous form of architecture known as the Triadic Architectural Style. This style dominated Preclassic architecture from about 300 BC until about AD 150 and was used sporadically throughout subsequent Maya history. The ideological framework suggested by art and architecture reinforced the legitimacy of early rulers; its successful exploitation established an architectural legacy of unprecedented proportions.

GEOGRAPHIC AND CULTURAL CONTEXT

The Mirador Basin is located in the extreme north-central Petén of Guatemala and the southernmost part of Campeche, Mexico (figure 5.1). The Mirador Basin is part of the Buena Vista Formation of early Eocene age (Force and Dohrenwend 2008) and is an uplifted plateau circumscribed by a range of karstic hills on its north, east, and south and somewhat lower and less-pronounced elevations on its western edge. It is a triangular-shaped depression of seasonal swamps, or *bajos*. Drainage near the northern section of the Mirador Basin extends toward the Candelaria River drainage system in Campeche and Tabasco, a possible contact route with the complex societies in the Gulf Coast region during the Middle Preclassic Period.

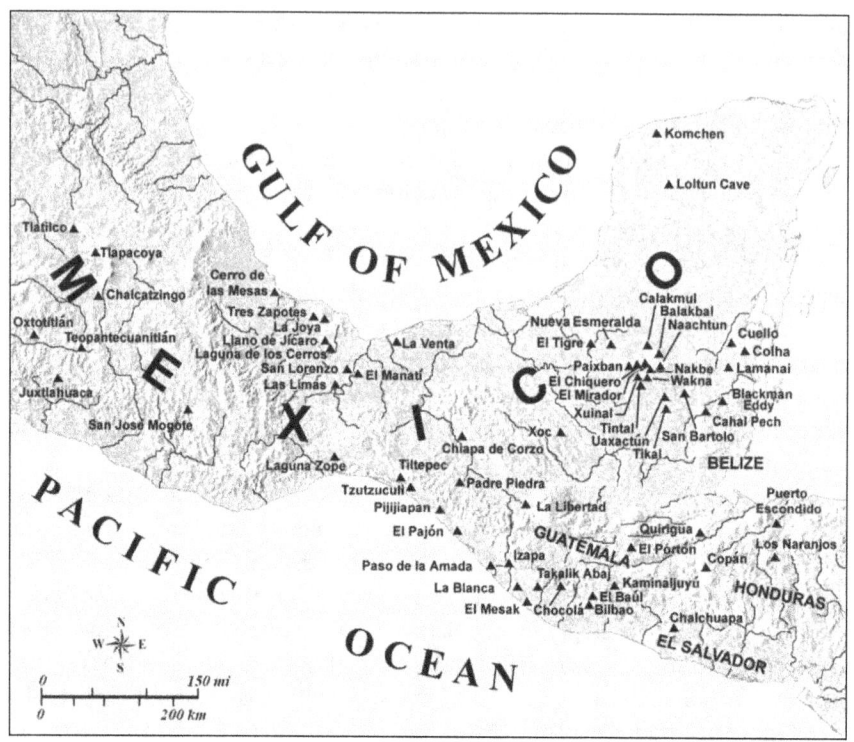

5.1. *Map of Mesoamerica showing the Mirador Basin region and other archaeological sites. By Rusty van Rossmann, after Clark and Pye 2000.*

Bajos comprise the majority of the surface area (figure 5.2). The bajo is one of the unique geological features of the basin and represents the result of a slow-moving accumulation of water with hydrologic pressure from the higher karstic ridges surrounding the basin on all sides. The soils of the Mirador Basin consist of clay types known as Uaxactún, Macanché, and Yaloch; are of poor to medium fertility (Simmons, Tarano, and Pinto 1959 ; Stevens 1964; FYDEP 1968); and are distinct from soils to the west and east of the basin. The Mirador Basin is also known to have rare or uncommon minerals (Dixon, Jacob, and White 1994).

Explorations by the Carnegie Institution in the 1920s and 1930s identified several major sites within the Mirador Basin (Morley 1938; Ruppert and Denison 1943). Subsequent work by Ian Graham in the 1960s and 1970s resulted in the first maps of major sites such as El Mirador and Nakbé (Graham 1967). The first systematic survey work was conducted by Bruce Dahlin and Ray Matheny between 1978 and 1983 and defined a major Preclassic presence at El Mirador (Dahlin, Foss, and Chambers 1980; Matheny, Hansen, and Gurr 1980; Dahlin 1984; Matheny 1986, 1987a, 1987b). In 1987, investigations on a regional scale

KINGSHIP IN THE CRADLE OF MAYA CIVILIZATION

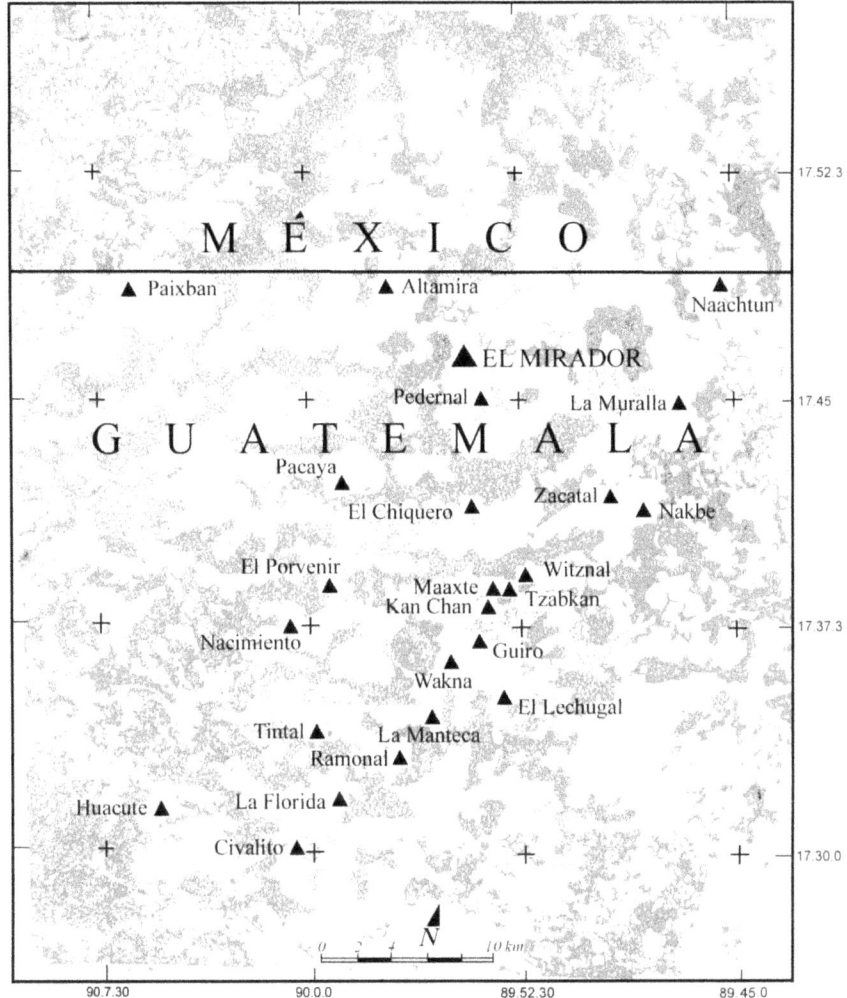

5.2. *Map of the Mirador Basin with bajos stippled, showing their relationships with the major ancient centers. By Richard D. Hansen and E. Ortega, after Hansen 1992a: 276.*

in the Mirador Basin began with the birth of the UCLA RAINPEG (Regional Archaeological Investigation of the North Petén, Guatemala) Project, which gradually transformed into the Mirador Basin Project, under my direction. Extensive work has identified the antiquity and range of occupation within the Mirador Basin (Forsyth 1989, 1992, 1993; Hansen 1990, 1991, 1992a, 1992b, 1992c, 1996, 1998, 2000, 2001, 2005; Balcarcel 1999; Hansen, Howell, and Guenter 2008). The Mirador Basin Project has now mapped thirty-five major and minor sites within Guatemala, and work by Nikolai Grube and Ivan Sprajc in southern

Campeche has further identified numerous Preclassic sites on the Mexican side of the border (e.g., Sprajc 2005).

Within the Mirador Basin are structures rivaling the largest in the Western Hemisphere, older than most Maya centers of the Middle and Late Preclassic Periods. Even more enigmatically, in contrast to models proposed for complex societies throughout the ancient world and even for initial Maya settlements on riverine systems (Puleston and Puleston 1971), the precocious political and economic dynamics of the Mirador Basin coalesced in the most distant locations possible from riverine or coastal regions. The rise of kingship in the Mirador Basin therefore represents a geographical, geological, cultural, and ecological anomaly that deserves investigation.

Systematic investigations at thirty-five sites within the Mirador Basin have incorporated more than 700 separate excavation operations. These include broad architectural exposures; horizontal exposures of early floors, platforms, residences, monuments, and architectural facades; coring projects; tunnels; and test pits. Through all this work, a fair chronological assessment of the Mirador Basin archaeological sites and their associated architecture has been acquired. Architectural sampling included not only large public architecture (Matheny, Hansen, and Gurr 1980; Hansen 1984, 1990; Matheny 1986, 1987a, 1987b; Stutz-Landeen 1986; Howell and Copeland 1989; Balcarcel 1999; Hansen et al. 2004a, 2004b; Hansen, Suyuc-Ley, Linares et al. 2005; Hansen, Suyuc-Ley, Morales et al. 2007) but also Preclassic and Classic residences of varying sizes and dimensions.

The recovery of archaeological materials from stratified contexts has allowed a refined ceramic chronology for what were formerly considered large blocks of time. In like manner, the ceramics associated with architecture have allowed a chronological seriation of architecture and settlement in the Mirador Basin. This has been correlated with fine-grained studies of the pollen sequences and associated AMS radiocarbon dates from more than seventeen vertical meters of highly stratified cylindrical cores from deep-water lakes along the western edge of the Mirador Basin (Wahl, Byrne, et al. 2006; Wahl, Schreiner, et al. 2007a, 2007b). These stratified pollen samples are believed to accurately reflect the Mirador Basin's cultural and ecological sequences, since the predominant winds come from the east, carrying pollen from agricultural or natural botanical sources.

Numerous radiocarbon assays and chronologically distinctive pottery suggest that the earliest permanent occupation of the Mirador Basin occurred somewhere near 1000 BC, particularly at the site of Nakbé (figure 5.7) and possibly at Xulnal (Forsyth 1993; Hansen 1998, 2001, 2005). At Nakbé the initial sedentary occupation corresponds to a period dubbed the "early Ox" Phase. Ceramics include red washed rims on unslipped tecomate bodies and punctuated, unslipped bodies with red slipped, restricted rims. Some ceramics incorporate incised lines on everted rims. A chert blade technology existed, but there is no evidence of obsidian importation or other outside contact at this earliest time. It appears that there was only a limited occupation at Nakbé, although extensive quarrying at the site during later periods has destroyed much evidence of earlier settlements. The earliest known residences had hard-packed clay floors or postholes carved into bedrock. Some form of settlement nucleation had begun by this time.

Pollen data (Wahl 2000, 2005; Wahl, Byrne, et al. 2006; Wahl, Schreiner, et al. 2007a, 2007b) and stable isotope data (Jacob 1994; Hansen et al. 2002) demonstrate that the seasonal swamps around Nakbé and El Mirador were open, grass-covered, wetland marshes known as *civales*. Aquatic and forest wildlife would have been attracted to such a location, and the abundance of such resources may have also been an attraction for the first Maya pioneers.

The civales ultimately became crucial factors in the rise of kingship because of the rich, organic marsh mucks that were farmed and ultimately transported to terraces, providing the economic abundance needed for incipient kingships to flourish. Phytoliths recovered from ancient field surfaces have demonstrated the production of corn, squash, gourds, palms, and possibly cotton and cacao (Bozarth 2000; Bozarth and Hansen 2001).

EARLY MIDDLE PRECLASSIC EMERGENCE OF KINGSHIP

By the Early Middle Preclassic Period (1000–600 BC) there are ample variations in residence size and structural sophistication at several sites in the Mirador Basin, including small, stone-lined residential platforms with packed clay floors, wattle-and-daub residences, as well as major platforms with vertical stone walls. The labor marshaled into public construction projects during this time was controlled by administrative elites, not only in the Mirador Basin but elsewhere in the Maya Lowlands as well (Estrada-Belli 2006; Garber, Hartman, and Brown 2002). During this period an embryonic leadership and status hierarchy in the Mirador Basin is suggested by the importation and distribution of exotic goods such as obsidian, jade, and basalt from the Maya Highlands, imported chert artifacts, and seashells from the eastern coast. The symbols representative of rank and the status of a patron elite also appear.

The importation of shell appears to have had singular importance at this time. Small shells (*Margenellidae: Prunum apicinum*) were brought into the Mirador Basin, and shell ornaments were being worked. But some of the most significant imports into Nakbé and other Middle Preclassic sites in the interior Maya Lowlands were the *Strombus* shells (*Strombus costatus* sp.) and other gastropods (*Turbinella angulata*) from the Caribbean Sea (figure 5.3); most of these shells were cut and drilled conically (unidirectionally) or occasionally bi-conically (bi-directionally), leaving the spines and natural protuberances of the shell intact. These shells are exclusive to the Early Middle Preclassic Period and have not been found in any deposits of subsequent periods, either in the

5.3. *Strombus shells from Early Middle Preclassic deposits from the Mirador Basin. Photo by Richard D. Hansen.*

Mirador Basin or at Tikal, Uaxactún, and numerous sites in Belize. The unique presence of the shells in Early Middle Preclassic deposits of a ritual and elite character suggests that they represented an important economic symbol or perhaps even a currency. *Strombus* shells do not appear in any of the extensive Late Preclassic contexts in the Mirador Basin, suggesting that the shell's function may have been as specialized as it was temporally restricted. Their presence is useful as a period marker as well as a possible demonstration of economic and political prowess.

Other exotic imports during the Middle Preclassic Period include obsidian—primarily from San Martín Jilotepeque (Kunselman 2000)—jade, and coral. The obsidian was transported as nodules with cortex and initially worked into prismatic blades at the local sites. This can be interpreted as a mechanism encouraging craft specialization and the control of exotic-foreign commodities by an emerging elite. By 800 to 600 BC, symbols of hierarchical status included cranial deformation, dental inlay of hematite disks, jade beads, sherds with the woven mat motif, and enlarged platform constructions (Hansen 2001).

LATE MIDDLE PRECLASSIC KINGSHIP MATURATION

By the Late Middle Preclassic Period, 600 to 400 BC, kingcraft had evolved to the point where pyramidal structures up to 18 m high were constructed at Nakbé,

5.4. *Roughly hewn stones from an Early Middle Preclassic wall at the base of Nakbé Structure 5, ca. 900–800 BC. Photo by Richard D. Hansen.*

Xulnal, Wakna, El Pesquero, and, on a lesser scale, at La Florida. A ballcourt was built at Nakbé during this time, consistent with the Middle Preclassic ballcourt discovered at Takalik Abaj (Schieber de Lavarreda 1994). However, with the maturation of kingship, a major new focus became the economic and social organization of massive labor forces to construct ritually significant architecture. Blocks quarried throughout the ancient centers changed radically in size from small, roughly hewn stones (figure 5.4) to those 1.4 m long, 0.50 m high, and 0.50 m wide (figure 5.5), indicating that specialist development and procurement were clearly in place by this time (Sidrys 1978).

Ritual Architecture

One of the most important architectural formats has been called the E-Group (figure 5.6), named after Group E at Uaxactún where the ritual pattern was first detected in 1924. This standardized structural format consists of a dominant pyramidal structure on the west side of a plaza, frequently with quadripartite stairways, while an elongated platform structure is placed on the east side of the plaza (Laporte and Fialko 1993, 1995; Laporte and Valdés 1993; Chase and Chase 1995; Hansen 1998, 2000, 2001, 2005; Estrada-Belli 2006).

5.5. *Major block wall from Late Middle Preclassic Structure 35 at Nakbé showing the long axis of the stones parallel to the wall alignment. Blocks are 1.0–1.2 m long. Photo by Richard D. Hansen.*

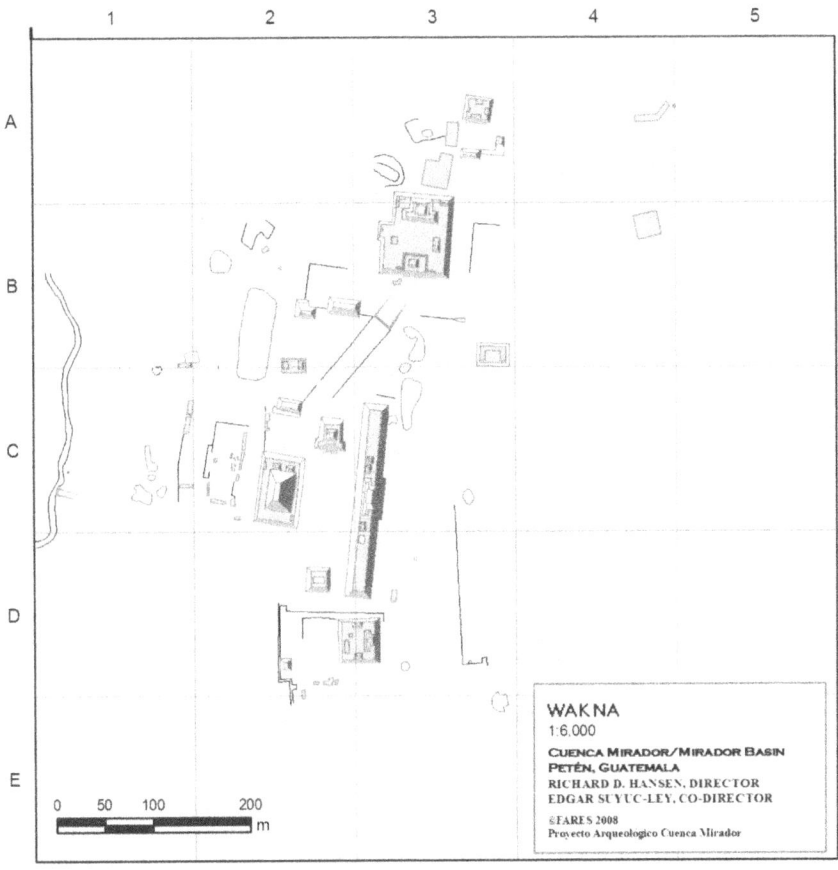

5.6. *Map of a portion of the site of Wakna showing the E-Group in Quadrants C 2 and C 3. By Hector Mejia, © FARES 2008.*

Occasionally, but not always, one or several structures appear on the platform of the eastern elongated structure. The E-Group pattern of architecture can be considered the earliest consistent ritual format that spread throughout Preclassic Mesoamerica; it most likely originated among the Lowland Maya (Hansen 2005, n.d.a). It is found in Eb and Tzec Phase architecture within Structure 5C–54 at Tikal (Laporte and Valdés 1993; Laporte and Fialko 1995) and Group D at Uaxactún (Renaldo Acevedo, personal communication, 1998) and also appears prior to 700 BC at Nakbé in Str. 51 Sub 1. Through a combination of cosmology and ritually consistent architecture, administrative authority was justified and solidified. The ideological importance of this architectural group was so substantial that it endured well into the Classic Period.

Richard D. Hansen

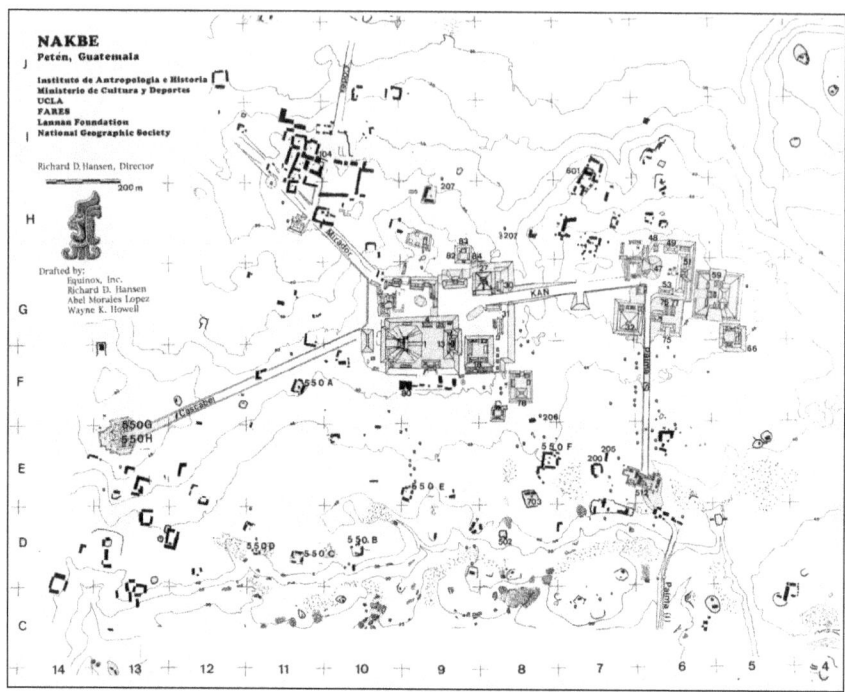

5.7. Map of Nakbé showing inter- and intra-site causeways, after Hansen et al. 2002: 285.

Elite Residential Architecture

Large platform constructions lined with smaller structures have been found adjacent to major religious-ceremonial architecture, such as Group 18 at Nakbé, located directly east of the largest pyramid on the primary platform in the West Group of the city (figure 5.7). Excavation of these platforms suggests that this compound was the residence area for an elite hierarchy of Middle and Late Preclassic Nakbé, either for priests who functioned in the sacred precinct immediately to the west or for the king and his court (Clark and Hansen 2001).

Causeways

Causeways at Nakbé whose earliest levels date to the Late Middle Preclassic Period are the Kan, Palma, and Mirador causeways. These indicate that organized labor had been marshaled into intra-site (Kan, Palma) and inter-site (Mirador-Nakbé and Mirador-Tintal) efforts (figure 5.7). Subsequently, Late Preclassic floors were added to these original constructions. Major causeways, 24 to 40 m wide and 2 to 6 m high, connote massive amounts of labor as well as political, economic, and social cohesion between the major sites of the Mirador Basin. Hierarchical structure (i.e., kingship) in the Mirador Basin, to judge from the major architectural innovations commissioned during this time, was growing strongly.

Agriculture

If socio-political and economic complexity and a developed authoritative hierarchy permeated Maya society in the Mirador Basin by the Early and Late Middle Preclassic Periods, how were they financed? Pollen and isotope data indicate that the majority of the Mirador Basin was covered with civales, or perennially wet marshes, rich in aquatic and faunal resources.

Because the first settlers would have faced considerable obstacles in felling large trees, the presence of which is evident in the pollen samples, the initial settlements probably occurred along the edges of the marshes. This observation is consistent with evidence from other sites such as Tikal, where the majority of Early Middle Prelassic (Eb) materials were found to the east of the site near the Bajo de Santa Fé (Coe 1965a, 1965b; Harrison 1986).

The potential of the swamp soils would have been evident to the incipient farmers (Martínez et al. 1999; Bozarth 2000; Hansen, Martínez, et al. 2000, Hansen, Bozarth, et al. 2002; Bozarth and Hansen 2001). A system of imported mud fields, terraces, residential gardens, and dams has been identified in the site center of Nakbé (Martínez, Hansen, and Howell 1996; Martínez et al. 1999; Hansen et al. 2002: 289). There is also evidence of unusual lineal formations in the bajos to the southwest and west of El Mirador, suggesting a marsh utilization—perhaps chinampa-style—by Preclassic farmers. Research is ongoing through large horizontal excavations in the bajos supervised by Dr. Thomas Schreiner of UC Berkeley and Enrique Hernandez of the Universidad de San Carlos. The discovery of imported soil fields, check dams, and artificial terrace constructions suggests that intensive agriculture had been incorporated into Maya society of the Mirador Basin by the Late Middle Preclassic Period, if not earlier. Such innovative farming practices provided the economic surpluses needed to propel the accumulating or "aggrandizing" elite into the more sophisticated dynamics of the succeeding Late Preclassic Period.

EMPIRICISM OF HIERARCHY: STONE MONUMENTS

Carving stone monuments is a universal kingship strategy. The social and political ideology of monument erection in key locations legitimizes regal authority and suggests the immortality of the governing elite (Kappelman 1997). However, in the case of the Early Maya in the Mirador Basin, the earliest monuments do not directly depict rulers but rather display deity portraits or cosmic monsters, perhaps to pay homage to an all-governing deity pantheon. Such homage would have served emergent rulership well because it demonstrated that even kings were subservient to cosmological laws; therefore, the general populace should also be subject to "divine" governance.

The earliest carved monument recovered to date in the Mirador Basin is believed to be Stela 1 at the site of La Isla (figure 5.8), located on an "island" of elevated terrain in the bajo between Nakbé and El Mirador (figure 5.2). This monument is an unmodified limestone slab stone 1.67 m high with an upward-peering saurian creature incised on its face. The early date for the monument is based on style and theme rather than archaeological context, since it appears that the monument had been reset in its discovery position. The earliest securely dated monument is Altar 4 at Nakbé, placed in the centerline axis of Middle Preclassic architecture—directly associated with Middle Preclassic ceramics and with uncorrected carbon dates of between 800 and 600 BC, which usually implies an even earlier actual date (Hansen 1992a, n.d.b).

The presence of an emergent elite with possible connections to kingship is suggested by the stone monuments; woven mat symbols on ceramics; status items such as dental inlays (figure 5.10) of hematite (Mata Amado and Hansen 1992); exotic imported items of an exclusive nature such as *Strombus* shells, obsidian, coral, basalt, and jade; as well as evidence of cranial deformation and symbols of royalty on figurines (Hansen 1992b, 1992c, n.d.a). By the end of the Middle Preclassic Period between 600 and 400 BC, on the basis of ceramics and radiocarbon dates, there was an amalgamation of architectural specialists by an emerging and powerful elite—as suggested by the construction of massive platforms and monumental architecture, the building of the first causeways, variations in the size and sophistication of residences, dramatic changes in the shape and form of stones used in architecture, and the presence of stone monuments, including monuments of increasing size and complexity (see Justeson and Mathews 1983).

One of the most notable monuments is Nakbé Stela 1, nearly 5 m high, featuring two standing protagonists in royal costumes with elaborate headdresses and ceremonial belts with jade plaques, belt heads, and spools. The scene likely represents an early king acknowledging his source of authority from the founding father of the dynasty (Hansen n.d.b; Hansen et al. 2007). The legitimization of authority must be established *before* the exercise of economic and political power through massive labor expenditures, public works constructions, and inter-polity integrations, as were to follow in the Late Preclassic Period; monuments depicting kings were powerful tools for displaying the legitimization of power.

Middle Preclassic Period kingship and political centralization can be inferred from the use of sculptured stone monuments, increasing lime production and stucco utilization, agricultural intensification, and major transformations in the size and form of limestone blocks used in architectural constructions. Cultural-social-political innovations may have been fueled by differential access to wealth, organized exploitation of natural resources, implementation of systematic, intensive agriculture, and increasing labor intensification and specialist production

5.8. *La Isla, Stela 1, a Middle Preclassic monument. Photo by Richard D. Hansen.*

systems. Such radical transformations served to consolidate the economic and political power of an emerging administrative elite. One of the consolidants that fused society was a rigid cosmological ideology in the public manifestations of power, represented by such architectural forms of ritual and ideological importance (Hansen 1998) as the Middle Preclassic E-Group compounds at Nakbé, Xulnal, possibly Wakna, Tikal (5C–54 Sub), and Uaxactún (Group D).

LATE PRECLASSIC PERIOD KINGSHIP APOGEE

By the Late Preclassic Period (300 BC–AD 150) in the Mirador Basin, human populations and administrative authority reached an apogee. Major centers saw a maximum of settlement occupation, with population densities unmatched in subsequent periods. During this period maximum manifestations of kingship also became apparent through massive architectural constructions and dense nucleation of monumental architecture. Orchestrated public works projects were completed by populations apparently so large as to require residence constructions within marginal living areas such as the bajos and along the edges of escarpments. The size of the architecture may be a direct reflection of kingly power as well as a manifestation of the sophistication of the religious authority at the time.

Kingship and Stone Monuments

The ideology of kingship continued with stone monument placement, but by the Late Preclassic Period monument size had decreased dramatically (Hansen n.d.b; Hansen et al. 2007). Stones that had previously ranged from 4 to 5 m in height were reduced to small monuments less than 80 cm to 1 m tall. They were carved with symbols of kingship with a new twist: incised writing (Hansen 1991, 2001). Monuments such as Stela 2 at El Mirador, Monument 3 at Pedernal, El Chiquero Stela 1 (figure 5.9), and La Toronja Stela 1 were all carved in miniature fashion but with texts (Hansen 1991, 2001, n.d.b; Hansen et al. 2007). Subsequent monuments believed to be from the Mirador Basin, such as the Hauberg Stela, continued this small sculptural pattern (Schele 1985; Guenter 2002). Other miniature monuments lack carved texts (Chambers and Hansen 1996). It is ironic that while the largest pyramids in the Maya world were being built, displays of kingship on associated stone monuments were reduced to small banner stones. The use of writing, however, established a new immortality of kingly ideology.

Kingship and Sacbeob

Causeways, or sacbeob ("white roads"), of massive fill and topped with thick layers of plaster united major centers throughout the Mirador Basin. The

5.9. *Late Preclassic miniature Stela 1, El Chiquero, showing eroded glyph panel. Drawing by E. Ortega and Richard D. Hansen.*

Tintal-Mirador causeway was rebuilt on at least four separate occasions. These constructions, ranging from 2 to 6 m high and 24 to 40 m wide, extended up to 25 km in length. The precise engineering of the causeways is evident in their straight alignments over upland areas and through the bajos. There is little doubt that the causeways also controlled water systems for the irrigation of raised fields and what may be a chinampa-style agricultural system in the bajos to the north, west, and south of the civic center of El Mirador and on the southern side of Nakbé.

While the more obvious functions of the causeways can be reliably interpreted, such as trade and commodity transport, inter-site alliances, military movements, and political and economic homogeneity, the ideological concepts that initiated causeway construction and maintenance should also be considered as viable denominators of royal power postures. Alfred M. Tozzer (1941) and Arthur G. Miller (1974) reported a fascinating account of a Yucatec myth noted as the *kusansum* pathway, with a reference to the strategic and cosmological importance of the causeways. According to Maya informants near Valladolid, in the first period of world existence there

> was a road suspended in the sky, stretching from Tuloom [sic] and Coba to Chichén Itzá and Uxmal. This pathway was called *kusansum* or *sabke* [sic] (white road). It was in the nature of a large rope (*sum*) supposed to be living (*kusan*) and in the middle flowed blood. It was by this rope that the food was sent to the ancient rulers who lived in the structures now in ruins. For some reason, this rope was cut, the blood flowed out, and the rope vanished forever. (Tozzer 1907: 153, cited in Miller 1974: 172)

In this sense, the causeways served as an umbilical cord or lifeline over which rulers were able to send and receive food, trade goods, and similar commodities.

155

Richard D. Hansen

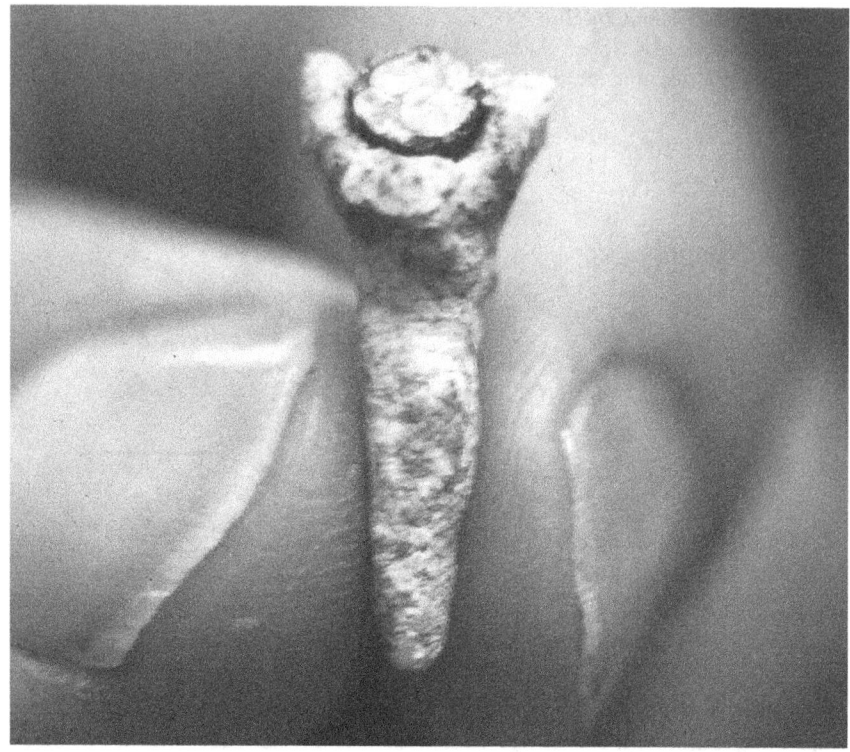

5.10. *Human incisor with hematite disk inlay, Early Middle Preclassic, ca. 800 BC. Photo by Richard D. Hansen.*

However, Miller also notes the strong representations of the umbilical cord as lineage markers, certainly a primary concern of ancient kingship, particularly in the *Codex Vindobonensis Mexicanus* and the *Codex Laud* (Miller 1974: 175–176). The causeways may have represented the life blood of sacred Maya kingship, meaning they allowed for the kinds of societal cohesion and control that were so important for the acceptance and maintenance of royal power. They also, however, could have represented a cosmic dimension to "express the formation of two contrasting and once connected worlds: the natural world and the supernatural world" (Miller 1974: 172), implied by the relationship with the umbilical cord and the "Cosmic Roads" referred to in the *Popul Vuh* (Tedlock 1985: 334). The *cahib xalcat be* were the celestial crossroads, associated with cardinal direction colors, that interacted with the Milky Way as part of the "complex system navigation" through the ideological and cosmological labyrinth of Maya ideology. In every functional sense the causeways provided the economic, political, and social benefits that enhanced rulers' administrative capabilities and formed a key element in the maintenance and coordination of the ideology of kingship.

Kingship and Triadic Architecture

Another crucial component by the early Late Preclassic Period (early Cycle 7) was the advent of the Triadic Architectural Style. The vast majority of the monumental architecture at the major sites throughout the Mirador Basin was constructed in the triadic format (figure 5.11): three structures placed atop a major platform, a single, central, dominant structure flanked by two smaller structures facing each other (see Graham 1967: 45–46; Hansen 1984, 1990, 1992a, 1998, 2001; Hansen, Howell, and Guenter 2008). This was the most ubiquitous architectural form in the Late Preclassic Period in the Maya Lowlands and was replicated on special occasions or at special events for centuries later, as at Uaxactún Str. A-V and the interior precincts of the North Acropolis at Tikal (Strs. 5D-22, 5D-23, 5D-24). Specialized triadic structures may have continued in use by the Historic Lowland Maya. Nicholas Hellmuth (1977: 425) noted that Nicolas de Valenzuela referred to a triadic pattern of "community houses" in the seventeenth-century Lacandón village of Sac Balam, Chiapas. Late Classic kings such as Chan Bahlum II replicated the thousand-year-old triadic architectural form in the Palenque Cross Group as a personal statement of royal authority, genealogical privilege, and regal power following the demise of Pacal the Great (Hansen 1992a: 149ff, 1998: 77ff). At El Mirador alone, more than twenty-six monumental structures—including nearly all of the largest structures—and the largest structures at Tintal, Xulnal, Wakna, and Nakbé are all in Triadic Architectural Style. The triadic pattern was thus a very important denominator of royal architecture.

Outside the Mirador Basin, the Cross Group at Palenque provides a case of a triadic style format complete with one of the largest compilations of hieroglyphic texts in the Maya world. I have suggested elsewhere (Hansen 1992a: 149–152) a possible correlation between this triadic architectural arrangement and its Preclassic antecedents. The Cross Group's radical departure from the standard Palenque architectural agenda of earlier centuries suggests that the ruler Chan Bahlum was reaching deep into the historic past to legitimize his royal position at that site. As David Freidel and Linda Schele (1988b: 67) have noted: "The choice of archaic costume and the emphasis on the Gods of the Triad, so prevalent in the Early Classic cache complex, was deliberately evoked as the basis of political sanction; it legitimized the Palenque lineage at the most ancient and most orthodox level of Maya political and religious thought and cosmology."

Another important clue as to the meaning of the triadic format may have been retained by the contemporary Maya. During a translation of the *Popul Vuh* with the aid of Quiché shamans, Barbara and Dennis Tedlock noted that the three stars Alnitak, Saiph, and Rigel, located in the constellation of Orion (lower belt star and the two knees), represent the celestial hearth as a metaphor for the three hearthstones of the Maya kitchen (Tedlock 1985: 261). The nebula contained within these three stars, Nebula M42, represents the ash and embers

5.11. *Triadic architecture: hypothetical reconstruction of Structure 34, El Mirador. Courtesy, Fernando Paiz, Studio C, Guatemala.*

of the fires of creation. In traditional Maya households, the three stones of the typical Maya hearth stabilize the *comal* and the cooking pots. Every morning Maya women fan the fires of the previous day's cooking activities into active use, bringing light and sustenance to the Maya family. The triadic format may represent a metaphoric statement or symbolic depiction of the creation, universally accepted and recognized by Maya populations. The rigorous manipulation and control of labor by the administrative elite during the Late Preclassic Period for the construction of the massive architectural triads, even if ultimately based on the three hearth stones, was unequaled throughout all subsequent Maya history.

Kingship and Formal Tombs

Another clear advent of kingship and associated ideology is the placement of formal tombs in architecture. Royal tomb placement in the Mirador Basin is not consistent with later, Classic Period tomb location patterns outside it. Thousands of Preclassic structures have been looted throughout the Mirador Basin, with a general lack of success in finding tomb locations despite major damage to monumental architecture. Tombs have been scientifically located at several Middle and Late Preclassic Period Maya Highland sites (Sharer and Sedat 1987: plate 4.3). Lowland royal burials of similar age, however, are extremely scarce, with locations known from Tikal (Burials 164, 166, 167, 85, 117, and 125; Coe and McGinn 1963; Coe 1965a, 1965b), San Bartólo (William Saturno, personal communication, 2005), and Wakna (Hansen 1998: 90–95). In the case of Wakna, three mortuary chambers were found, with two burials directly at the base on each side of a triadic style major structure, while the third burial was located in the centerline axis of the dominant structure of the triadic style building. However, numerous excavations in triadic structures of similar size, shape, and antiquity have failed to locate funerary constructions in identical locations, thus frustrating attempts to define consistent funerary patterns in Preclassic kingships.

Architectural Art

In addition to the causeways, Triadic Architectural Style, tombs, and monuments, the incipient Maya kings of the Late Middle and early Late Preclassic Periods commissioned sophisticated and complex ideological masks flanking stairways on structural facades (figure 5.11). Early masks were sculpted from stone, while later ones were modeled in plaster directly over roughly hewn stone armatures. The plastic medium of lime plaster was crucial in the depiction of the elements and symbols of kingship and royal authority, and extensive studies have documented the production and use of this medium (Schreiner 2001, 2002, 2003). Early versions of this art depict a standardized theme of J-scrolls and brackets with monumental masks and panels in rich colors of red, cream, and black.

Late Middle Preclassic/early Late Preclassic masks have been discovered at Rio Azul and have recently been found inside Structure 34 at El Mirador on the facade of Structure 34 Sub 1. The depiction of royal authority in such imposing art forms at Mirador Basin sites (El Mirador, Nakbé, El Pesquero, Wakna, Tintal), as well as outside the Mirador Basin (Uaxactún, Tikal, San Bartólo, and Cival), clearly indicates the universal status of architecture as a billboard for king craft, skillfully tied into religious ideology to wield secular and religious control over expanding populations. As the architectural art evolved, it began to include subtle references to explicit individuals. For example, Late Middle Preclassic art on Structure 1 at Nakbé and Structure 34 Sub 1 at El Mirador depicts deity portraits and associated symbolisms, while the Late Preclassic art on the facade of Structure 34 at El Mirador depicts deity masks, but with jaguar paw panels that may be associated with names and titles of specific individuals. In this case, the personage depicted would possibly be the thirteenth ruler of an identified sequence of Preclassic kings from the Mirador Basin known as Yi'chaak K'ak (Guenter 2002, 2004, 2007).

CONCLUSION

H. B. Nicholson was a giant within Mesoamerican studies. He was one of the primary reasons I selected UCLA for graduate school, and I profited much from his insights and observations. His interests spanned the Mesoamerican chronological gamut, ranging from the Preclassic Period (Nicholson 1976) to the Spanish

Conquest (Nicholson 1974). A primary concern of his was the need to consider socio-ideological and cosmological themes when interpreting culture history:

> Precisely what is conspicuously lacking in . . . analysis of major evolutionary trends in Mesoamerican civilization is any genuinely adequate consideration of the religious-ritual-divinatory ideology that constituted such a massive dimension of the history of this area co-tradition . . . [I]deology and esthetics are precisely those dimensions that provided most of the distinctive cultural personality of this great area co-tradition and most clearly set it apart from any other in world history. (Nicholson 1976: 3, 6)

The advantage of long-term and comprehensive investigations on a regional scale is that they facilitate a broad, multidisciplinary perspective based on multiple lines of evidence. This notwithstanding, my review of cultural developments in this chapter has never strayed too far from the ideological and aesthetic dimensions that meant so much to Dr. Nicholson. The Mirador Basin monuments and buildings are silent witnesses to a unique saga of human history that began during the Middle Preclassic Period and existed vibrantly until several hundred years after the time of Christ, when construction programs and occupation began to wane. Although there must have been subsequent kings in the Mirador Basin, shortly after AD 150 the entire area appears to have suffered a large-scale depopulation. This is corroborated by the pollen data (Wahl 2000, 2005; Wahl, Schreiner, and Byrne 2005; Wahl, Byrne, et al. 2006; Wahl, Schreiner, et al. 2007a, 2007b). Jungle returned to cover the great Preclassic structures, and only limited and dispersed populations then lived amid the ruins (Hansen 1996; Hansen, Howell, and Guenter 2008).

The Preclassic kings of the Mirador Basin created a built environment unrivaled in the Maya Lowlands at any period of time. The great sites of the Mirador Basin must have been the objects of pilgrimages for centuries, as suggested by incense burners on the summits of the largest pyramids and the preponderance of unique artistic and thematic Late Classic ceramics, such as the codex style pottery painted between ca. AD 680 and AD 740 by scribes residing among the ruins of the great Preclassic cities (Robicsek and Hales 1981; Hansen, Bishop, and Fahsen 1991). Late Classic codex style ceramics from the Nakbé region (figure 5.12) found their way into royal burials such as that found at Calakmul Structure 2. During the Late Middle and Late Preclassic Periods, ca. 500 BC–AD 150, the Mirador Basin kings created a state-level society, the Kan kingdom. Strategic causeways linking the kingdom's major cities symbolize the economic and political alliances between them. Causeways also facilitated the construction of the largest platforms, palaces, and pyramidal structures in most of the major sites within the study area.

Ongoing epigraphic, iconographic, and archaeological research on the advent of kingship in the Kan polity should expand this preliminary work. If

KINGSHIP IN THE CRADLE OF MAYA CIVILIZATION

5.12. *Late Classic codex-style vessel manufactured in Nakbé, found in Burial 2, Structure 2, Calakmul. Photograph by R. D. Hansen.*

my chronological and cultural interpretations of Mirador Basin developments are correct, then this area could be considered the cradle of Maya civilization. And, if properly conserved, the tangible legacy of ancient Maya kings, their monuments of stone, mud, and stucco, will stand as proud sentinels within the enshrouding tropical forest for centuries to come.

REFERENCES CITED

Balcarcel, Beatriz
    1999   Excavaciones en Residencias Preclásicas de Nakbé, Petén. In *XII Simposio de Investigaciones Arqueológicas en Guatemala, 1988*, ed. Juan Pedro Laporte, Héctor L. Escobedo, and Ana Claudia Monzon de Suasnavar, pp. 337–351. IDAEH, Guatemala.

2000   Excavaciones en Residencias Preclásicas, Nakbé, Petén. In *Investigaciones Arqueológicas y Ecológicas en la Cuenca Mirador, 1998: Informe de la Temporada de Campo*, ed. Richard D. Hansen and Judith Valle, pp. 297–329. PRIANPEG, Guatemala.

2006   Investigaciones en la Acopolis Central, Edificio 313, El Mirador, Proyecto Arqueológico Cuenca Mirador, Petén, Guatemala: Informe Final de la Temporada 2005. In *Investigacion y Conservacion en los sitios arqueológicos El Mirador, La Muerta, Wakna, El Porvenir, El Guiro, La Iglesia, La Sarteneja, Chab Ché y la Ceibita: Informe Final de la Temporada 2005*, ed. Edgar Suyuc and Richard D. Hansen, pp. 520–583. Idaho State University, Foundation for Anthropological Research and Environmental Studies.

2007   Acrópolis Central: Excavaciones en la Estructura 313, El Mirador, Petén, Guatemala. In *Proyecto Arqueológico Cuenca Mirador: Investigacion y Conservación en los Sitios Arqueológicos El Mirador, La Muerta, Tintal, La Tortuga, Tamazul, La Llorona, Camarón, El Desencanto, Lechugal, Icotea, Los Chuntos, y El Laurel, Informe 2006*, ed. Nora M. López, pp. 248–281. IDAEH, Guatemala.

Balcarcel, Beatriz, and Francisco Lopez

2001   Excavaciones y Rescate de la Estructura 1 de La Florida, Petén. *Abstractos del XV Simposio de Investigaciones Arqueológicas en Guatemala* (July 16–20): 27. Museo Nacional de Arqueologia y Etnologia.

2002   Excavaciones y rescate de la Estructura 1, La Florida, Petén. In *Investigaciones Arqueológicas y Ecológicas en la Cuenca Mirador: Rescate y Excavaciones en el sitio La Florida, Informe Final de la Temporada 2001–2002*, ed. Richard D. Hansen and Edgar O. Suyuc-Ley, pp. 60–120. IDAEH, Guatemala.

Bozarth, Steven

2000   Analisis de Fitolitas de Opalo en un Jardín de la Realeza de Nakbé, Sitio Maya Preclasico, Guatemala. In *Investigaciones Arqueológicas y Ecológicas en la Cuenca Mirador, 1998: Informe de la Temporada de Campo*, ed. Richard D. Hansen and Judith Valle, pp. 567–598. PRIANPEG, Guatemala.

Bozarth, Steven, and Richard D. Hansen

2001   Estudios Paleo-Botánicos de Nakbé: Evidencias Preliminares de Ambiente y Cultivos en el Preclásico. In *XIV Simposio de Investigaciones Arqueologicas en Guatemala*, ed. Juan Pedro Laporte, Ana Claudia de Suasnavar, and Barbara Arroyo, pp. 419–436. IDAEH, Guatemala.

Chambers, Mary Elizabeth, and Richard D. Hansen

1996   El Monumento 18 de El Mirador: El Contexto Arqueológico y la Iconografia. In *IX Simposio de Investigaciones Arqueológicas en Guatemala*, ed. Juan Pedro Laporte and Hector L. Escobedo, pp. 313–329. IDAEH, Guatemala.

Chase, Arlen Frank, and Diane Z. Chase

1995   External Impetus, Internal Synthesis, and Standardization: E Group Assemblages and the Crystallization of Classic Maya Society in the Southern Lowlands. In *The Emergence of Lowland Maya Civilization: The Transition from the Preclassic to the Early Classic*, ed. Nikolai Grube, pp. 87–101. Verlag Anton Saurwein, Möckmühl, Germany.

Clark, John E.
  1991   The Beginnings of Mesoamerica: Apologia for the Soconusco Early Formative. In *The Formation of Complex Society in Southeastern Mesoamerica*, ed. William R. Fowler, pp. 13–26. CRC Press, Boca Raton, LA.
  1994   The Development of Early Formative Rank Societies in the Soconusco, Chiapas, Mexico. PhD dissertation, Department of Anthropology, University of Michigan, Ann Arbor.

Clark, John E., and Michael Blake
  1994   The Power of Prestige: Competitive Generosity and the Emergence of Rank Societies in Lowland Mesoamerica. In *Factional Competition and Political Development in the New World*, ed. Elizabeth M. Brumfiel and John W. Fox, pp. 17–30. Cambridge University Press, New York.

Clark, John E., and Richard D. Hansen
  2001   The Architecture of Early Kingship: Comparative Perspectives on the Origins of the Maya Royal Court. In *Royal Courts of the Ancient Maya, Volume 2: Data and Case Studies*, ed. Takeshi Inomata and Stephen D. Houston, pp. 1–45. Westview, Boulder, CO.

Clark, John E., and Mary E. Pye, eds.
  2000   *Olmec Art and Archaeology in Mesoamerica*. National Gallery of Art, Washington, DC, and Yale University Press, New Haven, CT.

Coe, William R.
  1965a   Tikal, Guatemala, Emergent Maya Civilization. *Science* 147 (3664): 1401–1419.
  1965b   Tikal: Ten Years of Study of a Maya Ruin in the Lowlands of Guatemala. *Expedition* 8 (1): 5–56. University Museum, University of Pennsylvania, Philadelphia.

Coe, William R., and John J. McGinn
  1963   Tikal: The North Acropolis and an Early Tomb. *Expedition* 5 (2): 24–32.

Dahlin, Bruce H.
  1984   A Colossus in Guatemala: The Preclassic Maya City of El Mirador. *Archaeology* 37 (5): 18–25.

Dahlin, Bruce H., John E. Foss, and Mary Elizabeth Chambers
  1980   Project Acalches: Reconstructing the Natural and Cultural History of a Seasonal Swamp at El Mirador, Guatemala: Preliminary Results. In *El Mirador, Petén, Guatemala: An Interim Report*, ed. Ray T. Matheny, pp. 37–57. Papers of the New World Archaeological Foundation 45. Brigham Young University, Provo, UT.

Dixon, J. B., J. S. Jacob, and G. N. White
  1994   Todorokite in Manganese Oxide Nodules of a Guatemalan Vertisol. Paper presented at the Annual Meeting of the Soil Science Society of America, November 13–18, 1994. Seattle, WA.

Estrada-Belli, Francisco
    2006   Lightning, Sky, Rain, and the Maize God: The Ideology of Preclassic Maya Rulers at Cival, Petén, Guatemala. *Ancient Mesoamerica* 17: 57–78.

Fields, Virginia M.
    1989   The Origins of Divine Kingship among the Lowland Classic Maya. PhD dissertation, Department of Latin American Studies, University of Texas, Austin.

Fomento y Desarrollo del Petén, Guatemala (FYDEP)
    1968   *Mapa de los Suelos de El Petén. Proyecto de Evaluación Forestal FAO-FYDEP*. Fomentos y Desarrollo del Petén and Instituto Geográfico Nacional, Guatemala.

Force, Eric, and John Dohrenwend
    2008   Geologic and Geomorphologic Analysis of the Area of the Mirador Basin Archaeological Project. Manuscript on file, FARES, Rupert, ID, June 25.

Forsyth, Donald W.
    1989   *The Ceramics of El Mirador, Petén, Guatemala*. Papers of the New World Archaeological Foundation 63. Brigham Young University, Provo, UT.
    1992   Un Estudio Comparativo de la Cerámica Temprana de Nakbé. In *IV Simposio de Arqueología Guatemalteca, Julio 1990*, ed. Juan Pedro Laporte, Hector L. Escobedo, and Sandra V. de Brady, pp. 45–56. IDAEH, Guatemala.
    1993   The Ceramic Sequence at Nakbé. *Ancient Mesoamerica* 4: 31–53.

Freidel, David A.
    1981   Civilization as a State of Mind: The Cultural Evolution of the Lowland Maya. In *The Transition to Statehood in the New World*, ed. Grant D. Jones and Robert R. Kautz, pp. 188–227. Cambridge University Press, Cambridge.
    1985   Polychrome Facades of the Lowland Maya Preclassic. In *Painted Architecture and Polychrome Monumental Sculpture in Mesoamerica*, ed. Elizabeth Boone, pp. 5–30. Dumbarton Oaks, Washington, DC.
    1986   The Monumental Architecture. In *Archaeology at Cerros, Belize, Central America, vol. 1: An Interim Report*, ed. Robin A. Robertson and David A. Freidel, pp. 1–22. Southern Methodist University Press, Dallas, TX.

Freidel, David A., and Linda Schele
    1988a   Kingship in the Late Preclassic Maya Lowlands: The Instruments and Places of Ritual Power. *American Anthropologist* 90 (3): 547–567.
    1988b   Symbol and Power: A History of the Lowland Maya Cosmogram. In *Maya Iconography*, ed. Elizabeth Benson and Gillett Griffin, pp. 44–93. Princeton University Press, Princeton, NJ.

Garber, James F., Christopher J. Hartman, and M. Kathryn Brown
    2002   The Kanocha Phase (1200–850 B.C.) on Structure B1: Results of the 2001 Field Season at Blackman Eddy. In *The Belize Valley Archaeology Project: Results of the 2001 Field Season*, ed. James F. Garber, M. Kathryn Brown, and Christopher J. Hartman, pp. 42–75. Southwest Texas State University, San Marcos.

Graham, Ian
    1967   Archaeological Explorations in El Petén, Guatemala. *Middle American Research Institute Publication* 33. Tulane University, New Orleans, LA.

Guenter, Stanley Paul
    2002   La Estela Hauberg y el reino Preclásico Kan. In *Investigaciones Arqueológicas y Ecológicas en la Cuenca Mirador: Rescate y Excavaciones en el sitio La Florida, Informe Final de la Temporada 2001–2002*, ed. Richard D. Hansen and Edgar O. Suyuc-Ley, pp. 305–319. IDAEH, Guatemala.
    2004   Gobernantes Preclásicos de la Cuenca Mirador. In *Abstractos de la XVIII Simposio de Investigaciones Arqueológicas en Guatemala*, p. 78. IDAEH, Guatemala.
    2007   Discovering the Snake Kingdom: The Epigraphy of the Mirador Basin. Paper presented at the 72nd Meeting of the Society for American Archaeology, Austin, TX.

Hansen, Eric F.
    2000   Ancient Maya Burnt Lime Technology: Cultural Implications of Technological Styles. PhD dissertation, Archaeology Program, UCLA, Los Angeles.

Hansen, Richard D.
    1982   Excavations in the Tigre Pyramid Area, El Mirador, Guatemala: A New Evaluation of Social Process in the Preclassic Maya Lowlands. In *Abstracts of the 44th International Congress of Americanists, Past and Present in the Americas: A Compendium of Recent Studies*, ed. John Lynch, pp. 133–134. Manchester University Press, Manchester, England.
    1984   Excavations on Structure 34 and the Tigre Area, El Mirador, Petén, Guatemala: A New Look at the Preclassic Lowland Maya. MS thesis, Department of Anthropology, Brigham Young University, Provo, UT.
    1990   *Excavations in the Tigre Complex, El Mirador, Petén, Guatemala*. Papers of the New World Archaeological Foundation 62. Brigham Young University, Provo, UT.
    1991   *An Early Maya Text from El Mirador, Guatemala*. Research Reports on Ancient Maya Writing 37. Center for Maya Research, Washington, DC.
    1992a   The Archaeology of Ideology: A Study of Maya Preclassic Architectural Sculpture at Nakbé, Petén, Guatemala. PhD dissertation, UCLA, Los Angeles.
    1992b   El Proceso Cultural de Nakbé y el Area del Petén Nor-Central: Las Epocas Tempranas. In *V Simposio de Investigaciones en Guatemala*, ed. Juan Pedro Laporte, Hector L. Escobedo, and Sandra V. de Brady, pp. 81–96. IDAEH, Guatemala.
    1992c   Proyecto Regional de Investigaciones Arqueológicas del Norte de Petén, Guatemala: Temporada 1990. In *IV Simposio de Arqueología Guatemalteca, Julio 1990*, ed. Juan Pedro Laporte, Hector L. Escobedo, and Sandra V. de Brady, pp. 1–36. IDAEH, Guatemala.
    1996   El Clásico Tardío del Norte de Petén. *U tz'ib* 2 (1): 1–15. Asociacion Tikal, Guatemala.
    1998   Continuity and Disjunction: The Pre-Classic Antecedents of Classic Maya Architecture. In *Function and Meaning in Classic Maya Architecture*, ed. Stephen D. Houston, pp. 49–122. Dumbarton Oaks, Washington, DC.
    2000   Ideología y Arquitectura: Poder y Dinámicas Culturales de los Mayas del Período Preclásico en las Tierras Bajas. In *Arquitectura e Ideología de los Anti-*

           guos Mayas: Memoria de la Segunda Mesa Redonda de Palenque, ed. Silvia Trejo, pp. 71–108. CONACULTA-INAH, México, DF.
2001   The First Cities—The Beginnings of Urbanization and State Formation in the Maya Lowlands. In *Maya: Divine Kings of the Rain Forest*, ed. Nikolai Grube, Eva Eggebrecht, and Matthias Seidel, pp. 50–65. Könemann Verlag, Cologne, Germany.
2005   Perspective on Olmec-Maya Interaction in the Middle Formative Period. In *New Perspectives on Formative Mesoamerican Cultures*, ed. Terry Powis, pp. 51–72. BAR International Series 1377, Oxford.
n.d.a   Architecture, Economy, Ideology and the First Maya States: A Perspective from the Lowlands. In *The Origins of Maya States*, ed. Robert J. Sharer, and Loa Traxler. University of Pennsylvania Press, Philadelphia; in press.
n.d.b   Yax Lakamtun: Perspectives of the First Monuments in the Maya Lowlands and the Implications for the Ideological Depictions of Kingship of the Preclassic Maya. In *The Place of Sculpture in Mesoamerica's Preclassic Transition*, ed. John E. Clark, Julia Guernsey, and Barbara Arroyo. Dumbarton Oaks, Washington, DC; in preparation.

Hansen, Richard D., Ronald L. Bishop, and Federico Fahsen
1991   Notes on Maya Codex-Style Ceramics from Nakbé, Petén, Guatemala. *Ancient Mesoamerica* 2: 225–243.

Hansen, Richard D., Steven Bozarth, John Jacob, David Wahl, and Thomas Schreiner
2002   Climatic and Environmental Variability in the Rise of Maya Civilization: A Preliminary Perspective from Northern Petén. *Ancient Mesoamerica* 13: 273–295.

Hansen, Richard D., and Stanley P. Guenter
2005   Early Social Complexity and Kingship in the Mirador Basin. In *Lords of Creation: The Origins of Sacred Maya Kingship*, ed. Virginia M. Fields and Dorie Reents-Budet, pp. 60–61. Los Angeles County Museum of Art, Los Angeles, and Scala Publishers Ltd., London.

Hansen, Richard D., Wayne K. Howell, and Stanley P. Guenter
2008   Forgotten Structures, Haunted Houses, and Occupied Hearts: Ancient Perspectives and Contemporary Interpretations of Abandoned Sites and Buildings in the Mirador Basin, Guatemala. In *Ruins of the Past: The Use and Perception of Abandoned Structures in the Maya Lowlands*, ed. Travis W. Stanton and Aline Magnoni, pp. 25–64. University Press of Colorado, Boulder.

Hansen, Richard D., Gustavo Martínez, John Jacob, and Wayne K. Howell
2000   Cultivos Intensivos: Sistemas Agrícolas de Nakbé. In *Investigaciones Arqueológicas y Ecológicas en la Cuenca Mirador, 1998: Informe de la Temporada de Campo*, ed. Richard D. Hansen and Judith Valle, pp. 687–700. PRIANPEG, Guatemala.

Hansen, Richard D., Edgar Suyuc-Ley, and Beatriz Balcarcel, eds.
2004   *Investigación, Conservación y Desarrollo en El Mirador, Petén, Guatemala: Informe 2003*. IDAEH, Guatemala.

Hansen, Richard D., Edgar Suyuc-Ley, Wayne Howell, and Abel Morales López
    2004a   Investigaciones en el Sitio Arqueológico El Mirador: Excavaciones Recientes. In *Abstractos del XVIII Simposio de Investigaciones Arqueológicas en Guatemala*, p. 62. IDAEH, Guatemala.
    2004b   Investigaciones en el Sitio Arqueológico El Mirador: Excavaciones Recientes. In *Abstractos del XVIII Simposio de Investigaciones Arqueológicas en Guatemala*, p. 62. IDAEH, Guatemala.

Hansen, Richard D., Edgar Suyuc-Ley, Adriana Linares, Carlos Morales Aguilar, Beatriz Balcarcel, Francisco López, Antonieta Cajas, Abel Morales López, Enrique Monterroso Tun, Enrique Monterroso Rosado, Carolina Castellanos, Lilian de Zea, Adelzo Pozuelos, David Wahl, and Thomas Schreiner
    2005   Investigaciones en la zona cultural Mirador Petén. In *XIX Simposio de Investigaciones Arqueológicas en Guatemala*, ed. Juan Pedro Laporte, Barbara Arroyo, and Hector E. Mejía, pp. 867–876. IDAEH, Guatemala.

Hansen, Richard D., Edgar Suyuc-Ley, Abel Morales López, Carlos Morales, Thomas Schreiner, Enrique Hernandez, and Douglas Mauricio
    2007   La Cuenca Mirador: Avances de la Investigación y Conservación del Estado Kan en los períodos Preclásico y Clásico. In *XX Simp. de Investigaciones Arqueológicas en Guatemala*, ed. Juan Pedro Laporte, Barbara Arroyo, and Hector E. Mejía, pp. 349–362. IDAEH, Guatemala.

Harrison, Peter D.
    1986   Tikal: Selected Topics. In *City-States of the Maya: Art and Architecture*, ed. Elizabeth P. Benson, pp. 45–71. Rocky Mountain Institute for Pre-Columbian Studies, Denver, CO.

Hellmuth, Nicholas
    1977   Cholti-Lacandon (Chiapas) and Petén-Ytza Agriculture, Settlement Pattern and Population. In *Social Process in Maya Prehistory: Studies in Honour of Sir Eric Thompson*, ed. Norman Hammond, pp. 421–448. Academic Press, New York.

Helms, Mary W.
    1993   *Craft and the Kingly Ideal: Art, Trade, and Power*. University of Texas Press, Austin.

Hohmann, Bobbi, and Terry Powis
    1996   The 1995 Excavations at Pacbitun, Belize: Investigations of the Middle Formative Occupation in Plaza B. In *Belize Valley Preclassic Maya Project: Report on the 1995 Field Season*, ed. Paul F. Healy and Jaime Awe, pp. 98–117. Trent University Occasional Papers in Anthropology 12. Peterborough, Ontario, Canada.

Howell, Wayne K., and Denise Ranae Evans Copeland
    1989   *Excavations at El Mirador, Petén, Guatemala: The Danta and Monos Complexes*. Papers of the New World Archaeological Foundation 60 and 61. Brigham Young University, Provo, UT.

Jacob, John
    1994   Evidencias para Cambio Ambiental en Nakbé, Guatemala. In *VII Simposio Arqueológico de Guatemala*, ed. Jose Pablo Laporte, Hector L. Escobedo, and Sandra V. de Brady, pp. 275–280. IDAEH, Guatemala.

Justeson, John S., and Peter Mathews
    1983   The Seating of the Tun: Further Evidence Concerning a Late Preclassic Lowland Maya Stela Cult. *American Antiquity* 48 (3): 586–593.

Kappelman, Julia Guernsey
    1997   Of Macaws and Men: Late Preclassic Cosmology and Political Ideology in Izapan-Style Monuments. PhD dissertation, Department of Art History, University of Texas, Austin.

Kunselman, Raymond
    2000   Yacimiento Mesoamericano de Obsidiana: Estudios de Utilización, Conexiones y Contactos en Nakbé. In *Investigaciones Arqueológicas y Ecológicas en la Cuenca Mirador, 1998: Informe de la Temporada de Campo*, ed. Richard D. Hansen and J. Valle, pp. 630–644. PRIANPEG, Guatemala.

Laporte, Juan Pedro, and Vilma Fialko
    1993   El Preclásico de Mundo Perdido: Algunos Aportes sobre los Orígines de Tikal. In *Tikal y Uaxactún en el Preclásico*, ed. Juan Pedro Laporte and Juan Antonio Valdés, pp. 9–42. UNAM, México, DF.
    1995   Un Reencuentro con Mundo Perdido, Tikal, Guatemala. *Ancient Mesoamerica* 6: 41–94.

Laporte, Juan Pedro, and Juan Antonio Valdés, eds.
    1993   *Tikal y Uaxactún en el Preclásico*. UNAM, México, DF.

Marcus, Joyce, and Kent V. Flannery
    1996   *Zapotec Civilization: How Urban Society Evolved in Mexico's Oaxaca Valley*. Thames and Hudson, London.

Martínez, Gustavo, Richard D. Hansen, and Wayne K. Howell
    1996   Cultivos Intensivos: Sistemas Agrícolas de Nakbé. Paper presented at the X Simposio de Investigaciones Arqueológicas en Guatemala, July 24, Guatemala.

Martínez, Gustavo, Richard D. Hansen, John Jacob, and Wayne K. Howell
    1999   Nuevas Evidencias de los Sistemas de Cultivo del Preclasico en la Cuenca El Mirador. In *XII Simposio de Investigaciones Arqueológicas en Guatemala, 1988*, ed. Juan Pablo Laporte, Hector L. Escobedo, and Monzon de Suasnavar, pp. 327–335. IDAEH, Guatemala.

Mata Amado, Guillermo, and Richard D. Hansen
    1992   El Diente Incrustado Temprano de Nakbé. In *V Simp. de Invest. Arq. en Guatemala*, ed. Juan Pedro Laporte, Hector L. Escobedo, and Sandra V. de Brady, pp. 115–118. IDAEH, Guatemala.

Matheny, Ray T.
   1986   Investigations at El Mirador, Petén, Guatemala. *National Geographic Research* 2: 332–353.
   1987a   Early States in the Maya Lowlands during the Late Preclassic Period: Edzna and El Mirador. In *City States of the Maya: Art and Architecture*, ed. Elizabeth P. Benson, pp. 1–44. Rocky Mountain Institute for Pre-Columbian Studies, Denver, CO.
   1987b   El Mirador: An Early Maya Metropolis Uncovered. *National Geographic* 172 (3): 316–339.

Matheny, Ray T., Richard D. Hansen, and Deanne L. Gurr
   1980   Preliminary Field Report, El Mirador, 1979 Season. In *El Mirador, Petén, Guatemala: An Interim Report*, ed. Ray T. Matheny, pp. 1–23. Papers of the New World Archaeological Foundation 45. Brigham Young University, Provo, UT.

Miller, Arthur G.
   1974   The Iconography of the Painting in the Temple of the Diving God, Tulum, Quintana Roo, Mexico: The Twisted Cords. In *Mesoamerican Archaeology: New Approaches*, ed. Norman Hammond, pp. 167–186. University of Texas Press, Austin.

Morley, Sylvanus G.
   1938   *Inscriptions of Petén*, vols. 1–5. Publication 437. Carnegie Institution of Washington, Washington, DC.

Nicholson, H. B.
   1974   Tepepulco, the Locale of the First Stage of Fr. Bernardino de Sahagún's Great Ethnographic Project. In *Mesoamerican Archaeology: New Approaches*, ed. Norman Hammond, pp. 145–154. University of Texas Press, Austin.
   1976   Introduction. In *Origins of Religious Art and Iconography in Preclassic Mesoamerica*, ed. H. B. Nicholson, pp. 1–6. UCLA Latin American Center Publication 31. Ethnic Arts Council of Los Angeles, Los Angeles, CA.

Puleston, Dennis E., and Olga S. Puleston
   1971   An Ecological Approach to the Origins of Maya Civilization. *Archaeology* 24 (4): 330–336.

Reese-Taylor, Kathryn V.
   1996   Narratives of Power: Late Formative Public Architecture and Civic Center Design at Cerros, Belize. PhD dissertation, Department of Anthropology, University of Texas, Austin.

Reilly III, F. Kent
   1994   Visions to Another World: Art, Shamans, and Political Power in Middle Formative Mesoamerica. PhD dissertation, Department of Art History, University of Texas, Austin.

Robicsek, Francis, and Donald M. Hales
   1981   *The Maya Book of the Dead: The Ceramic Codex*. University of Virginia Art Museum, Charlottesville.

Richard D. Hansen

Ruppert, Karl, and John H. Denison Jr.
    1943   *Archaeological Reconnaissance in Campeche, Quintana Roo, and Petén*. Publication 543. Carnegie Institution of Washington, Washington, DC.

Schele, Linda
    1985   The Hauberg Stela: Bloodletting and the Mythos of Maya Rulership. In *Fifth Palenque Round Table, 1983*, vol. 7, gen. ed. Merle G. Robertson, vol. ed. Virginia M. Fields, pp. 135–149. Pre-Columbian Art Research Institute, San Francisco, CA.

Schieber de Lavarreda, Christa
    1994   A Middle Preclassic Clay Ball Court at Abaj Takalik, Guatemala. *Mexicon* 16: 77–89.

Schreiner, Thomas
    2001   Fabricación de Cal en Mesoamerica: Implicaciones para los Mayas del Preclásico en Nakbé, Petén. In *XIV Simposio de Investigaciones Arqueologicas en Guatemala*, ed. Juan Pedro Laporte, Ana Claudia de Suasnavar, and Barbara Arroyo, pp. 405–418. IDAEH, Guatemala.
    2002   Traditional Maya Lime Production: Environmental and Cultural Implications of a Native American Technology. PhD dissertation, Architecture Department, University of California, Berkeley.
    2003   Aspectos Rituales de la Producción de Cal en Mesoamérica: Evidencias y Pespectivas de las Tierras Bajas Mayas. In *XVI Simposio de Investigaciones Arqueológicas en Guatemala, 2002*, ed. Juan Pedro Laporte, Barbara Arroyo, Hector L. Escobedo, and Hector E. Mejía, pp. 487–494. IDAEH, Guatemala.

Sharer, Robert J., and David W. Sedat
    1987   *Archaeological Investigations in the Northern Maya Highlands, Guatemala: Interaction and the Development of Maya Civilization*. Museum Monographs 59. University of Pennsylvania, Philadelphia.

Sidrys, Raymond
    1978   Megalithic Architecture and Sculpture of the Ancient Maya. In *Papers on the Economy and Architecture of the Ancient Maya*, ed. Raymond Sidrys, pp. 155–183. Monograph 8. Institute of Archaeology, UCLA, Los Angeles, CA.

Simmons, Charles S., José Manuel Tarano, and José Humberto Pinto
    1959   *Clasificación de Reconocimiento de los Suelos de la República de Guatemala*. Editorial del Ministerio de Educación Pública, Guatemala.

Sprajc, Ivan
    2005   More on Mesoamerican Cosmology and City Plans. *Latin American Antiquity* 16 (2): 209–216.

Stevens, Rarfred L.
    1964   The Soils of Middle America and Their Relation to Indian Peoples and Cultures. In *Natural Environment and Early Cultures*, ed. Robert C. West, pp. 265–315. Handbook of Middle American Indians, vol. 1, Robert Wauchope, gen. ed. University of Texas Press, Austin.

Stutz-Landeen, Ellen
    1986   Excavations on a Late Preclassic Plaza Unit at El Mirador, Petén, Guatemala. MA thesis, Department of Anthropology, Brigham Young University, Provo, UT.

Tedlock, Dennis, trans.
    1985   *Popol Vuh: The Definitive Edition of the Mayan Book of the Dawn of Life and the Glories of Gods and Kings.* Touchstone, New York, and Simon and Schuster, London.

Tozzer, Alfred M., ed.
    1941   *Landa's Relación de las Cosas de Yucatan: A Translation.* Papers of the Peabody Museum 18. Harvard University, Cambridge.

Wahl, David
    2000   A Stratigraphic Record of Environmental Change from a Maya Reservoir in the Northern Petén, Guatemala. MA thesis, Department of Geography, University of California, Berkeley.
    2005   Climate Change and Human Impacts in the Southern Maya Lowlands: A Paleoecological Perspective from the Northern Petén, Guatemala. PhD dissertation, Department of Geography, University of California, Berkeley.

Wahl, David, Roger Byrne, Thomas Schreiner, and Richard Hansen
    2006   Holocene Vegetation Change in the Northern Petén and Its Implications for Maya Prehistory. *Quaternary Research* 65: 380–389.

Wahl, David, Thomas Schreiner, and Roger Byrne
    2005   La secuencia paleo-ambiental de la Cuenca Mirador en Petén. In *XVIII Simposio de Investigaciones Arqueológicas en Guatemala, 2004*, ed. Juan Pablo Laporte, Barbara Arroyo, and Hector E. Mejía, pp. 53–58. IDAEH, Guatemala.

Wahl, David, Thomas Schreiner, Roger Byrne, and Richard Hansen
    2007a   Paleoecological Record from a Late Classic Maya Reservoir in the North Petén. *Latin American Antiquity* 18 (2): 212–222.
    2007b   Palaeolimnological Evidence of Late-Holocene Settlement and Abandonment in the Mirador Basin, Petén, Guatemala. *The Holocene* 17 (6): 813–820. http://hol.sagepub.com/cgi/content/abstract/17/6/813; accessed March 12, 2009.

6

YAXCHILÁN STRUCTURE 23: THE HOUSE OF IX K'AB'AL XOK

Sandra L. Orellana

Little is known about the rulers of Yaxchilán[1] until the reign of Itzamnah B'ahläm ("Shield Jaguar"),[2] who ruled from AD 681 to 742 (figure 6.1). Yaxchilán was a small city prior to this time, but monuments of early rulers do record warfare with nearby cities such as Piedras Negras and Bonampak. Aj Wäktun Yaxun B'ahläm ("Six-Stone Bird Jaguar"), the father of Itzamnah B'ahläm, became ruler of Yaxchilán in AD 629 and reigned until around AD 669. Most of what is known about him comes from later monuments carved long after his death by his son and grandson, who hoped to enhance their legitimacy and the continuity of their dynasty. There is a gap in the history of Yaxchilán prior to the accession of Itzamnah B'ahläm in AD 681. This may indicate a period of subordination for the city that could have extended for some time into the reign of Itzamnah B'ahläm. Yaxchilán may have been dominated by Piedras Negras or by Palenque and Toniná, the latter two cities having had influence along the Usumacinta River during the vacant years of Yaxchilán's history (see Martin and Grube 2000: 117–123 for a discussion of Yaxchilán's early rulers).

Roberto García Moll (2004: 268) believes that, beginning in AD 652, Yaxchilán increased its trade contacts and that the archaeology reveals a great diversity of non-local products from Central Mexico and Central America. Despite this, Itzamnah B'ahläm did not begin his construction program until the early 720s. He then demonstrated Yaxchilán's growing power in the Usumacinta region

6.1. *Yaxchilán and the Maya region. Illustration by Rusty Van Rossmann.*

YAXCHILÁN STRUCTURE 23

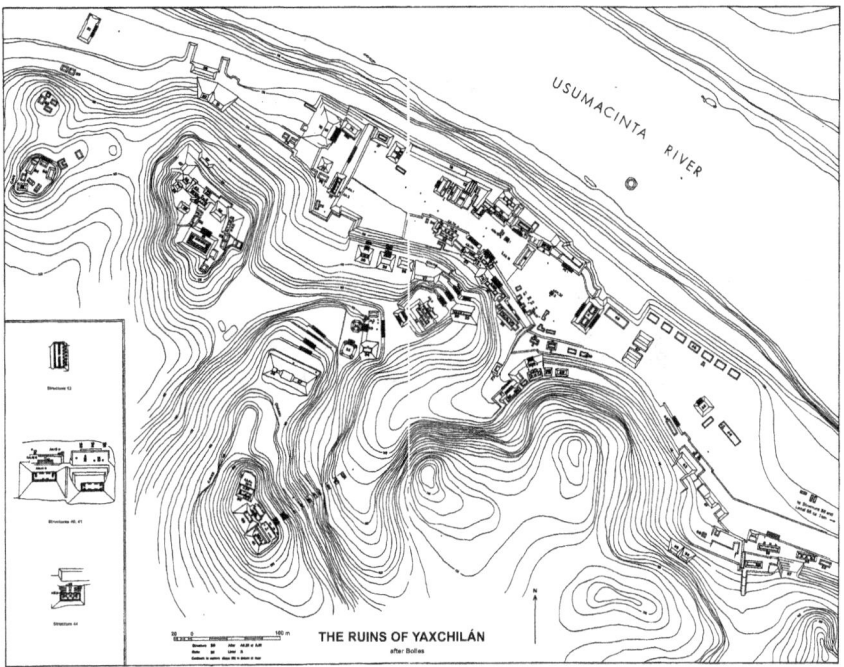

6.2. *Site map of Yaxchilán, by Ian Graham and Eric Von Euw. (1977 Volume 3, Part 1:6). Courtesy, the President and Fellows of Harvard College.*

by building and dedicating new structures and monuments that connected the B'ahläm Dynasty to the cosmic realm of the deities and ancestors. This ambitious building program enhanced the prestige of Yaxchilán.

THE BUILDING

Simon Martin and Nikolai Grube (2000: 123) suggest that if greater autonomy resulted in greater revenue from the Usumacinta River trade, then this may have allowed Itzamnah B'ahläm to eventually finance his construction projects. One of the first buildings he erected was Structure 23. Most of the surviving buildings and monuments of Itzamnah B'ahläm (figure 6.2) celebrate his military victories or show him performing traditional ritual functions. Structure 23 is different from his other buildings because it was dedicated to, owned by, and featured a royal woman (died 749) named Ix K'ab'al Xok ("Lady? Shark"),[3] one of Itzamnah B'ahläm's wives. Recent epigraphic research has stimulated new interpretations of Classic Maya rituals and mythology, enabling a more comprehensive understanding of this atypical building.[4] Comparative data from other Maya cities and from as far away as Teotihuacan help clarify the meaning and importance Structure 23 had for the early eighth–century Maya of Yaxchilán.

175

Sandra L. Orellana

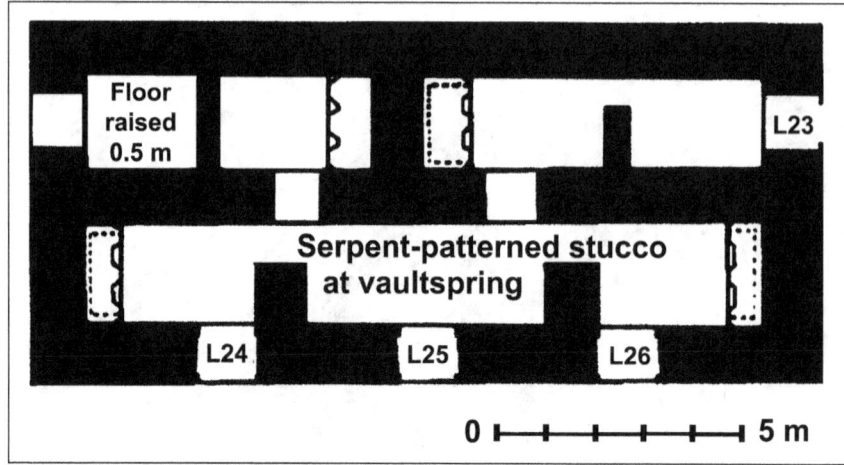

6.3. Plan of Yaxchilán Structure 23, by Carolyn E. Tate. Lintel locations (L) numbered. Courtesy, University of Texas Press.

I will demonstrate that Structure 23, the House of Ix K'ab'al Xok, was a Founder House constructed to commemorate the accession and dynastic refounding rites of Itzamnah B'ahläm. These rites allowed him to reactivate the B'ahläm Dynasty and renew the power of Yaxchilán. I will also show that the three figural lintels were associated with the three stones of Creation and portray scenes enacted by the royal couple that illustrate the ritual domains codified by each of the stones (Looper 2003: 158–164). The Tlaloc-Venus war cult[5] figured prominently in these rites, which involved bloodletting, conjuring the War Serpent, communicating with an ancestor, and receiving symbols of war and rulership. The role of Ix K'ab'al Xok was magnified because of the political situation in Yaxchilán, which required the participation of a royal woman in accession and dynastic rites. I will also show that the costumes worn by Itzamnah B'ahläm and Ix K'ab'al Xok provide important information that clarifies the ritual scenes portrayed on the monuments and relates them to sacrifice, creation, and war.

Yaxchilán Structure 23 (figure 6.3) is located on a terrace approximately 3 m above the main plaza (Tate 1986: 12). It had two parallel vaulted rooms, but today little of the roof remains. Three doorways face north-northeast toward the river, and three figural lintels once spanned these openings. Two other doorways are located at the southeast and southwest;[6] a lintel containing only texts[7] was placed over the latter doorway (Tate 1992: 112, 203; McAnany and Plank 2001: figure 4.4, 111; Josserand 2007: 305–307). The building's exterior cornice frieze featured stucco masks of long-nosed supernaturals[8] (Tate 1986: 12). Carolyn Tate reports (ibid., 1992: 203) that traces of stucco decoration of a serpent body still exist on the central pier of the rear wall in the front room, below the vault spring.

Traces of paint also remain in that room, suggesting that it once contained polychrome scenes. García Moll notes (2004) that two internal doors lead from the first interior room to two smaller rear ones. The first room has two internal buttresses supporting the outer walls, dividing it into three areas corresponding to the three front entrances. The two side rooms (Rooms 1 and 3) have benches and niches, some set into the walls. The central space (Room 2) gives access to the small rear rooms. Tombs located in Rooms 2 and 3 contain burials presumed to be those of Ix K'ab'al Xok and Itzamnah B'ahläm, respectively.

Buildings were rarely dedicated to or owned by royal women in ancient Maya cities, but during Itzamnah B'ahläm's reign, at least two such women owned their own houses (*y-otot*,[9] "her house") at Yaxchilán. The other woman is not portrayed on any surviving monuments and is mentioned only on the front edge of Lintel 56 (McAnany and Plank 2001: 113–114). Structure 23 was the most important building at Yaxchilán owned by a royal woman.

David Stuart suggests (1998: 374–375) that most of the surviving Classic Maya inscriptions are "dedication texts," indicating the importance the Maya gave to activating ritual things and spaces. These dedications involved "fire-entering," or bringing fire into the building to vivify and ensoul it (ibid.: 417–418). Buildings may actually have been "alive" from the Maya perspective, and personal names[10] were bestowed on them (Webster 1998: 29). The fact that most of the dedications at Yaxchilán dating to Itzamnah B'ahläm's reign relate to Structure 23 points to the special nature of this building.

THE LINTELS

Scenes of Maya courtly life were often found on pottery and also possibly in painted books. Maya monumental sculpture, however, was rather limited in scope and subject matter. Large stone monuments varied stylistically from city to city, but most focused on warfare, period-ending rites, and ritual enactments. Mary Miller suggests (1998: 194) that "the goal of Maya architecture is to promote a specific set of memories and then to enter them time and again on the mental slate through both visual images and written texts." The memories the Maya wished to preserve were often anchored to historical events, but they were based on mythology. Because of this, buildings and carved monuments cannot be understood strictly as factual memorials or mere political propaganda but as a means to enhance royal prestige and the power of the architecture. The scenes on monuments may represent the ideal situation, while an actual event may not have taken place in the way pictured on the monument or may never have taken place. If royalty are shown performing actions, then, for the Maya, it was the same as if those actions had actually been done. On carved monuments rulers attempted to empower their dynasties and foster continuity of rule by connecting themselves to the supernatural realm.

The carved lintels of Structure 23 are examples of such idealized, mythical enactments depicting rituals that were important to the B'ahläm Dynasty. The scenes were drawn from the cycle of cosmic mythology fundamental to Maya thought. Tate suggests (1992: 108–110) that the use of Calendar Round dates, such as those on the three lintels of Structure 23, may indicate the circularity of time. If so, the scenes were repeatable episodes from the cosmic cycle. She states that the ideal mode of behavior depicted was appropriate for events taking place in the present and simultaneously in the past and future. Each scene is part of a large nonlinear cycle, so it is difficult for us to know where the story begins. We can assume that each scene shows actions deemed appropriate to the event referenced by the texts and dates on the lintels. Kathryn Josserand (2007: 303) states: "Although the Calendar Round dates of Lintels 24–26 place the three events pictured at widely spaced moments in time, they seem to commemorate successive stages of three different instances of the same ritual, since they appear to have a narrative structure, reading from left to right."

Lintel 24: Underside

Lintel 24 has one date on the underside: 9.13.17.15.12 5 Eb' 15 Mak (AD October 26, 709). This date (figure 6.4) was close to Itzamnah B'ahläm's twenty-eighth accession anniversary and to the eighty-year (four *k'atuns*) accession anniversary of his father, Aj Wäktun Yaxun B'ahläm (Tate 1992: 120). This day occurred during a conjunction between Jupiter and Saturn. Conjunctions seem to have been important to Itzamnah B'ahläm, as a later one was mentioned on Stela 18 (Tate 1992: figure 145; Harris and Stearns 1997: 138). Celebrating his accession anniversary along with an important accession anniversary of his father at the time of an important astronomical event may have been designed to bridge the gap in dynastic continuity that occurred between Aj Wäktun's death and his own accession and is probably the reason for the scene shown on Lintel 24. Linda Schele and David Freidel (1990: 270–271) proposed that Lintel 24 shows actions the royal couple performed in support of their son and heir, Yaxun B'ahläm ("Bird Jaguar," r. AD 752 to 768). However, no heir is mentioned on Lintel 24, and more current information (Martin and Grube 2000: 127; Josserand 2007: 307–308) suggests that Yaxun B'ahläm was not Itzamnah B'ahläm's direct heir and that he may have been succeeded by another son. The three figural lintels of Structure 23 are accession commemorations, which portray ideal ritual behavior designed to enhance Itzamnah B'ahläm's legitimacy. The main text[11] of the underside of Lintel 24 reads: "On 5 Eb' 15 Mak he is shown sacrificing at his fiery arrival or birth (*hu-lu*),[12] his penance, the Four K'atun Lord, Itzamnah B'ahläm, Master of Aj Nich,[13] Holy Lord of Yaxchilán."

6.4. *Yaxchilán Lintel 24, Itzamnah B'ahläm (left) and Ix K'ab'al Xok (right). Drawing by Ian Graham and Eric Von Euw (1977 Volume 3, Part 1:53). Courtesy, the President and Fellows of Harvard College.*

Sandra L. Orellana

Itzamnah B'ahläm

On Lintel 24 Itzamnah B'ahläm does not appear in the typical war costume he wears on several other monuments, such as Lintel 26. His Lintel 24 costume is not seen on any other monument at Yaxchilán, and I suggest that it may represent archaic regalia dating to his father's time or even earlier and that it linked his reign with that of his predecessors. He wears greenstone jewelry[14] consisting of a large beaded necklace with a Sun God pectoral, wristlets trimmed with shell danglers or possibly jade skull beads (Dillon and Christensen 2005), knee bands with beaded danglers, a nosepiece, and a floral top piece. He may also wear a jaguar pelt or possibly bloody bark paper, sandals, and a rope collar signifying self-sacrifice. His hair is tied up in a cloth band. The hank of hair pulled through the floral top piece hangs over his forehead in the style worn by those engaging in self-sacrifice, and feathers are attached to his hair. A small head is tied at his crown with a strip of cloth or a headband (Schele and Miller 1986: 186–187). Flora Simmons Clancy (2002: 29, 31) interprets this as the head of Aj Nich ("Flower Lord"), his most important captive, identified by the flower in his ear. The head wears the hairstyle of a sacrificial victim. Severed heads of captives were preserved as trophies (Miller and Taube 1993: 173); the shrunken head was the ideal way for a ruler to provide sustenance for the gods through taking a captive in war.

Itzamnah B'ahläm wears a loincloth decorated with the same quatrefoil-knot design seen on the gown of Ix K'ab'al Xok on Lintel 25. The quatrefoil was an ancient sign used as far back as Olmec times (Schele and Mathews 1998: 45). The rounded four-lobed quatrefoil with the central knot inside was used during the reign of Itzamnah B'ahläm on garments portrayed on Lintels 24, 25, and 46 and on Stela 8. Mary Miller and Simon Martin suggest (2004: 222) that the quatrefoil represents a window or portal into a supernatural cave. Beings from the underworld could be seen in these portals (Looper 2003: 54). The quatrefoil was also used to represent the *ol*[15] portal, or crack, in the back of the cosmic turtle, which represented the surface of the earth from which maize was reborn during the time of the Creation (Freidel, Schele, and Parker 1993: 215). According to Matthew Looper (2000: 20–21), quatrefoils represent flowers associated with the watery underworld. They relate textiles to the underworld, birth, and water. The quatrefoils on the loincloth have a central knot sign (Elisabeth Wagner [2000a: 37–39] discusses the knot sign). Looper demonstrates (2000: 21, figure 31a–c) that the knot, which he calls the interlace, and the crossbands sign commonly seen within quatrefoils reinforce their relationship to water, as both are frequently associated with flowers and water lilies elsewhere in Maya art. Itzamnah B'ahläm also wears a herringbone-patterned sash above his loincloth. The quatrefoil-knot and herringbone designs are also seen together on vases that are painted like textiles (Reents-Budet 1994: figures 1.12, 2.12). Perhaps the herringbone, or zigzag, pattern is another metaphor for water (Looper 2000: 24–25).

The design on his long fringed cape has the same meaning as the quatrefoil-knot sign and again relates to the underworld, birth, and water. The cape is tied over his chest and is fringed along the edges. The quatrefoils are straight-sided and are surrounded by bifurcated scrolls, indicating fragrance (Looper 2000: 19). The quatrefoils are intersected by two diagonals (crossbands), which may also relate to water. The intersection point could also represent the center of the ol portal, the *tan ol k'ab'*, or world center (Taube 1998: figure 96). Itzamnah B'ahläm's costume on Lintel 24 links him to sacrifice, war, and the creative powers of the underworld that allowed the rebirth of deities and ancestors. The fiery torch in the scene may indicate that the sacrificing occurred at night or in a dark interior space (Schele and Miller 1986: 186; Miller and Martin 2004: 100). It is also possible that this scene portrays actions that originally occurred in the darkness that existed at the time of the Creation. Itzamnah B'ahläm may be burning an offering of his blood in the torch. The torch may relate him to the fiery god K'awil.

Ix K'ab'al Xok

The short text behind the ruler refers to Ix K'ab'al Xok: "She is shown sacrificing, Lady Self-Sacrificer Xok, Ix K'ab'al Xok, Lady Kolomte." The smaller text below this refers to the dedication and emplacement of the lintel. She kneels before her husband and pulls a thorned rope through her tongue, the ideal way for royal women to auto-sacrifice in an effort to raise and provide sustenance for the gods. Blood oozes from her wound and flows over her cheek and chin.

While performing this sacrifice, Ix K'ab'al Xok wears a Teotihuacan-style headdress. One-tiered and rectangular, it sits atop a cloth cap. This headdress was related to war, sacrifice, and high nobility at Teotihuacan and was worn by Tlaloc, the god of war, storm, and lightning, an important deity at that city (Pasztory 1997: 117–121; Coggins 2002: 56–57; Manzanilla 2003). Versions similar to that worn by Ix K'ab'al Xok were worn by men at other Maya cities (Coe 1975: 25–26 and color plate), and Yaxun B'ahläm wears one on Lintel 17 (Graham and Von Euw 1977: 43). On the Dallas Altar two royal women are shown, and one wears a Teotihuacan-derived headdress. David Freidel and Stanley Guenter (2003: 3) state that the iconography relating to this woman indicates "the role of royal women in bringing war gods into this world to wreak havoc on their enemies." Bloodletting served to nourish the gods and to vivify and bring them forth from the supernatural realm, and sacrifice by royal women was an important part of accession and dynastic refounding rites. On top of her headdress is a goggle-eyed Tlaloc head, which sits in front of two Mexican Year signs[16] with a feather bundle on top. Her greenstone jewelry consists of a mosaic collar with a Sun God medallion, mosaic wristlets trimmed with shell danglers, and floral with square-nosed serpents as stamens (Looper 2000: 23).

Ix K'ab'al Xok's gown is bordered at the sides with a skyband composed of symbols that reinforce the aquatic symbolism prevalent in the main field of the garment (Looper 2000: 31, plate 8). The skyband is edged with delicate feathers that have tiny beads, possibly pearls, at the tips. The diamond net pattern of her gown contains crosses enclosed by smaller diamonds bordered by a serrated aquatic design. The diamond net with enclosed crosses could represent a variation of the Venus sign (Macri and Looper 2003b: 230), relating her to warfare. However, the diamond net pattern is most often related to aquatic imagery, particularly the turtle shell and the water lily pad (Looper 2000: 27). As the turtle shell represented the earth's surface, the design may also reference the earth and its ol portal to the underworld. The water-related imagery on her gown also relates Ix K'ab'al Xok to the procreative powers of the underworld.

Miller and Martin suggest (2004: 25–26) that women began to be portrayed more often on monuments around AD 700, possibly the result of increased warfare. Female dynastic lines may have gained political significance, giving women greater power. At this time some women were represented in ways that were usually restricted to men (see, for example, Josserand 2002: figure 8.9). On Lintel 24 Ix K'ab'al Xok wears a Teotihuacan-style headdress more commonly worn by men elsewhere in the Maya area. Her costume links her to sacrifice and the powers of creation and war.

The scene on Lintel 24 shows Itzamnah B'ahläm and Ix K'ab'al Xok portraying the ideal way for a royal couple to engage in sacrifice to feed and conjure the gods. He wears the shrunken head of a decapitated war captive and a rope collar illustrating self-sacrifice. She performs tongue sacrifice, letting her blood, which falls on paper contained in a basket at her knees. Lintel 24 features sacrifice, particularly that of Ix K'ab'al Xok.

Looper suggests (2003: 161) that "the triadic structure of Maya architecture could codify the same domains of royal power as the three stones of Creation." I propose that Structure 23 is a "three-stone" place and that the three lintels of Structure 23 also embody the domains codified by the stones. Looper demonstrates (2000: 11, 2002: 192–193, 199, 2003: 106, 158) that the snake platform/throne, one of the three stones set up at the time of the Creation, codified bloodletting and ancestor communication and was associated with the serpent-footed god K'awil and conjuring. This platform/throne was linked to the female gender because of its relationship to the rebirth of deities and ancestors. This was likened to the female role as mother. Sacrifice and communication with the ancestors was therefore the canonical ritual domain of women.

Palenque's Temple of the Foliated Cross, the easternmost building of the Cross Group, features K'awil in his role as provider of sustenance (Freidel, Schele, and Parker 1993: 145, 194). Yaxchilán Lintel 24 is over the eastern doorway of Structure 23, and it focuses on sacrifice as a means of sustenance and conjuring. A bloodletting, probably by a female, was mentioned in the texts of the Temple of the Foliated Cross but was not shown on the wall panels (Schele and Freidel 1990: figure 6.15). On Lintel 24 female sacrifice is prominent. Itzamnah B'ahläm did not build three buildings, as was done by Kàan B'ahläm ("Snake Jaguar," r. AD 684 to 702) at Palenque, but he used the three doorways of Structure 23—one of his most important buildings—to convey ideas that were fundamental to Maya rulership.

Lintel 24: Front Edge

The front edge of Lintel 24 was lost in the nineteenth century (Miller and Martin 2004: 106), so it can no longer be read. It probably contained information on dedications relating to Structure 23, as did the front edges of Lintels 25 and 26.

Lintel 25: Underside

The central lintel of Structure 23, Lintel 25, refers to Itzamnah B'ahläm's accession day, 9.12.9.8.1 5 Imix 4 Mak (AD October 21, 681; figure 6.5). Lintel 25 may be his primary accession monument, as no other surviving lintel or stela can be certainly identified as recording his accession.[17] However, Lintel 25 was not set in place until much later. The only other remaining mention of his accession day is given on Hieroglyphic Step III (figure 6.6) of Hieroglyphic Stairway 3 of Yaxchilán Structure 44 (Graham and Von Euw 1982: 169).

The text of Lintel 25 is carved in mirror, or reversed, image to the usual left-to-right reading order.[18] Some of the texts of Structure 10L–11 at Copán are partly reversed, so Lintel 25 is not unique in this aspect. The mirror image text emphasizes Lintel 25, as the texts on Lintels 24 and 26 are not reversed. The main text of the underside of Lintel 25 reads:[19] "On 5 Imix 4 Mak he conjured his god (K'awil), his 'flint and shield' (*Tok'-Päkal*), the Fiery One of O-Chahk (Aj K'akh O-Chahk), conjuring his holy arrival (or birth) (hu-lu),[20] the Four K'atun Lord, Itzamnah B'ahläm, Master of Aj Nich, Holy Lord of Yaxchilán, First in the World (*B'akab'*). The image of the Nawal (Na-Wa-La) of the Founder House (*Wi-Te-Na*)."[21]

The text mentions a Founder House. In the Maya area these houses were usually associated with dynastic founders who introduced the Tlaloc-Venus war cult into a city. The rituals conducted in these houses connected dynastic leaders to Teotihuacan (Martin and Grube 2000: 192; Looper 2003: 36). Several Maya cities, such as Palenque (Freidel, Schele, and Parker 1993: 434n54), Copán (Martin and Grube 2000: 192–193), and Tikal (Schele and Mathews 1998: 79), had these Founder Houses, which also served as accession houses. Looper says (2003: 177) that accession was an important transition, as it represented a renewal of the basic patterns of space and time first established at the Creation when the gods

6.5. *Yaxchilán Lintel 25, with Ix K'ab'al Xok at right. Drawing by Ian Graham and Eric Von Euw (1977 Volume 3, Part 1: 56). Courtesy, the President and Fellows of Harvard College.*

6.6. *Yaxchilán Hieroglyphic Stairway 3, Step III: Itzamnah B'ahläm's accession day. Drawing by Ian Graham and Eric Von Euw (1982 Volume 3, Part 3: 169). Courtesy, the President and Fellows of Harvard College.*

set three stones. Founder Houses in other cities may have employed some of the same iconography as is seen on the lintels of Structure 23.

Because of the break in dynastic continuity between his reign and that of his father, Itzamnah B'ahläm engaged in "refounding" rites during his accession, either building or rebuilding Structure 23 as part of them. At other Maya cities, such as Naranjo and Sak Nikté, women from more powerful cities—Dos Pilas and Calakmul, respectively—had an important role in refounding rites. They brought with them the powers of creation and war to refound the dynasties at the two subordinate cities (Martin and Grube 2000: 74–75; Freidel and Guenter 2003: 3–4). On the Yaxchilán Structure 23 lintels, Ix K'ab'al Xok is shown participating in these rites.

It is possible that Ix K'ab'al Xok's male relatives played a major role in Itzamnah B'ahläm's fight for independent rule and that, because of this, her family was prominent at Yaxchilán. The situation at Yaxchilán was unusual. A gap in the historical record from AD 669, when Aj Wäktun probably died, to AD 681, when Itzamnah B'ahläm acceded to the throne, may represent a period of subordination for Yaxchilán (Martin and Grube 2000: 122–123). Or perhaps there was another ruler (Josserand 2007: 307–308). Little is known of Ix K'ab'al Xok's early background. One of her female relatives, Ix Päkal Xok, the wife of Aj Wäxtun and the mother of Itzamnah B'ahläm, had the *janab'* ("Flower") sign in her name, as did Janab' Päkal ("Flower ? Shield,"

r. AD 615 to 683), the great ruler of Palenque, and Ix Päkal Xok was a female lord (*ix ajaw*) (McAnany and Plank 2001: 112). Perhaps she was of the Palenque Dynasty. If so, then Ix K'ab'al Xok may also have been connected by her clan affiliation with Ix Päkal Xok to the ruling line at that city. If she was of Palenque's ruling dynasty, then her status might have strengthened Itzamnah B'ahläm's claim to the throne. Her status, however derived, was high enough for her to play a prominent role in her husband's accession and refounding rites.

The main text seems to focus on Itzamnah B'ahläm's earlier conjuring while the scene shows the result of hers. Two bloodletting bowls are shown on Lintel 25 with the serpent hovering over hers. This bowl contains a rope, a lancet, and bloodstained paper. It must be the one used by Ix K'ab'al Xok, as men are not shown pulling a rope through their tongues at Yaxchilán. The bowl she holds in her hand contains a lancet, a stingray spine, and bloody paper. This was the bowl of Itzamnah B'ahläm. Each bowl contains items used in bloodletting, and the blood dripped onto the paper strips. Itzamnah B'ahläm is the subject of the main text, and the smaller text refers to Ix K'ab'al Xok. Clancy (1986: 26) points out that the text of a monument does not always dictate the iconographic content of the scene but may relay additional information. Josserand notes (2002: 136) that sometimes the text describes another part of the ritual and not the one shown in the image. This is what seems to be happening on Yaxchilán Lintel 25.

B'olon K'awil Aj K'ahk O-Chahk

The main text of Lintel 25 states that Itzamnah B'ahläm conjured his K'awil and his *tok'-päkal*, Aj K'ahk O-Chahk ("the Fiery One of O-Chahk") (figure 6.7). A deity named O-Chahk was mentioned on the Early Classic Lintel 35 at Yaxchilán (Graham and Von Euw 1979: 79), so this god had been known at the city for a long time. In Itzamnah B'ahläm's time the name O-Chahk was combined with K'awil,[22] or B'olon K'awil, and Aj K'ahk.

B'olon means "Nine or Many" (Macri and Looper 2003b: 263) and modifies K'awil, indicating the Maya belief that this god had many spirit companions (ibid.: 67). K'awil is often depicted with a serpent leg, a visual manifestation of his transforming ability. In the Late Classic Period K'awil and Chahk, or O-Chahk, were often conflated, with K'awil shown as the smoking, or fiery, lightning ax held by O-Chahk. This ax was a weapon of decapitation sacrifice, which often involved war captives (Freidel, Schele, and Parker 1993: 202). Karl Taube (1992a: 73–76, 79) suggests that K'awil was a conflation of a flaming serpent and a lightning ax and that the composite K'awil O-Chahk functioned as a form of Chahk. The Teotihuacan Tlaloc is sometimes shown holding a similar ax. Tlaloc was a god of storm, lightning, lineage, and war, like the various Maya Chahks (Coggins 2002: 52, 56–57). Therefore, O-Chahk shared some characteristics with Tlaloc.

YAXCHILÁN STRUCTURE 23

6.7. *The Maya deity O-Chahk. Drawing by Rusty Van Rossmann (after Robicsek [1979:112]).*

The "flint and shield" (tok'-päkal), or war emblem, according to Timothy Knowlton (2002: 10), was a paired metaphor for military efficacy. In the main text of Lintel 25 both K'awil and tok'-päkal refer to Aj K'ahk O-Chahk, the fiery lightning ax of O-Chahk, whose leg could be manifested in the form of many serpents. The serpent shown on Lintel 25 is one of these serpents and appears to combine some features of the Feathered Serpent and the War Serpent headdress seen on the Temple of the Feathered Serpent at Teotihuacan. The War Serpent, according to Taube (1992b: 82), was identified predominantly with fire and warfare. Either as a headdress, often shown covered with mosaic platelets, or as a complete serpent, it occurs in the context of war (Miller and Taube 1993: 163; Taube 1992b: figure 6). In the Maya area the War Serpent was associated with rulership and was a patron of the Tlaloc-Venus war cult (see John Carlson 1993: 209 for the patrons of the Teotihuacan Tlaloc-Venus war cult). This serpent is the one that is conjured on Lintel 25.

On monuments at some Maya cities, such as Tikal and Copán, the Maya War Serpent is called Waxäkläju'n Ub'ah Chan ("Eighteen Serpent Heads"), but this name was not used at Yaxchilán. This name relates the War Serpent to the Temple of the Feathered Serpent at Teotihuacan, where the terraces on each side of the stairway have eighteen heads of this deity (Schele and Mathews 1998:

345n1). Eighteen sacrificed warriors were buried on the south side of this pyramid, and they were accompanied by hundreds of small, rectangular platelets like those known later to compose warrior headdresses (Coggins 2002: 51–52). Taube says (2002) that the War Serpent was conjured and pulled out of the Temple of the Feathered Serpent, a Five-Flower Mountain, by the Feathered Serpent, the god of wind and breath. The War Serpent is clearly of Teotihuacan origin. A similar scene is seen on the frieze of the entablature of the West Building of the Nunnery Quadrangle at Uxmal (Schele and Mathews 1998: 283–284).

The undulating shape of the War Serpent on Lintel 25 associates it with lightning. The serpent leg of K'awil was equated with a lightning bolt (Miller and Martin 2004: 293), and the War Serpent was also linked to lightning. The War Serpent is decorated with feather fans with crenellated edging (Taube 2000b: 283), circles, and serpent segments (crosshatched or dark diamonds) on the fleshed parts of its body. An S-shaped scroll rises up behind the Serpent, representing a cloud (Macri and Looper 2003b: 189) and the possibility of rain. The cloud sign is marked by two symbols, a Venus sign and a crossed-bands sign.[23] The Maya War Serpent may have been part skeletonized serpent and part centipede (Martin and Grube 2000: 125; Macri and Looper 2003b: 59–60). Taube states (2000b: 324) that among the Classic Maya, the War Serpent was strongly serpentine, and that is true for its image on Lintel 25. Looper points out (2003: 235n22) that among the ancient Maya, centipedes belonged to the same class as snakes.

A jawless Tlaloc head wearing a Tlaloc-Venus war headdress and mask with blood flowing from its mouth (Schele and Mathews 1998: 416) is located at the War Serpent's lower head. At Teotihuacan jawless Tlaloc figures on headdresses were related to sacrifice of captives in battle who had their lower jaws removed (García–Des Lauriers 2000: 136). The head on Lintel 25 wears an ear flare similar to that worn by the rear head of the Cosmic Monster (Schele and Miller 1986: figure 22). This ear flare relates to blood sacrifice and the transformation and rebirth of the sun. Its presence on the Tlaloc head on Lintel 25 points to the role of sacrifice and transformation in the rebirth of warriors from the underworld.

Itzamnah B'ahläm

The identity of the warrior emerging from the larger head of the War Serpent has been interpreted in various ways. Tate suggests (1986: 18) that the warrior represents the ruler as "the living God K" (K'awil). Some years later she said (1992: 89) that the warrior represents "Shield Jaguar." Peter Mathews notes (1997: 155, 159) that the profile of the warrior resembles that of Escudo (Shield)-Jaguar (Itzamnah B'ahläm) and may picture him. Freidel, Schele, and Parker (1993: 308) posit that the warrior is the founder (of the B'ahläm line). Martin and Grube think (2000: 125) the figure is "a warrior masked as . . . Tlaloc" and represents "the king himself as defender of the city." Miller and Martin suggest (2004: 100) that the warrior is the ruler himself. Josserand states (2007: 303): "The conjured warrior may ... be one of Lady Xok's ancestors rather than an ancestor of her husband (and because of the patterns of wife exchange between lineages, it may be an ancestor common to both of them)."

I agree with Freidel, Schele, and Parker (1993) that the emerging warrior is the founder of the B'ahläm lineage. In the Maya area dynastic founders were sometimes pictured wearing the Tlaloc-Venus war costume (cf. Martin and Grube 2000: 35, 202), and they were associated with Founder Houses (Freidel, Schele, and Parker 1993: 434n54; Schele and Mathews 1998: 79; Martin and Grube 2000: 192–193). As the lineage founder is a B'ahläm, this may account for his resemblance to Itzamnah B'ahläm. Perhaps the rite involved the ruler merging with the spirit of the local patron deity of the Tlaloc-Venus war cult (the founder) to reactivate his dynasty and renew his obligation to defend Yaxchilán by pursuing war. During rituals, Maya rulers could merge with supernatural entities, physically and psychologically transforming into them (Looper 2003: 28). During such transformations, the ruler was believed to be transported through time and space to relive cosmic events that originally took place at the time of Creation.[24] During his accession rites, a new ruler was believed to experience a ritual death and rebirth. Lintel 25 may portray Itzamnah B'ahläm at the moment he is reborn as the human incarnation of the founder of his dynasty, the local Yaxchilán patron god of the Tlaloc-Venus war cult. This, perhaps, is the moment he became ruler and regenerated his city as a military power. My interpretation explains why he seems to be absent from the central lintel of the building.

The dynastic founder is dressed in Tlaloc-Venus regalia, a costume not portrayed on any other known Yaxchilán monuments, probably because of its Teotihuacan origin. He wears a Tlaloc-Venus "balloon" style headdress probably made of stuffed deerskin (Miller and Martin 2004: 165–166). The headdress is dotted with blood and is decorated with bead and bone signs, possibly indicating rain. It has two knots at the front and one at the back; the triple knot symbolizes ritual bloodletting (Schele and Miller 1986: figure 4.1; Looper 2003: 172). There are two Mexican Year signs on the front of the headdress, the upper one topped by a feather bundle. A Tlaloc mask floats in front of the founder's face. This goggle-eyed jawless mask with blood flowing from its mouth was worn by warriors (García–Des Lauriers 2000: 136) and dynastic founders. Schele and Mathews (1998: 223) suggest that the round eye rings were read as *ch'ok*, which can be read as "sprout" (Macri and Looper 2003b: 106). Taube (2000b: 274) suggests that the round goggles of the mask resemble the eye orbits of skulls, and Carlson (1993: 210n3) thinks the goggles derive from the ring eyes of the Teotihuacan War Emblem Owl. The headdress and mask are similar to those worn by the Tlaloc head located before the lower head of the War Serpent.

The founder wears a greenstone mosaic collar trimmed with beads and shells, which is decorated with medallions that have faces with *k'in* (sun) signs on the foreheads. Disk and pendant ear flares with floral danglers complete his jewelry. His round shield may be decorated with the face of the Jaguar War God like the one on the shield on the central wall panel in the Temple of the Sun at Palenque (Schele and Freidel 1990: figure 6.13). The short spear has flint tips at both ends, and it is dotted with blood. The crossed spears that accompany the shield in the Temple of the Sun panel are also flint-tipped.

Stela 35, a later monument, also shows the War Serpent, but a Tlaloc head emerges from its jaws (Schele 1991: figure 144). On a stucco relief from Structure 21, the building that contains Stela 35 (ibid.: figure 150; Tate 1992: 197), Itzamnah B'ahläm and Ix K'ab'al Xok are shown along with Yaxun B'ahläm and two of his wives. The War Serpent appears in the scene with a Tlaloc head wearing the war headdress and mask at one end while another Tlaloc head emerges from the open jaws of the other head. As a Tlaloc head emerges from the jaws of the War Serpent on Stela 35, this links the identity of the emerging warrior on Lintel 25 to Tlaloc and his war cult. The Tlaloc head on the relief also confirms this. On Stela 6 from Copán, a Tlaloc head is also seen in association with the War Serpent (Schele 1991: 173). The image on Lintel 25 differs only in the fact that the local patron deity is pictured in human form.[25]

Ix K'ab'al Xok

On Lintel 25 Ix K'ab'al Xok is shown in the lower, and therefore secondary, position (Houston 1998: 343). The inscription enclosed by the top of the cloud sign refers to her. It can be translated as "Ix K'ab'al Xok, Scatterer,[26] foot of the tree of[27] Tan-Ha' Yaxchilán" "in-the-center-of/in-front-of-the-water-Yaxchilán" (McAnany and Plank 2001: 107).

She wears a greenstone mosaic collar decorated with one central medallion in the front that has the face of the sun. Besides the mosaic collar, she wears greenstone floral ear flares, a large bead necklace, a small string of beads over her forehead, and a bar pectoral. Bar pectorals have been linked to Teotihuacan imagery by Claudia García–Des Lauriers (2000: 81). Her gown is decorated with the quatrefoil-knot sign, which relates to birth, water, and portals to the underworld (Looper 2000: 18–23, plate 9). The bottom of the gown is bordered with beads. She wears two items associated with auto-sacrifice: a strip of bark paper dotted with blood is attached to her hair, and a bark paper sash is tied around her waist. The sides of her gown are fringed, and crosshatched, or dark, panels are separated by narrow bands of stripes; its bottom is beaded.

The final costume elements of Ix K'ab'al Xok are her headband and a flexible bar, which she presents to the founder.[28] The headband has a serpent head at one end and a skull at the other. A flayed body joins the two heads. The skull has the same ear flare seen on the Tlaloc head located before the smaller head of the War Serpent. The headband and flexible bar are similar in conception to the Cosmic Monster at other cities such as Piedras Negras, Quiriguá, and Palenque on accession monuments (Looper 2003: 172–176, 237n13). At Yaxchilán the Cosmic Monster appears on Hieroglyphic Step III of Hieroglyphic Stairway 3, the only other surviving reference to Itzamnah B'ahläm's accession (Graham and Von Euw 1982: 169). On Lintel 25 the War Serpent substitutes for the Cosmic Monster. On the headband and bar the serpent head substitutes for the front head of the Cosmic Monster, and the skull is similar to the rear skeletal head usually seen in Cosmic Monster representations (see Schele and Miller 1986: figure 22). The Cosmic Monster was related to the god Itzamnah, the watery surface of the underworld, the water platform/throne, and to accession (Looper 2003: 174–176). The flexible bar Ix K'ab'al Xok balances on her right arm is not rigid like typical Late Classic ceremonial bars (Miller and Taube 1993: 150), so this may be another example of archaizing. From the serpent head a "hocker" (quadrupedal animal), possibly a frog or a toad, emerges. It may be associated with water as, outside of textile contexts, it is usually linked to aquatic imagery (Looper 2000: 29). The skull at the other end of the bar wears an ear flare like that of the rear head of the Cosmic Monster and has water lily foliage sprouting behind it, relating it to the watery surface of the underworld (Looper 2003: 133). The serpent head depicts rebirth and life and the skull death and the underworld. On Lintel 25 it was Ix K'ab'al Xok's role to communicate with the ancestor and witness the most important moment of her husband's accession and refounding rites.

The scene on Lintel 25, the central lintel of the House of Ix K'ab'al Xok, focuses on the arrival of the War Serpent and the rebirth of the dynastic founder—the local patron deity of the Tlaloc-Venue war cult, who was conjured on Itzamnah B'ahläm's accession day. This image represents the ideal accession and dynastic refounding moment when the new ruler either merged with the spirit of the founder or otherwise received the authority to rule, allowing him to accede to power and reactivate the B'ahläm Dynasty. She presents the new ruler with the double-headed flexible bar, the symbol of his status as king. On Lintel 25 the dynastic founder represents the powers of war and to Ix K'ab'al Xok the forces of creativity.

The water platform/throne codifies birth and resurrection and is associated with accession, the god Itzamnah, and the Cosmic Monster/War Serpent. As it is the youngest stone, it is also associated with youth (Looper 2002: 191, 199, 2003: 175). At Palenque the water platforms/throne was located in the central position on the Palace Tablet depicting the accession of K'än Joy Chitam II ("Precious/Yellow Tied Peccary," r. AD 702 to 711) (Looper 2002: figure 10.9). His parents are shown seated on jaguar and snake platform/thrones while he, as the newly acceded ruler, sits on the water throne. Yaxchilán Lintel 25 is located in the central position in Structure 23. Palenque's Temple of the Cross, the central building of the Cross Group, featured birth and accession in its texts (Schele and Freidel 1990: 246–247) and was associated with a deity that had aquatic characteristics, just as Tlaloc did.

Lintel 25: Front Edge

The text of the front edge of Lintel 25 begins by stating that it had been forty-two years since the conjuring of K'awil at Tan-Ha' Yaxchilán.[29] The text focuses on actions that occurred on 9.14.11.15.1 3 Imix 14 Ch'en (AD August 5, 723). On that day Ix K'ab'al Xok dedicated the sculpture, or "carving," of her house. This carving may refer either to the plaster sculpture around the roof of the building (Schele 1991: 95; McAnany and Plank 2001: 105) or to its inscriptions (Josserand 2007: 303). The final glyphs of the text refer to "his earth, his cave." This phrase has been discussed by Knowlton (2002: 10–12) and McAnany and Plank (2001: 108–110). According to Knowlton, it refers to a residence, in this instance the residence, or city, of Itzamnah B'ahläm. The dedication of the House of Ix K'ab'al Xok was done under the auspices of "Itzamnah B'ahläm" (Josserand 2007: 303).

Lintel 26: Underside

There is one date (figure 6.8) on the underside of Lintel 26, 9.14.12.6.12 12 Eb' O Pop (AD February 12, 724; Graham and Von Euw 1977: 57), the day the lintel was dedicated and set in place. This date is found in the small text[30] located above and to the left of Itzamnah B'ahläm's head. It reads: "On 12 Eb' O Pop the carving of K'awil Chahk of Sak Ok was set up." Sak Ok was another city, so the sculptor was not from Yaxchilán (Martin and Grube 2000: 126). The lintel was put in place on New Year's Day and is another accession commemoration. The main text in the T-shaped area says: "His image as king with the water head [dress],[31] First Jaguar Paw Throne, Seven Sun-Faced Lord,[32] Four K'atun Lord, Master of Aj Nich, Itzamnah B'ahläm, Holy Lord." First Jaguar Paw Throne may refer to the jaguar platform/throne associated with war. Linda Schele and Nikolai Grube (1994: 155–156) call it the jaguar paw/throne glyph. David Stuart (2004: 1n2) calls it the "paw-and-pillow" logogram and says it may signify accession to office.

Itzamnah B'ahläm

On Lintel 26 Itzamnah B'ahläm faces Ix K'ab'al Xok and wears his customary war costume. He also wears the "Jester God" headband (*Säk Hunal*, "White Headband"),[33] signifying his accession to the throne (Taube 1998: 454–462). This headband is composed of jade rosettes and a jade "jester head," which personi-

6.8. *Yaxchilán Lintel 26, with Itzamnah B'ahläm (left) and Ix K'ab'al Xok (right). Drawing by Ian Graham and Eric Von Euw (1977, Volume 3, Part 1: 57). Courtesy, the President and Fellows of Harvard College.*

6.9. *Yaxchilán Lintel 4, Itzamnah B'ahläm. Drawing by Ian Graham and Eric Von Euw (1977, Volume 3, Part 1: 19). Courtesy, the President and Fellows of Harvard College.*

fies the royal headband and has aquatic characteristics (Looper 2003: 41, 105). In his right hand he holds his flint spear point, ready for hafting, and he reaches for his headdress with his left hand.

On other monuments Itzamnah B'ahläm appears with his Water Jaguar war headdress already on his head (see, for example, Stela 20 in Tate [1992: 247] and the lintel in Schele [1991: figure 120]). On Lintel 26 Ix K'ab'al Xok holds the Water Jaguar headdress. Lintel 4 of Structure 34 (Graham and Von Euw 1977: 19) shows Itzamnah B'ahläm wearing the Water Jaguar headdress and holding the same type of spear point seen on Lintel 26 (figure 6.9). His flexible shield is in front of him, but it is not possible to see who holds it, as the other section of Lintel 4 is too eroded. He wears the same war costume as is seen on Lintel 26. Lintel 4 was found in the debris in front of the middle chamber of Structure 34, and no other lintels have been found in this building (Maler 1901–1903: 166–167; Tate 1992: 227). The text of Lintel 4 is badly eroded, and there is no readable date other than that stating that Itzamnah B'ahläm was a Five K'atun Lord. This indicates that Lintel 4 is later than Lintel 26, where he is called a Four K'atun Lord. Lintel 4 may represent another later accession commemoration. The dedication date of Lintel 56, which mentions another royal woman who may have been a wife of Itzamnah B'ahläm, fell during the time when he was a Five K'atun Lord (McAnany and Plank 2001: 113). Ix K'ab'al Xok may have handed him his flexible shield, or the woman mentioned on Lintel 56 or another wife may have done so.

Itzamnah B'ahläm's war headdress represents a jaguar that has been referred to as the Water Jaguar (Taube 1998: figure 8) or the Water-Lily Jaguar (Milbrath 1999: 120–124; Looper 2003: 87).[34] This jaguar is prominent in Maya mythology, and it appears on the upper part of the "Cosmic Plate" that depicts the structure of the Maya cosmos (Wagner 2000b: figures 451, 452). The Water Jaguar is also often seen on jaguar platforms/thrones (Looper 2003: 187; Miller and Taube 1993: 104). The Water Jaguar was associated with decapitation sacrifice. On pottery it is sometimes pictured wearing a sacrificial neck scarf (Milbrath 1999: figure 4.2d and e). On one vessel the Water Jaguar holds a bleeding, decapitated human head (Reents-Budet 1994: figure 6.21:252). Wearing the Water Jaguar headdress strongly related Itzamnah B'ahläm to war, death, sacrifice, and the underworld. Among the Maya, the headdress could relate to the wearer's identity or affiliation (Coggins 2002: 51n27). The glyphs for b'ahläm ("jaguar") are T751a and 751b, and these two signs are identical except that the latter shows a jaguar with water lily foliage on top of its head (Macri and Looper 2003b: 80). This is the glyph that refers to the Water Jaguar. As Itzamnah B'ahläm's headdress has the foliage on top, it refers to the Water Jaguar, the closely related alter ego of b'ahläm—the jaguar without the foliage—which is part of his name.

Another important component of the royal war costume is the long scarf covering the front of Itzamnah B'ahläm's body. On some of his monuments, such as Lintels 45 and 46, where he is shown in the act of taking captives, this scarf appears to be bulky and heavy (Graham and Von Euw 1979: 99, 101). Andrea Stone notes (1989: 160) that a "neck garment or cotton armor" was worn by God N (Pawahtun) and other characters on vases and in ceramic figurines. Something that looks similar is carried by two warriors shown on Register C of the Lower Temple of the Jaguars at Chichén Itzá. Schele and Mathews call (1998: 251–252) these "large bags," but they could be local versions of the war scarf.

Linda Schele and Mary Miller (1986: 211) write that the "armor he dons over his jerkin is a tufted garment that may have been made of feathers or unspun cotton." A war costume similar in construction to the scarf on Lintel 26 appears on a Jaina warrior figurine. Schele and Miller suggest (ibid.: 223–224, see also plate 79) that this costume is made of feathers and that it is a bird costume. On Yaxchilán Lintels 45 and 46 the scarf looks too heavy to be made of feathers. It could be made of feathers or unspun cotton, although it does not look like the feathered or cotton armor shown on some Maya and Teotihuacan figurines (see García–Des Lauriers 2000: 209–212). This scarf covered the ruler's vital organs, and I think it may be composed of shells, which would have provided better protection for his body. A close inspection of the scarf shown on Lintel 45 and Stela 18 shows the small holes at the base of each element composing it (Tate 1992: 246, 256). These holes are also seen at the base of the shells dangling from his wristlets on Lintel 26. A spondylus-shell vest was buried with Ruler 3 of Piedras Negras (Houston 2004: 275), so shell garments were known in the Usumacinta region in the Classic Period. If the scarf was made of shells, then it represented aquatic imagery.

On his upper body Itzamnah B'ahläm wears a vest made out of reed twisted into a pattern that looks like the *jäl* glyph, translated as "plait" or "weave" (Macri and Looper 2003b: 228). Looper (2000: figure 31b) considers this another version of the "interlace" or knot sign, which reinforces the association of his headdress and scarf with water. The vest is decorated with six round stones and a band of step frets and wavy lines across the chest. The wavy lines indicate water, and stepped frets are often found in association with water iconography (Looper 2000: 24–27). The vest provided additional protection for Itzamnah B'ahläm's upper body. Below the scalloped border of the vest, he wears a beaded belt bordered at the bottom with dangling shells. At his knees he wears greenstone or shell knee bands, and his wristlets, made of the same material, are trimmed with shell danglers. Sandals and a rope collar complete his costume. His body seems overly exposed for battle, but he will use his long, flexible shield to protect himself.[35] On Lintel 26 Itzamnah B'ahläm's costume not only clearly reflects his status and power as a warrior, but it also associates him with sacrifice, water, birth, and the underworld.

Ix K'ab'al Xok

Ix K'ab'al Xok wears a headband with two visible birds and flowers wound around her head. The birds may be hummingbirds,[36] as Tate (1992: 72) has suggested, or possibly *cotingas*, which were worn in the headdresses of warriors at Seibal and Chichén Itzá (Schele and Mathews 1998: 192, 224). The birds suck nectar from the flowers on the headband, a metaphor for sacrificial bloodletting. On both Lintel 26 and Stela 35 the royal women wear the birds-and-flowers headband, and both perform or have performed sacrifice. On Lintel 26 blood is flowing from Ix K'ab'al Xok's cheek. As was the case with other headbands and headdresses, the birds-and-flowers headband could be worn by men as well as women (see Justin Kerr [1989: 66] for an example of a man wearing this headband). Ix K'ab'al Xok wears a greenstone necklace and medallion with a human face in the center, floral ear flares, and mosaic wristlets with shell danglers; hanks of her hair are pulled through greenstone tubes. Her gown is bordered by a skyband edged with feathers terminating in small beads. The skyband motifs reinforce the aquatic symbols on the main area of the garment (Looper 2000: plate 7). The main design is composed of a diamond net pattern bordered by a zigzag band. At the bottom of the gown is a border of stepped frets and a lower band of half-quatrefoils. Both of these designs may be related to water (Looper 2000: 26–27). Inside the diamonds are "hockers," possibly representing frogs or toads, lying on a crosshatched or dark field. The interior bodies of the animals are also crosshatched. The crosshatching may signify the murky waters of the underworld. A similar design is seen on an Early Classic tripod vessel from Waxäktun with a turtle on its lid (Reents-Budet 1994: figure 6.10: 243; Looper 2000: 29), possibly representing the earth's surface and the interface between the sky and water. On the vessel water is represented by dots and circles over a dark background. Similar dots are found on Lintel 26.

A scene portrayed on a vase from Tikal is very similar to the ones shown on Yaxchilán Lintels 4 and 26. The Tikal vase dates to AD 794 and was excavated from Structure 5D-44 in the Central Acropolis (Kahn 1994: figure 17). Two women are shown handing the ruler Nuk Yax Ahin II ("First Great Alligator," r. AD 768 to 794) his war shield and mask. The woman closest to him wears a gown decorated with quatrefoils and fragrance scrolls, and she offers a mask. The other woman holds a large shield with a ch'ok face, indicating that it is a Tlaloc-Venus war shield. This vase suggests that the Lintel 26 scene was part of the commonly shared mythological cycle that served as a basis for ritual scenes during important events, such as accessions and their subsequent commemorations. Ix K'ab'al Xok's costume once again relates her to sacrifice and the procreative powers of the waters of the underworld.

The headdress and shield were important items that conferred the power of rule and were given to a new ruler by close family members. On Lintel 26 Ix K'ab'al Xok, Itzamnah B'ahläm's wife, presents him with symbols of his rule—the war headdress and flexible shield. At Palenque Janab' Päkal and his wife are shown on the Palace Tablet with their son K'än Joy Chitam II sitting between them. Päkal presents his son with the "drum major" headdress on his accession day, while his mother presents him with an effigy of the tok'-päkal. Each sits on one of the three platforms/thrones. On the Palenque Oval Palace Tablet Ix Säk K'uk ("Lady Resplendent Quetzal"), the mother of Päkal, presents him with the "drum major" headdress as he sits on a double-headed jaguar platform/throne (Martin and Grube 2000: 161, 171). On Lintel 26 and the Tikal vase the ruler receives a Tlaloc-Venus war shield and his headdress or mask. All these scenes are local variants of an important part of the Maya accession ceremony.

The jaguar platform/throne represents the canonical masculine domain of warfare, and it was the first stone set up at the time of the Creation (Looper 2003: 158, 163). The war imagery on Lintel 26 relates the lintel to this stone, and the water iconography of the costumes relates to the Tlaloc-Venus war and the underworld into which sacrificed warriors descend to be reborn. The West was associated with war, and Lintel 26 was over the western door of Ix K'ab'al Xok's house. Palenque's Temple of the Sun, the westernmost building of the Cross Group, also featured war imagery. This building was dedicated to the god GIII, the Palenque version of the Jaguar War God. On Yaxchilán Lintel 26 the Water Jaguar, an avatar of the Jaguar War God, is featured as a headdress. On the central panel of the Temple of the Sun, crossed flint-tipped spears and a Jaguar War God shield rise from a platform/throne that has two snake heads and two Water Jaguar heads, indicating sacrifice and war. In this temple Kàan B'ahläm appears on one of the outer panels holding a jaguar on a small throne and on the other wearing a Tlaloc-Venus war costume. On the central panel he holds a personified tok'-päkal. A text that mentions his accession is located above the Jaguar War Shield (Schele and Freidel 1990: 243–245). Much of the imagery seen in the Temple of the Sun also occurs on Yaxchilán Lintel 25 and Lintel 26. The Temple of the Sun panel and the two lintels all relate to the ruler's accession. Above all, Itzamnah B'ahläm saw himself as a war leader, and it was under the floor of Room 3, spanned by Lintel 26, that his burial was found (García Moll 2004: 269–270).

Lintel 26: Front Edge

The date on the front edge of Lintel 26 contains an error and should agree with the one given for the same dedication on Lintel 23, which is 9.14.14.13.17 6 Kab'an 15 Yaxk'in (AD June 23, 726; McAnany and Plank 2001: 105). This was the date of the dedication of the House of Ix K'ab'al Xok when fire or incense was brought into the building to form a hearth, thereby investing it with heat and strength and animating the structure (Stuart 1998: 417–418). June 23 was near the summer solstice and was the date of a lunar eclipse, which may have been relevant in the selection of this date for dedicating the building. The front edge of Lintel 26 is somewhat eroded, but after the dedication date the name of Structure 23, the name of Ix K'ab'al Xok, her titles, and the "his earth, his cave" phrase can be read. The text ends with the name of Itzamnah B'ahläm and his title "Holy Yaxchilán Lord." On AD June 23, 726, Structure 23, the House of Ix K'ab'al Xok, was completely finished and activated.

CONCLUSION

The House of Ix K'ab'al Xok was a special structure at Yaxchilán where Itzamnah B'ahläm commemorated his accession and dynastic refounding rites. It may have been built or renovated to celebrate these events, which reactivated the city as a power and restored the continuity of the B'ahläm Dynasty. Although owned by a woman, this building was also a Founder House where the new ruler and his wife engaged in rituals that linked his dynasty to the Tlaloc-Venus war cult and Teotihuacan, reinforcing its power. Royal women played a particularly important role in Maya dynastic refounding rites.

Each of the three figural lintels that spanned the front doorways of the House of Ix K'ab'al Xok was associated with one of the three stones of Creation, which codified ritual domains fundamental to Maya thought. These lintels connected Itzamnah B'ahläm and Ix K'ab'al Xok to the supernatural realm, portraying them engaging in scenes based on the Maya mythological cycle. These scenes commemorate Itzamnah B'ahläm's accession and refounding rites, enhancing the legitimacy and continuity of rule by showing the royal couple performing actions canonized by the three stones of Creation. Archaic and foreign costume elements served to establish a connection with the past and with foreign military power and to emphasize the special nature of these rites. Costume elements on all three lintels associate the actors with the watery surface of the underworld, rebirth, sacrifice, and war.

Lintel 24 focuses on sacrifice and illustrates the ideal way for a ruler and his wife to conjure and provide sustenance for the gods. Itzamnah B'ahläm wears a rope collar indicating self-sacrifice and a decapitated head signifying sacrifice of a captive taken in war. Ix K'ab'al Xok pulls a thorned rope through her tongue, letting her blood and simultaneously performing the act that will bring forth the War Serpent. Lintel 24 is associated with the snake platform/throne, which codifies bloodletting and ancestor communication and is associated with K'awil and conjuring. This platform/throne is linked to the female gender because of women's role in birth.

Lintel 25 portrays the pivotal accession/refounding ritual. The War Serpent has been conjured and is shown with the founder of the Itzamnah B'ahläm Dynasty (the local patron of the Tlaloc-Venus war cult), emerging from the jaws of its larger head. This may also be the moment of rebirth of the new ruler who, by merging with the spirit of the founder of his dynasty, accepted the obligation of war and reactivated his city and his line. Ix K'ab'al Xok communes with the ancestor and witnesses this important event, having previously conjured the War Serpent with her husband. She presents him with the flexible ceremonial bar held by kings at accession. Lintel 25 is associated with the water platform/throne, which codifies birth and resurrection and is linked to accession, Itzamnah, the Cosmic Monster/War Serpent, and to youth because it is the youngest stone. Ordinarily, it is the Cosmic Monster that is shown on accession monuments, but the War Serpent takes its place on Lintel 25.

Lintel 26 focuses on the investiture of the new ruler. Itzamnah B'ahläm receives items that embody the power of rule and war from Ix K'ab'al Xok during his accession rites. The scene on Lintel 26 is a Yaxchilán variation of the same ceremony seen at other Maya cities such as Palenque and Tikal. Lintel 26 is associated with the jaguar platform/throne, which codifies the masculine domain of war. This platform/throne is linked to the Jaguar War God.

Ix K'ab'al Xok owned and dedicated a Founder House and played a prominent role in her husband's accession and dynastic refounding rites. At other Maya cities, such as Naranjo and Sak Nikté, prominent royal women from other cities arrived to refound local dynasties. They carried the powers of creation and war. These women, like Ix K'ab'al Xok, were important in the Tlaloc-Venus war cult and in the rites that reestablished the dynasties at those cities. It was the role of important royal women to perform sacrifice. This was the canonical female ritual role codified by the snake platform/throne, one of the three stones set up at the time of the Creation, although the ruler also performed sacrifice on important occasions.

Ix K'ab'al Xok may also have had important family ties that gave her the status and power to help refound her husband's dynasty and ensure his accession.

Her male relatives from Yaxchilán may have gained in power during Itzamnah B'ahläm's struggle for independence and rule. Increasing warfare in the Maya area may have led to the increasing significance of female dynastic lines and greater power for women. Perhaps at marriage she received the Founder House and the right to picture herself participating in Itzamnah B'ahläm's accession rites; in return, he received loyal supporters in his fight to gain the throne. It is possible that her maternal line had links to Palenque, as the iconography of the lintels of her house is somewhat similar to that of the buildings in the Cross Group at that city. Limited information on her family background prevents a more complete understanding of her connection with any outside city. Notwithstanding her possible origins as an outsider, her status at Yaxchilán was an exalted one no previous or subsequent royal woman attained.

NOTES

1. Martin (2004: 4, 6) translates the Yaxchilán emblem glyph as *pa' chan* ("split/broken sky"). In this chapter Maya word spelling and translations of hieroglyphs are taken from Macri and Looper (2003b) whenever possible. These authorities (2003b: 7) note that phonetic and morphological evidence suggests that most of the Classic Period inscriptions are best understood as a Ch'olan language rather than Yukatekan.

2. See Macri and Looper for the meanings of the hieroglyphs for *itzamnah* (2003b: 170) and *b'ahläm* (80). The English translation of Itzamnah B'ahläm has been popularly rendered as "Shield Jaguar," but *itzamnah* may mean "obsidian mirror," alluding to divination.

3. See Macri and Looper for the meanings of the hieroglyphs for *ix* (2003b: 134), *k'a* (ibid.: 126), *b'a* (ibid.: 181), *al* (*la*) (ibid.: 69), and *xok* (ibid.: 53). See Josserand (2007: 297) for a discussion of the name Ix K'ab'al Xok.

4. Many explanations have been proposed for the function of Structure 23. McAnany and Plank (2001: 111, 119) see it as a women's house in the court of Itzamnah B'ahläm, a place where he would go to receive "political and military empowerment that perhaps only a royal woman can provide," but few buildings were owned and dedicated by royal women. Linda Schele and David Freidel (1990: 270–271) view Structure 23 as an example of "a grand compromise" by Itzamnah B'ahläm, who wished to honor an alliance with Ix K'ab'al Xok's family but designate as his heir a son born to another wife from Calakmul. New data suggest that he did not designate the son of his foreign wife as his heir and that another son succeeded him (Martin and Grube 2000: 127; Josserand 2007: 307–308). Several studies have discussed or portrayed Structure 23's history (García Moll and Juárez Cossío 1986; Tate 1986, 1992; Mathews 1988, 1997; Clancy 2002), political significance (Schele and Freidel 1990: 265–282), genealogical and kinship information (Jones, Jones, and Marhenke 1990; Robin 2001; Josserand 2007), monuments (García Moll 1977, 1978; Graham and Von Euw 1977, 1979, 1982), its place in the royal court of Yaxchilán (McAnany and Plank 2001: 99–124), and its burials (García Moll 2004). An analysis of its hieroglyphic texts is found in McAnany and Plank (2001: 103–124), Schele (1991), and Tate (1986, 1992). Tate (1992) provides a study of the entire site.

5. The Tlaloc-Venus war cult was adopted by the Maya. It originated in the Central Mexican city of Teotihuacan, and by the time of Itzamnah B'ahläm, Maya cities had

their own versions of this cult. Looper (2003: 40) defines the Tlaloc-Venus war cult as "a martial complex of ritual and iconography adopted by the Maya from Teotihuacan." Geoffrey Braswell (2003: 138) says this war cult is called "Star war," "Venus war," or "Tlaloc-Venus war." According to David Freidel, Linda Schele, and Joy Parker (1993: 296), Tlaloc-Venus warfare involved the conquest of territory and the taking of captives for sacrifice. Battles were sometimes timed to coincide with the cycles of Venus (Harris and Stearns 1997: 129–135). War costumes were characterized by such Mexican elements as the balloon headdress (Schele and Freidel 1990: 146–148), the Mexican Year sign (Carlson 1993: 209, 212), goggle-eyed Tlaloc masks, flexible shields, the round shield emblazoned with the face of the Jaguar War God (Jaguar God of the Underworld; Miller and Martin 2004: 165), the mosaic platelet War Serpent headdress (Stone 1989: 158), and the *tok'-päkal* (flint and shield; Knowlton 2002: 10–11). The Classic Maya saw these elements as foreign and used the war cult to reinforce the power of their dynasties. The appearance of the Tlaloc-Venus war cult in the Maya area coincides with the regimes of particularly powerful and ambitious rulers, and the use of the Tlaloc-Venus war costume is tied to periods of political expansion (Stone 1989: 164).

6. The fact that Structure 23 has five doorways could indicate a connection to the supernatural location called *Ho'-Janab' Witz* ("Five-Flower Mountain"). Looper (2003: 68–71) refers to "Five-Flower place." This was believed to be the place where the rebirth of maize and the War Serpent occurred. Because of this association with rebirth, buildings with tombs of important royalty could be called Five-Flower Mountain (Wagner 2000a: 34; Taube 2002; Escobedo 2004: 277). Such tombs were found in Structure 23 (García Moll 2004) and the War Serpent was conjured there, so it is possible that Structure 23 was seen as a Five-Flower Mountain.

7. The text of the underside of Lintel 23 mentions Itzamnah B'ahläm's twenty-fifth accession anniversary, his titles, the "fire-entering" of Structure 23, its name, Ix K'ab'al Xok's titles, and Itzamnah B'ahläm's name. The front edge mentions a doorway modification and dedication by Ix K'ab'al Xok. For translations, see also Jones, Jones, and Marhenke (1990); Josserand (2007: 300–306); Schele (1991: 96–98, 110–112); Tate (1986: 11–12, 1992: 276).

8. Schele and Mathews (1998: 46–47) suggest that long-nosed deities of architectural sculpture could depict several gods. It is not clear how these masks originally looked, but it is possible that they represented one of the rain deities, possibly the lightning spirits *Yo'at/Yo'pat* mentioned by Looper (2003: 4, 29, 231n6). These lightning spirits cracked open the back of the cosmic turtle at the time of the Creation so that maize could be reborn. Structure 23 was an accession building, and these were symbolic places of rebirth (ibid.: 237n13). Another possibility is that the masks represented O-Chahk, a local deity. Looper believes (ibid.: 29) that the Chahks "can be grouped into a single complex, based on their shared iconography and associations with thunderstorms and the portals between realms of the cosmos." García Moll reports (2004: 268) that today little remains of the exterior stucco decoration of Structure 23, so it may not be possible to reconstruct its original appearance.

9. *Otot* refers to a house that was owned by someone, while a *na* (or *nah*) is the more general term for "structure." It is not clear whether *otot* denoted a residential building because some were owned by gods or had other functions (McAnany and Plank 2001: 100–101; Stuart 1998: 376–378). Structure 23 is described as Ix K'ab'al Xok's otot on the lintels of the building (*y* or *y-otot*).

10. The name of Structure 23, possibly *Ok K'in Hul-Nal*, is given on Lintel 23 (Graham and Von Euw 1982: 136; Schele 1991: 110–111). *Okol K'in* has been translated as "Entering Sun" or "Sunset" (Coggins 1988: 70); John Montgomery (2002: 154) offers "? Sun Water-Place" as an alternative meaning. I suggest the name may refer to a place of arrival or rebirth in the West, but the precise meaning of the name of the building is unclear. See Macri and Looper (2003b: 238) for the "moon sign" in its meaning of *hul*, or "arrive."

11. The text of the underside of Lintel 24 has been translated by Michael Coe and Mark Van Stone (2001: 138), Schele (1991: 84–89), and Tate (1986: 10, 1992: 276).

12. The meaning of *hu-lu* in the main text is probably "arrival." His "fiery arrival" must refer to the War Serpent, a fiery being, who was conjured up during Itzamnah B'ahläm's accession and refounding rites. See the discussion of the War Serpent under Lintel 25: Underside. See also note 20.

13. Flora Clancy (2002: 31–32) discusses the meaning of the name Aj Nich ("Flower Lord"); Montgomery (2001: 135–136) says Aj Nich's capture was significant in Itzamnah B'ahläm's campaign to achieve independence for Yaxchilán. Aj Nich was sacrificed just prior to Itzamnah B'ahläm's accession, and his importance could result from the fact that he was the previous ruler of Yaxchilán or a rival for the throne. In the Maya area the ritual death of a ruler through a surrogate human sacrifice was followed by his mystical rebirth (Looper 2003: 105–106). Aj Nich appears to have played the role of surrogate in Itzamnah B'ahläm's accession and dynastic refounding rites.

14. The jewelry worn by figures on the lintels of Structure 23 may have been made of jade, but the Maya used other greenstones in making jewelry. Sometimes stuccoed ceramic beads were also used. Some of these were found in a necklace from a female burial at Altar de Sacrificios, along with similarly made disks and pendants (Bruhns and Stothert 1999: 14–15). Such jewelry may have been heirlooms.

15. Macri and Looper (2003a: 288–289) discuss the *(y)óol* (often written *ol*), which they say exists in the Yukatekan and Nahua languages but not in Ch'olan. It is usually translated as "heart" in Classic Maya inscriptions but refers specifically to the abstract concept of "life, energy, spirit." It may mean "half" or "middle" from the Ch'ol word *ojlil*, or "hole," "well," "opening," "cave," or "door" from the Itzaj word *hol*, or "almost" from the Yukatek *óolak*.

16. Carlson believes (1993: 209, 212–213) that when the Mexican Trapeze-and-Ray Year sign appears in the Tlaloc-Venus warfare complex, often as a warrior's headdress element, it represents a *xiuhmolpilli*, a "binding of the years" bundle—specifically the binding of eight years—symbolizing the five-Venus cycle/eight-year Venus Almanac. This sign is a conflation of the binding straps of a year bundle with the interwoven symbols for the solar year, the "ray," and the Venus cycle, the "trapeze." Whoever wears this insignia embodies the Venus Almanac and becomes the divine personification of the Tlaloc-Venus war cult.

17. According to Tate (1992: 117, 243), Stela 19, which was located at the center of the lower terrace of Structure 41, is another possibility for Itzamnah B'ahläm's accession monument. It is likely that he commissioned this stela to record his accession and consequently emplaced it at the highest point of the city, in front of Structure 41. Stela 19 is another retrospective monument, and it is earlier than Structure 23.

18. There are several explanations for mirror image texts. Houston posits (1998: 341–342) that gods are sometimes shown in reverse order, the underworld court being a

mirror image of palace life in dynastic centers. He explains the text of Lintel 25 as reversed because "the reader approaches through a doorway to gaze up at glyphs that have been reoriented to face the viewer." Looper indicates (2003: 23) that mirror image texts "may imply that the texts were meant to be read through the walls or from the sky, that is, by a divine audience." Palka notes (2002: 432) "that the mirrored or reversed designs were intended by the artists to make the sculptures, their creators, and the people depicted more unique, powerful, and in closer contact with deities, ancestors, and sacred realms." The mirror image text of Structure 10L-11 at Copán has scenes of ancestors called up to participate in an accession (Schele and Miller 1986: 124). Houston states (1998: 342) that these texts were oriented so they faced a corridor entrance.

19. The text of the underside of Lintel 25 has been translated by Freidel, Schele, and Parker (1993: 208, 308–309), Mathews (1997: 155, 159), McAnany and Plank (2001: 107), Schele (1991: 69–79), and Tate (1986: 10, 1992: 276).

20. *Hu-lu* has been translated as "perforator" by Schele (1991: 76), but Lintel 24 has a text similar to that of Lintel 25 (Graham and Von Euw 1979: 93), and the glyph used there is the one meaning "to be born" or "to arrive" (Macri and Looper 2003b: 64–65). Therefore, I think the text on Lintel 25 is saying that what is being conjured is the "arrival" or "birth" of the War Serpent.

21. "The image of Ix Ol of the Founder House" is the way this phrase has customarily been translated. *Ix Ol* has been rendered as Lady of the "Heart" or "Center" (McAnany and Plank 2001: 107). According to Stuart (cited in McAnany and Plank 2001: 107n6), it is odd that the phrase is not carved nearer to the kneeling figure of Ix K'ab'al Xok, as names of carved figures often are, and that it is possible that it refers to something or someone else in the figural scene. On Stela 6 at Itzimté a female holding a serpent she has conjured has similar glyphs in her headdress that, in this case, probably give her name, Ix Yohl (Mejía, García Campillo, and Laporte 2005: 39). Schele (1991: 71) proposed a different translation of *na wa la*, or *nawal*, a Nahua word similar in meaning to *way* in the Maya area. Way, or nawal, is the name for the animal and spirit companions who shared the souls of human beings (Schele and Mathews 1998: 417). Schele (1991: 71) believes the phrase relates to the War Serpent. This solves the problem of the location because if it refers to the War Serpent, then it is in the right place, close to the larger head. This eliminates speculation as to whether the phrase refers to the emerging warrior or to Ix K'ab'al Xok, and it places the focus of the scene on the War Serpent, the largest figure on the monument. I believe this translation provides the best and most meaningful translation and that the phrase should read "The image of the Nawal of the Founder House." *Wi-Na* has been translated by Schele and Mathews (1998: 79) as "Root Structure" or "Origin Structure." *Wi-Te-Na* is translated as "Root Structure" or "Origin Tree Structure." These structures were Founder Houses.

22. Looper (2003: 103–104) indicates that, as a scepter, K'awil seems to have had particularly close associations with royal blood and bloodlines. This symbolism is particularly conveyed by means of the transformation of its leg into a serpent. Karl Taube states (2000a: 268) that K'awil embodied the manifestation and rebirth of gods and ancestors. The god O-Chahk is shown on the knobbed end of a bone perforator found in the tomb of Itzamnah B'ahläm (García Moll 2004: 270; Miller and Martin 2004: 112–113). Other carved bones were found in his tomb: incised on one was the name "B'olon Ka-la Chahk." Bone perforators were put through slits made during bloodletting rites when

gods or ancestors were conjured from the supernatural realm (Schele 1991: 76–77, 190–191), and therefore O-Chahk, who held the fiery decapitation ax associated with conjuring, was a good choice for the head of a perforator.

23. Venus signs resembling the Maya sign for zero were also used at Tikal. Schele and Mathews (1998: 72) suggest that the signs are related to the "star" and "Venus" symbols used at Teotihuacan and other western Mesoamerican sites. The crossed-bands sign represents a pectoral element that also occurs in the Quadripartite Badge (Looper 2003: 164–165), and it is also infixed within quatrefoils (Looper 2000: 18). The eye of the front head of the Cosmic Monster often includes a Venus or a crossed-bands sign (Schele and Miller 1986: figure 22). Therefore, these signs point to the War Serpent's relationship to the Cosmic Monster.

24. Susan Milbrath (1999: 297) states that on Itzamnah B'ahläm's accession day, Venus appeared high in the sky as the evening star and was passing by Antares, a star in Scorpius. If so, this may have been considered an auspicious time to conjure the spirit of the dynastic founder. Another astronomical event that may have influenced the selection of his accession day and the summoning of the local patron of the Tlaloc-Venus war cult was the Orionid meteor shower, which occurs every year between October 16 and October 22 (ibid.: 56). In Central Mexico and the Maya area, meteors were related to the War Serpent, weapons, and warfare (Taube 2000b: 298–301).

25. At Chichén Itzá the origin of the War Serpent may be pictured on the walls of the South Temple, associated with the Great Ballcourt. Panels on the end walls appear to show the birth of the War Serpent during the Creation from the nose or breath of maize. It emerged with a standing warrior in its jaws (Schele and Mathews 1998: 244–245).

26. *Ch'ahom(a)* ("Scatterer," "Censer") (Macri and Looper 2003b: 142) was a common Classic Period title that referred to the scattering of drops of incense. It is likely, according to Looper (2003: 13), that blood and other precious substances were burned along with the incense.

27. Martin (2004: 3n5) translates the glyphs as *uyokte'el* ("foot of the tree of") Tan-Ha'Yaxchilán. This phrase might be metaphorical, meaning that Ix K'ab'al Xok is the "pillar" of the place. I suggest it may alternatively mean she is the pillar of the Founder House. Tan-Ha'Yaxchilán is the name of the location of her house.

28. Goddesses of the Postclassic codices wear a serpent headdress in several depictions (Vail and Stone 2002: figures 11.2f, 11.6a). This headband may have been adopted from Teotihuacan. A monumental relief carving at that city in the Street of the Dead Complex incorporates a double-headed serpent headdress (Carlson 1993: 215).

29. The text of the front edge of Lintel 25 has been translated by McAnany and Plank (2001: 105–107), Schele (1991: 94–95), and Tate (1986: 10–11, 1992: 276).

30. The texts of the underside and front edge of Lintel 26 have been translated by Schele (1991: 99–100) and Tate (1986: 11, 1992: 276–277).

31. Schele (1991: 100) translated the glyphs as *xe ki ba le* or *xekbal*, but the meaning of this is not known. Another possible translation is *b'ak* or *jol* ("head") *b'a-le(l)* ("watery"?), which may refer to the Water Jaguar headdress (see Macri and Looper 2003b: 155, 181–182). The same glyphs also appear on a lintel from another city that shows Itzamnah B'ahläm wearing the headdress on his head (ibid.: figures 104, 120).

32. The *K'inich*, or "Sun-Faced," title (Macri and Looper 2003b: 162) used by the Maya rulers refers here to the setting sun because the Jaguar War God, who was associ-

ated with the underworld sun, embodied the number seven. The day sun was the lord of the number four (Milbrath 1999: 103). Looper says (2003: 27) "sun-faced," or "sun-eyed," refers to the searing heat and brilliant light believed to emanate from a ruler's face or eyes.

33. David Freidel and Charles Suhler (1999: 266) translate Säk Hunal as "White Eternity, White Oneness." Montgomery gives (2002: 213) *säk* as "white," "resplendent," or "pure."

34. In the Postclassic *Dresden Codex* the Water-Lily Jaguar appears with the name glyph prefixed by T109, "red" or "great" (Milbrath 1999: 120). Taube interprets (2000a: figure 411) this as Chak (Chahk) B'alhäm.

35. Flexible shields could be rolled up for carrying and were part of the war costume at several Maya cities such as Toniná (Miller 1998: 213–214), Palenque (Schele and Freidel 1990: 243), and Tikal (Montgomery 2001: 78).

36. Mary Miller and Karl Taube state (1993: 98) that the act of sacrificial bloodletting was commonly compared to the hummingbird sucking nectar from a flower. In the Lower Temple of the Jaguars at Chichén Itzá, a hummingbird is shown piercing the heart of a man emerging from a flower. Looper notes (2003: 165) that the hummingbird had martial and ancestral associations in Aztec culture, and among the Maya there is some evidence for similar associations. Birds-and-flowers headbands are seen on Teotihuacan figurines, especially female ones, after AD 450 (Schele and Mathews 1998: 229), so this headband may have been adopted from that city.

REFERENCES CITED

Braswell, Geoffrey E.
    2003   Understanding Early Classic Interaction between Kaminaljuyu and Central Mexico. In *The Maya and Teotihuacan: Reinterpreting Early Classic Interaction*, ed. Geoffrey E. Braswell, pp. 105–142. University of Texas Press, Austin.

Bruhns, Karen Olsen, and Karen E. Stothert
    1999   *Women in Ancient America*. University of Oklahoma Press, Norman.

Carlson, John
    1993   Venus-Regulated Warfare and Ritual Sacrifice in Mesoamerica. In *Astronomies and Cultures*, ed. C.L.N. Ruggles and N. J. Saunders, pp. 202–252. University Press of Colorado, Boulder.

Clancy, Flora Simmons
    1986   Text and Image in the Tablets of the Cross Group at Palenque. *Res* 11: 17–32.
    2002   Shield Jaguar's Monuments. *Res* 42: 23–33.

Coe, Michael D.
    1975   *Classic Maya Pottery at Dumbarton Oaks*. Dumbarton Oaks, Washington, DC.

Coe, Michael D., and Mark Van Stone
    2001   *Reading the Maya Glyphs*. Thames and Hudson, London.

Coggins, Clemency Anne
    1988   Classic Maya Metaphors of Death and Life. *Res* 16: 63–84.
    2002   Toltec. *Res* 42: 34–85.

Dillon, Brian Dervin, and Wes Christensen
  2005 The Maya Jade Skull Bead: 700 Years as a Military Insignia? In *Archaeology without Limits: Papers in Honor of Clement W. Meighan*, ed. Brian Dervin Dillon and Matthew A. Boxt, pp. 369–388. Labyrinthos, Lancaster, CA.

Escobedo, Hector L.
  2004 Tales from the Crypt: The Burial Place of Ruler 4, Piedras Negras. In *Courtly Art of the Ancient Maya*, ed. Mary Miller and Simon Martin, pp. 277–279. Fine Arts Museum of San Francisco. Thames and Hudson, New York.

Freidel, David, and Stanley Guenter
  2003 Bearers of War and Creation. Electronic document, http://www.archaeology.org/magazine.php?page=online/features/siteq2/index.

Freidel, David, Linda Schele, and Joy Parker
  1993 *Maya Cosmos: Three Thousand Years on the Shaman's Path*. William Morrow, New York.

Freidel, David, and Charles Suhler
  1999 The Path of Life: Toward a Functional Analysis of Ancient Maya Architecture. In *Mesoamerican Architecture as a Cultural Symbol*, ed. Jeff Karl Kowalski, pp. 250–273. Oxford University Press, London.

García-Des Lauriers, Claudia
  2000 Trappings of Sacred War: The Warrior Costume of Teotihuacan. MA thesis, Department of Anthropology, University of California, Riverside.

García Moll, Roberto
  1977 Los escalones labrados del edificio 33, Yaxchilán, Chiapas. *Revista Mexicana de Estudios Antropológicos* 23: 395–423.
  1978 Conservación de monumentos en Yaxchilán, Chiapas. *Revista Mexicana de Estudios Antropológicos* 24: 257–286.
  2004 Shield Jaguar and Structure 23 at Yaxchilán. In *Courtly Art of the Ancient Maya*, ed. Mary Miller and Simon Martin, pp. 268–270. Fine Arts Museum of San Francisco. Thames and Hudson, New York.

García Moll, Roberto, and Daniel Juárez Cossío
  1986 *Yaxchilán. Antología de su descubrimiento y estudios*. INAH, Serie Arqueología, México, DF.

Graham, Ian, and Eric Von Euw
  1977 *Corpus of Maya Hieroglyphic Inscriptions*, vol. 3, Part 1: *Yaxchilán*. Peabody Museum of Archaeology and Ethnology, Harvard University, Cambridge, MA.
  1979 *Corpus of Maya Hieroglyphic Inscriptions*, vol. 3, Part 2: *Yaxchilán*. Peabody Museum of Archaeology and Ethnology, Harvard University, Cambridge, MA.
  1982 *Corpus of Maya Hieroglyphic Inscriptions*, vol. 3, Part 3: *Yaxchilán*. Peabody Museum of Archaeology and Ethnology, Harvard University, Cambridge, MA.

Harris, John F., and Stephen K. Stearns
  1997 *Understanding Maya Inscriptions: A Hieroglyphic Handbook*. University of Pennsylvania Museum of Archaeology and Anthropology, Philadelphia.

Houston, Stephen D.
    1998   Classic Maya Depictions of the Built Environment. In *Function and Meaning in Classic Maya Architecture*, ed. Stephen D. Houston, pp. 333–372. Dumbarton Oaks, Washington, DC.
    2004   The Acropolis of Piedras Negras: Portrait of a Court System. In *Courtly Art of the Ancient Maya*, ed. Mary Miller and Simon Martin, pp. 271–276. Fine Arts Museum of San Francisco. Thames and Hudson, New York.

Jones, Tom, Carolyn Jones, and Randa Marhenke
    1990   Blood Cousins: The Xok-Balam Connection at Yaxchilán. *U Mut Maya* 3: 99–114.

Josserand, J. Kathryn
    2002   Women in Classic Maya Hieroglyphic Texts. In *Ancient Maya Women*, ed. Traci Ardren, pp. 114–151. Altamira, Walnut Creek, CA.
    2007   The Missing Heir at Yaxchilán: Literary Analysis of a Maya Historical Puzzle. *Latin American Antiquity* 18: 295–318.

Kahn, Anna Lee
    1994   Some Themes Concerning the Icon of Woman in Maya Vessel Painting. *U Mut Maya* 5: 140–158.

Kerr, Justin, ed.
    1989   *The Maya Vase Book*, vol. 1. Kerr and Associates, New York.

Knowlton, Timothy
    2002   Diphrastic Kennings in Mayan Hieroglyphic Literature. *Mexicon* 24: 9–14.

Looper, Matthew
    2000   *Gifts of the Moon: Huipil Designs of the Ancient Maya*. Textile Reconstructions by Thomas Tolles. San Diego Museum of Man, San Diego, CA.
    2002   Women-Men (and Men-Women): Classic Maya Rulers and the Third Gender. In *Ancient Maya Women*, ed. Traci Ardren, pp. 171–202. Altamira, Walnut Creek, CA.
    2003   *Lightning Warrior*. University of Texas Press, Austin.

Macri, Martha J., and Matthew G. Looper
    2003a   Nahua in Ancient Mesoamerica: Evidence from Maya Inscriptions. *Ancient Mesoamerica* 14: 285–297.
    2003b   *The New Catalog of Maya Hieroglyphs*, vol. 1: *The Classic Period Inscriptions*. University of Oklahoma Press, Norman.

Maler, Teobert
    1901–1903   *Researches in the Central Portion of the Usumatsintla Valley: Report of Explorations for the Museum, 1898–1900*. Memoirs of the Peabody Museum of Archaeology and Ethnology 2. Harvard University, Cambridge, MA.

Manzanilla, Linda
    2003   Teotihuacan and Maya Relations: A Review of Archaeological Data. Paper presented at the Tenth Annual Maya Weekend, Institute of Archaeology, UCLA, Los Angeles, CA, October 11.

Martin, Simon
    2004   A Broken Sky: The Ancient Name of Yaxchilán as *Pa' Chan*. *PARI Journal* 5 (1): 1–7.

Martin, Simon, and Nikolai Grube
    2000   *Chronicle of the Maya Kings and Queens: Deciphering the Dynasties of the Ancient Maya*. Thames and Hudson, London.

Mathews, Peter
    1988   The Sculpture of Yaxchilán. Unpublished PhD dissertation, Department of Anthropology, Yale University, New Haven, CT.
    1997   *La escultura de Yaxchilán*. INAH, México, DF.

McAnany, Patricia A., and Shannon Plank
    2001   Perspectives on Actors, Gender Roles, and Architecture at Classic Maya Courts and Households. In *Royal Courts of the Ancient Maya*, vol. 1, ed. Takeshi Inomata and Stephen D. Houston, pp. 84–129. Westview, Boulder, CO.

Mejía, Héctor E., José Miguel García Campillo, and Juan Pedro Laporte
    2005   La Estela 6 de Itzimté, Petén, Guatemala. *Mexicon* 27: 37–40.

Milbrath, Susan
    1999   *Star Gods of the Maya: Astronomy in Art, Folklore, and Calendars*. University of Texas Press, Austin.

Miller, Mary
    1998   A Design for Meaning in Maya Architecture. In *Function and Meaning in Maya Architecture*, ed. Stephen D. Houston, pp. 187–222. Dumbarton Oaks, Washington, DC.

Miller, Mary, and Simon Martin
    2004   *Courtly Art of the Ancient Maya*. Thames and Hudson, New York.

Miller, Mary, and Karl Taube
    1993   *The Gods and Symbols of Ancient Mexico and the Maya: An Illustrated Dictionary of Mesoamerican Religion*. Thames and Hudson, London.

Montgomery, John
    2001   *Tikal: An Illustrated History*. Hippocrene Books, New York.
    2002   *Dictionary of Maya Hieroglyphs*. Hippocrene Books, New York.

Palka, Joel W.
    2002   Left/Right Symbolism and the Body in Ancient Maya Iconography and Culture. *Latin American Antiquity* 13 (4): 419–443.

Pasztory, Esther
    1997   *Teotihuacan: An Experiment in Living*. University of Oklahoma Press, Norman.

Reents-Budet, Dorie
    1994   *Painting the Maya Universe: Royal Ceramics of the Classic Period*. Duke University Press, Durham, NC.

Robicsek, Francis
    1979   Mythological Identity of God K. In *Tercera Mesa Redonda de Palenque, Palenque Round Table Series*, vol. 4, ed. Merle Robertson and Donnan Jeffers, pp. 111–128. PARI, Monterey, CA.

Robin, Cynthia
    2001   Kin and Gender in Classic Maya Society: A Case Study from Yaxchilán, Mexico. In *New Directions in Anthropological Kinship*, ed. Linda Stone, pp. 204–228. Rowman and Littlefield, New York.

Schele, Linda
    1991   *The Proceedings of the Maya Hieroglyphic Workshop*, March 9–10, 1991. University of Texas, Austin.

Schele, Linda, and David Freidel
    1990   *A Forest of Kings: The Untold Story of the Ancient Maya*. William Morrow, New York.

Schele, Linda, and Nikolai Grube
    1994   Tlaloc-Venus Warfare: The Peten Wars. In *Notebook for the XVIIIth Maya Hieroglyphic Workshop at Texas*, ed. Timothy Albright, pp. 79–167. Department of Art and Art History, College of Fine Arts, Center for Mexican Studies, and Institute of Latin American Studies, University of Texas, Austin, March 13–14.

Schele, Linda, and Peter Mathews
    1998   *The Code of Kings: The Language of Seven Sacred Maya Temples and Tombs*. Scribner, New York.

Schele, Linda, and Mary Ellen Miller
    1986   *Blood of Kings: Dynasty and Ritual in Maya Art*. Kimball Art Museum, Fort Worth, TX.

Stone, Andrea
    1989   Disconnection, Foreign Insignia, and Political Expansion: Teotihuacan and the Warrior Stelae of Piedras Negras. In *Mesoamerica after the Decline of Teotihuacan, A.D. 700–900*, ed. Richard A. Diehl and Janet Catherine Berlo, pp. 153–172. Dumbarton Oaks, Washington, DC.

Stuart, David
    1998   "The Fire Enters His House": Architecture and Ritual in Classic Maya Texts. In *Function and Meaning in Classic Maya Architecture*, ed. Stephen D. Houston, pp. 373–425. Dumbarton Oaks, Washington, DC.
    2004   New Year Records in Classic Maya Inscriptions. *PARI Journal* 5 (2): 1–6.

Tate, Carolyn E.
    1986   Maya Astronomical Rituals Recorded on Yaxchilán Structure 23. *Rutgers Art Review* 7: 1–20.
    1992   *Yaxchilán: The Design of a Maya Ceremonial City*. University of Texas Press, Austin.

Taube, Karl A.
- 1992a *The Major Gods of Ancient Yucatan.* Studies in Pre-Columbian Art and Archaeology 32. Dumbarton Oaks, Washington, DC.
- 1992b The Temple of Quetzalcoatl and the Cult of Sacred War at Teotihuacan. *Res* 21: 53–87.
- 1998 The Jade Hearth: Centrality, Rulership, and the Classic Maya Temple. In *Function and Meaning in Classic Maya Architecture*, ed. Stephen D. Houston, pp. 427–478. Dumbarton Oaks, Washington, DC.
- 2000a The Classic Maya Gods. In *Maya: Divine Kings of the Rain Forest*, ed. Nikolai Grube, pp. 262–277. Könemann, Cologne, Germany.
- 2000b The Turquoise Hearth: Fire, Self-Sacrifice, and the Central Mexican Cult of War. In *Mesoamerica's Classic Heritage: Teotihuacan to the Aztecs*, ed. Davíd Carrasco, Lindsay Jones, and Scott Sessions, pp. 269–340. University of Colorado Press, Boulder.
- 2002 The Symbolism of Music among the Classic Maya. Paper presented at the Ninth Annual Maya Weekend, Cotsen Institute of Archaeology, UCLA, Los Angeles, CA, October 6.

Vail, Gabrielle, and Andrea Stone
- 2002 Representations of Women in Postclassic and Colonial Maya Literature and Art. In *Ancient Maya Women*, ed. T. Ardren, pp. 203–228. Altamira, Walnut Creek, CA.

Wagner, Elisabeth
- 2000a An Alternative View of the Meaning and Function of Structure 10L–22a, Copan, Honduras. In *The Sacred and the Profane: Architecture and Identity in the Maya Lowlands*, ed. Pierre R. Colas, Kai Delvendahl, Marcus Kuhnert, and Annette Schubart, pp. 25–49. Acta Mesoamericana 10. Third European Maya Conference, University of Hamburg, November 1998. Verlag Anton Saurwein, Germany.
- 2000b Maya Creation Myths and Cosmography. In *Maya: Divine Kings of the Maya Rain Forest*, ed. Nikolai Grube, pp. 280–293. Könemann, Cologne, Germany.

Webster, David
- 1998 Classic Maya Architecture: Implications and Comparisons. In *Function and Meaning in Classic Maya Architecture*, ed. Stephen D. Houston, pp. 5–47. Dumbarton Oaks, Washington, DC.

7

SANTA ROSA, CHIAPAS: HUMAN SACRIFICE AND THE MESOAMERICAN BALLGAME

Alejandro Martínez Muriel and Emilie Carreón Blaine

Two of the most controversial research topics addressed by Americanist scholars are human sacrifice and the Precolumbian ballgame. Despite much academic inquiry, analysts have attained only a rudimentary grasp of the intricacies of both (cf. Blom 1932; Stern 1966; Van Bussel, Van Dongen, and Leyenaar 1991; Scarborough and Wilcox 1991). Since excavation data connecting the two have been hitherto nonexistent, scholarship has so far relied entirely on ethnographic, ethnohistoric, and iconographic sources for one of ancient Mesoamerica's most distinctive culture traits (Kelly 1943; Kirchhoff 1943). Few scholars have tackled this topic strictly thorough archaeological excavation; most have stressed the distribution or physical description of the ballcourt itself (cf. Quirarte 1975; Healy 1992; Schultz, Gonzalez, and Hammond 1994). Several analysts have considered the relationship among the Mesoamerican ballgame, human sacrifice, ritual decapitation, and trophy taking (Knauth 1961; Borhegyi 1969; Moser 1973; Cohodas 1975; Leyenaar and Parsons 1988; Berryman 2007; Koontz 2008). Only Marcia Castro Leal Espino (1972) has ever reported a human skull in situ within an ancient Mesoamerican ballcourt. This example reputedly comes from Ballcourt Number 2 at Tula, Hidalgo. Susan Gillespie (1991: 322) also accepts this claim. However, a careful review of all excavation data available for the archaeology of Tula failed to corroborate Castro Leal Espino's assertion, rendering this claim specious. To the best of our knowledge, fieldwork at Santa Rosa, Chiapas,

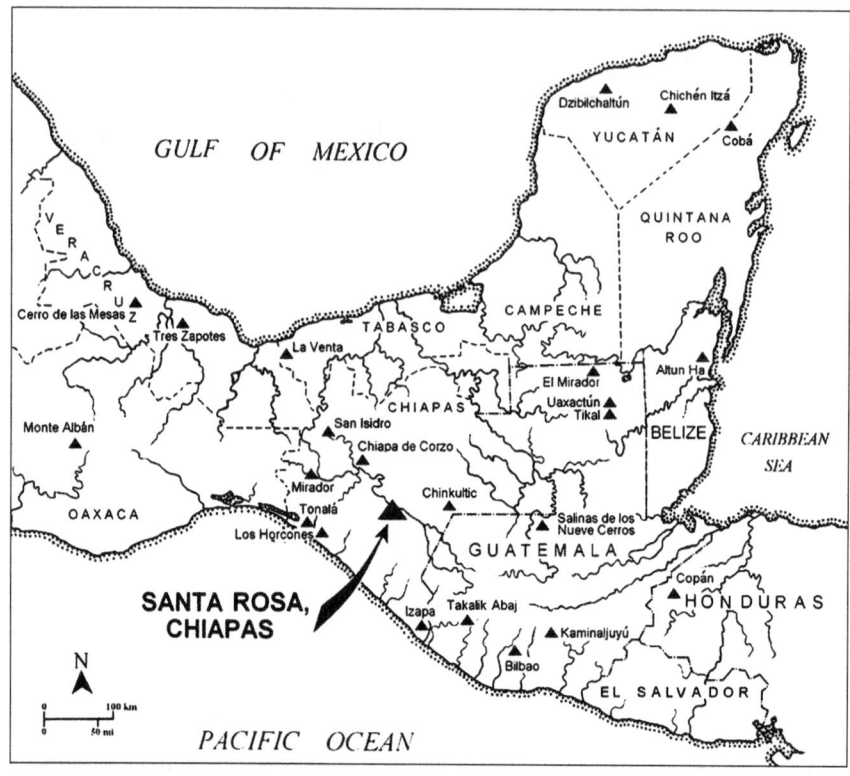

7.1. *Location of the Santa Rosa archaeological site (arrow) within the Maya area. Map by NWAF and Rusty van Rossmann.*

provides the very first documented example of human sacrifice and decapitation at a Mesoamerican ballcourt. Given H. B. Nicholson's interest in the subject and his lifelong dedication to Mesoamerican culture history, our presentation of the Santa Rosa data is particularly relevant to a volume honoring his memory.

RESEARCH BACKGROUND

The cultural significance of Santa Rosa and its environs was firmly established in the 1950s by a New World Archaeological Foundation (NWAF) research team. Gareth Lowe (1959) surveyed the territory from Chiapa de Corzo south to the Guatemalan border, dividing it into four sub-regions: Chiapa de Corzo, Acala, Chapatengo-Chejel, and Altos Tributarios. Controlled excavations at selected sites within these sub-regions, including Santa Rosa, revealed at least 3,000 years of human occupation, encompassing the Early Preclassic and Early Colonial Periods. Based on this research, Lowe (ibid.) concluded that Santa Rosa was the largest multi-component site on the Grijalva River between Chiapa de Corzo and

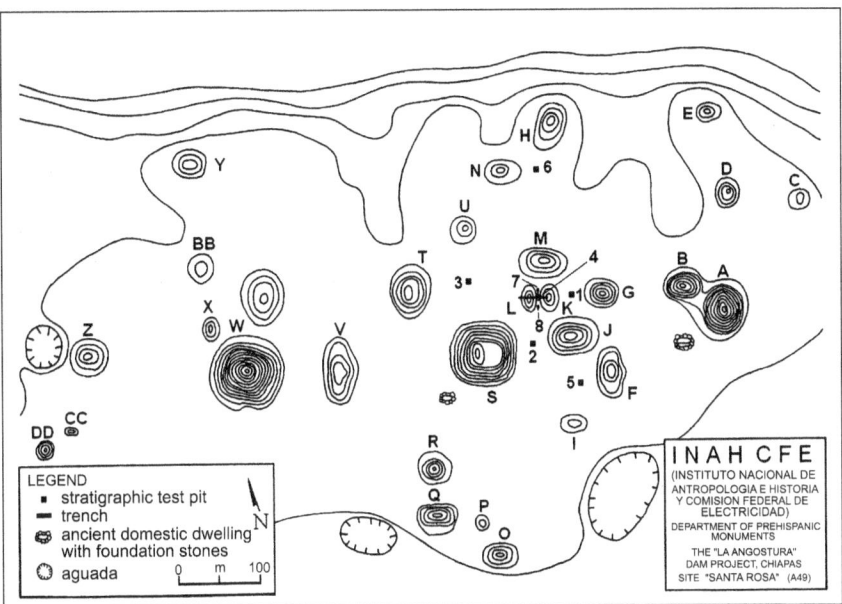

7.2. Site map of Santa Rosa, Chiapas, by Eduardo Martínez E., in Brockington 1967. Note the ballcourt Mounds K and L at right-center.

Guatemala. Santa Rosa (figure 7.1) was initially settled in the Early Preclassic, experienced a Protoclassic (400 BC–AD 100) fluorescence, was abandoned in the Early Classic, reoccupied in the Late Classic, and abandoned a second and final time during the Postclassic Period.

NWAF's pioneering efforts set the archaeological foundation for the present study. Throughout 1958, NWAF researchers worked extensively at Santa Rosa and produced the first topographic map of the site. Through the excavation of twenty-nine test pits throughout the site, Agustín Delgado (1965) and Donald L. Brockington (1961, 1967) confirmed Lowe's (1959) initial chronological assessment; the excavation of seventeen trenches further assessed the site's architectural component. Of paramount concern to the present study were the excavations at Mounds K and L (figure 7.2), which comprise the Santa Rosa ballcourt. Protoclassic fill from trenches at the summits of Mound K and Mound L originally suggested a Protoclassic age for construction of the ballcourt; more recent archaeological data indicate, however, that the structure was built between AD 650 and 900 in the Late Classic Period, using fill from earlier periods.

More than forty years ago, Alejandro Martínez Muriel, then an INAH archaeology student, participated in the Angostura Hydroelectric Dam Project—a major salvage archaeology effort focusing on the Chiapas Central Depression. Construction of the dam posed a significant threat to scores of archaeological sites; consequently, a team of investigators was entrusted to conduct mitigation and salvage activities in the inundation zone. Their objective was to inventory and record all archaeological sites before they were lost forever. Between 1970 and 1974 Martínez Muriel (1988) surveyed the Chapatengo-Chejel region, identifying upward of 170 sites between Angostura Canyon and the confluence of the San Gregorio and San Miguel Rivers. Archaeological fieldwork indicated that periods of intensive cultural occupation occurred during the Preclassic and Late Classic Periods. Relatively few Historic sites were identified, indicating that the Postclassic depopulation continued into Historic times and that the research area was a sparsely populated region that remained outside major Colonial era commercial routes. An extremely warm climate and unhealthy living conditions may explain why so few historical sites and archival documents are available for this region.

To date, 194 ballcourts have been recorded within the Chapatengo-Chejel region, the majority of which are located at coastal sites, within the Central Chiapas Depression, and at highland communities. In fact, more ballcourts have been identified in southern Chiapas than in any other sub-region of the Mesoamerican culture area (Taladoire 1981; Martínez Muriel 1988; Agrinier 1991). Some of Mesoamerica's oldest ballcourts have been recorded in southern Chiapas, including Finca Acapulco, San Mateo, and El Vergel. Thus, any discussion of the Precolumbian ballgame must consider the archaeology of the Chapatengo-Chejel region, including Santa Rosa, Chiapas. Not only was Santa Rosa situated in the region that boasted the greatest concentration of Mesoamerican ballcourts, but its period of peak use coincided with the era when the popularity of this enigmatic game probably reached its pinnacle (Agrinier 1991: 177).

SANTA ROSA, CHIAPAS: SITE DESCRIPTION

Prior to its destruction by the dam, the Santa Rosa archaeological site was located near the confluence of the Grijalva and Aguacate Rivers, on the second alluvial terrace above the Grijalva. The many mounds making up the site were set on a broad, grassy terrace that also supported ceiba and guanacaste trees. The archaeological site covered a surface area of 900 m by 600 m; over forty structures of varying sizes and shapes were recorded within its boundaries (see figure 7.2). Most Santa Rosa architecture was of rammed earth, but some buildings were irregularly faced, with cut stones and slabs. Most structures were aligned to an east-west axis and exhibit no obvious formal arrangements. Most centerlines were oriented 21° east of magnetic north, a characteristic alignment for Preclassic sites in southern Chiapas. Architectural features at Santa Rosa varied greatly in size: the largest structure stood 11 m tall and measured 80 by 50 m at its base. The numerous small, low-lying mounds probably functioned as foundations for domestic structures.

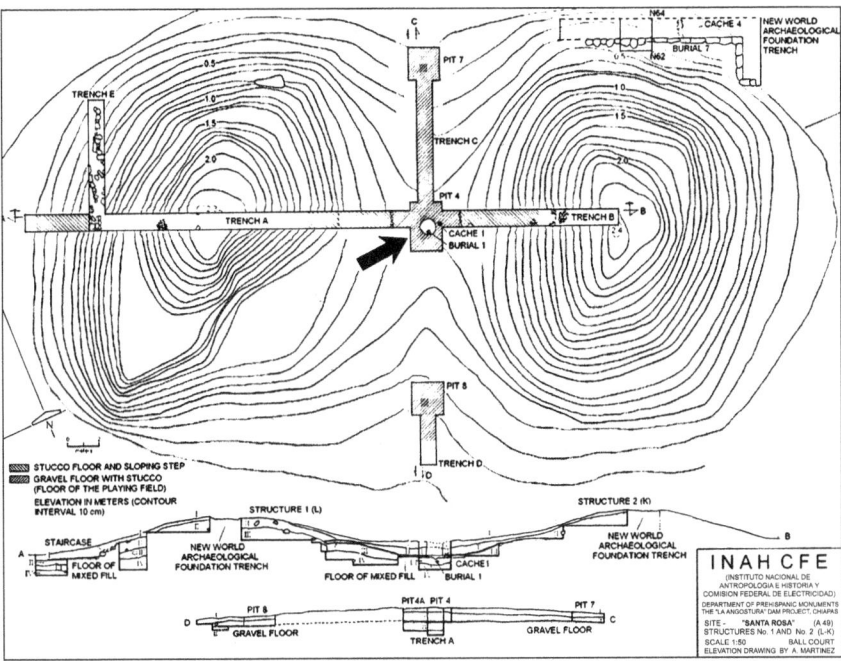

7.3. *Topographic map of excavations conducted at the Santa Rosa, Chiapas, ballcourt, by Alejandro Martínez Muriel. Note location of decapitated human skull (arrow) at center court.*

THE SANTA ROSA BALLCOURT

Given the constraints of time and money inherent in programs of salvage archaeology and with only eight days in which to complete fieldwork, our research efforts at Santa Rosa focused on the site's ballcourt. Initially, a stratigraphic test pit was excavated into the center of the presumed playing field. Next, three trenches were dug, extending outward from this first test pit. The first trench reached eastward, the second westward, each traversing one of the two parallel mounds that made up the court. Another exploratory trench was begun at right angles to the first two, in the hope of delineating the ballcourt's northern and southern boundaries (figure 7.3). Fortunately, these excavations produced the intended results, confirming not only the presence of an ancient ballcourt at Santa Rosa but also internal details, such as the playing alley, sloping aprons, stairs, and portions of an intact upper wall.

The Santa Rosa ballcourt was oriented in a north-south direction; its playing alley measured 26 m long by roughly 4.2 m wide. The playing floor was surfaced with a 20-cm-thick layer of coarse gravel and stucco. The sloping walls of Structure L and Structure K formed an apron, framing the playing field. Measuring about 2.5 m thick, these parallel apron walls were covered by a thin stucco veneer. A thickly applied surface of stucco was detected at the summit

7.4. *Excavation Trench B cutting into Mound K, one of the two parallel mounds that make up the Santa Rosa ballcourt. View toward west. Pit 4 is at lowest point in foreground. Photo by Alejandro Martínez Muriel.*

of Structures K and L, which may represent the remnants of an upper wall or cornice. The northern and southern boundaries of the ballcourt proved elusive; Structure M did not represent the court's northern end wall. Rather, Structures M, G, J, and S formed a kind of plaza group surrounding the court itself. The Structure K trench produced valuable data, enabling us to determine the dimensions of the sloping walls (figure 7.4). The northern end of Structure K, explored earlier by Brockington (1961, 1967), may represent the platform's northern boundary. Two or three rows of well-cut and purposefully aligned stones signify an ancient upper wall spanning 5.76 m from west to east, south for 2.55 m, and then turning east for 76 cm. The wall to the west incorporated rough and heavy stones, extending to the west for 3.81 m.

At approximately 80 cm below the present ground surface, crew members unearthed the remnants of a floor with traces of red paint. Soon thereafter, the partial remains of a mutilated skeleton were found, including the pelvis and assorted leg and feet bones; apparently, this burial had been damaged by ancient building renovation. To date, this individual has not been fully analyzed; however, its association with an Unslipped Polished Brown Incised ceramic vessel suggests a Middle Preclassic date for its internment and therefore probably predates the construction of the ballcourt.

The western boundary of the Santa Rosa ballcourt (Structure L) was determined by running a trench from the center of the playing field to the western exterior of Structure L. This excavation revealed several carefully aligned stone slabs, tentatively identified as stairs or risers, leading to its summit. Brockington (1967) identified four rows of aligned and hewn stones at the summit of Mound L, which may represent the remnants of a wall. Martínez Muriel discovered two cached ceramic vessels beneath the ballcourt's stucco floor. Both vessels were inverted and nested one inside the other. The Santa Rosa cache vessels are comparable in age, design, and form to well-defined regional pottery, including the *Cajetes de paredes recto-divergentes de fondo plano con tres soportes* type reported from Laguna Francesa (Uribe 1981: 77–79). The two Santa Rosa cache vessels also resemble Late Classic Phase X pottery from Chiapa de Corzo (ca. AD 600 to 900) and Tasajo rojo pottery that proliferated at Late Classic communities in the Alto Grijalva region (Bryant, Clark, and Cheetham 2005). Thus, the construction, or at least the final renovation, of the Santa Rosa ballcourt dates to the Late Classic.

Less than a meter to the east of the cached vessels, the INAH archaeologists observed an unusual circular depression or slump in the plaster floor of the playing alley (figure 7.5). This circular feature measured roughly 1 m in diameter and could have been the spot where a stone ballcourt marker once stood.[1] Although archaeological investigations at Santa Rosa produced no ballcourt markers, further excavation at the locality led to a truly remarkable find relating to the Precolumbian ballgame.

THE BALLCOURT SKULL

A disembodied skull was unearthed in Unit 4 (figure 7.6). No signs of disturbance were noted in the test pit; in fact, the same-textured construction fill that surrounded the skull was used to build the entire ballcourt alleyway. Once excavators exposed the Santa Rosa skull, it was apparent that it marked the center of the playing alley. The skull rested in a lateral position, facing north; it exhibited cranial deformation, dental mutilation, and visible signs of trauma on its forehead. We assumed that the individual had been decapitated, as the skull was found with articulated cervical vertebrae. Based on context and association, we assumed that this skull was cached prior to the completion of the Santa Rosa ballcourt and that it represented a distinctive primary burial.[2] Were we to end our chapter here, one might simply conclude that the Santa Rosa skull

7.5. *The Pit 4 excavation in the bottom of Trench B, revealing the ancient circular intrusive pit cut through the stucco floor of the ballcourt, possibly a socket for a stone marker. Photo by Alejandro Martínez Muriel.*

represented a trophy head related to a ballgame decapitation sacrifice (Coe and Koontz 2002). Since lives and reputations presumably were staked on the outcome of the game, it would be plausible to suggest that we had unearthed a professional Maya athlete who represented the losing (or winning?) captain of his team.[3] However, osteological analysis of the Santa Rosa ballcourt skull produced evidence contradicting most long-established notions about the Mesoamerican ballgame, human sacrifice, and their functional interconnection.

OSTEOLOGICAL ANALYSIS

Osteological analysis of the Santa Rosa skeletal remains was undertaken by Carmen M. Pijoan A. and Gerardo Valenzuela at the INAH Physical Anthropology

7.6. *The decapitated human skull found in the Pit 4 excavation at the bottom of Trench B under the stucco floor of the ballcourt, with associated Late Classic cache vessels at left. Photo by Alejandro Martínez Muriel.*

Laboratory in Mexico City. Pijoan A. and Valenzuela (2008) identified a disembodied human skull, including its mandible, and two cervical bones, the atlas and the axis. Based on craniometric measurements, they posited that the skull belonged to an adult woman, ranging in age from twenty-one to thirty-five. The front of her skull exhibits two healed wounds resulting from blunt-force trauma (figure 7.7). A circular-shaped injury to the left boss bone seems fresher and less fully healed than the elongated wound to the right part of her forehead. Her teeth were badly worn but also intentionally altered, presenting Type M and K dental mutilation, which are not local Maya forms. Pijoan A. and Valenzuela also noted unambiguous evidence of intentional head deformation. The back of the skull revealed clear indentations consistent with the application of knots associated with a head-binding apparatus. This meant that her malleable cranial vault was shaped into a tabular oblique form at a very young age.

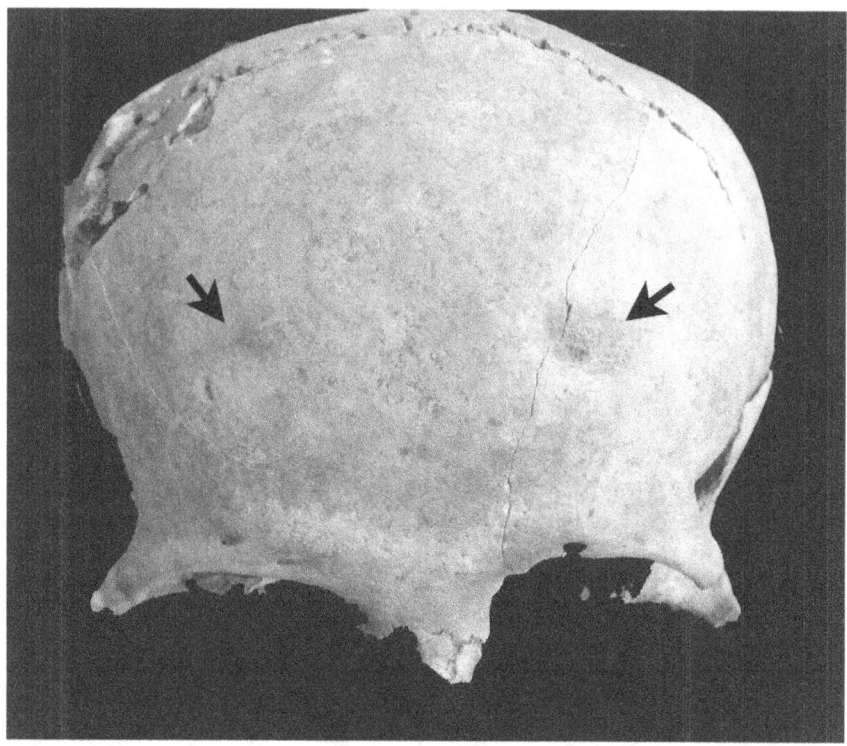

7.7. Frontal portion of the decapitated human skull found below the Santa Rosa ballcourt floor. Note tabular oblique cranial deformation and healed wounds (arrows) on forehead. Photo by INAH.

INTERPRETATIONS

The discovery of a female human skull in the center of the Santa Rosa ballcourt raises several questions: Who was this individual? Where did she come from? Was she foreign-born, a member of the ruling elite, a captive slave, or a ballplayer? Why was her disembodied head buried at center court? What prompted her death? Definitive answers to some of these questions remain beyond our ken. However, certain morphological features provide relevant clues about her life and death. The two healed head injuries indicate ante-mortem violence, perhaps foreshadowing her ultimate demise. These features simply are not normal anatomical quirks. Based on the location of her cranial injuries and the differential patterns of wound healing, we surmise that she lived a perilous existence over a lengthy period of time. Her injuries are consistent with someone who was not a stranger to violence, but whether this occurred on a battlefield, a playing field, or at home we cannot say. Judging from the evidence, we believe it is very unlikely that the Santa Rosa woman died of natural causes. The mandible and uppermost vertebra were in their correct anatomical position, suggesting that the head was severed from her body while still completely fleshed: in other words, decapitated. Since butcher-like cut marks were not detected on the skull and INAH archaeologists failed to recover any cutting tools—such as chert knives or obsidian blades—in association with the skull, the nature of her death and decapitation remains a mystery. Nevertheless, physical anthropologists concluded that her head was removed postmortem and, consequently, that decapitation was not the actual cause of death. Given that the mandible and first vertebrae were intact and in place, they speculated that her head must have been removed from the body with its ligaments attached and that the burial of the skull must have occurred shortly thereafter.

Pijoan A. and Valenzuela speculated that excessive dental wear resulted from a steady diet of corn processed on volcanic metates. Since Maya peoples in southern Chiapas consumed maize ground on limestone metates, their teeth were typically in better shape than those of Mesoamerican peoples who lived in highland volcanic regions (Romero Molina 1986). The Chiapas diet lacked substantial amounts of abrasive grit unintentionally added to food, which would otherwise damage the surfaces of teeth. The condition of the Santa Rosa woman's teeth, coupled with their distinctive pattern of dental modification, led Pijoan A. and Valenzuela (2008) to suggest that she was not born locally and may have come from a community in Central Mexico, such as Teotihuacan.[4] Once her gender was determined, the nature of her death became of paramount interest. We wanted to know whether she died prior to decapitation or if her death resulted from beheading.[5] Unfortunately, this issue could not be definitively resolved.

Based on the stratigraphic context of the skull, her death and interment coincided with the dedication of the ballcourt. But who was she? It is plausible to suggest she was a ballplayer. Since metric and morphological analysis of the remains strongly suggests that the individual was not male (figure 7.8), some of our notions about the Mesoamerican ballgame may require reassessment. A case in point is that since iconographic representations of ballplayers are typically male, most scholars overlook the possibility that women participated in this event (Stern 1966: 38, 57). Gonzalo Fernández de Oviedo y Valdés (1979), however, noted that women in the Greater Antilles played in the regional variant of the ballgame. Moreover, the notion of women ballplayers in Mesoamerica is supported by archaeological and historical (codex) evidence. Formative Period ballplayer clay figurines from Xochipala, Guerrero, are interpreted as female, while the *Codex Nuttall* (Nuttall 1975) depicts the decapitated Lady 11 Serpent standing on a ballcourt with blood issuing from her neck (Moser 1973: 36–37).

The multiple head wounds to the Santa Rosa skull may be indicative of the violent nature of the ballgame. But, alternatively, the woman may have been a soldier or a warrior captured in a raid or during battle. Judging from her age

Alejandro Martínez Muriel and Emilie Carreón Blaine

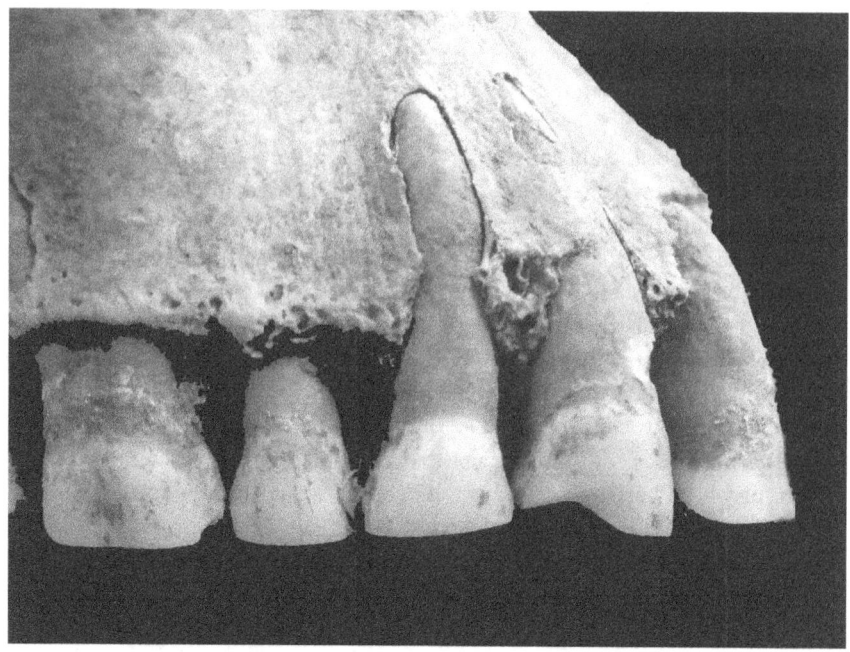

7.8. *Detail of dental mutilation and wear patterns on the teeth of the decapitated human skull found below the Santa Rosa ballcourt floor. The dental evidence suggests a Central Mexican origin for the female skull found at this Maya site. Photo by INAH.*

and apparent exposure/resilience to injury, she was able-bodied and potentially accustomed to combat. This possibility is not outlandish. Hieroglyphic studies of women's names or appellative phrases indicate that the term *na bate* (woman warrior) was bestowed upon select elite Maya women (Schele and Freidel 1990: 364–367; Hewitt 1999). Still, there is no clear evidence that this term literally means they were warriors; it does, however, imbue them with masculine qualities, which may have been exalted by the ancient Maya. Likewise, we observe a woman standing among numerous male warriors at the Temple of the Warriors in Early Postclassic Chichén Itzá. While it is worth exploring the possibility that ancient Maya and other Mesoamerican women were warriors, we have no unequivocal evidence at this time to satisfactorily resolve this issue.

There may be another explanation for her presence at Santa Rosa: she could have been sold as a captive or slave to a resident of Santa Rosa. Torture or violence might explain her head wounds; ritual human sacrifice would certainly explain her demise. In this context, it is well to remember the suggestion that elite captives were forced to play a ritualized version of the ballgame during much later periods (Schele and Miller 1986: 249–250). The ethnohistoric record indicates that Late Postclassic Central Mexican women's skulls were incorporated on the infamous *tzompantli* (skull rack) of Tenochtitlan (Sahagún 1985: 134; Mendoza 2007); based on the osteological analysis of the Tlatelolco tzompantli, Pijoan Aguadé and Mansilla Lory (1997) concluded that roughly 25 percent (43) of the 170 crania studied belonged to women. Since Mexica warriors took captives from the battlefield, we maintain that some of their prisoners might have been women soldiers. Finally and perhaps most significant, women were essential to Aztec religion and ritual. According to Alfredo López Austin (1996), female captives were "transformed" into living Mexica goddesses until their death; until then, they embodied the divine essence of a female deity.

CONCLUSION: AT CENTER COURT

The Santa Rosa skull represents one of the most interesting finds from five years of archaeological salvage work in the Central Chiapas Depression. After a concerted search for comparative archaeological examples, we began to appreciate the uniqueness of the discovery. Although images of human skulls and decapitated ballplayers proliferate on pottery, stone carving, and within pictorial manuscripts (e.g., *Codex Borbonicus* [Anders, Jansen, and Reyes García 1991: 19]; Tonalamatl Aubin [Seler 1900–1901: 19]; *Codex Nuttall* [Nuttall 1975: 4]; *Codex Magliabechiano* [Boone 1983: 68r]; *Codex Tudela* 67r [1980]), their archaeological counterparts are rare. To date, we have been unable to identify any other comparative excavated specimens deriving from controlled fieldwork.[6] We therefore remain less confident about the symbolic meaning of this specimen than we are about its age and burial context.

It is therefore fitting that we consult the writings of H. B. Nicholson regarding the interpretation of our find. In a notable article, Nicholson and Eloise Quiñones Keber (1991) review the salient images of ballcourts found in Mexican pictorial manuscripts, concluding that skulls, sacrificial knives, and deities highlight the games' ritual and symbolic underpinnings; they note that the center of the ballcourt was the standard location for depictions of human skulls. To understand why iconographic images of human skulls are located at the center of the ballcourt, they recount the myth of Huitzilopochtli at Coatepec, as described by Fernando Alvarado Tezozómoc (1980: 227–229), indicating a kind of well in the center of the court called *itzompan*, or "his place of skulls" (Nicholson and Quiñones Keber 1991: 131–132). These authorities suggest that the center of the court symbolizes an opening where the skull or the ball is placed and add that skulls "connote the sacrificial deaths, especially those by decapitation, that were clearly such a significant element in Mesoamerican ballgame ritual" (ibid.). Even if this assumption proves erroneous, the study of ballcourt imagery provides a means for interpreting the Santa Rosa specimen. We may never know precisely why a woman's skull was buried at center court in the Santa Rosa playing alley sometime during the Late Classic Period; the most plausible interpretation is that it was a cache associated with the dedication of a new, or at least renovated, ballcourt.

Our Santa Rosa research makes us question the supposition that only ballplayers, losers or winners, were sacrificed in the context of the ballgame. It is quite possible that iconographic decapitation scenes and skulls had more to do with the dedication of the ballcourt than they did with the outcome of the game itself. It is also possible that at least some ballplayers were women.

In conclusion, two points must be stressed. The first is the inherent value of osteological analysis, which has shed light on a hitherto truly murky subject and which archaeologists and art historians ignore at their peril. The second is that studies of the Mesoamerican ballgame cannot rely exclusively on ethnographic and iconographic evidence. Instead, a holistic approach, evaluating archaeological, ethnographic, ethnohistoric, iconographic, and osteological evidence together, should be employed for understanding this fascinating subject. Only more facts and less speculation will advance our knowledge of the ancient Mesoamerican ballgame, ancient human sacrifice, and decapitation. The female skull at the center of the Santa Rosa ballcourt forced us to question longstanding notions about sports, masculinity, gender, and power. Once the archaeological evidence had been thoroughly studied, we found that we had, as they say, a whole new ballgame.

NOTES

1. A smooth stone marker was a common feature among ballcourts in southern Chiapas, having been recorded at numerous Late and Terminal Classic Maya communities. Ballcourt markers vary throughout Mesoamerica, and their placement was not universal. For example, three flat, circular markers were aligned along the long axis of Copán's ballcourt. Older ballcourts, such as those reported at Vergel and San Mateo, Chiapas, exhibit rough-cut circular slab markers rising above the playing alley at center court (Agrinier 1991: 176). The carved marker found mid-court at Chapatengo exhibits a glyph band circling its edge (Lowe 1959; Agrinier 1991: 192). In contrast, ballcourt markers at Laguna Francesa (Uribe 1981), Ojo de Agua, and Tenam Rosario were plain (Agrinier 1991: 193).

2. We cannot disregard the possibility that a stone marker may have marked this spot. Comparative evidence from Chapatengo supports this notion. Here, beneath the central ballcourt marker, archaeologists unearthed a cache of Late Classic pottery, shells, and beads (Gussinyer 1972; Agrinier 1991: 192).

3. Ballgame symbols proliferate in the archaeological record, expressed in diverse contexts and media (e.g., Structure 33 at Yaxchilán, the La Esperanza ballcourt marker, Central Mexican codices, West Mexican ceramic figurines, a gold pendant from Tomb 7 of Monte Albán Oaxaca, and graffiti in Tikal, Guatemala [Leyenaar and Parsons 1988: 88]). Notable examples of decapitation exist on bas-reliefs (e.g., Chichén Itzá, El Tajín, and Las Higueras), stelae (e.g., Aparicio, Papaloapan, Santa Lucia Cotzumalguapa), miscellaneous stone artifacts (e.g., carved *hachas* of unknown proveniences and the ballcourt

ring at Comitán), pottery (Hammond 1976; cf. Tiquisate tripod vessels), and in codices. The *Codex Borbonicus* (Anders, Jansen, and Reyes García 1991: 19) and the Tonalamatl Aubin 19 (Seler 1900–1901), for example, depict a decapitated male and an I-shaped ballcourt. The *Borbonicus* shows a skull inside a playing alley; the skull displays a water symbol and seems to be moving or passing through one of the ballcourt rings at the center of the playing field. Additional examples of ballgame-related representations are found in the *Codex Borbonicus* (Anders, Jansen, and Reyes García 1991: 27), Historia Tolteca Chichimeca 16v (Kirchhoff, Odena Güemes, and Reyes García 1989), *Florentine Codex* (Sahagún (1954: fol. 91), Durán Atlas cap. 23 (Durán 1967), Colombino Codex 11 (Smith 1966), and the *Codex Nuttall* 80 (Nuttall 1975). In general, these examples depict a male protagonist—wearing ballplayer gear, carrying a severed head by the hair, and facing his prostrate victim, whose blood issues from his decapitated body in the form of serpents. These examples merely infer decapitation—the act of beheading someone is not represented. The focus of these images is the severed head and the postmortem treatment it receives, whether it is held by the hair, suspended by a cord, or worn around the neck. Taladoire (1981) reviews many ballgame scenes, and the consensus among most scholars is that ballplayers were male. Nevertheless, our understanding of the "rules of the game" is nominal. In reference to Monte Albán's renowned Danzantes, Coe and Koontz (2002: 97) state, "It is a measure of our ignorance of the early Mesoamerican mind that we are not sure whether these represent the victors or the vanquished!" Perhaps much of the sacrificial and death imagery commonly associated with ballcourts may not be directly related to the practice of the ballgame itself.

4. A Central Mexican individual at Santa Rosa might reflect regional economics and political alliances. Agrinier (1991: 178–179) posits that Los Horcones was a Teotihuacan trading outpost in southern Chiapas, maintaining commercial ties with Kaminaljuyú. Re-analysis of skeletal remains from this region may reveal the presence of other foreigners. A potential chronological conundrum is that Teotihuacan's heyday was in the Early Classic Period, and the Santa Rosa ballcourt may date to the successive Late Classic Period. This problem may be resolved if we consider that the fall of Teotihuacan and the beginning of the Maya Late Classic Period were more or less contemporaneous.

5. Decapitating a live person differs from beheading the dead, although the result is the same. Mesoamerican sacrificial victims were either dorsally extended or sat or kneeled in supplication; behind or above them loomed a knife-wielding sacrificer. Decapitation of the dead was normally done subsequent to heart extraction; these individuals were beheaded lying face-up. The ligaments that join the atlas to the occipital bone are particularly solid and resist when the body begins to decompose. Pereira and Stresser Pean (1995) note that connections between skull and vertebrae can well be interpreted as a sign of decapitation but have stressed that only the presence of the hyoid bones can fully confirm it. In the case of the Santa Rosa skull, excavated more than three decades ago, this element was not registered, and its discovery might possibly have resolved the question of how the woman met her death. Pre- or postmortem decapitation is an important issue that must be resolved prior to any discussion of funerary or sacrificial practices. It is very unlikely that the Santa Rosa woman died of natural causes.

6. A comparable iconographic example comes from Cobá, Quintana Roo (Uribe and Martínez Muriel 2002). There, the Group D central ballcourt marker displays a carved human skull, while another marker to the north exhibits a headless jaguar.

REFERENCES CITED

Agrinier, Pierre
    1991   The Ballcourts of Southern Chiapas, Mexico. In *The Mesoamerican Ballgame*, ed. Vernon L. Scarborough and David R. Wilcox, pp. 175–194. University of Arizona Press, Tucson.

Alvarado Tezozómoc, Fernando
    1980   *Crónica Mexicana*. Annotated by Manuel Orozco y Berra. Editorial Porrúa, México, DF.

Anders, Ferdinand, Maarten Jansen, and Luis Reyes García
    1991   *El libro del Ciuacoatl, Homenaje para el año de Fuego Nuevo, libro explicativo del llamado Códice Borbónico*. Fondo de Cultura Económica, México, DF.

Berryman, Carrie Anne
    2007   Captive Sacrifice and Trophy Taking among the Ancient Maya: An Evaluation of the Bioarchaeological Evidence and Its Sociopolitical Implications. In *The Taking and Displaying of Human Body Parts as Trophies by Amerindians*, ed. R. J. Chacon and D. H. Dye, pp. 377–399. Springer, New York.

Blom, Frans
    1932   The Maya Ball-Game *Pok-ta-Pok*. *Middle American Research Institute Publication* 4 (14): 485–530. Tulane University, New Orleans, LA.

Boone, Elizabeth Hill
    1983   *The Codex Magliabechiano and the Lost Prototype of the Magliabechiano Group*. University of California Press, Berkeley.

Borhegyi, Stephan F.
    1969   *The Precolumbian Ballgame: A Pan Mesoamerican Tradition. Verhandlungen des XXXVIII internationalen amerikanistenkongresses, Stuttgart-Munchen, agosto 1968*. Kommissionsverlag Klaus Renner, Munich.

Brockington, Donald L.
    1961   A Prolongation of the Preclassic Period Indicated by the Ceramics of Santa Rosa, Chiapas. In *Los Mayas del Sur y sus Relaciones con los Nahuas Meridionales*, pp. 85–92. VIII Mesa Redonda de la Sociedad Mexicana de Antropología Celebrada en San Cristobal Las Casas, Chiapas, September 1959. Sociedad Mexicana de Antropología, México, DF.
    1967   *The Ceramic History of Santa Rosa, Chiapas, Mexico*. Papers of the New World Archaeological Foundation 23. Brigham Young University, Provo, UT.

Bryant, Douglas Donne, John E. Clark, and David Cheetham
    2005   *Ceramic Sequence of the Upper Grijalva Region, Chiapas, Mexico*. Papers of the New World Archaeological Foundation 67. Brigham Young University, Provo, UT.

Castro Leal Espino, Marcia
    1972   La decapitación y el juego de pelota. In *Religión en Mesoamérica*, ed. J. Litvak King and Noemi Castillo Tejero, pp. 457–462. XII Mesa Redonda de la Sociedad Mexicana de Antropología. Sociedad Mexicana de Antropología, México, DF.

Codex Tudela
- 1980 *Códice Tudela, José Tudela de la Orden.* 2 vols. Ediciones Cultura Hispánica, del Instituto de Cooperación Iberoamericana, Madrid.

Coe, Michael D., and Rex Koontz
- 2002 *Mexico: From the Olmecs to the Aztecs.* Thames and Hudson, New York.

Cohodas, Marvin
- 1975 The Symbolism and Ritual Function of the Middle Classic Ballgame in Mesoamerica. *American Indian Quarterly* 2 (2): 99–130.

Delgado, Agustín
- 1965 *Excavation at Santa Rosa, Chiapas: Archaeological Research in Santa Rosa Chiapas and in the Region of Tehuantepec.* Papers of the New World Archaeological Foundation 13. Brigham Young University, Provo, UT.

Durán, Fray Diego
- 1967 *Historia de las Indias de Nueva España e Islas de Tierra Firma.* Á. María Garibay K. Porrúa, México, DF.

Gillespie, Susan
- 1991 Ballgames and Boundaries. In *The Mesoamerican Ballgame*, ed. Vernon L. Scarborough and David R. Wilcox, pp. 317–345. University of Arizona Press, Tucson.

Gussinyer, Jordi
- 1972 *Segunda temporada de Salvamento Arqueológico en la Presa de "La Angostura," Chiapas.* ICACH, Segunda época 5–6 (23–24): 41–56. Instituto de Ciencias y Artes de Chiapas, Tuxtla Gutiérrez.

Hammond, Norman
- 1976 A Classic Maya Ball-Game Vase. In *Problems in Economic and Social Archaeology*, ed. Gale de Giberne, Ian H. Longworth, and K. E. Wilson, pp. 101–108. Gerald Duckworth, the Old Piano Factory, London.

Healy, Paul
- 1992 The Ancient Maya Ballcourt at Pacbitun, Belize. *Ancient Mesoamerica* (3): 229–239.

Hewitt, Erika A.
- 1999 What's in a Name? *Ancient Mesoamerica* 10: 251–262.

Kelly, Isabel
- 1943 Notes on a West Coast Survival of the Ancient Mexican Ball Game. *Notes on Middle American Archaeology and Ethnology* 1: 26. Carnegie Institution, Washington, DC.

Kirchhoff, Paul
- 1943 Mesoamérica: Sus Límites Geográficos, Composición Étnica y Caracteres Culturales. *Acta Americana* 1 (1): 92–107.

Kirchhoff, Paul, Lina Odena Güemes, and Luis Reyes García, eds.
- 1989 *Historia Tolteca-Chichimeca.* Fondo de Cultura Económica, México, DF.

Knauth, Lothar
    1961   El Juego de Pelota y el Rito de Decapitación. *Estudios de Cultura Maya* 1: 183–198. Instituto de Investigaciones Filológicas, Centro de Estudios Mayas, UNAM, México, DF.

Koontz, Rex
    2008   Precolumbian Landscapes of Creation and Origin: Ballcourt Rites, Paradise, and the Origins of Power in Classic Verazruz. In *Pre-Columbian Landscapes of Creation and Origin*, ed. John E. Staller, pp. 11–29. Springer, New York.

Leyenaar, Ted J.J., and Lee A. Parsons, eds.
    1988   *Ulama: The Ballgame of the Mayas and Aztecs 2000 BC to AD 2000, from Human Sacrifice to Sport*, introduction by H. B. Nicholson. Spruyt, Van Mantgem, and De Does, Leyden, The Netherlands.

López Austin, Alfredo
    1996   Los mitos del tlacuache. *Caminos de la Mitología Mesoamericana* 2A: 178–180. UNAM, México, DF.

Lowe, Gareth W.
    1959   *Archaeological Exploration of the Upper Grijalva River, Chiapas, Mexico.* Papers of the New World Archaeological Foundation 2. Brigham Young University, Provo, UT.

Martínez Muriel, Alejandro
    1988   Prehistoric Rural Population Trends in Central Chiapas, Mexico. PhD dissertation, Department of Anthropology, UCLA, Los Angeles, CA.

Mendoza, Rubén G.
    2007   The Divine Gourd Tree: Tzompanlti Skull Racks, Decapitation Rituals, and Human Trophies in Ancient Mesoamerica. In *The Taking and Displaying of Human Body Parts as Trophies by Amerindians*, ed. Richard J. Chacon and David H. Dye, pp. 400–443. Springer, New York.

Moser, Christopher
    1973   *Human Decapitation in Ancient Mesoamerica.* Studies in Pre-Columbian Art and Archaeology 11. Dumbarton Oaks, Washington, DC.

Nicholson, H. B., and Eloise Quiñones Keber
    1991   Ball Court Images in Central Mexican Native Tradition Pictorial Manuscripts. In *The Mesoamerican Ballgame*, ed. Gerard W. Van Bussel, Paul Van Dongen and Ted J.J. Leyenaar, pp. 119–133. National Museum of Ethnology. Leyden, The Netherlands.

Nuttall, Zelia
    1975   *The Codex Nuttall: A Picture Manuscript from Ancient Mexico*, edited with new introductory text by Arthur G. Miller. Dover, New York.

Oviedo y Valdés, Gonzalo Fernández de
    1979   *Historia general y natural de las Indias, islas y Tierra firme del Mar Océano.* Centro de Estudios para la Historia de México, libro 6, cap. 2, folio LIX. Condumex, México, DF.

Pereira, Gregory, and Guy Stresser Pean
    1995   Un cas anormal de decapitation Huasteque á Vista Hermosa, Tamaulipas. *Journal de la Société des Américanistes* 81: 231–241. Musée de l'Homme, París.

Pijoan Aguadé, Carmen María, and Josefina Mansilla Lory
    1997   Evidencia de sacrificio humano, modificación ósea y canibalismo en el México prehispánico. In *El cuerpo humano y su tratamiento mortuorio*, ed. Elsa Malvido, Gregory Pereira, and Vera Tiesler, pp. 193–212. Colección Científica 344. INAH, México, DF.

Pijoan Aguadé, Carmen María, and Gerardo Valenzuela
    2008   *Informe del entierro num.1 de La Angostura, sitio A49 (Santa Rosa)*. Laboratorio de Antropología Física, INAH, México, DF.

Quirarte, Jacinto
    1975   The Ballcourt in Mesoamerica: Its Architectural Development. In *Pre-Columbian Art History: Selected Readings*, ed. Alana Cordy-Collins and Jean Stern, pp. 63–69. Peek Publications, Palo Alto, CA.

Romero Molina, Javier
    1986   *Catálogo de la colección de dientes mutilados prehispánicos*. 4 parte. Colección Fuentes, INAH, México, DF.

Sahagún, Fray Bernardino de
    1954   *Florentine Codex Book 8: Kings and Lords*. Translated from the Nahuatl with notes by Arthur J.O. Anderson and Charles E. Dibble. University of Utah Press, Salt Lake City.
    1985   *Historia general de las cosas de la Nueva España*, ed. Ángel Ma. Garibay. Colección "Sepan Cuántos" 300. Editorial Porrúa, México, DF.

Scarborough, Vernon L., and David R. Wilcox, eds.
    1991   *The Mesoamerican Ballgame*. University of Arizona Press, Tucson.

Schele, Linda, and David Freidel
    1990   *The Forest of Kings: The Untold Story of the Ancient Maya*. William Morrow, New York.

Schele, Linda, and Mary Ellen Miller
    1986   *The Blood of Kings: Dynasty and Ritual in Maya Art*. Kimbell Art Museum, Fort Worth, TX.

Schultz, Kevin C., Jason J. Gonzalez, and Norman Hammond
    1994   Classic Maya Ballcourts at La Milpa, Belize. *Ancient Mesoamerica* 5: 45–53.

Seler, Eduard
    1900–1901   *The Tonalamatl of the Aubin Collection. An Old Mexican Picture Manuscript in the Paris National Library*. Manuscrits Mexicains 18–19. Published at the Expense of His Excellency the Duke of Loubat, Berlin and London.

Smith, Mary Elizabeth
    1966   *Las glosas del Códice Colombino [The Glosses of the Codex Colombino]*. Sociedad Mexicana de Antropología, México, DF.

Stern, Theodore
 1966 *Rubber-Ball Games of the Americas*. University of Washington Press, Seattle.

Taladoire, Eric
 1981 *Les terrains de Jeu de Balle (Mesoamérique et Sud-Ouest des États-Unis), México*. Mission Archeologique et Ethnologique Francaise au Mexique, Études Mesoaméricaines, Centre d'Études Mexicaines et Centraméricaines, México, DF.

Uribe, María José
 1981 *Laguna Francesa*. Colección Científica 100. INAH, México, DF.

Uribe, María José, and Alejandro Martínez Muriel
 2002 Cobá. Entre caminos y lagos. *Arqueología Mexicana* 9 (54): 34–41.

Van Bussel, Gerard W., Paul Van Dongen, and Ted J.J. Leyenaar, eds.
 1991 *The Mesoamerican Ballgame*. Rijksmuseum loor Volkenkunde, Leyden, The Netherlands.

8

PIPIL ARCHAEOLOGY OF PACIFIC GUATEMALA

Frederick J. Bove, José Vicente Genovez, and Carlos A. Batres

Migrations of Nahua-speaking groups from Central Mexico and the Gulf Coast to the Soconusco region, the Pacific Coast of Guatemala, and lower Central America constituted one of the most important examples of large-scale population movements in New World culture history (Fowler 1989a, 1989b). They had a profound impact on much of Postclassic Mesoamerica and in particular the Pacific Coast of Guatemala (figure 8.1). While their dating is still debatable, most experts would probably agree that the historic, linguistic, and archaeological evidence indicates that the Nahua migrations to Central America were a complex series of population movements occurring from about AD 800 to AD 1350 (Torquemada 1969; Davies 1977; Justeson et al. 1985; Fowler 1989a; Voorhies 1989).

Concurrent with a newly increasing interest in migration and ethnicity is that on the relationship between style and ethnicity (Conkey and Hastorf 1990; Gosselain 1998; Sackett 1990; Stark 1998a). Domestic pottery and architecture have been studied elsewhere to identify ethnically specific styles and, in turn, cultural boundaries (Barth 1969; Conkey and Hastorf 1990; Jones 1997; Rouse 1986; Schortman 1986; Shennan 1994a; M. Stark 1998a); we hoped to do the same in Pacific Coastal Guatemala through our Pipil Research Project. Our project also represented a rare opportunity in Pacific Coastal archaeology to combine both documentary and archaeological research in a conjunctive approach.

Frederick J. Bove, José Vicente Genovez, and Carlos A. Batres

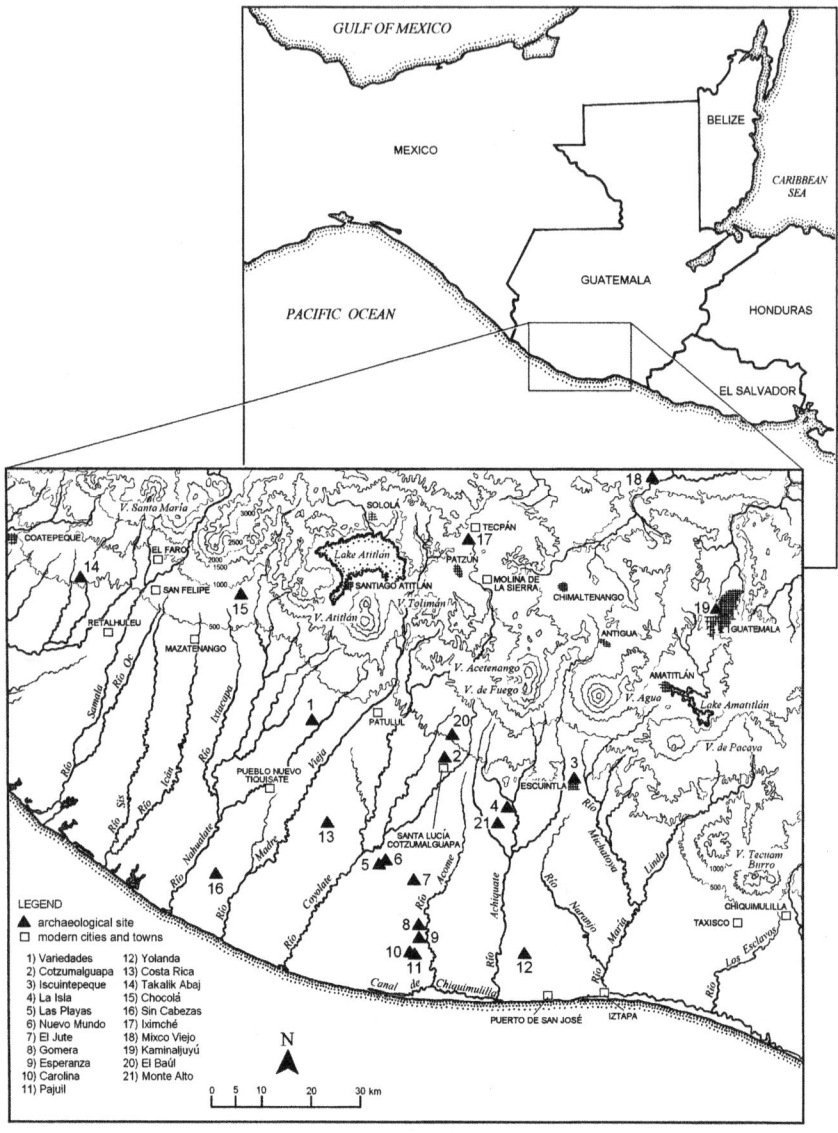

8.1. Map of the study area on the Pacific Coast of Guatemala, showing modern towns and archaeological sites. After Shook 1965, by Frederick J. Bove and Rusty van Rossmann.

THE PIPIL QUESTION

When the Spaniards conquered Coastal and Highland Guatemala in the early sixteenth century, they found Pipil populations inhabiting a limited area within what is the modern Guatemalan Department of Escuintla. Pedro de Alvarado destroyed their presumed capital, Iscuintepeque, but provided scant details on the city or the people (Alvarado 1924 ; Thompson 1948; Kelly 1971). Earlier, the Pipil had populated an area substantially larger than the one that existed at the time of the Conquest (Thompson 1948; Carmack 1965, 1973, 1981; Polo Sifontes 1979, 1989), but much of their territory had been overrun by the expansionist K'iche and Kakchiquel from the adjacent highlands during the later part of the Late Postclassic Period.

With considerable foresight, J. Eric Thompson (1948: 14) stated:

> Purely as a speculation one might suggest that the ruling families of Quiche and other highland Maya peoples who claimed Mexican (Toltec) ancestry might have descended from Pipil groups who conquered the highlands and established ruling families which were later absorbed by the Maya groups they ruled . . . A Pipil origin for the ruling families of the Guatemala highlands might be connected with an early expansion of the Pipil.

Dates of the Nahua-Pipil movements into southern Mesoamerica are ambiguous (Torquemada 1969). Stephan de Borhegyi (1965: 20, 31, 41–42) proposed three sequential movements: Teotihuacan-Pipil at AD 400–500, Tajín-Teotihuacan-Pipil at AD 700–900, and Nonoalca-Pipil-Toltec at AD 1000–1200. Although the earlier dates were speculative, the date ranges are in general agreement with William Fowler (1989a). Several decades of coastal research (Bove et al. 1993; Bove 1999, 2002a, 2002b; Neff and Bove 1999; Neff et al. 1999; Bove and Medrano 2003) suggest that Teotihuacan entry, eventual takeover, and colonization of the central Escuintla coast began within the Early Classic Colojate Phase. It culminated in a military incursion and colonization in the Middle Classic San Jerónimo Phase, concurrent with Borhegyi's hypothesized Teotihuacan-Pipil movements. Karen Dakin and Søren Wichmann (2000) believe the Teotihuacanos spoke Nahuatl. We follow Dakin and Wichmann in using *Nahuatl* to refer to the language, including all dialect variants, and *Nahua* to refer to the people speaking, regardless of whether the words end in *tl* or *t*.

Fowler (1989a: 42) believes the strongest indication of Late Classic Pipil migrations is the glotto-chronological evidence for Nahua divergence at about AD 650–850, reflecting early Pipil movements out of Central Mexico to the Gulf Coast and possibly Central America. Another active period of Nahua divergence, based again on glottochronology, is AD 900–1100 (Kaufman 1974: 49). There is strong evidence of Pipil migrations to El Salvador by the Epiclassic Period, which Fowler believes were associated with the collapse of Tula and which account for the major Early Postclassic Period centers of Cihuatán and Las Marías. Serious chronological, ethnic identity, and linguistic problems still exist concerning the "Toltec" issue. Some argue that the fall of Tula, now dated to about AD 1150–1200, instigated a late Nahua migratory movement onto the Guatemala–El Salvador Pacific Coastal Plain (Diehl and Berlo 1989; Wolfman

1990; Nicholson 2001). It is also possible that the Toltec "diaspora" instigated a late migratory movement by the "Nonoalca-Pipil," thought to have been a Nahuatisized group, the most powerful at Tula (Borhegyi 1965; Davies 1977; Fowler 1989a).

A striking new development, although somewhat speculative, is recent ethnohistoric research suggesting that the most important lineages at the K'iche capital of Q'umarkaaj claimed to have come from the Pacific Coast. The *Título de Sacapulas* is explicit about this and refers to the coastal city from which they came as "Four Hundred Ceibas, Four Hundred Temple-Pyramids" (Estrada and Niebla 1955; van Akkeren 2000). Bove (1989) has identified this city as the Middle Classic regional capital of Ixtepeque in the Tiquisate Zone. Ixtepeque is believed to be similar to the great Texas-Montana Complex 45 km east, possibly derived from a Teotihuacan movement and colonization of the Escuintla lower coast (Bove 1999, 2002a, 2002b; Bove and Medrano 2003). Based on other documentary evidence, Ruud van Akkeren suggests that the Toj lineage, the Late Postclassic rulers of Rab'inal in the Guatemalan Highlands, also originated from the Ixtepeque center (personal communication, 2004). Although serious chronological problems exist with these interpretations, much of the Central Mexican influence on the Postclassic K'iche and Kakchiquel cultures might possibly derive from the Middle Classic Pacific Coast, the proposed time of maximum Teotihuacan political control. The material culture of the Late Postclassic Highland K'iche strongly supports this interpretation (Brown 1985).

Fowler (1989a: 146–150) offers calculations for the Pipil population on the Guatemalan coast in 1519. His estimates range from 37,000 to 115,000, with a mid-range of approximately 78,000 persons occupying an area of about 4,000 km^2. These data and calculations are based on documentary sources, not archaeology, and suggest that the Pipil settlements were numerous and well organized, probably in the form of *altepetl* (Nahua city-states or ethnic-states). Regardless of the preceding conjectures, the Pipil presence on the Guatemalan Pacific Coast was indeed considerable. Documentary sources identify a number of Pipil towns occupied in the immediate aftermath of the Conquest (figure 8.2). The unpublished Cerrato Tasaciones de Tributos, a Spanish document containing economic and demographic data, provides information on nineteen Pipil towns in what are now Escuintla and Santa Rosa Departments and contains "the earliest intact set of tribute assessments in existence" (Fowler 1989a: 27, figure 2). Lawrence Feldman (1974) lists twenty-one Pipil tribute payers in the Early Colonial Period, and Sandra Orellana (1995) offers data on thirty towns. Feldman (1989) has demonstrated that a wealth of documentation exists for the research area apart from the better-known Archivo General de Central America (AGCA Guatemala City) and the Archivo General de Indios (Seville), both of which still contain vast quantities of un-cataloged documents. A host of useful records such as censuses, tax assessments, and land titles and disputes might still be available at municipalities

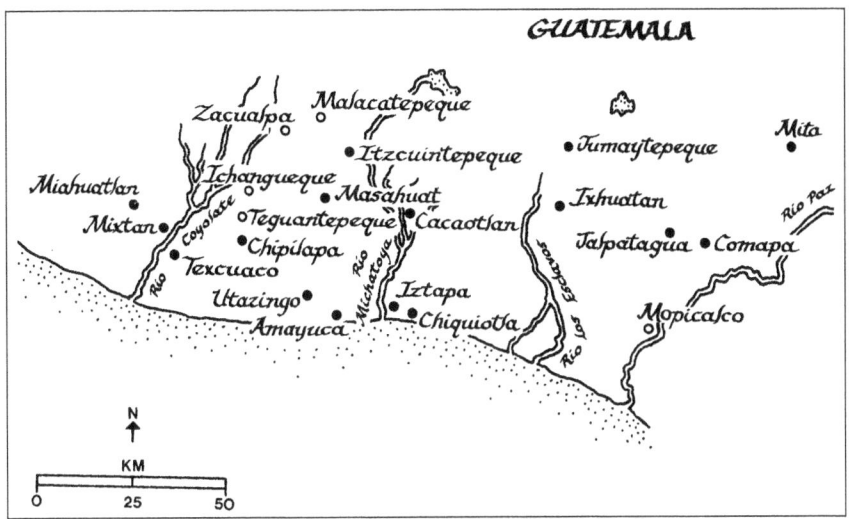

8.2. *Pipil towns on the Pacific Coast of Guatemala during the Spanish Colonial Period. After Fowler 1989a, figure 2. Open circles represent uncertain locations.*

and parish churches and should be examined to shed light on the probable existence and location of Contact Period sites and other valuable data.

DOCUMENTARY RESEARCH

We hoped to find links between archaeological sites and ethnohistoric ones, tying prehistory directly to Pipil ethnic identity. Dr. Ruud van Akkeren, a Dutch ethnohistorian, reviewed all known primary documents and searched for new texts in the AGCA to find Preconquest data on the social and political organization of Pipil towns such as Chipilapa, Teguantepeque, Utazingo, and Miahuatlán. He also looked for documentary accounts of Pipil culture—such as subsistence practices, craft specialization, and economic systems—to aid the identification of Pipil sites through strictly archaeological evidence.

An example of the material available for the Guatemalan Pipil region is *El Título de Ixhuatán*, an early–seventeenth-century manuscript written in a regional dialect of Nahuatl and difficult to translate. According to Feldman (personal communication, 2002) it contains data on the provinces of Escuintla and Guazacapa dating from the Prehistoric into the sixteenth century. A partial translation of the first part of the manuscript deals with the founding of various towns by the Preconquest Pipil and provides the names of various *caciques*, or chiefs. Most important, it names the towns as altepetl (Ichon and Grignon 1998). This strongly suggests that the Guatemalan Pipil emulated Nahua social and political organizations familiar from Postclassic Central Mexico.

Colonial documentation for the Escuintla Pipil is, unfortunately, scarce. Nevertheless, van Akkeren's research in the AGCA found two kinds of useful data. The first were Colonial documents detailing litigation about land issues or descriptions of social conflicts. Land disputes between Pipil towns or attempted usurpation (often successful) of Pipil lands by Spaniards who sought control over areas suitable for cattle raising or indigo production proved a good source of indigenous place names and lineage information. The second relates to linguistic identifications from numerous texts written in Nahuatl such as wills, a *cabildo* (town council) book written in Nahuatl in AD 1600, numerous passages about the importance of fishing to various Pipil towns, interrogations in the Mexican language, and numerous references to the *principales* of Pipil towns speaking *mejicana*. This research, together with appropriate data from the prior publications of Feldman (1974, 1980, 1992) and others, is too extensive to be detailed here.

Most, if not all, of the Pipil Colonial towns were not built over Prehispanic settlements but instead were the result of *reducciones*, where surviving remnants of Postconquest Pipil populations were forcibly moved and concentrated. This notwithstanding, at least some of the regional archaeological centers we believe to have been Pipil are either adjacent or in close proximity to the Colonial Pipil towns. This appears to be true in the cases of Carolina/Gomera-Chipilapa, Las Playas–Teguantepeque, Yolanda-Utazingo, and Costa Rica–Miahuatlán (see figure 8.2).

FIELDWORK GOALS, METHODS, AND LIMITATIONS

Our research goals were to (1) identify archaeological evidence of Pipil ethnicity, (2) describe the limits of Pipil settlement systems in time and space, (3) identify the nature and abundance of imported materials, (4) possibly identify craft production and economic specialization, and (5) describe subsistence practices. We hoped to be able to identify culturally specific Nahua traits introduced by in-migrating groups such as altepetl, *calpolli*, *chinamitl*, and *calli*.

We believe the best archaeological evidence by which Pipil ethnicity might be interpreted would be derived from controlled survey, surface collecting, and excavations in residential architecture. Because the Carolina-Gomera Complex represented two of the largest centers with associated residential areas, we intended originally to conduct 100 percent surface surveys of about 30 km^2 within a 2-km radius around and between these two sites, including the Pajuil, Esperanza, and Caulote sites as well (figure 8.3). Access, however, was denied to the two key areas of Caulote and Loma Linda, both large tracts of land adjacent to Carolina on the west and northwest sides. In addition, a relatively large area north and northwest of Gomera was either within urban Gomera or inaccessible. The inaccessible areas are shown in white in figure 8.3. Nevertheless, the area actually surveyed by the Pipil Project (shown in gray) was about 23 km². When combined with the Manantial area previously surveyed and excavated in 1991–1992 (shown in the southwest corner of figure 8.3), our survey area totaled approximately 27 km². We compensated for the un-surveyed zones to which we were denied access by expanding our research area to include the Las Playas site and surrounding area. Here we fortuitously discovered the large, previously unknown Nuevo Mundo village. We also surveyed and excavated El Jute, a small rural site 5.9 km southeast of Las Playas. Finally, we were also able to survey, sketch map, surface collect, and excavate a midden deposit at the Costa Rica site located at the probable western limit of the suspected Pipil-controlled region.

Our research area has been heavily impacted by modern agricultural operations. Most Late Postclassic residential structure remnants are no more than 5 to 20 cm high, almost invisible, especially in cattle pastures and all areas constantly plowed. We attempted to overcome the problem by using posthole diggers to test suspected mounds, with reasonably good success. It is also logical to assume that residential structures are underrepresented in our survey because of their destruction by annual plowing. One other example of the difficulties encountered was the survey of Potrero 2 at Carolina. The field was in *maicillo* (a type of sorghum) during our survey, and any ancient architecture had been plowed almost completely flat. The only evidence of occupation was heavy sherd concentrations on the mostly flat ground surface combined with several low mounds. Our explorations found that this single field contained the remains of about thirty structures, mostly elite residential.

Surveys in sugarcane fields were considerably easier, as ground surfaces were exposed following the cane harvest. These surveys were conducted 100 percent on foot. The field season ran from late October 2003 to mid-May 2004, much longer than originally anticipated. This resulted entirely from the scheduling of the sugarcane harvest, which, in turn, was complicated by the early arrival of the rainy season that then caused further delays in the harvest. Most sites were mapped with a total station and GPS unit directed by Lic. Carlos A. Batres, now a graduate student at Southern Illinois University. Data from maps, air and satellite photos, site surveys, and appropriate artifact information are being input into the regional GIS. To provide some idea of the scope of the project, about 400 individual structures were recorded during the field season.

Although we expected to find intact household architecture, burials, undisturbed charcoal samples, and intact trash deposits in domestic contexts under sealed floors, instead, almost all of the cultural remains we encountered were shallow and heavily disturbed. We estimate that 80 to 90 percent of all artifacts recovered were in the upper 30 to 40 cm and well within the plow zone. Although artifact densities were often quite high, most of the pottery and other artifacts were very fragmented. Our response was to excavate a larger number of test

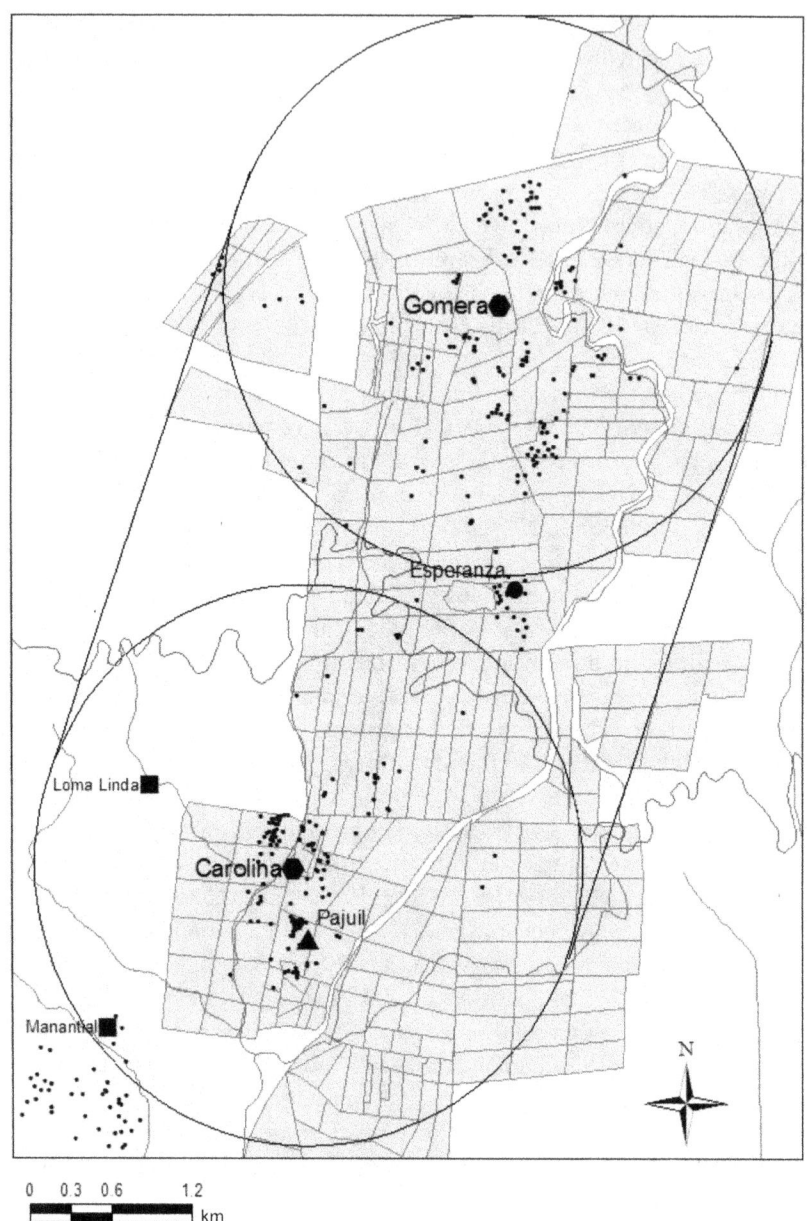

8.3. *The Carolina-Gomera study region. Gray shaded areas were surveyed, white areas were not. Carolina and Gomera regional centers (hexagons), Pajuil secondary center (triangle), Esperanza tertiary center (large circle). Pipil rural sites are small circles, including those shown in the southwest corner of the map that are Classic Period sites adjacent to Manantial and reoccupied by the Pipil. Other centers are shown as rectangles. By Frederick J. Bove and Carlos A. Batres.*

pits at a considerably larger number of sites than originally planned to obtain a larger sample. The shallow deposits permitted the relatively rapid excavation of 2m by 2 m test pits, even though all material was passed through 0.25-inch mesh screens. We also searched for deposits near fence lines and roads where the plows could not reach, finding several intact deposits and burials this way. In May 2004 we completed our first season's fieldwork of the Pipil Project on the Guatemalan Central Pacific Coast. We believe the Late Postclassic sites we have identified as regional centers are Nahua-Pipil, based on both documentary and archaeological evidence.

ARCHAEOLOGICAL SITE DESCRIPTIONS

Carolina

Bove discovered the Carolina site during his 1979 dissertation research. It was then recognized as the only major Late Postclassic regional center known on the Pacific Coast. The central nucleus of Carolina is compact, with a series of long, low mounds surrounding twin pyramids in the center and four sides, with the Zanjón San Pedro acting as the western boundary (figure 8.4). The Carolina site constructions are typically small and low, a general characteristic of all Ixtacapa Phase sites. It is the only known Late Postclassic coastal site with a twin pyramid complex that is highly reminiscent of the twin temples at Tenochtitlan. The trait may reflect some degree of contact with the Mexica-controlled Xoconusco in the Late Postclassic Aztec period. The Carolina twin temples are aligned north-south, unlike those in the adjacent highlands at Cahyup, Jilotepeque Viejo, and Los Cimientos–Tulumajillo, which are oriented east-west (Fox 1981: figure 3).

In 1982 a group of University of San Carlos, Guatemala, archaeology students under Bove's direction excavated at the site. All artifacts were shallow, stratigraphically speaking, with no evidence of multi-period occupancy; they were clearly intrusive (Bove 2002a). The ceramic and obsidian materials recovered represented the largest controlled collection of Ixtacapa Phase artifacts from any site on the Pacific Coast until the recent Pipil Project and were enormously valuable in the early definition of the Ixtacapa Phase. Our surveys recorded eighty-seven mounds or occupied areas outside the site center, including about thirty in Potrero 2 on the west side of the Zanjón San Pedro. We excavated nineteen mounds, including ten in Carolina central and nine in Potrero 2.

The elite nature of these two areas is shown by the fact that they contained 88.9 percent (n=24) of all the copper artifacts and 78.6 percent (n=11) of all the green obsidian ear spool fragments found at all the sites investigated by the Pipil Project. The copper artifacts include sewing needles, fishhooks, rings, strips, and several alloy nuggets. The most interesting discoveries were made in Operation 13–1, a low mound at the northern edge of Carolina central that contained 45.8

Frederick J. Bove, José Vicente Genovez, and Carlos A. Batres

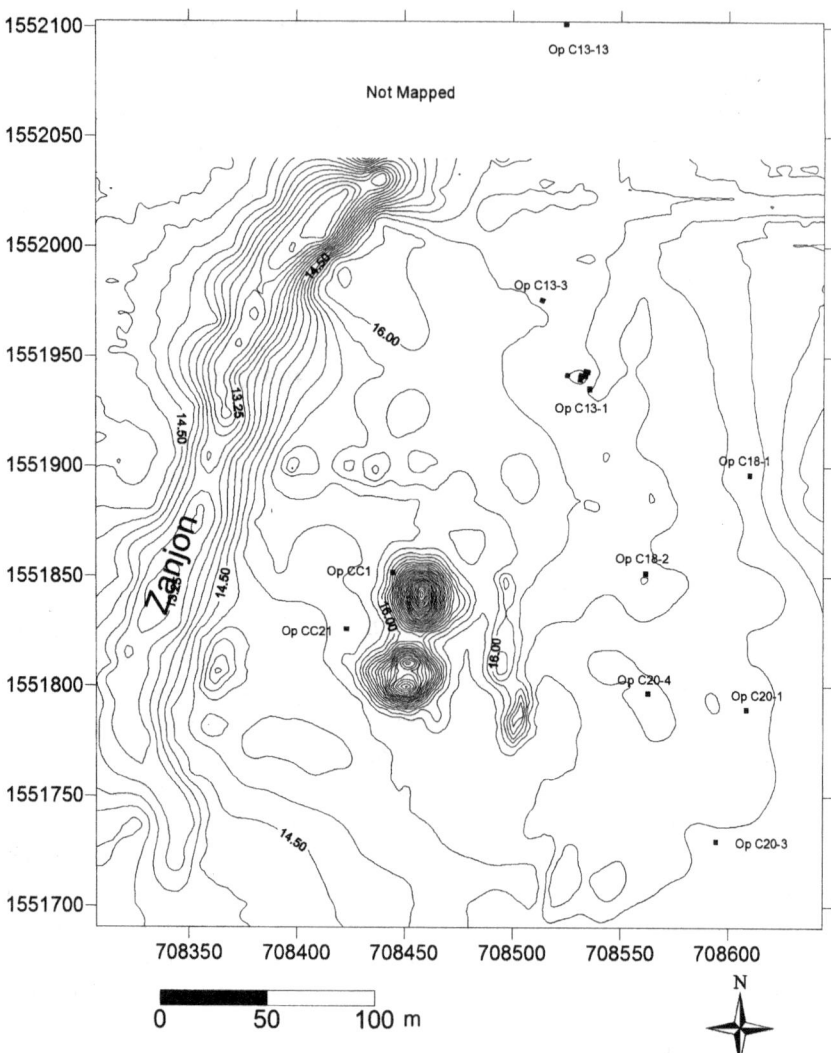

8.4. *The central part of the Late Postclassic Carolina archaeological site, showing mounds and excavations.*

percent (n=11) of all the copper artifacts found at Carolina. Here we also uncovered an enormous quantity of pottery and obsidian artifacts, including numerous small projectile points, many imported exotics, much Chinautla Polychrome, Fortress White-on-Red, Santa Rita Micaceous wares, and several caches containing obsidian cores. Another cache offering was a Teotihuacan-style candelero and a Teotihuacan figurine head, possibly heirlooms or perhaps an indication that the Texas-Montana colonists (whose gigantic complex is only 2.8 km southwest) were Nahua as proposed by Dakin and Wichmann (2000).

The percentage of imported exotics, along with very high densities of ceramics and obsidian, leave little doubt that the Potrero 2 zone as well as Mounds 13-1 and 18-2 were occupied by elites. The elite-occupied area is concentrated close to the nuclear center, although there is no recognizable elite-ritual group in Potrero 2. The surface and excavated collections suggest a single Ixtacapa occupational phase, although some Classic Period sherds were found in mound fill—especially on the west side of Potrero 2, the portion of the site nearest the Middle Classic Loma Linda Complex. A test pit into the eastern side of the base of the northern twin pyramid (Operation CC1) revealed several construction phases, although all the pottery found in the mound fill was Ixtacapa Phase. It is possible that a second pyramid was added at a later date than the original, but we cannot confirm this until excavations are expanded. Three radiocarbon age determinations are available from Carolina: two from Operation 13-1 and one from Operation 20-1 (table 8.1). They place the Carolina Complex and Ixtacapa Phase squarely within the Late Postclassic Period, a placement supported by other evidence.

Caulote

This archaeological site (figure 8.5) was discovered in 1979. Caulote is unusual in that it contains the remains of four elite-ritual architectural groups aligned north-south on the west bank of the Zanjón San Pedro. All identifiable material from the sparse surface collections made is Ixtacapa Phase. Caulote's architecture is almost identical to that of Pajuil. We believe the buildings represent the seat(s) of a lineage or corporate group, although the number, clustered as they are, is unusual, as is their separation from the nearest residential zone in Potrero 2 to the south.

Pajuil

The Pajuil site groups (figure 8.6) were first identified in 1982–1983 during surveys by a University of San Carlos field class. The Pajuil area was explored again in 2000 and thoroughly mapped and investigated in 2003 during the Pipil Project. The site complex is located 800 m south of Carolina and contains two elite-ritual groups (P1 and P2) plus about twenty-five residential structures. We believe the site represents a chinamitl. Extensive survey and test excavations suggest a domestic rural center because of the complete absence of imported exotics such as copper and green obsidian ear spool artifacts. The residential area associated with P1 contained the usual domestic pottery, many small obsidian projectile points, fired-clay net weights, burned animal bone, and several heavily disturbed burials. All cultural materials were shallow, in the upper 30 to 40 cm,

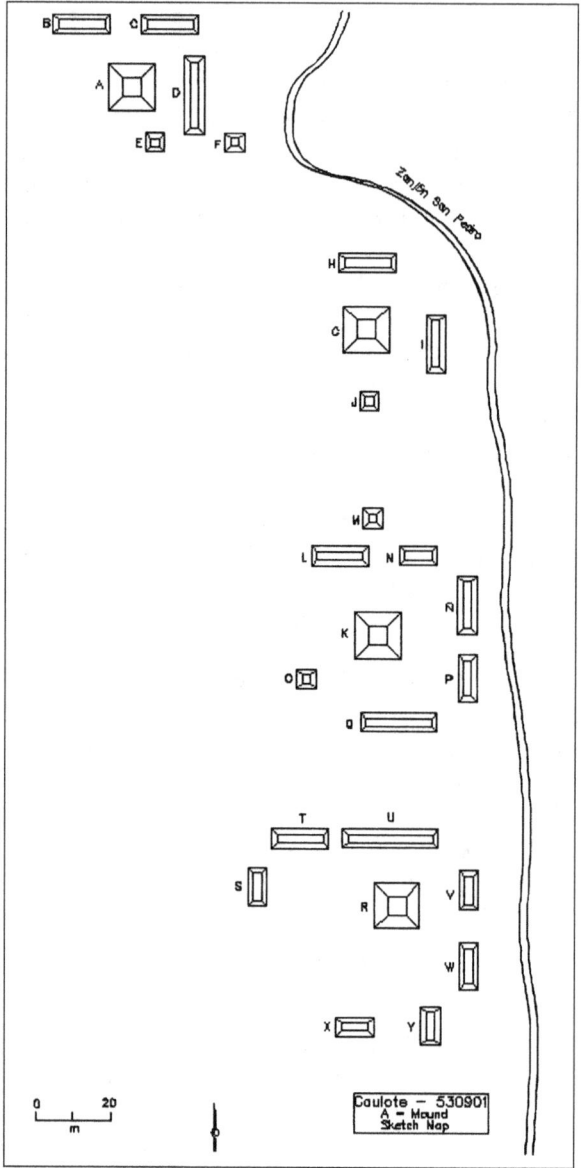

8.5. *The Late Postclassic Caulote archaeological site. Drawings by Frederick J. Bove and Carlos A. Batres.*

and Ixtacapa Phase. Imported ceramics in relatively low frequencies included Chinautla Polychrome, Santa Rita Micaceous, and Fortress White-on-Red. Their presence in certain households may represent higher status.

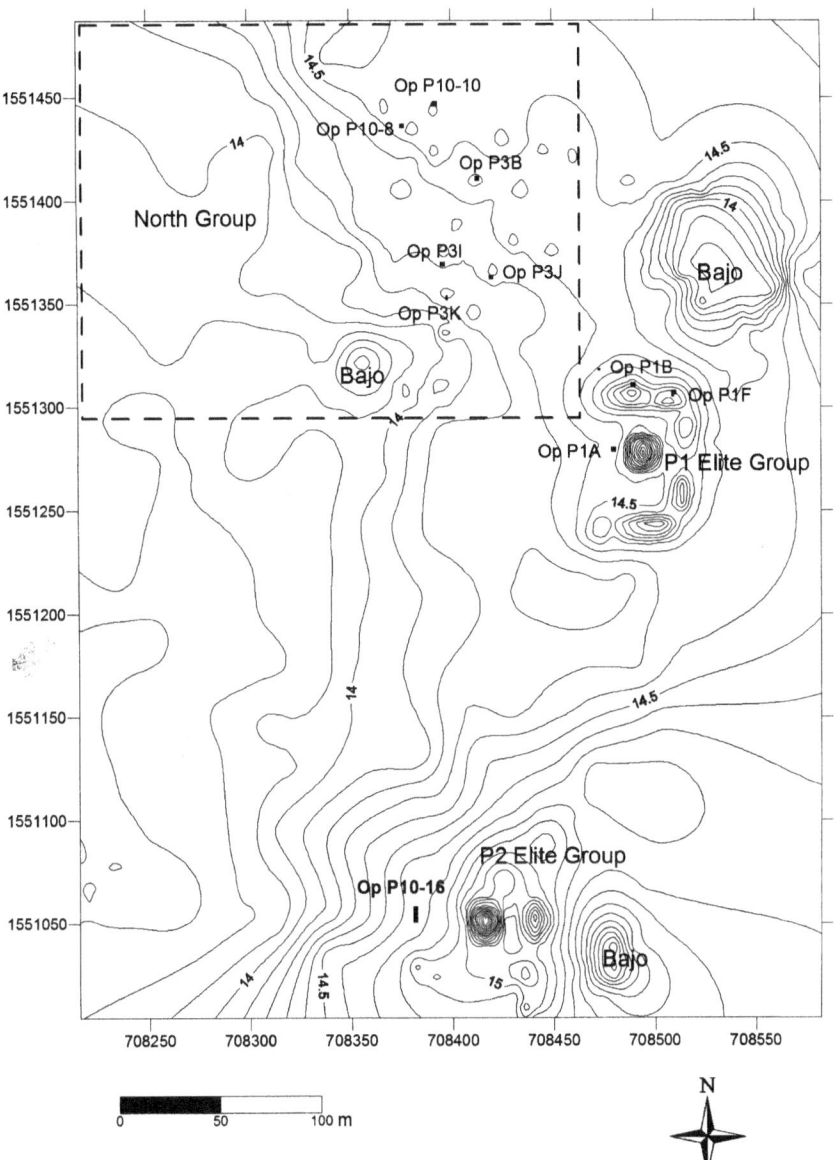

8.6. *The Late Postclassic Pajuil site, showing mound locations and excavation operations. By Frederick J. Bove and Carlos A. Batres.*

Esperanza

This site, first discovered in 2002, is located between Carolina and Gomera about 2.5 km northeast of the Carolina site center. Fourteen extremely low mounds or surface sherd concentrations and a single elite-ritual group (E1-Group) were found. We excavated eight test pits, including three adjacent to the central area near what are probably elite residential structures. Cultural materials are always no more than 30 to 40 cm in depth. Some imported ceramics were found, including Chinautla Polychrome, Santa Rita Micaceous, and Fortress White-on-Red, but in very small quantities. We believe Esperanza represents a chinamitl, although one considerably smaller than Pajuil. All mounds and surface sherd scatters lie atop sterile sands. This sand horizon was apparently the result of catastrophic flooding just prior to the Pipil arrival.

Gomera

The Gomera archaeological site is located principally on the Finca Los Cerritos and adjacent fincas to its east and south about 2 km south of the modern town of La Gomera. Gustav Eisen (1888), despite not having visited the ruins, nevertheless reported that sculptures in what we now recognize as Cotzumalguapa Style purportedly came from the Gomera site. Edwin Shook studied aerial photographs in 1967 showing long mounds forming a court, but he did not visit the site either. No archaeologist visited, mapped, or collected the site until February 2000, with the arrival of Bove's GIS survey project.

Historic sources report that an Indian town named Chipilapa (Nahuatl: place of the Chipilines) was located about 1 km from the town of La Gomera. The indigenous population was moved from its place of origin to Chipilapa in 1611 (AGCA, A1, expediente, legajo 210; Aucar 1987). Other sources dated to 1676 state that the inhabitants of Chipilapa spoke mejicana (Nahuatl), and there seems little doubt that they were Pipil. It is tempting to think that the Gomera archaeological site is ancient Chipilapa because of its proximity to modern La Gomera. However, modern Chipilapa is 1 to 2 km north, not south, of La Gomera where the Gomera archaeological site is located. The Chipilapa area has not been investigated, and it is possible that during the Spanish reduction process the surviving population of the Gomera site was moved to Chipilapa, perhaps also with that of the Carolina zone. It is highly unusual to find two major archaeological centers as close together as Carolina and Gomera. Perhaps both in combination constituted the major regional center on the lower central coast, with the overall complex possibly defined as a "capital zone" (Alexander 1997; Stark 1997, 1999).

Unfortunately, Gomera has been largely destroyed. We estimate that the nuclear zone and nearby residential area originally contained about seventy-five structures in addition to a possible elite-ritual center to the southeast. We recorded an additional thirty-six Late Postclassic occupied areas on the nearby Finca Vista Hermosa to the northeast, all dated to the Ixtacapa Phase. Surface collections and twenty excavations made within the site center and nearby domestic structures revealed, once again, a shallow, single-phase occupation.

The Gomera site center, as at Carolina, lacked artifacts suggestive of ritual or administrative activities. Evidence of multiple constructions was noted at Operation G8 (several floors) and at Operation G7 (burned adobe floors and a complex series of constructions); all were apparently completed within a relatively short period of time.

Las Playas

The Las Playas regional center was discovered by Shook, Hatch, and Bove during a reconnaissance of the general area in 1978. Las Playas is located 500 m south of the Río Cristóbal and north of modern Cerro Colorado. The archaeological site contains at least twenty-five mounds, many still with a river cobble covering. Unique within all known Ixtacapa Phase regional centers is a sunken *palangana* style I-shaped ballcourt oriented 22°. Mound 2, the tallest surviving structure, is only 2.5 m high (figure 8.7). Las Playas is located about 3 km west of the Finca Teguantepeque, the undoubted location of the Early Historic town of San Miguel Teguantepeque. We believe the surviving Pipil population from Las Playas was forcibly moved to Teguantepeque during the reduction process following the Conquest. Later, what few people were left were transported to Santa Lucía Cotzumalguapa about AD 1600, according to the sources (Fuentes y Guzman 1932–1933). The current Finca Teguantepeque was originally part of the extensive Finca San Jerónimo formed in 1560 (Gavarrete Escobar 1980; Aucar 1987).

Mounds near the site center were found to be almost devoid of artifacts. Surface artifacts were sparse, yet almost all identifiable sherds were Ixtacapa Phase. Trenching revealed that the ballcourt walls were made of river cobbles and some shaped stones set with mud or adobe mortar. These walls were stepped with two vertical risers separated by a narrow horizontal section, not slanted as is typical of Maya courts. The ballcourt floor was thin, fragile clay resting on sterile sands. All architectural evidence clearly pointed to a rapid, single-phase construction.

The obvious question of why only a single ballcourt is known from all the regional centers cannot be answered at present. The scarcity of Late Postclassic ballcourts, particularly at peripheral coastal sites (Agrinier 1988; Leyenaar and Parsons 1988), is well-documented. Barbara Voorhies and Janine Gasco (2004: 182) also note that they are rare at Late Postclassic Soconusco sites. The Las Playas nuclear zone may be somewhat earlier than the others, although recovered ceramics are predominately Ixtacapa Phase. The proximity of the nearby large Nuevo Mundo village, with its overwhelming inventory of Pipil ceramics, as well as the nearby probable location of Early Historic San Miguel Teguantepeque, makes it extremely likely that Las Playas was a Pipil regional center.

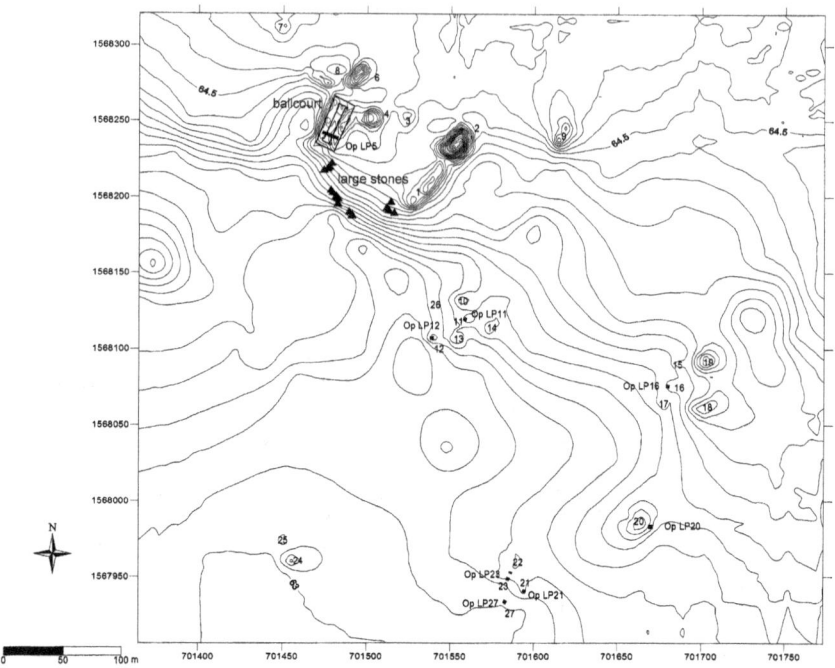

8.7. *The Late Postclassic Las Playas archaeological site, showing mound designations and excavation operations. Note the ballcourt at the top left. By Frederick J. Bove and Carlos A. Batres.*

Nuevo Mundo

Nuevo Mundo, discovered in 2004, is a large archaeological village, possibly a calpolli, only about 700 m northeast of Las Playas. The site consists of about seventy mounds, many with river cobble bases. A possible elite-ritual group has been almost destroyed. Surface collections and excavations revealed dense artifact concentrations. At least some of these are probably trash dumps close to residential households. No copper artifacts or green obsidian ear spools were found, and Chinautla Polychrome and Fortress White-on-Red imported ceramics were rare. Somewhat higher frequencies of Santa Rita Micaceous are present but still in small quantities. Nuevo Mundo seems to have played a purely domestic role similar to Esperanza, Pajuil, and El Jute. Pottery is identical to that from sites such as Carolina and Gomera, believed to be the central zone of the Escuintla Pipil.

El Jute

This small site, located 8 km southeast of Las Playas, was accidentally discovered in 1989 during a survey of the nearby Middle-Late Formative Los Limones regional center. It consists of nine or ten small mounds around an irregular elite-ritual group. Many of the mounds were surfaced with river cobbles. We excavated an apparent altar, one of two small altars within the elite-ritual plaza, and found a thick layer of river cobbles overlaying mound fill containing mostly Ixtacapa Phase material. Excavations down the center of the tallest mound (J6) suggested multiple construction activity. With the exception of some Middle-Late Formative sherds in mound fill probably incorporated from the nearby Los Limones site, all ceramics from domestic contexts are Ixtacapa Phase. The El Jute elite-ritual grouping is less architecturally rigid than those found at Caulote or Pajuil and more similar to those found at Nuevo Mundo and Esperanza.

Costa Rica

This site was discovered by Shook in 1977 through examination of aerial photographs. Surface collections from the adjoining sugarcane finca to the south and west were made as far as 1 to 1.5 km west of Costa Rica, and all seemed to be Ixtacapa Phase. Surveys in 2002 of a newly cleared area on the Finca Santa Julia 1 km northwest also found Ixtacapa Phase sherds atop large platform structures. In 1991 Bove photographed a small stone sculpture with a carved Tlaloc face on a farm in the Obero zone 70 km east, brought there from the Costa Rica site by the former owner (Bove 2002a: figure 7). We finally obtained permission in 2004 to map and surface collect the Costa Rica site and surrounding areas. We recorded fifty-six surviving mounds in the site's central portion. Locals told us of many other mounds formerly in the cane fields surrounding Costa Rica but since destroyed. We also excavated a rich, albeit partially looted, midden deposit accidentally discovered by finca workers. An enormous quantity of pottery came from this excavation plus a charcoal sample (see table 8.1). The dates are entirely consistent with those from the Carolina site. The Costa Rica site pottery appears to be a variant of Ixtacapa Phase, especially since most of the *comales* lacked the composite wall of Prado examples, although some are identical to central coastal Prado examples. The Remanso Ceramic Group is a bit different at Costa Rica, with *guacamaya* (parrot) effigy supports predominating. That may be significant, since eagle and jaguar supports predominate in the central zone. Most of the Costa Rica comales are similar to those from the Tzutujil capital of Chuitinamit in the adjacent highlands and are now housed in the "ceramoteca" at the Museo Nacional in Guatemala City.

The Costa Rica site is located on the South Coast directly south of the Tzutujil Maya area. Costa Rica was near the Colonial town of Miahuatlán, which, like Teguantepeque, has never been located. In Nahuatl, *Miahuatlán* means "place of the maize flower"; the meaning is the same in Tzutujil Maya. Van Akkeren (2000) believes members of the Tzutujil confederation came from the Miahuatlán Pipil region at a date earlier than the Late Postclassic Period. Orellana (1984) describes incursions to the coastal area near the Miahuatlán region by the Tzutujil Maya in the Late Postclassic Period. Ethnohistoric sources note a Late Postclassic alliance between the Pipil and Tzutujil against the Kakchiquel Maya. We suspect the Miahuatlán area may have been multiethnic, based on the different comales and somewhat different Remanso Group pottery.

Yolanda

The Yolanda archaeological site is the southernmost regional center thus far known. Located 2 km east of the Rió Achiguate and 6 km from its mouth on the Pacific Coast (see figure 8.1), the site was discovered by a survey crew in 1991. Yolanda was revisited in 2000 and 2003, as we originally planned to include it in the Pipil Project, but at the last minute access was denied. The site is large, with two enormous groups forming huge plazas and the probable remnants of a third on the north. Three of the highest mounds reach 5 m. Yolanda site architecture is different from that at other regional centers, which are better interpreted as altepetls. All Yolanda pottery is Ixtacapa Phase, with Prado comales, Remanso, and Chontel well represented. No surveys were conducted outside the main architectural groups, but it is probable that extensive residential zones lie within 1 km. Yolanda may have been located to control salt production along the coastal littoral, as well as coastal canoe commercial traffic. Yolanda is only 2 km southeast of the Early Colonial Period town of Utazingo (Otacingo). Colonial Utazingo was a cacao tribute payer in that period and is probably the town where Pipil survivors of the Spanish Conquest from the Yolanda region were forcibly moved (Bergman 1959; Carmack 1965; Feldman 1974; Feldman and Walters 1980).

Iscuintepeque

This is the assumed Pipil capital destroyed by Alvarado and his allies in 1524, although we now believe the Carolina-Gomera capital zone also could have served as a major power center. Lic. Francis Polo Sifontes and Bove tried to locate Iscuintepeque in 1981, based on Polo Sifontes's interpretation of descriptions in the *Título de Alotenango*, but without success. It has either been incorporated into modern Escuintla or possibly could be on or near the Finca Las Chagüites area to the north (Polo Sifontes 1979, 1989).

La Isla

The La Isla site, located on the west bank of the Río Achiguate 14 km west of modern Escuintla, was discovered by Oswaldo Chinchilla in 1996. Access to La Isla for inclusion in our Pipil Project was denied by the landowners. Nevertheless, using a GPS unit, we mapped and surface collected the site in 2001, finding twenty low mounds in irregular patio groups between two Classic Period platform mounds. Ceramics are principally Ixtacapa Phase pottery with some local variation. The Remanso Group is well represented, but sherds are thicker, with surface treatments not as well prepared as those from Carolina and other major centers. Some sherds are decorated with red-on-buff paint with small white circles and are similar to several sherds observed in ceramic collections from the Santa Rosa area in eastern Guatemala (Estrada Belli 1999; Kosakowsky, Estrada Belli, and Pettit 2000; Kosakowsky 2002). Much ceramic material appears to be provincial variants of Remanso, Prado, and Chontel. Some sherds may represent trade pottery from the highlands.

Variedades

The Variedades site and several artifacts were described by Shook (1965). In 2000 our survey team visited the area, located on the Finca Variedades, now a large sugarcane farm. Although hampered by high sugarcane growth, we were able to locate three separate sectors with cultural materials. The collection areas were named Variedades 1, 2, and 3. We collected numerous Ixtacapa Phase sherds from relatively flat areas at Variedades 1 and 2 where sherd concentrations indicated subtle rises, probably the remains of low domestic structures. Variedades 3 is located 1 km south of Variedades 1 and 2 and is a large, modified natural hill forming a platform structure around which were collected an Ixtacapa Phase metate and sherds that suggest a probable domestic occupation adjacent to the platform structure.

Cotzumalguapa

Chinchilla's research, aided by Sonia Medrano, within the greater Cotzumalguapa area over the past decade has revealed some areas containing Ixtacapa Phase pottery, especially Santa Rita Micaceous, Santa Rita Jabonoso, and Masagua Reddish-Brown comales. These are from the general areas of Bilbao, El Baúl, and the El Castillo groups (Chinchilla 1996; Chinchilla and Medrano 1997). There is no question of a substantial Late Postclassic presence within the zone, but it is complicated by the existence of both Pipil and Kakchiquel Early Historic communities in close proximity. The Kakchiquel supposedly occupied El Convento, and the Pipil were at nearby San Juan Perdido only 2 km northeast. In spite of relatively high frequencies of Ixtacapa Phase pottery within certain limited areas in the zone, no major Late Postclassic center has been found and we remain doubtful that one existed.

ARCHAEOLOGICAL EVIDENCE FOR PIPIL ETHNICITY

The strongest indications of Prehistoric intrusive migratory groups are discontinuities in three kinds of archaeological evidence: (1) domestic ceramics, (2) household architecture, and (3) settlement patterns (Schortman 1986; Creamer

1987; Shennan 1994a, 1994b; Jones 1997; Stark, Elson, and Clark 1998). The Pipil Late Postclassic on the Guatemalan Escuintla coast saw the arrival of a completely new set of ceramic styles, household architecture, and settlement patterns. Preexisting patterns of obsidian procurement were also abandoned and new ones substituted, and further evidence for the chronological placement of a proposed Pipil intrusion is supported by chronometric age determinations.

Radiocarbon Age Determinations

Our project produced the first radiocarbon dates from any Postclassic site on the Pacific Coast. Consequently, chronologies were based predominantly on cross-ceramic comparisons and the few stratigraphic excavations that took place in 1982 at the Carolina site. These were later augmented by the 1991–1992 excavations of Classic Period residential structures in the Texas-Montana area southwest of Carolina with Late Postclassic remains within their upper strata. We now have four radiocarbon age determinations in hand from stratigraphic excavations at two of the sites studied by the Pipil Project (see table 8.1). All samples were run at the University of Arizona NSF laboratory, all were charcoal, and all are AMS corrected for isotopic fractionation. All have been calibrated at 2δ (95.4 percent) with the CALIB 5.0 program (Stuiver and Reimer 1993; Stuiver et al. 1998; Stuiver, Reimer, and Reimer 2005) for conversion to AD dates in the Christian calendar.

Ixtacapa Phase Ceramics

The Pacific Coastal Late Postclassic Ixtacapa Ceramic Complex (AD 1200/1250–1500) is distinguishable not only from local Classic Period antecedents but from contemporary coastal Xinca and Highland Kakchiquel (at Iximché and Chitak Tzak) Ceramic Complexes as well (Navarrete 1962; Parsons 1967; Wauchope 1970; Robinson 1994, 1998; Estrada Belli 1999; Kosakowsky, Estrada Belli, and Pettit 2000; Bove 2002a; Kosakowsky 2002; Nance, Whittington, and Borg 2003; Bove et al. n.d.). Domestic pottery usually derives from household production and is usually a quite conservative artifact assemblage. It tends to reflect local ethnic identity much more than elite or trade items (Rouse 1986; Creamer 1987; Jones 1997; Stark 1998a). We have identified several domestic pottery types probably diagnostic of Pipil ethnicity at sites that are almost assuredly Pipil (Bove 2002a; Bove et al. n.d.). The best identification resulted from comparative analysis and spatial distribution studies of that most basic Late Postclassic domestic pottery form: the flat comal.

Several different comal types are found in the Ixtacapa Phase on the Pacific Coast: Prado Black, Masagua Reddish-Brown, Santa Rita Micaceous, and Santa Rita Jabanoso. Prado Black comales are ubiquitous at Carolina, Gomera, Las

Table 8.1. Pipil Project radiocarbon age determinations

Site	Laboratory No.	Lot No.	RAUD*	14C Years BP	AD Age Range
Carolina	AA60822	C13-1-06-06	0.57653	566 ± 42	1299–1370
			0.42347		1381–1432
Carolina	AA60821	C13-1-08-06	0.190279	519 ± 42	1318–1353
			0.809721		1389–1446
Carolina	AA60824	C20-1-05-05	0.575332	676 ± 42	1267–1324
			0.424668		1345–1354
Costa Rica	AA60823	CR-04-1	0.213563	522 ± 42	1317–1354
			0.786437		1389–1446

*Relative area under distribution

Playas, Nuevo Mundo, El Jute, Esperanza, and Yolanda and are present in lesser frequencies at Costa Rica, all believed to be Pipil or Pipil-dominated centers. They are rarely found in the Late Postclassic Piedmont Cotzumalguapa regional sites to the north, nor are they reported at Xinca sites to the east. The most distinguishing feature of Prado Black comales, apart from color and paste composition, is their form: open plates with thin composite silhouette walls. This form represents 85 percent of all Prado comales analyzed previous to our Pipil Project. A sample of fifteen of these specimens was analyzed using Instrumental Neutron Activation Analysis (INAA) at the Missouri University Research Reactor (MURR) laboratories. Eleven are from the lower coastal zone sites of Carolina, Las Playas, and Yolanda, and four are from the Cotzumalguapa zone. All were sourced to the lower coast most likely near the Carolina site.

The only Postclassic form with a profile similar to the Prado comal is reported from the Texcoco and Chalco-Xochimilco regions, Mexico, in the Late Toltec Period (Parsons 1971: figure 71l–n; Parsons et al. 1982: figure 100a–d). The Late Toltec Period under Parsons's old system is the Mazapan Phase, approximately AD 950–1150. In general, however, the Tollan Ceramic Complex at Tula, dated to AD 950–1150/1200, bears no resemblance to Pipil Ixtacapa Phase ceramics. Some types with effigy supports are similar to the Marihua type at Cihuatán, El Salvador, and include Macana Red-on-Brown: Macana variety and probably Manuelito Plain Brown ware excluding the comales (Cobean 1990; Mastache, Cobean, and Healan 2002: figure 3.1).

Masagua Reddish-Brown comales are significantly different than Prado, as they do not have the distinctive composite silhouette (or s/z angle) profile. Instead the forms are open/out-slanting or rounded-wall dishes or plates representing 94 percent of all identified forms. Masagua surface treatments and paste composition are completely different from Prado as well. Masagua comales are found in high frequencies at Cotzumalguapa area sites but are completely absent from the Pipil centers on the central and lower coast. Ten specimens were analyzed at MURR, and all were sourced within the upper Piedmont Cotzumalguapa zone. Masagua comal forms are similar to those reported at Highland Kakchiquel centers such as Chitak Tzak, Iximché, the Antigua Basin, and others—all of which have profiles significantly different than the composite silhouette of Prado. Gosselain (1998: 92) has shown that "distribution of [ceramic] fashioning techniques generally coincides with linguistic boundaries" (but see Shennan 1994a; Jones 1997). Both Prado and Masagua comales undoubtedly had similar functions but are of completely different styles; we believe this is a result of ethnic differences (Sackett 1977, 1990).

Yet another example is the spatial distribution and forms, including comales, of the Santa Rita Ceramic Group, which includes Santa Rita Micaceous and Santa Rita Jabonoso. Santa Rita is the most abundant ceramic group in the Cotzumalguapa region during the Ixtacapa Phase and is usually considered a Late Postclassic to Protohistoric diagnostic marker (Bove 2002a; Bove et al. n.d.). Mica or Micaceous ware is widely distributed at highland sites and is dominant there (Navarrete 1962; Robinson 1994, 1998). All Santa Rita Micaceous types are rare at the lower coastal Pipil sites. Only 2.243 kg of Santa Rita ceramics were found in all of our Pipil Project excavations, just 0.0017 percent of the 1,322.3-kg total ceramic weight excavated.

Twelve Santa Rita Micaceous and ten Santa Rita Jabanoso sherds were analyzed at MURR, and all were found to have been produced from raw material sources near the upper Piedmont Cotzumalguapa zone or perhaps at higher elevations. Significantly, the comal forms, particularly vessel profiles of both Santa Rita types, are also markedly different from Prado examples. About 83 percent have open/out-slanting or rounded walls. None has a composite silhouette profile. Striking differences in the spatial distribution of other key ceramic types exist with the Remanso, Chontel Unslipped, and Pajuil Ceramic Groups that were found in high frequencies in all domestic contexts at Carolina, Gomera, Nuevo Mundo, El Jute, Esperanza, and Yolanda but that were largely or totally absent from the Cotzumalguapa and Xinca regions. In summary, it appears that the domestic pottery assemblage of the sites we believe to have been Pipil can be specifically linked to Pipil ethnic identity.

Settlement Patterns and Architecture

Ethnic identity can sometimes be discerned through site layout and domestic architecture (Stark 1998a, 1998b; Stark, Elson, and Clark 1998). As with domestic pottery, Late Postclassic Period Pipil architecture and settlement patterns incorporate distinctive features that distinguish them from Xinca, Kakchiquel, and K'iche patterns. New patterns attributable to the intrusive Pipil include the general lack of monumental architecture at most sites studied, the reduced size of central places, the long, low-range structures surrounding plazas within the regional centers, the absence of large platform structures, small building size, and an entirely different residential pattern represented by what we term elite-ritual architectural patio groups, a hallmark of Pipil sites.

Pipil elite-ritual patio groups are usually from five to seven low, small structures surrounding a rectangular patio with a temple shrine in the center. They cluster into larger groups that can be interpreted as Pipil social organizations, such as chinamitl (sub-wards), calpolli (wards), and probably to the next highest level, the altepetl, the fundamental political and territorial building block; all such organizations were presumably imported from Postclassic Central Mexico. The elite-ritual patio groups are clearly identified with the Pipil regional centers and are not reported at Xinca centers in the adjoining territory to the east (Campbell et al. 1975; Feldman and Walters 1980; Estrada Belli 1999). Xinca architecture and household form are completely different and are built around large groupings of up to fourteen or fifteen small-range structures formally arranged around a rectangular plaza, with the larger sites composed of several clusters. Arranged informally around these clusters are households in a relatively dense pattern but lacking formal spatial regularity.

In contrast, Kakchiquel and K'iche political centers were built around three ruling lineages and manifested archaeologically by three distinct civic plazas at their capitals (Hill 1996). The Highland Late Postclassic civic plazas are oriented east-west, usually with temples on the east and west sides. None of these characteristics fits the known Pipil regional centers. Architecture at the Kakchiquel Chitak Tzak site does not resemble any of the Pipil centers except in the presence of long, low structures, a trait that appears to be pan-Mesoamerican (Robinson 1994, 1998).

Obsidian

Major changes in obsidian procurement, exchange, tool manufacturing, and use are probably associated with the intrusive Pipil groups during the drastic restructuring that took place in the Classic-Postclassic transition. During the Formative and Classic Periods the principal obsidian sources were El Chayal (EC) and San Martín Jilotepeque (SMJ) in the adjacent highlands, whose proportions varied across space and time. Pachuca green obsidian was only found in Early Classic contexts and accounted for 2.2 percent of the Balberta site total. The largest amount of Ixtepeque obsidian before the Postclassic Period was only 1.4 percent from the Late Terminal Classic Cotzumalguapa area. At Late Postclassic Carolina, Ixtepeque obsidian increased dramatically to 91 percent of the total (n=587) recovered during the limited 1982 project. An uncontrolled collection from Las Playas (n=50) shows 54 percent Ixtepeque, 25 percent EC, and 22 percent SMJ. At the time of the Conquest there is strong evidence that the Pipil controlled the Ixtepeque source near the El Salvador border. Fowler

(1989a, 1989b) suggests that a Pipil state was established at Asunción Mita in the eastern Guatemala Piedmont to control the Ixtepeque obsidian trade. Sheets (1984) believes the Pipil expansion into Central America represented a concerted effort to gain control of obsidian sources and trade routes.

INTERPRETATIONS

Our documentary and field research was guided by a number of working hypotheses derived from migration and ethnicity theory and our own experience in the regional archaeology of Pacific Guatemala. We interpreted the archaeological and archival evidence produced by our Pipil Research Project by applying more than a half-dozen alternative explanations as work proceeded, rejecting some, modifying others, and developing new ones. The hypothetical interpretations we considered, described next, are kept separate through numeration.

1. Pipil migrations to Coastal Guatemala might have consisted of short-distance movements following a wave-of-advance model (Haggett 1965; Hodder and Orton 1976). Unfortunately, such a model does not appear to agree with historical documentation for the Nahua "diaspora."

2. The Pipil migrations might first have been led by pioneers such as "pochteca," or mercenaries. If Middle Classic Texas-Montana Teotihuacan colonists were such pioneers, they occupied some of the most productive land on the Guatemalan Pacific Coast close to the Carolina-Gomera Complex of the Postclassic Period. Arguing against this, however, is the abrupt discontinuity in settlement pattern and ceramics between the Terminal Classic and Late Postclassic Periods and the fact that no fancy Tohil Plumbate or other artifact assemblage spans the break. Another possible scenario is suggested by the spatial distribution of *hachas*, yokes, and I-shaped palangana-type ballcourts, presumably originating on the Gulf Coast and diffused through the "Peripheral Coastal Lowlands" (Parsons 1969, 1978) during the Late Terminal Classic Period. These traits could have been brought by early pioneering Nahua groups. But this argument is at variance with the lack of green Pachuca obsidian at the Pipil centers. Green obsidian is found often at Early Postclassic centers in southern Mesoamerica, including western El Salvador (Gasco 1987; Clark 1989; Fowler 1989a). The lack of green obsidian at Late Postclassic Pipil centers during this period is probably a result of the late Pipil movement (after AD 1150–1200) and even later blockage of coastal commercial routes by the K'iche who conquered the western Guatemala coast in the late Late Postclassic (Carmack 1973, 1981).

3. The Pipil migrations might have been small-scale movements or infiltration over a long period, perhaps several centuries. Archaeological evidence supporting Pipil infiltration over several centuries would be the sequential development and occupation of major centers, with rural sites settled later than the major regional centers. Such an interpretation does not seem supported by the results of fieldwork completed so far.

4. The Pipil migrations might have been large-scale, of functioning communities with imbedded hierarchical structures, and occurring over short periods of time—less than several centuries. Archaeological expectations for this alternative would be short archaeological time depth at centers and a significant discontinuity from earlier periods in settlement patterns, ceramics (especially domestic pottery), and economic organization, as well as new patterns of obsidian procurement, tool manufacturing, and use. Nahua organizational structures such as the alteptl should be imported essentially intact. Such large-scale migrations would most easily have as their destinations previously unoccupied ground. This alternative seems well supported by the archaeological and ethnohistoric evidence so far in hand. Similarly, large-scale migration should "leapfrog," whereby large areas are bypassed (Anthony 1990). The archaeological correlates should resemble cultural islands of settlement. Ethnohistoric evidence slightly favors this hypothesis, as no Pipil settlements are presently known west of Escuintla to the Mexican border and the Xinca occupied most of the eastern Guatemala coast as far as El Salvador.

5. Another theoretical explanation for the Pipil entry to Coastal Guatemala is selective migration. Unstable conditions such as war, catastrophic environmental changes, economic stress, and persecution might produce large migratory groups of specific age and sex (such as young male warriors) rather than a more general population range. Such a process might have resulted in the Toltec "diaspora," the Nonoalca-Pipil Late Postclassic migrations, or both. Only the osteological analysis of extensive burial populations to determine age-gender compositions over space and time might support such a hypothesis, and such analyses are insufficient at present.

6. The Pipil migrations might have been into uncontested areas. None of the Late Postclassic Pipil settlements on the Guatemalan central coast appear to be fortified. All are easily accessible and lack obvious defensive walls, moats, or other fortifications. This is striking, given the ethnohistoric accounts of warfare between the Pipil and Kakchiquel, and it contrasts sharply with the adjacent highlands where the major regional capitals are fortified and located on defensible terrain (Guillemin 1965; Carmack 1973, 1981). Alternatively, if Pipil migrations were into populated areas, there should be some evidence of Early Postclassic site destruction, disruption, or abandonment. The difficulty here is that there appears to be severe depopulation during the period immediately preceding the Late Postclassic Pipil arrival. Even if a residual indigenous population remained, we are incapable at present of recognizing it since there are no recognizable houses or centers, diagnostic markers, or any evidence of occupation that can be confidently dated to between about AD 1000 and 1200. This being the case, all the evidence suggests that the Late Postclassic Pipil migrated into what had been an Early Postclassic population vacuum.

7. Sometimes the migration is a two-way street (Anthony 1990, 1997; Burmeister 2000). The strength of return is high if conditions are similar at the source and destination areas. But this process probably does not apply to Escuintla, given the documentary evidence stressing the pernicious and violent persecution of the Nahua migrants resulting either from the Toltec "diaspora" or the continual nature of the Olmeca-Xicalanca conflict (Thompson 1948; Jiménez Moreno 1966; Davies 1977; Fowler 1989a).

A major question remains, why are there no Early Postclassic sites within our study area? Many years ago Shook (1965: 190) observed that

> most of the Pacific Coastal plain underwent a drastic population shift at the end of the Late Classic. Scores of known major Late Classic centers down to the smallest rural village seemingly were abandoned. There is no certain record to date of an Early Postclassic site in the 0–300 m elevation zone of the South Coast. Sporadic finds of Tohil Plumbate sherds on the surface and a few other diagnostics of the period do occur but are conspicuous by their rarity.

If the Pipil passed through Pacific Coastal Guatemala during the Terminal Classic–Early Postclassic and settled in El Salvador, building the impressive Cihuatán and Las Marías centers, why didn't some of them stay on in Guatemala? Recent excavations at Cihuatán yielded plentiful Tohil Plumbate and a calibrated radiocarbon date whose 2δ range is AD 1030–1240, squarely within the Early Postclassic Period. Why was the Guatemala Pacific Coast seemingly abandoned for several centuries of the Early Postclassic Period, or between about AD 1000 and 1250 or so? Is the lack of Early Postclassic remains simply the result of our inability to identify ceramic and other markers for the period, as suggested by many researchers (cf. Voorhies and Gasco 2004)?

In the Cotzumalguapa region, Parsons (1967: 25) proposed an Early Postclassic occupational hiatus. In El Salvador, Fowler (1989a: 47–48) argued that the Nonoalca Pipil pushed into Central America only after around AD 1250–1300, suggesting that the Pipil of Cuscatlan may have been an "epigonic" Toltec group involved in the Nonoalca migrations or that their immediate origins may lie within El Salvador. Fowler (ibid.) noted that a number of other "western and central Salvadoran sites have pure Late Postclassic or Protohistoric components with no Early Postclassic antecedents," possibly representing "archaeological evidence of the last wave of Pipil migrations." Paul Amaroli's (1986) archaeological survey of Antiguo Cuscatlan (the former location of the Pipil center) found Late Postclassic materials distributed over an area of approximately eighty-five hectares but no evidence of Early Postclassic occupation.

If van Akkeren's research on the Pipil origins and lineage links with the K'iche, Rabinal, and Tzutujil Maya has any validity, why are we then unable to identify the presumably Early Postclassic coastal Pipil sites? Were these links established instead in the Classic Period, suggesting the existence of Nahuatl speakers at the Teotihuacan-controlled centers of Texas-Montana and Ixtepeque in the Tiquisate region? Two arguments favor this interpretation. First, the Late Postclassic Escuintla Pipil settled precisely within what we believe to have been the earlier, Teotihuacan-controlled heartland. The Texas-Montana capital is only 2.8 km southwest of the Carolina-Gomera Complex, and the site of Manantial forms a northern portion of this gigantic capital. Although the site was occupied principally in the Middle and Late Classic Periods, we found that a large number of residential structures at Manantial were reoccupied during the Late Postclassic Period. Second is the question of what language or languages were spoken at Teotihuacan (Bove 2002a: 206–208). Recently, two Mesoamerican linguistic specialists stated flatly: "It is likely Nahuatl was spoken by inhabitants of the city of Teotihuacan" (Dakin and Wichmann 2000: 67). Yet another recognized Postclassic authority argued that "even if Nahua was not spoken at Teotihuacan . . . it is possible that Teotihuacan expansion in southern Mesoamerica was responsible . . . for the first Nahua movements to Central America" (Fowler 1989a: 39).

Finally, returning to the Early Postclassic problem, it has recently been proposed that a terrible drought affected the lower Guatemalan Pacific Coast in the Early Postclassic Period, thereby accounting for its apparent abandonment. Yet the very large Early Postclassic site of Cihuatán in El Salvador, presumably with the same or similar environmental conditions, was not affected (Bruhns 1976, 1977, 1980a, 1980b, 1986, 1987, 1996, 2006; Bruhns, Amaroli, and Avila 2004; Neff et al. 2006).

CONCLUSIONS

The Pipil occupation on the Guatemalan Pacific Coast is shallow, and it seems obvious that Pipil sites, architecture, and artifacts are intrusive into the area, with no local antecedents. Drastic changes in obsidian procurement strategies suggest the same conclusion. Some ceramic variations may be a result of slight chronological differences or perhaps, as in the case of the Miahuatlán area, a multiethnic society or even local emulation by surviving pre-Pipil groups. The Escuintla Pipil incorporated many Late Postclassic Mesoamerican indicators. These included an abundance of copper items, green (Pachuca) obsidian ear spools, obsidian arrowheads in quantity, and net weights of clay, and were in common with Naco, Honduras (Wonderley 1981), Laguna de On in Belize (Masson 2000), and the Chiapas Soconusco coast (Voorhies and Gasco 2004). The Escuintla Pipil also maintained trade relations with nearby groups, as demonstrated by ceramics imported from the Piedmont and nearby highlands including Chinautla Polychrome, Santa Rita Micaceous wares, and Fortress White-on-Red. In the context of domestic pottery, however, the Escuintla Pipil had a completely different set of cooking and food preparation utensils. The distinctive Prado Black comales are present in significantly high percentages at all central Pipil sites except the Cotzumalguapa area and the Costa Rica site. Santa Rita Micaceous and Santa Rita Jabonoso comales are extraordinarily scarce at Pipil sites, and Masagua Reddish-Brown comales, found in high frequencies at Cotzumalguapa sites, are not found at all in Pipil sites. The very common Pipil Remanso Ceramic Group, with its distinctive decorative designs and effigy supports, is not found in the highlands; nor is the equivalent from Kakchiquel sites found at Pipil sites.

We believe the Pipil migrations into the Central Guatemalan Pacific Coast were large-scale, community-sized movements occurring within a relatively short time in the Late Postclassic Period. The Central Mexican Nahua were apparently unified not by politics but rather by a shared culture through their common language. According to James Lockhart (1992) the altepetl, or "Ethnic State," lay at the heart of the Nahua world and is defined as an organization of people holding sway over a given territory. Did the Late Postclassic Escuintla Pipil socio-political organization mirror the Nahua city-state, or altepetl, familiar from Central Mexico (Smith and Hodge 1994; Hodge 1997; Hare 2000)? Is there evidence of Nahua modularity (Hare 2000; Lockhart 1992)? Timothy Hare (2000) believes archaeological expressions of Nahua modularity seem to conform to individual calpolli or altepetl. Fowler (1989a, 1989b) also suggests that the Nicarao-Pipil organization was similar to the Nahua calpolli. We conclude that the reason all of the known Pacific Coastal Guatemalan Pipil regional centers we have studied have different architectural arrangements yet essentially the same material remains is because each represents a different altepetl.

Acknowledgments. It was 1981, and I (Bove) had finally finished the first complete draft of my dissertation. As I was heavily influenced by the then "new" archaeology, the dissertation reeked with jargon such as "rank-size distributions," "Spearman's Coefficient of Correlation," Central Place Theory, Lösch, Christaller, jackknife procedures, discriminate analysis, lattice structures, Nearest Neighbor Analysis, multiplier effects, canonical variables, and Mahalanobis distances. *American Antiquity* had just published my paper "Trend Surface Analysis and the Lowland Maya Collapse" (Bove 1981), causing Merle Greene Robertson, the eminent Mayanist, to ask, "who would have thought that the Maya collapse could be explained by a computer?" Anyway, Nick looked over the dissertation draft and dryly commented with these memorable words: "You know, Fred, you could have put something in there about the people."

Well, it's taken more than a quarter-century, but I did finally got around to the *people*, only in this case it's the *Pipil*, not people. I've even been reading ethnohistoric material, documents like the *Relaciones Geográficas* and tribute lists. In the end, a teacher can only hope to leave something of himself with his students, and I have tried to emulate, in a small way, some of Nick's passion and dedication to the field. Nick's excellence in scholarship distinguished him from the archaeological hordes looking for the flavor of the month, and here I have to include myself in my earlier obsession with the "New Archaeology." Since then has come the "New Old Archaeology," "Postprocessual Archaeology," "Post-Postprocessual Archaeology," and so forth and so on. Through it all, Nick's steadfast approach to scholarship was unperturbed, surpassing all the fads, and it survived intact as it will survive throughout time. Nick, thank you.

REFERENCES CITED

Agrinier, Pierre
    1988   The Ballcourts of Southern Chiapas, Mexico. In *The Mesoamerican Ballgame*, ed. Vernon L. Scarborough and David R. Wilcox, pp. 175–194. University of Arizona Press, Tucson.

Alexander, Rani T.
    1997   Comments on Settlement Hierarchies, Some Pesky Questions. Paper presented at the Third Biannual Complex Society Group, University of Arizona, Tucson.

Alvarado, Pedro de
    1924   *An Account of the Conquest of Guatemala in 1524*. Cortes Society, New York.

Amaroli, Paul
    1986   En la busqueda de Cuscatlán: Un proyecto etnohistórico y arqueológico. Unpublished manuscript, Patronato Pro-Patrimonio Cultural, San Salvador.

Anthony, David W.
    1990   Migration in Archaeology: The Baby and the Bathwater. *American Anthropologist* 92: 895–914.
    1997   Prehistoric Migration as Social Process. In *Migration and Invasions in Archaeological Explanation*, ed. John Chapman and Helena Hamerow, pp. 21–32. BAR International Series 664, Oxford, England.

Aucar, Jorgé
    1987   *Carolina: sitio Precolumbino en la costa sur y su desarrollo: Un estudio arqueológico-historico*. Tesis de Licenciatura, Escuela de Historia, Arqueología, Universidad de San Carlos, Guatemala.

Barth, Fredrik, ed.
    1969   *Ethnic Groups and Boundaries: The Social Organization of Culture Difference*. Little, Brown, Boston, MA.

Bergman, John F.
    1959   The Cultural Geography of Cacao in Aboriginal America and Its Commercialization in Early Guatemala. PhD dissertation, Department of Geography, UCLA, Los Angeles, CA.

Borhegyi, Stephan F. de
 1965 Archaeological Synthesis of the Guatemalan Highlands. In *Archaeology of Southern Mesoamerica*, Part 1, ed. Gordon R. Willey, pp. 3–58. Handbook of Middle American Indians, vol. 2, Robert Wauchope, gen. ed. University of Texas Press, Austin.

Bove, Frederick J.
 1981 Trend Surface Analysis and the Lowland Maya Collapse. *American Antiquity* 46 (1): 93–112.
 1989 Reporte preliminar de las investigaciones en las regiones Tiquisate y La Gomera/Sipacate, Costa Sur de Guatemala. In *Investigaciones Arqueológicas en la Costa Sur De Guatemala*, ed. D. Whitley and M. Beaudry, pp. 38–81. Monograph 31. Institute of Archaeology, UCLA, Los Angeles, CA.
 1999 Prólogo. In *Taller arqueología de la región de la costa sur de Guatemala*, ed. Christa Schieber de Lavarreda, pp. v–vii. IDEAH, Guatemala.
 2002a The Archaeology of Late Postclassic Settlements on the Guatemala Pacific Coast. In *Incidents of Archaeology in Central America and Yucatan: Essays in Honor of Edwin M. Shook*, ed. Michael Love, Marion Popenoe de Hatch, and Hector Escobedo, pp. 179–216. University Press of America, Lanham, MD.
 2002b La dinámica de la interacción de Teotihuacan con el Pacífico de Guatemala. In *Las memorias de la Primera Mesa Redonda de Teotihuacan*, ed. Maria E.R. Gallut, pp. 685–713. Centro de Estudios Teotihuacanos, México, DF.

Bove, Frederick J., and Sonia Medrano
 2003 Teotihuacan, Militarism, and Pacific Guatemala. In *Teotihuacan and the Maya: Reinterpreting Early Classic Interaction*, ed. Geoffrey E. Braswell, pp. 45–79. University of Texas Press, Austin.

Bove, Frederick J., Sonia Medrano, Brenda Lou, and Bárbara Arroyo, eds.
 1993 *The Balberta Project. The Terminal Formative–Early Classic Transition on the Pacific Coast of Guatemala*. Memoirs in Latin American Archaeology 6. University of Pittsburgh, Pittsburgh, PA.

Bove, Frederick J., Hector Neff, Bárbara Arroyo, Sonia Medrano, and José Genovez
 n.d. The Archaeological Ceramics and Chronology of Pacific Coastal Guatemala: Formative to Postclassic. Manuscript in Project Laboratory, Guatemala.

Brown, Kenneth L.
 1985 Postclassic Relationships between the Highland and Lowland Maya. In *The Lowland Maya Postclassic*, ed. A. F. Chase and P. M. Rice, pp. 270–281. University of Texas Press, Austin.

Bruhns, Karen O.
 1976 Investigaciones Arqueológicas en Cihuátan. *Anales del Museo Nacional "David J. Guzmán"* 49: 75–92 plus fold-out map. San Salvador.
 1977 Archaeology of Cihuatán in El Salvador. *Calgary Archaeologist* 5: 7–10.
 1980a *Cihuatán: An Early Postclassic Town of El Salvador. The 1977–1978 Excavations*. Monographs in Anthropology 5. University of Missouri, Columbia [reprinted 1983].

1980b   Investigations at Cihuatán, an Early Postclassic Town of El Salvador. *Mexicon* 2 (1): 6–8. Berlin.
1986   The Role of Commercial Agriculture in Early Postclassic Developments in Central El Salvador: The Rise and Fall of Cihuatán. In *The Southeast Mesoamerican Periphery*, ed. Patricia A. Urban and Edward M. Schortman, pp. 296–312. University of Texas Press, Austin.
1987   Settlement Archaeology at Cihuatán, El Salvador. In *The Periphery of the South Eastern Classic Maya Realm*, ed. Gary Pohl, pp. 55–65. Latin American Center, UCLA, Los Angeles.
1996   El Salvador and the Southwestern Frontier of Mesoamerica. In *Paths to Central American Prehistory*, ed. Frederick Lange, pp. 285–296. University Press of Colorado, Niwot.
2006   Housekeeping in Postclassic El Salvador. In *Reconstructing the Past: Recent Studies in Maya Prehistory*, ed. David M. Pendergast and Anthony P. Andrews, pp. 119–134. BAR International Series 1529, Oxford, England.

Bruhns, Karen O., Paul Amaroli, and Vladimir Avila
2004   Test Excavations in the Burned Palace of Cihuatán, El Salvador. *Mexicon* 26 (4): 72.

Burmeister, Stefan
2000   Archaeology and Migration. *Current Anthropology* 41: 539–567.

Campbell, Lyle, Lawrence H. Feldman, John M. Jessen, Payson D. Sheets, Edwin M. Shook, Gayla Spicknall, Ginger Stuemke, and Thomas T. Taylor
1975   *Papers on the Xinca of Eastern Guatemala*. Museum Brief 19. Museum of Anthropology, University of Missouri, Columbia.

Carmack, Robert M.
1965   The Documentary Sources, Ecology, and Cultural History of the Prehispanic Quiche Maya of Guatemala. PhD dissertation, Department of Anthropology, UCLA, Los Angeles, CA.
1973   *Quichean Civilization: The Ethnohistoric, Ethnographic, and Archeological Source*. University of California Press, Berkeley.
1981   *The Quiché Mayas of Utatlán: The Evolution of a Highland Guatemala Kingdom*. University of Oklahoma Press, Norman.

Chinchilla, Oswaldo F.
1996   Settlement Patterns and Monumental Art at a Major Pre-Columbian Polity: Cotzumalguapa, Guatemala. PhD dissertation, Department of Anthropology, Vanderbilt University, Nashville, TN.

Chinchilla, Oswaldo F., and Sonia Medrano
1997   *Proyecto de salvamento arqueológico El Baúl. Informe final de trabajo del campo temporada 1996–1997 y propuesta de area protegida para el sitio El Baúl*. IDEAH, Guatemala.

Clark, John E.
1989   Obsidian Tool Manufacture. In *Ancient Trade and Tribute: Economies of the Soconusco Region of Mesoamerica*, ed. Barbara Voorhies, pp. 215–228. University of Utah Press, Salt Lake City.

Cobean, Robert H.
    1990   *La cerámica de Tula, Hidalgo*. Estudios sobre Tula 2, Serie Arqueología. INAH, México, DF.

Conkey, Margaret W., and Christine A. Hastorf, eds.
    1990   *The Uses of Style in Archaeology*. Cambridge University Press, Cambridge, England.

Creamer, Winifred
    1987   Evidence for Prehistoric Ethnic Groups in the Sula Valley, Honduras. In *Interaction on the Southeast Mesoamerican Frontier*, ed. Eugenia J. Robinson, pp. 357–384. BAR International Series 327, Oxford, England.

Dakin, Karen, and Søren Wichmann
    2000   Cacao and Chocolate: A Uto-Aztecan Perspective. *Ancient Mesoamerica* 11: 55–75.

Davies, Nigel
    1977   *The Toltecs, Until the Fall of Tula*. University of Oklahoma Press, Norman.

Diehl, Richard A., and Janet C. Berlo, eds.
    1989   *Mesoamerica after the Decline of Teotihuacan A.D. 700–900*. Dumbarton Oaks, Washington, DC.

Eisen, Gustav
    1888   On Some Ancient Sculptures from the Pacific Slope of Guatemala. *Memoirs, California Academy of Sciences* 2 (2): 9–20.

Estrada, Juan de, and Fernando de Niebla
    1955   Descripción de la Provincia de Zapotitlán y Suchitepéquez. *Anales de la Sociedad de Geografía e Historia* 28: 68–83 plus map.

Estrada Belli, Francisco
    1999   *The Archaeology of Complex Societies in Southeastern Pacific Guatemala: A Regional GIS Approach*. BAR International Series 820, Oxford, England.

Feldman, Lawrence H.
    1974   *Papers of Escuintla and Guazacapan. A Contribution to the History and Ethnography of South-Eastern Guatemala*. Occasional Publications in Mesoamerican Anthropology 7. Museum of Anthropology, University of Northern Colorado, Greeley.
    1980   *Las tacaciones y tributos de Guatemala 1514–1599. Informe I*. Museum of Anthropology, University of Missouri, Columbia.
    1989   In Back of the Beyond: Colonial Documentation for a Rural Backwater. In *New Frontiers in the Archaeology of the Pacific Coast of Southern Mesoamerica*, ed. Frederick J. Bove and Lynette Heller, pp. 243–256. Anthropological Research Papers 39. Arizona State University, Tempe.
    1992   *Indian Payments in Kind: The Sixteenth-Century Encomiendas of Guatemala*. Labyrinthos, Culver City, CA.

Feldman, Lawrence H., and Gary Rex Walters, eds.
    1980   *The Anthropology Museum's Excavations in Southeastern Guatemala, Preliminary Reports*. Miscellaneous Publications in Anthropology 9, Special Reports 1 and 2. Museum of Anthropology, University of Missouri, Columbia.

Fowler, William R., Jr.
    1989a   *The Cultural Evolution of Ancient Nahua Civilizations: The Pipil-Nicarao of Central Mexico*. University of Oklahoma Press, Norman.
    1989b   The Pipil of Pacific Guatemala and El Salvador. In *New Frontiers in the Archaeology of the Pacific Coast of Southern Mesoamerica*, ed. Frederick J. Bove and Lynette Heller, pp. 229–242. Anthropological Research Papers 39. Arizona State University, Tempe.

Fox, John W.
    1981   The Late Postclassic Eastern Frontier of Mesoamerica: Cultural Innovation along the Periphery. *Current Anthropology* 22: 321–346.

Fuentes y Guzman, Francisco Antonio de
    1932–1933   *Recordación florida. Discurso historical y demostración natural, material, militar y política del Reyno de Guatemala*, 3 vols. Biblioteca Goathemala 6–8. Sociedad de Geografía e Historia, Guatemala.

Gasco, Janine
    1987   Cacao and the Economic Integration of Native Society in Colonial Soconusco, New Spain. PhD dissertation, Department of Anthropology, University of California, Santa Barbara.

Gavarrete Escobar, Juan
    1980   *Anales para la historia de Guatemala, 1497–1811*. Editorial José de Pineda Ibarra, Guatemala.

Gosselain, Olivier P.
    1998   Social and Technical Identity in a Clay Crystal Ball. In *The Archaeology of Social Boundaries*, ed. Barbara Stark, pp. 78–106. Smithsonian Institution, Washington, DC.

Guillemin, Jorge E.
    1965   *Iximché: Capital del antigua reino Cakchiquel*. IDEAH, Guatemala.

Haggett, Peter
    1965   *Locational Analysis in Human Geography*. Edward Arnold Ltd., London.

Hare, Timothy S.
    2000   Between the Household and the Empire. In *The Archaeology of Communities: A New World Perspective*, ed. M. A. Canuto and J. Yaeger, pp. 78–101. Routledge, London.

Hill, Robert M.
    1996   Eastern Chajoma (Cakchiquel) Political Geography: Ethnohistorical and Archaeological Contributions to the Study of a Late Postclassic Highland Maya Polity. *Ancient Mesoamerica* 7: 63–87.

Hodder, Ian, and Clive Orton
 1976 *Spatial Analysis in Archaeology*. Cambridge University Press, Cambridge, England.

Hodge, Mary G.
 1997 When Is a City-State? Archaeological Measures of Aztec City-States and Aztec City-State Systems. In *The Archaeology of City-States: Cross-Cultural Approaches*, ed. Deborah L. Nichols and Thomas H. Charlton, pp. 209–227. Smithsonian Institution Press, Washington, DC.

Ichon, Alain, and Rita Grignon
 1998 El título de Ixhuatán y el problema Xinca en Guatemala. In *Memoria del 2da Congreso Internacional de Mayistas, 1992*, pp. 327–338. UNAM, México, DF.

Jiménez Moreno, Wigberto
 1966 Mesoamerica before the Toltecs. In *Ancient Oaxaca*, ed. John Paddock, pp. 1–82. Stanford University Press, Palo Alto, CA.

Jones, Siân
 1997 *The Archaeology of Ethnicity: Constructing Identities in the Past and Present*. Routledge, London.

Justeson, John S., William M. Norman, Lyle Campbell, and Terrence Kaufman
 1985 *The Foreign Impact on Lowland Mayan Language and Script*. Middle American Research Institute Publication 53. Tulane University, New Orleans, LA.

Kaufman, Terrence
 1974 *Idiomas de Mesoamérica*. Seminario de Integración Social, Ministerio de Educación, Guatemala.

Kelly, John E.
 1971 *Pedro de Alvarado conquistador*. Kennikat Press Scholarly Reprints. Kennikat Press, Port Washington, NY [reprint of 1932 edition].

Kosakowsky, Laura J.
 2002 The Ceramics of the Southeastern Pacific Coast of Guatemala: A Summary View. In *Incidents of Archaeology in Central America and Yucatán: Essays in Honor of Edwin M. Shook*, ed. Michael Love, Marion Popenoe de Hatch, and Hector Escobedo, pp. 129–145. University Press of America, Lanham, MD.

Kosakowsky, Laura J., Francisco Estrada Belli, and Paul Pettit
 2000 Preclassic through Postclassic. Ceramics and Chronology of the Southeastern Pacific Coast of Guatemala. *Ancient Mesoamerica* 11: 199–215.

Leyenaar, Ted J.J., and Lee A. Parsons
 1988 The Ballgame in the Peripheral Coastal Lowlands. In *Ulama: The Ballgame of the Mayas and Aztecs*, ed. Ted J.J. Leyenaar and Lee A. Parsons, pp. 22–61. Spruyt, Van Mantgem and De Does, Leiden, The Netherlands.

Lockhart, James
 1992 *The Nahuas after the Conquest: A Social and Cultural History of the Indians of Central Mexico, Sixteenth through Eighteenth Centuries*. Stanford University Press, Palo Alto, CA.

Masson, Marilyn A.
  2000 *In the Realm of Nachan Kan: Postclassic Maya Archaeology at Laguna de On, Belize*. University Press of Colorado, Boulder.

Mastache, Alba Guadalupe, Robert H. Cobean, and Dan M. Healan, eds.
  2002 *Ancient Tollan: Tula and the Heartland*. University Press of Colorado, Boulder.

Nance, C. Roger, Stephen L. Whittington, and Barbara E. Borg
  2003 *Archaeology and Ethnohistory of Iximché*. University Press of Florida, Gainesville.

Navarrete, Carlos
  1962 La cerámica de Mixco Viejo. *Cuadernos de Antropología, No. 1*. Instituto de Investigaciones Historicas, Universidad de San Carlos de Guatemala.

Neff, Hector, and Frederick J. Bove
  1999 Mapping Ceramic Compositional Variation and Prehistoric Interaction in Pacific Coastal Guatemala. *Journal of Archaeological Science* 26: 1037–1051.

Neff, Hector, James W. Cogswell, Laura J. Kosakowsky, Francisco Estrada Belli, and Frederick J. Bove
  1999 A New Perspective on the Relationships among Cream Paste Ceramic Traditions of Southeastern Mesoamerica. *Latin American Antiquity* 10: 281–299.

Neff, Hector, Deborah M. Pearsall, John G. Jones, Bárbara Arroyo de Pieters, and Dorothy E. Freidel
  2006 Climate Change and Population History in the Pacific Lowlands of Southern Mesoamerica. *Quaternary Research* 65 (3): 390–400.

Nicholson, H. B.
  2001 *Topiltzin Quetzalcoatl: The Once and Future Lord of the Toltecs*. University Press of Colorado, Boulder.

Orellana, Sandra L.
  1984 *The Tzutujil Mayas: Continuity and Change, 1250–1620*. University of Oklahoma Press, Norman.
  1995 *Ethnohistory of the Pacific Coast*. Labyrinthos, Lancaster, CA.

Parsons, Jeffrey R.
  1971 *Prehistoric Settlement Patterns in the Texcoco Region, Mexico*. Memoirs of the Museum of Anthropology 3. University of Michigan, Ann Arbor.

Parsons, Jeffrey R., Elizabeth Brumfiel, Mary H. Parsons, and David J. Wilson
  1982 *Prehispanic Settlement Patterns in the Southern Valley of Mexico: The Chalco Xochimilco Region*. Anthropological Museum Memoirs 14. University of Michigan, Ann Arbor.

Parsons, Lee A.
  1967 *Bilbao, Guatemala: An Archaeological Study of the Pacific Coast Cotzumalhuapa Region*. Publications in Anthropology 11 (1). Milwaukee Public Museum, Milwaukee, WI.
  1969 *Bilbao, Guatemala: An Archaeological Study of the Pacific Coast Cotzumalhuapa Region*. Publications in Anthropology 12 (2). Milwaukee Public Museum, Milwaukee, WI.

1978 The Peripheral Coastal Lowlands and the Middle Classic Period. In *Middle Classic Mesoamerica: A.D. 400–700*, ed. Esther Pasztory, pp. 25–34. Columbia University Press, New York.

Polo Sifontes, Francis
  1979 *Título de Alotenango*, 2nd ed. José de Pineda Ibarra, Guatemala.
  1989 Titulo de Alotenango, 1565: A Contribution to the Archaeology of the South Coast of Guatemala. In *New Frontiers in the Archaeology of the Pacific Coast of Southern Mesoamerica*, ed. Frederick J. Bove and Lynette Heller, pp. 257–264. Anthropological Research Papers 39. Arizona State University, Tempe.

Robinson, Eugenia J.
  1994 Chitak Tzak: Un centro regional postclásico tardío de los mayas Kaqchkeles. In *VII Simposio de Investigaciones Arqueológicas en Guatemala*, ed. J. van Pedro Laporte and Hector Escobedo, pp. 175–184. Ministerio de Cultura y Deportes, Guatemala.
  1998 Organización del estado Kaqchikel: El centro regional de Chitak Tzak. *Mesoamérica* 35: 49–71.

Rouse, Irving
  1986 *Migrations in Prehistory: Inferring Population Movement from Cultural Remains*. Yale University Press, New Haven, CT.

Sackett, James R.
  1977 The Meaning of Style in Archaeology: A General Model. *American Antiquity* 42: 369–380.
  1990 Style and Ethnicity in Archaeology: The Case for Isochrestism. In *The Uses of Style in Archaeology*, ed. M. Conkey and C. Hastorf, pp. 32–43. Cambridge University Press, Cambridge, England.

Schortman, Edward M.
  1986 Interaction between the Maya and Non-Maya along the Late Classic Southeast Maya Periphery: The View from the Lower Motagua Valley, Guatemala. In *The Southeast Maya Periphery*, ed. Patricia A. Urban and Edward M. Schortman, pp. 114–137. University of Texas Press, Austin.

Sheets, Payson D.
  1984 The Prehistory of El Salvador: An Interpretative Summary. In *The Archaeology of Lower Central America*, ed. F. W. Lange and D. Z. Stone, pp. 85–112. University of New Mexico Press, Albuquerque.

Shennan, Stephan J.
  1994a *Archaeological Approaches to Cultural Identity*. Routledge, London.
  1994b Introduction: Archaeological Approaches to Cultural Identity. In *Archaeological Approaches to Cultural Identity*, ed. Stephan J. Shennan, pp. 1–32. Routledge, London.

Shook, Edwin M.
  1965 Archaeological Survey of the Pacific Coast of Guatemala. In *Archaeology of Southern Mesoamerica*, Part 1, ed. Gordon R. Willey, pp. 180–194. Handbook

of Middle American Indians, vol. 2, Robert Wauchope, gen. ed. University of Texas Press, Austin.

Smith, Michael E., and Mary G. Hodge
- 1994 An Introduction to Late Postclassic Economies and Polities. In *Economies and Polities in the Aztec Realm*, ed. Mary G. Hodge and Michael E. Smith, pp. 1–42. Institute for Mesoamerican Studies 6. State University of New York, Albany.

Stark, Barbara L.
- 1997 Settlement Hierarchies, Some Pesky Questions. Paper presented at the Third Annual Complex Society Group, University of Arizona, Tucson.
- 1999 Formal Architectural Complexes in South-Central Veracruz, Mexico: A Capital Zone? *Journal of Field Archaeology* 26: 197–225.

Stark, Miriam T., ed.
- 1998a *The Archaeology of Social Boundaries*. Smithsonian Institution Press, Washington, DC.
- 1998b Technical Choices and Social Boundaries in Material Culture Patterning: An Introduction. In *The Archaeology of Social Boundaries*, ed. Miriam T. Stark, pp. 1–11. Smithsonian Institution Press, Washington, DC.

Stark, Miriam T., Mark D. Elson, and Jeffery J. Clark
- 1998 Social Boundaries and Technical Choices in Tonto Basin Prehistory. In *The Archaeology of Social Boundaries*, ed. Miriam T. Stark, pp. 208–231. Smithsonian Institution Press, Washington, DC.

Stuiver, M., and P. J. Reimer
- 1993 Extended 14C Database and Revised CALIB Radiocarbon Calibration Program Version 5.0. *Radiocarbon* 35: 215–230.

Stuiver, M., P. J. Reimer, E. Bard, J. W. Beck, G. S. Burr, K. A. Hughen, B. Kromer, F. G. McCormac, J. v.d. Plicht, and M. Spurk
- 1998 INTCAL98 Radiocarbon Age Calibration 24,000 Cal BP. *Radiocarbon* 40: 1041–1083.

Stuiver, M., P. J. Reimer, and R. W. Reimer
- 2005 Quaternary Isotope Laboratory, University of Washington. Electronic document, http://calib.qub.ac.uk/calib/calib/html, accessed February 25, 2005.

Thompson, J. Eric S.
- 1948 *An Archaeological Reconnaissance in the Cotzumalhuapa Region, Escuintla, Guatemala*. Publication 574, Contribution 44. Carnegie Institution of Washington, Washington, DC.

Torquemada, Juan de
- 1969 *Monarquía indiana*, 3 vols. Editorial Porrúa, México, DF.

van Akkeren, Ruud
- 2000 *Place of the Lord's Daughter. Rab'inal, Its History, Its Dance Drama*. CNWS Publications 91. Research School, University of Leiden, The Netherlands.

Voorhies, Barbara, ed.
    1989   *Ancient Trade and Tribute: Economies of the Soconusco Region of Mesoamerica.* University of Utah Press, Salt Lake City.

Voorhies, Barbara, and Janine Gasco
    2004   *Postclassic Soconusco Society: The Late Prehistory of the Coast of Chiapas, Mexico.* Institute for Mesoamerican Studies Monograph 14. State University of New York, Albany.

Wauchope, Robert
    1970   Protohistoric Pottery of the Guatemala Highlands. In *Monographs and Papers in Maya Archaeology*, ed. William R. Bullard Jr., pp. 89–244. Peabody Museum Papers 61. Peabody Museum, Cambridge, MA.

Wolfman, Daniel
    1990   Mesoamerican Chronology and Archaeomagnetic Dating, A.D. 1–1200. In *Archaeomagnetic Dating*, ed. J. Eighmy and R. Sternberg, pp. 216–391. University of Arizona Press, Tucson.

Wonderley, Anthony W.
    1981   Late Postclassic Excavations at Naco, Honduras. Latin American Studies Program, Dissertation Series. Cornell University, Ithaca, NY.

9

UNDER GROUND IN ANCIENT MESOAMERICA

James E. Brady

Since my graduate student days at UCLA, I have been involved in the development of the subdiscipline of Maya cave archaeology. In a recent book on the subject (Brady and Prufer 2005: 6), I noted that one of the hallmarks of this emerging discipline is its pan-Mesoamerican approach. Here the influence of H. B. Nicholson is clear and direct. The pan-Mesoamerican focus Nick encouraged me to take was critical to the development of one of the central theories of cave archaeology: that caves were essential to the validation of Precolumbian settlement. This grew out of the recognition of a number of instances of caves associated with major site architecture (figure 9.1). J. Eric Thompson (1959: 128) was perhaps the first to draw attention to this phenomenon in the first synthesis of Maya cave data: "Mention should [be] made of caverns beneath buildings, notably the High Priest's Grave at Chichén Itzá, but discussion of them would vastly extend our subject."

The statement is intriguing because it suggests that Thompson was aware of multiple examples that would require an extended discussion. How did Thompson interpret this phenomenon? We are given no clue except that the quote comes near the end of the paper, so it would appear that he considered the matter less important than the other uses that formed the core of the article.

Sixteen years later, it appears that Thompson had decided that cave-architecture relationships were not important. In his introduction to the reprint

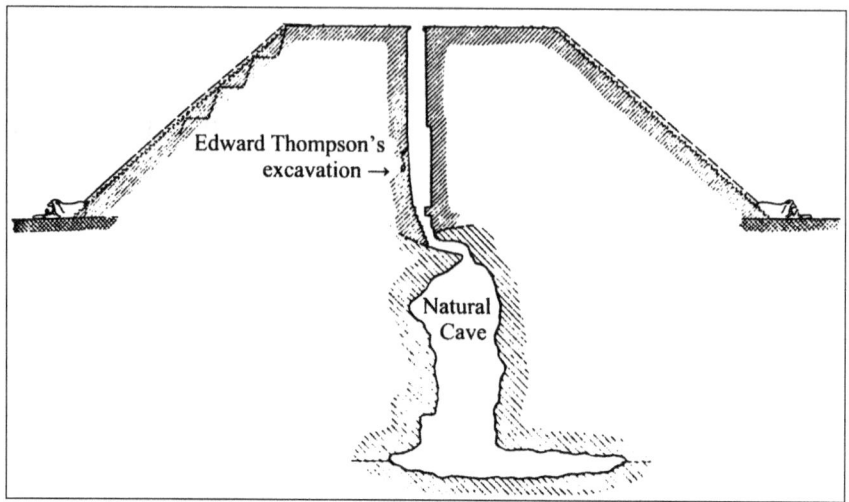

9.1. *In 1896, Edward Thompson excavated a pit into the center of the structure now called the High Priest's Grave at Chichén Itzá and discovered that the pyramid had been built on top of a cave. After Thompson 1938.*

edition of Henry Mercer's *The Hill-Caves of Yucatan* (1975 [1896]), where space certainly was available to elaborate on the topic, Thompson (1975: xlii) relegated the issue to "Other Uses" and simply said: "One should also note Maya structures built over caverns, of which the High Priest's Grave at Chichén Itzá is the most important because of the human bones, worked jades, pearls, and vase of Mexican onyx, all seemingly thrown into the cavern before the aperture was closed." The tone is striking because it is the artifacts that had become important, not the cave or its relationship to architecture.

Edward Thompson does not mention any examples other than the High Priest's Grave (E. H. Thompson 1938). This is curious because cave-architecture relationships had already been explicitly recognized at Tulum (Lothrop 1924: 109–110), Cozumel (Mason 1927: 278; Sanders 1955: 191–192), and Polol (Lundell 1934: 177; also see Patton 1987) in publications by the Carnegie Institution, for which Thompson also worked.

Another had been noted at Pusilha (Joyce et al. 1928; Joyce 1929). It is possible that none of the examples other than the High Priest's Grave was sufficiently spectacular to suggest that something important might be occurring. In this respect, it is particularly unfortunate that Thompson appears to have been unaware of the discovery of the cave beneath the Pyramid of the Sun at Teotihuacan, which had been published (Heyden 1973) two years before the appearance of his second synthesis, because it certainly was spectacular.

The same year J. Eric Thompson's introduction to Mercer's classic work appeared, Doris Heyden's (1975) "An Interpretation of the Cave underneath the

9.2. *The cave (*dark line at bottom*) beneath the Pyramid of the Sun at Teotihuacan. After Heyden 1975.*

Pyramid of the Sun in Teotihuacan, Mexico" was published in English. Heyden's approach was very different because she was attempting to explain what she saw as a unique discovery: the placement of a single feature at a particular site. The cave, which started at the central stairway of the pyramid, was probably supposed to terminate under the center point (figure 9.2). Her work focused on the meaning and significance of caves. For Heyden, the placement of the pyramid over the cave could only be understood in the context of the role of caves in myth and cosmovision. Very important, Heyden (ibid.: 134) directly addresses the question of the social context of caves in a section entitled "The Importance of Caves in Mesoamerica." Because of the prevalence of *"-oztoc"* (Nahuatl for cave) in the site names of Central Mexico and the presence of the cave motif in place glyphs, Heyden (ibid.) concluded that "they constitute an important element in town sites." The series of articles on the cave beneath the Pyramid of the Sun is particularly noteworthy because the articles ascribed an importance to caves that was of an entirely different order than anything suggested in the literature at that time (Heyden 1973, 1975, 1981). While Heyden was cautious in her wording, others recognized the implications of her argument. René Millon (1981: 235), for example, said explicitly: "Nevertheless, the stubborn fact remains: the pyramid must be where it is and nowhere else because the cave below it was the most sacred of sacred places. Whether or not the Teotihuacanos believed that the sun and the moon had been created there, the rituals performed in the cave must have celebrated a system of myth and belief of transcendent importance."

On the negative side, the division of Mesoamerica into Central Mexico and the Maya area is quite apparent. Heyden never cites Edward H. Thompson's synthesis in any of her articles, although it is far from certain that Thompson's mention of other cases would have led Heyden to see the Teotihuacan cave as part of a wider pattern of utilization. In a later discussion of the Teotihuacan cave, Heyden (1981: 14) was clearly aware of the High Priest's Grave but missed the implications completely, stating, "This of course, presupposes a cave per structure, which is doubtful."

CAVE-ARCHITECTURE RELATIONSHIPS

When I came to UCLA in the early 1980s, I began to grapple with interpreting the significance of the few known examples of cave-architecture relationships. Nick was instrumental in pointing out Fernando Alvarado Tezozómoc's (1975: 63) description of the founding of Tenochtitlan in which the eagle with the serpent in its claws was perched on a cactus that grew on top of a cave from which two springs flowed. There is no doubt that this was a legitimizing symbol. Eduardo Matos Moctezuma (1987: 191) writes: "As Mircea Eliade has noted, the founding or first settlement of every city is accompanied by signs and, in general, the sacred space is made into a defined area that transforms it into an 'inexhaustible source' of sacralty. This place is always 'discovered' by humans through certain symbols laden with mystic meaning, among which frequently occurs the presence of some animal."

The eagle and serpent motif has been repeated so often that it has blinded us to the fact that they were simply markers of the symbols that were really important to the Aztecs: the cave and springs. The Templo Mayor is supposedly built on this spot, and the dual temples at the top model the two springs. Whether the myth was true was unimportant. I immediately saw that the Aztecs were invoking precisely the same image as the cave beneath the Pyramid of the Sun, with its system of drains that fed water into the cave that would run out the entrance. When I later learned that the pyramid at Cholula is also supposedly built over

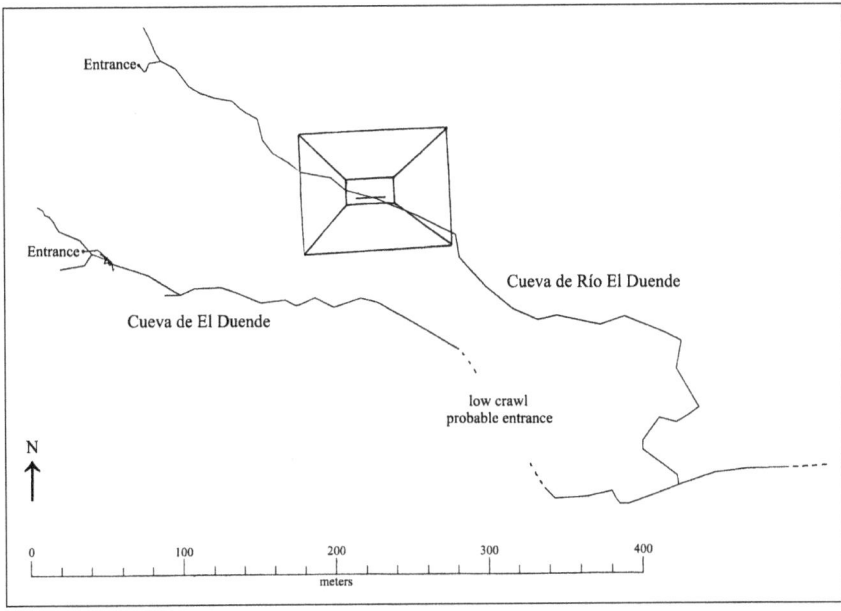

9.3. *The El Duende Complex at Dos Pilas, Guatemala. The hill contains two caves, including one running directly under the temple shown. Map by John Fogarty and Allan Cobb.*

a spring and a cave (McCafferty 1996: 3, 5, 13), it became clear that this was a primary legitimizing symbol for Central Mexican settlement.

CAVES AND ARCHITECTURE AT DOS PILAS

I was unable to do more than note the cave-architecture connection in my dissertation (Brady 1989: 64–71), but I subsequently directed a project at Dos Pilas, Guatemala, explicitly designed to look for cave-architecture relationships. The first year was fraught with frustration, but during the second season we discovered one cave after another. The pattern that emerged suggested that the ancient Maya architecture was deliberately placed above cave entrances. Results of this research have been detailed elsewhere (Brady 1997), but a few outstanding examples are worth mentioning. The largest pyramid at Dos Pilas, the El Duende Complex, is a modified natural hill on which a temple and several stelae had been erected (figure 9.3). The toponym on the stelae suggested that the place was called K'inalha', "sun faced water" (Stuart and Houston 1994: 84–85). Stephen Houston believed the water in the name referred to an intermittent spring because the temple at the top appears to be aligned with this feature. In 1991 we discovered a new cave running directly under the hill; this cave contains a subterranean lake, the largest body of standing water at the site (figure 9.4).

James E. Brady

9.4. *The subterranean lake located directly under the pyramid of the El Duende Complex at Dos Pilas, Guatemala. Ann Scott (left), Charley Savvas (right). Photo by Barbara Luke.*

Artifacts in the cave prove that the Maya had used it, and the toponym indicates that the entire complex was named for this cave.

Here again, a pan-Mesoamerican approach allows us to appreciate the significance of this discovery. I have argued for several years that archaeologists have imposed a Western bias on Mesoamerican cosmology through over-attention to celestial deities. Such bias overlooks the fact that a noteworthy feature of Amerindian religion is the importance of earth as a sacred and animate entity. Several years ago I noted that caves and mountains can be united into a single symbol representing earth and that the most sacred locations are those that combine the fundamental elements of earth and water into a unified expression of the power of earth. In this regard we can see an underlying Mesoamerican approach to human settlement. In Nahuatl human settlements are called *altepetl*, which literally means "water-filled mountain" (Broda 1996: 460), while the Yucatec Maya name is *chan ch'een*, "sky cave." In both cases human settlement is defined in relation to these important terrestrial features. Returning to the Dos Pilas El Duende Complex, we can see that it is literally a water-filled mountain. In Nahuatl it would be the altepetl, the very symbol of community.

A second cave runs under the Dos Pilas Bat Palace, an important architectural complex containing the residence of the site's rulers and a large pyramid: its entrance lies just below the platform on which the complex is built. The cave itself is the termination of a many-kilometers-long subterranean river system, so after heavy rains water issues from it with such force that the sound is audible

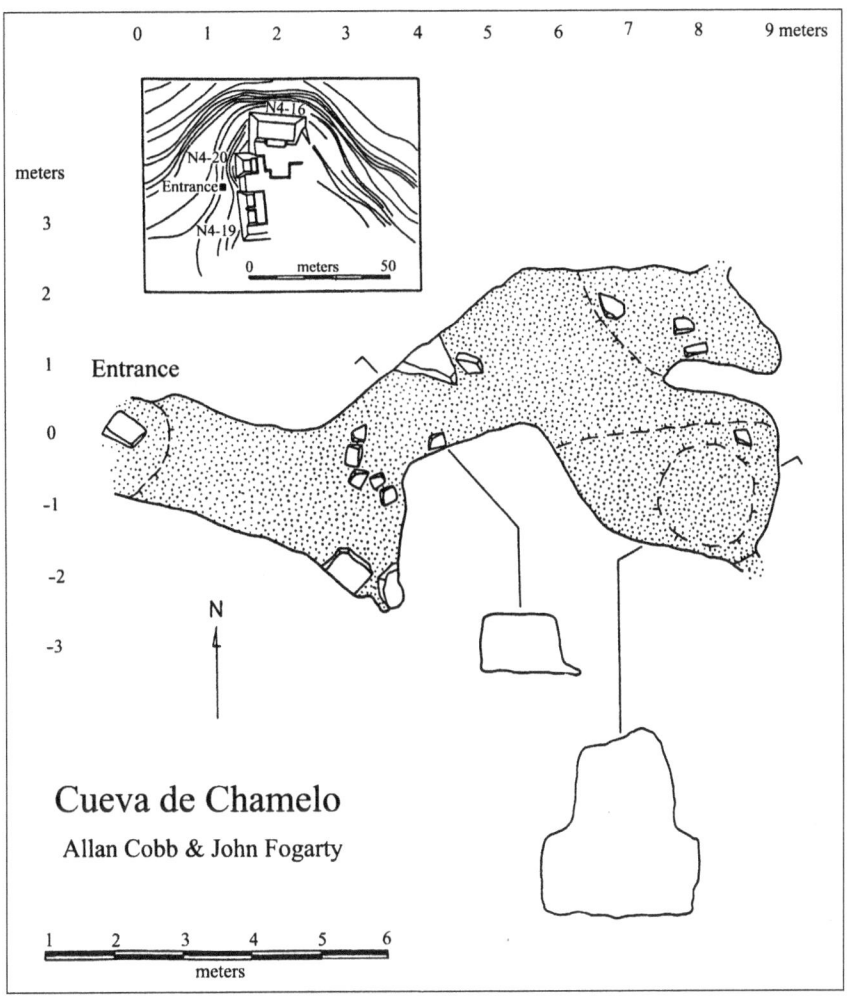

9.5. *The Cueva de Chamelo at Dos Pilas, Guatemala. Map by Allan Cobb and John Fogarty.*

for more than half a kilometer. It was certainly no accident that the rulers of Dos Pilas appropriated this spot to build their palace, since the cave appears to be dramatically proclaiming the rulers' control over water—a claim rulers may have been making for over a millennium, as we see in the "El Rey" panel from Chalcatzingo (Grove 1989: 133, figure 7.6).

One additional Dos Pilas example is of interest. The cave beneath Structures N4–19 and 20 is small, and the structures on top are not particularly imposing. What is important is that the spacing of the three structures on the platform is not uniform; rather, a large space has been left between Structures N4-19 and 20 to provide access to the cave entrance just below (figure 9.5). This is a

9.6. *Maya workman emerging from the diminutive opening of the Cueva de Sangre at Dos Pilas, Guatemala. This is the beginning of a 3.5-km-long cave. Photo by James E. Brady.*

clear architectonic statement, not only of the builders' acknowledgment of the presence of the cave but also of its importance. A number of other examples of small caves were incorporated into simple residential structures at the site, so we appear to be looking at a pattern of utilization rather than a multiplicity of accidents.

CAVES AND SURFACE ARCHAEOLOGY

Even though I had proposed that cases of architecture built in relation to caves would be found, I was frankly surprised to find so many examples at all levels of construction, from those of private residences to large, public structures. My first question was why we had found so many caves when two previous projects in the Dos Pilas area had not reported any. This resulted at least in part from the fact that many of our caves had extremely small entrances, so that from the archaeological perspective they were holes rather than caves (figure 9.6). In the tropics, poking around in holes is asking for trouble. Many things can reside in these holes, and most of them are nasty.

More recently, I have concluded that if the members of a field project are not looking for caves, they are unlikely to find them. When surface archaeologists state that there are no caves in their study area, it sometimes reveals, more than anything else, how little they know about their areas. A case in point is Reiko Ishihara's 2002 cave survey at Caracol for the Western Belize Regional

Cave Project. Despite more than a decade of previous research at the site, intensive mapping of surface features, and assurances from the archaeologist that all the caves had been found, Ishihara documented at least ten previously unknown caves (Ishihara 2003).

Just as repeated subsurface tunneling excavations over a half-century missed the cave under the Pyramid of the Sun at Teotihuacan (detailed in Millon, Drewitt, and Bennyhoff 1965), so have many surface archaeological surveys throughout Mesoamerica missed significant underground features. I am pressing this issue because reservations about the cave-architecture hypothesis have tended to be based on negative evidence that there are no caves in a particular area, that no caves had been discovered at several of the most intensively investigated sites such as Tikal and Uaxactún, or, finally, that if such a pattern existed, it would certainly have been noted by now with all the archaeological work that has been done. All of these arguments are predicated on the assumption that surface archaeologists have done a competent job of both discovering and documenting caves. Unfortunately, recent research strongly suggests the opposite.

Archaeological cave surveys at Cuyamel (Healy 1974), in Alta Verapaz (Pope and Sibbernsen 1981; Carot 1989), at Oxkintok (Bonor Villarejo 1987, 1989), Copán (Scott 1992), the Vaca Plauteau (Reeder 1993; Reeder, Brady, and Webster 1998), Dos Pilas (Brady 1997), Yalahau (Rissolo 2001), the Maya Mountains (Prufer 2002), and the Sibun Valley (Peterson 2002) have documented cave frequencies on a different order of magnitude than anything produced by surface projects with the possible exception of the Carnegie Mayapan Project. These cave-specific surveys make it clear that most surface archaeology has done such a poor job of identifying and documenting caves that no argument based on negative evidence can be taken seriously.

CAVES AND THE LEGITIMIZATION OF SPACE IN MESOAMERICA

The unprecedented number of cave-architecture relationships at Dos Pilas brought home to me the need to understand on a much deeper level and in clearer terms why caves were so important to the legitimization of settlement for Mesoamerican peoples. That importance can still be seen today. For one Yucatec Maya group, "Community members inherit the responsibility of venerating and caring for the sacred cross in the cave, which is thought to be the home of the supernatural owner of the community's land" (Villa Rojas 1946: 16).

This suggests that a kind of unwritten contract may exist between the members of the settlement and the earth in which the community's right to the land is validated by cave ritual (Brady 1997: 604). Angel García-Zambrano's study of Precolumbian rituals of foundation provides additional explanation. He notes that in founding new settlements, Mesoamerican people searched for a place with attributes of a particular ideal landscape (1994: 217–218):

> Essentially, Mesoamerican migrants searched for an environment with specific characteristics that comprised several symbolic levels . . . Such a place had to recall the mythical moment when the earth was created: an aquatic universe framed by four mountains with a fifth elevation protruding in the middle of the water. The mountain at the core had to be dotted with caves and springs, and sometimes surrounded by smaller hills. A setting like this duplicated, and forever would freeze, the primordial scene when the waters and the sky separated and the earth sprouted upwards. (García-Zambrano 1994: 217–218)

Geographer Erich Isaac (1962), in attempting to explain which types of societies practice large-scale religious landscape modification, states that, as ideal polar opposites, there are two very different justifications for human existence. One resides in a divine covenant and the other in the act of creation. Covenant-based religions continually refer back to the covenant. The Judeo-Christian tradition clearly falls in this category, and for that reason we have failed to appreciate the tremendous importance of the act of creation for religions in the other category. Mircea Eliade (1959: 81) recognized this in saying: "The paramount time of origins is the time of the cosmogony, the instant that saw the appearance of the most immediate of realities, the world. This . . . is the reason the cosmogony serves as the paradigmatic model for every creation, for every kind of doing."

For these societies the moment of creation becomes the model for religious landscape modification. As Isaac (1962: 12) says, "The attempt will be made to reproduce the cosmic plan in the landscape with greater or lesser effect upon the land, depending on the elaborateness of reproduction attempted."

Elements of this model have been recognized for some time, but not in a complete or integrated form. Robert F. Heizer concluded after excavations at La Venta (Drucker, Heizer, and Squier 1959) that the great pyramid at that site represented a kind of "sacred mountain"—hardly an original idea, as this interpretation has been around ever since Europeans began studying Mesopotamian ziggurats more than a half-century before the UC Berkeley excavations in Tabasco. Evon Vogt (1964a, 1964b) continued the "sacred mountain" analogy forward over time to include the Classic Maya. The cave, however, has not been recognized as part of the complex, but García-Zambrano (1994: 218) states: "A natural cave had to contain water or be surrounded by it. Many times, the grotto was manually excavated to approximate its shape to that of the mythological cave with internal niches. The grotto alluded to the mythological place of origin."

The cave, then, *is* the symbol of human creation. No wonder García-Zambrano (ibid.) concludes: "These cavities, when ritually dedicated to the divinities[,] became the pulsating heart of the new town, providing the cosmogonic referents that legitimized the settlers' rights for occupying that space and for the ruler's authority over that site."

PROBLEMS, DOUBTS, AND OBJECTIONS

Despite mounting evidence (Pugh 2001, 2005; King and Shaw 2003; Brown 2005; Halperin 2005; Prufer and Kindon 2005) for the appropriation of caves in Meoamerican settlement as an indispensable part of the process of site legitimization or even as a basic reason for original site location, the basic hypothesis is not well accepted. Why should this be? The first problem is simply that many archaeologists have ceased to be anthropologists. For more than fifty years the archaeological literature has seen ever-increasing expressions of a basic mistrust of ethnographic analogy. As a result, archaeology has been cut off from living people, especially, in some cases, those historically related to the ancient cultures being reconstructed.

It is therefore not surprising that many archaeological models of settlement have tended to be simplistic and ethnocentric. First, archaeologists tend to model settlement selection among agriculturalists as concerned primarily with maximizing agriculture potential to the exclusion of ideological concerns. Ethnography and ethnohistory have shown that this is not the case. Gertrude Duby and Frans Blom (1969: 292) note that a group of Lacandon Maya settled in an area with poor soil specifically to be near a sacred cave the sun was considered to enter at night. Ethnohistoric sources record the fact that ecologically favored areas might be bypassed if they did not contain specific features important to the cosmology (García-Zambrano 1994: 217).

Second, as Western, generally secular scholars, archaeologists find it difficult to relate to the importance of the highly religious ideology and cosmology that characterize non-Western, non-industrialized societies. When one looks at the actual behavior of modern Mesoamerican peoples, however, one begins to appreciate the importance of religion in the lives of real people. Major portions of the *Popul Vuh* (Recinos, Goetz, and Morley 1950) are devoted to descriptions of people and supernaturals living underground in the land of Xibalba, Guatemala's karstic Alta Verapaz, where present-day Kekchi Indians still worship cave-dwelling deities (Pope and Sibbernsen 1981). Mesoamerican peoples name their settlements after caves and mountains (Villa Rojas 1946: 16, 1947: 579; Toor 1947: 35; Holland 1963: 27; Heyden 1975: 134; Dillon 1977: 7; Broda 1996; Garza 2005); in some cases they take their surnames from their caves (Vogt 1976: 25) and continue to conduct rituals at caves and treat them as sacred places (Andrews 1970; Monaghan 1995; Wilson 1995). To my colleagues who find this difficult to accept I will simply say, "Wake up! This is the way real people actually behave."

A more legitimate objection grows out of a vague uneasiness with the types of alignments between caves and architecture I have outlined. I have presented the clearest examples. The El Duende Complex was selected precisely because an indigenous text appears to refer to the cave. What happens when no text is available? Can one be sure the ancient peoples recognized the relationship?

9.7. *Vilma Fialko stands in "Cave" 1 at Utatlán, Guatemala. A manmade tunnel over 100 m long, this was a major engineering feat. Photo by James E. Brady.*

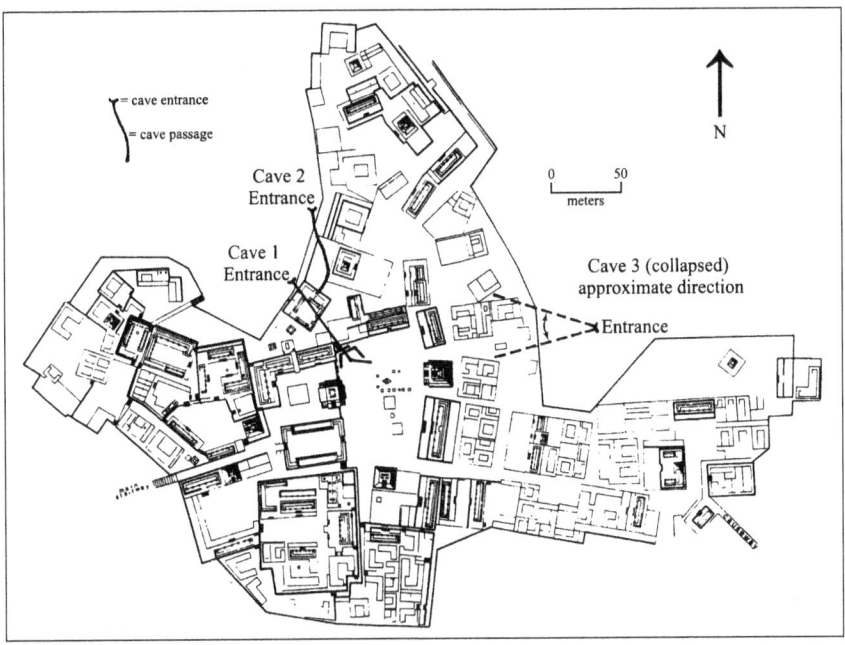

9.8. *Late Postclassic Utatlán, Guatemala, showing "cave" (actually manmade tunnel) locations. Modified from Wallace and Carmack 1977.*

Admittedly the argument becomes more difficult, and archaeologists are trained to be both critical and skeptical. Cave archaeology has also hurt its own cause by becoming a technical subdiscipline so that most work is done by specialists. This means we have made few converts through the process of "seeing is believing," that is, surface archaeologists discovering caves at their sites and recognizing relationships with surface architecture.

INTENTIONAL CAVE-ARCHITECTURAL ALIGNMENTS

I believe the relationships between caves and architecture in Mesoamerica were intentional and the meaning I have attached to them is correct. When I returned to Guatemala in 1988 to conduct my dissertation research, I had the opportunity to visit caves in the Maya Highlands at Utatlán (Gumarcaaj or Q'umarkaaj), Mixco Viejo, and Esquipulas. While the "caves" at Utatlán had long been recognized as manmade (Fox 1978: 24), when I found that others were as well, I realized that a previously unrecognized pattern of tunneling or "cave construction" existed (figure 9.8). As I investigated further, French archaeologist Alain Ichon showed me an example he had investigated at La Lagunita (Ichon and Viel 1984; Ichon and Arnauld 1985), and I discovered other examples at Zacuelu, Iximché,

Llano Largo, and a number of other sites (Brady 2004). These finds indicated that caves were such important features that they were regularly constructed in non-karstic areas where caves do not naturally occur. Later, Linda Manzanilla and colleagues (1994) reported that the "cave" under the Pyramid of the Sun at Teotihuacan was artificial, as were caves at Xochicalco (Hirth 2000) and a number of sites my colleagues and I examined in Puebla (Aguilar et al. 2005). Once again the distribution indicates a pan-Mesoamerican pattern of artificial cave construction.

The implications of artificial caves are profound. Because the location, length, and form of artificial caves reflect decisions of their makers rather than the whim of nature, the relationship between artificial caves and other cultural features can reflect the cultural ideal far more faithfully than do natural caves. This is indeed what we see. At Teotihuacan, the cave began at the base of the original central stairway and was supposed to end under the center of the Pyramid of the Sun. There is absolutely no doubt here that the Teotihuacanos intended the cave and the pyramid to be linked as a single unit. Archaeologists have been slow to accept this point. For instance, there are a number of manmade passages behind the Pyramid of the Sun that Manzanilla and colleagues (1996: 246) label "quarry tunnels," but they state that "the plazas of the [pyramid] complexes seem to be deliberately located on top of these tunnels." Curiously, they seem not to recognize that this is precisely the same idea expressed in the cave beneath the Pyramid of the Sun.

At the Guatemalan Highland site of La Lagunita, the cave begins at the central stairway of one of the principal pyramids and terminates in the center of the central plaza. It appears that the largest cave at Utatlán was also supposed to terminate in the middle of the central plaza, and side passages were apparently designed to terminate under other structures that border the plaza (see figure 9.8). Because this type of measurement was quite complicated, it did not actually achieve this. Nevertheless, these examples of artificial caves clearly demonstrate that ancient Mesoamericans deliberately made tunnels, essentially artificial caves, as part of architectural complexes. There is little doubt that this practice was based on natural prototypes. Thus, while the spatial relationship between architecture and natural caves is not as "neat" as it is with artificial caves, it seems certain that Mesoamerican peoples were intentionally linking their constructions with natural caves.

Because the form of artificial caves reflects decisions of their makers, elaborate caves may also provide important insights into exactly what the structures were designed to represent. Ichon argued that the single passage at La Lagunita was supposed to represent the cave of origin, but no data actually supported that interpretation. At Utatlán (Brady 1991), however, the seven passage terminations in Cave 1 make it a model of the cave of origin of the K'iche' people (figure 9.9). At Acatzingo Viejo in Puebla, Mexico, we recorded six tunnels or "artificial

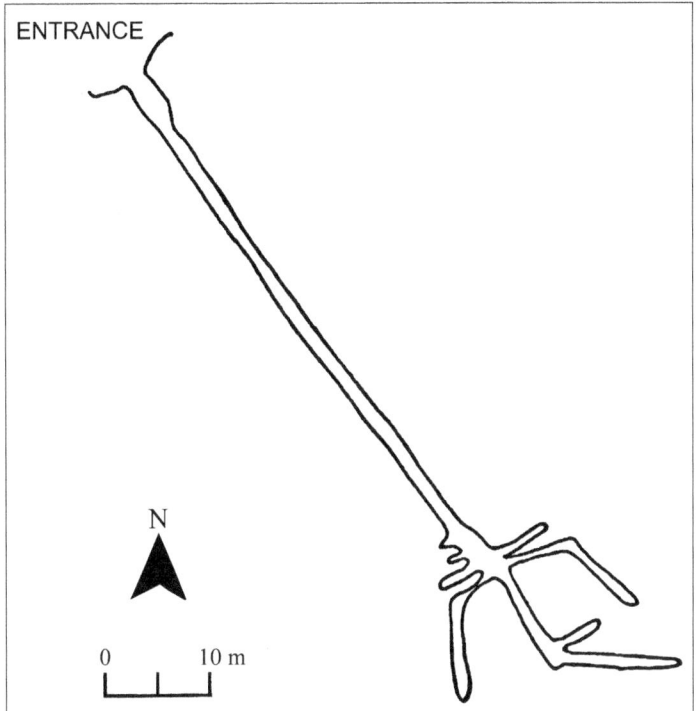

9.9. *Cave 1 (actually a tunnel), Utatlán, Guatemala. Map by George Veni and Allan Cobb.*

caves" excavated along a small escarpment, and local informants verified that a seventh had been destroyed by the construction of a road (figure 9.10). In our analysis we noted that the linear arrangement of the caves is very reminiscent of the drawing of the Chicomoztoc (figure 9.11), the seven mythic caves of origin of the Nahuatl-speaking people, in the *Codex Vaticanus A* (Aguilar et al. 2005). It is clear that these caves, in the words of García-Zambrano (1994: 218), "alluded to the mythological place of origin." I would suggest, based on the importance of the act of creation in Mesoamerican cosmology, that the major caves found in site centers carried this meaning.

CONCLUSIONS

The pan-Mesoamerican approach H. B. Nicholson encouraged his students to employ was critical to my recognition of that pattern of linking surface architecture with caves (Brady and Prufer 2005; Prufer and Brady 2005). Enough examples have been provided in this chapter to clearly demonstrate that these were not simply idiosyncratic occurrences. Although more examples had been documented in the Maya area, the Central Mexican occurrences were more

James E. Brady

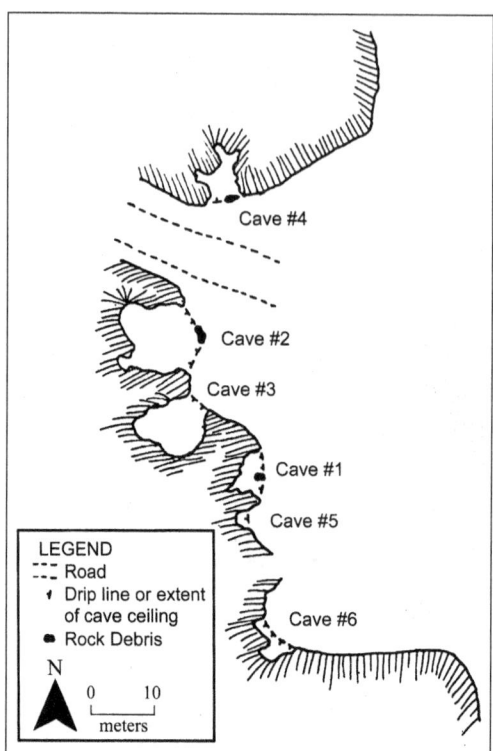

9.10. *The caves of Acatzingo Viejo, Puebla, Mexico. Map by John Fogarty and Allan Cobb.*

easily interpreted. The cave beneath the Pyramid of the Sun was a compelling example in Heyden's (1975) analysis simply in terms of the power the cave appeared to have in structuring settlement at Teotihuacan. The significance of the cave motif was clearly related to site validation in the Tenochtitlan foundation myth. By drawing data from the two areas, a clear pattern of fundamental importance emerged. When this model was tested at Dos Pilas (Brady 1997), examples of cave-architecture relationships were documented throughout the site and involved a range of forms, from the largest public structures to small residential units. The discovery of an unsuspected pattern of intentional artificial cave construction provided critical confirming evidence. The spatial relationships proposed between natural caves and architecture were more clearly produced in artificial caves where the intentionality was unquestionable.

García-Zambrano's (1994) study of foundation rituals provides an elegant and well-documented model in which the role of caves is clear in the validation of settlement. His examples from Mesoamerica reinforce the unity of the culture area. Finally, by drawing together the artificial cave data from across Mesoamerica, it is possible to produce examples of seven-chambered caves from both Central Mexico and the Maya area. These elaborate cases of the material-

9.11. *The linear arrangement of the mythical Aztec Chicomoztoc, as depicted in the* Codex Vaticanus A. *Drawing by Mario Dávila, from Aguilar et al. 2005.*

ization of cosmology provide persuasive evidence for suspecting that the major caves found in site cores represented the original places of origin for the ancient cities themselves.

REFERENCES CITED

Aguilar, Manuel, Miguel Medina Jaen, Tim M. Tucker, and James E. Brady
    2005   Constructing Mythic Space: The Significance of a Chicomoztoc Complex at Acatzingo Viejo. In *In the Maw of the Earth Monster: Mesoamerican Ritual Cave Use*, ed. James E. Brady and Keith M. Prufer, pp. 69–87. University of Texas Press, Austin.

Alvarado Tezozómoc, Fernando
    1975   *Crónica mexicáyotl*, 2nd ed. Traducción directa del náhuatl por Adrián León. Instituto de Investigaciones Históricas, UNAM, México, DF.

Andrews IV, E. Wyllys, ed.
    1970   *Balankanche, Throne of the Tiger Priest*. Middle American Research Series Publication 32. Tulane University, New Orleans, LA.

Bonor Villarejo, Juan Luis
    1987   Exploraciones en las grutas de Calcehtok y Oxkintok, Yucatán, México. *Mayab* 3: 24–31.
    1989   Las cuevas de Oxkintok: Informe preliminar. In *Memorias del Segundo Coloquio Internacional de Mayistas*, pp. 303–309. UNAM, México, DF.

Brady, James E.
    1989   An Investigation of Maya Ritual Cave Use with Special Reference to Naj Tunich, Petén, Guatemala. PhD dissertation, Archaeology Program, University of California, Los Angeles.
    1991   Caves and Cosmovision at Utatlán. *California Anthropologist* 18: 1–10.
    1997   Settlement Configuration and Cosmology: The Role of Caves at Dos Pilas. *American Anthropologist* 99: 602–618.
    2004   Constructed Landscapes: Exploring the Meaning and Significance of Recent Discoveries of Artificial Caves. *Ketzalcalli* 1: 2–17.

Brady, James E., and Keith M. Prufer, eds.
  2005   In the Maw of the Earth Monster: Mesoamerican Ritual Cave Use. University of Texas Press, Austin.

Broda, Johanna
  1996   Calendarios, cosmovisión y observación de la naturaleza. In *Temas Mesoamericanos*, ed. Sonia Lombardo and Enrique Nalda, pp. 427–469. INAH, México, DF.

Brown, Clifford T.
  2005   Caves, Karst, and Settlement at Mayapán, Yucatán. In *In the Maw of the Earth Monster: Mesoamerican Ritual Cave Use*, ed. James E. Brady and Keith M. Prufer, pp. 373–402. University of Texas Press, Austin.

Carot, Patricia
  1989   Arqueología de las Cuevas del Norte de Alta Verapaz. *Cuadernos de Estudios Guatemaltecos* 1. Centre D'Etudes Mexicaines et Centraméricaines, México, DF.

Dillon, Brian Dervin
  1977   *Salinas de los Nueve Cerros, Guatemala: Preliminary Archaeological Investigations*. Ballena Press Studies in Mesoamerican Art, Archaeology and Ethnohistory 2, ed. John A. Graham. Ballena Press, Socorro, NM.

Drucker, Philip, Robert F. Heizer, and Robert J. Squier
  1959   *Excavations at La Venta, Tabasco, 1955*. Bureau of American Ethnology Bulletin 170. Smithsonian Institution, Washington, DC.

Duby, Gertrude, and Frans Blom
  1969   The Lacandon. In *Ethnology*, ed. Evon Z. Vogt, pp. 276–297. Handbook of Middle American Indians, vol. 7, Robert Wauchope, gen. ed. University of Texas Press, Austin.

Eliade, Mircea
  1959   *The Sacred and the Profane: The Nature of Religion*. Trans. Willard R. Trask. Harcourt Brace Jovanovich, New York.

Fox, John W.
  1978   *Quiche Conquest: Centralism and Regionalism in Highland Guatemalan State Development*. University of New Mexico Press, Albuquerque.

García-Zambrano, Angel J.
  1994   Early Colonial Evidence of Pre-Columbian Rituals of Foundation. In *Seventh Palenque Round Table, 1989*, ed. Merle Greene Robertson and Virginia Field, pp. 217–227. Pre-Columbian Art Research Institute, San Francisco, CA.

Garza, Sergio
  2005   Ethnographic Models of Cave-Community Relations. Paper presented at the 70th Annual Meeting of the Society for American Archaeology, Salt Lake City, UT, April 1.

Grove, David C.
    1989   Chalcatzingo and Its Olmec Connections. In *Regional Perspectives on the Olmec*, ed. Robert J. Sharer and David C. Grove, pp. 122–147. Cambridge University Press, Cambridge, England.

Halperin, Christina T.
    2005   Social Power and Sacred Space at Actun Nak Beh, Belize. In *Stone Houses and Earth Lords: Maya Religion in the Cave Context*, ed. Keith M. Prufer and James E. Brady, pp. 71–90. University Press of Colorado, Boulder.

Healy, Paul
    1974   The Cuyamel Caves: Preclassic Sites in Northeast Honduras. *American Antiquity* 39 (3): 435–447.

Heyden, Doris
    1973   ¿Un chicomóstoc en Teotihuacan? La cueva bajo la pirámide del Sol. *Boletín del Instituto Nacional de Antropología e Historia* 2 (6): 3–18.
    1975   An Interpretation of the Cave underneath the Pyramid of the Sun in Teotihuacan, Mexico. *American Antiquity* 40: 131–147.
    1981   Caves, Gods, and Myths: World-View and Planning in Teotihuacan. In *Mesoamerican Sites and World-Views*, ed. Elizabeth P. Benson, pp. 1–39. Dumbarton Oaks Research Library and Collection, Washington, DC.

Hirth, Kenneth
    2000   *Archaeological Research at Xochicalco*, vol. 1: *Ancient Urbanism at Xochicalco: The Evolution and Organization of a Pre-Hispanic Society*. University of Utah Press, Salt Lake City.

Holland, William R.
    1963   *Medicina Maya en los altos de Chiapas: Un estudio del cambio socio-cultural*. Instituto Nacional Indigenista, México, DF.

Ichon, Alain, and Marie Charlotte Arnauld
    1985   *Le Protoclassique á La Lagunita, El Quiché, Guatemala*. Centre National de la Recherche Scientifique, Institut d'Ethnologie, Paris.

Ichon, Alain, and René Viel
    1984   *La Periode Formative á La Lagunita et dans le Quiché Meridional, Guatemala*. Centre National de la Researche Scientifique, Institut d'Ethnologie, Paris.

Isaac, Erich
    1962   The Act and the Covenant. *Landscape* 11: 12–17.

Ishihara, Reiko
    2003   Are There Any Holes around Here? A Preliminary Report on the Caracol Cave Survey. In *The Belize Valley Archaeological Reconnaissance Project: A Report of the 2002 FICLO Season*, ed. Jaime J. Awe and Carolyn M. Audet, pp. 64–82. Institute of Archaeology, National Institute of Culture and History, Belmopan, Belize.

Joyce, Thomas A.
    1929   Report on the British Museum Expedition to British Honduras, 1929. *Journal of the Royal Anthropological Institute* 59: 439–459.

Joyce, Thomas A., Thomas Gann, Edward L. Gruning, and Richard Charles Edward Long
  1928   Report on the British Museum Expedition to British Honduras, 1928. *Journal of the Royal Anthropological Institute* 58: 323–349.

King, Eleanor M., and Leslie C. Shaw
  2003   A Heterarchical Approach to Site Variability. In *Heterarchy, Political Economy, and the Ancient Maya*, ed. Vernon L. Scarborough, Fred Valdez Jr., and Nicholas Dunning, pp. 64–76. University of Arizona Press, Tucson.

Lothrop, Samuel Kirkland
  1924   *Tulum: An Archaeological Study of the East Coast of Yucatan*. Publication 335. Carnegie Institution of Washington, Washington, DC.

Lundell, Cyrus Longworth
  1934   Ruins of Polol and Other Archaeological Discoveries in the Department of Petén, Guatemala. Contribution 8. Carnegie Institution of Washington, Washington, DC.

Manzanilla, Linda, Luis A. Barba, Rene Chávez, Andrés Tejero, Gerardo Cifuentes, and Naycli Peralta
  1994   Caves and Geophysics: An Approximation to the Underworld of Teotihuacan, Mexico. *Archaeometry* 36: 141–157.

Manzanilla, Linda, Claudia López, and Ann Corinne Freter
  1996   Dating Results from Excavations in Quarry Tunnels behind the Pyramid of the Sun at Teotihuacan. *Ancient Mesoamerica* 7: 245–266.

Mason, Gregory
  1927   *Silver Cities of Yucatan*. G. P. Putnam's Sons, New York.

Matos Moctezuma, Eduardo
  1987   Symbolism of the Templo Mayor. In *The Aztec Templo Mayor*, ed. Elizabeth Hill Boone, pp. 185–209. Dumbarton Oaks Research Library and Collection, Washington, DC.

McCafferty, Geoffrey G.
  1996   Reinterpreting the Great Pyramid of Cholula, Mexico. *Ancient Mesoamerica* 7: 1–17.

Mercer, Henry C.
  1896   *The Hill-Caves of Yucatan*. J. B. Lippincott, Philadelphia; reprinted 1975, University of Oklahoma Press, Norman.

Millon, René
  1981   Teotihuacan: City, State, and Civilization. In *Archaeology*, ed. Jeremy A. Sabloff with the assistance of Patricia A. Andrews, pp. 198–243. Supplement to the Handbook of Middle American Indians, vol. 1, Victoria Reifler Bricker, gen. ed. University of Texas Press, Austin.

Millon, René, Bruce Drewitt, and James A. Bennyhoff
  1965   *The Pyramid of the Sun at Teotihuacan: 1959 Investigations*. Transactions of the American Philosophical Society, New Series 55, Part 6. Philadelphia, PA.

Monaghan, John
    1995   *The Covenant with Earth and Rain: Exchange, Sacrifice, and Revelation in Mixtec Sociality*. University of Oklahoma Press, Norman.

Patton, James L.
    1987   The Architecture and Sculpture of Polol, El Petén, Guatemala. MA thesis, Department of Anthropology, San Francisco State University, San Francisco.

Peterson, Polly A.
    2002   Caves of the Sibun-Manatee Karst. In *Sacred Landscape and Settlement in the Sibun River Valley: XARP 1999 Survey and Excavation*, ed. Patricia A. McAnany, pp. 83–98. Institute of Mesoamerican Studies Occasional Papers 8. State University of New York, Albany.

Pope, Kevin O., and Malcolm Sibbernsen
    1981   In Search of Tzultacaj: Cave Explorations in the Maya Lowlands of Alta Verapaz, Guatemala. *Journal of New World Archaeology* 4 (3): 16–54.

Prufer, Keith M.
    2002   Communities, Caves and Ritual Specialists: A Study of Sacred Space in the Maya Mountains of Southern Belize. Unpublished PhD dissertation, Department of Anthropology, Southern Illinois University, Carbondale.

Prufer, Keith M., and James E. Brady, eds.
    2005   *Stone Houses and Earth Lords: Maya Religion in the Cave Context*. University Press of Colorado, Boulder.

Prufer, Keith M., and Andrew Kindon
    2005   Replicating the Sacred Landscape: The Ce'en at Muklebal Tzul. In *Stone Houses and Earth Lords: Maya Religion in the Cave Context*, ed. Keith M. Prufer and James E. Brady, pp. 23–46. University Press of Colorado, Boulder.

Pugh, Timothy W.
    2001   Flood Reptiles, Serpent Temples, and the Quadripartite Universe: The Imago Mundi of Late Postclassic Mayapan. *Ancient Mesoamerica* 12: 247–258.
    2005   Cracks in the Carapace: Underworld Metaphors in Late Postclassic Maya Ceremonial Groups. In *Stone Houses and Earth Lords: Maya Religion in the Cave Context*, ed. Keith M. Prufer and James E. Brady, pp. 47–69. University Press of Colorado, Boulder.

Recinos, Adrian, Delia Goetz, and Sylvanus G. Morley
    1950   *Popul Vuh: The Sacred Book of the Ancient Quiche Maya*. University of Oklahoma Press, Norman.

Reeder, Philip
    1993   Cave Exploration and Mapping on the Northern Vaca Plateau. *National Speleological Society News* 51: 296–300.

Reeder, Philip, James E. Brady, and James Webster
    1998   Geoarchaeological Investigations on the Northern Vaca Plateau, Belize. *Mexicon* 20: 37–41.

Rissolo, Dominique A.
- 2001 Ancient Maya Cave Use in the Yalahau Region, Northern Quintana Roo, Mexico. Unpublished PhD dissertation, Department of Anthropology, University of California, Riverside.

Sanders, William T.
- 1955 An Archaeological Reconnaissance of Northern Quintana Roo. *Current Report* 24. Carnegie Institution of Washington, Washington, DC.

Scott, Ann M.
- 1992 Cave Reconnaissance in the Copan Valley. Report presented to the Instituto Hondureño de Antropología e Historia, Copan Ruinas, Honduras.

Stuart, David, and Stephen Houston
- 1994 *Classic Maya Place Names*. Studies in Pre-Columbian Art and Archaeology 33. Dumbarton Oaks Research Library and Collection, Washington, DC.

Thompson, Edward H., ed.
- 1938 *The High Priest's Grave, Chichen Itza, Yucatan, Mexico*. Anthropology Series 27 (1). Field Museum of Natural History, Chicago, IL.

Thompson, J. Eric S.
- 1959 The Role of Caves in Maya Culture. *Mitteilungen aus dem Museum für Völkerkunde im Hamburg* 25: 122–129.
- 1975 Introduction to the Reprint Edition. In *The Hill-Caves of Yucatan [by Henry C. Mercer]*, pp. vii–xliv. University of Oklahoma Press, Norman.

Toor, Frances
- 1947 *A Treasury of Mexican Folkways*. Crown, New York.

Villa Rojas, Alfonso
- 1946 *Notas sobre la etnografía de los indios Tzeltales de Oxchuc, Chiapas, México*. University of Chicago Microfilms, Manuscripts on Middle American Cultural Anthropology 7. Chicago.
- 1947 Kinship and Nagualism in a Tzeltal Community, Southeastern Mexico. *American Anthropologist* 49: 578–587.

Vogt, Evon
- 1964a Ancient Maya and Contemporary Tzotzil Cosmology: A Comment on Some Methodological Problems. *American Antiquity* 30 (2): 192–195.
- 1964b Some Implications of Zinacantan Social Structure for the Study of the Ancient Maya. In *Actas y Memorias del XXXV Congreso Internacional de Americanistas*, vol. 1, pp. 307–319. México, DF.
- 1976 *Tortillas for the Gods: A Symbolic Analysis of Zinacantelo Rituals*. Harvard University Press, Cambridge, MA.

Wallace, Dwight T., and Robert M. Carmack
- 1977 *Archaeology and Ethnohistory of the Central Quiche*. Institute for Mesoamerican Studies Publication 1. State University of New York, Albany.

Wilson, Richard
- 1995 *Maya Resurgence in Guatemala: Q'eqchi' Experiences*. University of Oklahoma Press, Norman.

PART III
CENTRAL MEXICO

10

THE MIXTECA-PUEBLA TRADITION AND H. B. NICHOLSON

Pablo Escalante Gonzalbo

In 1956 H. B. Nicholson presented his paper "The Mixteca-Puebla Concept in Mesoamerican Archaeology: A Re-examination" to a rapt audience at the Fifth International Congress of Anthropological and Ethnological Sciences in Philadelphia, Pennsylvania. This was the first public dissemination of a theme that would interest him throughout his entire professional career (Nicholson 1960, 1961, 1977, 1982). Nicholson's fascination with the Mixteca-Puebla tradition reached its apogee with the publication of the landmark volume *Mixteca-Puebla: Discoveries and Research in Mesoamerican Art and Archaeology* (Nicholson and Quiñones Keber 1994). H. B. Nicholson precisely determined the scope of the Mixteca-Puebla Concept by limiting it to the analysis of a stylistic and iconographic tradition. He established the basic characterization of the style, identified its principal iconographic traits, and offered hypotheses on the critical issue of where and when this tradition first appeared. As we shall see, all of these issues warrant continued study.

Nicholson's original 1956 paper had the great merit of converting previously imprecise terminology into a scientific definition with great explanatory potential for the study of Prehispanic Mexican art. After offering his initial criteria for the concept, Nicholson refined and strengthened them in the context of a long debate sustained with Donald Robertson. This rigorous, sometimes even heated exchange generated one of the greatest contributions to the field of

Mesoamerican studies (Robertson 1959, 1963, 1968; Nicholson 1960, 1961, 1982). Every time a contemporary student works with the Mixteca-Puebla Concept, he or she is following the trail blazed by H. B. Nicholson. This study reviews the development of the Mixteca-Puebla Concept, summarizes its content, and is offered as a tribute to the memory of H. B. Nicholson.

ORIGIN OF THE MIXTECA-PUEBLA CONCEPT

For more than 600 years Teotihuacan exerted a great centrifugal force, scattering its metropolitan traits hundreds of kilometers from the Valley of Mexico. As the Teotihuacan system crumbled around AD 600, it appears that a kind of reversal took place, similar to what physicists call centripetal force. Now the cultures on the periphery of the Teotihuacan system began to make their presence felt on the Meseta Central and joined in interesting processes of intermingling and cultural synthesis. This amalgamation became characteristic of the Late Classic Period (AD 600–900). The different artistic traditions of the Epiclassic Period are critical for understanding the rise of unified expression in thought and material culture in the succeeding, final period of Prehispanic Mesoamerican culture history.

Around AD 1000 a new kind of polychrome pottery appeared, shared, with some regional variation, by the many diverse peoples of the Meseta Central and Oaxaca. Simultaneously, a new style of mural painting and low-relief sculpture also emerged. Groups of Nahuatl speakers, Popolucas, Mixtecs, Zapotecs, Otomí, and others, used these new art forms and adopted them as a common means of communicating and documenting their religious thoughts and history.

The first investigator who attempted to explain this phenomenon was George C. Vaillant (1938), introducing the term *Mixteca-Puebla* as a general reference to what was variously termed a "culture," a "civilization," or both. According to Vaillant, Mixteca-Puebla was characterized by such traits as a clearly defined political system, use of the *tonalpohualli* and the fifty-two–year calendar, the presence of stylized pictorial writing, ruling lineages, formalized warfare, and specific ceremonial practices (Vaillant 1940: 299, 1941: 84). Vaillant believed this culture's traits had extended throughout all of Mesoamerica, but he used the term *Mixteca-Puebla* to refer to two zones in particular—the Mexican State of Puebla and the Mixteca—because he felt it was there that Mixteca-Puebla had flowered with the greatest intensity.

In 1942 Wigberto Jiménez Moreno made another significant contribution to the Mixteca-Puebla Concept by linking historical accounts with archaeological evidence. In his classic work "El enigma de los olmecas," Jiménez Moreno (1942) hypothesized that the Olmeca-Xicalanca were responsible for the kinds of cultural features Vaillant had described as "Mixteca-Puebla." In his 1942 publication and again in his great later study of Mesoamerican history prior to the rise of Toltec Tula (1959), Jiménez Moreno suggested the Mixteca Baja as the birthplace of Mixteca-Puebla traits. Nicholson built upon this earlier work in his 1956 presented paper and 1960 publication, striving for a more precise and explicit Mixteca-Puebla trait enumeration. He proposed:

> **1.** That Mixteca-Puebla should be an analytical concept specific to a stylistic and iconographic tradition, not to a single culture or civilization.
> **2.** From the stylistic point of view, the determining characteristics of the Mixteca-Puebla tradition are the almost-geometric precision in the delineation of figures, the rigorous standardization of the symbols employed, the use of an extensive range of colors, and the portrayal of figures as caricatures with some traits greatly exaggerated.
> **3.** Characteristic Mixteca-Puebla inconographic symbols and motifs include: solar and lunar disks, terrestrial and celestial bands, the Venus symbol, skulls and skeletons, *chalchihuite* [precious stones], water, fire, the human heart, war symbols, mountains, flowers, starry eyes, segmented marine snails, the signs of the *tonalpohualli*, jaguars, deer, and rabbits. (Nicholson 1960: 615)

Three years after Nicholson presented his paper, Donald Robertson (1959) published *Mexican Manuscript Painting of the Early Colonial Period*. Robertson's book was basically devoted to the Colonial Period Nahua codices, including a definition of what he called the Mixtec Style (Robertson 1959: 9–24). Robertson used this definition as a counterpoint to Nicholson's Mixteca-Puebla Concept throughout all of his professional research and publication.

If Nicholson's position clearly favored the iconographic aspects of the Mixteca-Puebla tradition, then Robertson's ran in the opposite direction, giving the most weight to stylistic considerations. Furthermore, his deletion of the word "Puebla" from Mixteca-Puebla and consistent references to the style of the Prehispanic codices and polychrome ceramics as the creations of the Mixtecs became a position he would defend throughout his career, constantly affirming the Mixtecs' cultural leadership and superiority in artistic concerns over all the peoples of the Postclassic Period. Robertson's 1959 publication resulted in a rejoinder from Nicholson (1961), who objected to the use of the term *Mixtec* to the detriment of the original Mixteca-Puebla terminology. Nicholson felt suggesting the preeminence of any single ethnic group as the carrier of this tradition was premature, obscuring any potential understanding of the origin and diffusion of the Mixteca-Puebla Style. Two years later Robertson (1963) again returned to the subject, arguing much more explicitly and emphatically for the contribution of the Mixtec culture to the Mesoamerican Postclassic. Robertson concluded his article by stating that "the Mixtecs were the source of the highest artistic achievement that Cortés found in Mexico Tenochtitlan when he visited the great metropolitan center" (ibid.: 164). Robertson went on to say that the people of the city of Mexico were accustomed to draw upon the Mixtec city-states when they needed artists.

This time, Nicholson was late in replying. Finally, in 1977, he firmly corrected all who had overestimated the role of the Mixtecs in Postclassic Mesoamerican culture. In an obvious reference to Robertson, he stated: "I am aware of no passage in any primary source which indicates that Mixtec-speaking craftsmen from Oaxaca were ever brought to Mexico Tenochtitlan to practice their skills" (Nicholson 1982: 236).

Without diminishing the importance of the debate between Nicholson and Robertson, I should also note the important contributions of other scholars in the field of ceramic analysis and artifact classification to our understanding of the Mixteca-Puebla Concept. The first ceramic sequence worked out for the great metropolis of Cholula, perhaps the heir apparent to Teotihuacan in the centuries after the fall of that city, was undertaken by Eduardo Noguera (1954). Noguera's sequence was later modified by Florencia Müller (1970). In addition, the work of Michael Lind (1967, 1994) and James Ramsey (1975, 1982) is relevant for the classification and description of Cholulan archaeological data. Lind (1967) deserves much credit for having been the first to identify systematic distinctions between the polychrome ceramics from Cholula and those from the Mixteca. Although his initial work remains unpublished, some of his conclusions appeared in his article "Cholula and Mixteca Polychromes" (Lind 1994). Ramsey (1975) completed a stylistic analysis of pottery, jewelry, turquoise mosaics, and other artifacts for his doctoral dissertation and also published a summary of his conclusions in "An Examination of Mixtec Iconography" (1982).

The final major publication devoted to the Mixteca-Puebla question is *Mixteca-Puebla: Discoveries and Research in Mesoamerican Art and Archaeology*, edited by Nicholson and Quiñones Keber in 1994. This volume reflects the substantial advances made in the study of all those cultural manifestations George Vaillant grouped together under the label *Mixteca-Puebla* more than a half-century ago. Today the concept is generally understood in a form very similar to that which Nicholson tried to define.

1. There is general agreement that the term *Mixteca-Puebla* is more appropriate than the term *Mixtec* because the former incorporates both of the great geographic areas in which the phenomenon predominates, while the second refers to a single ethnic group out of many.

2. It is also accepted that the expression *Mixteca-Puebla Stylistic and Iconographic Tradition* is more useful and precise than Vaillant's ambiguous *Mixteca-Puebla Culture*.

3. In spite of Nicholson and Robertson's differences regarding the ethnic components of the phenomenon, today both scholars' proposals are fundamental to the understanding of the Mixteca-Puebla Concept. Nicholson made the more complete contribution to the iconographic definition of the tradition, while Robertson's comments on style are critical to all research on that subject. After all, Robertson was an art historian.

4. It is clear that Mixteca-Puebla traits had special force in ceremonial and elite contexts within the central and southern portions of the State of Puebla (from Huejotzingo to Tehuacán), the entire State of Tlaxcala, the great Mixtec region (Costa, Alta, and Baja), and the Valley of Oaxaca. But the demarcation of this principal or primary area in no way diminishes Mixteca-Puebla manifestations encountered in places far removed. Various investigators have noted the impact of Mixteca-Puebla traits in remote places, including some outside Mesoamerica proper.

5. It is an accepted fact, although little studied, that the unified Mixteca-Puebla tradition does not imply the absence of regional varieties in style any more than in iconography.

6. Although it is recognized that the Mixteca-Puebla tradition includes things such as architecture, mosaics, gold work, carved bones, and jewelry in general (Paddock 1982: 4–5; Ramsey 1982), its fundamental definition has been applied to polychrome ceramics and, to a lesser extent, mural painting and low-relief sculpture.

STYLE AND ICONOGRAPHY

It is possible to create a motif repertory to study Mixteca-Puebla iconography, just as one can study its symbolic meaning. It is important to remember, however, that in reality, both exist together. The jaguar and the stars are both common Mixteca-Puebla motifs, but they will always be rendered in similar fashion—through the use of thick black lines, uniform color areas, and other elements. Mixteca-Puebla art can only be defined through attention to both components. The iconographic component is immediately recognizable, but only because the style provides unity and comprehension of that iconography.

A list of Mixteca-Puebla stylistic and iconographic traits is presented below. In compiling this list I considered only ceramic decoration and mural painting, basing my analysis on polychrome ceramics from the Mixteca Alta, Mixteca Baja, ancient Tehuacán, Cholula, and Huejotzingo and from the archaeological sites within what is now the urban area of Tlaxcala. I also included mural painting from Tehuacán, Puebla, and Ocotelulco and Tizatlán, Tlaxcala.

Mixteca-Puebla expression is characterized by the use of a wide range of colors. Polychrome pottery (figure 10.1) is perhaps most representative of the Mixteca-Puebla tradition, which is logical: never before in Mesoamerica had such an immense quantity of polychrome vessels been produced as was the case under the influence of the Mixteca-Puebla tradition. The colors black, tan, dark brownish-orange, yellow, orange, red, and white predominate. Blue is rare in

Pablo Escalante Gonzalbo

10.1. *Tripod vessel from Nochixtlán with Mixteca-Puebla polychrome decoration. (Above): Photo from Westheim et al. 1969: 242; (below): rollout drawing from Seler 1993: 286.*

ceramic decoration but is very common in mural painting. Color areas (in both ceramics and mural painting) are bounded by thick, dark lines, usually black, which Robertson designated "frame lines." As opposed to lines used in shading, a frame line never varies in thickness and never serves to suggest volume or three-dimensional shading, only to isolate shapes. Color is applied with equal intensity over the entire surface, without darkening or lightening. The use of black frame lines and the intense and homogeneous color areas convey the impression that the objects represented are composed of semiautonomous parts, separated as in a puzzle.

Representations of human beings, animals, and other objects from the natural world, such as flowers, are made through a process of simplification resulting in relatively rigid stereotypes. The human figure has unnatural proportions, with the head alone accounting for a quarter to a third of its total height.[1] Faces tend to have large, projecting noses and prominent teeth; in par-

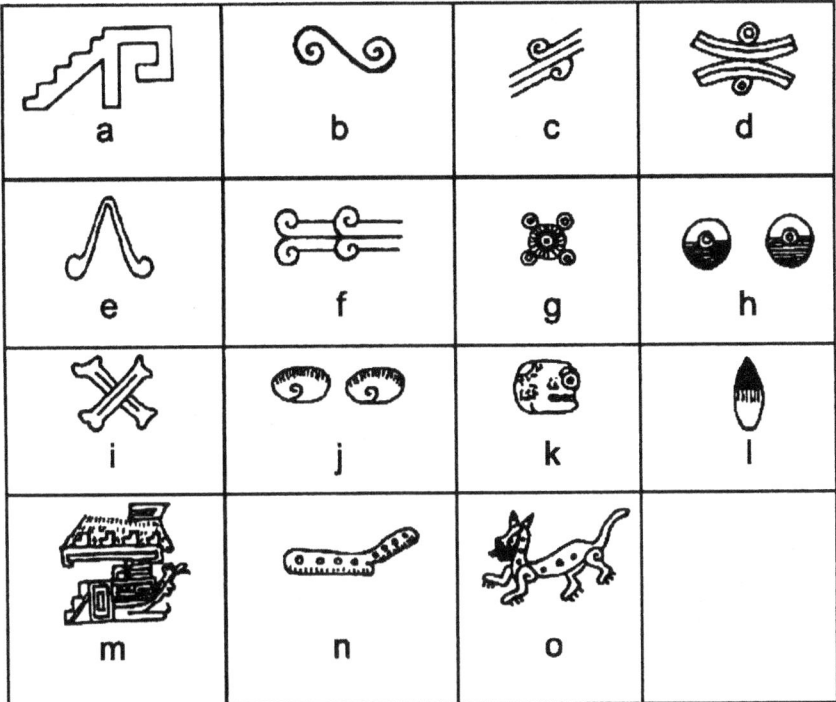

10.2. *Mixteca-Puebla iconographic elements. After Lind 1994: 94–95.*

ticular, the upper teeth are frequently exposed. Old age is depicted by leaving a single tooth visible (indicating that the elderly were nearly edentulate), and death is suggested by closed eyelids. Ears are presented in a rigid, schematic form I have called "mushroom ears." Fingernails are large and showy. Sandals are also prominently represented and are generally large in comparison to the thickness of the legs. Toes are shown as curved, projecting downward over the ends of the sandal soles.

One of the most salient characteristics of Mixteca-Puebla iconography is its affinity with human sacrifice and war. Representations of sacrificial knives are emphasized, with or without faces (figure 10.2l), as are hearts and skulls (figure 10.2k), crossed bones (figure 10.2i), downy sacrificial feather balls (figure 10.2j), shields (*chimallis*), the *teoatl-tlachinolli* symbol, and eagle and jaguar figures (figure 10.2o). Also depicted with regularity are stellar eyes or stars (figure 10.2h), the solar disk and sun rays (figure 10.2e), *chalchihuites* (figure 10.2g), segmented snails and the *ollin* sign (figure 10.2d), the *ilhuitl* (day symbol) (figure 10.2c), the step-fret (*xicalcoliuhqui*) (figure 10.2a), and scroll (*xonecuilli*) designs (figure 10.2b). The human figure, either complete or partial, can also appear, as do more or less schematic representations of mountains and architecture (figure 10.2m).[2]

There is a tendency to think of Mixteca-Puebla iconography as a homogeneous unit, lacking significant stylistic differences within the tradition. Nevertheless, the work of Michael Lind (1994) has signaled a change in this perception. Lind undertook a comparative analysis of the iconography of ceramic vessels from Oaxaca and Cholula, reaching some interesting conclusions. Apparently, Oaxacan pottery reflects nobility and palace life, with emphasis on motifs such as caves, images of the first Mixtecs and Lord 9 Wind, and themes such as ritual *pulque* drinking and the eating of psychotropic mushrooms. In contrast, Cholulan pottery, which emphasizes human sacrifice and blood offerings, is predominated by representations of bone awls, maguey spines, sacrificial knives, crossed bones, and feather down.

ORIGIN AND DIFFUSION OF THE MIXTECA-PUEBLA TRADITION

Two questions, still unresolved, always fascinated H. B. Nicholson (1982: 241). We may never know the precise geographical source of the Mixteca-Puebla tradition or the exact time of its initial spread throughout Mesoamerica. It may now be possible, however, to assemble clues pointing toward a solution to both problems. The typologies and chronologies formulated by Universidad de las Américas analysts, when linked to salvage data recovered by archaeologists working at dozens of sites in the city of Cholula, have dramatically improved our knowledge of Mixteca-Puebla ceramics. Today, we know that different polychrome ceramic types did not appear right at the end of the Classic Period, as Noguera (1954) had earlier thought (Suárez Cruz 1994: 49); nor, on the other hand, did they appear very late in the cultural sequence, as suggested by Müller (1970; see also McCafferty 1994). According to recent studies, the first Mixteca-Puebla polychrome vessels appeared during the Aquiahuac Phase (AD 950–1150; Lind 1994: 81), placing the start of the Mixteca-Puebla tradition at Cholula in the Early Postclassic Period. The fact that this date is not earlier than AD 900 agrees with what we know about the style and antiquity of the Cacaxtla site: Cacaxtla mural painting is not Mixteca-Puebla yet dates immediately prior to it, in the Late Classic Period, between AD 600 and 900.[3] If the Mixteca-Puebla Style had existed at this time, then it might have appeared at Cacaxtla.

The apparent consistency of the different polychrome ceramic types recovered from excavations in the Postclassic archaeological sites of Tlaxcala, Huejotzingo, Cholula, and Tehuacán convince us that this pottery is essentially typical and representative of the region. Complete and up-to-date ceramic sequences for the Mixteca and the Valley of Oaxaca are lacking; consequently, the precise relationship between the two great sectors of the Mixteca-Puebla remains hitherto undefined. With the information presently available, however, we can advance several arguments for the primacy of the Mixteca-Puebla tradition in the Puebla-Tlaxcala territory rather than that in the Mixteca and Oaxaca.

1. At present, the earliest dates proposed for Mixteca-Puebla pottery are from Cholula. The very few dates available from Oaxaca are later (Lind 1994: 81).

2. Cholula was a vibrant metropolis, a shrine that attracted pilgrims from remote regions throughout Mesoamerica, and a point of contact for migration streams that combined different ethnic components. This special situation made the artistic and technological synthesis at the heart of the tradition that took place there possible (Winter 1994: 218).[4]

3. Recent research in the Mixteca Baja indicates a major break in the cultural sequence at the end of the Classic Period, with abandonment of the urban centers, possibly resulting from a political crisis. Apparently, the political instability was resolved toward the end of the Early Postclassic. Soon thereafter the Mixteca Baja received the fully developed Mixteca-Puebla tradition. At present, no archaeological evidence supports a local genesis of the Mixteca-Puebla tradition in the Mixteca Baja (ibid.).[5]

4. Between AD 900 and 1000, the Mixteca Alta experienced a period of crisis and "high political fractionalization," which was similar yet subsequent to the disruptive events in the Mixteca Baja. During this period plain pottery from Puebla appeared in the Sierra (Pohl and Byland 1994: 197); the importation of these non-local wares could signal the start of the process that ultimately led to the adoption of Puebla-Tlaxcalan polychromes in the Sierra.

5. Maya influence may have been decisive in the development of Mixteca-Puebla polychrome ceramic decorative techniques (Lind 1994: 98). If this is the case, then (a) we should realize that during the Late Classic (AD 600–900) Maya influence was strongly felt on the Meseta Central, particularly in the city of Cacaxtla, yet we have no evidence of a similar situation in the Mixteca; (b) it is therefore likely that such Maya influence came through Tabasco and Veracruz so as to reach Puebla and Tlaxcala; (c) localities within the Puebla-Tlaxcala Zone (i.e., Tehuacán or Cholula) might have been the sites at which Maya ceramic techniques were combined with local techniques, designs, and artistic inspiration.

Regardless of which of the two sectors first adopted the Mixteca-Puebla tradition, it is an accepted fact that during the Late Postclassic Period the Mixteca and the Puebla-Tlaxcala Zone shared the same iconography and stylistic tradition. This can be explained with relative ease: the zones were neighbors, and between them there existed political alliances forged through royal marriage (Lind 1994: 96). The political ties, together with geographical proximity, fostered the exchange of cultural patterns. The fact that the elite alliances facilitated the diffusion of the Mixteca-Puebla tradition should not be surprising, given that the tradition was characteristically elitist: we are talking about ceremonial vessels, palace and temple wall paintings, and jewelry of the highest sophistication.

In the Mixtec cities no less than in those of the Puebla-Tlaxcala area, the Mixteca-Puebla tradition became the dominant form of expression throughout the entire Late Postclassic Period, right up to the Conquest. But what happened in other areas? The Mixteca-Puebla stylistic and iconographic tradition spread throughout Mesoamerica and left its traces at sites some distance from what we consider its original or primary area. This expansion was first studied by Vaillant (1940: 299–300) and was later emphasized by Robertson (1968), who referred to what he called the "Mixtec Style" as the "International Style of the Postclassic."

In fact, Mixteca-Puebla polychrome ceramics have been reported some distance from the Valley of Mexico (Batres 1990), at various Gulf Coast archaeological sites, as well as at Totonac and Huaxtec sites (Ochoa Salas 1979: lámina 13; Schávelzon 1980: 25–27). In West Mexico, from north to south, Mixteca-Puebla polychrome ceramics are known from Guasave, Sinaloa (Schávelzon 1980: 28) and Amapa, Nayarit (von Winning 1977). Mural paintings demonstrating strong Mixteca-Puebla influence have been discovered in San Luis Potosí (Du Solier 1946), at Tulum (Robertson 1968; Miller 1982), and at Santa Rita Corozal, Belize (Quirarte 1982).

At present, it is hard to say in which of these regions the Mixteca-Puebla tradition took root strongly enough to have been converted by the local elite into the dominant form of artistic expression. Among the Totonacs there seems to be a difference between locally made ceramics and those of Mixteca-Puebla Style (Schávelzon 1980: 27); yet in the West, particularly in Nayarit, Mixteca-Puebla ceramics were locally produced (von Winning 1977). In the Nayarit case it is interesting that while characteristic Mixteca-Puebla traits are well represented, these traits have been adapted to regional tastes through stylistic modification emphasizing straight lines and angularity in figures. A similar process of Mixteca-Puebla trait modification took place in the mural painting of San Luis Potosí and at the Maya sites of Tulum, Quintana Roo, México, and Santa Rita Corozal, Belize.

The mural paintings of Tulum and Santa Rita Corozal juxtapose Maya and Mixteca-Puebla traditions; the first impression on viewing these murals is that they do not correspond to normal Maya naturalistic conventions or to the habitual Maya compositional formulae. Mixteca-Puebla traits are identifiable at Santa Rita Corozal, including the abundance of straight lines, the use of uniform color areas surrounded by thick black lines, and details such as sandal knots and decorations. Mixteca-Puebla stylistic traits at Tulum include the curvature of the feet and prominent sandals, the arrangement of the legs and the posturing of individuals who bear offerings, the presence of a ceramic vessel suspended between two individuals, and the depiction of a metate and the woman who is grinding on it.[6] Santa Rita Corozal was not the final stop in the southward movement of Mixteca-Puebla influence. The Mixteca-Puebla tradition had a profound imprint on Central American ceramics, especially in the Nicoya region of southern Nicaragua and northern Costa Rica (Stone 1982; Day 1994).

If a scarcity of tangible information makes it difficult to explain the precise relationship between Puebla-Tlaxcala and the Mixteca, then it is even more challenging to explain the presence of the Mixteca-Puebla tradition on the Yucatán Peninsula and in northern Belize. In the case of Tulum and Santa Rita, however, the identification of an exotic art style may simply have resulted from foreign merchants visiting this locale; its presence need not mean the movement of large Central Mexican populations into the Maya area. But in the cases of Nicoya and Amapa, it seems much more likely that we are faced with local elites adopting a prestigious new foreign tradition and encouraging the development of the new and specialized art form, with new ideas and new preferences.

Usually, when we encounter a Mesoamerican style or iconographic repertoire many kilometers from its presumed place of origin, we explain such displacement by making reference to some other faraway metropolis that spawned it. We therefore believe, surely with good reason, that the presence of Teotihuacan-style iconography at Tikal resulted from imperial vigor in commercial or even colonial contexts; we explain Early Postclassic Chichén Itzá by alluding to Tula, the probable place of origin of its refounders, and we explain the artistic characteristics of Castillo de Teayo in reference to Mexica military expansionism.

CONCLUSION

So from which metropolis came the Mixteca-Puebla expansion? The most recent investigations point to Cholula, which was suggested almost seventy years ago by Jiménez Moreno (1942: 128–129) and over thirty years ago by Nicholson (1977: 117).[7] It is not necessary to assume that political expansion by Cholula, the city of the Great Pyramid, was the means by which the style was spread. There were already two means of influence inherent in its historical tradition and in the composition of its population: Cholula was a great shrine that attracted pilgrims from diverse regions. In particular, elite groups worshipped at the gigantic Temple of Quetzalcoatl (McCafferty 1994: 58). In addition, Cholula was one of the principal seats and religious centers of the pochtecah, who aggressively forged Postclassic commercial routes throughout Mesoamerica (ibid.). Pilgrims and merchants might have been primarily responsible for the diffusion of the Mixteca-Puebla tradition, but never without the approval, interest, and patronage of local elites. These elites, after developing an appetite for imported Mixteca-Puebla art, would then have commissioned similar decoration on locally made ceremonial pottery vessels, mosaics, jewelry, and mural paintings.

Among many good reasons why the elites of Nayarit and Nicoya, of the Huaxteca and the Valley of Mexico adopted the Mixteca-Puebla tradition is perhaps the most important: the Mixteca-Puebla Style was instrumental in the development of pictographic communication and was an excellent vehicle for the precision and clarity of expression required by the pictographic system. Mixteca-Puebla symbols efficiently represent much broader belief systems related to Postclassic Period religious rituals (cf. Smith and Heath-Smith 1980). In fact, one of the most important contributions of Mixteca-Puebla material culture was the pictographic codices, in which were recorded marriage alliances (e.g., Mixtecos of Coixtlahuaca and the Nahuas of Teotitlán and Tehuacán) and sacrificial rituals, including heart extractions as depicted in the Amapa paintings and Ocotelulco murals.

The Mixteca-Puebla Concept is a model. It serves as one of the most useful tools in the study of Postclassic cultural interaction, artistic production, the pictographic manuscripts, and the complete Colonial transformation of native artistic expression. As noted at the outset, H. B. Nicholson's work in building the concept was decisive.

NOTES

1. In other words, the canon varies between 1:3 and 1:4.
2. This list is not exhaustive and includes only painted representations on ceramics and in murals. If codex examples were included, it would greatly expand.
3. I refer only to those murals presently visible, not to the earlier examples obscured by later construction.
4. Marcus Winter (1994: 218) states: "With its ample cultivable land, with its contacts with groups from Oaxaca, Teotihuacán, the Gulf Coast and even the Maya—as seen in the Cacaxtla murals—Cholula was a powerfully great center, whose leaders were able to borrow elements from diverse groups so as to crystallize them into a new style."
5. Winter (1994: 218) suggests: "Perhaps the Mixtec of Oaxaca did not contribute as much to the origin of the Mixteca-Puebla Style as to its diffusion and development."
6. Paintings from different phases are present at Tulum. The majority of the Mixteca-Puebla traits are found in the final phase, after AD 1400. Arthur Miller (1982: 71) has also connected these latest paintings with the codices and has stated, following Robertson, that they correspond to the "International Late Postclassic Style."
7. Nicholson and Quiñones Keber (1994) provide the most up-to-date synthesis of this subject.

REFERENCES CITED

Batres, Leopoldo
    1990   Exploraciones en las calles de las escalerillas. In *Trabajos arqueológicos en el Centro de la Ciudad de México*, 2nd ed., ed. Eduardo Matos Moctezuma, pp. 11–167. INAH, México, DF.

Day, Jane Stevenson
    1994   Central Mexican Imagery in Greater Nicoya. In *Mixteca-Puebla: Discoveries and Research in Mesoamerican Art and Archaeology*, ed. H. B. Nicholson and Eloise Quiñones Keber, pp. 235–248. Labyrinthos, Culver City, CA.

Du Solier, Wilfredo
    1946   Primer fresco mural huasteco. *Cuadernos Americanos* 5 (6): 151–159.

Jiménez Moreno, Wigberto
    1942   El enigma de los olmecas. *Cuadernos Americanos* 1 (5): 113–145.
    1959   Síntesis de la historia pretolteca de Mesoamérica. In *Esplendor del México Antiguo*, vol. 2, ed. Carmen Cook de Leonard, pp. 1019–1096. Centro de Investigaciones Antropológicas de México, México, DF.

Lind, Michael
    1967   Mixtec Polychrome Pottery: A Comparison of the Late Pre-Conquest Polychrome Pottery from Cholula, Oaxaca, and Chinantla. MA thesis, Department of Anthropology, University of the Americas, México, DF.
    1994   Cholula and Mixteca Polychromes: Two Mixteca-Puebla Regional Sub-Styles. In *Mixteca Puebla: Discoveries and Research in Mesoamerican Art and Archaeology*, ed. H. B. Nicholson and Eloise Quiñones Keber, pp. 79–99. Labyrinthos, Culver City, CA.

McCafferty, Geoffrey G.
    1994   The Mixteca-Puebla Stylistic Tradition at Early Postclassic Cholula. In *Mixteca Puebla: Discoveries and Research in Mesoamerican Art and Archaeology*, ed. H. B. Nicholson and Eloise Quiñones Keber, pp. 53–78. Labyrinthos, Culver City, CA.

Miller, Arthur G.
    1982   *On the Edge of the Sea: Mural Painting at Tancah-Tulum, Quintana Roo, México*. Dumbarton Oaks, Washington, DC.

Müller, Florencia
    1970   La cerámica de Cholula. In *Proyecto Cholula*, ed. Ignacio Marquina, pp. 129–142. INAH, México, DF.

Nicholson, H. B.
    1960   The Mixteca-Puebla Concept in Mesoamerican Archaeology: A Re-examination. In *Fifth International Congress of Anthropological and Ethnological Sciences, 1956*, ed. Anthony F. Wallace, pp. 612–617. University of Pennsylvania Press, Philadelphia.
    1961   The Use of the Term "Mixtec" in Mesoamerican Archaeology. *American Antiquity* 26 (3): 431–433.
    1977   The Mixteca-Puebla Concept in Mesoamerican Archaeology: A Re-examination [reprint of Nicholson 1960]. In *Pre-Columbian Art History: Selected Reading*, ed. Alana Cordy-Collins and Jean Stern, pp. 113–119. Peek Publications, Palo Alto, CA.
    1982   The Mixteca Puebla Concept Revisited. In *The Art and Iconography of Late Post-Classic Central Mexico: A Conference at Dumbarton Oaks, October 22nd and 23rd, 1977*, ed. Elizabeth H. Boone, pp. 227–254. Dumbarton Oaks, Washington, DC.

Nicholson, H. B., and Eloise Quiñones Keber, eds.
1994 *Mixteca-Puebla: Discoveries and Research in Mesoamerican Art and Archaeology.* Labyrinthos, Culver City, CA.

Noguera, Eduardo
1954 *La cerámica arqueológica de Cholula.* Editorial Guarania, México, DF.

Ochoa Salas, Lorenzo
1979 *Historia prehispánica de la Huaxteca.* UNAM, México, DF.

Paddock, John
1982 Mixteca-Puebla Style in the Valley of Oaxaca. In *Aspects of the Mixteca-Puebla Style and Mixtec and Central Mexican Culture in Southern Mesoamerica: Papers from a Symposium Organized by Doris Stone*, pp. 3–6. Occasional Paper 4. Middle American Research Institute, Tulane University, New Orleans, LA.

Pohl, John M.D., and Bruce Byland
1994 The Mixteca-Puebla Style and Early Postclassic Socio-Political Interaction. In *Mixteca Puebla: Discoveries and Research in Mesoamerican Art and Archaeology*, ed. H. B. Nicholson and Eloise Quiñones Keber, pp. 189–200. Labyrinthos, Culver City, CA.

Quirarte, Jacinto
1982 The Santa Rita Murals: A Review. In *Aspects of the Mixteca-Puebla Style and Mixtec and Central Mexican Culture in Southern Mesoamerica: Papers from a Symposium Organized by Doris Stone*, pp. 43–59. Occasional Paper 4. Middle American Research Institute, Tulane University, New Orleans, LA.

Ramsey, James
1975 An Analysis of Mixtec Minor Art. PhD dissertation, Department of Art History, Tulane University, New Orleans, LA.
1982 An Examination of Mixtec Iconography. In *Aspects of the Mixteca-Puebla Style and Mixtec and Central Mexican Culture in Southern Mesoamerica: Papers from a Symposium Organized by Doris Stone*, pp. 33–42. Occasional Paper 4. Middle American Research Institute, Tulane University, New Orleans, LA.

Robertson, Donald
1959 *Mexican Manuscript Painting of the Early Colonial Period.* Yale University Press, New Haven, CT.
1963 The Style of the Borgia Group of Mexican Pre-Conquest Manuscripts. In *Latin American Art, and the Baroque Period in Europe. Studies in Western Art: Acts of the Twentieth International Congress of the History of Art*, vol. 3, pp. 148–164. Princeton University Press, Princeton, NJ.
1968 The Tulum Murals: The International Style of the Late Postclassic. *XXXVIII Internationalen Amerikanisten Kongresses (Stuttgart-Munich) Verhandlungen* 2: 77–88. Stuttgart, Germany.

Schávelzon, Daniel
1980 *El Complejo Arqueológico Mixteca-Puebla. Notas para una Redefinición Cultural.* UNAM, Coordinación de Extensión Universitaria, México, DF.

Seler, Eduard
    1993   Some Excellently Painted Old Pottery Vessels of the Sologuren Collection from Nochistlan and Cuicatlan in the State of Oaxaca. In *Collected Works in Mesoamerican Linguistics and Archaeology*, ed. J. Eric S. Thompson and Francis B. Richardson, vol. 4, pp. 285–290. Gen. ed. Frank E. Comparato. Labyrinthos, Culver City, CA.

Smith, Michael E., and Cynthia M. Heath-Smith
    1980   Waves of Influence in Postclassic Mesoamerica? A Critique of the Mixteca-Puebla Concept. *Anthropology* 4 (2): 15–50.

Stone, Doris
    1982   Cultural Radiations from the Central and Southern Highlands of Mexico into Costa Rica. In *Aspects of the Mixteca-Puebla Style and Mixtec and Central Mexican Culture in Southern Mesoamerica: Papers from a Symposium Organized by Doris Stone*, pp. 61–70. Occasional Paper 4. Middle American Research Institute, Tulane University, New Orleans, LA.

Suárez Cruz, Sergio
    1994   El Policromo Laca de Cholula, Puebla. In *Mixteca-Puebla: Discoveries and Research in Mesoamerican Art and Archaeology*, ed. H. B. Nicholson and Eloise Quiñones Keber, pp. 45–51. Labyrinthos, Culver City, CA.

Vaillant, George C.
    1938   A Correlation of Archaeological and Historical Sequences in the Valley of Mexico. *American Anthropologist* 40 (4): 535–573.
    1940   Patterns in Middle American Archaeology. In *The Maya and Their Neighbors: Essays on Middle American Anthropology and Archaeology*, ed. Clarence L. Hay, Ralph L. Linton, Samuel K. Lothrop, Harry L. Shapiro, and George C. Vaillant, pp. 295–305. D. Appleton-Century, New York.
    1941   *Aztecs of Mexico: Origin, Rise and Fall of the Aztec Nation*. Doubleday, Garden City, NY.

von Winning, Hasso
    1977   Rituals Depicted on Polychrome Ceramics from Nayarit. In *Pre-Columbian Art History: Selected Readings*, ed. Alana Cordy-Collins and Jean Stern, pp. 121–134. Peek Publications, Palo Alto, CA.

Westheim, Paul, Alberto Ruz, Pedro Armillas, Ricardo de Robina, Alfonso Caso, and Román Piña Chán, eds.
    1969   *Cuarenta Siglos de Plástica Mexicana*, vol. 1: *Arte Prehispánico*. Editorial Herrero, S.A., México, DF.

Winter, Marcus
    1994   The Mixteca Prior to the Late Postclassic. In *Mixteca-Puebla: Discoveries and Research in Mesoamerican Art and Archaeology*, ed. H. B. Nicholson and Eloise Quiñones Keber, pp. 201–221. Labyrinthos, Culver City, CA.

11

OBSIDIAN BUTTERFLY AND FLOWERY TREE: AN EFFIGY VESSEL FROM COXCATLÁN

Edward B. Sisson

I knew H. B. Nicholson long before I met *Nick*. As a graduate student in the late 1960s, I read with great interest Nicholson's article "Religion in Pre-Hispanic Central Mexico" for the Handbook of Middle American Indians. It was circulated and became a classic before its actual publication in 1971. Forty years later, as I sit here at my desk, I can see the handbook on a nearby shelf. Most of the original volumes still have their paper wrappers, which are in near-pristine condition. A notable exception is volume 10, of which I have two copies for some reason. Neither copy has its paper wrapper. The wrappers were shredded and lost long ago as I pulled the volumes from the shelf to consult Nicholson's article on religion. I find it as useful today as it was forty years ago.

I was also aware of Nicholson's 1957 dissertation, "Topiltzin Quetzalcoatl of Tollan: A Problem in Mesoamerican Ethnohistory." I remember Gordon Willey speaking of Nicholson and the excellence of his scholarship. Whether he meant them to be or not, Willey's comments about the quality of Nicholson's research were intimidating. How was one to live up to this standard? Since my primary interest at the time was in the Olmec, I did not consult this classic until its publication by the University of Colorado Press in 2001.

In the early 1970s, when I began work on the Late Postclassic in the Tehuacán Valley, two articles by Nicholson proved very important for my research. One was "The Mixteca-Puebla Concept in Mesoamerican Archaeology: A Re-examination,"

Nicholson's (1960) detailed appraisal of George C. Vaillant's Mixteca-Puebla Concept. The second was his 1955 article "The Temalacatl of Tehuacán," in which Nicholson succinctly summarized the information then accessible on the ethnohistory of the Tehuacán Valley.

I was consequently well aware of H. B. Nicholson's intellectual reputation and scholarly publications when I joined the Dumbarton Oaks Summer Research Seminar on the Codices of the Borgia Group in 1982. For me, with my limited knowledge of Central Mexican ethnohistory and iconography, this seminar was an intense, eye-opening, and productive two months. The principal participants were Ferdinand Anders, Carlos Arostegui, Elizabeth Boone, John Carlson, Maarten Jansen, H. B. Nicholson, Peter van der Loo, and me; but other scholars dropped by for brief visits to give presentations and to participate in a final conference. In spite of the many accomplished scholars who participated in the event, there was no doubt from the very beginning that the seminar would be guided by Nicholson. Nicholson and Boone were the organizers and had selected the participants, and Nicholson was the dominant force that summer.

During the course of the seminar, I got to know Nick. I found him a kind person and a generous colleague. He freely shared his knowledge with us all; after the seminar was over, he generously supported our continuing research. My wife, Penny, spent part of that summer in Washington; whenever she was with the group, Nick quickly put her at ease and included her in the conversation. She still speaks of his kindness in including her and not dismissing her as an outsider ignorant of what we were doing.

As I reflect on the last twenty-five years, my only regret is that I did not call upon Nick more often for advice and assistance. For example, there were a number of polychrome vessels from Coxcatlán Viejo and later from Tehuacán Viejo that I always intended to show him. I knew he would have been interested in their iconography and that he could have provided valuable insights into their interpretation. If only I had not procrastinated. If only . . . But all is not lost. Nick not only left us a legacy of fine scholarly publications, he also left a large cadre of students to carry on his work and who might help me if I make illustrations of the vessels available to them. One such vessel was from the plaza atop the southernmost ridge within Coxcatlán Viejo. Its final function was to hold cremated human remains, remains that may have represented one of the many Coxcateca who might have died as a consequence of diseases introduced by the Spaniards.

HISTORY OF COXCATLÁN AND THE TEHUACÁN VALLEY

The scant data on the late Precolumbian and Early Colonial history of Coxcatlán and the Tehuacán Valley have been summarized by Peter Gerhard (1993: 260–264, 314–319), Nicholson (1955: 116–118), and Joaquin Paredes Colín (1953, 1960). The *Anales de Cuauhtitlán* (Velázquez 1975: 15) reports that the Tehuacán Valley

OBSIDIAN BUTTERFLY AND FLOWERY TREE

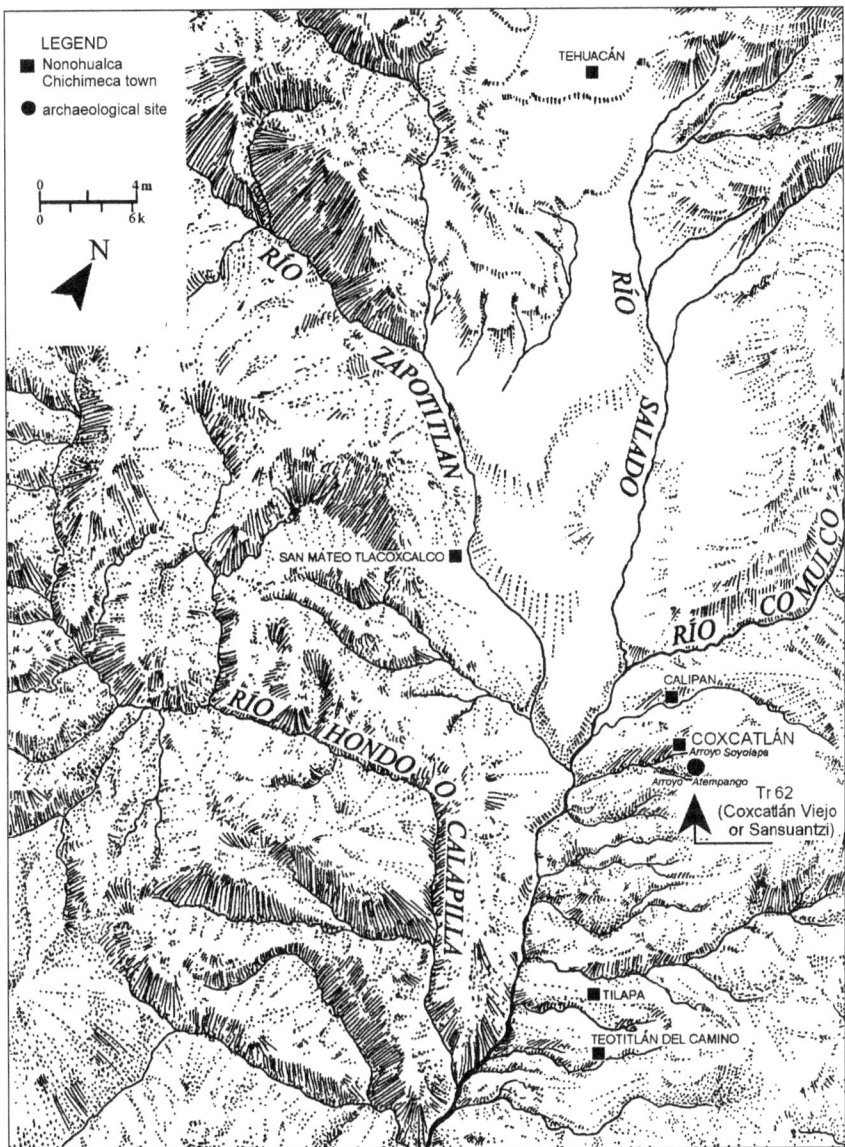

11.1. *The Nonohualca Chichimeca towns of Tehuacán, Coxcatlán, and Teotitlán del Camino. The Coxcatlán Viejo or Sansuantzi archaeological site (Tr 62) is indicated by the black arrow. Original Tehuacán Valley map by MacNeish and Nelken-Turner 1972: figure 2; additions by Rusty van Rossmann.*

was invaded by migrants from Tollan at the beginning of the thirteenth century (figure 11.1). The *Historia Tolteca-Chichimeca* provides more specific information (Kirchhoff, Odena Güemes, and Reyes García 1989: 134–138). Having fought with the Tolteca-Chichimeca, the Nonohualca Chichimeca fled Tollan; after a long migration they arrived in Tenpatzacapan near Coxcatlán. Here the Nonohualca divided into seven groups, each of which founded a town either in the Tehuacán Valley or in the Sierra de Zongólica to the east. One of these groups, the Coxcateca, founded the town and *cacicazgo* of Coxcatlán. In Coxcatlán and the other valley towns of Tehuacán and Teotitlán del Camino, these Nahuatl-speaking Nonohualca displaced local Popoloca or Mazatec elites. Their towns, however, probably maintained a multiethnic population.

Alfonso Caso (1977–1979) summarized genealogical data for the existence of marriage alliances between these Nonohualca elites of Tehuacán and Coxcatlán and the Chocho elites of Ihuitlán in the Coixtlahuaca Valley. Likewise, Mary E. Smith and Ross Parmenter (1991: 22, 54, 56) argued that marriage alliances were established between the Mixtec elites of Acatlán and the Nonohualca elites of Tehuacán as early as the thirteenth century. John Pohl and Bruce Byland (1994: 195–197) have argued that the Nonohualca cacicazgos of the Tehuacán Valley were members of a confederation of polities, or an "alliance corridor," that united Tolteca-Chichimeca, Mixtec, and Zapotec royal houses from Tlaxcala in the north to the Valley of Oaxaca in the south. Following a suggestion of Elizabeth Brumfield, Pohl and Byland argued that the members of these elite houses emulated one another and communicated through a shared symbolic vocabulary manifested in part by painting on polychrome pottery and codices.

Although Robert Barlow (1949) suggested that the Tehuacán Valley towns, including Coxcatlán, were independent allies of the Mexica, Nigel Davies (1968: 14–16, 1987: 213) and Ross Hassig (1988: 165, 170, 195, 319, 329–330) have argued persuasively that the valley was conquered and incorporated into the empire in the 1460s during the reign of Motecuhzoma Ilhuicamina.

In 1520 the elite of Coxcatlán and Tehuacán sent representatives to Tepeaca (present-day Segura de la Frontera) to pledge their fealty to Hernán Cortés (Gerhard 1993: 260). As early as 1534, Tehuacán and Teotitlán del Camino were a single *corregimiento* and Coxcatlán was a separate corregimiento (Gerhard 1993: 261–262). In the mid-1530s Franciscan friars from Huexotzinco established the church and convent of Concepción de Nuestra Señora at the foot of the mesa below Tehuacán. Sometime before 1579 a church was constructed in Coxcatlán. If this church was built in close proximity to the contemporary church location, it was across the Arroyo Soyolapa southwest of the Precolumbian site.

THE COXCATLÁN VIEJO ARCHAEOLOGICAL SITE

The Late Postclassic site of Coxcatlán Viejo is locally known as Sansuantzi, a name derived from *San Juan* plus the Nahuatl honorific *tzin* (figure 11.2). The patron of the modern town is St. John the Evangelist. The archaeological site is located immediately east of and across the Arroyo Soyolapa from the modern

OBSIDIAN BUTTERFLY AND FLOWERY TREE

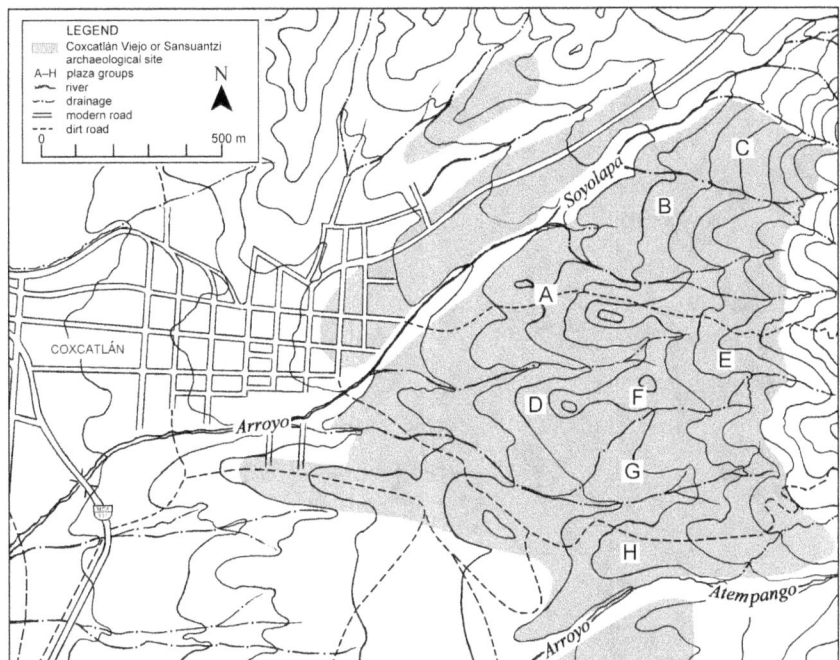

11.2. *Map of the Coxcatlán Viejo archaeological site (shaded area), showing its relationship to the modern town of Coxcatlán. Plaza groups are indicated by capital letters. Original map by Fowler and MacNeish 1972: 333, figure 137; additions by Rusty van Rossmann.*

town. The site covers an area of approximately 100 hectares (ca. 247 acres) and occupies a narrow band of gently sloping land along the Arroyo Soyolapa and a series of small, fingering ridges descending from a major ridge between the Arroyo Soyolapa and the Arroyo Atempango. The slopes of these smaller ridges are terraced. Those terraces that have been excavated contain small shrines and residential structures. Each ridge is dominated by a plaza complex at its highest point. Minimally, these complexes consist of a plaza with a pyramidal platform and a temple at its eastern end. The largest plaza with the pyramid known as Sansuantzi is located in the narrow, relatively flat band of land along the Arroyo Soyolapa.

THE GROUP H PLAZA

The Group H Plaza rests atop the southernmost ridge of the Coxcatlán Viejo site, overlooking the deep cut of the Arroyo Atempango. On the Group H Plaza's eastern side is a small pyramidal structure. Facing this pyramid, on the opposite, western side of the plaza, is a low rectangular platform mound. Another low

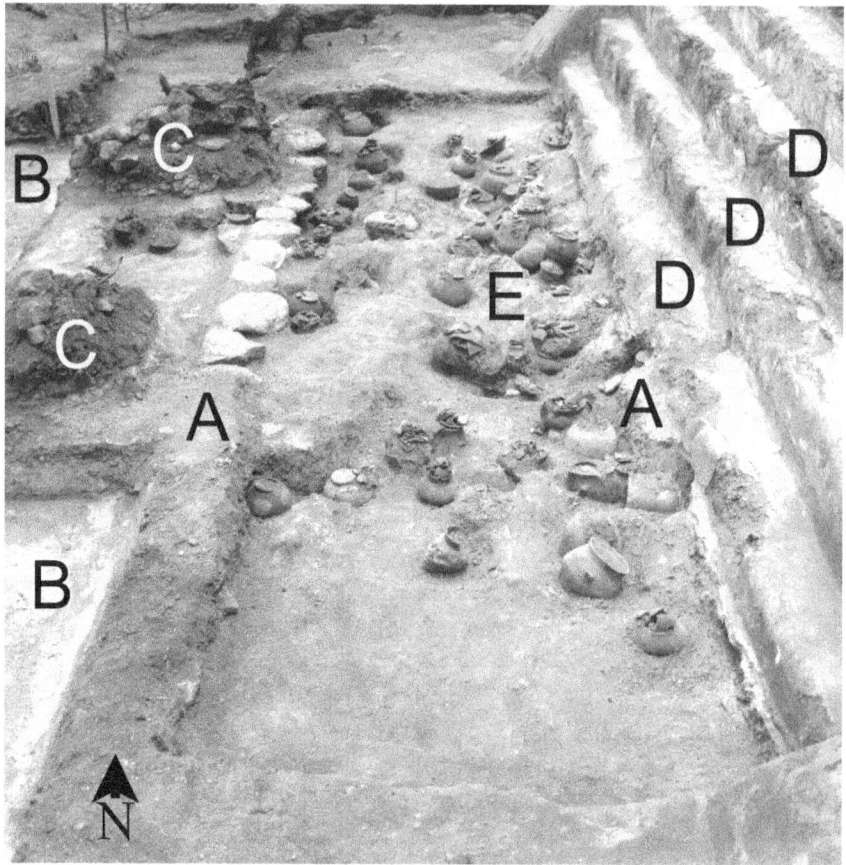

11.3. *Ceramic vessels containing cremated human remains beneath apron in front of pyramid on the east side of the Group H Plaza, revealed after removal of stucco floor. A: stucco floor remnant of apron, B: stucco floor of Group H Plaza, C: remains of stationary incensarios flanking pyramid stairway, D: lower steps of stairway; E: vessels with cremated human remains atop bedrock. Photo by Edward B. Sisson.*

platform flanks the plaza on the south; a fourth structure, a platform similar to that on the south, may have existed on the north side of the plaza, but, unfortunately, it has been completely destroyed (figure 11.3).

The preserved portion of the eastern structure measures 7.6 m wide on its western face by at least 3.84 m high. A stairway 5.8 m wide flanked by simple balustrades 88 cm wide is located on its western face; portions of seven steps are preserved. The sidewalls of the platform are nearly vertical. The building atop this platform was destroyed by looters. Fallen stone cylindrical column elements indicate that this superstructure had twin columns in a doorway opening to the west. This design is consistent with small Late Postclassic temples atop pyramidal bases found elsewhere in the Tehuacán Valley. The larger examples of these temples have two small rooms, one behind the other.

At the base of the eastern mound on its north, west, and south sides is a low, continuous artificial terrace approximately 1.4 m wide. At the centerline of the structure on its west or plaza side, the terrace has an extension 3.4 m wide projecting a meter further into the plaza. Near the north and south edges of this extension are preserved the bases of two stationary incense burners 80 and 84 cm in diameter. To the west of this extension, on the plaza floor, is a poorly preserved hearth approximately 80 cm in diameter. Beneath this terrace, concentrated and aligned with the centerline of the pyramid, excavations revealed a cache of seventy-six ceramic vessels containing cremated human remains. Two of these vessels took the form of human skulls. Of the seventy-six vessels, thirty-eight contained a single greenstone bead, three contained two greenstone beads, one contained a single turquoise bead, two contained a single white-stone bead, one contained one greenstone bead and an obsidian ear spool, one contained one greenstone bead and copper tweezers, and one contained a greenstone bead and nine copper bells. The remaining twenty-nine vessels had no associated offerings.

The platform on the west side of the plaza was at least 30 cm high and measured 8.88 m from north to south and 5.8 m from east to west. The building atop the platform had been destroyed completely, but the locations of cylindrical column stones indicate that it was entered from the east through a colonnaded entranceway. There was a low terrace or apron 1.6 m wide and 10 cm high across the front, or east, side of the structure. An extension 1.72 m (north-south) by 1.0 m (east-west) was added to the center of the east side of this apron. From beneath this apron, excavations revealed sixty-nine additional ceramic vessels with cremated human remains. One of these is a human skull effigy and the subject of this chapter. Of the sixty-nine vessels, thirty-eight contained a single greenstone bead, one contained two greenstone beads, and one contained a small rectangular stone pendant. The remaining twenty-nine vessels had no associated offerings.

Of the seventy-six vessels associated with the pyramidal platform on the east, at least one was buried in the collapsed debris from the temple. Those buried beneath the aprons in front of the two platforms were placed in holes punched through the stuccoed plaster floors. In many cases the holes were never resealed by a fresh layer of stucco. These conditions suggest that at least some of the vessels were deposited after the platforms and temple ceased to be maintained. This probably indicates the continued use of the plaza and its ritual structures for some time after the Spanish Conquest. The large number of vessels and the casual manner of their interment may well reflect the hurried burial of a large number of dead from the infectious diseases introduced at the beginning of the Early Colonial Period. One can imagine the smoke from cremation fires

11.4. *Rear, side, and front views of the effigy vessel from the Group H Plaza, Coxcatlán Viejo archaeological site. Photo by Edward B. Sisson.*

and the smell of burning flesh wafted from these plazas down to the new center of Coxcatlán, with its church.

THE GROUP H PLAZA POLYCHROME EFFIGY VESSEL

The polychrome effigy vessel associated with the low platform structure on the west was in poor condition when recovered (figure 11.4). The annular base, a portion of the rim, and the left ear were missing. The broken edge of the rim was eroded as if it had been exposed for some time. This, plus the fact that the small Coxcatlán Gray bowl used as the vessel's stopper sat comfortably in its mouth, indicates that the breakage preceded the vessel's final function as the repository of cremated human remains. The paint on the surface of the vessel was poorly preserved also; much of it had flaked off. All of this is consistent with the interpretation that the vessel's use as a cremation urn was secondary to some earlier function. Within the effigy vessel were found ash and small bone fragments, representing cremated human remains, and a single greenstone bead.

The vessel takes the form of a partially flensed human skull, portions of which are fleshless, other portions retaining yellow-orange flesh. Supporting the vessel is an annular base of indeterminate height and diameter. Crowning the skull is the vessel's out-flaring rim, its painted decoration forming a kind of headdress that consists of four parallel bands or zones, each separated from the other by a thin black line.

The first, or lowest, of these bands contains a white ground with small, irregular, yellow-orange and black patches. Part of this band frames the face on the vessel's front. Just posterior to the ears, this band turns down at a right angle to pass behind the ears on each side of the face. The second band is red to red-brown in color and completely encircles the neck of the vessel. The third band is yellow-orange in color, the same color as the upper portion of the effigy's face. It, too, completely encircles the neck of the vessel. Rising above and from the third of these bands is the fourth band consisting of a design of repeated, vertical standing blades on a red background, which takes up the vessel's out-flaring rim. These painted blades are personified with eyes, eyebrows, mouths, upper lips, and prominent incisors. The upper half of their incisors is painted red, the lower half white. The upper part of each "face" is painted red, the lower part white with three red stripes from just below the level of the eye to the bottom of the teeth; two red stripes also exist on the "chin." The eyes on these blades are formed by two concentric circles, the innermost circle representing the pupil. The eyes are painted white with the exception of a small area of red on the outside edge. A black area is painted around the outside edge of the eyes. Each upper lip is shown as a straight yellow-orange band above the mouth that droops down on each side of the mouth, then turns upward in a curl.

The face of the effigy vessel is modeled and painted with prominent arched eyebrows in a very dark red to black color with darker line work representing details. The eyes are sunken with bulging white eyeballs on which three concentric black circles are painted. The innermost circle is painted solid black and represents the pupil. The outer 20 percent of the right eye is painted red, and the outer 20 percent of the left eye is the same yellow-orange color as the upper part of the effigy's face. There is a narrow horizontal black band across the face at the level of the eyes. The band passes from in front of each ear to the outer edge of each eye and then from the inner edges of the eyes across the bridge of the nose. The nose is depicted as fleshless. Seen from the front, the nose is painted with an inverted "V." The margins of the V are straight black lines. Between these lines, the V is painted red. The area between the red inverted arms of the V is painted the same yellow-orange as the face. Painted on this yellow-orange ground are irregular red dots and dashes.

Beneath the level of the nose and the prominent modeled cheekbones and at the level of the middle of the ear flares is a horizontal white band reaching across the face from one ear to the other. This white band is outlined on the upper side by a narrow black line. Below this white band, the face is painted black. The black paint ends beneath the ears on both sides of the face and in front of the white band, with irregular patches descending behind each ear. Superimposed on the black ground is the white mandible with rectangular white teeth. Above the mandible is an upper row of similar rectangular teeth. Eleven teeth are shown in the upper row. Each is separated from its neighbor by a vertical black line. Another black line separates the teeth on their lower edge from a narrow "lip" with red paint. On their upper edge, these teeth are bounded by the black ground of the lower face. A sunken depression representing the slightly open mouth separates this upper row of teeth from the lower teeth of the mandible. The open mouth has traces of red paint inside it.

The eleven rectangular teeth of the lower jaw are separated from one another by black vertical lines. Horizontal black lines on the upper and lower edges of the tooth row separate the teeth from the red mouth above and the white mandible below. The mandible is white, with five round circles painted on its anterior edge between the ascending rami. Each of these round circles is painted yellow-orange. The color is lighter than that of the upper portion of the face, as if painted in a thinner wash on the underlying white of the mandible. Approximately eleven solid red dots appear on each of these yellow-orange circles. Each ascending ramus has two prominent, rounded projections. The outer one is slightly larger. Three round circles with red dots are painted on each ascending ramus. The one on the outer projection is larger than the other two. The top of these projections reaches up to the level of the top of the upper tooth row. These circles on the mandible represent putrefying flesh (*tlaxapochtli*).

The ear and ear flare on the right side of the skull are missing. The ear on the left side of the skull is rectangular with a rounded upper corner. It is painted the same color as the upper part of the face and has a single thick black band on its upper edge and two horizontal black bands below the upper edge. The lower portion of the ear is obscured by a round ear flare painted black with a small yellow circle in its center. A single red dot is painted in the lower exterior part of this yellow circle. Dark lines add detail to the ear flare.

Framing the face behind each ear are white painted bands outlined by black lines. These vertical bands are continuous with the one framing the face on the front of the vessel. The surface of these vertical bands is painted with pendant ovals open at the top. Four to six vertical black lines are painted within these ovals, giving them a textured appearance. Irregular dots in yellow-orange and black are painted on the white ground and the pendant ovals. Small rectangular protrusions outlined in black extend from the rear side of these bands. Attached to each protrusion is a stylized flower. The flowers identify the bands as the trunk or the limbs of a tree enclosing the face of the effigy. The bases of the two bands, or the roots of the tree, are painted black and yellow-orange.

Eight stylized flowers issue from the trunk of the tree and appear upon a solid white ground, the back of the skull. The flowers are virtually identical to one another. The base of each is a yellow-orange circle with details in red lines. In the center of each is a small circle from which four lines radiate. Between the radiating lines are red dots. Above this base is a flaring cup or calyx with red, black, and white horizontal bands. Two pairs of vertical black lines are painted on the red and white bands. Above this cup are four petals. The two central petals are vertical, and the two lateral petals flop down to the outside. The petals are painted the same yellow-orange as the face and have irregular red and black dots on them. Above the first flower and between each of the lower flowers are round jewels, four on each side. Those on the right are dark blue or black. Those on the left are dark blue or black, yellow, and red.

On the white ground of the back of the skull and descending from the yellow-orange and red bands that encircle the neck of the vessel is a stream of dark red blood. Superimposed on this flow are four broad, black horizontal bands. Two thinner black bands occur between each of the broad bands. Partially overlapping and superimposed upon the second, third, and fourth broad bands and the red of the blood above them are three large jewels that are circular with a yellow-orange center surrounded by a thick black circle. Beneath the lowest of the thick black bands, the stream of blood splits into three smaller flows that have two horizontal black bands across them.

On each side of the stream of blood, there are six smaller jewels attached to the flow and painted on the white ground of the skull. On the left side, from top to bottom, the colors of these jewels are black, blue, yellow, black, yellow, and black. On the right side, from top to bottom, they are red or yellow, dark blue, uncertain, blue, blue, and black. On five of these jewels, a small inner circle can be seen that is similar in form to those of the larger jewels on the blood flow. The back of the skull, consequently, might best be interpreted as decorated with a flow of precious (jeweled) blood coming down from the evening or morning sky (the red and yellow-orange bands) between two sections of a flowering tree.

ICONOGRAPHY

In a previous article (Sisson 1997) I have argued that the figure on the front of the vessel represents Itzpapalotl, the obsidian butterfly, patron of the sixteenth day of the *tonalpohualli* and the fifteenth *trecena*. This identification is based on similarities with depictions in the *Codex Borgia* identified by Eduard Seler (1963) as Itzpapalotl and on similarities with depictions in the *Codex Telleriano-Remensis* (Quiñones Keber 1995) and the *Codex Vaticanus A* (1979) identified by their Colonial annotators as Itzpapalotl. For example, features shared by the vessel and the depictions in the *Codex Borgia* (Seler 1963), pages 11 and 66, include

1. The thin black band across the face at the level of the eyes.
2. The lower face painted black.
3. The pronounced, dark eyebrows.
4. The outer third of the eyes painted red and the rest white.
5. The lipless teeth.
6. The red and yellow bands are found on the lower fringe of the figure's cape (or wings) rather than encircling the top of the skull.
7. Rather than a "crown" of flint knives, the figures have a skirt whose lower hem has a fringe of flint knives; in the *Codex Borgia* (11, 66), the *Codex Telleriano-Remensis* (13r), the *Codex Vaticanus A* (32r), and the *Codex Borbonicus* (15).

8. Itzpapalotl always appears with a broken and bleeding flowering tree interpreted as representing Tamoachan by Seler (1963: 1: 137). If this is the same tree on the back of the effigy vessel, it would strongly support the identification of the figure as that of Itzpapalotl.

Prominent features of the effigy that do not appear in the codex figures are

9. The fleshless nose.
10. The fleshless jaw.
11. The putrefying flesh (tlaxapochtli).

The most noticeable feature of the figures in the codices that does not appear on the effigy vessel is the white face with red stripes. Instead, the upper part of the effigy's face is yellow-orange and the lower part is black. The (9) fleshless nose, (10) fleshless jaw, and (11) putrefying flesh that do not appear in depictions of Itzpapalotl in the codices do, however, appear on depictions of Mictlantecuhtli. Other features shared between the Coxcatlán Viejo ceramic effigy and depictions of Mictlantecuhtli in the codices include:

3. The pronounced, dark eyebrows.
4. The outer third of the eyes painted red and the rest white.
5. The lipless teeth.

A representation of Mictlantecuhtli in the *Codex Telleriano-Remensis* shares

1. The thin black band across the face at the level of the eyes.
2. The lower face painted black.

Thus, there are strong reasons for connecting the effigy vessel with the god Mictlantecuhtli. Important features of Mictlantecuhtli that are missing from the effigy include the tangled, chaotic hair with "night eyes" and the human hand as an ear ornament.

Because of the many similarities between the ceramic effigy vessel and Mictlantecuhtli and the fact that the back of the skull is white where not obscured, it is tempting to suggest that the effigy represents a mask of Itzpapalotl overlying a depiction of Mictlantecuhtli or, perhaps better, his consort Mictecacihuatl. Nicholson (1971: 421–422) includes Itzpapalotl in his "earth-mother goddess" category. He also argues that the earth-mother goddesses, especially Cihuacoatl and Coatlicue, with their death imagery, were linked to Mictecacihuatl because the earth represented both womb and tomb. The effigy also shares notable features with Xiuhtecuhtli, including

1. The thin black band across the face at the level of the eyes.
2. The lower face painted black.
4. The outer third of the eyes painted red and the rest white.

The effigy, however, lacks the descending bird on the forehead that is so distinctive of Xiuhtecuhtli. Finally, the effigy shares a number of features with Tlahuizcalpantecuhtli, especially when he is depicted with a skeletal head. They include

1. The thin black band across the face at the level of the eyes.
3. The pronounced, dark eyebrows.
4. The outer third of the eyes painted red and the rest white.
5. The lipless teeth.
9. The fleshless nose.
10. The fleshless jaw.

The effigy lacks several of the diagnostic features of Tlahuizcalpantecuhtli, such as the *quincunx*, yellow hair, and unspun cotton ear ornaments.

The identification of the flowering tree and the flow of blood on the back of the effigy vessel as a representation of Tamoanchan and Xochitlicacan is also based on Seler's identification of similar depictions in the *Codex Borgia* and on the Colonial annotators' descriptions of similar depictions in the *Codex Telleriano-Remensis* and the *Codex Vaticanus A*. All of the depictions from the codices include a flowering tree with a wound from which blood issues. In the *Codex Telleriano-Remensis* and *Codex Vaticanus A*, the wounds in the trees are bounded by a red band and a yellow scalloped band. In the case of the effigy vessel, the blood issues from red and yellow bands that encircle the neck of the vessel and then falls between two joined trunks of flowering trees. Beyond this, there is a great deal of variation in the representations within the codices and between them and the representation on the effigy vessel. The tree of the effigy vessel shares the hatched roughened bark with the trees of the *Borgia* and the more naturalistic flowers with the *Codex Telleriano-Remensis* and *Codex Vaticanus A*.

Perhaps persuaded by their color, I once suggested (Sisson 1997: 136) that the flowers on the tree of the effigy vessel represented *cempohualxochitl*, marigolds, the flowers associated with death and the Day of the Dead. I no longer believe that to be the case. The size of the plant and the small number of petals—only four depicted—do not seem consistent with the many petals of the marigold. A more likely possibility is that the tree is a *cacaloxochitl*, or frangipani (*Plumeria rubra*), but this, too, is uncertain. Characteristics that favor this identification, either because they resemble effigy vessel design motifs or because of possible associations with Tamoanchan, include a long-stemmed flower with only five petals; the white and yellow, red, and yellow colors of the flowers; the scars left on the trunk and branches where attached leaves had been removed; the pungent, sweet smell of the flower; and the fact that the flower opens in the late afternoon and at night, attracting hawkmoths as pollinators (Haber 1984).

CONCLUSION

If the identifications suggested in this chapter are correct and the Coxcatlán Viejo effigy vessel represents Itzpapalotl and Tamoanchan, what, if anything, can it tell us that we don't already know? Perhaps we should first evaluate what we think we know about Itzpapalotl and Tamoanchan.

Citing various sources, Seler (1963: 1: 135–142) argued that Itzpapalotl was an ancient Chichimec earth-mother goddess, a symbol of the aged, a companion of Mixcóatl, a stellar goddess, one of the gods ejected from the heavens for their transgression, the first sacrificed, the first to die by arrow sacrifice, the first to die in war, the goddess of women who died in childbirth, a *tzitzimime*, an aspect of Cihuatéotl, a *cihuateteo*, a goddess of the West. She is the patron of the sixteenth day, Coxcacuauhtli, and the fifteenth trecena beginning with the day 1 Calli.

Again citing various sources, Seler (1963: 1: 137–142) argues that Tamoanchan Xochitlicacan is the paradise of the West and home of the gods of the earth and maize; the place of origin; the place of birth; the thirteenth and highest heaven; the abode of the gods of life, Tonacatecuhtli and Tonacacíhuatl; the place of flowers and abundance; the place from which both newborns and the demonic tzitzimime and cihuateteo descend; the evening sky from which comes darkness. Seler challenged Konrad Pruess's (1903) identification of Tamoanchan as located in the interior of the earth.

Alfredo López Austin (1993: 53–59) argued that, for the Aztec, Tamoanchan was the mythic space in which the totality of time was present; that the gods, time, transgression, punishment, and mankind all came into being in this space. On the other hand, the gods' transgressions led to the rupturing of the tree of Tamoanchan and the production of a flow of precious blood, "the divine effluvium," "the daily descent of divine forces to earth," "the liberation of the divine force and the establishment . . . of the alliance between a god and his people" (ibid.). Hermann Beyer (1965: 40) tentatively suggested a relationship between the tree of Tamoanchan and the Milky Way. López Austin's and Beyer's ideas taken together appear to suggest that the divine force linking mankind and the gods flows from the tree of Tamoanchan and down the Milky Way and that it is an axis mundi.

Returning to the effigy vessel, if it does represent Itzpapalotl and Tamoanchan, there are several striking differences with the representations in the codices. For example, the flowering tree of the ceramic effigy does not show a wound. The stream of blood on the back of the skull flows from the bands encircling the neck of the vessel and not directly from the tree. A second difference is the greater number of characteristics associated with Mictlantecuhtli than is found in the codices. Finally, the effigy vessel appears to share more features with Tlahuizcalpantecuhtli than do the representations in the codices.

Although there are no "night eyes" or stars, I suggest that the three bands encircling the out-flaring neck of the effigy—a band of knife blades, a yellow-orange band, and a red band—represent the late evening or early morning sky. With the exception of the lack of "night eyes," these bands closely resemble representations of the night sky in the *Codex Borgia*, especially the section that depicts the world directions and their respective sky bearers (49–52). Interestingly, two of the sky bearers share characteristics with the effigy. The sky bearer of the West is Tlahuizcalpantecuhtli, and the sky bearer of the north is Mictlantecuhtli. Other than Itzpapalotl, the effigy shares the most characteristics with these two deities.

If these bands do represent the night sky, then the blood flow issues forth from this dark sky rather than from the flowering tree. In previous interpretations of the effigy vessel, I have argued that the blood flows from the tree because it lies between the tree's two vertical trunks or branches. This may not be the case, however. The fact that the tree is a precious flowering plant is indicated by the stylized flowers and jewels. This is consistent with it representing Tamoanchan, as depicted in the codices and described in poems recorded in the Colonial Period. Earlier in this chapter I suggested that the flowering tree may represent a frangipani (*Plumeria rubra*), whose pungent, sweet-smelling, hawkmoth-pollinated flowers open in the late evening when the sun is setting in the West and at night. Perhaps the strange anthropomorphic insect (Seler 1963: 1: 137) that appears with the tree in the *Codex Vaticanus B* (63, 92) is a hawkmoth. Since the blood flows between the two trunks or branches of the tree, a tree associated with the paradise of the West, it, too, comes down from the heavens in the West. As López Austin (1993) suggests, the blood may define this as mythic space where present, past, and future are simultaneously present and where divine forces manifest as Itzpapalotl, the tzitzimime, the cihuateteo, and others come down, joining heaven and earth and the underworld. The tree itself may serve a cognate function, unifying space and time as a Central Mexican axis mundi. The similarities between the effigy vessel and Tlahuizcalpantecuhtli in the codices may reflect their common origin as Chichimec stellar deities. But why are the most similarities, other than those with Itzpapalotl, with Mictlantecuhtli, regent of underworld's place of death—Mictlan?

Nicholson suggested that, as an earth-mother goddess, Itzpapalotl was related to the Mictlantecuhtli Complex, since the earth is both tomb and womb. The strong similarity may also reflect Itzpapalotl's identification with the tzitzimime and cihuateteo, women who died in childbirth. Although they were dead and it is appropriate that they be shown with death imagery, these women accompanied the sun from midday until sunset in the West. They did not reside in the underworld of Mictlan. Instead, they resided in Tamoanchan, the paradise of the West, the paradise of women and fertility. However, if López Austin is correct in his interpretation that Tamoanchan is a unifying mythic space, then perhaps Itzpapalotl as the goddess most identified with Tamoanchan brings together in her person both death and fertility, the underworld and the heavens,

Edward B. Sisson

Mictlan and Tamoanchan. To paraphrase Nick, in her person both tomb and womb are brought together.

REFERENCES CITED

Barlow, Robert H.
    1949   *The Extent of the Empire of the Culhua Mexica*. Ibero-American 28. University of California Press, Berkeley.

Beyer, Hermann
    1965   Tamoanchan, El Paraiso De Los Antiguos Mexicanos. In *Mito y simbología del México antiguo*, ed. Carmen Cook de Leonard, pp. 39–43. El Mexico Antiguo 10. Sociedad Alemana Mexicanista, México, DF.

Caso, Alfonso
    1977–1979   *Reyes y reinos de la Mixteca*, 2 vols. Fondo de Cultura Económica, México, DF.

Codex Borbonicus
    1974   *Codex Borbonicus*. Commentary by Karl A. Nowotny and Jacqueline de Durand-Forest. Akademische Druck- u. Verlagsanstalt, Graz, Austria.

Codex Vaticanus A
    1979   *Codex Vaticanus 3738 ("Cod. Vat. A," "Cod. Ríos") der Biblioteca Apostolica Vaticana. Farbreproducktion des Codex in Verkleinertem Format*. Akademische Druck- u. Verlagsanstalt, Graz, Austria.

Davies, Nigel
    1968   *Los senoríos independientes del imperio Aztec*. INAH, México, DF.
    1987   *The Aztec Empire: The Toltec Resurgence*. University of Oklahoma Press, Norman.

Fowler, Melvin L., and Richard S. MacNeish
    1972   Excavations in the Coxcatlán Locality in the Alluvial Slopes. In *Prehistory of the Tehuacán Valley*, vol. 5: *Excavations and Reconnaissance*, ed. Richard S. MacNeish, Melvin L. Folwler, Angel Garcia Cook, Frederick A. Peterson, Antoinette Nelken-Terner, and James A. Neely, pp. 219–340. Robert S. Peabody Foundation, Phillips Academy, Andover, NH, and the University of Texas Press, Austin.

Gerhard, Peter
    1993   *A Guide to the Historical Geography of New Spain*. University of Oklahoma Press, Norman.

Haber, William A.
    1984   Pollination by Deceit in a Mass-Flowering Tropical Tree: *Plumeria rubra* L. (Apocynaceae). *Biotropica* 16 (4): 269–275.

Hassig, Ross
    1988   *Aztec Warfare: Imperial Expansion and Political Control*. University of Oklahoma Press, Norman.

Kirchoff, Paul, Lina Odena Güemes, and Luis Reyes García, eds. and trans.
    1989   *Historia Tolteca-Chichimeca*, 2nd ed. Centro de Investigaciones Superiores, Fondo de Culture Económica, México, DF.

López Austin, Alfredo
    1993   *The Myths of the Opossum: Pathways of Mesoamerican Mythology*. Trans. Alfredo López Austin and Bernard R. Ortiz de Montellano. University of New Mexico Press, Albuquerque.

MacNeish, Richard S., and Antoinette Nelken-Terner
    1972   Introduction. In *Prehistory of the Tehuacán Valley*, vol. 5: *Excavations and Reconnaissance*, ed. Richard S. MacNeish, Melvin L. Fowler, Angel Garcia Cook, Frederick A. Peterson, Antoinette Nelken-Terner, and James A. Neely, pp. 219–340. Robert S. Peabody Foundation, Phillips Academy, Andover, NH, and University of Texas Press, Austin.

Nicholson, H. B.
    1955   The Temalacatl of Tehuacán. *El México Antiguo* 8: 95–134.
    1957   Topiltzin Quetzalcoatl of Tollan: A Problem in Mesoamerican Ethnohistory. PhD dissertation, Department of Anthropology, Harvard University, Cambridge, MA.
    1960   The Mixteca-Puebla Concept in Mesoamerican Archeology: A Re-examination. In *Men and Cultures: Selected Papers of the Fifth International Congress of Anthropological and Ethnological Sciences, Philadelphia, 1956*, ed. Anthony F.C. Wallace, pp. 612–617. University of Pennsylvania Press, Philadelphia.
    1971   Religion in Pre-Hispanic Central Mexico. In *Archaeology of Northern Mesoamerica*, Part 1, ed. Gordon F. Ekholm, and Ignacio Bernal, pp. 395–446. Handbook of Middle American Indians, vol. 10, Robert Wauchope, gen. ed. University of Texas Press, Austin.
    2001   *Topiltzin Quetzalcoatl: The Once and Future Lord of the Toltecs*. University of Colorado Press, Boulder.

Paredes Colín, Joaquín
    1953   *Apuntes históricos de Tehuacán*. Ayuntamiento Municipal de Tehuacán, Tehuacán.
    1960   *El Distrito de Tehuacán*. Tipográfico Comercial "Don Bosco," México, DF.

Pohl, John M.D., and Bruce E. Byland
    1994   The Mixteca-Puebla Style and Early Postclassic Socio-Political Interaction. In *Mixteca-Puebla: Discoveries and Research in Mesoamerican Art and Archaeology*, ed. H. B. Nicholson and Eloise Quiñones Keber, pp. 189–199. Labyrinthos, Culver City, CA.

Pruess, Konrad T.
    1903   Die Fuergötter als Ausgangpunkt zum Verständnis der mexicanischen Religon, in ihrem Zusammenhänge. *Mitteilungen de Antropologischen Gesellschaft in Wien* 33 (129): 233.

Quiñones Keber, Eloise
    1995   *Codex Telleriano-Remensis: Ritual, Divination, and History in a Pictorial Aztec Manuscript*. University of Texas Press, Austin.

Seler, Eduard
    1963   *Comentarios al Códice Borgia*, 3 vols. Trans. Mariana Frenk. Fondo de Cultura Económica, México, DF.

Sisson, Edward B.
    1997   La muerte en el cacicazgo de Coxcatlán. In *Simposium internacional Tehuacán y su entorno: Balance y perspectiva*, ed. Eréndira de la Lama, pp. 129–147. INAH, México, DF.

Smith, Mary E., and Ross Parmenter
    1991   *The Codex Tulane*. Publication 61. Middle American Research Institute, Tulane University, New Orleans, LA.

Velázquez, Primo Feliciano, ed. and trans.
    1975   *Códice Chimalpopoca: Anales de Cuauhtitlán y Leyenda de los Soles*. UNAM, México, DF.

12

NICK AT NIGHT: COSMIC ASPECTS OF TOPILTZIN-QUETZALCOATL

Anthony F. Aveni

The most detailed account of an astronomically observable manifestation of the myth of Quetzalcoatl is surely the one that appears in a passage in the *Anales de Cuauhtitlan* (Bierhorst 1992: 36):

> The old people said that he was changed into the star that appears at dawn. Therefore they say that it came forth when Quetzalcoatl died, and they called him Lord of the Dawn. What they say is that when he died he disappeared for four days. They said he went to the dead land then. And he spent four more days making darts for himself. So it was after eight days that the morning star came out, which they said was Quetzalcoatl. It was then that he became lord, they said.

The motion of the planet Venus provides the obvious celestial metaphor for acting out the career of the hero who disappears in the desert, is cremated by his servitors, and then becomes resurrected in the eastern sky as the morning star from the smoke that issues from his body, as Nick (Nicholson 2001: 16) tells it. Unlike the other bright planets, Venus always stays close to the horizon, and once it disappears in the West as the Evening Star it returns to our world just ahead of the rising sun in the East, becoming most luminous in the first few days after it reappears as the morning star—a perfect visual fit with the narrative of the Quetzalcoatl myth.

What is striking about the passage from the *Anales* is the specific reference to the eight-day period of disappearance in the underworld. Astronomically speaking, it refers to the interval surrounding inferior conjunction, when the planet is lost from view in the glare of the sun as it passes from its evening to its morning star aspect. When I (Aveni 1992) did a study of the actual movement of Venus on the sky as it might pertain to specific prognostications in the Maya Venus Table in the *Dresden Codex* (Codex Dresdensis 1975) and its relationship to the lunar eclipse table in the same document, I discovered that Venus disappearance intervals around inferior conjunction actually vary, depending largely upon the season of the year in which they occur. The variations I computed ranged between zero and twenty-six days, the former generally occurring in February and the latter in August (Aveni 2001: 94, figure 41). This variation occurs because the zodiacal band of constellations, which traces the path of Venus among the stars, tilts at different angles relative to the horizon at various times of rising/setting of the planet over the year. This effect either hastens or delays its progress through the disappearance interval. I was surprised to discover that the long-term average disappearance period around inferior conjunction turns out to be precisely eight days. This implies that the celestial reference in the *Anales* cannot be casual. Rather, it must have been based upon extensive sky observations of a fairly rigorous and precise nature. Thus, this interesting passage about the heroic demi-god who is transformed so as to become a denizen of the Mexica cosmos yields unanticipated information about the nature of precise astronomical knowledge within that culture.

Further Venerean computations revealed a connection between Venus and the *tonalpohualli*. It turns out that the time Venus spends in the sky as the morning star, which is also highly variable, averages 263 days, the same being true for its evening star aspect (Aveni 2001: 87). This result helped validate an interesting statement about Venus I heard about thirty years ago from Doris Heyden. It was first discussed in a publication by Zelia Nuttall (1904) over a century ago.

In reference to Toribio de Benavente Motolinía's 1555 (1971) writings, Nuttall (1904: 498) suggests that the Mexica were well aware of the astronomical basis of the sacred day count:

> Next to the sun they adored and made more sacrifices to this star than to any other celestial or terrestrial creature. The astronomers knew on what day it would appear in the east after it had lost itself or disappeared in the west, and for the first day they prepared a feast, warfare, and sacrifices. The ruler gave an Indian who was sacrificed at dawn, as soon as the star became visible . . . In the land *the star lingers and rises in the east as many days as in the west—that is to say, for another period of 260 days*. Some add thirteen days more, which is one of their weeks . . . The reason why this star was held in such esteem by the lords and people, and the reason why they counted the days by this star and yielded reverence and offered sacrifices to it, was because the deluded natives

thought or believed that when one of their principal gods, named Topiltzin or Quetzalcoatl, died and left this world, he transformed himself into that resplendent star [emphasis added].

Here is yet another instance in which an ethnohistoric document implies that care and precision in the observation of nature were employed in framing a myth in a visible celestial context. That the Mexica would undertake such an enterprise makes sense given the elaborate nature of their rituals and the fact that most of them were conducted out of doors amid an assembled throng in the large open spaces fronting their ceremonial buildings. In these natural theaters a reenactment of the mythic past plays out beneath a planetarium-like sky. In such a social setting the role of the professional skywatcher would have been to see to it that the celestial luminaries made their appointments on the ritual stage at the appropriate times and in their proper places. (For examples involving other ritually timed celestial events, see Aveni 2001: chapter 5.)

I had not read Nick's PhD dissertation until it was published by the University Press of Colorado in 2001. From it I culled out no fewer than fourteen pages referring to the Venus/morning star metaphor of the story of Topiltzin Quetzalcoatl. One of the passages that caught my eye bears on the problem of the nature of indigenous precise astronomical knowledge I had been exploring. In it Nick traces the chronology of the myth in detail. He divides it into seventeen successive episodes, of which I quote here only the parts in which specific time periods are mentioned:

> (8) Quetzalcoatl's happy reign of 160 years is interrupted by the appearance of a rival, the god Tezcatlipoca, who is bent on mischief; (9) after disguising himself as a pauper, transforming himself into various fearful shapes, stealing and hiding Quetzalcoatl's powerful rain-producing magic mirror, and destroying his effigy in the temple dedicated to him, Tezcatlipoca succeeds in his goal of driving Quetzalcoatl and his people from Tollan; (10) the latter and a few attendants travel to Tenanyocan, where they reside for some time, then to Colhuacan for an even longer time, then over the mountains of Cuauhquechollan, where Quetzalcoatl successfully establishes himself, adored as their sole god, for 290 years; (11) leaving behind a lord named Matlacxochitl, Quetzalcoatl moves on to Chololan, where the Great Pyramid, built by the giants, is raised in his honor; (12) after 160 years in Chololan, he flees to Cempohuallan, where he resides 260 years before his old antagonist, Tezcatlipoca, arrives to further persecute him. (Nicholson 2001: 16)

Then comes the final episode in which Quetzalcoatl disappears from the scene.

While I have yet to find an interpretation of the numbers 160 and 290 in the context of observable Venus periods, I believe it is quite likely that the last number, read as 260 *days of real time* instead of *years of mythic time*, was intended to map out the movement of the planetary deity over the precise interval during which he appears in the evening sky as seen from a fixed location, in this instance

Cempohuallan. I believe this statement is yet another example of embedding precise astronomy in what we would regard as a mythic tale.

A medieval medical manual from Baghdad yields data about a supernova; an inscribed sherd in the rubble fill from a wall in Uruk records a statement in cuneiform testifying to knowledge of the retrograde motion of Jupiter. Finding surprising things in unanticipated places constitutes one of the joys of research on the history of astronomy. I had not suspected that a connection between real-time astronomy and the great Tollan tale would be tucked away in Nick's book.

At the end of his thorough and penetrating explorations of *The Once and Future Lord of the Toltecs*, Nick raises the question of the historicity of the myth (ibid.: 255–267), telling us that "the mere presence of 'impossible' supernaturalistic incidents or improbable apocryphal material in an account of the career of an historical figure in itself by no means negates his/her historicity" (ibid.: 255). This statement, made by the wise *tlatoani* of Mexica studies, validates my inquiry. Moreover, it encourages me to look still further into mythic tales as repositories of ancient knowledge about scientific astronomy.

All of us who knew Nick were acquainted with his curious quirk of sometimes lecturing with his eyes shut. I used to think: *he doesn't even need to look at the image—it's seared in his mind—or that man has amazing concentration!* Now, having had the opportunity to report my little discovery in this celebration of the work of a great scholar and friend, I wonder if, once he closed his eyes, in that dark field of view before him, Nick was instead taking a peek at the stars.

REFERENCES CITED

Aveni, Anthony F.
    1992   The Moon and the Venus Table: An Example of Commensuration in the Maya Calendar. In *The Sky in Mayan Literature*, ed. Anthony F. Aveni, pp. 87–101. Oxford University Press, New York.
    2001   *Skywatchers: A Revised, Updated Version of Skywatchers of Ancient Mexico*. University of Texas Press, Austin.

Bierhorst, John, trans.
    1992   *The History and Mythology of the Aztecs: The Codex Chimalpopoca*, trans. John Bierhorst. University of Arizona Press, Tucson.

Codex Dresdensis
    1975   *Codex Dresdensis: Sächsische Landesbibliothek Dresden (Mscr. Dresd. R 310)*. Kommentar, Helmut Deckert, zur Geschichte der Dresdner Maya-Handschrift; Ferdinand Anders, die Dresdner Maya-Handschrift kodikologische Beschreibung. Akadem. Druck- u. Verlagsanstalt, Graz, Austria.

Motolinía, Toribio de Benavente
    1971   *Memoriales o Libro de las cosas de la Nueva España y de los naturales de ella. Nueva transcripción paleográfica del manuscrito original, con inserción de las porciones*

de La historia de los indios de la Nueva España que completan el texto de Los memoriales. Edición, notas, estudio analítico de los escritos históricos de Motolinia y apéndices. Apéndice documental, con inclusión de la carta que dirigió Motolinia al emperador Carlos V en 1555, y de otras piezas provenientes de o relativas a Motolinia, y un índice analítico de materiales, ed. Edmundo O'Gorman. UNAM, Instituto de Investigaciones Históricas, México, DF.

Nicholson, H. B.
    2001   *Topiltzin Quetzalcoatl: The Once and Future Lord of the Toltecs*. University Press of Colorado, Boulder.

Nuttall, Zelia
    1904   The Periodical Adjustments of the Ancient Mexican Calendar. *American Anthropologist*, new series 6 (4): 486–500.

13

THE XIPE TÓTEC CULT AND MEXICA MILITARY PROMOTION

Carlos Javier González González

Of all the Mesoamerican gods, Xipe Tótec has probably stimulated the most interest and controversy among contemporary culture historians. Just the name, composed of two Nahuatl words, exemplifies this controversy. Originally translated by Eduard Seler (1990–1998: 2: 245) as "Our Lord the Flayed One," meaning someone stripped of his skin, Alfredo López Austin (1998: 119) more recently translated it as "[Our Lord] the Owner of Skin," exactly the opposite meaning. We are now coming to see Xipe as somebody who has gained or obtained a new dermic wrapping, not lost one. Skinning sacrificial victims in this god's honor was a ritual associated with the *veintena*, or twenty-day month festival dedicated to him. This festival in Nahuatl was called tlacaxipehualiztli, or "flaying of people." Xipe Tótec the god was invariably represented wearing a flayed human skin (figure 13.1).

The veintena dedicated to Xipe Tótec was of enormous importance in Tenochtitlan. Although that twenty-day period spanned March 5–24, its climax occurred during the final three days, coinciding with the spring equinox (González González 2006: 153–155). The three-day climax of the tlacaxipehualiztli festival was known as the tlahuahuanaliztli, or "scratching." In this ceremony the most courageous or distinguished war captives fought, virtually defenseless, against fully armed Mexica warriors atop a great circular stone, or *temalácatl*. As a consequence, sixteenth-century European authors referred to this as the "gladiatorial sacrifice" (figure 13.2).

13.1. *Xipe Tótec as portrayed in the* Codex Borgia, *wearing a flayed human skin. From Seler 1963: 3: 49.*

The tlacaxipehualiztli was also reserved for celebrating the Mexicas' most recent military conquests because the best time for war in Mesoamerica was the dry season, beginning in November once the corn harvest had been completed, and ending in February or March, in time for planting (González González 2006: 211–213). The victims sacrificed during the tlacaxipehualiztli were war captives, men by definition. After death, their bodies were flayed so that others could wear their skin.

The correlation between the festival of Xipe Tótec and the spring equinox, as well as its close relationship with the skinning of victims and the representations of the deity wearing a human skin, caused Seler to interpret Xipe Tótec as a god of spring and of the earth. According to the German scholar, the flaying was symbolically associated with the renewal of plant life as a prelude to the sowing of corn (Seler 1900–1901: 100, 1990–1998: 2: 244, 5: 76). Seler's ideas have been endorsed and subsequently repeated by many Mesoamericanists; consequently, very little further research has been conducted on this subject.

This notwithstanding, H. B. Nicholson (1971: 422–424) was one of the few scholars to reexamine the cult of Xipe Tótec, contributing valuable insights and raising new and relevant questions. Nicholson refers to Xipe Tótec as a notable god whose precise nature continues to be obscure and identifies him with three great themes of the Mesoamerican religious universe: rain, humidity, and agricultural fertility. Nicholson stresses the broad distribution of Xipe Tótec

13.2. *The tlahuahuanaliztli, or gladiatorial sacrifice. According to Fray Diego Durán 1967: I.*

throughout Mesoamerica and his close relationship with the earth-mother goddess, evidenced above all by the skinning of the victims, suggesting that Xipe's origins might be located within what are now the Mexican states of Oaxaca or Guerrero. Nicholson questions Seler's interpretation of flaying human victims as symbolic of the renewal of plant life, first because it is not supported by indigenous testimonies and second because this mortuary practice was not restricted to the worship of that deity alone (Nicholson 1972: 216; cf. Broda 1970: 261–262).

In point of fact, skinning human victims was equally characteristic of a festival dedicated to Toci or Tlazeoltéotl, the Mother Goddess. This festival, called *Ochpaniztli* (*barredura*, or "sweeping"), was celebrated in September; here, women were sacrificed instead of men. Ritual human flaying was also carried out during the festivities of Tepeílhuitl (Hill Festival), *Tecuhilhuitontli* (Small Festival of the Lords), and *Xócotl Huetzi* (Fruit Fall), where the victims represented Xochiquétzal (another manifestation of the Mother Goddess), Xochipilli (the God of Song and Dance), and probably Huehuetéotl-Xiuhtecuhtli, the Fire God (Gómez de Orozco 1945: 44; Durán 1967: 1: 155; Cervantes de Salazar 1985: 35; Anders, Jansen, and Reyes García 1996: 98v).

Nicholson's (1961) excellent study of the rock art on the cliffs of Chapultepec Hill reveals that the petroglyphs were commissioned by several Mexica *tlatoque*. According to primary sources, three of the four final rulers of Tenochtitlan—Axayácatl, Ahuítzotl, and Motecuzoma II—ordered that their images, costumed as Xipe Tótec, be carved there. Such attire was very significant, as it was donned by the Tenochca Hueitlatoani when commanding their armies during military campaigns.

THE BIRTH AND SPREAD OF THE XIPE TÓTEC CULT

Xipe Tótec was probably a deity with deep ancestral roots in Mesoamerica. The wide geographic distribution of the Xipe Tótec cult during the final part of the Prehispanic era was most likely the result of considerable time depth (cf. Nicholson 1972, 1976: 165). Although there is no specific information about the age and origin of Xipe Tótec, it has been suggested that two Late Classic ceramic vessels discovered by Alfonso Caso at Monte Albán, Oaxaca, depict an unquestionable iconographic relationship with later images of the god (González González 2006: 24–27). Archaeological evidence takes the form of a funerary urn (figure 13.3) found in Tomb 103 at that site, corresponding to the beginning of Phase III B (ca. AD 600), and a *brasero* (figure 13.4) found in Tomb 58, deposited at the end of the same phase (ca. AD 800). The iconographic complexity of Caso's Monte Albán Tomb 103 urn (figure 13.3) does not suggest an early manifestation of the deity but instead an evolved one; therefore, it is reasonable to assume even earlier antecedents.

To the north, a deity wearing a flayed human skin appears within the Basin of Mexico at least four centuries before the founding of Mexico-Tenochtitlan. This is clearly demonstrated by the discovery of a beautiful ceramic sculpture by Sigvald Linné around 1932 at Teotihuacan (figure 13.5). This artifact was associated with Mazapa ceramics, and the pottery effigy itself is of that ceramic type (Linné 1934: 64–86). According to the modern chronological sequence for the Basin of Mexico, this ceramic sculpture would correspond to the first part of the Second Intermediate Phase, or what is generally termed the Early Postclassic, from AD 950 to 1150 (Sanders, Parsons, and Santley 1979: 461–463, 465; González González 2006: 28–29).

THE XIPE TÓTEC CULT AND MEXICA MILITARY PROMOTION

13.3. *Late Classic funerary urn from Monte Albán Tomb 103, showing a personage wearing a flayed human skin. Height 50.8 cm. Courtesy, Museo Nacional de Antropología, México, Sala de Oaxaca.*

Archaeological evidence for an Early Postclassic "Flayed God" in the Basin of Mexico is significant in light of the academic tenacity of the idea that Xipe Tótec was a god "imported" by the Mexicas through military conquest only after AD 1430 (Garibay K. 1995: 178–180; cf. Heyden 1986).[1] Garibay may be assuming that the first celebration of the tlacaxipehualiztli ceremony, in the

13.4. *Late Classic brasero from Monte Albán Tomb 58, an early example of a deity wearing a flayed human skin. Height 35.3 cm, width 33.5 cm. Courtesy, Museo Nacional de Antropología, México, Sala de Oaxaca.*

fifteenth year of the rule of Motecuzoma I, around AD 1455 (cf. Durán 1967: 2: 171–175; Alvarado Tezozómoc 1987: 318–323), was also the first appearance of Xipe Tótec in the Basin of Mexico.

THE LATE POSTCLASSIC XIPE CULT

Both archaeological and documentary evidence lead to the conclusions that Xipe Tótec was *not* an "imported god" of the mid-fifteenth-century Mexicas, that he had ancestral roots relevant to that group, and that he was also a member of the pantheon worshipped in the Basin of Mexico centuries before the founding of Tenochtitlan. The enormous importance of the tlacaxipehualiztli festival in the last great city in Mesoamerica is consequently better appreciated in light of the chronological depth and geographic distribution of the worship of Xipe Tótec. Additional mythical-religious references to the god and his festival underline that importance through his association with the creation of the Fifth Sun, or Quinto Sol.

Documentary evidence also contradicts Garibay's view that the Xipe cult was imported into the Anahuac Basin. Yopico, the *calpulli* of Tenochtitlan with Xipe Tótec as its patron god, is mentioned as one of the seven social entities that left Aztlan-Chicomóztoc on the Mexica pilgrimage to the Basin of Mexico (Durán 1967: 2: 28–29; Alvarado Tezozómoc 1987: 14–15, 26; Chimalpain Cuauhtlehuanitzin 1991: 25). A temalácatl and a temple already dedicated to "Our Lord the Flayed" in the calpulli of Tlacocomoco (one of Yopico's neighbors) was renewed and consecrated in AD 1425, during the rule of Chimalpopoca

13.5. *Early Postclassic ceramic sculpture of a figure wearing a flayed skin, found by Sigvald Linné at Teotihuacan. Height 109 cm, width 33 cm. Photo by Michel Zabé, in Matos Moctezuma 2001: 276. Courtesy, Museo Nacional de Antropología, México, Sala de Teotihuacán.*

but before the beginning of the "Imperial" stage of Tenochtitlan (Anderson and Schroeder 1997: 1: 231; Chimalpain Cuauhtlehuanitzin 1997: 131; Torquemada 1943: 1: 126; cf. González González 2005). In some versions of the Mexica tradition Tlalcocomoco appears as a place closely related to the history of Cópil and to the very origins of the Mexica capital (Durán 1967: 2: 38; Alvarado Tezozómoc 1992: 44). Finally, information from several sources suggests that Tlalcocomoco and, in general, the area of Moyotlán—the southwestern portion of Tenochtitlan—was the location of the city's first founding during the second half of the thirteenth century, much earlier than the founding in its southeastern portion, Teopan, in the first half of the fourteenth century (González González 2005: 51–54).

The *Anales de Cuauhtitlan* contains a brief passage narrating the mythical origin of the tlacaxipehualiztli, or "flaying of people," the specific ritual dedicated to

Xipe Tótec. This source locates the event in a 13 Reed year and at a place called Texcalapan (Bierhorst 1992: 40). According to the *Anales de Cuauhtitlan* (ibid.: 26), the *History of the Mexicans through Their Paintings* (García Icazbalceta 1941: 215–216), and the calendar glyph inscribed in the *Piedra del Sol*, the mythical creation of the Fifth Sun, also called *Nahui Ollin* or "4 Movement," took place in the year 13 Wind—in other words, the sun of the current era that was emblematic for the Mexicas.

On the other hand, the name Texcalapan has two possible translations— "Place of the Cliff" or "Place of the Bonfire"—since the word *texcalli* means "cliff or steep rock" as well as "oven or bonfire" (Molina 1992: 112v). The foregoing makes it possible to establish a relationship with the *teutexcalli*, or "divine oven," in which the prodigious transformation of Nanahuatzin into the Fifth Sun took place, according to known versions of the myth (Bierhorst 1992: 149–151; Muñoz Camargo 1998: 148–149; Sahagún 2000: 2: 694–697).

Fray Bernardino de Sahagún collected oral testimony from his Indian informants about the same mythical event, in which we find Xipe Tótec and Ehécatl-Quetzalcóatl, the Wind God, performing a stellar role (Sahagún 2000: 2: 694–697). According to the story, all the gods gathered at Teotihuacan, their goal being to create the sun to light up the world. Nanahuatzin and Tecuciztecatl threw themselves consecutively on the divine bonfire, or teutexcalli, and the gods kneeled to be able to see the place where Nanahuatzin would emerge as the sun. The gods faced toward the four cosmic directions based on their premonitions; finally, the star rose from the East, proving that those who had looked in that direction were right. The source says verbatim:

> They say that the [gods] who looked toward the east were Quetzalcóatl, who is also known as Ecatl [Ehécatl], and the other who is called Tótec, and by another name Anáhuatl Itécuh, and by another name Tlatláhuic Tezcatlipuca [Tlatlauhqui Tezcatlipoca]; and by others who are called mimixcóah, which are innumerable. And four women: one is called Tiacapan; the other, Teicu; the third one, Tlacoehua; the fourth, Xocóyotl. (Sahagún 2000: 2: 696)

Xipe Tótec appears in the account as the Red Tezcatlipoca or Tlatlauhqui Tezcatlipoca, for he was one of the principal manifestations of that deity, together with Mixcóatl-Camaxtli (cf. Nicholson 1971: 398, 426). The exceptional importance of both "Our Lord the Flayed One" and Quetzalcoatl in the account assumes greater significance when the calendrical implications of both gods are considered. The Fifth Sun was called Nahui Ollin (4 Movement), and it began its motion on the day 4 Movement, having been immobile for four days after its creation (Bierhorst 1992: 148; Muñoz Camargo 1998: 149; Sahagún 2000: 2: 697). Taking into account the sequence of the days in the *tonalpohualli* (260-day ritual-divinatory calendar of the ancient Nahuas), the foregoing means the transformation of Nanahuatzin into the new sun took place on a day Ce Ocelotl or

THE XIPE TÓTEC CULT AND MEXICA MILITARY PROMOTION

13.6. *Calendrical glyph 13 Cane from the* Piedra del Sol, *Tenochtitlan, in Matos Moctezuma 1992: 127. Courtesy, Museo Nacional de Antropología, México, Sala Mexica.*

1 Jaguar, the calendrical name for the Red Tezcatlipoca and the first day of the second trecena (thirteen-day period) of the tonalpohualli, which was presided over by Quetzalcoatl (Seler 1900–1901: 41–42; Caso 1961: 92).

With what has been said previously, the image of Xipe Tótec presides over the fourteenth trecena of the *tonalámatl* of the *Codex Borbonicus*; here he appears dressed as the Red Tezcatlipoca with the calendar glyph *Nahui Ollin* attached to his left foot (figure 13.7).[2] In this context the references by Durán and Alvarado Tezozómoc about a magnificent celebration of tlacaxipehualiztli performed in the time of Axayácatl, in which "Our Lord the Flayed" was honored as the Red Tezcatlipoca, make better sense (Durán 1967: 2: 275–279; Alvarado Tezozómoc 1987: 413–417). The testimony of Alvarado Tezozómoc suggests that the investiture of the god on that occasion was an unprecedented event, referring to the Tlatlauhqui Tezcatlipoca as the "new god unknown" or the "New Idol God *Tlatlauhquitézacatl*" (Alvarado Tezozómoc 1987: 414, 416).[3] Elsewhere (González González 2006: 216–219) I have proposed that this lavish celebration probably took place in 1479, which would have been very meaningful because in the indigenous count that date corresponded to a year 13 Cane, coinciding with the same mythical year in which the Fifth Sun was created and the tlacaxipehualiztli ceremony originated.

13.7. *Representation of Xipe Tótec as the Red Tezcatlipoca wearing a flayed skin. From Paso y Troncoso 1993: 14.*

This discussion facilitates the understanding of why the festival the Mexicas dedicated to Xipe Tótec had such great importance within the society's warrior context. The tlahuahuanaliztli (*rayamiento*), the ritual fight or gladiators' sacrifice's main symbolic content, was the mythical massacre of the 400 *mimixcoa* and the institution of the sacred war, as Michel Graulich (1979: 3: 580–625) explained from the *Legend of the Suns* (cf. Bierhorst 1992: 149–151). Graulich also noted that the immense majority of the sacrificed victims were war captives.

THE XIPE TÓTEC CULT AND MEXICA MILITARY PROMOTION

Nevertheless, one salient aspect of the Xipe Tótec festival that has received little scholarly attention despite its obvious significance is the distinction awarded to certain Mexica warriors during the ceremony, a phenomenon in which tlahuahuanaliztli played a key role. Durán, for example, notes the importance of those who contributed captives and briefly describes a celebration of tlacaxipehualiztli in the time of Motecuhzoma II. After referring to the gladiatorial sacrifice, he tells us:

> Motecuhzoma [II] ordered that all his men who had taken part in that war be brought there, *especially* those that had performed outstanding feats and had brought prisoners to be sacrificed at that time [tlahuahuanaliztli], thus honoring the gods. For this purpose a proclamation was made, it was announced all over the city, and as a result a large number of soldiers and officers gathered in the appointed places, each one designated for the men according to their rank and record. (Durán 1967: 2: 483; emphasis added)

The first step in this process of distinction was selecting victims for the ceremony. Documentary sources indicate that only captives of high status or those who had demonstrated great courage on the battlefield were worthy of the tlahuahuanaliztli. Among sixteenth-century authors, Juan Bautista de Pomar described the process with the greatest clarity, explaining the supreme ruler's role in that process: "They made sacrifices to the other idol called Xipe . . . of the bravest Indians, who had been chosen by the king, after conducting many enquiries and proceedings on the effort and spirit of each one, and on his courage, because if they were not [brave], they did not die in the sacrifice to this idol" (Pomar 1986: 63).

Pomar (1986: 23) also reveals that the victim selection process enhanced the captors' prestige, explaining that it was done "to make famous those that captured them." Contributing victims for the so-called gladiators' sacrifice for the festival of Xipe Tótec was also a necessary requirement for Mexica warriors who wanted to be promoted up through the ranks of their military hierarchy.

The day before the celebration of the tlahuahuanaliztli, the war captives who had not been selected to participate were sacrificed in the Temple of Huitzilopochtli through the normal procedure of having their hearts extracted at the *techcatl*, the sacrificial stone located at the top of the temple. Afterward their bodies were cast down the stairway, landing on the lower platform of the temple (Sahagún 2000: 1: 180). Most significant, the victims' bodies were skinned then and there, on the lower part of the Temple of Huitzilopochtli. The flayed bodies were then taken to the Calpulco, or precinct, of the warrior who had offered them as sacrifices, transported by a group of priests-officials called *cuacuacuiltin* (shaved heads) under the service of the supreme hierarchy, or *hueitlatoani* (Sahagún 2000: 1: 180–181; cf. González González 2006: 232–236).

343

According to documentary sources, tlahuahuanaliztli took place on the temalácatl located at the foot of the temple dedicated to Xipe Tótec or Yopico (Durán 1967: 1: 99, 2: 173; Alvarado Tezozómoc 1987: 321–322, 415–416, 621–622; Sahagún 2000: 1: 181–182). The victims were selected on the basis of their prestige or courage, which would reflect positively on their captors.

These differences were echoed in the details of the ceremony and in the mortuary treatment of those who died in the process. According to Sahagún (2000: 1: 182), the Mexica warriors danced and concentrated on the temalácatl while their captives were subjected to the tlahuahuanaliztli. The greater the captive's courage as he fought his sacrificers on the temalácatl, then doubtless the greater the prestige the captors acquired as a result of such bravery. Pomar (1986: 65) is very clear on this point: "It turned out that many . . . then surrendered to death and sacrifice, which made those who had conquered them less famous; so that the greater the effort and spirit shown fighting in this sacrifice, the greater the fame as a valiant [warrior] was gained by those who had vanquished and captured them in war, and brought them to sacrifice."

In this case, the heart sacrifice was made on the edge of the temalácatl. The warrior who provided the victim received the blood in a gourd decorated with feathers, then offered it to the gods personified in effigy. Afterward, he returned for the body of his captive.

However, germane to our discussion are the facts that the warrior himself was responsible for taking the body to his Calpulco, without any involvement of the cuacuacuiltin, and, above all, that the skinning took place in the Calpulco (Sahagún 2000: 1: 183). This is different from the case described previously, where the skinning took place in the same part of the Temple of Huitzilopochtli and the flayed body was then removed to the Mexica warrior's territory. In the second example, the cadaver arrived with skin intact at his captor's calpulli, or neighborhood, and the skinning took place in the community area, the Calpulco. This latter place, according to Sahagún (1989: 20–21), was "a large palace-like house that they used in each barrio to hold meetings among those who governed the neighborhood."

Once the body had been flayed, the Mexica warrior took it to his home to provide the usual ritual banquet with human flesh (Sahagún 2000: 1: 183). The skin remained in the Calpulco, becoming an object to be claimed by the entire community of the calpulli to which the warrior belonged. Sahagún translated Nahuatl texts written by his Indian informants that confirm this description:

> The skin of the captive belonged to the one who had captured him, and he would let *others* borrow it so they could *wear it* and they could *go around* the streets with it, as if it were a wolf's head. And everybody would give something to the person that was wearing it, and he would give all of it to the owner of the skin, who would divide it as he wished among *those* that had been wearing it. (Sahagún 2000: 1: 184; emphasis added)

As can be seen from the italicized words in the quote, the warrior loaned the skin to different individuals who took turns wearing it. With it they collected valuables on the warrior's behalf, delivering them to him and then sharing in the proceeds. The comment "The skin of the captive belonged to the one who had captured him" is of great interest because it carries a European concept of property that is not entirely applicable in the Mesoamerican context. Turning to the original Nahuatl text, the phrase involves the verb *pialtia*,[4] translated by Molina as "to deposit or give somebody something for safekeeping" (Molina 1992: 81v, Nahuatl-Spanish). In light of this, a more accurate translation would have been "The skin of the captive was kept by the one who had captured him," which agrees better with the fact that the victims of the tlahuahuanaliztli were skinned in the Calpulcos. Therefore, the Mexica warrior served as the custodian of a collective or community asset (the skin), acquiring the privilege of its disposition.

Simultaneously with the collection of valuables for the benefit of the victim's captor (as described by Sahagún), a system of investiture obligations and reciprocity was established. The means by which the rank of *tecuhtli* was attained by the Nahua of Tlaxcala, Huexotzinco, and Cholula was linked to the worship of Xipe. The advancement process is described fundamentally by Motolinia (1996: 469–474) and in a study by Pedro Carrasco (1966: 134–139). Both sources note that for the candidate to obtain the rank of tecuhtli, he or his parents would collect in advance a wealth of goods that would pay for the process as well as for the feasts offered by the aspirant, which took place both at the beginning and the end of the process. The two sources differ somewhat; Motolinia only mentions the involvement of candidate's parents in raising such wealth, while Carrasco refers to two banquets at the beginning of the process in which the candidate spent what he had been able to raise previously, followed by a fast that would last until he was able to amass the necessary wherewithal once again to be able to offer new feasts. The suppliers in this second collection of valuables were the *macehuales*, the candidate's followers or supporters, linked with the future tecuhtli (Carrasco 1966: 136).

As part of the celebration of Xipe Tótec by those who borrowed the skin of the Mexica warrior, valuables were collected for twenty days (Durán 1967: 2: 175; Sahagún 2000: 1: 186–187). This was done following the ritual banquet offered immediately after the sacrifice of the victim, at which his flesh was eaten. Sahagún (2000: 1: 187) also clearly explains that the warrior offered a second banquet at the conclusion of the twenty days, which served a promotional function (cf. González González 2006: 257–258). Alternatively, the *Relación Geográfica de Acolman* suggests that everything collected by the person who donned the skin of the victim sacrificed in the tlacaxipehualiztli was consumed at a banquet offered by the victim's "owner" once the twenty days had transpired (Castañeda 1986: 227).

The human skins obtained through the tlahuahuaniztli played an integral role in the military promotion process. From the moment their captives were selected for the ceremony, the principals in this process were the distinguished warriors themselves. Furthermore, as we will see shortly, it is possible that specific captives were selected because their captors had already been "short-listed" for the military rank of tequihua.[5]

Pomar (1986: 63–64) states that when the tlahuahuanaliztli was performed, the captives were organized in rows; at the side of each one stood the warrior who had captured him, as well as another warrior who had already achieved the rank of tequihua. This is of special interest because it implies that the donor warrior was aspiring to this rank, while the man escorting him acted as a kind of sponsor. Pomar explains that becoming a tequihua required the capture of four enemies, and he describes the ceremony in which that position was conferred: "that then, with certain padrinos [godfathers] and in the main temple, in the oresence of the lord or king, they gave him the rank of knight, shaving him and giving him certain feather tassels as an insignia of his position and knighthood" (ibid.: 85).

A final comment is necessary about the participation of the god Xipe Tótec in this process of military promotion. This process probably occurred from the very origins of the sacrificial ceremony, for that act was dedicated to the god and constituted the liturgic climax of his festival. The people charged with collecting goods for the warrior donor and who donned the skin of his captive became living images of the deity by that mere act.[6] This being the case, it was the god himself who collaborated in the warrior's promotion as his sponsor.

The role of "Our Lord the Flayed" as promoter and protector of those warriors elevated to a new military rank or social status was one of his main attributes, one shared with the Fire God, Huehuetéotl-Xiuhtecuhtli. In fact, according to Sahagún (2000: 1: 396–397), the festival held for the election of a new ruler was carried out in the fourteenth trecena of the tonalpohualli, starting on the day 1 Dog, or Ce Itzcuintli, precisely because it was the sign of the Fire God, portending prosperity for the initiate. However, as mentioned earlier, Xipe Tótec was the regent god of the thirteenth "month," according to the codices and divinatory almanacs or "books of fate," known as tonalámatl;[7] for that reason, Alfonso Caso (1961: 88) regarded Ce Itzcuintli as the principal calendrical name of this deity.

Xipe Tótec was present at diverse events involving social promotion. According to Motolinia, for a newly elected *tlatoani* to truly assume power and acquire the right to wear the ornaments, clothes, and badges corresponding to his new status, it was necessary for him to carry out a military campaign and take his first captive. This captive was sacrificed and skinned, then the skin was stuffed with cotton and hung from the house of the newly appointed leader (Motolinia 1996: 486–487). In addition, Alvarado Tezozómoc (1987: 584) describes Motecuhzoma II dressed up as Xipe Tótec during his investiture military campaign. In Tenochtitlan, one of the places the new tlatoani had to visit during his investiture, with the object of making offerings and extracting blood from his body, was the Temple of Xipe Tótec, the Yopico. The same thing happened—at least in regard to the offerings—in the case of a merchant, or pochteca, when he was about to celebrate his banquet and spend lavishly to enhance his prestige (Durán 1967: 2: 302; Alvarado Tezozómoc 1987: 439; Sahagún 2000: 2: 819). Finally, in achieving the rank of tecuhtli among the Nahuas from Tlaxcala, Huexotzinco, and Cholula, the candidate was initially received at the temple by five priests who represented as many gods, among them Xipe Tótec, and at the conclusion of the process he was dressed as "Our Lord the Flayed One" to receive the honor so eagerly sought (Carrasco 1966: 135, 138).

CONCLUSION

It is now clear that Xipe Tótec was an ancestral deity in Mesoamerica and not merely a Mexica god imported to the Basin of Mexico as a consequence of military conquest. The importance of this god's festival in Tenochtitlan is explained in large measure by his identification with the Red Tezcatlipoca and his symbolic links with the creation of the Fifth Sun, a primordial mythical event to the so-called People of the Sun, the Mexica. Status distinctions accorded to specific warriors during Xipe's festival are revealed by unique characteristics in the mortuary treatment of the victims sacrificed at the tlahuahuanaliztli. These distinctions have expanded our understanding of the role the flayed human skins and Xipe Tótec played in a ritualized process of military promotion for the warriors involved.

Although my focus has been devoted mainly to the warlike symbolism of the Tlacaxipehualiztli and the means by which that ceremony served as a specific process for the social and military advancement of the warriors involved, the festival's agricultural character was equally important. Its relevance for a successful corn harvest is a connection I have discussed elsewhere (González González 2006). Suffice it to say here that the most distinguished and capable warriors, both the captives sacrificed at the temalácatl and their captors who obtained military promotion for having offered them as victims, were symbolically linked with the ceremonial selection of the best ears of corn. This corn was destined for use as seed for the future harvest and was also offered to Xipe Tótec on his festival. If we believe Durán, these ears were consecrated to him from the moment of their selection at the conclusion of the harvest (Durán 1967: 1: 243–244). The polarity between war and agriculture, characteristic of the worship of this god, must have been what led H. B. Nicholson to attempt to define the precise nature of Xipe Tótec, no matter how obscure. If the present work helps clarify that nature a little more, it will serve as a tribute to the memory of a great scholar.

13.8. *Xipe Tótec wearing a flayed skin in the* Tonalámatl of Aubin. *From Aguilera 1981: 14.*

NOTES

1. This opinion persists in an even more recent work on Mesoamerican religion by Miller and Taube (1993: 188).

2. Xipe Tótec is also associated with the Nahui Ollin glyph in the *Tonalámatl of Aubin* (figure 13.8). No other image of a ruling deity in the *Codex Borbonicus* has associated calendar glyphs.

3. Only six references to tlacaxipehualiztli celebrations in Tenochtitlan can be found in the documentary sources (cf. González González 2006: 214–216).

4. "Auh yn ieoaio qujmopialtiaia in tlamanj" (Sahagún 1953–1982: 2: 54).

5. The rank of tequihua was the highest rank in the Mexica military hierarchy. To earn it, one must have captured four enemy warriors (Sahagún 2000: 2: 783). According to Durán, both noblemen, or *pillis*, and commoners, or macehuales, could attain the rank. There were several differences in the procedure and dress in each case (Durán 1967: 1: 113–116). Pomar (1986: 80) states that the supreme ruler (*tlatoani*) could only wear the badges of a tequihua if he was, in fact, legitimately one.

6. With respect to this, see López Austin (1996: 1: 433–435).

7. Among them should be mentioned the codices of the so-called Borgia Group, the *Tonalámatl of Aubin*, the *Codex Borbonicus*, and the *Codex Vaticanus* 3738. In the *Codex Borbonicus* Xipe Tótec appears as the Red Tezcatlipoca and is linked to the Fifth Sun's day sign, Nahui Ollin.

REFERENCES CITED

Aguilera, Carmen,
 1981 *El Tonalámatl de la Colección de Aubin*. Estudio introductorio de Carmen Aguilera. Diagramas de cada lámina y tablas explicativas de Eduard Seler. Antiguo Manuscrito Mexicano en la Biblioteca Nacional de París, Manuscrit Mexicain 18–19. Estado de Tlaxcala, México, DF.

Alvarado Tezozómoc, Fernando
 1987 *Crónica Mexicana*, 4th ed. Editorial Porrúa, México, DF.
 1992 *Crónica Mexicáyotl*. Instituto de Investigaciones Históricas, UNAM, México, DF.

Anders, Ferdinand, Maarten Jansen, and Luis Reyes García, eds.
 1996 *Códice Ixtlilxóchitl. Apuntaciones y pinturas de un historiador. Estudio de un documento colonial que trata del calendario naua*. Akademische Druck- und Verlagsanstalt, Graz, Austria, and Fondo de Cultura Económica, México, DF.

Anderson, Arthur J.O., and Susan Schroeder, eds. and trans.
 1997 *Codex Chimalpahin: Society and Politics in Mexico Tenochtitlan, Tlatelolco, Texcoco, Culhuacan, and Other Nahua Altepetl in Central Mexico*, 2 vols. University of Oklahoma Press, Norman.

Bierhorst, John
 1992 *History and Mythology of the Aztecs: The Codex Chimalpopoca*. University of Arizona Press, Tucson.

Broda, Johanna
 1970 Tlacaxipeualiztli: A Reconstruction of an Aztec Calendar Festival from 16th Century Sources. *Revista Española de Antropología Americana* 5: 197–273. Universidad de Madrid.

Carrasco, Pedro
 1966 Documentos sobre el rango de Tecuhtli entre los nahuas tramontanos. *Tlalocan* 5 (2): 133–160.

Caso, Alfonso
 1961 Nombres calendáricos de los dioses. *El México Antiguo* 9: 77–100. Sociedad Alemana Mexicanista, México, DF.

Castañeda, Francisco de
 1986 Relación de Acolman. In *Relaciones geográficas del siglo XVI: México*, vol. 7, ed. René Acuña, pp. 223–232. Instituto de Investigaciones Antropológicas, UNAM, México, DF.

Cervantes de Salazar, Francisco
 1985 *Crónica de la Nueva España*. Prólogo por Juan Miralles Ostos. Editorial Porrúa, México, DF.

Chimalpahin Cuauhtlehuanitzin, Domingo Francisco de San Antón Muñón
 1991 *Memorial breve acerca de la fundación de la ciudad de Culhuacan*. Estudio, paleografía, traducción, notas, e índice analítico por Víctor M. Castillo F., i–lxviii. Instituto de Investigaciones Históricas, UNAM, México, DF.

    1997   *Primer amoxtli libro. 3ª Relación de las Différentes Histoires Originales.* Estudio, paleografía, traducción, notas, repertorio, y apéndice de Víctor M. Castillo F. Instituto de Investigaciones Históricas, UNAM, México, DF.

Durán, Fray Diego
    1967   *Historia de las Indias de Nueva España e islas de la tierra firme,* 2 vols. Editorial Porrúa, México, DF.

García Icazbalceta, Joaquín, ed.
    1941   *Nueva Colección de Documentos para la Historia de México. Pomar. Zurita. Relaciones Antiguas (Siglo XVI).* Editorial Salvador Chavez Hayhoe, México, DF.

Garibay K., Ángel María
    1995   *Veinte himnos sacros de los nahuas.* Instituto de Investigaciones Históricas, UNAM, México, DF.

Gómez de Orozco, Frederico
    1945   Costumbres, Fiestas, Enterramientos y Diversas Formas de Proceder de Los Indios de Nueva España. *Tlalocan* 2 (1): 37–63.

González González, Carlos Javier
    2005   Ubicación e importancia del templo de Xipe Tótec en la parcialidad tenochca de Moyotlan. *Estudios de Cultura Náhuatl* 36: 47–66.
    2006   Relaciones de una Deidad Mesoamericana con la Guerra y el Maíz. El Culto de Xipe Tótec entre los Mexicas. PhD thesis, Facultad de Filosofía y Letras, UNAM, México, DF.

Graulich, Michel
    1979   *Mythes et Rites des Vingtaines du Mexique Central Préhispanique,* 3 vols. Thèse présentée pour l'obtention du grade de Docteur en Philosophie et Lettres, Université Libre de Bruxelles.

Heyden, Doris
    1986   Xipe Tótec: ¿Dios nativo de Guerrero o hijo adoptivo? In *Arqueología y Etnohistoria del estado de Guerrero,* pp. 373–387. INAH and Gobierno del Estado de Guerrero, México, DF.

Linné, Sigvald
    1934   *Archaeological Researches at Teotihuacan, Mexico.* New Series Publication 1. Ethnographical Museum of Sweden, Stockholm.

López Austin, Alfredo
    1996   *Cuerpo humano e ideología. Las concepciones de los antiguos nahuas,* 2 vols., primera reimpresión. Instituto de Investigaciones Antropológicas, UNAM, México, DF.
    1998   *Hombre-dios. Religión y política en el mundo náhuatl,* 3rd ed. Instituto de Investigaciones Históricas, UNAM, México, DF.

Matos Moctezuma, Eduardo
    1992   *La Piedra del Sol. Calendario Azteca.* Editorial Fondo de Cultural Económico, México, DF.

2001   Teotihuacan. In *Descubridores del Pasado en Mesoamérica*, pp. 255–283. Océano, DGE Ediciones, Antiguo Colegio de San Ildefonso, México, DF.

Miller, Mary E., and Karl Taube
1993   *The Gods and Symbols of Ancient Mexico and the Maya: An Illustrated Dictionary of Mesoamerican Religion.* Thames and Hudson, London.

Molina, Fray Alonso de
1992   *Vocabulario en Lengua Castellana y Mexicana y Mexicana y Castellana*, 3rd ed. Estudio preliminar de Miguel León-Portilla. Editorial Porrúa, México, DF.

Motolinia, Fray Toribio de Benavente
1996   *Memoriales (Libro de oro, MS JGI 31).* Edición crítica, introducción, notas, y apéndice por Nancy Joe Dyer. El Colegio de México, México, DF.

Muñoz Camargo, Diego
1998   *Historia de Tlaxcala (Ms. 210 de la Biblioteca Nacional de París).* Paleografia, introducción, notas, apéndices, e índices analíticos de Luis Reyes García, con la colaboración de Javier Lira Toledo. Gobierno del estado de Tlaxcala, Centro de Investigaciones y Estudios Supiores en Antropología Social, and Universidad Autonoma de Tlaxcala, Tlaxcala.

Nicholson, H. B.
1961   The Chapultepec Cliff Sculpture of Motecuhzoma Xocoyotzin. *El México Antiguo* 9: 379–444.
1971   Religion in Pre-Hispanic Central Mexico. In *Archaeology of Northern Mesoamerica*, Part 1, ed. Gordon F. Ekholm and Ignacio Bernal, pp. 395–446. Handbook of Middle American Indians, vol. 10, Robert Wauchope, gen. ed. University of Texas Press, Austin.
1972   The Cult of Xipe Totec in Mesoamerica. In *Religión en Mesoamérica*, ed. J. Litvak King and Noemi Castillo Tejero, pp. 213–217. 7th Mesa Redonda de la Sociedad Mexicana de Antropología. Sociedad Mexicana de Antropología, México, DF.
1976   Preclassic Mesoamerican Iconography from the Perspective of the Postclassic: Problems in Interpretational Analysis. In *Origins of Religious Art and Iconography in Preclassic Mesoamerica,* ed. H. B. Nicholson, pp. 157–175. UCLA Latin American Center Publications, Los Angeles, CA.

Paso y Troncoso, Francisco del
1993   *Códice Borbónico.* Descripción, historia, y exposición del Códice Borbónico, con un comentario explicativo por Ernest T. Hamy. Siglo Veintiuno Editores, México, DF.

Pomar, Juan Bautista de
1986   Relación de la ciudad y provincia de Tezcoco. In *Relaciones geográficas del siglo XVI*, vol. 8, ed. René Acuña, pp. 23–113. Instituto de Investigaciones Antropológicas, UNAM, México, DF.

Sahagún, Fray Bernardino de
1953–1982 *Florentine Codex: General History of the Things of New Spain*, 12 vols. Translated from the Aztec into English, with notes and illustrations, by Charles E.

Dibble and Arthur J.O. Anderson. Monographs of the School of American Research and the Museum of New Mexico, Santa Fe. School of American Research, Santa Fe, and University of Utah, Provo.

1989   *Breve compendio de los ritos idolátricos que los indios de esta Nueva España usaban en tiempos de su infidelidad.* Presentación, paleografía, y notas de María Guadalupe Bosch de Souza. Departamento del Distrito Federal y Lince Editores, México, DF.

2000   *Historia general de las cosas de Nueva España,* 3 vols. Versión íntegra del texto castellano del manuscrito conocido como *Códice florentino.* Estudio introductorio, paleografía, glosario, y notas por Alfredo López Austin and Josefina García Quintana. Cien de México, Consejo Nacional para la Cultura y las Artes, México, DF.

Sanders, William T., Jeffrey R. Parsons, and Robert S. Santley

1979   *The Basin of Mexico: Ecological Processes in the Evolution of a Civilization.* Academic Press, New York.

Seler, Eduard, ed.

1900–1901   *The Tonalamatl of the Aubin Collection: An Old Mexican Picture Manuscript in the Paris National Library (Manuscrits Mexicains No. 18–19).* Printed by Hazell, Watson, and Viney, Berlin and London.

1963   *Comentarios al Códice Borgia,* 3 vols. Fondo de Cultura Económica, México, DF.

1990   *Códice Durán.* Arrendadora Internacional, México, DF.

1990–1998   *Collected Works in Mesoamerican Linguistics and Archaeology,* 6 vols., ed. J. Eric S. Thompson and Francis B. Richardson; Frank E. Comparato, gen. ed. Labyrinthos, Culver City, CA.

Torquemada, Juan de

1943   *Monarquia Indiana,* 3 vols. Editorial Salvador Chavoz Hayhoe, México, DF.

PART IV
ETHNOHISTORY

14

PREHISPANIC K'ICHE-MAYA HISTORIOGRAPHY

Robert M. Carmack

This chapter was inspired by an unpublished essay written by H. B. Nicholson in 1969 entitled "Pre-Hispanic Central Mexican Historiography" (see also Nicholson 1967, 1975). I will attempt to discuss the same historiographic issues for the K'iche Maya that Nicholson had investigated for the Central Mexicans. I never published the original essay, and this festschrift in honor of Nicholson seemed to provide a fortuitous opportunity to finally bring it to light. I do so with the utmost esteem and respect for my mentor in Mesoamerican ethnohistory. Except for stylistic changes, I have left the essay as it was written over thirty years ago at a strategic time in my academic career when Nicholson's influence on my thinking remained profound. To indicate some of the new information and interpretations of K'iche history that have appeared since I first wrote the essay, I have added endnotes where appropriate.

In an early work, Nicholson (1955) included the K'iche and Kaqchikel among groups in Mesoamerica whose documentary corpus is rich by Mesoamerican standards. With the goal of contributing to the study of the Highland Maya corpus of documents, I have attempted through the years to exploit these sources and thus contribute to the now extensive collection of synthetic ethnohistories of Mesoamerican peoples. The focus of the present chapter is on one small aspect of Prehispanic K'iche-Maya culture, that of historiography. A secondary goal of the essay is to provide some of the textual evaluation and critique of the documentary sources Nicholson so strongly advocated over his long and productive scholarly career as a Mesoamerican ethnohistorian.

The K'iche documentary corpus is too extensive to be described here in detail.[1] Key sources relevant to K'iche historiography consist of fifty or so sixteenth-century native documents scattered throughout the world in various publications, libraries, archives, and private collections. The sources vary tremendously with respect to the kind of historical and cultural information they contain, although for convenience of study they might be classified into three categories, in descending richness of content:

1. In this first category would be the *Popol Wuj* (hereafter abbreviated as *PW*), easily the most extensive and important of all the K'iche native sources. Also of supreme importance, although written in the Kaqchikel rather than the K'iche language, is the Annals of the Kaqchikels (abbreviated as Annals). As will be explained, these two documents contain considerable history, and the latter may be considered a genuine historical chronicle.[2]

2. A second category consists of sources that contain important but limited information on Prehispanic history and culture of the K'iche and related K'ichean groups. The sources in this category would include the *Rabinal Achí* (although the date of composition is somewhat late);[3] accounts by the Nijaib, Tamub, and Kanil branches of the K'iche; three documents written by the Xpantzay branch of the Kaqchikel; one account each by the Tzutujil and Poqomam; and small documents from the K'iche of Santa Clara la Laguna, Zapotitlán, Quezaltenango, and Santa Cruz del Quiché.[4]

3. A third category consists of brief documents with little substantive material, although they contain scattered references to Prehispanic cultural features. This category would include two minor documents written by the Nijaib K'iche and another by the K'iche from Retalhuleu, Santa María Chiquimula, and Santa Cruz del Quiché.[5] In addition, there exists a pictorial and brief inscription in K'iche attached to a document from Momostenango, a testament from Suchitepéquez, and additional minor documents from groups closely related to the K'iche—including two from the Xpantzay Kaqchikel, one from the Chajoma Kaqchikel, and one each from the Mam and Tzutujil.

An approximation of Prehispanic K'iche historiography can be reconstructed from these native documents, a corpus that will be added to as documents are uncovered from time to time. Additional limited references to K'iche history and culture can be found in Spanish sources, especially in the writings of Bartolomé de Las Casas, Francisco Ximénez, and Antonio Fuentes y Guzmán.[6]

GENERAL FEATURES OF K'ICHE HISTORY

When the PW is examined from the point of view of K'iche historiography, several interesting patterns are revealed. In the first place, one finds that K'iche history appears as an emergent or developmental process. The first, and most lengthy, phase refers to the acts of gods and demi-gods, who are only vaguely specified temporally (to a pre-human period) and spatially to a spiritual world (Recinos 1947: 81–173). This first phase of K'iche "history" might be referred to as mythological.[7]

With the creation of the forefathers, the K'iche considered that human history had begun (Recinos 1947: 174–224). Recorded acts are of men, but they tend to be generalized (that is, events usually refer to groups rather than to individuals, as, for example, references to the sacrifice of "the tribes") and are interconnected with the miraculous (for example, references to a parting of the sea and to the transformation of gods into men). Temporal references are primarily to the creation of humans but also to a mysterious unspecified "dawning." Spatial placement appears more important for this phase, and references are to places that were still known at the time of the Spanish invasion (for example, Chipixab, Jaqawitz).[8]

The second phase of K'iche history closely parallels native accounts from Central Mexico that Ángel Garibay (1953: 463ff) classified as "sagas." The accounts in the PW for this phase take the form of a series of heroic tales strung together, with dialogue employed as a prominent mode of explication.[9]

For the third and final phase of K'iche history (Recinos 1947: 224–228), the acts of humans are recorded in detail, with specification as to names of individual and group participants, their numbers, and the social organizations to which they belonged. Temporal placement, although not calendrical, is precise. It is represented by references to the ruling line: for example, "K'otuja, Q'ukumatz, and all the lords arrived there; and the fifth point in the line (le) of succession began" (Villacorta C. 1962: 333; author's translation from the K'iche text). Spatial placement is also precise, the sources not only providing information on the territories and settlements where actions took place but in some cases specifying the very buildings within which the events unfolded. Thus, it can be seen that there is a historical unfolding, with increasing specificity of eventful detail and spatial-temporal placement.[10] This last phase of K'iche history may properly be referred to as chronological history.

A second feature of K'iche history as revealed by the PW concerns its emphasis on political events. After the mythological section, most of the events described are patently political: military conquests, internal conflicts between officials and lineages, ceremonies of royal investiture, and successions of rulers. Ritual is important but is almost always associated with the names of political rulers (for example, no named priest is given who is not also an important official in the political system). And, as pointed out earlier, the continuous and most important temporal specification of events is through reference to nodes along the ruling line.

A further feature of K'iche history, only adumbrated in the PW, is the tendency to record events in cyclic sequences. This pattern is primarily confined to the use of the names (or titles) of rulers, which in some cases are repeated from the beginning of history to the end. But it is also present in the accounts of recurring political visitations to the East and the continuous migrations and cyclic founding of political capitals in the Highlands. This type of repetition in K'iche history, combined with the absence of a refined chronology, makes historical reconstructions based on the PW difficult.[11]

History as revealed in the Annals is also emergent, although compared to the PW it is less mythological in the first part but more chronological in the last part. The Annals lack a strictly mythological section comparable to the PW, for the account begins with the founding fathers already in existence. The first sections of the document (Recinos 1950: 47–87) reveal a pattern similar to the second, saga-like phase of history, as recorded in the PW. Events are generalized and integrated with miraculous occurrences associated with the founding ancestors. There are also similar temporal and spatial specifications of several places known at the time of Spanish contact, as well as of important "dawnings." As the account unfolds, events become more detailed, and specification of Kaqchikel forefathers and rulers is supplemented by references to K'iche rulers (Recinos 1950: 87–105).

After the Kaqchikel separated from the K'iche, events in the Annals become patently historical (Recinos 1950: 105ff). Descriptions contain elaborate details about participants, including quotations from them, their names and numbers, and many specific features about the acts they performed. As in the last phase of the PW, spatial placement becomes so precise that specific sections of the Kaqchikel capital are described; consequently, an archaeologist working at the site has been able to use the Annals to identify sections and structures of the ruins.[12] Even more impressive, however, is the calendrical dating that appears in the Annals. In the first two cases of dating, reference is to days in the 260-day calendar (13 Iq', the day of separation from the K'iche'; 10 Tz'i', the day an important war began against the K'iche). After the revolt of the Tuquchee, nearly all entries are dated relative to that important event. Each year that elapsed after the revolt is recorded, and this continues into the Postconquest period, eventually becoming a yearly chronicle (ending in AD 1603).[13]

Like the PW, the Kaqchikel account is decidedly political throughout. No important occurrence disassociated with K'iche or Kaqchikel rulers is recorded. The pages are filled with accounts of wars, political successions, conflicts over office, investitures of authority, and similar events. This is also true for the more strictly chronological phase of history: of about thirty-five entries for the period between the Tuquchee revolt and the Spanish invasion, fully twenty-five directly refer to political matters (especially wars), and the other ten references are indirectly political (such as signs or omens preceding the Spanish invasion or the "royal" genealogy of the authors of the Annals). This political orientation continues into the Posthispanic Period, where we find a surprisingly strong interest in and knowledge of the political affairs of the Spanish *audiencia* (court).

Historical repetition is less pronounced in the Annals than in the PW, although it is evident in the earliest phase of Kaqchikel history (as indicated by the multiple "dawnings," migrations, and visits to the East). A more pronounced characteristic of this early phase of history in the Annals is the attempt to describe a pre-civilized cultural condition for the peoples of the Highlands (that is, pre-agricultural, pre-family, pre-weaving, and so on). Similar descriptions are found in the PW, suggesting that references to a "pre-civilized" condition become an additional leitmotif in K'iche history.

A comparison between the documents from the second category and the PW and Annals of the first category reveals their fundamental historical similarity. They generally show a progressive historicity, although none contains a strictly mythological section as found in the PW. Most of these documents contain saga-like accounts, followed by a more detailed and chronological section at the end (in some cases the detailed accounts are of the Spanish invasion). Again, most of the documents, whether K'iche or Kaqchikel, specify time by referring to the K'iche ruling line, but there is no use of calendrical chronology.[14] The most important specifications appear to be spatial, with placement (if any) given in terms of the successive political centers occupied by the K'iche and Kaqchikel.

In every case political events completely dominate the contents of these documents, with a similar concentration on warfare and political succession. However, they differ from accounts in the PW and Annals in that they generally deal with events directly affecting the political situation in the local areas where they were written. They are not entirely provincial, however, for almost always some connection is made with rulers from K'iche capitals. At the same time, ruling lines of descent, whether local or central, are rather confused, and in most cases the events are loosely clustered around either the reigns of the K'iche founding fathers, the famous ruler K'iq'ab, or Tekum, the traditional K'iche hero of the Spanish invasion period.

The tendency to employ cyclic patterning in K'iche history is more evident in the provincial documents than in the PW or the Annals. Thus, based on documents largely from this category, I have elsewhere pointed to the recurring epi-Toltec legitimization in K'iche history and to the reworking of facts surrounding the rule of Q'ukumatz to recapitulate the Quetzalcoatl tradition of Mexico (Nicholson 1957; Carmack 1966a).[15] Even with this additional evidence of historical repetition, however, it must be emphasized that most K'iche history is linear rather than cyclic.

One document in the second category, written by the Poqomam from San Cristóbal Verapaz (Crespo 1967), is of special comparative interest. The Poqomam of this area were never under strong K'iche influence, and at the time of the Spanish invasion they were entirely independent. Thus, their history provides an interesting and largely independent case that contrasts with the K'iche situation. Accordingly, the Poqomam account is more provincial than most of the K'iche documents, its history beginning with the birth of the village forefathers from the very hills of San Cristóbal. Throughout, only events are recounted that occurred within the confines of a small territory that included San Cristóbal and four nearby settlements (Tukurub, Taltique, Chinautla, and Rabinal). Most of the events described are political in nature, and the sequential ruling line is recorded at the end. The account is very generalized (much like the second phase of K'iche history), and there is almost no placement of events in terms of points along a ruling line. A fairly strong specification of place is recorded, but almost none with respect to time. In fact, it is not possible to arrange many of the events in chronological order, even in such gross terms as to whether they occurred before or after the Spanish invasion. In sum, the Poqomam document throws into relief such general characteristics of K'ichean history as its Catholicism, specificity of detail, and use of chronology.

Documents in the third category contain little information and nothing of much significance concerning aboriginal K'iche historiography. The Spanish sources, however, do shed additional light, especially with respect to the mode of writing used to record K'iche history (discussed later).

Father Bartolomé de Las Casas (1958: 346) argued that the K'iche were well accomplished at writing history:[16]

> They [the Indians of Guatemala] had notice of the origins of all things, including religion, the gods, and their ritual; the founding of towns and cities, how many lords had passed away, their works, achievements, and memorable acts, both good and bad, how they governed, whether good or bad, the good and great men, and valorous captains, the wars they had, and how they distinguished themselves in them. Also [they kept track] of the customs of the first inhabitants, and how they changed later for good and ill, and all that which pertains to history, so that there would be an understanding and memory of the things of the past [translation by author].

Father de Las Casas further intimates that they used a dating system in keeping their history, but in his brief summary of that history he makes no further reference to it.

The Creole chronicler Francisco de Fuentes y Guzmán (1932–1934: 7: 107–112) was well acquainted with K'iche historiography through access to several native documents written shortly after the Spanish invasion, which he claims show that the K'iche expressed their history in writing. The native sources in his possession, as best can be determined, were not basically dissimilar to the ones discussed earlier in this chapter (although no doubt they had suffered errors in translation and a certain hispanization in his hands). In fact, some of de Fuentes y Guzmán's confused interpretations of these sources can be attributed to the nature of K'iche history itself, as discussed earlier; namely, the absence of a standard chronology, the tendency to repeat the names and titles of rulers, and the provincial distortions of ruling lines. These features are probably all partly responsible for de Fuentes y Guzmán's hopelessly garbled reconstruction of the K'iche ruling line. Nevertheless, his account of a political "bride capture" and the resulting wars between the K'iche and the Tzutujil, largely rejected by scholars as spurious, is not inconsistent in degree of detail or specificity with the chronological phase of K'iche history found in the sources described previously (which is not to argue, however, that de Fuentes y Guzmán did not distort the facts of native history in this and other instances, for he certainly did, most notably with respect to native population figures).[17]

Father Francisco Ximénez (1929) believed the K'iche had a developed historical tradition that was transmitted in both written and oral forms. He argued, however, that the keeping of history was mainly confined to the royal court officials. Furthermore, he minimized the historicity of (third-category) accounts coming from the provinces, specifically criticizing de Fuentes y Guzmán for basing his reconstructions of K'iche history on such sources. For Ximénez, the PW provided the correct and official version of K'iche history.

THE WRITTEN TRANSMISSION OF K'ICHE HISTORY

There can be little doubt that the K'iche transmitted their history partly in writing. According to the PW, the ancestors to the K'iche and other Highland peoples brought books (*u tz'ibal*) and calendars (*chol q'ij, may q'ij*) with them when they returned to the Highlands following a visit to "Tulan." In fact, the PW was written, we are told, because the "book of the council (*popol wuj*), as it is called, cannot be seen any more" (Villacorta C. 1962: 16).[18] Unfortunately, none of these Prehispanic codices have survived into modern times, although de Las Casas saw some of them while he resided in Guatemala (ca. 1540). He describes them (de Las Casas 1958: 346) as consisting of "figures and characters by which they could signify everything they desired; and . . . these great books are of such acuteness and subtle technique that we could say our writing does not offer much of an advantage."

Father de Las Casas goes on to explain that they were partially phonetic, apparently based on the rebus principle. This points to a system of writing closer to that of the Aztecs than the lowland Maya hieroglyphic system, and the few K'iche pictorial fragments that have come down to us from the Colonial Period reinforce this conclusion.

Francisco de Fuentes y Guzmán describes two native documents in his possession that bear on the topic. One was a map showing the territory of the K'iche state, drawn prior to the Spanish invasion (although a few characters were added to it after that important event). His description (Fuentes y Guzmán 1932–1934: 7: 108) makes it clear that the document was almost exclusively pictographic, although lines in the form of the spokes of a wheel connecting various *caciques* were used as an ideographic representation of a political pact or agreement. The provenience of the second "writing" is not given, but de Fuentes y Guzmán (ibid.: 112) included a copy of it in his book. If we accept his interpretation of the characters, it suggests that at least this particular script was basically Mexican. It was primarily pictographic, although it also contained signs that were ideographic (for example, numbers) and rebus-based (for example, the names of conquered settlements). It is interesting that the characters were arranged in vertical positioning, a technique more characteristically Maya than Mexican.[19]

Two other "paintings" or "cloths" are mentioned in a sixteenth-century document that records a dispute over leadership in Santiago Atitlán (Archivo General de Centroamérica [AGCA] n.d.a). The cloths were painted by Tzutujil lords from that community, but there is no indication as to whether they were produced before or after the Spanish invasion. Apparently, the contents were exclusively pictorial, in which fifteen Tzutujil rulers and their residences were represented. The pictorials were used in connection with the dispute as mnemonic signs for the names of the fifteen rulers and their hierarchical rankings. It is noteworthy that the map of the Lake Atitlán region attached to the Relación Geográfica from there (Gall 1963: 87) appears to be based on Prehispanic models. It is similar in style to the geographic portion of an early pictorial from Momostenango.[20]

Other early pictorials include two second-category documents from Momostenango, two additional pictorials incorporated in the *Título K'oyoi* (Carmack 1973: 265ff), and a map from Sacapulas (AGCA n.d.b).[21] The two Momostenango pictorials reveal strong Spanish influence in style, although their pictographic forms are probably a reflection of aboriginal patterns (they are similar in this regard to the Lake Atitlán map mentioned earlier). The Sacapulas map, on the other hand, is highly schematic and appears to show little or no Spanish influence. It was drawn in the form of three concentric circles, the outermost of which is segmented into twenty-eight sections, and in each section the name of a place in the Sacapulas area was inscribed.[22] It is possible that the idea for the map came from aboriginal representations of the calendar in disc form, as with the Aztec *Calendar Stone* and other maps from the Central Mexico area.[23] In fact, one of the intriguing problems connected with K'iche writing remains that of establishing the form in which the aboriginal calendars were recorded (discussed later).

J. Eric Thompson (1965: 647) noted that a K'iche 260-day calendar from the eighteenth century was represented in the form of a circular disc or wheel, and he suggests a connection between this form of representation and aboriginal forms. Of related interest are two jade pieces in the Rossbach Collection in the museum at Chichicastenango, which appear to have circular calendars incised on them. Regrettably, their provenience is not known, except that they came from the Department of Quiché and therefore might be K'iche artifacts. A possible clue to the origin of these "calendar stones" is a statement by a former resident of Santa Cruz del Quiché, Juan de León (1955: 85), who stated that a jade stone with an incised circular calendar similar to that of the Aztecs was found in the ruins of San Andrés Sajcabajá in 1911 and was later given to President Estrada Cabrera. With the information available, it is not possible to determine either the date or the precise provenience of the Chichicastenango jade pieces.[24]

The engravings on the Chichicastenango jade pieces consist of three concentric circles, the outer two divided into eleven and eighteen sections, the latter sections possibly representing the eighteen months of the Mesoamerican calendar system. The inner circle contains a blocked-out face with pendants hanging down on both sides, apparently representing the sun (as in the Aztec *Calendar Stone*). A preliminary examination of the characters within the concentric circles suggests that they are more pictorial than glyphic and therefore perhaps more reminiscent of Mexican than of the highly abstract lowland Maya characters.[25] In addition, de León's (1955: 82–84) informants from Santa Cruz del Quiché were able to use the Aztec calendar disc as a mnemonic device for describing the Maya calendar system, and this resulted in a valuable list of K'iche astronomical and calendrical terms. Unfortunately, we are not told the extent to which his list was based on local tradition.

Apart from the uncertain calendar stones, the other fragments of K'iche "writing" described previously provide little indication of the style in which they were originally produced. In fact, the only substantial clue as to style comes not from the documents at all but instead from the archaeological record: that is, the painted murals at Iximché (Guillemin 1965: 16–17) and the stone carvings at Chuitinamit (Lothrop 1933: 80–85).[26] Based on these two sites alone, it would appear that the K'iche expressed their symbols artistically within the Mixteca-Puebla Style.[27] This is indicated by the use of such features as the symbolic importance given to colors, the caricaturistic portrayal of persons, and the use of well-known standardized symbols such as the skull and crossbones, human figures in moving postures, and the exaggeration of prominent body features (Nicholson 1960).

K'ICHE CALENDRICS

Unquestionably, the calendar formed an important component of the K'iche written corpus. As mentioned, we are told that they brought calendars with them from "Tulan" (Villacorta C. 1934: 186). From transcriptions made in the seventeenth and eighteenth centuries (Berendt n.d.a [1685], n.d.b [1722]; Cortez y Larraz 1958: 157), we learn that the K'iche were using a written calendar well into the Colonial Period, presumably perpetuating a feature derived from aboriginal culture (see also Ximénez 1929: 101–102). The fact that the calendars were recorded, even if in a new format, probably reflects the aboriginal pattern of calendrical representations. The suggestion by some scholars that the original calendars may have existed in hieroglyphic form seems unlikely, given the pictorial mode of writing employed by the K'iche. Both the 260-day divinatory (*chol q'ij*) and the 365-day solar (*junab*) calendars were recorded, and both have persisted through oral tradition in modern K'iche-speaking communities (García Elgueta 1962). René Acuña (1966) has called attention to the basic relationship between the 260-day and 365-day calendars of the Kaqchikel and other Mesoamerican peoples.[28]

There is uncertainty as to whether the K'iche employed a "long-count" calendrical system and, if they did, to what extent it was used to chronologize historical events. As noted, the Annals demonstrate that a long-count concept existed among the Kaqchikel, but it was recorded only late in their history, post–AD 1493 (Recinos 1950: 35, 111). After that date it was used extensively to date all major events, both before and after the Spanish invasion. It was a vigesimal system, based on the accumulation of units of single days (*q'ij*), 20 days (*winal*), 400 days (*a* or *junab*), and 8,000 days (20 × 400) (*may*). The zero starting point in the Annals was the Tuquchee revolt of 1493, suggesting that perhaps starting points could be reassigned at different times in history as important events occurred (Long 1934: 62–63; cf. Miles 1965: 272).

Because of the close cultural relationship between the K'iche and Kaqchikel peoples (there were, however, calendrical as well as other cultural differences [Miles 1965: 272–274]), it is to be expected that the K'iche might have had knowledge of a similar long-count system. This is further suggested by references in the K'iche sources to the same vigesimal units employed by the Kaqchikel. However, in the only case where long-count units are associated with specific historical events by K'iche scribes, they state that "it is not possible to give dates in the units of 400 days (junab) or 8,000 days (may)" (Recinos 1957: 30). The general absence of calendrical dating in the native documents (other than the Annals) is surprising, although the evidence available is sufficient at least to leave the question open as to whether in Prehispanic times the K'iche had a similar "chronicle consciousness" to that of the Central Mexicans (Nicholson 1955).

If a long-count system was employed Prehispanically by the K'iche and Kaqchikel, this would probably implicate Maya rather than Mexican cultural influence. The lowland Maya, however, employed the 360-day *tun* rather than the K'iche 400-day unit, and their starting point was fixed. Furthermore, the chronologically important *katun* unit was absent among the Highland K'ichean Maya. Thompson (1965: 657) discovered a 400-day unit in southern Veracruz, suggesting a possible place of origin for this K'iche and Kaqchikel calendrical feature. In Central Mexico a long count was apparently never adopted, and most historical events there were recorded in the chronicles in yearly or 52-year cycles (Caso 1939, 1967; Velázquez 1945).²⁹

The "dawnings" simultaneously observed by most of the Highland Maya groups were possibly geared to important permutations of their calendrical system. One possible interpretation is that these dawning celebrated the beginning of 52-year cycles (the Mesoamerican "century") and perhaps the initiation of new cultural eras (the Central Mexican "Suns"). Like the "New Fire Ceremony," which in Central Mexico was calibrated to the beginning of each 52-year cycle, the PW (Villacorta C. 1962: 264–266) describes how a "dawning" was preceded by a period of anxious awaiting. Observations were made from the mountaintops of "stars" that precede the coming of the sun, along with offerings of copal in gratitude for the renewed light and rejoicing over the appearance of the sun. Along with the dawning came the renovation of life, especially the lives of animals and birds. While the K'iche dawning is probably generically related to the "New Fire Ceremony," it does not appear to be identical with it. Apparently missing were such features as the destruction and replacement of household utensils, the danger believed to exist for pregnant women and children, and the dramatic rekindling of fire. Possibly, for the K'iche the dawnings were associated with the beginning not only of a new 52-year cycle but also of a larger new era. This is suggested in the PW (ibid.: 267–268) by the cosmogonic effects of the first new sun: it dried the earth of a flood from a previous era, turned the gods and supernaturally powerful animals to stone, and made life possible for humans.

Unfortunately, this interpretation of the K'iche dawning must remain uncertain because the documents make no other direct references to it after the first one, except for a prior dawning at a time when the forefathers were still in the East (ibid.: 250). In all probability the K'iche recognized a 52-year cycle throughout their history, but perhaps it was little used to date events and thus was not directly mentioned in the sources.³⁰

K'ICHE HISTORIANS

From Father de Las Casas (1958: 346) we learn that the K'iche had special scribes in charge of keeping official history:

> Among other offices and officials were those who served as chroniclers and historians. They had notice of the count of the days, months, and years . . . [they] were never lacking because this office was derived from father to sons, and it was an office greatly esteemed in the Republic. At all times this man instructed two or three brothers or relatives of that family in those things related to history and had them exercise in the task while he was [still] living [translation by author].

Assuming that Father de Las Casas's statement is accurate, it would appear that writing and interpreting history were in the hands of specialists who transferred this knowledge and office within the lineage patriline. Unfortunately, the title or titles of the office are not given, nor is there any indication of how many patrilines provided such officials. Nevertheless, it can be surmised that the term *ajtz'ib*, meaning "scribe" or "painter" (Saenz de Santa María 1940; Vico n.d.), was the general title applied to them, while *ajmay wuj* ("he of the 8,000-day calendar book") and *ajchol q'ij*, or "he who counts the days" (that is, the days of the 260-day calendar) (Recinos 1957: 168), were employed to refer to the calendrical side of their duties.

The number of patrilines with books and guardian officials to maintain them can be estimated by examining the various *títulos* (Colonial native documents dealing with land titles and other matters) written in the first decades following the Spanish invasion. It is reasonable to assume that only the major politico-descent groups of the K'iche and related peoples had such officials, perhaps twenty to thirty in all (Kaweq, Tamub, Nijaib, Kanil, Tzutujil, Kejnay, Xajil, Xpantzay, and others). The assumption is that the capacity of a lineage group to initiate a detailed historical K'iche document while under Spanish rule depended on the prior existence in the group of Prehispanic codices and historians to interpret them. While this was probably not true in all cases, it was likely valid in a general way. The relevant Posthispanic documents would be those classified as belonging to the first and second categories.

One of the reasons we know so little about the K'iche "historians" is that shortly after the Spanish invasion most of them ceased to function as they had in aboriginal K'iche society. In almost every case, the sixteenth-century títulos were written by the heads of aboriginal political divisions and not by the trained historians. This was probably the result of over-specialization: the historians had been trained specifically to read and interpret the books and calendars, both of which were closely associated with native religion. Father de Las Casas (1958: 246) tells us that "these books were seen by the friars, who had them burned because it seemed to them that they dealt with religious matters." One possible exception was the PW. Its principal authors may have remained anonymous precisely because they were religiously oriented historians rather than political leaders. This would explain their apparent close adherence to a Prehispanic codex of some kind and the presence of an extensive mythological section in the PW (both of which contrast with the more limited mythology in the other títulos).[31]

Many of these historians and other priestly officials, of course, continued clandestinely to maintain aboriginal traditions through divination and other forms of ritual. They must have formed part of the corps of shamans and diviners (*ajitz*, *ajq'ij*) mentioned so frequently in the Colonial sources (Edmonson 1964: 268–269). Through time, however, their knowledge and expertise were reduced largely to memorizing the 260-day calendar for divinatory purposes (even today, hundreds of priest-shamanic practitioners in certain K'iche communities have this kind of knowledge; Carmack 1966–1967). Undoubtedly, knowledge of the complex myths recorded in the aboriginal documents was also considerably reduced, as indicated by its relative scarcity in the folklore of native K'ichean communities today.[32]

ORAL TRANSMISSION OF K'ICHE HISTORY

Father de Las Casas (1958: 346) states that in areas of Guatemala where the codices were not kept, there were "historians" especially trained to memorize the "knowledge of ancient things" and to pass these traditions on from "one to another, from hand to hand." He adds that the method was defective, and we also know it was greatly debilitated by the events of the Spanish invasion and colonization. Nevertheless, a general cultural tradition did continue to be orally transmitted by the K'iche, and in the eighteenth century Ximénez (1929: 5) refers to it as a "doctrine which they imbibed from the time they first nursed." Today in the rural areas of K'iche-speaking communities of Highland Guatemala, a similar cultural transmission continues to take place, communicated partly by the family and partly by the clan and lineage priests during ceremonial reunions (Schultze Jena 1933).[33]

A pronounced characteristic of this generalized oral transmission of tradition is its lack of historicity. Even narration of historical events of the clans and lineages themselves is scarce and shallow in time depth, while legend and myth are also surprisingly attenuated. For example, in the K'iche community of Momostenango, lineage genealogy rarely goes back more than a few generations, while historical memory is largely restricted to legends about the founding of the Colonial town center or the role of Tekum in the Spanish invasion. This loss of historical memory can be explained largely in terms of the breakdown by the Spaniards of the aboriginal state structure that overarched the descent groups and institutionalized the recording of historical traditions and institutions.

Of much greater importance for K'iche oral transmission were the ceremonial presentations in drama, dance, divination, and song. For convenience, I refer to them all as "ceremonial dramas." The documents indicate that this form of transmission was fully operational during the aboriginal period, and ethnographic studies have shown acculturated ceremonial dramas to be one of the most important mechanisms by which "folk history" has been expressed and retained in modern times. Munro Edmonson (1964) in particular has drawn attention to continuities between Prehispanic K'iche dances and the ceremonial dramas carried out during the Colonial and modern periods.

While it appears that the Posthispanic ceremonial dramas are not strongly historical in content, they can be divided into two broad categories on historiographic grounds. The category of least historical interest would be the rituals representing the great cyclic themes about nature and society; namely, agricultural productivity and fertility, hunting of wild game, successive deaths of political officials, and similar topics. Ceremonial dramas of this type—some of the names of which have come down to us—include "Song of the Kamuku" (Recinos 1947: 217), "Dance of the Deer" (Termer 1957), "Dance of the Serpent" (ibid.), "Dance of Corn" (Armas Lara 1964: 22lff), *Waxaqib Batz* (Goubaud Carrera 1935), and others (see Termer 1957: 209–211). Edmonson (1964) has suggested that these dramas were based on calendrical rituals, regulated by the 20-day names of the K'ichean calendars. While such a Prehispanic base may be correct, it appears that in most cases calendrical correlations were hopelessly lost through time.[34]

Ceremonial dramas of the second category are more like sagas, representing well-known historical or legendary events, in contrast with the more ritually patterned acts of the dramas described earlier. The most famous of these dramas is the *Rabinal Achí* ("Dance of the Tun"), which portrays the capture and sacrifice of a K'iche Kaweq prince by the Rabinal people (Brasseur de Bourbourg 1862).[35] Similarly, the conquest and sacrifice of Tolq'om by the Kaqchikel was celebrated in drama and ritual in Prehispanic times (Recinos 1950: 78).[36] Ximénez (1929: 78) and de Fuentes y Guzmán (1932–1934: 7: 388) were convinced that the dance called *Quiché Vinac* also portrayed historical events occurring before the Spanish invasion. The ceremonial dramas representing events of that invasion—for example, the *Zaqi K'axol* ("Dance of the Conquest") and the "Dance of the Volcano"—although written after contact with Spanish culture, appear to contain many aboriginal elements. Armas Lara (1964: 75), for example, claims that the *Zaqi K'axol* was written by a Dominican missionary in 1542. If that is true, the missionary must have drawn information from native informants, since the narrative of the drama clearly does not give the Spanish version of the "Conquest."[37]

The dramas of this second category apparently also became associated with the ritual calendar, at least in the case of the Tolq'om drama (Recinos 1950: 78). Apart from their function in ritual, they served as an important medium for the transmission of historical tradition in aboriginal times. The priests in charge of historical traditions no doubt used the chants accompanying such dramas to flesh out the skeletal texts provided by the codices. This technique has been well described for the peoples of Prehispanic Mexico, who called on special priests to check the accuracy of the songs and chants used to interpret the codices (León Portilla 1961). For commoners who did not have access to state historians, ceremonial dramas must have provided a simplified but vivid view of K'iche history. It may have been their most important source of historical (or legendary) information and perhaps was the ultimate source for the more widespread tradition of cultural inheritance taking place within partriarchal families and lineages.[38]

FUNCTIONS OF ABORIGINAL K'ICHE HISTORY

Although we know little about the Prehispanic K'iche codices, it nevertheless seems clear that they functioned somewhat differently from the native documents written during the first decades of Spanish colonization. Father de Las Casas (1958: 346) describes the native codex as a kind of "book of the state," containing precedence for public ritual and policy:

> Among other offices and officials were those who served as chroniclers and historians ... and they came to him [the chief historian] when they were doubtful about any articles or steps of history; not only those new historians but also the kings, lords, and priests [came] about doubts they might have with respect to the ceremonies and precepts of religion, festivals, the gods, and any other thing related to ancient government and profane things of quality; each one consulted in that sphere which pertained to him [translation by author].

As noted by Ximénez (1929: 54), in its aboriginal form the PW was just such a book of state. In fact, its etymology is roughly equivalent: the term *popol* can be glossed as "reunion," "community," or "council"; while the term *wuj* is glossed as "paper" (made from the bark of the Amatle tree) or "book" (Saenz de Santa María 1940; Vico n.d.). The root word of *popol* is *pop*, glossed as "mat."[39] Special mats were placed in public buildings and became a metanymic symbol of the authority and public action of rulers who sat upon them. This symbolism parallels usage in Central Mexico, where the Nahua term *petatl* had the double meaning of "mat" and "office of authority." An accurate translation of *Popol Wuj*, therefore, would be "book of the official council," the reference being to the official or ruling council as described by Las Casas (1958: 242, 251).

This etymology of *Popol Wuj* is confirmed by the context within which the Prehispanic codex of the K'iche state is described: "Great lords and wonderful men were the marvelous kings ... They knew if there would be war, and everything was clear before their eyes; they saw if there would be death and hunger, if there would be strife. They knew well that there was a place where it could be seen, that there was a book which they called the Popol Wuj" (Recinos, Goetz, and Morley 1950: 225).

The evidence from the documentary sources suggests these functions of K'iche "history" in Prehispanic times:

1. The codices themselves served as remarkable symbols of the power and esoteric knowledge of the K'iche rulers. There is some indication that the Prehispanic PW was periodically viewed (probably at a distance) by subject lords during visits to the K'iche capital to pay homage and tribute to rulers there (Recinos 1947: 238–239). The very fact of having produced or at least possessed such documents must have been inspiring, and this was intensified by the pomp and ceremony that apparently surrounded their guardianship. Today in many Highland Guatemalan communities the elders derive considerable prestige and influence as a result of their control and guardianship of Colonial land titles and other documents. Furthermore, impressive ceremony is connected with the periodic transfer of such documents from one set of officials to another.[40]

2. Certain historical and legendary accounts in the codices functioned to legitimize and sacralize the political supremacy of the K'iche state. Much of the second phase of history (quasi-legendary) found in the PW no doubt existed in the Prehispanic codices, and this was the ultimate source for parts of similar accounts recorded in other documents of categories one and two. It would appear from those accounts that legitimization primarily consisted of linking up the founders of the ruling lines with the epi-Toltecs, in ascribing miraculous powers to them—for example, the miraculous transformations of the ruler Q'ukumatz (Recinos 1947: 232–233)—and in recounting the long series of conquests by which the K'iche state became the major political power of the Highlands. Undoubtedly, aspects of this feature in K'iche history were recounted to the various subject peoples of the state during periodic public ceremonies (Carrasco 1967; Las Casas 1958).[41]

3. A divinatory function for the "book of state" is emphasized in the statement from the PW quoted earlier; that is, the council book somehow provided answers to questions about the desirability of war, the likelihood of natural disasters, and probably other issues as well. Abundant evidence from many sources (for example, Berendt n.d.b [1722]; Ximénez 1929) indicates that most K'iche divination was based on the 260-day calendar and its permutations with other calendars, and apparently this was an important function of the calendars included in Prehispanic K'iche codices.[42]

4. The mythological and possibly some of the legendary sections of the codices functioned as repositories for the ideas and tales behind the public rituals of K'iche society. Thus, for example, it is probable that the PW accounts of the demi-gods (for example, Junajpu, Ixbalanke) were based on representations in the codices and served as the primary source for ceremonial dramas. The same may be true of the *Rabinal Achí* (Edmonson 1964: 263, 272). Apparently, the priests consulted these accounts to clarify detail, assure correct recitation and chanting, and interpret the accompanying ritual (see the earlier quotation from Las Casas).[43]

5. Finally, the codices no doubt contained elements that functioned primarily as explanatory statements ("charters") of the existing socio-political order. Apparently, well-known social conditions had come to be explained and represented in standardized ways and were probably woven into the legendary and historical sections of the codices (they more than likely corresponded with the second phase of K'iche history found in the PW). Key examples from the PW would include the relationships between the K'iche and their earliest Wuqamaq' neighbors, symbolized by the episodes about K'iche youth begging for fire and their seduction by neighboring maidens (Recinos 1947: 186ff, 206ff); the genealogical relations between the Kaqchikel clans and lineages, symbolized by the metaphor of a red tree (Recinos 1957: 157); the relations of dominance over subject towns by the K'iche rulers, possibly represented in special maps (perhaps with signs for the towns [Fuentes y Guzmán 1932–1934: 7: 108; Recinos 1950: 62]). If indeed such topics were recorded in Prehispanic K'iche history, it was because they constituted a genre of historical memory and at the same time explained and represented in a culturally meaningful way social and political relations of continuing significance.[44]

The appearance of just one aboriginal K'iche codex would tell us much more than we now know from all the accounts written after the Spanish invasion. However, if the previous reconstruction is reasonably accurate, K'iche history before the Conquest appears to have been highly symbolic, providing primarily political and ritualistic functions. History, in the sense of a chronological record of past events, was present but must have been more limited than in the case of Central Mexico.[45]

FUNCTIONS OF EARLY POSTHISPANIC K'ICHE HISTORY

We are on much firmer ground in assigning functions to the native accounts (títulos) written after contact with the Spaniards. Not only do they contain many additional narratives that can be examined, but also in most cases the specific purposes for which they were written were made explicit by the authors. In general, the overriding function of these documents was political; that is, they were written as titles to land and office, as claims to the privileges of *cacicazco* (chiefdomship), and as attempts to lighten the burden of the Spanish subjugation.

Edmonson (1964: 257–263) has emphasized the way the native documents functioned as lineage land titles, but I suggest some modifications to this analysis. First, in some cases it is a distortion to classify the documents as strictly "lineage" accounts. K'iche political organization was more complex than the "tribal" or lineage explanations suggest, and as land titles these documents often refer to social groups that were more complex than any lineage organization (Carmack 1966b).[46] Second, some of the documents were not designed primarily as land titles, and in a few cases land was not an issue at all (for example, Recinos 1947: 249–251; Tzutujil 1952 [1571]). A good case can be made that many of the earliest Posthispanic K'iche documents were not written primarily as land titles; only later were they brought forward to settle contests over lands that had increasingly fallen into short supply (for one such case, see Carmack 1967).[47]

Land claims were nevertheless an important part of many of the documents, including the PW and the Annals, and such claims were almost the sole purpose of some of the second-category and most of the third-category documents (Recinos 1957: 120–129; Gall 1963). As noted by Edmonson (1964: 259), rights to land were divided, and competing claims could be made by different social units. Most of the claims in the documents refer to either local rights of administration or to state tributary rights. The former claims were usually based on mythic and legendary associations between the lands and the local groups (such as the association between a particular *nagual* [totem] and the salt springs at Sacapulas) (Crespo 1967) or on territorial occupancy, in which cases land boundaries and markers were recorded (see Crespo 1956). Claims to tribute were often based on the narration of territorial conquests and subsequent instances of tributary payments.[48]

The contrast between manifest land claims of third-category documents and the larger first-category and second-category documents suggests that these latter two types of documents had important additional functions. One of these functions was to support claims to special cacique privileges for members of the aboriginal K'iche ruling class. Documents of this type were generally written in the 1550s, possibly in response to the Spanish Crown's attempt at that time to limit the tributary rights and other privileges of the caciques (Gibson 1964: 197; Carmack 1981: 305–320). Under increasing pressure for acceptable verification of ties to native nobility, the Spanish courts demanded that the caciques supply documentary evidence demonstrating their ties to Prehispanic noble genealogical lines and historical events. This was a fairly reasonable policy, for, as noted earlier, direct access to the aboriginal historical tradition was confined to the ruling class. Only members of the nobility would have had access to the codices and adequate knowledge of their contents or control over former priests with such knowledge. Further, it appears that only members of the native ruling class were taught to write in Latin characters, making it possible for them to compose the necessary documents required by the Spanish courts (Sociedad de Geografía e Historia de Guatemala [SGHG] 1935: 191).[49]

The documents clearly indicate that the most direct path to cacique standing was through the ruling K'iche line at Q'umarkaaj. There were several ways by which that connection could be established: by demonstrating genealogical relations or political collaboration with past rulers, through recognized possession of Prehispanic titles and insignia, or by acquiring the testimonial signatures of living descendants of the royal lines.

An important feature of almost all the documents was the genealogy of native authorities (chiefs [caciques], governors [*gobernadores*], mayors [*alcaldes*]) in the local area. To demonstrate linkages between local officials and the K'iche ruling line, two simplifications were widely employed. One was to focus primarily on specific links between the local authorities and the K'iche ruling line (see the genealogical foreshortening that resulted from this in Recinos 1947: 249–251, 1957: 152–169). A related technique was to focus on ties between the rulers of the local area and only the most revered of the K'iche rulers; that is, ties to either the founding fathers (Balam Kitze and others), Q'ukumatz, K'iq'ab, or Tekum (Umam).⁵⁰ As a result of such simplifications, attention was ineluctably drawn to ties with the K'iche nobility and ipso facto to the right of cacique privileges.

In some Posthispanic documents, local authorities supported their claims to status by referring to prior military collaboration with the K'iche state in carrying out conquests of the provincial areas. For example, members of a Kaqchikel branch claimed credit for the success of many of the K'iche conquests, apparently in an attempt to ingratiate themselves with Spanish overlords by arguing that they had been pressured into abandoning their otherwise peaceful ways (Recinos 1957: 132–149). In other cases, the claimed relationship with the K'iche was one of tributary subjugation, a type of relationship that made it possible for local leaders to obtain recognition from important Posthispanic K'iche lords (as in the Sacapulas título, AGCA n.d.c).

The titles of the highest K'iche offices (*ajpop*, *q'alel*) were widely granted within the territory of the aboriginal K'iche state, and evidence of their continuing possession under Spanish rule became an important means of claiming caciqueship. In one document the significance of such titles is made explicit:

> Behold the authority of the lord Don Francisco Izquín, who has the double honor of *q'alel* and *ajpop*. No Bishop conceded to him this lordship, nor any President . . . Judge [*Oidor*] . . . Minister . . . *Alcalde Mayor* . . . Governor . . . *Alcalde* . . . nor did his vassals concede this authority to him . . . I, don Juan Cortés [a direct descendant of a K'iche ruler], king and gentleman, before all the great ones, give it to you with your brother in the name of the towns that were conquered. (Recinos 1957: 203)

The approving witnesses and signatures of K'iche rulers accompanied most of the documents. In a few cases rulers from many provinces were brought together, as if to ensure the claim to cacique status by weight of numbers (see especially the documents in Recinos 1957). Often, too, local officials and elders signed the documents, apparently to demonstrate their acceptance of the caciqueships being recognized by the Spaniards (for example, Crespo 1956; Recinos 1957: 115). All of these signatures helped establish Colonial high status for the descendants of Prehispanic rulers and allowed them to retain traditional K'iche titles (as distinct from local Spanish titles).⁵¹

In varying degrees, all of the native documents show evidence of Christian influence (Contreras R. 1963). This indicates the process of acculturation taking place but also another important function of the documents: they represented pleas by the K'iche subjects for the Spaniards to relax tributary demands, in exchange for which the natives promised to be faithful followers of the Christian religion. In many cases, based on teachings by the Spanish missionaries, the historical migrations of the K'iche founding fathers were linked to the dispersion of the Israelites from Babylon, presumably hoping in this way to be considered the children of God by their Spanish overlords and thus worthy of all of God's (and the Spaniards') blessings.[52] In other cases the events of the Spanish invasion are portrayed in such a way as to portray the native rulers giving ready acceptance of Christianity (for example, Recinos 1957: 91–93) or providing special assistance to the conquistadors (Recinos 1957: 89; Gall 1963). Furthermore, almost without exception, the former K'iche rulers at the time of the Spanish invasion are described as faithfully carrying out their Christian duties: attending masses, providing for the material well-being of the Spanish priests, occupying positions in the Church organization, and performing similar duties (Gall 1963).

The "good Christian" appeal to the Spaniards seems implicit in all of the documents and is made explicit in some of them (for example, Tzutujil 1952 [1571]). In the Tzutujil account the elders from Santiago Atitlán argue their case for relief from Spanish demands. They support their claim by citing (1) the aid they had given the Spaniards during the battle against the rebellious K'iche, (2) the excessive tributary burdens placed on them despite their continued fidelity to the Church, and (3) the extra contributions and work they had given to build the highly ornamented local cathedral.[53]

CONCLUSION

All of the functions of the documents discussed in this chapter—as land titles, testimonials to cacique standing, and pleas for relaxation of Spanish demands—were directly related to the Spanish domination of the K'iche natives. At the same time, however, the native documents continued to serve some of the same functions provided by the Prehispanic histories. Like the Prehispanic K'iche codices, for example, the Posthispanic documents themselves became important symbols of power and were guarded with ceremonial care. In addition to the function of backing cacique claims, the documents continued to serve as legitimizers of local authorities within the traditional political structure. Some of the accounts, for example, refer only to the legitimacy of district (*chinamit*) or lineage positions (Recinos 1950: 195–207, 1957: 165–169).[54] Certainly, too, the native documents continued to function as explanatory statements about the tenuous socio-political order of the sixteenth century. With the breakdown of the K'iche state by the Spaniards, intercommunity relations of significance were greatly diminished, and as a result the social "charters" that appear in the documents often refer to internal lineage and district divisions within K'iche communities (for example, Recinos 1950: 205–206, 1957: 24–67). The glories of lineages and other local structures were widely extolled and their relationships to other social units specified.[55]

Because native religious activities were suppressed by the Spaniards, the documents of the sixteenth century did not continue to function as divinatory texts or as repositories for myth and ritual. The latter function may have been served by the original PW for a short time, but for the most part native ritual was lost or continued only in attenuated form through ceremonial drama. Divination was practiced away from the surveillance of the Spaniards, and the only written expressions we have of it come from copies of calendrical texts made long after the Spanish Colonial Period (Berendt n.d.a [1685], n.d.b [1722]). After the Spanish invasion, divinatory knowledge and procedures appear to have been transmitted orally (Carmack 1966–1967).[56]

Finally, a close examination of the functions of K'iche history—both Pre- and early Posthispanic—suggests that the kind of history that purports to contain a chronological record of past events played only a limited role. Nevertheless, this form of so-called true history was important in the Annals and perhaps in the PW and can be detected in limited ways in most of the other documents of categories one and two. Since all of our K'iche documentation is Posthispanic, it is difficult to say to what extent chronological history was a carryover from aboriginal historiography rather than derived primarily from Spanish influence. In the case of the Annals, the late appearance of the dating system there and its close association with events of the Spanish invasion make the latter explanation more plausible. Surely the natives were greatly impressed with the recordkeeping of the Spanish scribes and with the historical accounts taught to them from the Bible.[57]

As explained previously, there was ample inducement from the Spaniards for the K'iche natives to produce documents containing accounts of their aboriginal condition, and this was intensified by the almost continuous demands by the Crown to have native history and customs recorded (such demands began in Guatemala at least as early as 1555) (Hernández Sifontes 1965: 176). The resulting K'iche documents of the early Posthispanic Period were largely indigenous in content and style, but they already revealed subtle traces of Spanish influence relative to every aspect of native life, including the degree to which chronological history was recorded.[58]

NOTES

1. A fuller discussion of the K'iche sources can be found in Carmack (1973), Edmonson (1985), and van Akkeren (2000).

2. Important new translations of the PW have appeared since this chapter was first written, including into English by Edmonson (1971) and D. Tedlock (1985). A new translation and analysis of the Annals by Judith Maxwell and Robert Hill II (2006) has now been published. To this should be added the *Título de Totonicapán*, translated into Spanish by Carmack and Mondloch (1983, 2007) based on the discovery of a copy of the original manuscript.

3. See the elegant translation of the *Rabinal Achí* from K'iche to Spanish and English by Breton (1999, 2007), the extensive translations and analysis of the same document by

Robert M. Carmack

van Akkeren (2000), and the recent English translation and exegesis by Dennis Tedlock (2003).

4. The *Título de Yax*, found with the collection of documents that contained the *Título de Totonicapán* manuscript, should be included in this second category; see Carmack and Mondloch (1989).

5. Five other category-three documents were found with the *Título de Totonicapán* and have been translated and published along with the Yax document by Carmack and Mondloch (1989).

6. Numerous Spanish administrative documents also provide useful information on aboriginal K'iche political, legal, demographic, and other cultural features (see Carmack 1973: 81ff). New information from Spanish sources on the Prehispanic K'iche continues to be found in the archives, such as a map prepared by Nahuatl-speaking warriors who assisted the Spaniards during the invasion of Highland Guatemala. Florine Asselbergs (2002) and Ruud van Akkeren (2007) have published analyses of the document along with color facsimiles of it.

7. Any attempt to understand the historical phases of the K'iche as found in the PW faces formidable difficulties. For much more sophisticated discussions of this issue than the account in this chapter, see the comments by Garrett Cook (2000) on K'iche cosmology of Momostenango and Dennis Tedlock (1985) in his discussion of history in the PW.

8. The locations of these early K'iche foundation settlements have been identified ethnographically in the northeastern zone of Santa Cruz del Quiché (Carmack 1981), although the validity of this finding is still contested by scholars such as Dennis Tedlock (1993) and Ruud van Akkeren (2000).

9. Dennis Tedlock (1985: 63), in the introduction to his translation of the PW, speaks of a transition from myth to history and in broad terms characterizes the PW as "mythistory." Ruud van Akkeren (2000: 3ff) goes farther than Tedlock in denying the historicity of K'iche documents such as the PW. He claims they were based primarily on oral myths and tales, the scribes only "mingling historical facts into myths." Van Akkeren (ibid.: 4) labels this kind of writing "mytho-historiography . . . a method that yields a history in writing that describes the past as it should have been rather than as it was."

10. The specificity of time and place in the K'iche sources makes it possible to relate the events of K'iche history to specific times and places, especially at Q'umarkaaj (Utatlán) (Carmack 1981).

11. For examples of recent discussions about conflicting views on K'iche history, see Carmack (1999, 2003a) and van Akkeren (2000).

12. Jorge Guillemin (1965, 1967); see also the recent description of the archaeology and ethnohistory of Iximché by Nance, Whittington, and Borg (2003).

13. For a study of chronology and errors in the Annals, see Timothy Smith (2002).

14. These observations hold as well for the recently discovered second-category K'iche document, the *Título de Yax*, from Totonicapán (Carmack and Mondloch 1989).

15. Nicholson's invaluable doctoral dissertation on the influence of the Quetzalcoatl tale throughout Mesoamerica, including the Highland Maya area, has finally been published (Nicholson 2001).

16. It is important to determine when Las Casas is referring specifically to the K'iche and when more generally to K'ichean peoples of the Highland Guatemalan region.

Nevertheless, many of the Highland peoples, including the Poqomam and K'iche, broadly shared cultural patterns (see Miles 1957).

17. The Guatemalan historian Severo Martínez P. (1970) has demonstrated that de Fuentes y Guzmán was the prototypical creole propagandist. He glorified the K'iche of the past but denigrated the colonized K'iche of his day.

18. While originally preparing this essay, I worked directly from the K'iche text published by Villacorta C. (1962), despite its defective orthography. More accurate versions of the text have been provided since then by Edmonson (1971), Estrada Monroy (1973), and Sam Colop (2001), among others. Colop and Carlos López (Marshall University) are currently preparing even more accurate transcriptions of the original text based on in situ study at the Newberry Library in Chicago.

19. Dennis Tedlock (1985: 28, 32) has suggested that the original PW manuscript may have included "an occasional hieroglyph" and argues that it might have been similar to the four Maya hieroglyphic books that have come down to us.

20. For commentary on the Tzutujil map, see Orellana (1984). The controversial Momostenango pictorial has an inscription in the K'iche language bearing the message that the K'iche ruler had received two of Motecuzoma's daughters in marriage. The version of the pictorial found at Buenabaj, Momostenango (Carmack 1995) reveals an iconography that appears to be more Spanish than K'iche, but it may be a copy of an earlier, more authentic original.

21. The *Título K'oyoi* document was listed as Quiché 103 in the Robert Garett Collection at Princeton University at the time I consulted it (Carmack 1973: 265ff). Important pictorials were included in the *Título de Totonicapán* manuscript discovered in that town (Carmack and Mondloch 1983), especially one portraying buildings in the Q'umarkaaj central plaza. This manuscript is a copy of an earlier sixteenth-century version, and accordingly the art style had clearly been altered. Several additional pictorials found in a series of documents in the Totonicapán collection evidently are also copies significantly altered from the original manuscripts (Carmack and Mondloch 1989).

22. For a scholarly reconstruction of the Prehispanic K'iche culture of Sacapulas, see Hill and Monaghan (1987).

23. The Quauhquecholan map produced by Nahuatl speakers from Puebla who accompanied Jorge de Alvarado in the Spanish invasion of Guatemala (Asselbergs 2002; van Akkeren 2007), along with the Tlaxcala pictorial (Acuña 1984), provide graphic examples of how Central Mexicans portrayed places and events subsequent to the Spanish invasion of Highland Guatemala. It is possible that such pictorial documents exercised stylistic and substantive influence on Early Colonial K'iche documents.

24. Archaeological investigations in the Sajcabajá area by A. Ledyard Smith (1955), and more recently by Ichon and other French scholars (Arnauld 1993; Ichon 1993), have identified several possible K'iche sites from the Late Postclassic Period.

25. At the time I observed the two Chichicastenango jade stones in the 1970s, I had hoped to send photographs of them to J. Eric Thompson for his comments, but with the passing of time I failed to do that. To my knowledge these pieces have never been analyzed by professional archaeologists. It is possible, of course, that they are not authentic.

26. The SUNY Albany Utatlán project uncovered additional painted murals similar in style to the paintings at Iximché (Carmack 1995). Unfortunately, in a recent summary

of the archaeology of the Iximché site (Nance, Whittington, and Borg 2003), the painted murals there are not discussed.

27. Michael Smith and other scholars of Mesoamerica prefer the more general term "Postclassic international styles" over the traditional Mixteca-Puebla designation (Smith and Berdan 2003).

28. For more recent studies of K'ichean calendrics, see B. Tedlock (1982), Edmonson (1988), and Carmack (1995: 87–89).

29. For a more recent description of Central Mexican calendrics, see Townsend (1992: 122ff).

30. Dennis Tedlock (1985: 60) argues that 52-year cycles were important in K'iche history and suggests that the composition of the Posthispanic text of the PW around 1558 corresponded with a new 52-year cycle in June of that same year. Furthermore, Tedlock (ibid.: 46, 54, 58) associates the K'iche "dawnings" with Venus cycles, which became the symbolic time frame for major developments in K'iche history (the trip to the underworld by the twin heroes, the return trip to the East by the sons of the founders of the K'iche "kingdom," later ritual fasts, and similar events). Tedlock (ibid.: 32) speculates that the original PW might have contained Venus tables indicating the rising and setting of that planet. Van Akkeren (2000: 348) claims to find evidence in the K'iche and Kaqchikel sources of a dating system based on 13-year cycles celebrated in a major calendrical ceremony (known as the *pokob*). Four such cycles would culminate in a 52-year "century" celebration such as the one organized by K'iq'ab in 1426(?) (ibid.: 354). I have argued elsewhere (Carmack 2003b), however, that van Akkeren's calendrical reconstructions have insufficient documentary support.

31. The identity of the authors of the PW has been the source of considerable debate among scholars. Adrián Recinos (1947) argued that Diego Reynoso was one of the authors of the PW. The *Título de Totonicapán* specifically states that this same K'iche lord authored at least one section of that document (Carmack and Mondloch 1983: 15). Dennis Tedlock (1985: 60–61) proposes that the "Great Toastmasters" (*Nim Ch'okoj*) mentioned at the very end of the PW text might be the authors, since they are identified as "mother-fathers" (*chuchqajaw*), which is to say, lineage spokesmen. Van Akkeren (2001) asserts that Diego Reynoso could not have been one of the authors of the PW because he belonged to an internal faction that opposed those who composed the PW text. Instead, he agrees with Tedlock that (a faction of) Ch'okoj officials were the authors of the PW. Van Akkeren's claim that these authors belonged to a lineage faction struggling to support the Kaweq version of K'iche history seems reasonable, but his assertion that they did not have access to a Prehispanic codex but instead relied on oral tradition seems dubious.

32. Myths are certainly not totally absent in modern K'ichean communities, as revealed in numerous ethnographic accounts; see especially Carmack (1979: 353ff), Cook (2000), and Shaw (1972).

33. I have written extensively on this topic (see especially Carmack 1995, 2003a). The oral transmission of tradition among the K'iche and related K'ichean peoples in Highland Guatemala has been studied in great detail by many other anthropologists, among the most important of which are David Carey (2001), Robert Carlsen (1997), Garrett Cook (2000), Edward Fischer (2001), Barbara Tedlock (1982), and John Watanabe (1984).

34. Garrett Cook (2000) has increased our understanding of K'iche ceremonial drama with his exegesis of tale and ritual in Momostenango. Edmonson (1985: 107ff)

has also further elaborated on his ideas about K'iche ceremonial dramas in an important summary; for example, he concludes that "it will be some time before the measured formality, farcical and sometimes satirical humor, sense of tradition and duty, and sense of time disappear from the discourse of the heirs of the *Popol Vuh*" (ibid.: 130).

35. Van Akkeren (2000) has made the Rabinal ceremonial drama the centerpiece of his complex reanalysis of Highland K'iche ethnohistory. He argues that the drama portrays a major "Poqob Dance" organized around the 52-year calendrical cycle. Also important are the new translations of the *Rabinal Achí* and elegant commentaries by Alain Breton (1999) and Dennis Tedlock (2003).

36. Again, van Akkeren (2000: 337) offers a unique interpretation of the Tolq'om ceremonial drama, arguing that the key ritual act was an "arrow sacrifice" derived from Central Mexican practices. It could also be performed as part of the so-called Poqob Dance.

37. See Edmonson (1985, 1997) for a comprehensive study of the cultural significance of the *Zaqi K'axol* drama. Edmonson (1997: 5) points out that the drama was also a dance and that it expressed traditional K'iche interest in "the play of fate" and "the element of human sacrifice."

38. I have described the way these ceremonial symbols served to integrate the commoners with the elite at the K'iche capital of Q'umarkaaj (Carmack 1981: 199ff). This is also one of the main arguments made by van Akkeren (2000) in his study of ritual symbols in Rabinal. Cook (2000) suggests that rural K'iche commoners were primary receptacles of traditional symbolism and ceremony, both in Prehispanic times and down to the present.

39. Many K'iche natives today, especially followers of the deceased charismatic intellectual Adrián Chávez, refer to the PW as *Pop Wuj* ([TIMACH] Centro de Estudios Mayas Adrián Chávez 1999, 2003). This is based on an entry in the Ximénez transcription of the PW text that by mistake left off the adjectival form *-al*. Although not linguistically defensible, use of the term *pop wuj* has come to symbolize the right of the K'iche themselves to interpret their own history and culture.

40. I witnessed such guardianship rites in Totonicapán and Momostenango (Carmack and Mondloch 1983; Carmack 1995). The ceremonial transfer of documents in Totonicapán has been studied by the Norwegian anthropologist Stener Ekern (2006) in his dissertation research on rural politics in Totonicapán.

41. This form of legitimization of authority was endemic to the Mesoamerican world (see Boone 2003: 207ff).

42. The best scholarly study of K'iche divination is by Barbara Tedlock (1982).

43. The ceremonial dramas were themselves undoubtedly a source for the codices, and vice versa. For more ambitious attempts to understand the relationships among mythology, ceremonial drama, and text in Prehispanic K'iche society, see van Akkeren's (2000) study of the *Rabinal Achí* document and Edmonson's (1985) general summary of K'iche literature.

44. I have explored the significance of these PW accounts for K'iche socio-political structure in detail (Carmack 1981: 148ff). Recently, Geoffrey Braswell (2003) has offered an alternative interpretation of these structural features based largely on archaeological information.

45. Alas, no K'iche codex has been found, and it is unlikely that one will ever come to light. Nevertheless, Colonial K'iche títulos unknown to the scholarly world probably

still exist in isolated communities of Highland Guatemala—among them, perhaps, even the original text of the PW transcribed by Ximénez.

46. Ruud van Akkeren (2000) makes the same oversimplification as Edmonson in arguing that the lineages were the main operative units in K'iche society. Braswell (2003) makes a similar interpretation in his account of Prehispanic K'iche political organization. As the PW and other K'iche documents make clear (Carmack 1995), the basic unit of K'iche society was the lineage-district organization. Elite lineages (*nim ja*) exercised political control over local territorial districts (*chinamit, calpules*), and these structures constituted the basic elements of the K'iche polities (and of other Mesoamerican polities as well).

47. For additional examples, see the Totonicapán documents (Carmack and Mondloch 1983, 1989).

48. The Sacapulas documents (Hill and Monaghan 1987) provide clear examples of such relationships, as do the Totonicapán documents (Carmack and Mondloch 1983, 1989) and Colonial documentation from Santa Cruz del Quiché (Carmack 1981: 305ff).

49. The dates of many of the early Posthispanic K'iche documents and the reasons for their preparation are discussed in greater detail in Carmack (1973: 11ff, 1981: 305ff), D. Tedlock (1985: 59–60), and van Akkeren (2000).

50. The ties to both royal Kiche lines and local leaders are amply illustrated by the Totonicapán documents (Carmack and Mondloch 1983, 1989). It might also be mentioned in the context of these documents that Tekum apparently resided in the Totonicapán area. As has been pointed out (Carmack 1979: 179ff), the term widely added in references to Tekum, "*umam*," is in fact a reference to Tekum's kinship relationship with the K'iche ruler (as "grandson") rather than to his name per se.

51. For discussion of the legitimization of authority in various K'iche communities carried out by descendants of Prehispanic rulers, see Carmack (1973, 1983, 1995) and van Akkeren (2000).

52. The Totonicapán documents (Carmack and Mondloch 1983, 1989) are the most explicit in making the connection between biblical traditions and Prehispanic K'iche history, although the connection is also made more briefly in other K'iche and Kaqchikel títulos. The newly discovered *Título de Totonicapán* has a long preface taken directly from Vico's *Theologia Indorum* (copies of which are located in various international archives, including the Biblioteque National in Paris) and was clearly designed to link K'iche with biblical history.

53. Documents found in Momostenango (Carmack 1995) provide additional information on the many ways the Posthispanic native authorities in that community, such as Cacique Diego Vicente, served the Spanish Church.

54. Other examples of traditional authorities continuing to function in the Colonial Period can be found in documents from Santa Cruz del Quiché (Carmack 1981), Momostenango (Carmack 1995), Sacapulas (Hill and Monaghan 1987), and from the Kaqchikel (Hill 1992) and Tzutujil (Orellana 1984) communities.

55. The survival of K'iche lineages into the Colonial and modern periods is documented in detail in my political ethnohistory of Momostenango (Carmack 1995, 2003a, 2003b).

56. The two most important sources on K'ichean divination are based on ethnographic studies carried out in the twentieth century by Colby and Colby (1981) and Barbara Tedlock (1982).

57. The general issue of interaction between Spanish and native historiographic processes deserves much more attention than could be devoted to it in this essay on K'iche historiography. Two of the most enlightening discussions on the issue for Mesoamerica are by Burkhart (1989) and Restall (2003).

58. In the original manuscript on which this chapter is based, an attempt was made to compare K'iche historiography with that of the Yucatec Maya. I pointed out in the earlier essay that Yucatec Maya historiography was heir to a Classic lowland Maya tradition that was more ritualistic and calendrical than the legacy received by the K'iche. Nevertheless, influence in Yucatán from the Itzá and other "Mexican" groups introduced political and historical tendencies into the area similar to those found in Mexican and K'iche historiography. This, in turn, suggests that the so-called Toltec (actually epi-Toltec) influence on the K'iche peoples probably played a central role in determining the chronological and political nature of K'iche historiography. Since my original essay was written, both epigraphic studies of the Classic lowland Maya (e.g., Schele and Freidel 1990; Grube 2001) and ethnohistoric studies of the Postclassic Yucatecan Maya (e.g., Freidel 1985; Quezada 1993) have suggested to Maya scholars that both Classic and Postclassic lowland Maya historiography was profoundly both chronological and political.

REFERENCES CITED

Acuña, René
 1966 El Junab Cakchiquel. La Palabra y el Hombre. *Universidad Veracruzana, Revista* 39: 427–439.
 1984 Tlaxcala. *Relaciones Geográficas del Siglo XVI*, vols. 2 and 3. UNAM, México, DF.

Archivo General de Centroamérica (AGCA)
 n.d.a Land Dispute from Santiago Atitlan, 1563. AI: 5946 (legajo)–53042 (expediente).
 n.d.b Map of Santo Domingo Sacapulas, and Fragment of Titulo (in K'iche). AI: 337–7091.
 n.d.c Título de Sacapulas (in Spanish). AI: 6025–53126.

Armas Lara, Marcial
 1964 *El renacimiento de la Danza Guatemalteca, y el origen de la marimba*. Ministerio de Educación Pública, Guatemala.

Arnauld, Marie-Charlotte
 1993 Los territorios políticos de las cuencas de Salamá, Rabinal y Cubulco en el Postclásico. In *Representaciones del espacio político en las Tierras Altas de Guatemala*, ed. Alain Breton, pp. 43–109. Cuadernos de Estudios Guatemaltecos 2, México, DF, and Guatemala.

Asselbergs, Florine
 2002 La conqista de Guatemala: Nuevas perspetivas del Lienzo de Quauhquecholan. *Mesoamerica* 44: 1–53.

Berendt, C. H.
 n.d.a Calendario de los Indios de Guatemala, Cakchiquel (1685). Copy of the original manuscript in the University of Pennsylvania Museum Library, Philadelphia.

n.d.b   Calendario de los Indios de Guatemala, K'iche (1722). Copy of the original manuscript in the University of Pennsylvania Museum Library, Philadelphia.

Boone, Elizabeth
   2003   A Web of Understanding: Pictorial Codices and the Shared Intellectual Culture of Late Postclassic Mesoamerica. In *The Postclassic Mesoamerican World*, ed. Michael E. Smith and Francis Berdan, pp. 207–224. University of Utah Press, Salt Lake City.

Brasseur de Bourbourg, Charles E.
   1862   *Grammaire de la Langue Quichée et RabInal-Achi. Collection de documents dans les langues Indigenas de l'Amérique ancienne*, vol. 2. Arthus Bertrand, Paris.

Braswell, Geoffrey
   2003   Highland Maya Politics: K'iche'an Origins, Symbolic Emulation, and Ethnogenesis in the Maya Highlands, A.D. 1450–1524. In *The Postclassic Mesoamerican World*, ed. Michael E. Smith and Francis Berdan, pp. 45–49. University of Utah Press, Salt Lake City.

Breton, Alain
   1999   *Rabinal Achi. Un drama dinástico maya del siglo XV*. Centro Francés de Estudios Mexicanos y Centroamericanos, México, DF.
   2007   *Rabinal Achi: A Fifteenth-Century Maya Dynastic Drama*. University Press of Colorado, Boulder.

Burkhart, Louise
   1989   *The Slippery Earth: Nahua-Christian Moral Dialogue in Sixteenth-Century Mexico*. University of Arizona Press, Tucson.

Carey, David
   2001   *Our Elders Teach Us: Maya-Kaqchikel Historical Perspectives*. University of Alabama Press, Tuscaloosa.

Carlsen, Robert
   1997   *The War for the Heart and Soul of a Highland Maya Town*. University of Texas Press, Austin.

Carmack, Robert
   1966–1967   Notes and Documents Gathered in Santiago Momostenanago. Papers in possession of the author.
   1966a   El ajpop quiché, K'uk'umatz: Un problema de la sociología histórica. *Antropología e Historia de Guatemala* 18: 43–50.
   1966b   La perpetuación del clan patrilineal en Totonicapán. *Antropología e Historia de Guatemala* 19: 43–60.
   1967   Análisis histórico-sociológico de un antiguo título quiché. *Antropología e Historia de Guatemala* 19: 3–13.
   1973   *Quichean Civilization: The Ethnohistoric, Ethnographic, and Archaeological Sources*. University of California Press, Berkeley.
   1979   *Historia social de los quichés*. Seminario de Integración Social Guatemalteca 38, Guatemala.

1981   *The Quiché Mayas of Utatlán: The Evolution of a Highland Guatemala Kingdom.* University of Oklahoma Press, Norman.

1983   Spanish-Indian Relations in Highland Guatemala, 1800–1944. In *Spaniards and Indians in Southeastern Mesoamerica: Essays on the History of Ethnic Relations,* ed. Murdo D. MacLeod and Robert Wasserstrom, pp. 215–252. University of Nebraska Press, Lincoln.

1995   *Rebels of Highland Guatemala: The Quiche-Mayas of Momostenango.* University of Oklahoma Press, Norman.

1999   El sistema político k'ichee según el Popol Wuj. In *Memorias del Segundo Congreso sobre el Popol Wuj,* pp. 253–260. Centro de Estudios Mayas, TIMACH, Quetzaltenango, Guatemala.

2003a Historical Anthropological Interpretations of Prehispanic K'iche-Mayan History. In *Misceláneas . . . en honor a Alain Ichon,* ed. M.-Charlotte Arnauld, Alain Breton, Marie-France Fauvet-Berthelot, and Juan Antonio Valdes. Centro Francés de Estudios Mexicanos y Centroamericanos and Asociación Tikal, Caudal, Guatemala.

2003b La política maya desde una perspectiva histórica. In *Memorias del Tercer Congreso Internacional sobre el Popol Wuj,* pp. 144–153. Centro de Estudios Mayas, TIMACH, Quetzaltenango, Guatemala.

Carmack, Robert, and James Mondloch

1983   *El Título de Totonicapán: Su texto, traducción y comentario.* Fuentes para el Estudio de la Cultura Maya 3. UNAM, Instituto de Investigaciones Filologicas, Centro de Estudios Mayas, México, DF.

1989   *Título de Yax, y otros documentos quichés de Totonicapán, Guatemala.* Fuentes para el Estudio de la Cultural Maya 8. UNAM, Instituto de Investigaciones Filologicas, Centro de Estudios Mayas, México, DF.

2007   *Uwujil Kulewal aj Chwi Miq'ina'. El Título de Totonicapán.* Cholsamaj, Guatemala.

Carrasco, Pedro

1967   Don Juan Cortés, cacique de Santa Cruz Quiché. *Estudios de Cultura Maya* 6: 251–266.

Caso, Alfonso

1939   La correlación de los Años Azteca y Cristiano. *Revista Mexicana de Estudios Antropológicos* 3 (1). México, DF.

1967   *Los calendarios prehispánicos.* UNAM, México, DF.

Colby, Benjamin, and Lore Colby

1981   *The Daykeeper: The Life and Discourse of an Ixil Diviner.* Harvard University Press, Cambridge, MA.

Colop, Sam

2001   *Popol Wuj. Versión poética del texto k'iche'.* Cholsamaj, Guatemala.

Contreras R., Daniel J.

1963   Temas y motivos bíblicos en las crónicas Indígenas de Guatemala. *Antropología e Historia de Guatemala* 15 (2): 46–58.

Cook, Garrett
    2000   *Renewing the Maya World: Expressive Culture in a Highland Town.* University of Texas Press, Austin.

Cortes y Larraz, Pedro
    1958   Descripción goegráfico-moral de la diócesis de Goathemala (1778–1780). *Biblioteca Goathemala de la Sociedad de Geografía e Historia* 20. Sociedad de Geografía e Historia, Guatemala.

Crespo, Mario
    1956   Títulos Indígenas de tierras. *Antropología e Historia de Guatemala* 8 (2): 10–15.
    1967   Títulos Indígenas de Guatemala. Unpublished thesis, Facultad de Humanidades, Universidad de San Carlos, Guatemala.

Edmonson, Munro S.
    1964   Historia de las tierras altas mayas, según los documentos indígenas. In *Desarrollo Cultural de los Mayas*, pp. 255–278. Seminario de la Cultura Maya, México, DF.
    1971   *The Book of the Counsel: The Popol Wuh of the Quiché Maya of Guatemala.* Middle American Research Institute (MARI) Publication 35. Tulane University, New Orleans, LA.
    1985   Quiché Literature. In *Literatures*, ed. Munro S. Edmonson, pp. 107–132. Supplement to the MARI, vol. 3, gen. ed. Victoria R. Bricker. University of Texas Press, Austin.
    1988   *The Book of the Year: Middle American Calendrical Systems.* University of Utah Press, Salt Lake City.
    1997   *Quiché Dramas and Divinatory Calendars.* MARI Publication 66. Tulane University, New Orleans, LA.

Ekern, Stener
    2006   Making Government: Community and Leadership in Mayan Guatemala. Faculty of Social Sciences, University of Oslo, Oslo, Norway.

Estrada Monroy, Agustín
    1973   *Popol Vuh. Traducido de la lengua quiché a la castellana por el R.P. fray Francisco Ximénez.* Editorial José de Pineda Ibarra, Guatemala.

Fischer, Edward
    2001   *Cultural Logics and Global Economics: Maya Identity in Thought and Practice.* University of Texas Press, Austin.

Freidel, David
    1985   New Light on the Dark Age: A Summary of Major Themes. In *The Lowland Maya Postclassic*, ed. Arlen Chase and Prudence Rice, pp. 285–309. University of Texas Press, Austin.

Fuentes y Guzmán, Francisco A. de
    1932–1934   *Recordación florida. Discurso historical y demostración natural, material, militaria y política del Reyno de Guatemala,* 3 vols. Biblioteca Goathemala 6–8. Sociedad de Geografía e Historia de Guatemala, Guatemala.

Gall, Francis
    1963   *Título de Ajpop Huitzitzil Tzunun. Probanza de méritos de los de León y Cardona.* Ministerio de Educación Pública, Guatemala.

García Elgueta, Manuel
    1962   *Descripción geográfica del Departamento de Totonicapán.* Guatemala Indígena 8, Guatemala.

Garibay, Ángel María
    1953   *Literatura nahuatl (primera parte).* Editorial Porrúa, México, DF.

Gibson, Charles
    1964   *The Aztecs under Spanish Rule: A History of the Indians of the Valley of Mexico, 1519–1810.* Stanford University Press, Palo Alto, CA.

Goubaud Carrera, Antonio
    1935   El "Guajxaquip Batz" ceremonia calendárica Indígena. *Anales de la Sociedad de Geografía e Historia de Guatemala* 12 (1): 39–52. Guatemala.

Grube, Nicholas, ed.
    2001   *Maya: Divine Kings of the Rain Forest.* Könemann, Cologne.

Guillemin, Jorge F.
    1965   *Iximche, capital del antiguo reino cakchiquel.* IDEAH, Guatemala.
    1967   The Ancient Cakchiquel Capital of Iximché. *Expedition* 9: 22–35.

Hernández Sifontes, Julio
    1965   *Realidad jurídica del indígena guatemalteco.* Ministerio de Educación Pública, Guatemala.

Hill, Robert
    1992   *Colonial Cakchiqueles: Highland Maya Adaptation to Spanish Rule, 1600–1700.* Case Studies in Cultural Anthropology. Harcourt Brace Jovanovich, New York.

Hill, Robert, and John Monaghan
    1987   *Continuities in Highland Maya Social Organization: Ethnohistory in Sacapulas, Guatemala.* University of Pennsylvania Press, Philadelphia.

Ichon, Alain
    1993   Los sitios postlclásicos de la cuenca de San Andrés Sajcabajá (El Quiché, Guatemala). In *Representaciones del espacio político en las tierras altas de Guatemala*, ed. Alain Breton, pp. 111–161. Cuadernos de Estudios Guatemaltecos 2, México, DF, and Guatemala.

Las Casas, Bartolomé de
    1958   *Apologética historia de las Indias.* Biblioteca de Autores Españoles 106, Madrid.

León, Juan de
    1955   *Diccionario Quiché-Español.* Editorial Landívar, Guatemala.

León Portilla, Miguel
    1961   *Los antiguos mexicanos a través de sus crónicas y cantares.* Fondo de Cultura Económica, México, DF.

Long, Richard C.E.
 1934   The Dates in the Annals of the Cakchquels and a Note on the 260-Day Period of the Maya. *Journal of the Royal Anthropological Institute* 64: 56–68.

Lothrop, Samuel K.
 1933   *Atitlán: An Archaeological Study of Ancient Remains on the Borders of Lake Atitlán, Guatemala.* Publication 444. Carnegie Institution of Washington, Washington, DC.

Martínez P., Severo
 1970   *La patria del criollo: Ensayo de interpretación de la realidad colonial guatemalteca.* Editorial Universitaria, Guatemala.

Maxwell, Judith M., and Robert M. Hill II, trans. and exegesis
 2006   *Kaqchikel Chronicles: The Definitive Edition.* University of Texas Press, Austin.

Miles, Susanna W.
 1952   An Analysis of Modern Middle American Calendars: A Study in Conservation. In *Acculturation in the Americas*, ed. Sol Tax, pp. 273–284. Twenty-Ninth International Congress of Americanists. University of Chicago Press, Chicago, IL.
 1957   *The Sixteenth-Century Pokom-Maya: A Documentary Analysis of Social Structure and Archaeological Setting.* Transactions of the American Philosophical Society 47, Philadephia, PA.
 1965   Sculpture of the Guatemala-Chiapas Highlands and Pacific Slopes, and Associated Hieroglyphs. In *Archaeology of Southern Mesoamerica*, Part 1, ed. Gordon R. Willey, pp. 237–275. Handbook of Middle American Indians, vol. 2, Robert Wauchope, gen. ed. University of Texas Press, Austin.

Nance, Roger, Stephen Whittington, and Barbara Borg
 2003   *Archaeology and Ethnohistory of Iximché.* University Press of Florida, Gainesville.

Nicholson, H. B.
 1955   Native Historical Traditions of Nuclear America and the Problem of Their Archaeological Correlation. *American Anthropologist* 57: 519–613.
 1957   Topiltzin Quetzalcoatl of Tollan: A Problem in Mesoamerican Ethnohistory. Unpublished PhD dissertation, Department of Anthropology, Harvard University, Cambridge, MA.
 1960   The Mixteca-Puebla Concept in Mesoamerican Archaeology: A Re-examination. In *Men and Cultures: Selected Papers from the Fifth International Congress of Anthropological and Ethnological Sciences (1956)*, pp. 612–617. University of Pennsylvania Press, Philadelphia.
 1967   The Concept of History in Pre-Hispanic Mesoamerica. Unpublished paper presented at the Congres International des Sciences Anthropologiques et Ethnologiques, Paris.
 1975   Middle American Ethnohistory: An Overview. In *Guide to Ethnohistorical Studies*, Part 4, ed. H. F. Cline, pp. 487–505. Handbook of Middle American Indians, vol. 15, Robert Wauchope, gen. ed. University of Texas Press, Austin.
 2001   *Topiltzin Quetzalcoatl: The Once and Future Lord of the Toltecs.* University Press of Colorado, Boulder.

Orellana, Sandra
    1984   *The Tzutujil Mayas: Continuity and Change, 1250–1630*. University of Oklahoma Press, Norman.

Quezada, Sergio
    1993   *Pueblos y caciques yucatecos, 1550–1580*. Colegio de México, México, DF.

Recinos, Adrián
    1947   *Popol-Vuh: Las antiguas historias del Quiché*. Fondo de Cultura Económica, México, DF.
    1950   *Memorial de Sololá, Anales de los Cakchiqueles. Título de los Señores de Totonicapán*. Fondo de Cultura Económica, México, DF.
    1957   *Crónicas Indígenas*. Editorial Universitaria, Guatemala.

Recinos, Adrián, Delia Goetz, and Silvanus G. Morley
    1950   *Popol Vuh, the Sacred Book of the Ancient Quiché Maya*. English translation of the Recinos Spanish version. University of Oklahoma Press, Norman.

Restall, Matthew
    2003   *Seven Myths of the Spanish Conquest*. Oxford University Press, Oxford, England.

Saenz de Santa María, Carmelo
    1940   *Diccionario cakchiquel-español*. Sociedad de Geografía e Historia de Guatemala, Guatemala.

Schele, Linda, and David Freidel
    1990   *A Forest of Kings*. William Morrow, New York.

Schultze Jena, Leonard
    1933   *Leben Glaube und Sprache der Quiché von Guatemala*. Indiana I, Jena, Germany.

Shaw, Mary
    1972   *Según nuestros antepasados . . . textos folklóricos de Guatemala y Honduras*. Instituto Lingüístico de Verano, Guatemala.

Smith, A. Ledyard
    1955   *Archaeological Reconnaissance Central Guatemala*. Publication 608. Carnegie Institution of Washington, Washington, DC.

Smith, Michael E., and Francis Berdan, eds.
    2003   *The Postclassic Mesoamerican World*. University of Utah Press, Salt Lake City.

Smith, Timothy
    2002   Skipping Years and Scribal Errors: Kaqchikel Maya Timekeeping in the 15th, 16th, and 17th Centuries. *Ancient Mesoamerica* 13 (1): 65–78.

Sociedad de Geografía e Historia de Guatemala (SGHG)
    1935   *Isogoge histórica apologética de las Indias Occidentales*. Biblioteca Goathemala 13, Guatemala.

Tedlock, Barbara
    1982   *Time and the Highland Maya*. University of New Mexico Press, Albuquerque.

Tedlock, Dennis
    1985   *Popol Vuh: The Definitive Edition of the Mayan Book of the Dawn of Life and the Glories of Gods and Kings*. Simon and Schuster, New York.

- 1993   Breath on the Mirror: Mythic Voices and Visions of the Living Maya. Harper, San Francisco, CA.
- 2003   Rabinal Achi: A Mayan Drama of War and Sacrifice. Oxford University Press, New York.

Termer, Franz
- 1957   Etnología y etnografía de Guatemala. Seminario de Integración Social Guatemalteca 5, Guatemala.

Thompson, J. Eric
- 1965   Maya Hieroglyphic Writing. In *Archaeology of Southern Mesoamerica*, Part 2, ed. Gordon R. Willey, pp. 632–658. Handbook of Middle American Indians, vol. 3, Robert Wauchope, gen. ed. University of Texas Press, Austin.

(TIMACH) Centro de Estudios Mayas Adrián Chávez
- 1999   Memorias del Segundo Congreso. Centro de Estudios Mayas Adrián Chávez, Quetzaltenango, Guatemala.
- 2003   Memorias del Tercer Congreso Internacional sobre el Pop Wuj. Centro de Estudios Mayas Adrián Chávez, Quetzaltenango, Guatemala.

Townsend, Richard
- 1992   The Aztecs. Thames and Hudson, London.

Tzutujil
- 1952   Relación de los caciques y principales del pueblo de Atitlán (1571). Anales de la Sociedad de Geografía e Historia de Guatemala 26, Guatemala.

van Akkeren, Ruud
- 2000   Place of the Lord's Daughter: Rab'inal, Its History, Its Dance Drama. Research School of Asian, African, and American Studies, University of Leiden, Leiden, The Netherlands.
- 2001   Authors of the Popol Wuj. Unpublished manuscript essay.
- 2007   La visión indígena de la conquista. Serviprensa, Guatemala.

Velázquez, Primo Feliciano
- 1945   Codice Chimalpopocatl: Anales de Cuauhtitlán y Leyenda de los Soles, vol. 1. Instituto Histórico, México, DF.

Vico, Fray Domingo de
- n.d.   Quiché-Spanish Dictionary. Copy of original in the Biblioteque National, Paris. Ayer Collection, no. 1586, Newberry Library, Chicago, IL.

Villacorta C., J. Antonio
- 1934   Memorial de Tecpán-Atitlán (Anales de los Cakchiqueles). Tipografía Nacional, Guatemala.
- 1962   Popol-Vuh, de Diego Reinoso. Ministerio de Educación Pública, Guatemala.

Watanabe, John
- 1984   Maya Saints and Souls in a Changing World. University of Texas Press, Austin.

Ximénez, Fray Francisco
- 1929   Historia de la provincia de San Vicente de Chiapa y Guatemala. Biblioteca Goathemala de la Sociedad de Geografía e Historia de Guatemala, vol. 1, Guatemala.

15

CONNECTING NAHUA AND MIXTEC HISTORIES

Kevin Terraciano

One of H. B. Nicholson's many contributions to the study of Mesoamerica was his work on the Mixteca-Puebla Style. In a brief but influential essay entitled "The Mixteca-Puebla Concept in Mesoamerican Archaeology: A Re-examination" (1960), Nicholson revisited three studies published by George Vaillant (1938, 1940, 1941) that outlined what he called a "culture" or "culture coplex" in the region of Puebla (Cholula, really) and the Mixteca of northeastern Oaxaca after the decline of Teotihuacan. Vaillant (1941: 83) considered the "civilization" that developed in this part of Highland Mesoamerica "the source and inspiration of Aztec civilization," filling a void created by the "Chichimec interregnum" in the Valley of Mexico and spreading beyond Central and Southern Mexico. Of course, subsequent excavations in Tula showed the extent of Toltec influences on the Valley of Mexico during this same period and the profound Tolteca-Chichimeca influences on the development of Aztec culture. Still, Nicholson revived Vaillant's construct in this essay and referred to it more precisely as a "style." The *Codex Borgia* and the decorative devices on Cholulan polychrome wares seemed to epitomize this style, which included numerous standardized symbols such as the stepped fret and the twenty *tonalpohualli* signs, vivid colors, a precision in delineation, and a bold exaggeration of prominent features reminiscent of the "modern caricature and cartooning of the Disney type" (Nicholson 1960: 614).

After defining and suggesting a number of sub-styles, Nicholson went on to argue that the Mixteca-Puebla Concept might also be called a "horizon style" in its broad spatial distribution (from Sinaloa to Central America), its narrow temporal distribution (not very narrow, actually, as it appears throughout much of the Postclassic Period), and its stylistic complexity and uniqueness. As to how such a style came about, Nicholson envisioned one possible scenario: "It is probable that, as both the Teotihuacan and Monte Albán traditions were sputtering out, a new stylistic synthesis was taking place (in which Xochicalco may have played an important role) somewhere to the east and south of the Valley of Mexico, possibly centered in Cholula" (ibid.: 616).

Ultimately, a "southern tradition" emerged, centered in Cholula and the Mixteca, that survived the breakup of Tula and continued to exert a strong influence on the Valley of Mexico during the Aztec ascendancy. In his unique writing style and authoritative tone, Nicholson proposed a "tentative reconstruction" of Vaillant's hypothesis that was as sweeping as the original idea and was, as he expected, bound to be "significantly modified by further analysis and excavation" (ibid.).

After the appearance of this stimulating article, Nicholson (1982) refined some of his ideas, and excavations at Cholula have confirmed the importance of this site for eastern and southern Highland Mesoamerica. Nicholson and Eloise Quiñones Keber (1994) edited a collection of essays that represent the most thorough treatment of the concept to date. In the introductory essay to this anthology, the editors observed that the diffusion of art style has been "closely correlated with the imperialistic expansion of polities" but that this "mechanism would not seem to be particularly applicable to the Mixtec-Puebla situation" (ibid.: xiv). They concluded that a combination of mechanisms, such as interdependent exchange and communication networks, contributed to the widespread diffusion of the tradition. Despite the importance of Cholula, there was no dominant center from which the style emanated. One multi-author essay in this collection (Neff et al. 1994) found the existence of multiple production centers of Late Postclassic polychrome vessels decorated with imagery similar to that featured in the *Codex Borgia Group* and the Mixtec codices.

In recent years, nobody has contributed more to this scholarship on the Mixteca-Puebla Concept than John Pohl, a student of Nicholson's at UCLA. Pohl views Cholula as a vital link in an extended network of communities, from Nahua Central Mexico to the Mixteca and the Valley of Oaxaca, that participated in a royal marriage alliance system. Gifts and trade goods, ideologies and rituals, and people circulated along this "alliance corridor," which linked many eastern Nahua communities (places such as Tlaxcala, Cholula, Huexotzinco, Cuauhtinchan, Tecamachalco, Tecali, and Acatlán) with the Mixteca Baja and Alta (including Tecomaxtlahuaca, Juxtlahuaca, Coixtlahuaca, Apoala, Yanhuitlan, Tlaxiaco, Tilantongo, and Teozacualco) and the Valley of Oaxaca (Cuilapan,

Zaachila, Mitla). Eventually, Tenochtitlan and Tetzcoco in the Valley of Mexico and Tututepec on the Coastal Pacific Plain represented the most extreme points of the network before Mexica expansion and the Spanish invasion interrupted the system.

Pohl's alliance system was more extensive and enduring than the Mexica Empire, which had only begun to make a direct impact on many of the above-mentioned places when the Spaniards arrived. In some places, such as Tlaxcala, the Mexica presence was minimal. Pohl (2004b: 398) downplays the archaeological and ideological importance of the Aztec capital, eschewing a tendency in Mesoamerican studies to attribute art and iconography, ideology and innovation to large military states. Pohl argues that what is often called Aztec actually predates in origin the rise of the Mexica capital by more than a century. He "de-centers" the empire when he argues that "there is no evidence that the Aztec ever contributed anything in the way of a great art or architectural style, much less a significant ritual program, to Mesoamerica, despite their extraordinary success in enriching themselves through conquest tribute" (ibid.).

Pohl argues that communities along this alliance corridor shared certain structural features, especially the prominence of *teuctli*, or lordly lineages, that were engaged in a marital alliance system that promoted the production and exchange of goods for ritual and consumption purposes. The writing systems in this multilingual area relied on widely recognized conventions and iconographic symbols that cut across ethnic and linguistic boundaries rather than on phonetic script based on a particular language (Pohl and Byland 1994: 197; Winter 1994:217). Donald Robertson (1959) called it the "International Style," in contrast to older Maya and Zapotec systems of writing, which relied on a single linguistic base. Pohl is more inclined to call the Mixteca-Puebla Style a "culture," returning to Vaillant's original terminology, because the interactions of so many people across such a wide area, and the multiple influences of these communities on each other, go beyond the stylistic traits found in codices and on ceramics. The culture was so dispersed throughout Nahua Central Mexico that Pohl (2004a: 41) has adopted the term *Nahua-Mixteca* to describe what has been called Mixteca-Puebla.

Working primarily with alphabetic Nahuatl-language texts written in the Colonial Period, James Lockhart has also looked beyond the conglomeration of tribute-paying states that made up the Mexica "Empire" to locate deeper, more constant cultural forms and modes of organization in the Nahua world. Lockhart (1992: 14) focused on the vitality and autonomy of the *altepetl*, the local ethnic state. In the extended Nahua sphere, centered in Central Mexico, he identified an "eastern Nahua area," most notable for the size and strength of the institution of the *teccalli* (literally "lordly house") in altepetl around Tlaxcala, Huexotzinco, and Cholula (Lockhart 1992: 102–109; see also Carrasco 1976 and Offner 1983: 132). Here Lockhart observed that every teuctli within an altepetl headed a teccalli, and every *pilli* (hereditary elite) belonged to a teccalli, approaching an organization by lineage that is rarely seen elsewhere among the Nahuas. In the west, including the entire Valley of Mexico, the term *teccalli* does not appear a single time in Nahuatl documents; instead, *tecpan* (literally, "where a lord is") was used, and the tecpan was generally restricted to the establishments (relatives, followers, buildings, and lands) of altepetl *tlatoque* (plural of *tlatoani*, hereditary ruler of altepetl). *Teteuctin* (plural of *teuctli*), are hardly mentioned, and the lands and dependents of lords seem to be part of the *calpolli* (subdivision of altepetl) structure. Some teccalli contained dozens of *pipiltin* (plural of *pilli*), so not every pilli was likely the child of a teuctli. Collateral relatives must have maintained a noble status, high-ranking mothers were important, and the female line was used to reckon descent for purposes of succession. Marriage would have occurred both within and outside the teccalli, making alliances with other teccalli.

Lockhart observed that the teccalli was so strong in some places that it seemed to overshadow the calpolli as the basic unit of socio-political organization within the altepetl. The teccalli seemed to exist apart from the calpolli, holding land as a corporation and considering a vast majority of the commoners (*macehualtin*, plural of *macehualli*) teccalli dependents, as in Cuauhtinchan and Tecali. In Huexotzinco, for example, whereas calpolli macehualtin had lands of their own, teccalli mecehualtin as dependents of teteuctin did not possess lands. But Lockhart hesitates to draw decisive conclusions as to how these differences ultimately affected the structure of the altepetl and its subunits, the calpolli or *tlaxilacalli*, indicating as many similarities as differences between the tecpan in the west and the teccalli in the east. Still, lordly establishments were notably different in the eastern Nahua world.

THE MIXTECA

My research on the Mixteca region of western Oaxaca, using Mixtec-language alphabetic and pictorial texts and Spanish-language legal records, has made comparisons between the two cultural regions more fruitful because now we are able to go beyond the Spanish terminology used to describe indigenous socio-political structures in the Mixteca (figure 15.1). I found many similarities between the structure and ideology of Nahua and Mixtec socio-political organization that I interpret as evidence of extensive contact between Nahua and Mixtec (and other) populations not related to Mexica imperial expansion (Terraciano 2000, 2001). The core area of my study, the Mixteca Alta, had begun to pay tribute to the Mexica Empire only two decades before the arrival of the Spaniards. Shared concepts and areal features reflect multiple generations of interaction.

The Mixtec-language corpus of archival sources with which I have worked includes more than twenty types of writing genres produced by *escribanos* of native *cabildos* (municipal councils), including last wills and testaments, crimi-

15.1. *Western Oaxaca and adjacent Puebla, showing the geographic divisions of the Mixteca and some locations mentioned in the text. After Terraciano 2001: 49. Map redrawn by Rusty van Rossmann.*

nal records, land transactions, cabildo election results, and petitions to Spanish authorities. Extant Mixtec-language sources span three centuries, from the 1560s to the first decade of the nineteenth century, covering the entire culture area from the Mixteca Baja to the Valley of Oaxaca, not including the Pacific Coast. Most of the Mixtec-language writings come from the Mixteca Alta, especially from the jurisdiction (*alcaldía mayor*) of Teposcolula and Yanhuitlan. This one jurisdiction consisted of several dozen communities in the Colonial Period.

In working with this documentation, I am especially concerned with the words and concepts the Mixtecs used themselves for their own communities, social relations, governing institutions, land tenure systems, and many other aspects of their internal organization. The repetition of familiar cultural patterns and conceptual vocabulary in each sub-region has allowed certain general conclusions that apply to the Mixteca as a whole. The same key concepts appear in native-language documents from three of the four sub-regions of the Mixteca: Alta, Baja, and Valley. Native terminology for an entire range of cultural categories, from socio-political organization to land tenure, is consistent in each region. When variation was observed, I noted the difference and searched for additional examples. Despite the importance of local exceptions to regional and cross-regional patterns, the exceptions do not alter the general picture.

Native-language writings reveal much of the ordinary vocabulary people used on a daily basis. The texts make repeated references to indigenous categories and concepts, which in many ways are valid for the immediate Preconquest and Postconquest periods. Inventing new categories, if Spanish-influenced, normally involved extending an existing etymon to the new concept, in which meaning was extended by metaphor or identification or relied on the use of a Spanish loanword. Mixtec escribanos continued to refer to fundamental concepts when they wrote documents and letters intended primarily for other native speakers. Some categories faded or disappeared by the time native-language writing was fully developed, such as slaves taken in warfare, but few totally new or transformed categories appear in the texts. Most new categories, concepts, and items can be identified readily as literal translations of Spanish introductions into Mixtec, such as *dzini ñuu*, "head town," for *cabecera*. Another strategy for handling introductions was to extend an existing etymon to the new concept, applying *ydzu*, or "deer," to the horse and mule, for example, and *ydzundeque*, "horned deer," to oxen. Yet another strategy was to extend a known equivalent and to use the word *castilla* to modify the new item, such as *tiñoo castilla* (Castilian turkey) for a chicken. Thus, terms for introductions tend to stand out in the Early Colonial *vocabularios* documenting the translation process from one language to the other.

One concept that stands out especially in writings from the Mixteca Alta and the Valley of Oaxaca is the repeated use of the self-ascribed term *ñudzahui* (pronounced ñudawi or ñudawi). The term means "the rain place" or "place of Dzahui," the rain deity.[1] Writers used this term to refer to people, their language, the region, communities, flora and fauna, and artifacts associated with their cultural zone. I observed the term *ñudzahui*, also written as "ñudzavui" or "ñudzaui," in the earliest and latest native-language texts from the Colonial Period, whereas I did not find the term *Mixtec* used in any of the same texts.

The English "Mixtec" and the Spanish "Mixteco" come from "Mixteca," the plural form of the Nahuatl *mixtecatl*, meaning "people of the cloud place," a Nahuatl term assigned to the people of this region by Nahuas and then reiterated and reinforced by Spaniards. I examined how specific social and cultural contexts influenced an individual's use of the term to address broader issues of ethnicity and identity. Ñudzahui people were surrounded by other groups and communities for whom they had specific names, including Nahuas (*tay ñucoyo*), Zapotecs (*tay ñucuisi*), and Chochos (*tay ñucuij*). Despite the existence of this more inclusive cultural and ethnic term, most people identified primarily with their home communities, as elsewhere in Mesoamerica. The next section compares selected Mixtec or Ñudzahui cultural concepts, structures, ideologies, and modes of organization with those of the Nahuas, beginning with some of the topics mentioned earlier in relation to Lockhart's study of the altepetl in the Early Colonial Period.

COMMUNITIES

In their own language, Ñudzahui or Mixtec writers in the Colonial Period referred to all settled places as *ñuu*. Many place names contain *ñuu* as a prefix, often reduced to *ñu*, such as Ñunduhua, Ñundaa, and Ñundecu. Mary Elizabeth Smith (1973: 38–39) discusses the use of this term in place names. In the Colonial Period and beyond, people continued to use their own names for places that were renamed by Nahuas and Spaniards in the sixteenth century; for example, the three places mentioned earlier were known to Spaniards as Guaxaca or Oaxaca (from the Nahuatl name Huaxyacac), Texupa or Tejupan (from the Nahuatl name Texocpan), and Achiutla (from the Nahuatl name Achiotlan), respectively. Mixtec writers always used the original Mixtec names for places rather than the Nahuatl-based place names the Spaniards adopted; some communities never were assigned Nahuatl-based place names and thus retained their original names. By whatever name, the ñuu was as central to local indigenous organization and identity as the altepetl in Central Mexico.

Many of the most prominent and populous ñuu in the Mixteca, however, were better known as *yuhuitayu* and were referred to as ñuu only in the most general sense as a settled place. A yuhuitayu resulted from the marriage of a hereditary lord (*yya*) and lady (*yya dzehe*), each of whom represented the lordly establishment of a separate ñuu. For example, in the mid–sixteenth century Doña María de Guzmán represented Ñundecu (Achiutla) and Dón Felipe de Saavedra represented Disinuu (Tlaxiaco); the yuhuitayu resulting from their marriage joined the resources of both ñuu until both rulers died (Archivo Judicial de Teposcolula [hereafter AJT], Civil, leg. 7, exp. 654). When Dón Felipe gave his last will and testament in 1573, he confirmed that his wife was to rule the yuhuitayu until she died, when the couple's eldest daughter would inherit

Dón Felipe's part belonging to Disinuu. A yuhuitayu could not exist without a married ruling couple.

The yuhuitayu is represented in Preconquest-style codices and Postconquest pictorial writings as a royal couple facing one another, seated on a *petate* (reed mat). The term *yuhuitayu* is a metaphorical doublet: *yuhui* is "reed mat" and *tayu* is "seat" or "pair," depending on tone (Mixtec is a tonal language); as a writing convention in the codices, *tayu* is a tone pun for both the seat of rulership and the married ruling couple. *Tayu* is given for "pair" (*par*) in the *Vocabulario*, and the term for "marido y muger casados" is *tay nicuvui tayu* (those who were paired or seated together) (Alvarado 1962 [1593]: ff. 161, 146). This familiar glyph represents a royal marriage but also a place and its rulers. The *petate* was a Mesoamerican symbol of authority. Nahua authors of the *Florentine Codex* and *Primeros Memoriales* associated the reed mat throne (*petlatl icpalli*) with the altepetl and its rulers. Whereas the Nahua tlatoani is depicted in Central Mexican codices seated alone on a reed mat, the Mixtec man and woman shared the mat, facing and gesturing toward one another. Mixteca codices reflected a construction of hereditary rule based on direct descent from high-ranking male and female elites, assigning each a comparable elite status (Schroeder 1991: 180). The *Codex Mendoza* and the *Florentine Codex*, among many other sources, depict the Nahua tlatoani as a solitary, seated male figure. Alfonso Caso (1992: 1: 30) recognized this difference but did not elaborate on its symbolic meaning (see also Smith 1973: 29–31; Jansen 1982: 1: 59–60). Using Spanish-language documentation, Ronald Spores (1967: 131–154) was among the first scholars to recognize the legitimate rights of female *cacicas* to inherit the rulership. High-ranking women and the female line were important for reckoning descent among Nahua elites as well, but the yuhuitayu placed more emphasis on the alliance of two lordly establishments from two separate ñuu, each represented by a male or a female ruler.

The yuhuitayu survived the Conquest and persisted throughout much of the Colonial Period. The term appears in the earliest and latest extant native-language archival sources, dated 1571 and 1807, respectively (Archivo General de la Nación [hereafter AGN], Tierras, vol. 59, exp. 2; AJT, Civil, leg. 18, exp. 1578). In Fray Francisco de Alvarado's *Vocabulario en lengua mixteca*, printed in 1593, the yuvuitayu, or "tayu" for short, is associated with a number of Spanish terms: "ciudad" is *tayu canu* (large tayu), "cabecera del pueblo" is *sacaa tayu* (where there's a tayu), "comunidad" and "pueblo" are also yuvuitayu (Alvarado 1962 [1593]: ff. 63v, 174v, 40, 28, 135, 174v). The terms ñuu and yuhuitayu were used in all parts of the Mixteca represented by Mixtec-language documentation—the Valley of Oaxaca, the Mixteca Alta, and the Mixteca Baja around Huaxuapa (Ñuudzai) and Tonalá (Ñuuniñe). Not all ñuu were yuhuitayu, however. Only a ñuu represented by a royal couple was also called a yuhuitayu. In general, the term was not used in reference to smaller settlements that lacked a lordly

15.2. *1580 map of Amoltepec (Yucunama) Oaxaca, showing a ruling couple (yuhuitayu) seated inside their* aniñe, *or palace. Yucunama is identified by a semicircular band of place glyphs (left) and a river (right). The glyphic reference to Yucunama lies south of the church. Courtesy, Benson Latin American Collection, University of Texas, Austin.*

establishment. For example, one Mixtec official distinguished between the yuhuitayu of San Pedro y San Pablo Yucundaa (Teposcolula) and the nearby ñuu of Santiago Yodzonduhua in 1681 (AJT, Criminal, leg. 5, exp. 550). Likewise, Dón Domingo de Celís, who came from San Pedro Mártir Yucunama (figure 15.2) to make his testament in the cabecera of San Pedro y San Pablo Teposcolula (Yucundaa), consistently called the former place a ñuu and the latter a yuhuitayu (AJT, Civil, leg. 7, exp. 689).

Ñuu and yuhuitayu were divided further into smaller constituent parts; terminology for these subunits varied by region. In the Mixteca Alta around Teposcolula, Tamasulapa, and Tlaxiaco, the term *siqui* was used. In the Mixteca Baja the term for a subunit of the ñuu was *dzini*, and in the area of Yanhuitlan it was *siña*. The differences among these three terms, other than regional usage, are unclear. Like the ñuu, the siqui and its equivalents were also named units. In the Colonial Period the number of siqui in a given ñuu varied considerably, from several to dozens. The relationship between ñuu and smaller subunits was fluid and dynamic. Distinctions between ñuu and siqui could be unclear. For example, members of the largest siña of Yanhuitlan, Ayusi, often called their home a "ñuu siña." Apparently, a siqui could achieve ñuu status by becoming independent of the composite structure. The dynamic nature of these Conquest era structures, which existed throughout the Mixteca, reflected a complex socio-political organization.

The yuhuitayu, the ñuu, and its constituent siqui, siña, or dzini represent a complex scenario comparable to Nahua socio-political organization in many important ways. The organization of the ñuu is comparable to the Nahua altepetl.[2] In Central Mexico the altepetl consisted of a number of separate, self-contained units. There were three Nahua terms for subdivisions of the altepetl—*calpolli*, *tlaxilacalli*, and *chinamitl*.[3] As in the Mixteca, differences among the three Nahua names for the subunit may have been related to regional variation or structure. For example, subunits of the ñuu in the Mixteca Baja called dzini were often attached to the patrimonies of lords, similar to the teccalli of the eastern Nahua area. Mixtec and Nahua constituent units had distinctive names that resembled other place names. Unlike the names of ñuu and altepetl, however, siqui and calpolli names rarely included the word "hill" (*yucu* and *tepetl*, respectively).

In both cases, a subunit could conceivably break off and become a larger unit without changing its name or internal political arrangements. Some Nahua calpolli were contiguous and were either two parts of a former whole or participated in some type of dual organization. Terminological evidence for this phenomenon exists in siqui names designating upper and lower versions. Also, several ñuu contained a sub-entity of the same name, suggesting that the smaller entity lent its name to the larger. At the level of macro-units, the ñuu of a yuhuitayu alliance resembles the *tlayacatl altepetl*, or the constituent altepetl of a composite state in Central Mexico, as described by the Nahua historian Dón Domingo de San Antón Muñón Chimalpahin Quauhtlehuanitzin (Schroeder 1991: 131–136). In both forms of organization, each constituent had a separate ruler. But the ñuu of yuhuitayu were not united permanently or joined as contiguous units within a bounded territory, as were the four altepetl of Tlaxcala, for example. In fact, the constituent ñuu of a yuhuitayu might be separated by considerable distance.

The shifting, cross-regional nature of the yuhuitayu brought people from different ñuu into contact with one another; sometimes different language communities lived in the same ñuu, organized into respective subunits. There are numerous examples of multilingual ñuu in the Mixteca, especially in the Chocho-Mixtec areas of Coixtlahuaca and Tamasulapa, and in the Valley of Oaxaca among Zapotec-speaking peoples, especially around Cuilapan. Many Mixtec-speaking groups lived in the Puebla-Cholula area as well, but we know little about them, although John Chance's (1996, 1997, 2000, 2006) research in western Oaxaca and Puebla promises to shed light on this matter. As Fray Antonio de los Reyes noted in the introduction to his *Arte en lengua mixteca*, printed in 1593, dynastic marriages occasioned the movement of people, who were relocated to serve a lord's household or lands. For example, the yya of Tilantongo brought a group of people to Teposcolula, who settled into "barrios" there, when he married a high-ranking noblewoman of that yuhuitayu (Reyes 1976 [1593]: xii; see also the Relación Geográfica of Tilantongo in Acuña 1984: 2: 232–233). Likewise, a marriage between the lordly establishments of Zaachila and Almoloyas moved a contingent of people into the Valley of Oaxaca, who formed the basis of a Mixtec settlement around Cuilapa (ibid.: 157–158, 178–181).

The relocation of people was part of a normal socio-political arrangement based on the residence patterns of yuhuitayu alliances. Male yya or female yya dzehe who moved to reside in a spouse's palace would have been accompanied by dependents and relatives who might constitute the basis of another siqui (siña or dzini) in the new place of residence. Sometimes yya or yya dzehe sent groups of people to establish settlements on distant patrimonial lands. This process continued in the Colonial Period. For example, a Mixtec cacique of Tlaxiaco founded a settlement called Ñuyucu, near the ñuu of Malinaltepec, when he sent ten married couples to work and live on (*poblar y guardar*) his lands at the end of the sixteenth century (AJT, Criminal, leg. 3, exp. 275). The periodic migration of people based on the ambilocal residence patterns of dynastic lords, taking their portable objects with them, must have contributed in some way to the diffusion of the Mixteca-Puebla Style.

Colonial changes altered but did not transform the yuhuitayu-ñuu-siqui configuration beyond recognition; that is why we can detect the basic defining features of this organization. When the Spaniards arrived in the Mixteca, they encountered several hundred dispersed settlements, separated by the mountainous landscape and numerous small valleys. The tragic loss in population during the sixteenth century must have contributed to the general appearance of dispersal. Spaniards created more manageable units by moving some of the outlying settlements to the center, relocating settlements from hilltops and slopes down to level valleys and plains, and recreating the semblance of a Mediterranean city, with its rural hamlets. These activities were called *congregación*. The purpose of congregación was to shape larger settlements into cities, reorganized according to the *traza* layout with important civil and ecclesiastical buildings arranged around a central plaza. In general, Spaniards did not grasp, or were not concerned with understanding, the complex and dynamic nature of Mixtec socio-political organization. They envisioned the Mixteca in terms of dominant centers with nearby "barrios" and more dispersed "estancias." They created permanent administrative centers with subordinate satellite settlements by recognizing the most prominent ñuu in a given area as cabeceras and designating all smaller ñuu and siqui as either *sujetos* (subjects) or barrios of the cabecera. Thus, the original organization of settlements in the Mixteca was obscured by Spanish-language documentation, which tended to overlook the relations of all the units and subunits.

HEREDITARY LEADERS

Hereditary elites were a prominent group of men and women who represented their communities and organized relations among all social groups in the Mixteca. This section considers the relationship between lordly establishments and the socio-political structures discussed earlier, focusing especially on four Mixtec concepts and institutions: *toniñe*, aniñe, *ñuhu*, and *tniño*. Hereditary rulers of the yuhuitayu were called *yya toniñe* (male) and *yya dzehe toniñe* (female). High elites bore the general title of yya and were customarily addressed or referred to with honorific pronouns. The conception of *sa toniñe*, or "rulership," was in many ways the equivalent of the Nahua tlatocayotl (Alvarado 1962 [1593]: f. 80v under "dignidad o señorio"). Since a yuhuitayu could not exist without a yya toniñe and a yya dzehe toniñe, the ruling couple was an important symbol of high status. In several maps drawn during the sixteenth century, including those done for the *Relaciones geográficas* around 1580, many yuhuitayu from the Mixteca included images of their ruling couples as proof of autonomy. In 1583 officials from Santiago Yolomecatl, a "sujeto" and "estancia" of Teposcolula, argued for independence from the cabecera on the grounds that they had their own ruling couple. Juan Bautista Contuta (3-Water, based on the Mixtec version of the 260-day sacred calendar) informed Spanish officials through an appointed translator that his ñuu refused to pay tribute to the cabecera because "we have our own caciques, dón Pedro and doña Juana" (AJT, Criminal, leg. 1, exp. 40). Yolomecatl did not achieve autonomy from the cabecera of Teposcolula for another century.

Spaniards recognized local hereditary rulers in the Mixteca, including women. Colonial officials used the term *cacica* to designate a *señora natural* (native female lord) of a *cacicazgo*. Cacica was the feminine equivalent of "cacique," a term Spaniards adopted in the Caribbean islands and applied to all native rulers in New Spain. A cacicazgo was the "sum and combination of all traditional rights, duties, privileges, obligations, services and lands pertaining to the title of a native ruler" (Spores 1967: 117). In other words, the cacicazgo was the Spanish legal interpretation of toniñe. In recognition of the two constituent parts of the yuhuitayu, Spaniards applied the legal concept of "joint person" (*conjunta persona*) status, which recognized a union of royal patrimonies in marriage but specified when a male cacique derived his authority in a given place from his wife's position. For example, in 1566 Doña Catalina de Peralta and Dón Diego de Mendoza were called "caciques" of Teposcolula. However, the cacica, Doña Catalina, came from Teposcolula and inherited the rulership; her husband, Dón Diego, was from Tamasulapa. Their relationship was clarified when they were called "caciques of Teposcolula, Doña Catalina and the said Dón Diego as her joint person" (AGN, Tierras, vol. 24, exp. 6).

Spanish judges often interpreted native concepts in terms of their own cultural categories. For example, in the proceedings involving Doña Catalina and Dón Diego, one lawyer reasoned that Dón Diego had the right to be cacique of Teposcolula "as husband and lord of the dowry" (*como marido señor de los bienes dotales*), invoking the concept of a European dowry and the man as master in marriage. Judges and lawyers in legal cases over cacicazgos applied Spanish principles and ideas regarding inheritance and succession. As Woodrow Borah (1983: 46) observed, citing this same case from Teposcolula as an example, Castilian rules of inheritance could be imposed at the expense of local custom. Claimants appealed to Spanish principles of succession and tailored their descriptions of "ancient customs" to serve their own particular ends. In this same case, lawyers assailed the competing claims of a cacique of Tilantongo as "bestial and against all reason" and dismissed his pictographic writings as lies (AGN, Tierras, vol. 24, exp. 6, f. 10v).

The Spanish principle of "conjunta persona" entitled men to represent the yuhuitayu in legal proceedings, even when their separate patrimonies were not at issue. In fact, the term was invoked only when a cacique represented a cacica's patrimony; the reverse was not necessary in the Colonial legal system. Similarly, when a cacique and a cacica appeared together before Spanish officials, the male generally represented the couple in the proceedings. The Spanish legal system accorded native noblewomen properties and titles by virtue of their birth and marriage, but they seldom spoke in the record, hardly ever wrote, and were barred from the formal political arena within their communities. The accepted norms of Spanish public discourse privileged male actors in the legal and political realms. As with Spanish women, cacicas were especially prominent as widows in Spanish-language sources.

THE ANIÑE, OR ROYAL RESIDENCE

In the Mixteca, yya toniñe or rulers of yuhuitayu lived in royal residences called aniñe.[4] The aniñe was the palace of the yya, usually equated in Spanish-language documents with a *palacio* or a Nahua tecpan. The function, floor plan, and exterior décor of palaces in the Mixteca were similar to those in Central Mexico. In general, single-story stone and adobe structures, each with its separate entrance, were arranged around sunken patios.[5] The 1579 Map of Teozacualco (called Chiyocanu in Mixtec) depicts a palace next to the new church. Four separate structures are arranged around a central patio, each with its separate entrance, with one entrance to the entire compound. The arched doorways represent Spanish influence. A string of yuhuitayu couples proceeds upward from the aniñe, representing recent generations of the ruling dynasty of Teozacualco.

Several descriptions of palaces confirm the basic layout of the Teozacualco aniñe. The aniñe of Yanhuitlan (Yodzocahi in Mixtec) was described in early-sixteenth-century documents as a complex of large houses containing nine patios (AGN, Tierras, vol. 400, exp. 1, and vol. 985, exp. 2). When Dón Juan Manuel de Guzmán stayed with his wife in the aniñe of Yanhuitlan, his quarters were described in terms of an *aposento*, a large room or lodging, with a patio, separate from but connected to the rest of the palace (AGN, Tierras, vol. 985, exp. 2, f. 75). In the 1540s witnesses testified that various yya came together in the palace, called "las casas de la cacique" in the Spanish-language document, for all important matters, including sacred ceremonies and feasts.[6] In 1630 the Jesuit Bernabé Cobo noted that the main patio of the palace complex was large enough to run bulls.[7] The palace was such an important structure that each of the four surviving *Relaciones geográficas* maps from the Mixteca (Teozacualco, Amoltepec, Texupa, and Nochixtlan) depicts an aniñe at the center of the composition.

We know more about the aniñe of Teposcolula (Yucundaa in Mixtec) than any other palace in the Mixteca. The aniñe was described in a legal case in the Tierras section of the Archivo General de la Nación, written in the 1560s, as multiple structures arranged around several patios, including one large patio in front of the enclosed complex that exited to the street (AGN, Tierras, vol. 24, exp. 6, ff. 3–55). According to the AGN document, the aniñe of Yucundaa stood "facing the monastery of the pueblo," on the very same site where the "casa de la cacica" stands today.[8] It is possible that the palace was named after the cacica Doña Catalina de Peralta (introduced earlier), heiress to the rulership of Yucundaa, who claimed the palace that had once belonged to the cacique Dón Felipe de Austria (named, ironically, after the Hapsburg monarch Philip II of Spain). She laid claim to the palace with ancient paintings and the last will and testament of her uncle, Dón Pedro Osorio, which was written before sixty native witnesses in 1566. Spanish officials conferred cacique status upon her after hearing testimony and reviewing all titles and documentation pertaining to the case. She and her husband, Dón Diego de Mendoza, a lord of Tamasulapa, were confirmed and blessed by a priest in the church. A Spanish official then led them to the palace, where a door was unlocked, and led them by their hands into the complex. According to the document, the palace consisted of a building with several rooms and multiple contiguous structures arranged around sunken patios, each with its separate entrance.

When Doña Catalina took possession of her aniñe, she and Dón Diego walked through the entire complex with several yya and Spanish officials. The royal couple entered the main patio and, before all the witnesses, sat on a reed mat together as a sign of true possession. The ceremony personified the image of the yuhuitayu depicted in the codices: ruling figures seated on reed mats, usually inside or in front of a palace. The royal palace was the actual site of a reed mat throne, the seat of power where the lords lived and ruled. The act of seating was performed five times, once in each separate part or aposento of the complex. The couple sat on "petates y asientos de indios" (reed mats and Indian seats) or "petates e yquipales" (from the Nahuatl *icpalli*—the document was written in Spanish, using some Nahuatl loan vocabulary). The only part of the complex where they did not take a seat was the "aposento de cocina" (kitchen room), although the couple entered and took possession of it together. Doña Catalina and Dón Diego passed through the entire complex, opening and closing doors and windows and throwing stones from one side of a patio to another. Some doors were unlocked with a key. The couple then escorted everyone from the house, locking them out, as the final sign of true possession.

The ritual of slamming doors and throwing stones resembles typical Spanish ceremonial acts of possession in New Spain. The act was part of a legal proceeding that generated a written record and title, presided over by the Spanish *alcalde mayor* or an *audiencia* judge. Spanish influences on the ceremony also featured rituals of repetition and gesture, including the throwing of stones and slamming of doors. These acts emphasized the sanctity of private property in the sense that rightful owners could do as they pleased in their own houses. Similarly, kicking the sod, tearing up grass, and throwing sticks and stones were typical ceremonial acts associated with taking possession of land in Spain and New Spain. As a final act of "true possession," the owners threw the guests out of the palace and locked the door behind them.

Just as the ceremony combined Spanish and Mixtec gestures and rituals, the "casa de la cacica" blended multicultural architectural features, including European hinged doors and windows and Mixtec decorative facades and sunken patios. Recent excavations of the complex have revealed much more. Sebastián van Doesburg and Enrique Lastra (n.d.) are preparing a study of the structure and a description of its restoration. The principal structure that faces a road includes a fireplace and chimney, multiple rooms with walls supporting a wooden ceiling, arches, windows, doors—all in the European building tradition of the time. The stonework combines European and Mixtec techniques. However, adjacent structures were built in the Mixtec tradition: single-room dwellings with thick supporting pillars, traditional hearths, and a single entrance. The patio of the palace was so large that witnesses from Teposcolula claimed in 1639 that about 100 men and women had gathered there (AJT, Criminal, exp. 4, leg. 447).

The sprawling complex is located on a slope next to the Dominican church and convent. The palace is aligned almost directly with the outdoor open-air chapel of the church so that the new aniñe overlooked a new sacred site (Kiracofe 1995). When the settlement of Teposcolula was moved from the nearby hilltop to the valley floor, the lords needed a new residence. Spores and Nelly Robles

García (2007) have presented some startling preliminary findings of their excavations of the original Yucundaa, on top of the hill overlooking the colonial site of Teposcolula. The añine was constructed around the same time the church was being built. The Mixtec nobility and Spanish authorities must have reached an agreement over the construction of the buildings. Mixtecs also built a hospital and several other buildings in the new traza of the cabecera of San Pedro y San Pablo Teposcolula.

In the Mixteca the añine was assigned a specific name and attached to named lands within a named entity. The archival record contains numerous references to named palace structures that were located in named socio-political units. For example, in 1691 Doña Lázara de Guzmán, yya dzehe from a siqui of the yuhuitayu of Yucundaa (Teposcolula), described an añine in her testament in these terms: "attached to the siqui barrio [named] Yaasayhe is the lordly tayu palace [named] Ñuuñañu which belongs to this tayu cabecera" (*tnaha siqui bario yaasayhe yia tayu añine ñuuñañu maã tayu dzini ñuu yaha*) (AJT, Civil, leg. 4, exp. 417). She bequeathed the añine to her three sons: "I leave in the hands of my sons the tayu palace Ñuuñañu and all the cultivated lands of the palace and all the palace lands of Ñuuñañu" (*añine tayu ñuuñañu sihi nee cutu solar ñuhu añine sihi ndehe tacaca ñuhu añine ñuuñañu yaha ndehe yonachihindi ndaha dzayandi*). In 1572 Doña María de Paredes, cacica of Teposcolula, referred to her añine in the siqui called Tanduaa (AGN, Tierras, vol. 34, exp. 1, f. 82). As late as 1708, nearly two centuries after the Conquest, a group of nobles in Yolomecatl referred to the "palace of the lord Dón Agustín Carlos Pimentel y Guzmán called Dzahuico" (*añine yia don Agustin Carlos Pimentel y Gusman yonani dzahuico*).[9]

The location of añine in particular sub-entities of a community was also common in the Mixteca Baja. For example, Dón Jorge de la Cruz Alvarado's palace was located within a specific dzini of Tequistepec in 1678, which he called "my house palace in the dzini of ñuchiyo" (*huehiyu aniy dzini ñuchiyo*). Like most royal palaces, Dón Jorge's añine contained an archive of legal documents and paintings supporting the patrimonial claims of his lordly establishment. He possessed a *satno ñuhu tutu* (chest of land documents) that contained "the land documents and testaments of my grandparents" (*ñuhu tutu testamendo si siy sitnayu*) and "all the papers concerning lands and the cloths [i.e., *lienzos*] of the borders" (*dihi cutu tutu saha ñuhu dayu dzoo dzaño*).[10]

LAND AND HOUSEHOLD

One cannot speak of lordly establishments, called cacicazgos by Spaniards, without mentioning land. Land was called *ñuhu* in the general sense and *ytu* in reference to the cultivable plot. In general, land tenure and use was based on the *huahi* (house). The organization and structure of the huahi and *cahi* (house and patio) complex is similar in nearly all respects to the Nahua calli and ithualli, as discussed by Lockhart (1992). In both Central Mexico and the Mixteca Alta, several separate living quarters or "house structures," each with its own entrance, were arranged around a central patio. The Nahuatl calli and Mixtec huahi could refer to the single structures of a household or to the entire complex. The complex was often walled off to create an enclosure, with one shared entry, that united the household. The aniñe, the most elaborate huahi of the siqui or ñuu, conformed to this same pattern. Recently, two archaeologists working on separate field projects in the Teposcolula area, Verónica Pérez and Laura Diego Luna, have found evidence confirming my descriptions of houses and palaces, based on the documentary record.

The average land possession consisted of a main holding on which the house was located and a number of scattered plots; primary responsibility for separate plots was divided among household members. The site of the main land held by a household was called *ñuhu huahi*, or "house land," where the huahi and cahi (patio) complex was located. It was the site of a house as well as a sizable plot of cultivable land.[11] As the best and oldest plot passed down from one generation to the next, house land was usually associated with *ñuhu chiyo*, or "patrimonial land." Chiyo referred to an "altar" or a sacred, ancient site associated with ancestors. Lords used the term *chiyo* in reference to their *ñuhu aniñe*, or "palace lands." Beyond the house land, other fields, or ytu, were scattered within or outside the ñuu's borders.

Part of the ñuu's lands was controlled by its largest household, the aniñe, whose members relied on landless workers or dependent laborers (called *ñandahi*, the same term used for non-nobles or "commoners," who constituted about 90 percent of the native population) to cultivate its fields and provide other services and goods to the palace in return for a percentage of the yield. Distinctions between aniñe lands and corporate lands belonging to the ñuu (*ñuhu ñuu*) or siqui (*ñuhu siqui*) were sometimes unclear and contested. In contrast to the abundance of documents referring to the lands of lordly establishments, relatively few sources mention lands belonging to the siqui or ñuu. This fact may be in part a result of the prominence of caciques in the Colonial legal record, but the relative scarcity of information on corporate lands may also indicate that noble houses subsumed many of the corporate landholding responsibilities otherwise exercised by siqui and ñuu. The situation is comparable to the eastern Nahua culture area around Puebla and Tlaxcala, where teccalli may have subverted or replaced the structure and corporate powers of the altepetl and its subdivisions, the tlaxilacalli or calpolli (Lockhart 1992: 24, 102–109; Chance 1996: 475, 502). This tendency was especially pronounced in the Mixteca Baja, where lords frequently referred to the lands and laborers of entire dzini as part of their patrimonies.

References to ñuhu aniñe located in specific siqui or ñuu are common in the Colonial Period. Most yya and yya dzehe claimed significant amounts of land. Dón Gabriel de Guzmán, yya toniñe of Yanhuitlan, represents an extreme example; of the 102 plots of named land he claimed in 1580, 56 were located in communities outside his home ñuu of Yodzocahi (Yanhuitlan), indicating the extensive cross-regional nature of landholdings associated with the aniñe (AGN, Civil, vol. 516). Mixtec writers continued to refer to ñuhu aniñe (palace lands) in the late seventeenth and eighteenth centuries. In comparison, the use of Nahua terminology for nobles' lands in Central Mexico was rare by the later period; the term *tecpantlalli* does not appear in extant documents after the early 1600s (Lockhart 1992: 174–175). The term *tecpantlalli*, the equivalent of ñuhu aniñe, fell out of use in the early seventeenth century. In Coyoacan and Culhuacan, the term hardly appears at all (Cline 1986: 145–146; Lockhart 1992: 163; Horn 1997: 121; for Cuernavaca, see Haskett 1991: 72–73).

Even if nobles' lands in Central Mexico did not become entirely indistinguishable from corporate lands, the disappearance of these categories signifies changes in land tenure and use. These differences may be related to the relative strength of Mixtec and Nahua lordly establishments within corporate communities. Another decisive factor in the continued vitality of the Mixtec aniñe was the low rate of Spanish immigration to the Mixteca and the relatively slow development of Spanish estates in the region, which allowed many yya to consolidate properties and maintain continued access to labor, despite severe population loss. The Mixteca compares with the Valley of Oaxaca in this regard, where many cacicazgos remained relatively intact by the Late Colonial Period (Taylor 1972).

Unlike Central Mexico, Oaxaca was a relatively remote region of New Spain, with few Spanish residents. Population estimates for the Mixteca Alta indicate that only about 4 percent of households were not indigenous in 1746 (Spores 1984: 106–108). Teposcolula and Yanhuitlan had the highest percentage of non-native households. In contrast to the Valley of Mexico, many caciques and communities in the Mixteca were not forced to compete with aggressive Spanish interests for lands in the Late Colonial Period. If some caciques and cacicas suffered setbacks in the later Colonial Period, others adapted to Colonial changes and competition, avoided costly legal disputes with factions or won the support of audiencia judges, continued to profit from extensive landholdings, and, in some places, even maintained traditional labor arrangements.

The organization and tenure of land in the Mixteca resembled a general pattern described for the Nahuas. Mixtec land tenure categories included ñuhu huahi (house land), ñuhu chiyo (patrimonial land), ñuhu aniñe (palace land), ñuhu ñuu (land belonging to the ñuu), *ñuhu siña* (land belonging to the siña), and *ñuhu nidzico* (purchased lands). These categories correspond with the Nahua callalli, huehuetlalli, tecpantlalli, altepetlalli, calpollalli, and tlalcohualli, respectively, as discussed by Lockhart (1992) and Rebecca Horn (1997). The basic distinction between ñuhu aniñe and ñuhu ñuu in the Mixteca resembles the distinction between tecpantlalli and altepetlalli in Central Mexico. Inheritance patterns, the sale and purchase of lands, and many other features of land tenure, organization, distribution, and use are comparable to patterns described for the Nahuas. Likewise, tribute mechanisms, long-distance trade, and highly organized local market systems were common features in both culture areas.

TNIÑO, OR DUTY

The aniñe was a social entity as much as a building. It was the residence of a community's elites, providing room and board for the yya and *toho* (lesser nobles) who lived and ate there. Several yya stated in the sixteenth century that they fed and accommodated the "principales" who lived or stayed in the palace. For example, in 1573 Dón Gabriel de Guzmán, yya toniñe of Yanhuitlan, testified that many people periodically assembled and resided in his palace. He claimed he was obligated by ancient custom to serve them food and drink many times each week (AGN, Tierras, vol. 985, exp. 2, f. 47; vol. 400, exp. 1, f. 80v). To assist him in this obligation, he declared that he needed twelve men and twelve women (married couples) to prepare food and drink. He reminded Spanish officials that previous rulers had enjoyed many more servants and privileges. To feed themselves and others, caciques relied on a number of male and female ñandahi (commoners) to work in their palaces, in addition to the men and women who cultivated their lands and provided tribute items such as food and cloth. Normally, women prepared food and made tortillas, whereas men brought water, wood, and other materials to the palace and maintained the physical structure. Typically, married couples from the ñuu fulfilled this collective, rotating duty by serving for brief periods of eight to twenty days. Dón Gabriel reciprocated the couples' services by feeding them and giving them a daily quantity of cacao beans.

Before the Conquest, nobles gathered in the aniñe to organize the community's tniño. The concept of tniño encompassed an entire range of activities governing the assessment, paying, and collection of tribute, labor, and services. Tniño is very similar to the Nahuatl *tequitl* or *coatequitl* and can be translated as "work" or "duty." Tniño also refers to civic responsibility and the charge of office. As a form of labor organized at the household and corporate levels, tniño was the basis of everything the community produced. After the Conquest, Spaniards introduced a form of local municipal government by elected native officials called the *cabildo*. The cabildo drew upon existing forms of organization and incorporated many Preconquest political functions, from administering local justice to collecting taxes, as Charles Gibson (1964: 172–173), Robert Haskett (1991), and Lockhart (1992: 38) have shown for the Nahuas. Continuities were important for the rapid transition to Spanish-style government, which took root by the 1560s in most cabeceras of the region. Normally, the hereditary male ruler occupied the highest office of governor, while other elected positions rotated among the highest male lords and nobles from various constituents of the yuhuitayu. Women were excluded from the official political decision-making functions of the cabildo.

In the Early Colonial Period, the functions of the cabildo were associated with the performance of tniño. Mixtec-language terminology ascribed to cabildo offices is revealing for its conscious choice of native equivalences, indicating how the roles of the native municipal council were interpreted in the light of Preconquest practices. Alvarado (1962 [1593]: f. 40) noted that cabildo members were called *tay natnay tniño* (those who order/arrange the duty). The *Vocabulario* of 1593 defined "public office" as *tniño yuvuitayu* (yuhuitayu duty) and one's office simply as tniño (ibid.: ff. 174v and 166v). The term *tniño* was also associated with offices in the Colonial religious hierarchy; the "fiscal de la yglesia" was called *tay ñoho tniño huahi ñuhu*, or "person in charge of the church tniño" (ibid.: f. 111). In Teposcolula, elected cabildo officials were referred to as *yya toho coo tniño*, or "lords, nobles who arrange the tniño" (AJT, Criminal, leg. 6, exp. 705). According to Alvarado (1962 [1593]: f. 116) the highest cabildo officeholder, the governor, was "one who commanded the tniño" (*tay yotasi tniño*). One Mixtec writer who adopted the loan word "governador" in 1709 still used tniño as a qualifying term when he called the cacique and governor of Teposcolula "the ruler Dón Agustín Carlos Pimentel y Guzmán, tniño governor of the [yuhui] tayu of Teposcolula" (*yia toniñe don nagusti Carlo Pimentel y Guzmán tniño gobernador teyu yucundaa*) (AJT, Civil, leg. 6, exp. 586).

Terminology for the office of governor includes references to sheltering and providing cover for people, in the spirit of social relations. In addition to one who orders the tniño, a governor was defined as "one who guards the tayu" (*tay yondadzi tayu*), one who "provides cover" and "protects" people, employing the verbs *dzadzahui* and *dzaquete* (Alvarado 1962 [1593]: f. 116). Another entry is *tay yocuvui ñuu*, which could mean "one who is in front" or "one who is the face, the eyes," perhaps in reference to leadership. These descriptive acts resemble the "shade and covering" metaphor of the Nahuatl difrasis *in pochotl in ahuehuetl* (cyprus and silk cotton tree), used in reference to a governor's responsibility toward his people. This phrase was used repeatedly in Nahua election documents from Cuernavaca in reference to the governor's protection of his community (Haskett 1991: 88). Like the Mixtec use of "tniño" for cabildo offices, Nahuas used the word *tequitl* for these duties.[12]

The association of tniño with political and religious office indicates that yya and toho elites performed specific duties or work on behalf of their communities. The important service-oriented nature of cabildo offices, representing the community internally and externally, qualifies the premise that the nobility was exempt from labor service. Lords and commoners alike owed specific tniño and responsibilities to the community. Before the Conquest, elites offered tribute in goods but not in manual labor; however, they performed other types of tniño involving ritual warfare, religious ceremony, political office, and civil administration. In the Colonial Period male elites served on the cabildo, performing a range of tasks and labor essential to the functioning and representation of the community, including the very important charge of organizing tniño. In many places the building in which the cabildo met, called the audiencia or *la casa de la comunidad* in Spanish, and the aniñe were one and the same building. Just as yya and toho convened to discuss community affairs in the aniñe in Preconquest times, the Colonial cabildo often continued to meet in the palace.[13]

CONCLUSION

In anthropology and art history, mutual influences in style and various shared conventions in Central Mexico and Oaxaca have been recognized by the term *Mixteca-Puebla*. This chapter explores other manifestations of influence that reflect extensive contact between Nahuas and Mixtecs and other language groups in Highland Mexico. In 1994 Nicholson and Quiñones Keber called for additional archaeological evidence to understand the concept's diffusion: I have indeed found this in the documentary record. Similarities in the socio-political organization of communities, in terminology for social hierarchies and relations among elites and commoners, in the structural design of palace and household complexes, in terminology for land tenure classifications, and in concepts of labor and tribute owed to a community—all are too alike to be coincidental. Such close similarities suggest deeper, more profound processes of cultural interaction that predated the Mexica Empire and outlasted the Spanish Conquest. Colonial records, especially native-language documents, can reveal cultural patterns rooted in the Preconquest period. In this chapter I have attempted to follow Nahua and Mixtec footprints across the sands of time, detecting patterns and traces of contact. Nahuas and Mixtecs were not entirely alike, of course; there were significant local differences even within each language group. People who spoke what we call Nahuatl and Mixtecan languages shared many traditions, practices, and beliefs that transcended language differences and local variations. No doubt, other Mesoamerican groups contributed to this dynamic interaction, such as the Chocho (called "Ngiwa" in their own language) of the Coixtlahuaca Valley area (Parmenter 1982; Castillo-Tejero 1994; Doesburg and van Buren 1997; Rincón Mautner 1999; Doesburg 2003) and the Zapotecs of the Valley of Oaxaca (Oudijk 2000).

In addition, I have said nothing about sacred matters, another fertile common ground. Religious practices and beliefs represent a complex synthesis of shared Mesoamerican features and local differences. A prominent sacred force associated with rain, Dzahui, is a Ñudzahui version of the Nahua Tlaloc. Dzahui was (and still is in some places) among the most prominent numina in the Mixteca, while Tlaloc shared the Templo Mayor of Tenochtitlan with the

Mexica patron deity Huitzilopochtli. Sacred books from the Mixteca Alta depict Postclassic pilgrimages Mixtec ancestors made to Central Mexico, to Tollan and Cholollan (Jansen and Pérez Jiménez 2007). Codices feature sacred figures well-known in Central Mexico yet ascribe unique local characteristics and bestow separate names based on the Mixtec version of the Mesoamerican 260-day sacred calendar. Quetzalcoatl was known as 9 Wind in the Mixteca; his legendary story is told from a decidedly local perspective, despite his pan-Mesoamerican fame. Cecelia Klein's (1980) study of Tlaloc and Nicholson's (2001) of Quetzalcoatl probe the complexities of these rich topics.

Detailed comparisons of Mixtec and Nahua cultures seem to dispel the idea that the Nahuas and a prominent group at the time of the Spanish arrival, the Mexica or "Aztecs" of Tenochtitlan, had surpassed the peoples of adjacent culture areas in their political and cultural development. The Mixteca was not a province of petty chiefdoms on the periphery of an empire with a more sophisticated center. Centuries of interaction and mutual influence had a profound influence on both culture areas, and the evidence of this contact is as palpable in the documentary record of the sixteenth century as it is in the archaeological record of the Late Postclassic Period. In this densely populated, multi-ethnic Highland area of Mexico, local and regional variations on shared cultural and ideological themes were the rule rather than the exception. It is only appropriate that these connected Nahua and Mixtec histories be manifest in many ways, not only in terms of art style. I conclude, as Nicholson did in his work on the Mixteca-Puebla Concept—further analysis is needed.

NOTES

1. The term *place of Dzahui* refers to the rain deity (or deities), comparable to the Nahua Tlaloc(s). Early Colonial Period Inquisition records from Yanhuitlan reveal that the rain deity was a supreme sacred force in this area. In the Colonial Period the most typical alternate spelling was "dzavui" or "davui." Some friars who studied the language and attempted to develop and promote a standardized orthography in the Mixteca Alta distinguished *vui* from *hui* and wrote *dzavui* instead of *dzahui*; according to this scheme, *vu* plus a vowel was distinguished from *hu* plus a vowel in that the latter marked a medial glottal before [w]. But "dzahui" was a common form used by native escribanos in documents written during the Colonial Period. The phonetic value of *dz* ranged from [d] to [ɖ] in this period, depending on the area. This term is still used by many Mixtecan speakers in reference to themselves in many parts of the Mixteca, and it is spelled and pronounced many different ways, as it was in the Colonial Period. I found no references to the term *ñudzahui* in native-language records from the Mixteca Baja. The amount of extant documentation from the Baja is limited in comparison to the collection from the Alta. No other equivalent term has been observed in the Baja. The coastal region is entirely unrepresented in the native-language corpus, and people from the Alta referred to them as *tay ñundevui*. However, many native speakers from the coastal region call themselves "nusawi" today.

2. Even though *yuhuitayu*, *ñuu*, and *dzini* were the operative terms for sociopolitical entities in the Mixteca Baja, I have also seen the term *yucunduta*, "hill and water," the semantic equivalent of the Nahua altepetl, used in documentation from this area. I have not seen "yucunduta" elsewhere in the Mixteca, except in Alvarado's *Vocabulario*, which seems to have drawn on many different manuscript sources from friars who had worked throughout the Mixteca.

3. Similarly, few concrete distinctions have been made among the three Nahua terms. The Nahua annalist Chimalpahin tended to associate tlaxilacalli with subdivisions of an established altepetl and calpulli with subdivisions of wandering ethnic groups (Schroeder 1991: 210).

4. The words *toniñe* and *aniñe* are apparently related, similar to the way the Nahuatl *tecpan* (palace, literally "place of the lord[s]") is derived from *teuctli* (lord). In Mixtec the prefix "a" usually refers to a place or a "place within," and the term *niñe* itself is associated with royalty and perhaps blood (*neñe*).

5. On palace structures in Central Mexico, see Evans (1991) and Kubler (1948). Book XI of the *Florentine Codex* (Sahagún 1982) and the *Codex Mendoza* (f. 62, for example) feature Nahua representations of the tecpan (Berdan and Anawalt 1997).

6. AGN (Inquisición, vol. 37, exp. 10, f. 195v). Spanish writers normally used "casas" in reference to a large structure with multiple components.

7. Letter of March 7, 1630, reproduced in Jiménez Moreno and Mateos Higuera (1940: 49).

8. AGN (Tierras, vol. 24, exp. 6, ff. 29–40). For a fuller treatment of this document, see Terraciano (2000: 16–19, 2001: 160–164) and Restall, Sousa, and Terraciano (2005: 81–86).

9. AJT (Civil, leg. 8, exp. 724). *Dzahuico* means either "rain cloud" or "feast of Dzahui" (the rain deity).

10. AGN (Tierras, vol. 245, exp. 2, f. 85). *Huehi* (house) and *aniy* (palace) were Mixteca Baja variant spellings of *huahi* and *aniñe* in the Teposcolula area of the Mixteca Alta.

11. Ñuhu huahi resembles the Nahua category of land called callalli, which usually referred to the most fertile, valuable land of the household. For discussions of Nahua land tenure in the Colonial Period, see Cline (1986: 125–159), Gibson (1964: 257–299), Horn (1997: 111–143), and Lockhart (1992: 141–176).

12. Molina's *Vocabulario* (1977 [1571]: f. 90) defines "oficio publico" as *altepetequipanoliztli*, or "altepetl working." Interestingly, in the Late Colonial Period Nahua nobles had the same tribute obligations as commoners when not holding office (Lockhart 1992: 132).

13. The *Vocabulario* refers to the "place where the cabildo meets" as the *huahi tniño* (duty house). The "audiencia" was the *huahi sini tniño* (duty hearing house), or the place where speeches and petitions were heard. Alvarado (1962 [1593]: ff. 30, 40). The term *audiencia* could refer to the building as much as to the body of electors.

REFERENCES CITED

Acuña, René
    1984   *Relaciones geográficas del siglo XVI: Antequera*, 2 vols. UNAM, México, DF.

Alvarado, Fray Francisco de
    1962 [1593] *Vocabulario en lengua mixteca*, ed. Wigberto Jiménez Moreno. INAH, México, DF.

Berdan, Frances F., and Patricia Rieff Anawalt
    1997 *The Essential Codex Mendoza*. University of California Press, Berkeley.

Borah, Woodrow
    1983 *Justice by Insurance: The General Indian Court of Colonial Mexico*. University of California Press, Berkeley.

Carrasco, Pedro
    1976 Los linajes nobles del Mexico antiguo. In *Estratificación Social en la Mesoamérica Prehispánica*, ed. Pedro Carrasco and Johanna Broda, pp. 19–36. Centro de Investigaciones Superiores, INAH, México, DF.

Caso, Alfonso
    1992 *Reyes y Reinos de la Mixteca*, 2 vols. Fondo de Cultura Económica, México, DF.

Castillo-Tejero, Noemí
    1994 Los Popolocas y la Region Mixteca-Puebla. In *Mixteca-Puebla: Discoveries and Research in Mesoamerican Art and Iconography*, ed. H. B. Nicholson and Eloise Quiñones Keber, pp. 175–188. Labyrinthos, Culver City, CA.

Chance, John K.
    1996 The Caciques of Tecali: Class and Ethnic Identity in Late Colonial Mexico. *Hispanic American Historical Review* 76 (3): 475–502.
    1997 The Mixtec Nobility under Colonial Rule. In *Códices, Caciques, y Comunidades*, ed. Maarten Jansen and Luis Reyes García, pp. 161–178. Cuadernos de la Historia Latinoamericana 5. Asociación de Historiadores Latinoamericanistas Europeos, Leiden, The Netherlands.
    2000 The Noble House in Colonial Puebla, Mexico: Descent, Inheritance, and the Nahua Tradition. *American Anthropologist* 102 (3): 485–502.
    2006 Marriage Alliances among Colonial Mixtec Elites: The Villagómez Caciques of Acatlan-Petlalcingo. Paper presented at the Annual Meeting of the American Society for Ethnohistory.

Cline, Susan L.
    1986 *Colonial Culhuacan, 1580–1600: A Social History of an Aztec Town*. University of New Mexico Press, Albuquerque.

Doesburg, Sebastian van
    2003 El siglo XVI en los lienzos de Coixtlahuaca. *Journal de la Société des Américanistes* 89 (2): 67–96.

Doesburg, Sebastian van, and Enrique Lastra
    n.d. *La casa de la cacica en Teposcolula: Arquitectura mixteca del siglo XVI*. Fundación Alfredo Harp Helú A.C., Oaxaca.

Doesburg, Sebastian van, and Olivier van Buren
    1997 The Prehispanic History of the Valley of Coixtlahuaca, Oaxaca. In *Códices, Caciques, y Comunidades*, ed. Maarten Jansen and Luis Reyes García, pp. 103–

160. Cuadernos de la Historia Latinoamericana 5. Asociación de Historiadores Latinoamericanistas Europeos, Leiden, The Netherlands.

Evans, Susan T.
    1991   Architecture and Authority in an Aztec Village: Form and Function of the Tecpan. In *Land and Politics in the Valley of Mexico*, ed. H. R. Harvey, pp. 63–92. University of New Mexico Press, Albuquerque.

Gibson, Charles
    1964   *The Aztecs under Spanish Rule: A History of the Indians of the Valley of Mexico, 1519–1810*. Stanford University Press, Stanford, CA.

Haskett, Robert
    1991   *Indigenous Rulers: An Ethnohistory of Town Government in Colonial Cuernavaca*. University of New Mexico Press, Albuquerque.

Horn, Rebecca
    1997   *Postconquest Coyoacan: Nahua-Spanish Relations in Central Mexico, 1519–1650*. Stanford University Press, Stanford, CA.

Jansen, Maarten
    1982   *E.R.G.N. Huisi Tacu: Estudio interpretativo de un libro mixteco antiguo: Codex Vindobonensis Mexicanus I*, 2 vols. Centrum voor Studie en Documentatie van Latijns Amerika, Amsterdam, The Netherlands.

Jansen, Maarten, and Aurora Pérez Jiménez
    2007   *Encounter with the Plumed Serpent: Drama and Power in the Heart of Mesoamerica*. University Press of Colorado, Boulder.

Jiménez Moreno, Wigberto, and Salvador Mateos Higuera, eds.
    1940   *Códice de Yanhuitlán*. Edición en facsímile con un estudio preliminar. INAH, México, DF.

Kiracofe, James B.
    1995   Architectural Fusion and Indigenous Ideology in Early Colonial Teposcolula. The Casa de la Cacica: A Building at the Edge of Oblivion. *Anales de Instituto de Investigaciones Estéticas* 66: 45–84.

Klein, Cecelia
    1980   Who Was Tlaloc? *Journal of Latin American Lore* 6 (2): 155–204.

Kubler, George
    1948   *Mexican Architecture of the Sixteenth Century*, 2 vols. Yale University Press, New Haven, CT.

Lockhart, James
    1992   *The Nahuas after the Conquest: A Social and Cultural History of the Indians of Central Mexico, Sixteenth through Eighteenth Centuries*. Stanford University Press, Stanford, CA.

Molina, Fray Alonso de
    1977 [1571]   *Vocabulario en lengua castellana y mexicana y mexicana y castellana*. Editorial Porrua, México, DF.

Neff, Hector, Ronald Bishop, Edward Sisson, Michael Glascock, and Penny Sisson
    1994   Neutron Activation Analysis of Late Post Classic Polychrome Pottery from Central Mexico. In *Mixteca-Puebla: Discoveries and Research in Mesoamerican Art and Iconography*, ed. H. B. Nicholson and Eloise Quiñones Keber, pp. 117–142. Labyrinthos, Culver City, CA.

Nicholson, H. B.
    1960   The Mixteca-Puebla Concept in Mesoamerican Archaeology: A Re-Examination. In *Fifth International Congress of Anthropological and Ethnological Sciences*, ed. Anthony F. Wallace, pp. 612–617. University of Pennsylvania Press, Philadelphia.
    1982   The Mixteca-Puebla Concept Revisited. In *Art and Iconography of Late Post-Classic Central Mexico*, ed. Elizabeth H. Boone, pp. 227–254. Dumbarton Oaks, Washington, DC.
    2001   *Topiltzin Quetzalcoatl: The Once and Future Lord of the Toltecs*. University Press of Colorado, Boulder.

Nicholson, H. B., and Eloise Quiñones Keber, eds.
    1994   *Mixteca-Puebla: Discoveries and Research in Mesoamerican Art and Iconography*. Labyrinthos, Culver City, CA.

Offner, Jerome
    1983   *Law and Politics in Aztec Texcoco*. Cambridge University Press, Cambridge, England.

Oudijk, Michel
    2000   *Historiography of the Benizaa: The Postclassic and Early Colonial Periods (1000–1600 A.D.)*. Research School of Asian, African, and Amerindian Studies, Leiden, The Netherlands.

Parmenter, Ross
    1982   *Four Lienzos of the Coixtlahuaca Valley*. Dumbarton Oaks, Washington, DC.

Pohl, John M.D.
    2004a   Nahua Drinking Bowl with an Image of Xochiquetzal. *Princeton University Art Museum Record* 63: 41–45.
    2004b   Screenfold Manuscripts of Highland Mexico and Their Possible Influence on Codex Madrid: A Summary. In *Codex Madrid: New Approaches to Understanding an Ancient Maya Manuscript*, ed. Gabrielle Vail and Anthony Aveni, pp. 367–413. University of Colorado Press, Boulder.

Pohl, John M.D., and Bruce Byland
    1994   The Mixtec-Puebla Style and Early Postclassic Socio-Political Interaction. In *Mixteca-Puebla: Discoveries and Research in Mesoamerican Art and Iconography*, ed. H. B. Nicholson and Eloise Quiñones Keber, pp. 189–200. Labyrinthos, Culver City, CA.

Restall, Matthew, Lisa Sousa, and Kevin Terraciano
    2005   *Mesoamerican Voices: Native-Language Writings from Colonial Mexico, Oaxaca, Yucatan, and Guatemala*. Cambridge University Press, Cambridge.

Reyes, Fray Antonio de los
    1976 [1593] *Arte en lengua mixteca.* Publications in Anthropology 14. Vanderbilt University, Nashville, TN.

Rincón Mautner, Carlos
    1999 Man and the Environment in the Coixtlahuaca Basin of Northwestern Oaxaca, Mexico: 2000 Years of Historical Ecology. PhD dissertation, Department of Geography, University of Texas, Austin.

Robertson, Donald
    1959 *Mexican Manuscript Painting of the Early Colonial Period: The Metropolitan Schools.* Yale University Press, New Haven, CT.

Sahagún, Fray Bernardino de
    1982 *Florentine Codex Book 11: Earthly Things.* Translated from the Nahuatl with notes by Arthur J.O. Anderson and Charles E. Dibble. University of Utah Press, Salt Lake City.

Schroeder, Susan
    1991 *Chimalpahin and the Kingdoms of Chalco.* University of Arizona Press, Tucson.

Smith, Mary Elizabeth
    1973 *Picture Writing from Ancient Southern Mexico: Mixtec Place Signs and Maps.* University of Oklahoma Press, Norman.

Spores, Ronald
    1967 *Mixtec Kings and Their People.* University of Oklahoma Press, Norman.
    1984 *The Mixtecs in Ancient and Colonial Times.* University of Oklahoma Press, Norman.

Spores, Ronald, and Nelly Robles García
    2007 A Prehispanic (Postclassic) Capital Center in Colonial Transition: Excavations at Yucundaa Pueblo Viejo de Teposcolula, Oaxaca, Mexico. *Latin American Antiquity* 18 (3): 333–353.

Taylor, William
    1972 *Landlord and Peasant in Colonial Oaxaca.* Stanford University Press, Stanford, CA.

Terraciano, Kevin
    2000 The Colonial Mixtec Community. *Hispanic American Historical Review* 80 (1): 1–42.
    2001 *The Mixtecs of Colonial Oaxaca: Ñudzahui History, Sixteenth through Eighteenth Centuries.* Stanford University Press, Stanford, CA.

Vaillant, George C.
    1938 A Correlation of Archaeological and Historical Sequences in the Valley of Mexico. *American Anthropologist* 40 (4): 535–573.
    1940 Patterns in Middle American Archaeology. In *The Maya and Their Neighbors*, ed. Clarence L. Hay, Ralph Linton, Samuel K. Lothrop, Harry L. Shapiro, and George C. Vaillant, pp. 295–305. D. Appleton-Century, New York.

1941   *Aztecs of Mexico. Origin, Rise and Fall of the Aztec Nation.* Doubleday, Garden City, NY.

Winter, Marcus
1994   The Mixteca Prior to the Late Postclassic. In *Mixteca-Puebla: Discoveries and Research in Mesoamerican Art and Iconography*, ed. H. B. Nicholson and Eloise Quiñones Keber, pp. 201–222. Labyrinthos, Culver City, CA.

PART V
THE COLONIAL PERIOD

16

THE FINAL TRIBUTE OF TENOCHTITLAN

Lawrence H. Feldman

INTRODUCTION: 1519–1521

When the Spaniards first arrived in Tenochtitlan in November 1519, they examined everything they saw. They dismounted from their horses, remounted, but then dismounted again and again so as not to miss anything of interest. When the Spaniards entered the Royal House, they placed Motecuhzoma under guard and kept him under their vigilance. After the Spaniards were installed in the palace, they asked Motecuhzoma about the city's resources and reserves and about the warriors' ensigns and shields. They questioned him closely and then demanded gold. Motecuhzoma guided them to it. They formed a circle around him and crowded close with their weapons while he walked in the center of the circle. When they arrived at the treasure house called Teucalco, the riches were brought out to them: ornaments made of quetzal feathers, richly worked shields, disks of gold, the necklaces of the idols, gold nose plugs, gold greaves, bracelets, and crowns. The Spaniards immediately stripped the feathers from the gold shields and ensigns. They gathered all the gold into a great mound and set fire to everything else, regardless of its value. Then they melted down the gold into ingots. As for the precious greenstones, they took only the best of them; the rest were snatched up by the Tlascaltecas. The Spaniards searched through the entire treasure house, questioning and quarreling as they did so, and seized every object they thought was beautiful.

Next they went to Motecuhzoma's storehouse in the place called Totocalco, where his personal treasures were kept. The Spaniards grinned like little beasts and patted each other with delight. When they entered the hall of treasures it was as if they had arrived in paradise. They searched everywhere and coveted everything; they were slaves to their own greed. All of Motecuhzoma's possessions were brought out: fine bracelets, necklaces with large stones, ankle rings with little gold bells, the royal crowns, and all the royal finery—everything that belonged to the king and was reserved for him only. The Spaniards seized these treasures as if they were their own, as if this plunder were merely a stroke of good luck. When they had taken all the gold, they heaped everything else in the middle of the patio.

This situation did not last, for Cortés had to return to the Caribbean Coast to defeat a Spanish rival and the Aztecs, provoked by a massacre during his absence, rose up against the Spanish garrison. The return of Cortés resolved nothing; his attacks were evaded or repulsed, and Cortés then left Tenochtitlan. The retreat quickly turned into a massacre on the causeway leading out of the city through the waters of the great lakes, and very few Spaniards escaped with their lives. The Aztecs gathered up everything the Spaniards had abandoned in their terror. When a man saw something he wanted, he took it and it became his property; he hefted it onto his shoulders and carried it home. They also collected all the weapons that had been left behind or fallen into the water: the cannons, arquebuses, swords, spears, bows and arrows, along with the steel helmets, coats of mail and breastplates, and shields of metal, wood, and hide. They also recovered the gold ingots, gold disks, tubes of gold dust, and *chalchihuite* collars with their gold pendants.

The Spanish reconquest of the great Aztec city would consume more than another year and would not be completed until 1521, after many thousands of lives had been lost. When the Spaniards regained Tenochtitlan, they recovered some of the gold they had previously abandoned in their flight, but much remained lost.

ARCHIVAL TREASURE: 1981

In 1981 I was doing research at the Archivo General de Indias in Seville, Spain. This was a repository founded in the late eighteenth century with records from the Archivo de Simancas (near Valladolid). It contained the earliest information on the sixteenth-century Spanish conquests in the New World. There were descriptions of the lands and, most important, administrative detail of the lands under Spanish rule. The records are generally very detailed from the time of the viceroys (1540s), but I learned that there are also significant data from an earlier era.

A section of special interest in the Archivo but neglected by most was called the Contaduria (what today we would term "accounting"). The Contaduria contained the tribute records, or what the Indians paid in-kind to the Spanish overlords. It began for the area I was then interested in, the Audiencia of Guatemala, in the late 1540s. By using these records one could learn the amount individual Indian towns paid to the Spaniards. This was a good way to discover which places, for example, were ceramic manufacturing centers or where the gold-producing areas were located.

A large section dealing with the Audiencia de Mexico had similar but somewhat older data. The Mexican Contaduria began in the 1530s. At the time this did not concern me. What was of interest, however, and what startled me greatly was a *legajo* (bundle of papers) from one part of Contaduria that began in 1521, the final year of the initial Conquest of Central Mexico, which listed the earliest tribute given to the Spaniards by various Indian embassies. There were sections from the "Province of Michoacan," the independent State of Tehuantepec, various Mexica provinces, and—most important—Tenochtitlan. Most surprising, there were thirty-three objects obtained during the "taking" of the City of Tenochtitlan, recorded on the "23rd day of August of 1521."

I never got around to publishing this list of thirty-three objects, and, as far as I know, no one else has done so. Therefore, I thought this might be an appropriate offering in memory of H. B. Nicholson, who did so much with the Mexica past. Here, then, is the last tribute of Tenochtitlan, obtained during the "taking" of the City of Tenochtitlan, recorded on the twenty-third day of August of 1521:

1. One head of a small duck with a greenstone in the head; weight: 3 pesos, 4 tomins[1]
2. Another large head of a duck with a greenstone and another blue; weight: 39 pesos and 4 tomins
3. Two pieces of gold with greenstones; total weight: 12 pesos and 4 tomins
4. One flower of greenstone mounted in a gold bell; total weight: 24 pesos and 4 tomins
5. One death head of greenstone with some trimmings of greenstone mounted in gold; total weight: 25 pesos
6. One gold piece with a greenstone that has the open mouth of an owl; weight: 22 pesos, 4 tomins
7. One crab of greenstones and gold; weight: 14 pesos
8. Another greenstone mounted in gold, which has two moving pieces of gold; weight: 38 pesos, 4 tomins
9. Another greenstone mounted in gold, with green marble with a gold trimming; weight: 12 pesos
10. Another perforated greenstone mounted in gold; total weight: 26 pesos, 4 tomins
11. A head of gold hair that has a face of greenstone; weight: 17 pesos, 4 tomins

12. Another head of greenstone with two ears of the same stone, with some attached trimmings in gold; weight: 14 pesos and 4 tomins
13. A piece of white snail shell with a greenstone with gold trimmings at its extremities and gold thread; not weighed
14. Two pieces of gold one puts in one's ears, with some red and blue stones; total weight: 10 pesos
15. A necklace of green peach stones that come from a flower, with the flowers and weight of gold; there are thirty-two pieces in the string; total weight: 119 pesos
16. Two trimmings, each of which has four silver claws of an eagle of silver and gold; not weighed
17. Two other trimmings that have four greenstones framed in gold; not weighed
18. Another trimming of gold that has ten pieces like reeds that have two nails of greenstone framed in gold; not weighed
19. An armlet of ocelot hide that has four green pieces and four low-quality gold sweepings (?); not weighed
20. Three green beads with small tubes of gold balls inside them; not weighed
21. A square piece of greenstone mounted in gold, with trimming of greenstone and gold; weight: 31 pesos
22. A shell like a scallop mounted in gold, with a greenstone in the middle; not weighed
23. Another large shell mounted in gold, with a green face and stones from the neck of a blue and yellow face; not weighed
24. A gold butterfly with mica wings and body and head of greenstone; not weighed
25. Another scallop mounted in gold, with owl eyes and a greenstone for the head; not weighed
26. Another scallop of the same kind, with a red beak and blue ears; not weighed
27. Two other scallops, one purple and the other yellow, with a path of stones in the middle and blues mounted in gold; not weighed
28. Another white scallop like a brush mounted in gold; not weighed
29. A yellow snail head mounted in gold; not weighed
30. A gold butterfly without stone, the eyes red and blue; weight: 11 pesos
31. Another small red scallop mounted in gold; not weighed
32. A gold eagle with trimmings and a greenstone in the middle; weight: 12 pesos
33. A monster of gold with a greenstone in the belly, with its trimmings; weight: 11 pesos and 4 tomins

CONCLUSION

The manuscript located in 1981 from which I made this translation is the AGI Contaduria 657, Cuenta de Estrada #3, Grupo I. I wrote to several people at the time regarding it, but, because of many other commitments, it ended up buried in my files for more than a quarter-century.

So much that came after 1521 in the New World overshadowed the initial Spanish wonder and amazement at the golden Aztec treasure. But the spark that lit the inferno of the Spanish Conquest that spread over the length and breadth of two American continents for the next three or four human generations was the early reports of the Aztecs' amazingly rich treasure. If these reports first began to spread like verbal wildfire in 1519, by 1521 the quasi-mythic early reports had become accepted as fact and were then being rendered by literate bean-counters.

Henry B. Nicholson was a champion of historical research and the historical method who managed to make his enthusiasm contagious. Archaeologists who have an overly narrow focus sometimes say that everything in history is already known and that significant discoveries about the past can only be made through excavation. My discovery of a long-forgotten document written literally while the wounds sustained in the final battle between the Aztecs and the Spaniards were still healing proves the fallacy of that statement. I publish this forgotten jewel of historical information, taken from the very first chapter of the story of the collision of cultures in Central Mexico, both in honor of Henry B. Nicholson and as a reminder that exciting discoveries can still be made—not only through excavation in the ground but also within manuscripts in literary archives.

NOTE

1. The Spanish peso, or "weight," of gold was the standard unit of value at the time of the Conquest and remained so throughout much of the Colonial Period. One-eighth of a peso was a tomin, and the famous Spanish "pieces of eight" reflects the use of eight parts when calculating monetary value rather than the modern decimal system.

SOURCES

Díaz de Castillo, Bernal
    1963   *The Conquest of New Spain*. Translated by John M. Cohen. Penguin Books, London.

León-Portilla, Miguel, ed.
    1962   *The Broken Spears: The Aztec Account of the Conquest of Mexico*. Beacon Press, Boston, MA.

Molina, Fray Alonso de
    1944 [1555]   *Vocabulario en Lengua Castellana y Mexicana*. Ediciones Cultura Hispanica, Madrid.

Lawrence H. Feldman

Real Academia Espanola
    1992   *Diccionario de la Lengua Espanola*. Editorial Espasa Calpe, S.A., Madrid.

Smith, Collins
    1972   *Collins Spanish-English, English-Spanish Dictionary*. Collins, London.

17

FEATHERED SERPENTS, PULQUERÍAS, AND INDIAN SEDITION IN COLONIAL CHOLULA

Geoffrey G. McCafferty

More than 100 years ago, Carl Lumholtz (1909) published a short study on an incised black on red vessel in *American Anthropologist* (figure 17.1). The globular jar (olla) featured six handles around its shoulder and was decorated with Mixteca-Puebla Style iconography typical of the Postclassic Period (AD 900–1520). Feathered serpents are the dominant theme in the main design panel, alternating between full-bodied examples and just the heads. A narrow neck panel features stylized butterflies (symbolic of death and resurrection) interspersed between a rectangular motif with a circle in the center. Another panel around the lower portion of the shoulder features the step-fret *xicalcoliuhqui* motif often associated with the god Quetzalcoatl. Lumholtz noted that the vessel was purchased in Cholula (Puebla, Mexico) and was later donated to the American Museum of Natural History.

The Lumholtz vessel obtains renewed significance through comparison with a nearly identical example recovered through recent salvage excavation in the urban center of Cholula. Cholula was an important religious and economic center in the Mexican Highlands, and in the Postclassic it was the center of the religious cult of Quetzalcoatl, the feathered serpent god associated with the wind, the planet Venus, and religious knowledge (Carrasco 1982; Nicholson 2001). Cholula was one of the largest cities in Mesoamerica at the time of the Spanish Conquest (McCafferty 2001b), and it continued as a center of indigenous

425

Geoffrey G. McCafferty

17.1. *The Lumholtz Cholula vessel, a San Pedro Black on Red Incised olla (height 25.6 cm, maximum circumference 80 cm). From Lumholtz 1909: 199. Redrawn by Robyn Lacy.*

culture through the Colonial Period, in contrast to the more European character of nearby Puebla (Bonfil Batalla 1973; Castillo Palma 2001). The modern city of Cholula covers the Precolumbian site, and while a major archaeological project was carried out during the mid-twentieth century (Marquina 1970), most archaeological investigation in the past forty years has taken the form of salvage archaeology in response to development projects. Consequently and unfortunately, one of the most important archaeological resources in Mexico is being whittled away by rampant development, with minimal effort devoted to recovering cultural information.

The R-106 rescue project at Cholula was directed by Sergio Suárez Cruz of the Puebla Regional Center of Mexico's National Institute of Anthropology and History (INAH) in collaboration with archaeologists from Brown University. This project was a valuable exception to the general lack of information resulting from archaeological salvage (McCafferty 1996; Reynoso Ramos 2004). A Classic Period house and associated deposits were explored; this remains the best-known

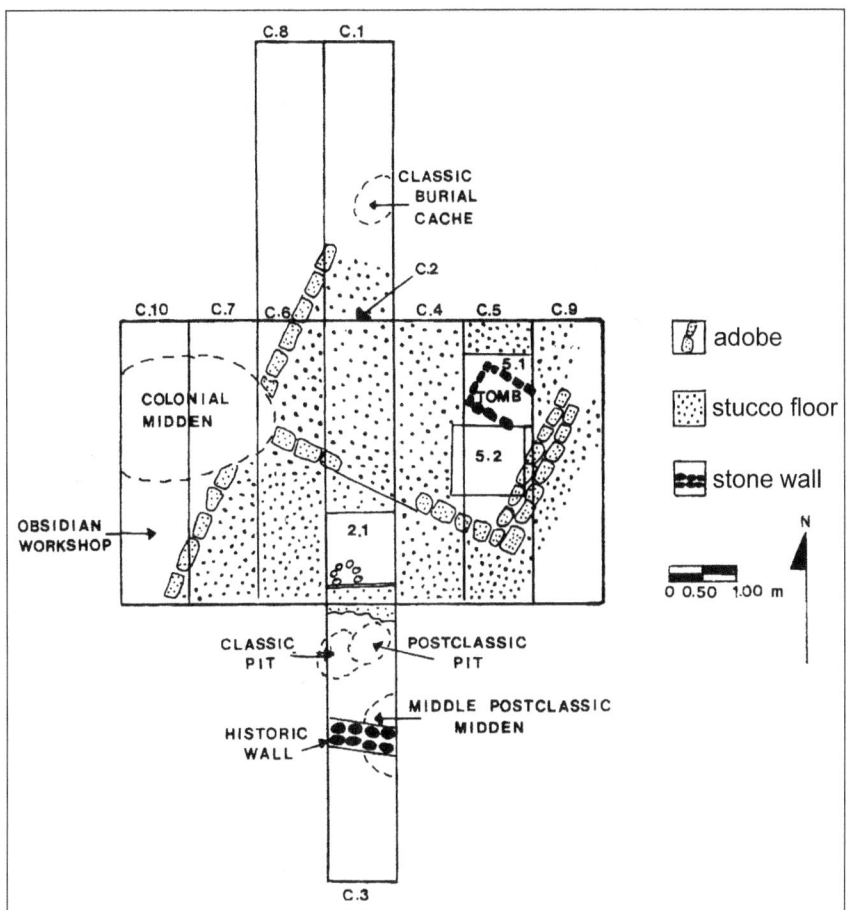

17.2. *Salvage excavations at El Tránsito (R-106), Cholula. Colonial Period trash pit (left). Plan view by Sharisse D. McCafferty.*

domestic site dating to the Late Classic Period (ca. AD 400–650). An intrusive trash pit penetrated through the west side of the Classic Period floor (figure 17.2). This pit contained midden with the bones of domesticated European animals and some Colonial glazed pottery; most of the ceramic assemblage was of indigenous earthenwares (McCafferty 1996; Reynoso Ramos 2004). Based on its majolica ceramics, Citlalli Reynoso Ramos (2004: 103) estimated the date of this intrusive midden to the end of the sixteenth century. San Pedro Polished Red decorated olla fragments (subtype Black on Red Incised) found in this midden are nearly identical to the Lumholtz vessel (McCafferty 2001a: 71–74): both have painted and incised images of a full-bodied feathered serpent and multiple loop handles on the shoulder (figure 17.3).

17.3. *Feathered serpent design on San Pedro Polished Red Incised pottery vessel from the El Transito (R-106) site, Cholula. Photo by Geoffrey G. McCafferty.*

CHOLULA CERAMICS

Postclassic Cholula was famous for its decorated polychrome pottery (Noguera 1954; McCafferty 2001a; Hernández Sánchez 2005), to the extent that the Aztec ruler Moctezoma II allegedly preferred to eat from Cholula wares over any others (Díaz del Castillo 1963 [1580]: 226). San Pedro Polished Red was a minor type in typical Postclassic assemblages (< 2 percent), and while it was locally produced, it probably relates to the more widespread *Guinda* tradition described by Michael Smith (1990: 154) for Postclassic Central Mexico. San Pedro Polished Red seems to have increased in popularity during the Colonial Period, as observed in deposits in a trash-filled well from the UA–1 site on the eastern edge of Prehispanic Cholula that also included European domesticated fauna and diagnostic glazed pottery (McCafferty 1992: 139, 2001a: 92–95). In Colonial Mexico City, comparable "Red Ware" utilitarian and serving wares were important components of household assemblages (Rodríguez-Alegría 2005: 561).

Black on red pottery has a long tradition in Puebla and continues to be produced in the city (Kaplan and Levine 1981; Kaplan 1994). When Colonial Puebla was founded in the early sixteenth century, potters from Cholula were relocated into the indigenous barrios of the budding capital city as one of several ploys to usurp economic power from the Precolumbian city. Flora Kaplan (1994: 3) has recognized black on red pottery as early as the mid–nineteenth century based on still-life art from that time period; at the time of her research, no historical archaeological studies were available for comparison. In her ethnoarchaeological study of the Puebla pottery tradition, Kaplan evaluates the potential meanings of a range of morphological and stylistic elements. She believes the combination of black and red surfaces, for example, is related to Quetzalcoatl symbolism (ibid.: 55).

One prominent element among contemporary potters is the distinction between "non-multiple vs. multiple ears" (handles). Non-multiple ear vessels are typically smaller and were used as individual serving vessels; they "relate to culturally defined Indian food categories" (Kaplan and Levine 1981: 879). Multiple ears are more typically associated with display and, at least in later time periods, were associated with *mestizo* and Mexican cultural identities. Kaplan and David Levine note that, when decorated, multiple ear pottery can include ideologically charged symbols such as the "eagle with serpent on cactus motif" representing the founding of Mexico.

The olla described by Lumholtz (1909) featured six handles (ears). The large fragment found at R-106 probably had an equal number based on the placement of those preserved on the potsherd. This was not a characteristic of Postclassic ollas, which typically had only two handles, if any. The multiple ears/handles support a Postcontact date for this vessel, consistent with the other Colonial Period contents of the R-106 midden deposit. The small olla vessel form is closely associated with the production and consumption of alcoholic *pulque* (Kaplan 1994: 57), the fermented sap of the agave plant that was a vitamin-rich staple of the indigenous diet.

If these are Colonial Period ollas, then it is telling that the prominent iconography of both vessels is that of the feathered serpent. Feathered serpents were important religious icons in Precolumbian mythology since at least the Middle Formative Period, ca. 1000 BC. They are represented in monumental sculpture and murals at such diverse sites as Teotihuacan, Uxmal, Chichén Itzá, Tula, Cacaxtla, Xochicalco (figure 17.4), and Tenochtitlan—but not at Cholula. This is surprising because Cholula was widely regarded as the center for the worship of Quetzalcoatl, literally "precious feather" plus "serpent" in the Nahuatl language of Central Mexico, at least as attested in Colonial Period ethnohistorical accounts (Durán 1971 [1576–1579]; Rojas 1927 [1581]; see also Carrasco 1982). These accounts also describe Precolumbian Cholula as a pilgrimage destination for religious festivals and for the investiture of visiting royalty by priests of the Quetzalcoatl temple.

In her detailed study of Late Postclassic iconography on Cholula "Codex style" pottery, Gilda Hernández Sánchez (2005) found little evidence of feathered

17.4. *Plumed serpent framing a seated human figure at Xochicalco. Photograph of the Pyramid of the Plumed Serpent by H. B. Nicholson; courtesy, H. B. Nicholson Photo Archive, California State University, Los Angeles.*

serpent imagery (3 examples out of a sample of 110), and none were on small ollas. Instead, metanymic elements associated with Quetzalcoatl are common; examples include the "cut shell" motif worn as a pendant or combinations of xicalcoliuhqui stepped frets appearing on his shield (figure 17.5). These symbols can be interpreted as a "shorthand" for representing Quetzalcoatl as an anthropomorphic deity but without reference to his persona as a feathered serpent. So why are feathered serpents, a prominent symbol of Prehispanic religion (but not at Cholula), represented on these later Colonial Period Cholulan vessels? The answer may be found in the archaeological evidence provided by the R-106 midden.

ARCHAEOLOGICAL EVIDENCE FROM CHOLULA

The R-106 archaeological site is located along the Camino Real, the royal highway linking Puebla and Mexico City, just as it enters Cholula. This would have been one of the most heavily traveled roads in New Spain during the Early Colonial Period. The midden artifact assemblage is distinctive. A large number of faunal remains were encountered, primarily from European domesticates. Of 296 bones, 61 were identifiable (Reynoso Ramos 2004: 114–115). Cow comprised the greatest proportion of the assemblage (57 percent), followed by sheep/goat (34 percent) and pig (7 percent). A single turkey bone represents the only native

FEATHERED SERPENTS, PULQUERÍAS, AND INDIAN SEDITION IN COLONIAL CHOLULA

17.5. *Quetzalcoatl, with stepped-fret motif on his shield. From Sahagún 1956: 4 (Atavíos de los Dioses, Ms. de Tepepulco [I]).*

species identified. While such faunal evidence suggests access to comparatively expensive meat resources, the skeletal elements (primarily tarsals, vertebrae, and cranial bones) actually indicate low-quality cuts, of types most amenable to stew rather than steak.

In addition to the large Black on Red Incised olla body sherd, there were also a few fragments of Colonial glazed pottery and other serving wares of indigenous styles that continued from the Late Postclassic Period. The glazed wares were of poor quality, with an incomplete glazed surface, while some of the indigenous-style polychromes were over-fired, giving the impression that they might be production "seconds."

Most ceramics recovered from the intrusive pit were indigenous-style earthenware utilitarian vessels. Of these, the most common were *comales*, the very shallow griddles used for heating tortillas, and small ollas (ibid.: 106–108). The relative proportions of these vessel forms vary radically from the domestic assemblages found in other Postclassic and Colonial contexts (McCafferty 1992). For example, comal rims made up 63 percent of the R-106 midden, roughly three times the frequency of a typical domestic assemblage. Small olla rims made up 13 percent of the assemblage, again about three times the expected frequency. Serving vessels such as bowls made up only 9 percent of the Colonial midden, about five times less than the expected frequency from a typical domestic assemblage. Because of these percentages, we believe the R-106 Colonial midden was probably not the result of domestic activities (see also Reynoso Ramos 2004: 149).

The large percentage of tortilla preparation vessels (comales) but low frequency of bowls in the Colonial Period midden is confusing, at least until the possibility of perishable drinking vessels is considered. In traditional Indian taverns, gourd bowls (*jícaras*) are often used for consuming liquids, especially pulque (Kaplan 1994: 56). These would be archaeologically invisible, thus skewing ceramic frequencies. Jícaras would have been lightweight and durable, perfect for travelers. The higher-than-expected frequency of small ollas would be consistent with the jugs from which pulque could have been served. Tortillas were a highly portable food easily combined with meats and sauces that would have been a perfect "fast food" along the highway.

In Prehispanic Mesoamerica, alcohol consumption was associated with ceremonial practice, especially religious feasts surrounding the ritual calendar. With the introduction of Spanish Colonial authority, restrictions against public drunkenness were relaxed, and secular taverns emerged. Serge Gruzinski (1993: 278) notes that in 1784 there were 600 taverns in Mexico City, which then had a population of about 200,000. He describes them as dirty and dangerous: "The *pulquería* was . . . on the fringes of the norms invoked by the Church and the Inquisition: a culture distinct from the façade of laws and constraints surrounding colonial power."

In a 1593 letter to the king of Spain, Juan de Pineda complained of forty taverns in Cholula and another fifty on its outskirts (Carrasco 1970: 180–181). They were frequented by indigenous merchants, for whom Cholula was famous. Pineda concluded that "they spent much on wine and other things, [the merchants] as well as their women and children, who would ordinarily be in the taverns day and night" (ibid.; translated by the author). The R-106 midden evidence may consequently represent an Early Colonial Period commercial establishment supplying food (tortillas) and drink (pulque?) to Indian travelers. By offering traditional indigenous foods so close to the Camino Real on the outskirts of the traditional pilgrimage center of Cholula, such a pulquería at the end of the first century of Conquest might have provided an atmosphere ripe for sedition. In this interpretive context, a brightly painted and iconographically charged olla decorated with a feathered serpent, multiple handles facilitating its suspension perhaps for public display, might have been a clandestine symbol of native resistance to acculturation.

CONCLUSION

In his study of Colonial Mexican foodways, Rodríguez-Alegría (2005: 551) argues that "both colonizers and Indians were aware of the social and political implications of their material lives and their eating practices." Then, as now, the pulquería was territory where priests feared to tread: "The pulquería was also a constant hotbed of anticlericalism and . . . it challenged the spiritual conquest of the Indian people by undertaking a process of acculturation and deculturation over which the Church had no hold" (Gruzinski 1993: 258).

Feathered serpent vessels in such establishments may have been nonverbal, covert statements of opposition to Colonial domination and unwillingness to embrace the new religious changes demanded by the conquerors. Within the relative safety of an indigenous tavern and surrounded by fellow travelers, gossip, boasts, jokes, and revolutionary mutterings were probably part of the daily

17.6. *Quetzalcoatl as depicted in the* Codex Magliabecchi. *From Nuttall 1903: 61.*

17.7. *Quetzalcoatl imagery and accoutrements. Folio 18r Codex Telleriano-Remensis. From Quiñones Keber 1995: 39.*

fare. Freed from Precolumbian ritual restrictions, overt alcoholism became a form of passive resistance (Burkhart and Gasco 2007: 216). Drunkenness was an easy escape from the physical and emotional conflicts brought about by Spanish domination.

The cult of Quetzalcoatl (cf. figures 17.6–17.8) was transformed in Colonial Period Mexico. Mythical accounts of the culture hero Topiltzin-Quetzalcoatl promised his return, and it was suggested that the Spanish conquistador Hernán Cortés may have become confused in this revitalization fable (Nicholson 2001). In the writings of Spanish chroniclers such as Diego Durán (1971 [1576–1579]; see also Lafaye 1976), Quetzalcoatl was compared to Jesus Christ and assumed Christian attributes of penitence and purity represented in Colonial codices in human form; little of the "feathered serpent" was left in the Colonial persona. Instead, the Colonial chronicler Bernardino de Sahagún (1950–1982 [1547–1585]: 11: 85) lists "quetzalcoatls," among other "earthly things," as a particular kind of venomous serpent with brightly colored feathers that flies on the wind. It is the completely indigenous icon that is represented on our two study vessels, similar in form to the illustration of the feathered quetzalcoatl (figure 17.9) depicted in Sahagún's *Florentine Codex* (ibid.: 276–277). A similar use of archaistic mythological images as a form of symbolic resistance is described by Anthony Wonderley (1986) at Naco, Honduras, where, in response to foreign domination, mythical bird motifs reappear on indigenous pottery after a hiatus of several centuries.

Our two study examples of incised black on red pottery can be interpreted as possibly symbolic of resistance to Spanish practices of forced acculturation in Central Mexico during the first generations after the Conquest. Perhaps, if we are correct, such opposition may have been part of a native revitalization

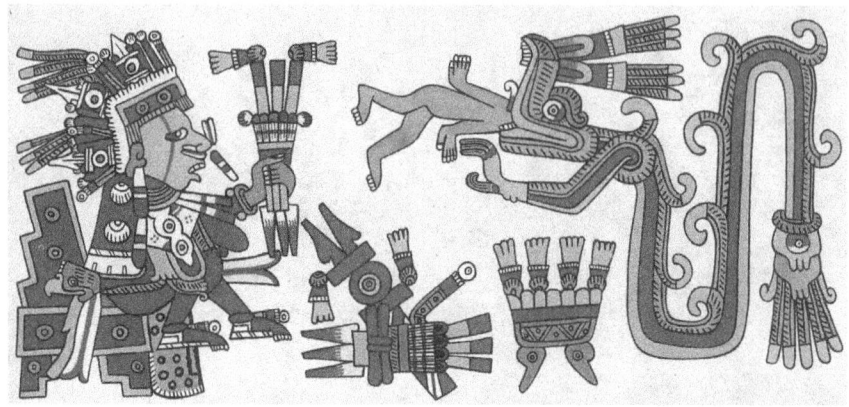

17.8. *Quetzalcoatl imagery on page 7 of the* Codex Borgia tonalpohualli. *From Díaz and Rodgers 1993: 11.*

17.9A AND 17.9B. *Feathered serpent, or Quetzalcoatl, depictions in Sahagún's* Florentine Codex. *From Sahagún 1963: 11: figures 276–277.*

movement invoking the return of a lost culture hero. Archaistic images of feathered serpents in Colonial Period Cholula recall much earlier icons and are not simply the unbroken continuation of a long-lived tradition, since feathered serpents were not found on Late Postclassic Cholula polychromes. The additional iconography on the Lumholtz vessel of xicalcoliuhqui frets was also a metanym for Quetzalcoatl. The butterfly imagery carried significance for resurrection (Berlo 1983), while the rectangle with circle may correspond to the stylization of "serpent skin" (Hernández Sánchez 2005: 70)—both fitting symbols for religious revival.

Dirt archaeology, especially Colonial Period historical dirt archaeology, reminds us that not everything going on at a given time and place always ends up documented in the historical records. A contextual "reading" of indigenous pottery from the Early Colonial Period, at least at our Cholula pulquería, offers tantalizing possibilities for the reconstruction of an Indian version of conquest and conversion, one in essential disagreement with that provided by literate Europeans.

REFERENCES CITED

Berlo, Janet Catherine
    1983   The Warrior and the Butterfly: Central Mexican Ideologies of Sacred Warfare and Teotihuacan Iconography. In *Text and Image in Pre-Columbian Art*, ed. Janet Catherine Berlo, pp. 79–118. BAR International Series 180, Oxford.

Bonfil Batalla, Guillermo
    1973   *Cholula: La Ciudad Sagrada en la Era Industrial*. Instituto de Investigaciones Historicas, UNAM, México, DF.

Burkhart, Louise M., and Janine Gasco
    2007   The Colonial Period in Mesoamerica. In *The Legacy of Mesoamerica: History and Culture of a Native American Civilization*, 2nd ed., ed. Robert M. Carmack, Janine Gasco, and Gary H. Gossen, pp. 182–221. Prentice-Hall, Upper Saddle River, NJ.

Carrasco, Davíd
    1982   *Quetzalcoatl and the Irony of Empire: Myths and Prophecies of the Aztec Tradition*. University of Chicago Press, Chicago, IL.

Carrasco, Pedro
    1970   Carta al Rey sobre la Ciudad de Cholula en 1593. *Tlalocan* 6: 176–192.

Castillo Palma, Norma A.
    2001   *Cholula: Sociedad Mestiza en Ciudad India*. Universidad Autónima Metropolitana Unidad Iztapalapa, México, DF.

Díaz, Gisele, and Alan Rodgers
    1993   *The Codex Borgia: A Full-Color Restoration of the Ancient Mexican Manuscript*, with an introduction and commentary by Bruce E. Byland. Dover, New York.

Díaz del Castillo, Bernal
    1963 [1580]   *The Conquest of New Spain*. Translated by J. M. Cohen. Penguin Books, Harmondsworth, Middlesex, England.

Durán, Diego
    1971 [1576–1579]   *The Book of the Gods and Rites and the Ancient Calendar*. Translated by Fernando Horcasitas and Doris Heyden. University of Oklahoma Press, Norman.

Gruzinski, Serge
    1993   *The Conquest of Mexico: The Incorporation of Indian Societies into the Western World, 16th–18th Centuries*. Translated by Eileen Corrigan. Polity, Cambridge, England.

Hernández Sánchez, Gilda
  2005 *Vasijas para Ceremonias: Iconografía de la Cerámica Tipo Códice del Estilo Mixteca-Puebla*. CNWS Publications Series 139, Leiden, The Netherlands.

Kaplan, Flora S.
  1994 *A Mexican Folk Pottery Tradition: Cognition and Style in Material Culture in the Valley of Puebla*. Southern Illinois University Press, Carbondale.

Kaplan, Flora S., and David M. Levine
  1981 Cognitive Mapping of a Folk Taxonomy of Mexican Pottery: A Multivariate Approach. *American Anthropologist* 83: 868–884.

Lafaye, Jacques
  1976 *Quetzalcóatl and Guadalupe: The Formation of Mexican National Consciousness, 1531–1813*. Translated by Benjamin Keen. University of Chicago Press, Chicago, IL.

Lumholtz, Carl
  1909 A Remarkable Ceremonial Vessel from Cholula, Mexico. *American Anthropologist* 11 (2): 199–201.

Marquina, Ignacio, ed.
  1970 *Proyecto Cholula*. Serie Investigaciones 19. INAH, México, DF.

McCafferty, Geoffrey G.
  1992 The Material Culture of Postclassic Cholula, Mexico: Contextual Analysis of the UA–1 Domestic Compounds. Unpublished PhD dissertation, Department of Anthropology, State University of New York, Binghamton.
  1996 The Ceramics and Chronology of Cholula, Mexico. *Ancient Mesoamerica* 7 (2): 299–323.
  2001a *Ceramics of Postclassic Cholula, Mexico: Typology and Seriation of Pottery from the UA–1 Domestic Compound*. Monograph 43. Cotsen Institute of Archaeology, UCLA, Los Angeles, CA.
  2001b Mountain of Heaven, Mountain of Earth: The Great Pyramid of Cholula as Sacred Landscape. In *Landscape and Power in Ancient Mesoamerica*, ed. Rex Koontz, Kathryn Reese-Taylor, and Annabeth Headrick, pp. 279–316. Westview, Boulder, CO.

Nicholson, H. B.
  2001 *Topiltzin Quetzalcoatl: The Once and Future Lord of the Toltecs*. University Press of Colorado, Boulder.

Noguera, Eduardo
  1954 *La Cerámica Arqueológica de Cholula*. Editorial Guaranía, México, DF.

Nuttall, Zelia
  1903 *Codex Magliabecchi: The Book of the Life of the Ancient Mexicans, Containing an Account of Their Rites and Superstitions: An Anonymous Hispano-Mexican Manuscript Preserved at the Biblioteca Nazionale Centrale, Florence, Italy*, reproduced in facsimile, with introduction, translation, and commentary by Zelia Nuttall. Part 1: Introduction and Facsimile. University of California, Berkeley.

Quiñones Keber, Eloise
    1995   *Codex Telleriano-Remensis: Ritual, Divination, and History in a Pictorial Aztec Manuscript*, with a foreword by Emmanuel LeRoy Ladurie and illustrations by Michel Besso. University of Texas Press, Austin.

Reynoso Ramos, Citlalli
    2004   Consumer Behavior and Foodways in Colonial Mexico: Archaeological Case Studies Comparing Puebla and Cholula. MA thesis, Department of Archaeology, University of Calgary, Calgary, Alberta.

Rodríguez-Alegría, Enrique
    2005   Eating Like an Indian: Negotiating Social Relations in the Spanish Colonies. *Current Anthropology* 46: 551–565.

Rojas, Gabriel de
    1927 [1581]   Descripción de Cholula. *Revista Mexicana de Estudios Historicos* 1 (6): 158–170.

Sahagún, Fray Bernadino de
    1950–1982 [1547–1585]   *Florentine Codex: General History of the Things of New Spain.* Edited and translated by Arthur J.O. Anderson and Charles E. Dibble, 13 vols. University of Utah Press and School of American Research, Salt Lake City and Santa Fe.
    1956   *Historia general de las cosas de Nueva España, escrita por Bernardino de Sahagún y fundada en la documentación en lengua mexicana recogida por los mismos naturales*, vol. 4: *La dispuso para la prensa en esta nueva edición*, with numeración, anotaciones, and apéndices by Ángel María Garibay K. Porrúa, México, DF.

Smith, Michael E.
    1990   Long-Distance Trade under the Aztec Empire. *Ancient Mesoamerica* 1 (2): 153–169.

Wonderley, Anthony W.
    1986   Material Symbolics in Pre-Columbian Households: The Painted Pottery of Naco Valley, Honduras. *Journal of Anthropological Research* 42 (4): 497–534. Albuquerque, NM.

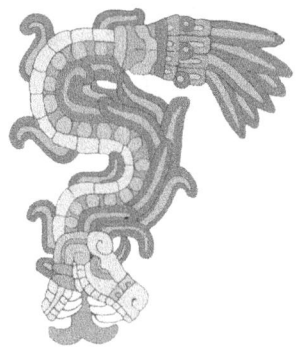

18

THE POSTHUMOUS HISTORY OF THE TIZOC STONE

Alfredo López Austin and Leonardo López Luján

Ancient stone monuments, preserved thanks to the tenacity of material almost immune to the passing of time, are testimonies to the thoughts and actions of vanished generations. They offer the illusion of clearly transmitted messages through the hardness of form, the perfection of contour, and the harmony of composition. Because we can see them, we also believe we can hear through them the distant voices of their creators. But we forget, at least momentarily, that the ancient message is not automatically crystallized within its stone medium and that the carved forms are simply triggers waiting to fire the imaginations of the varied beholders. Meanings are created and recreated differently depending upon their viewers' chronological and cultural position. Thus the objective appearance of any sculpture will continue to be subjectively transformed into idealizations: anthropomorphic figures will be turned into priests or warriors or philosophers or dancers, assumed functions will become astronomical or magical or recreational or commemorative, and volumetric quantity will becomes sacred flows, gods, demons, or simply mere collections of atoms. All such interpretations depend upon who is looking at the ancient monument and what his or her point of view is. This potential plurality of readings, even more mutable in the clash of cultures and the passing of centuries, is often the most important factor in the fate of individual monuments, for it will determine whether they survive.

Alfredo López Austin and Leonardo López Luján

18.1. *The Tizoc Stone with its distinctive basin and channel. The lateral face has fifteen conquest scenes. Photo by José Ignacio González Manterola.*

Such is the case of the Mexica monument that today bears the name Tizoc Stone, whose carving was ordered by this controversial sovereign of Tenochtitlan between AD 1481 and 1486. Its changing fate, like the fates of other, similar sculptures, has been marked by highly diverse assessments and a very unusual physical movement through the streets, plazas, and museums of Mexico City. The sculpture, currently in the Mexica Hall of the National Museum of Anthropology (inv. 10–162), is a squat cylindrical mass of andesite outstanding for its great size and weight: 94 cm high, 265 cm in diameter, and weighing about 9.5 tons (figure 18.1). The top and lateral faces of the cylinder are beautifully worked within the canons of the style that has been called "Imperial Mexica." The top surface bears the conventional representation of the sun. The lateral surface has a sequence of fifteen scenes or unbounded panel segments, each composed of a warrior subduing a deity who personifies a seigniorial domain identified with a toponymic glyph (see López Austin 2006; Matos Moctezuma 2009). The continuous design panel on the stone's side is bounded by two horizontal bands, one above, the other below, that respectively depict a nocturnal sky and a terrestrial reptile. In a disconcerting yet informative manner, a central concavity with a deep channel cuts through the carved reliefs, radially interrupting the solar disc on the upper surface and one of the conquest scenes on its side.

Today we know that the Tizoc Stone was an ideal instrument for the harsh exchanges between humans and gods. We have discussed its ritual function in the book *Monte Sagrado–Templo Mayor* (Sacred Mountain–Great Temple), identifying it as one of two large stone cylinders that formed a liturgical pair on the patio of the Temple of Yopico, a complex dedicated to the god Xipe Tótec and located on the southern end of the sacred precinct of Tenochtitlan (López Austin and López Luján 2009: 463–467). Both carved cylinders were destined for the *tlahuahuanaliztli*, or "striping," a ritual more commonly known in English as the "gladiatorial sacrifice." One of them, the *temalácatl*, was the small arena where the poorly armed captive fought the warrior sacrificers. The other, the *cuauhxicalli*, received the captive's wounded body for the inevitable removal of the heart and the subsequent offering of blood to the sun and the earth. The stone in our study was a cuauhxicalli, since it lacks the central spike sources attribute to the temalácatl, an appropriate element for attaching the cord that tethered the captive.

These impressive, paired cylinders also served as true memorials glorifying the feats of each sovereign, since they recorded on their sides inherited conquests as well as the sovereigns' own triumphs. This explains the Mexica obsession with constantly replacing the cuauhxicalli, the temalácatl, or both, thereby confirming the gradual expansion of the empire.

STONES DESTROYED, STONES BURIED

With the Spanish Conquest, the enormous ritual stage that formed the heart of Tenochtitlan was dismantled building by building and stone by stone. The great sculptures were profaned, desecrated, dispersed, and abandoned, each to its own destiny in the new course of history. The immediate fate of the cylindrical stones from the patio of Yopico differed, as described in the *Historia de los mexicanos por sus pinturas*, a document written between 1543 and 1544:

> En el año 136 [AD 1458] hizo Moteçuma el Viejo una rodela de piedra, la cual sacó R[odrig]o Gómez, que estava enterrada a la puerta de su casa, la qual tiene un agujero enmedio y es muy grande . . . Y en aquel agujero ponían los que tomavan en la guerra atados, que no podían mandar sino los braços, y dávanle una rodela y una espada de palo; y venían tres hombres: uno vestido como tigre, otro como león, otro como águila, y peleavan con él hiriéndole: luego tomavan un navajón y le sacavan el coraçón. Y así sacaron los navajones con la piedra debaxo de aquella rueda redonda y muy grande; y después los señores que fueron de México hicieron otras dos piedras, y las pusieron cada señor la

suya una sobre otra, y la una habían sacado y está hoy día debajo de la pila de bautizar, y la otra se quemó y quebró cuanto estuvieron los españoles. (*Historia de los mexicanos por sus pinturas* 2002: 72)

In the year 136 [AD 1458] Motecuhzoma the Elder made a stone round shield that Rodrigo Gómez removed, which was buried at the gate of his residence, which has a hole in the middle and is very large . . . And in that hole they used to attach those whom they took in battle, who could not move but his arms, and he was given a round shield and a club for a sword, and three men came, one dressed as a tiger, another as a lion, another as an eagle, and fought with him and wounded him, then they took out a large knife and removed his heart. And thus they took the knives with the stone under that very large and round wheel; and then the old lords of Mexico made two other stones, and each lord placed them one over the other, and the Spaniards removed one and today it is under the baptismal font, and the other was burned and broken when they came. (Authors' translation.)

Concerning the first case mentioned in this passage, the *Actas de Cabildo* (Mier y Terán Rocha 2005), the papers of Archbishop Juan de Zumárraga (García Icazbalceta 1947), and Francisco Guerrero's map of Mexico City (now in the Archivo General de Indias de Sevilla) make it clear that, between 1525 and 1526, the conquistador Rodrigo Gómez Dávila built his primary residence on the corner of Calle Real (Moneda Street today) and Calle del Agua (Seminario Street today) (figure 18.4) and that five years later the modest episcopal houses were built in an adjacent area to the east. Much later and after being constituted archiepiscopal, these houses expanded toward the west, occupying part of the old Gómez Dávila estate.

This causes us to speculate with good reason that the large "round shield with a hole in the middle" is none other than the famous Archbishop's Stone (figure 18.2), exhumed in 1988 and now displayed in the National Museum of Anthropology (inv. 10–393459). The archaeologists who discovered this temalácatl say they found it barely 30 cm away from a Colonial wall and under a layer of earth predominantly filled with fragments of Colonial Period ceramics (Pedro Francisco Sánchez Nava and Judith Padilla, personal communication, 2009). This and the fact that the Archbishop's Stone was not aligned to the Pyramid of Tezcatlipoca, whose stairway is situated a few meters to the east (see Matos Moctezuma 1997), confirms that it was moved from its original position or at least was noticed during the Colonial Period (figure 18.3[B]).

The other "round shield" that was not destroyed according to the *Historia de los mexicanos por sus pinturas* (2002) would have been buried after the fall of Tenochtitlan but rediscovered shortly afterward at a date we calculate between 1526 and 1532, when the first cathedral was built. There it would have remained under the baptistery chapel, at least until 1626, the year this small building with an east-west axis was demolished. Was the stone still buried underground?

THE POSTHUMOUS HISTORY OF THE TIZOC STONE

18.2. *The Archbishop's Stone lacks a channel. Eleven conquest scenes are arrayed along its side. Photo by José Ignacio González Manterola.*

THE TIZOC STONE IN THE SIXTEENTH AND SEVENTEENTH CENTURIES

Significantly, the Tizoc Stone comes from this same area. In "El libro de los ritos" (The Book of Rites) in the *Historia de las Indias de Nueva España* (History of the Indians of New Spain), Fray Diego Durán (1984: 1: 100) mentions that this sculpture

> era una que agora tornaron a desenterrar en el sitio donde se edifica la Iglesia Mayor de México, la cual tienen agora a la puerta del Perdón. A esta llamaban "batea" los antiguos, a causa de que tiene una pileta en medio y una canal por donde se escurría la sangre de los que en ella sacrificaban, los cuales fueron más que cabellos tengo en la cabeza. La cual deseo ver quitada de allí, y aun también de ver desbaratada la Iglesia Mayor y la nueva: es porque se quiten aquellas culebras de piedra que están por basas de los pilares, las cuales eran cerca del patio de Huitzilopochtli y donde sé yo que han ido a llorar algunos viejos y viejas la destrucción de su templo, viendo allí las reliquias, y plega a la divina bondad que no hayan ido allí algunos a adorar aquellas piedras y no a Dios. (Durán 1971: 181–182)

Alfredo López Austin and Leonardo López Luján

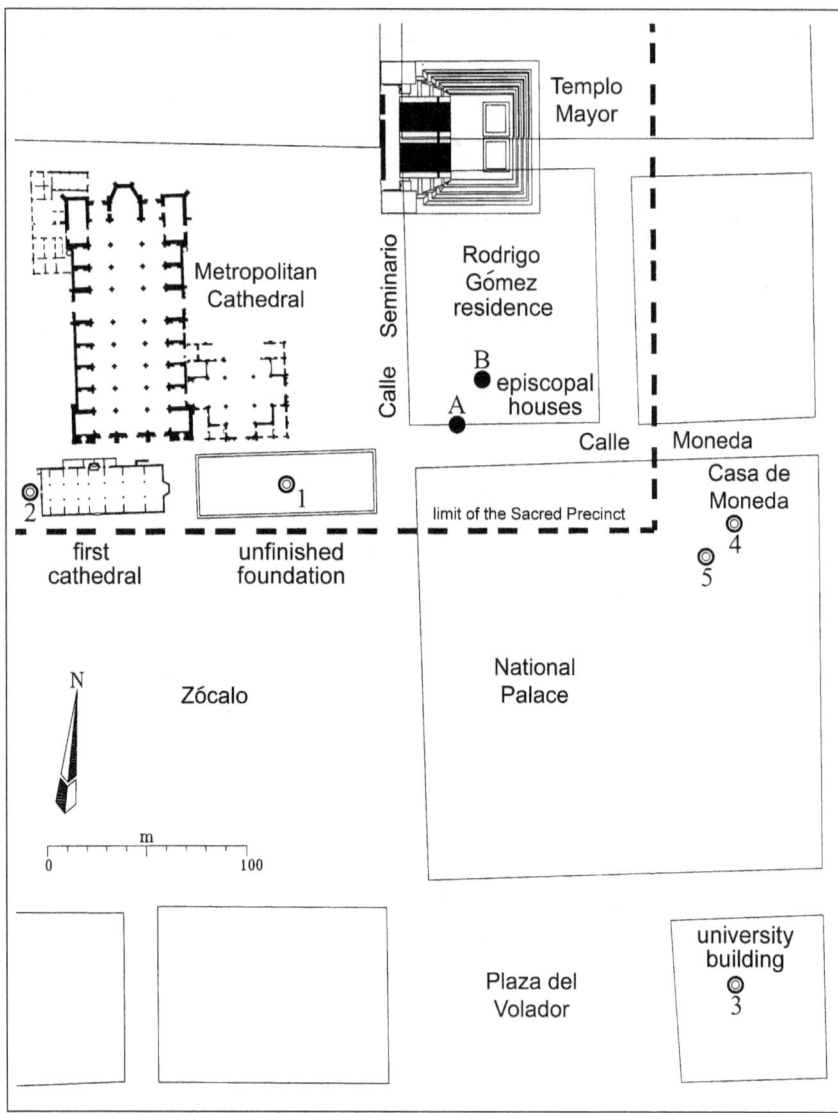

18.3. *Schematic map of the successive relocations of the Tizoc Stone (1–5) and the Archbishop's Stone (A–B), by Tenoch Medina.*

was the one that has been unearthed for the second time at the site where the Cathedral of Mexico City is being constructed. This stone now stands at the western doorway of the church. The ancients call this the "basin," because it had a concavity in the center and a channel through which ran the blood of the victims, which were more numerous than the hairs on my head. I would like to see this stone removed from the doorway of the church. And once

444

the old cathedral is torn down and the new one is erected, we should also remove the stone serpents which serve as the bases of the columns. These used to stand near the courtyard of Huitzilopochtli. I happen to know of old men and women who have gone there to weep over these relics because of the destruction of their temple. I trust that in His goodness our God has not permitted those Indians to go there and adore the stones and not God. (Authors' translation)

If we take into account the fact that the Dominican friar began this book around 1565 and had finished it by 1570, the area of the discovery would be located just east of the old cathedral, where an enormous pit was dug between 1562 and 1565 to construct the foundations of a new cathedral with seven naves that was intended to be as large as the one in Seville (figure 18.3, no. 1). This project was canceled, however, because of its high cost and the presence of a very shallow water table at the chosen site (Toussaint 1972). As it is well-known, a less ambitious project must have been initiated in 1570–1571, north of the old cathedral, which resulted in the current Metropolitan Cathedral.

What is important for our study is that for nearly six decades the Tizoc Stone remained exposed to the gaze of people passing in front of the so-called Puerta del Perdón (Portal of Forgiveness) of the first cathedral, that is, in front of the principal (west) entrance of the building, whose ruins lay beneath the southwest corner of the current cathedral complex (figure 18.3, no. 2). There it was seen by several privileged witnesses. For example, one of the indigenous artists of Fray Bernardino de Sahagún (1979, 9: fol. 7r) left an image of it depicted in the *Florentine Codex* between 1575 and 1577, without its sculpted reliefs but with its distinctive basin and channel (figure 18.5). It was located in the same place by Durán in his 1581 *Historia* (1984: 2: 395) and by the historian Hernando de Alvarado Tezozómoc in his 1598 *Crónica mexicana* (2001: 146, 404), the former calling it "piedra del sol" (sun stone) and the latter "piedra del sacrificio" (sacrificial stone).

More interesting still is the description by the young Francesco Carletti, who resided in Mexico City between June 1595 and March 1596. Carletti (2002: 69), a Florentine slave merchant, reported the Tizoc Stone's shape, location, and suspected functions in his *Razonamientos de mi viaje alrededor del mundo* (My Voyage around the World):

(Colegio [los jesuitas], el cual era una fábrica muy suntuosa y bella, tal como es también hermosísima aquella en donde vive el virrey, situada en una de las plazas, en donde está también la catedral, que en mis tiempos no estaba terminada de construir. Todavía se ve en ella una mesa de una piedra grande y gruesa trabajada en forma redonda, con varias figuras en medio relieve esculpidas dentro, con un canalillo en medio de ella, por el cual dicen que corría la sangre de aquellos hombres que se sacrificaban sobre ella en la época de su gentilidad mexicana, en honor de sus ídolos, cuyas reliquias se ven todavía por

445

Alfredo López Austin and Leonardo López Luján

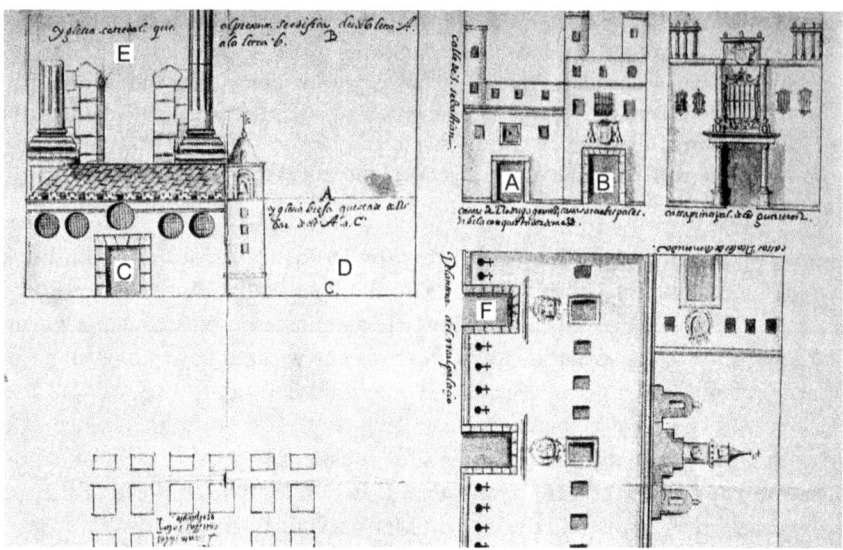

18.4. *Plan of central Mexico City in the sixteenth century. On the Calle Real (upper right) are (A) the residence of Rodrigo Gómez Dávila and (B) episcopal houses; on the Plaza de Armas (upper left) are (C) the first cathedral, (D) unfinished foundations, (E) the new cathedral; (lower right) (F) is the royal palace. By Francisco Guerrero, in the Archivo General de Indias, Seville.*

la ciudad fijadas por ellos en la pared, en las esquinas de las casas hechas por los españoles, puestas allí como triunfo de sus fundaciones). (Carletti 1964: 59)

[The Jesuit] College, a very sumptuous and beautiful fabric, as is that inhabited by the viceroy, which is located on one of the plazas in which there is also the cathedral, which had not been completed in my time. There one still sees a tablet formed from a huge, thick stone worked in a round shape on which are carved various figures in half-relief, and with a small gutter in the middle through which ran the blood of men who here were sacrificed in the times of the Mexican nobles, in honor of their idols, of which one sees the remains still throughout the city, walled up in the exterior walls of the buildings erected by the Spaniards, placed there to express the triumph of their foundation. (Authors' translation)

Visionary indeed is the testimony written between 1598 and 1600 by the chronicler Cristóbal del Castillo, who, when referring to the places conquered by the Mexica, says "están escritos en el malacate de piedra circular, la piedra de rayamiento, que está junto a la Iglesia Mayor de México" (they are written on the circular stone cylinder, the striping stone, which is next to the cathedral of Mexico City) (Castillo 1991: 136–137). In this enlightened manner he correctly interpreted its reliefs:

THE POSTHUMOUS HISTORY OF THE TIZOC STONE

18.5. *The Tizoc Stone as shown by one of Fray Bernardino de Sahagún's indigenous artists. Florentine Codex, Book 9, fol. 7r.*

(Aquel que está primero de pie, que tiene [al otro] por el cabello, es la imagen de los mecitin, y el otro hombre que está arriba, inclinado, ése es el poblador de los lugares que fueron conquistados, que es hecho cautivo. Allá está grabado sobre la piedra el nombre de cada población; en cada punto está esculpido, por todas partes, alrededor del lomo de la piedra discoidal. Y ya nadie sabe los que [eran] los nombres de nuestros lugares, pues en verdad han muerto todos los ancianos que sabían las historias de la escritura de la piedra.) (Castillo 1991: 136–137.)

The one at the bottom, who has the other by the hair, is the image of the Mexica [*mecitin*], and the other man who is above, inclined, is the settler of the places that were conquered, who is made a captive. Carved on the stone is the name of each settlement; and each point is sculpted, all over, around the back of the circular stone. And now nobody knows the names of our places, since all the elders who knew the stories of the writing on the stone truly have died. (Authors' translation)

Alfredo López Austin and Leonardo López Luján

THE TIZOC STONE IN THE LATE COLONIAL PERIOD

We do not know if the Tizoc Stone was intentionally buried in the seventeenth century or whether, as Francisco Sedano (1880: 292–294) stated, it was buried accidentally as a result of the great flood of 1629 and the subsequent earth filling done by the city's inhabitants until 1634 to raise the ground level above flood stage. The only certainty is that the stone reappeared on December 17, 1791, facedown, at least 42 cm below the surface. According to the astronomer and antiquarian Antonio de León y Gama (1832: segunda parte: 46):

> (Se iba abriendo la zanja para la atarjea que vá al primer arquillo inmediato al portal que llaman de los mercaderes, y pasa por la cerca del cementerio de la iglesia Catedral, en el sitio mismo donde estaba antiguamente una cruz, de madera pintada de verde sobre su peana de mampostería, que es donde formaba esquina la antigua cerca del cementerio y hace frente á las tiendas de cerería del Empedradillo.)

> The trench was still being dug for the water conduit that runs to the first small arch next to what they call the merchant's portal and passes right by the foundation of the Cathedral church, in the same spot where long ago there used to be a wooden cross painted green on a piled-stone pedestal, which formed the corner of the old foundation wall and faces the candle shops of the Empedradillo [Monte de Piedad Street today]. (Authors' translation)

In addition to commissioning a drawing by the engraver Francisco Agüera, León y Gama (ibid.) himself studied the relief at that time. He concluded (ibid.) that it was neither a temalácatl nor a cuauhxicalli but rather a solar monument registering Tenochtitlan's two zenithal passages, celebrated "con un divertido baile que representan los treinta danzantes, que de dos en dos están tan finamente grabados en la circunferencia cilíndrica" (with an amusing dance performed by thirty dancers who were so finely engraved in pairs on the cylindrical circumference).

The Flemish captain of dragoons, Guillermo Dupaix, also had occasion to examine and draw the stone. Dupaix came to the idea that it should not be called the Piedra del Sacrificio (Sacrificial Stone) or the Piedra de la Danza (Dance Stone), as his contemporaries proposed, but rather the Piedra Triunfal (Triumphal Stone):

> Pues este trozo cilíndrico muy precioso á la historia de ésta Nacion, dedicado á la posteridad, nos manifiesta palpablemente las Victorias que consiguió sobre 15 Provincias (o Reynos).

> For this cylindrical piece, quite precious to the history of this Nation, dedicated to posterity, palpably shows us the Victories achieved over fifteen Provinces (or Kingdoms). (Dupaix n.d.: fol. 1)

The top face, however, was disconcerting to him, and he ventured the opinion that its significance may have been astronomical.

THE POSTHUMOUS HISTORY OF THE TIZOC STONE

A few days after the discovery, the regent magistrate (*corregidor regente*) of Mexico City asked the dean of the cathedral to find an appropriate place to exhibit the monolith, as had been done with the Calendar Stone, placed by that time at the bottom of the new tower (see López Luján 2008). In spite of the spaciousness of the atrium, his response was negative, alleging that "no había paraje ni destino para poderla aplicar" (he had no spot or destination he could give it). Surprisingly, the regent magistrate communicated to the viceroy that he thought the same with respect to the city; therefore, it would be sufficient to have it "medir, dibuxar y describir si fuere posible para su futuro conocimiento" (measured, drawn, and described if possible for future knowledge) (AHGDF: n.d. fol. 4r–5r). So the Tizoc Stone was buried again, but this time with the solar disc facing upward at ground level, which resulted in the profound wear visible today on the top face. According to halberdier José Gómez (1986: 82), this occurred on September 3, 1793, "en el lugar que se ha de poner la santa cruz que estaba en el cementerio de la catedral" (on the spot where the holy cross that used to be on the cathedral foundation had been placed).

Sometime between 1803 and 1804, Dupaix gave his drawing of the Tizoc Stone's sequence of conquests to Alexander von Humboldt (1995: pl. 21), who was passing through the Colonial Mexican capital. The Prussian savant published a segment (figure 18.7) in his *Vues des Cordillères, et monuments des peuples indigènes de l'Amérique* (Views of the Cordilleras and Monuments of the Indigenous Peoples of America) (1810). There he says that the stone served as a temalácatl, for by then he was inclined toward the iconographic interpretation of the captain of dragoons and erroneously suggested that the Mexica warriors wore a sort of left shoe "terminado por una especie de pico que aparece destinado a la defensa" (ending in a kind of point that appears destined to defense) (Humboldt 1995: 136). Moreover, Humboldt (ibid.) claimed to have "confrontado la exactitud" (compared the accuracy) of Dupaix's drawing, thus implying that he had the rubble removed from the lateral face of the sculpture.

THE TIZOC STONE IN INDEPENDENT MEXICO

In 1823, following the War of Independence, the British showman William Bullock traveled to Mexico with his son (see Costeloe 2008). One of his goals was to produce the sketches for eventual paintings by John and Robert Burford for their View of Mexico City exhibition at the Leicester Square Panorama in London (Romero de Terreros 1959). Drawings and exhibitions composed of scenes from cities throughout the world were made using a procedure that was extremely ingenious for the period. The artist was located at a single point and reproduced from there everything in the surrounding landscape. The final images, of large dimensions, were exhibited on the smooth wall of a rotunda, producing a 360-degree view for spectators who, situated in the center with the painting at a sufficient distance,

18.6. *The Tizoc Stone (visible through grille) in the northeast corner of the patio of the Mexico City University in 1842. Detail of an oil painting by Pedro Gualdi.*

18.7. Two panels from the Tizoc Stone in an engraving published by Alexander von Humboldt (1810), based on a drawing by Guillermo Dupaix.

had the illusion of encountering the remote country from which the panoramic drawing had come. Bullock established his vantage point in the upper part of the cathedral and sketched in the round. In one of his sketches, which includes the southwest corner of the cathedral foundation at the bottom toward the right, we can see how the top face of the Tizoc Stone has surfaced (figure 18.8).

Another one of Bullock plans was to produce replicas destined for the Ancient Mexico exhibition in the Egyptian Hall (figure 18.9), a building on his property in Piccadilly (Bullock 1824a: 151, 335, 375–376). For this, he solicited the clerics at the cathedral to let him excavate around the contours of the sculpture, which they not only approved but for which they also assumed the cost. With great difficulty because of the elevated water table, he finally managed to free the monument. With the authorization of Lucas Alamán, minister of foreign and domestic relations, Bullock immediately took plaster molds and reproduced the reliefs (figure 18.10)—in "somewhat embellished" form, in the opinion of George Francis Lyon (1828: 2: 120). The following year Bullock (1824a: 335) recalled: "I have seen the Indians themselves, as they pass, throw stones at it; and I once saw a boy jump upon it, clench his fist, stamp with his foot, and use other gesticulations of the greatest abhorrence."

The location of the Tizoc Stone changed on November 10, 1824, when it was transferred to the no longer extant University building located in front of the Plaza del Volador (figure 18.3, no. 3). The following year the Mexican National

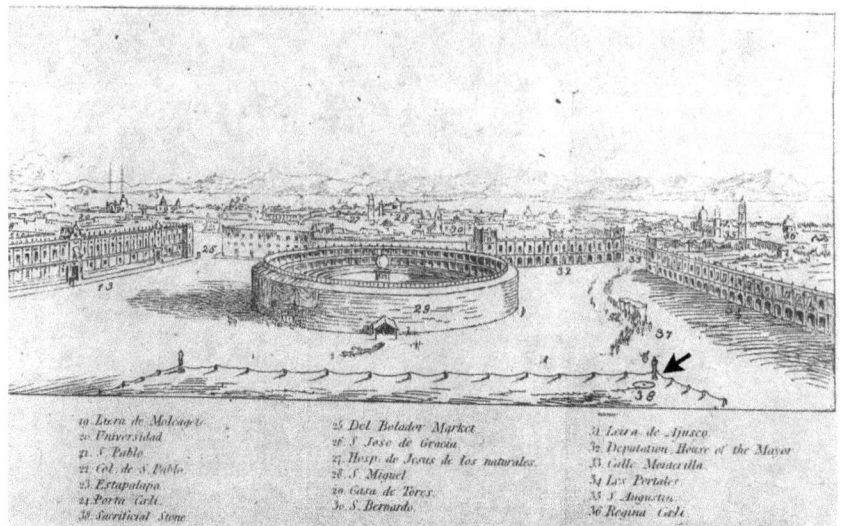

18.8. Sketch of the Mexico City Zócalo in 1823 by William Bullock for John and Robert Burford's Panorama. The Tizoc Stone (black arrow) is number 38. Romero de Terreros 1959.

Museum opened its doors there, an institution created by order of President Guadalupe Victoria. The travel logs of the American Edward T. Taylor (1959 [1825–1828]: 58) and the Englishmen Mark Beaufoy (1828: 198–199), as well as those of George Lyon (1828: 2: 120), agree that the sculpture was located on the corner of the extensive central patio behind a group of panels, sharing the enclosure with the massive Coatlicue sculpture (López Luján 2009: 148–150). This is confirmed in the renowned oil painting of the University patio created by the Italian artist Pedro Gualdi around 1842 (figure 18.6).

With the worked faces of the stone completely exposed, the activities of both illustration and interpretation gradually increased. For example, Carlos Nebel (1963) produced detailed lithographs (figure 18.11) that he published with an explanation in his *Viaje pintoresco y arqueológico sobre la parte más interesante de la República Mexicana* (Picturesque and Archaeological Journey over the Most Interesting Part of the Mexican Republic). We also recall the lithograph of Casimiro Castro (1855–1856), in which he brought together under the title "Antigüedades mexicanas" (Mexican Antiquities) the most spectacular pieces in the National Museum. This image (figure 18.13), in which the Tizoc Stone is strangely depicted at upper right, was included in *México y sus alrededores* (Mexico City and Its Surrounding Area). In this same lithographic album, José Fernando Ramírez (1855–1856) attributed to the monolith the character of a monument dedicated to the sun and commemorative of the victories of Tizoc.

Brantz Mayer (1844: 84), secretary of the US delegation to Mexico from 1841 to 1842, tells us that the stone was exhibited at that time with a rare addi-

18.9. *Detail of the frontispiece of the catalog for William Bullock's 1823 Ancient Mexico exhibition. Frontispiece, Bullock 1824b.*

tion: "a stone cross now erected in the middle to sanctify it." Madame Calderón de la Barca (1843: 51), in a fine display of imagination, evokes its ritual use, specifying down to the color of the officiants' attire: "We afterwards saw the Stone of Sacrifices, now in the courtyard of the university, with a hollow in the middle, in which the victim was laid while six priests, dressed in red, their heads adorned with plumes of green feathers . . . held him down while the chief priest cut open his breast, threw his heart at the feet of the idol."

Despite the fact that, in 1866, Emperor Maximilian ordered that the entire museum be moved to the old Casa de Moneda, located on the northeast corner of the palace, the transfer of the Tizoc Stone did not occur until 1873. At that time it occupied the center of the patio (figure 18.3, no. 4), among great palm

18.10. *Wax miniature of the Tizoc Stone, brought to London by William Bullock. Courtesy, British Museum.*

18.11. *Rollout of the Tizoc Stone conquest scenes on its side panel. Lithograph by Carlos Nebel, 1963.*

18.12. Detail of Ideal Reconstruction of a Ceremony *by Jean Frédéric Waldeck, ca. 1832. A gladiatorial sacrifice takes place on a temalácatl, and in the background a cuauhxicalli is visible. Oil painting, "Reconstrucción ideal de una ceremonia prehispánica," in Museo Soumaya, Mexico City.*

18.13. Mexican Antiquities of the National Museum. *Lithograph by Casimiro Castro, 1856. The Tizoc Stone is visible at upper right.*

18.14. *The Tizoc Stone at the center of the patio in the National Museum. Photo engraving published by Désiré Charnay, 1885.*

trees and very close to the Coatlicue. Thus it appears there in many photographs and in an engraving (figure 18.14) published by Désiré Charnay (1885: 41) in *Les anciennes villes du Nouveau Monde* (The Ancient Cities of the New World). From that period also date the interpretations of Manuel Orozco y Berra (1881), who saw in the Tizoc Stone a cuauhxicalli that posthumously celebrated the deeds of the said *tlatoani*, and of Jesús Sánchez (1886), who understood it as a votive monument with images of dancers who bore their captives for sacrificing to the fire in a feast held every four years.

In 1883 the Gallery of Monoliths was created in the back of the building, so the collection's most valuable works were no longer exposed to the inclement weather (López Luján 2009: 167–170). Notices mention that the bulk of the transfer took place between September of that year and August 1886. The Tizoc Stone went to the west end of the gallery, next to the Coyolxauhqui head (figure 18.3, no. 5). The maneuver was completed with the arrival of the Calendar Stone, which enabled President Porfirio Díaz to hold the inauguration of the gallery on September 16, 1887.

CONCLUSION

Since the story is so well-known, we will not elaborate on the transfer of the Tizoc Stone to its present location in the Mexica Hall at the National Museum of

18.15. *Replicas of the Tizoc Stone reliefs sold by Désiré Charnay to the Peabody Museum, Harvard University. The Musée du quai Branly, Paris, has the same four replicas. Photo by Barbara W. Fash, 2004.*

Anthropology in Chapultepec Park (Bosque de Chapultepec). This magnificent construction was inaugurated by President Adolfo López Mateos on September 17, 1964. Since that time it has been possible to view this cuauhxicalli from a new perspective, not only as a paradigmatic reflection of Mexican national history but also as a universally appreciated masterpiece of art. Finally, we note the irony hiding in plain sight: despite the "posthumous" nature of this muted monument, the Tizoc Stone remains very much alive, calling out to each successive generation, inspiring it to study the stone anew, and reopening the door to the distant Mexica Empire.

REFERENCES CITED

Alvarado Tezozómoc, Hernando de
    2001   *Crónica mexicana*. Dastin, Madrid.

Archivo Histórico del Gobierno del Distrito Federal (AHGDF), Ayuntamiento, Historia en general, vol. 2254, exp. 22.

Beaufoy, Mark
    1828   *Mexican Illustrations*. Carpenter and Son, London.

Bullock, William
    1824a   *Six Months' Residence and Travels in Mexico; Containing Remarks on the Present State of New Spain, Its Natural Productions, State of Society, Manufactures, Trade, Agriculture, and Antiquities, &c.* John Murray–Albemarle-Street, London.
    1824b   *A Description of the Unique Exhibition, Called Ancient Mexico; Collected on the Spot in 1823, by the Assistance of the Mexican Government, and Now Open for Public Inspection at the Egyptian Hall, Piccadilly.* London: printed for the proprietor.

Calderón de la Barca, Madame
    1843   *Life in Mexico during a Residence of Two Years in That Country*. Chapman and Hall, London.

Carletti, Francesco
    1964   *My Voyage around the World*. Translated by Herbert Weinstock. Pantheon, New York.
    2002   *Razonamientos de mi viaje alrededor del mundo, 1594–1606*. Edited and translated by Francisca Perujo. UNAM, México, DF.

Castillo, Cristóbal del
    1991   *Historia de la venida de los pueblos mexicanos y otros pueblos e Historia de la conquista*. Edited and translated by Federico Navarrete Linares. INAH, México, DF.

Castro, Casimiro
    1855–1856   *México y sus alrededores. Colección de vistas, trajes y monumentos por C. Castro, J. Campillo, L. Auda y G. Rodríguez*. Decaen, México, DF.

Charnay, Désiré
    1885   *Les anciennes villes du Nouveau Monde*. Hachette, Paris.

Costeloe, Michael P.
    2008   *William Bullock, Connoisseur and Virtuoso of the Egyptian Hall: Piccadilly to Mexico (1773–1849)*. HiPLAM, Bristol, UK.

Dupaix, Guillermo
    n.d.   Unpublished papers, Colleción Gómez Orozco 187. Biblioteca Nacional de Antropología e Historia, México, DF.

Durán, Fray Diego
    1971   *Book of the Gods and Rites and the Ancient Calendar*. Edited and translated by Fernando Horcacitas and Doris Heyden. University of Oklahoma Press, Norman.
    1984   *Historia de las Indias de Nueva España e islas de tierra firme*, 2 vols. Porrúa, México, DF.

García Icazbalceta, Joaquín
- 1947 *Don fray Juan de Zumárraga: Primer obispo y arzobispo de México*, 4 vols. Porrúa, México, DF.

Gómez, José
- 1986 *Diario curioso y cuaderno de las cosas memorables en México durante el gobierno de Revillagidedo (1789–1794)*. Edited by Ignacio González-Polo. UNAM, México, DF.

Historia de los mexicanos por sus pinturas
- 2002 In Rafael Tena, *Mitos e historias de los antiguos nahuas*, pp. 23–95. Consejo Nacional para la Cultura y las Artes, México, DF.

Humboldt, Alexander von
- 1810 *Vues des Cordillères, et monumens des peuples indigènes de l'Amérique*. Chez F. Schoell, Paris.
- 1995 *Vistas de las cordilleras y monumentos de los pueblos indígenas de América*, 2 vols. Siglo Veintiuno, México, DF.

León y Gama, Antonio de
- 1832 *Descripción histórica y cronológica de las dos piedras . . .* Alejandro Valdés, México, DF.

López Austin, Alfredo
- 2006 Mitos e íconos de la ruptura del Eje Cósmico: Un glifo toponímico de las piedras de Tízoc y del Ex Arzobispado. *Anales del Instituto de Investigaciones Estéticas* 89: 93–134.

López Austin, Alfredo, and Leonardo López Luján
- 2009 *Monte Sagrado–Templo Mayor: El Cerro y la Pirámide en la Tradición Religiosa Mesoamericana*. UNAM and INAH, México, DF.

López Luján, Leonardo
- 2008 El adiós y triste queja del gran Calendario Azteca. *Arqueología Mexicana* 91: 78–83.
- 2009 La Coatlicue. In *Escultura Monumental Mexica*, ed. Eduardo Matos Moctezuma and Leonardo López Luján, pp. 115–229. Fundación Conmemoraciones 2010, México, DF.

Lyon, George Francis
- 1828 *Journal of a Residence and Tour in the Republic of Mexico in the Year 1826. With Some Account of the Mines of That Country*, 2 vols. J. Murray, Albemarle Street, London.

Matos Moctezuma, Eduardo
- 1997 Tezcatlipoca, Espejo que Humea. In *Antiguo Palacio del Arzobispado*, pp. 27–41. Secretaría de Hacienda y Crédito Público, Espejo de Obsidiana Ediciones, México, DF.
- 2009 La Piedra de Tízoc y la del Antiguo Arzobispado. In *Escultura Monumental Mexica*, ed. Eduardo Matos Moctezuma and Leonardo López Luján, pp. 291–326. Fundación Conmemoraciones 2010, México, DF.

Mayer, Brantz
    1844   *Mexico as It Was and as It Is*. Winchester, New York.

Mier y Terán Rocha, Lucía
    2005   *La primera traza de la Ciudad de México, 1524–1535*, 2 vols. UNAM and Fondo de Cultura Económica, México, DF.

Nebel, Carlos
    1963   *Viaje pintoresco y arqueológico sobre la parte más interesante de la República Mexicana*. Manuel Porrúa, México, DF.

Orozco y Berra, Manuel
    1881   Cuauhxicalli de Tízoc. *Anales del Museo Nacional* 1: 3–39.

Ramírez, José Fernando
    1855–1856 Antigüedades mexicanas conservadas en el Museo Nacional de México. In *México y sus alrededores. Colección de vistas, trajes y monumentos por C. Castro, J. Campillo, L. Auda y G. Rodríguez*, pp. 33–37. Decaen, México, DF.

Romero de Terreros, Manuel
    1959   *México en 1823 según el Panorama de Burford*. Manuel Porrúa, México, DF.

Sahagún, Fray Bernardino de
    1979   *Códice Florentino*, 3 vols. Archivo General de la Nación, México, DF.

Sánchez, Jesús
    1886   Notas arqueológicas III: El Cuauhxicalli de Tizoc. *Anales del Museo Nacional de México* 3: 127–136.

Sedano, Francisco
    1880   *Noticias de México*. J. R. Barbedillo, México, DF.

Taylor, Edward T.
    1959   *Mexico 1825–1828: The Journal and Correspondence of Edward Thornton Taylor*. Edited by C. Harvey Gardiner. University of North Carolina Press, Chapel Hill.

Toussaint, Manuel
    1992   *La Catedral de México y el Sagrario Metropolitano*. Porrúa, México, DF.

19

THE *REAL EXPEDICIÓN ANTICUARIA* COLLECTION

Marie-France Fauvet-Berthelot, Leonardo López Luján, and Susana Guimarães

Born in New Orleans in 1799 to a family of French émigrés, young Latour Allard traveled to Mexico in 1824, where he acquired a collection of Precolumbian artifacts, a Prehispanic manuscript, and various contemporary manuscripts and drawings. His collection is preserved today in the Museum of Non-Western Arts of the Quai Branly in Paris. Allard could hardly have imagined that this purchase would place him—almost two centuries later—at the heart of an astonishing story. This chapter details the investigation its authors carried out in French, Mexican, and US archives to understand how artifacts collected for the king of Spain at the beginning of the nineteenth century ended up in France. Our story touches on some of the great men of the period: Marie-Joseph Paul Yves Roch Gilbert du Motier (Marquis de la Fayette), Jean-François Champollion, and Alexander von Humboldt. More specifically, our tale presents a cast of six fascinating characters: a captain of Flemish Dragoons who was also an enlightened amateur Prehispanic art enthusiast, an unscrupulous draughtsman, an obstinate magistrate, an enthusiastic if luckless young man, a patriotic spy, and, last but not least, a mysterious individual we shall refer to as "Mr. X."

THE DUPAIX-CASTAÑEDA *REAL EXPEDICIÓN ANTICUARIA*

Three manuscript notebooks and 140 drawings, some of which depict objects in the Latour Allard collection, make up the warp of our tapestry, woven in 1821. Our story unfolds while the Colony of New Spain was living out its final days and the new Mexican nation was being born. These drawings, representing Mexican artifacts, were published in three European books. Two appeared in the nineteenth century: *Antiquities of Mexico* was published in London in 1831 under the aegis of Lord Kingsborough, while *Antiquités mexicaines* was produced in Paris in 1834 by the abbot Jean-Henri Baradère. The third volume, *Expediciones acerca de los antiguos monumentos de la Nueva España: 1805–1808*, was published in Madrid in 1969 by José Alcina Franch. The drawings incorporated in all three volumes were made by Guillermo Dupaix (ca. 1750–1817) and José Luciano Castañeda (1774–ca. 1834), who drew them as part of the *Real Expedición Anticuaria*, commissioned by King Charles IV of Spain. The purpose of the *Royal Expedition in Search of Antiquities*, conducted between 1805 and 1809, was to collect documents pertaining to the antiquities of New Spain so the Spanish Crown might better know that distant colony's past and more greatly appreciate its artistic traditions.

As early as 1803 Ciriaco González Carvajal, a naturalist, antiquarian, and honorary member of the Royal Academy of San Carlos, wrote of New Spain: "The country abounds in monuments for which nobody cares, and which would still be quite useful to document its history." He added, for the benefit of Viceroy José de Iturrigaray (1742–1815): "I have heard of a captain of the Dragoons, don J. Dupée [*sic*], of Flemish nationality, who, without the help of anyone and motivated by his inquiring nature, has made many useful discoveries in this field, in spite of many difficulties and many dangers" (AGN, Historia, vol. 116).

Clearly, Dupaix was the man for the task. An Austrian born in Luxemburg, he received a French education. Dupaix arrived in New Spain in 1790, where "he enroll[ed] in the regiment of the Dragoons of Mexico, where he ha[d] a rather dull career without ever going into battle" (Estrada de Gerlero 1994: 191). A man with an inquiring mind, Dupaix had earlier traveled to Greece and Italy, knew Egyptian art, and was a connoisseur of the arts of ancient Mexico. He often manifested his displeasure over the way people in Europe talked about the ancient Mexican civilizations, especially Alexander von Humboldt, who at the time was rather influential in such matters and considered that the local populations were at best only half-civilized.

Dupaix accepted the royal mandate (*real comisión*) on October 4, 1804 (ibid.: 195), and asked Viceroy Iturrigaray "for a draughtsman versed in the drawing of objects and plans, for which [he] propose[d] Don José Castañeda, who has been a student at the Royal Academy of San Carlos in New Spain . . . as well as Don Juan Castillo, retired Dragoon Sergeant, to write up their accounts . . . also for two soldiers from the Dragoon corps, trusted men, to help them during their trek in difficult regions" (AGN, Historia, vol. 116).

With his four helpers, Guillermo Dupaix was entrusted with the mission of evaluating ancient sculptures and monuments throughout New Spain; he was to describe and make drawings of them while leaving them in situ. The results of his labors had to be written in triplicate, as ordered by the Spanish Crown for any official document it commissioned.

The *Real Expedición Anticuaria* incorporated three forays, exploring vast tracts of land throughout the country. Between campaigns, important work had to be done in Mexico City; there the field sketches and drawings were cleanly redrawn by Castañeda, and detailed descriptions of the monuments were written up from Dupaix's draft notes. The first of these expeditions lasted four months, from January 5 to May 9, 1805, and covered the present Mexican states of Puebla, Veracruz, and Morelos. A report on this first expedition, in triplicate, was remitted to the viceroy on January 17, 1806.

The second, much longer field expedition lasted fourteen months, from February 24, 1806, to April 1807. It focused on the Basin of Mexico, the present State of Morelos, and the ancient cities of Monte Albán, Zaachila, and Mitla in what is now the State of Oaxaca. The third and final campaign lasted even longer, seventeen months, from December 4, 1807, to May 1809. This exploration revisited Puebla and Oaxaca and, for the first time, included Chiapas: Ciudad Real (today's San Cristóbal de las Casas) and Palenque. An original version of the documents pertaining to the second and third expeditions was given to Viceroy Apodaca in January 1817, with the promise that the other two copies required by the Spanish Crown administration would be remitted at a later date. Dupaix died in June 1817 before he could finish that all-consuming task, but, thanks to Fausto de Elhuyar, the executor of his will, the results of those expeditions were preserved.

ELHUYAR: COLLECTING PATRIMONY

Always a careful man, Dupaix, having fallen gravely ill, wrote his will in July 1813, choosing as his executor his friend Fausto de Elhuyar (1755–1833). Elhuyar would play a key role in our story. He was the director of the Royal Tribunal of the Mines and the discoverer of wolfram. In his will, Guillermo Dupaix specified what should become of his possessions: "that, after my death, he [Elhuyar] should make the inventory of my possessions, sell or exchange what can be disposed of thus, and that the rest should be sold at public auction in the best conditions to obtain the best value" (UTBLAC G369).

Dupaix's inventory of his possessions was exact: personal drawings, some archaeological objects, and curios. He was careful to specify what had derived from the expeditions—"the objects pertaining to the Antiquities of this Kingdom, which he has collected during his Mission, as well as the Plans and descriptions he made of them, and which belong to the central government" (ibid.)—and to separate them from his own properties.[1]

When Guillermo Dupaix died in 1817, Elhuyar gathered everything that had belonged to him and moved it to the Real Seminario de Minas in Mexico

Marie-France Fauvet-Berthelot, Leonardo López Luján, and Susana Guimarães

19.1. *Greenstone figurine, 70 × 20 × 12 cm. Latour Allard collection (MQB 71.1887.155.13). Photo by Daniel Ponsard.*

City: "Since that person has passed away, I have had his papers and curios placed in a room set aside for that purpose in the Real Seminario de Minas, where they are kept very securely. I saw to it that the required triage was made and everything that pertains to the mentioned antiquities is preserved there, awaiting Your Excellency's decision about what should be done with them"[2] (ibid).

Elhuyar oversaw the completion of the second and third copies of the documents relating to the last two campaigns of the *Real Expedición Anticuaria*: "I think that one should first make sure that the three copies of the Drawings of the two Expeditions, still to be drawn, should be completed, together with their corresponding descriptions so that two sets can be sent to the Court, and the third can be kept in the capital, there to be carefully preserved and annexed to the documents from the first Expedition" (ibid.).

For that task he recommended José Luciano Castañeda, since "nobody can better be recommended than he who was part of the three Expeditions, doing the first drafts in front of the objects themselves" (ibid.). So Elhuyar gave the complete works their final form, with Castañeda's help. These various sets of drawings were remitted to the Colonial and Spanish governments. Some were used for the publications referred to previously.[3]

Elhuyar's efforts did not stop there. In 1818 and again in 1819, endorsed by Viceroy Juan Ruíz de Apodaca, Count of Venadito (1754–1835), he brought to the capital many of the pieces collected and drawn by Dupaix and Castañeda during the *Real Expedición Anticuaria*. When one reads documents in the American archives that mention those pieces, one is amazed at the remarkable organization of such a large-scale operation. A precise list was established of the "original American antiquities of medium size recognized by Don Guillermo Dupaix in various places of this Kingdom, and mentioned in the drawings and the descriptions of those three Expeditions" (ibid. G373) that were to be collected.[4]

Documentation during each campaign included a description of the objects, specifying their materials, dimensions, and provenience. The project tried to gather—in some cases to no avail—72 objects from 20 different places: 15 of these had been inventoried during the first expedition, 55 during the second, and 2 during the final campaign. There are 69 stone sculptures, 1 ceramic artifact, 1 of wood, and 1 of copper. The artifacts incorporate 27 human figures, 18 animals, 8 plant forms, 10 glyphs, and 9 ritual objects.[5]

The viceroy's endorsement allowed Elhuyar to enlist the help of local authorities to complete the operation. On December 14, 1818, he sent the list to the viceroy so the objects might be collected. Precise recommendations were made for recovery; if some objects were too heavy or the roads in too poor a state, it was specified that a stonecutter should chip away the part that was not sculpted: "as to the problem caused by their weights, I believe that in most cases it can be solved by cutting away matter, when the pieces are not sculpted on all sides or on all faces, a task that any stonecutter can perform on several of them" (ibid.).[6]

He continued:

> It has been indicated where certain monuments are integrated within the walls of the houses or of other buildings, from where they will have to be taken, to be replaced by other stones or even just by masonry; though these modifications are minor and can easily be done by the building owners themselves, the under-delegates will have to persuade them to do the work, showing them the collecting is done for the honor of the kingdom and of the Nation, which may even at the same time overcome the misgivings a number of them could have to see the pieces disappear. (ibid.)

Finally, Elhuyar even proposed bringing back pieces not mentioned by Dupaix, "and urged the sub-delegates to collect and send back monuments that are not in the inventory" (ibid.). The "sub-delegates" were the local representatives of the vice-regal government.

Events proceeded quickly. In January 1819 orders were sent to the intendants of Mexico City, Puebla, Veracruz, and Oaxaca, as well as to the governor of Ciudad Real de Chiapas. The intendant of Veracruz asked who was to pay for the costs of transportation, the one in Puebla said the monolith in Huauhquechula was too heavy and its weight could not be lightened because the stone was full of engravings, and the governor of Chiapas affirmed that one of the pieces requested had been stolen. The question also arose as to whether some of the pieces should be sent to Spain. The response was that royal finances would pay for transportation from Veracruz, that the monument in Huauhquechula would remain in place, and that, as far as Spain was concerned, all the antiquities would remain in Mexico (ibid. G245, G373).

LATOUR ALLARD'S ASTONISHING ACQUISITION

Once the artifacts arrived in Mexico City, their history becomes somewhat sketchy. This is understandable given that Mexico, recently independent, was in turmoil. One cannot tell for certain where the collection was deposited, although it is probable that it was combined with the documentation of the *Real Expedición Anticuaria* in the Real Seminario de Minas. However, after Mexico's independence, Fausto de Elhuyar, still faithful to the Spanish Crown, returned to Spain in 1822. According to Elena Estrada de Gerlero (1994: 194): "The material from the *Real Expedición*, as well as from the personal travels of the Flemish connoisseur of antiques, had been deposited by Elhuyar in a safe place within the Real Seminario de Minas; shortly after his departure from the country, it went on to form part of the new National Museum, created after the independence of Mexico by Lucas Alamán."

The artworks brought back to Mexico City would probably have been shipped to the Spanish king if New Spain had remained a colony. However, since Mexico had won its independence in 1821, the artifacts became the patrimony of the new Mexican nation. In fact, they should have been brought to the Mexican National Museum, founded in 1825. How was it that pieces collected for New Spain or for the Mexican nation ended up being sold to a private individual?[7]

Toward the end of 1824, Latour Allard, then age twenty-five, was traveling in Mexico and acquired at auction an archaeological collection that according to the description by Tomás Murphy, contained:

> 1st 180 idols, statues, some of them complete, some damaged, snakes and other animals and a number of low reliefs etc, 2nd 120 excellent drawings, very well done, representing the monuments found by Captain Dupaix in Palenque Viejo and in the palace in Mitla, in the province of Chiapa located between Oaxaca and Ciudad Real de Guatemala. There are also other drawings from various origins, among which a complete representation of the circular stone [Tizoc Stone] that is in the University in the city of Mexico. 3rd a book compris-

 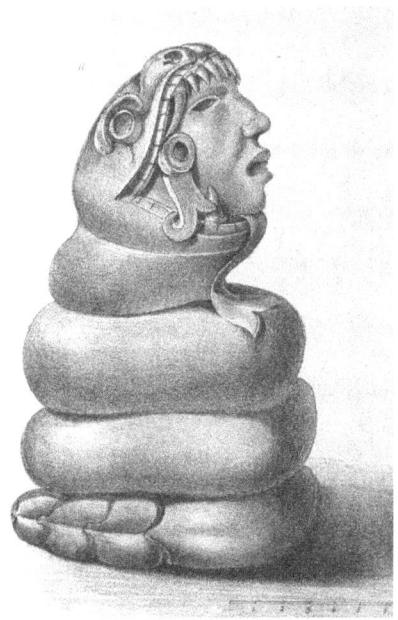

19.2A. *Coiled rattlesnake with human face emerging from mouth. Dense gray volcanic stone; 47.7 × 19.8 × 26.7 cm. Photo by Daniel Ponsard.*

19.2B. *Drawing by Aglio 1831. Latour Allard collection (MQB 71.1887.155.19).*

ing twelve folios in maguey paper, full of symbolic paintings . . . which once belonged to the famed Boturini. (AHSRE 3–3–3888, 1827)

We will meet Murphy again shortly. Latour Allard shipped his collection to France in 1825. But who did he buy it from, and how was it transported to France?

Thanks to a document that recently came to light in the archives of the Mexican Ministry for Foreign Affairs, we have been able to reconstitute the story of an astounding auction carried out by Castañeda. Indeed, it was he—the faithful draughtsman of the *Real Expedición Anticuaria*—who disposed of that collection of archaeological objects, manuscripts, and drawings, which by then had become the property of the new Mexican nation. Castañeda took advantage of Dupaix's death and of the profound changes occurring within the country to reimburse himself for the many hours of work he had put in without pay for the Spanish government.[8] The local situation must have been very murky indeed if he could organize such a public auction without question. Undoubtedly, Mexico's priorities at the time must have been other things. Castañeda's auction soon gained a certain fame, if not notoriety, and this is where a new character enters our story: Tomás Murphy.

TOMÁS MURPHY AND THE TROUBLED YOUNG MEXICAN REPUBLIC

Tomás Murphy was the son of an Irish expatriate with the same name. On February 26, 1824, he was sent to London, where Mexico had recently opened its first and only European embassy. He served as "first officer and under-secretary with the function of interpreter to the Legation of the Mexican Republic to His British Majesty" (AHSRE L-E–1614, 1824). Murphy still retained the post in 1826 (ibid. L-E–1617, 1826), but by 1831 he was living in France as head of the General Trade Agency of Mexico in Paris.

Murphy had been commissioned, in the name of the Mexican government, by Sebastián Camacho (1791–1847), minister of the Republic of the United States of Mexico in London, to make discreet inquiries about the purchase and subsequent shipment out of Mexico of Latour Allard's collection. Incensed by the auction, Murphy launched a formal police investigation to obtain all the evidence of that operation, even sending one of his acquaintances to interview Latour Allard. In a document sent to Camacho on February 1, 1827, Murphy reported that he could not objectively doubt the buyer's good faith:

> Mr. Latour does not hide any of the details of his purchase . . . He bought the collection towards the end of 1824 from the draughtsman or painter who accompanied Captain Dupaix during the mission he undertook for the governments of the Viceroys, financed by royal funds at the time, and, though I cannot be sure of his name . . . I believe he is called Cañedo or Castañedo. Mr. Latour says he was quite open in his bid, competing against English buyers who pushed him into paying a high price, the amount of which he has not unveiled; he says he took the crated collection to Veracruz where, in February of 1825, it was loaded on board of the French brigantine the *Éclair* bound for Bordeaux, without any difficulty or problem being caused either by the customs office of Mexico City or of Veracruz. (ibid. 3-3–3888, 1827)

Murphy continued:

> From all this, it is obvious that this man does not hide the origin of the operation, as evidenced in the description of the collection he had published in the *Revue encyclopédique*, tome 3 of 1826, n° 31, booklet 93 . . . where one can read, among other things: Mr. Dupaix having died shortly after having accomplished his mission, and political events having caused a breach in the relations between Mexico and Spain, the draughtsman thought he could dispose of the results of the works to which he had contributed so much. Thus, Mr. Latour has openly declared to the world that it is indeed the artist from the expedition who thought he had the right to sell that precious collection of Mexican antiquities. The sale was done out in the open, just as was effected the shipment of the pieces, all that being done in the presence of the Mexican government who was ruling in 1824, thereby depriving Mexican science of such a rich treasury. (ibid.)

Murphy recommended that "this national treasure, viciously bought, [should be recovered by buying it back from Latour Allard, who in turn] should

THE *REAL EXPEDICIÓN ANTICUARIA* COLLECTION

19.3A. *Chicomecoatl, goddess of maize and of all vegetable food. Grayish volcanic stone; 63.5 × 35 ×18.2 cm. Photo by Daniel Ponsard.*

19.3B. *Drawing by Aglio 1831. Latour Allard collection (MQB 71.1887.155.14).*

make a reasonable offer, or else be brought to justice, [as] under no circumstance these treasures should be allowed to belong to an employee of Captain Dupaix during his mission, whose works have been funded by the government" (ibid.).

Murphy raised the potential of legal action on the part of the Spanish government, which could argue "for its ancient rights over an operation which was conducted at the time of its dominion." Two days later, on February 3, Murphy added to this report the detailed inventory of the collection (appendix 3), together with its price: 70,000 francs for the set of archaeological pieces and 75,000 for the whole set of documents (ibid.).

Murphy's documents support the conclusion that Latour Allard bought the collection openly. The shadowy character in the story seems to have been Castañeda, but we lack additional information that could enlighten us as to the precise circumstances under which he took possession of the pieces and documents of the *Real Expedición Anticuaria*.

The auction that so troubled Murphy probably stimulated passage of a law to protect the Mexican national patrimony, enacted on November 16, 1827, prohibiting the export of any archaeological object. This law was mentioned by the Mexican consul in Bordeaux, who, in July 1835, asked that "our customs offices not let out illegally such precious objects which enrich the foreign museums to the detriment of our own, which remains so poorly endowed" (ibid. L-E-16-3-49, 1830–1838).

LATOUR ALLARD: THE IMPOSSIBLE RESALE

One wonders why Latour Allard bought the archaeological collection. Was it for his own delectation, because of a personal taste for Mexican antiquities? Or was he already thinking of proposing it, for his own profit, to a French institution? Or, possibly, had its purchase ruined him financially, forcing him ultimately to sell it? Few things are known about this individual.[9] Latour Allard came from a French family, originally from Alpine of Haute-Provence, who were among the founders of New Orleans. In 1830, following a bequest from the family, their plantation in Bayou Saint John became the city's first great park (Freiberg 1980: 218; López Luján and Fauvet-Berthelot 2005: 34–35). Born in New Orleans, Latour Allard studied in France but later wrote that he did not know that country's mores and customs. His letters reveal a young man, somewhat gauche. For five years he tenaciously attempted to sell his collection; any potential buyer was contacted. From documents in the Parisian archives, one finds him, year after year, ever more in need, lowering his expectations. It was all in vain.

Immediately after having bought the collection and upon its arrival in France, Latour Allard got in touch with the relevant institutions. The collection soon became famous in erudite circles, thanks largely to the noises made by its owner. The artist Jean-Frédéric Waldeck (1766–1875) mentioned it in his diary on January 22, 1826: "I went to the house of Mr. Latour to see a manuscript on agave paper, a collection of drawings among which I recognized a number of the same antiques I drew in lithographs for Bertou [sic]; and stone sculptures that were rather well preserved" (NL Ayer 1260a).

On January 10, 1827, Joel R. Poinsett (1779–1851), US minister plenipotentiary to Mexico, wrote to Peter S. Duponceau (1760–1844) of the American Philosophical Society to warn him that Latour Allard had taken copies of the texts and drawings of the *Real Expedición Anticuaria* to be reprinted in Paris (Freeman 1962: 532). Reports on the collection had also been published in the *Revue encyclopédique* (Anonymous 1826a) and the *Bulletin de la Société de Géographie* (Latour Allard 1828; Warden 1829: 45), of which Latour Allard was a correspondent. But when they arrived in Europe, the pieces selected by Guillermo Dupaix as reflections of the art of the great civilizations of ancient Mexico would lose their status as art objects and be diminished to testimonials merely of a certain level of human development. The weight of the opinion of a luminary such as Alexander von Humboldt (1769–1859) would soon prevail over the open-mindedness of a little-known captain of Dragoons.

Humboldt wrote to Latour Allard on July 28, 1826, in a letter that soon circulated widely among learned society:

THE *REAL EXPEDICIÓN ANTICUARIA* COLLECTION

> I cannot thank you enough, dear Sir, for the pleasure I received at seeing the objects you have collected in Mexico and which bring a new light to shine on an almost unknown part of the History of human genius. This is indeed the most complete collection of its kind and which relates so felicitously to the so happily conceived idea of following the progress of the arts among half barbarian peoples . . . It would be true to the munificence of a great monarch to deposit the Drawings of Mr. Dupaix, to whose scrupulous exactness I can bear witness, in some great Library. The naïve simplicity of these drawings themselves attests to the truthfulness of the testimony. (AHSRE 3-3-3888, 1826–1829; Anonymous 1826a, 1826b; ANP O/3/1417; CMR w/n; Dupaix 1834)

Humboldt added, as a note: "The Drawings of Mr. Dupaix, mentioned in the present letter, number one hundred and twenty and are part of Mr. Latour Allard's collection" (ibid.).

Comforted by this letter, Latour Allard wrote, as early as July 31, 1826, to Louis Nicolas Philippe Auguste, count of Forbin (1779–1841), the general director of the Royal Museums:

> Having arrived in Paris a few weeks ago, with a collection of objects of antiquity I brought back from Mexico, I would like to know, before I go with them to England, if it would not be deemed convenient by the French government to acquire them; born in America from French parents, having been educated in France, it seems natural to me that, by a sort of preference, I should make my offer first to this country. Up to now, the persons I have had to deal with in this affair seem to have been rather indifferent, and so I hope you will forgive the liberty I am taking today in writing directly to you. (ANP O/3/1427)

He added:

> As I am certain that nobody better than you, Sir, would be able to judge on this matter, and to report your findings to the Minister, I would consider myself extremely privileged if I could have the honor of receiving your visit in my home, and to show you my collection, which is undoubtedly not without interest, as you can judge by the letter I have received from Baron De Humboldt, a copy of which I send you enclosed. As I do not have any pressing business, I leave you free to decide the hour and the day of your visit. However, I would appreciate receiving written notice of it the day before. Please be assured, Sir, of my respect and distinguished consideration. (ibid.)

On August 8, 1826, the count of Forbin reported to Louis-François-Sosthène, viscount of La Rochefoucauld (1785–1864), in charge of the Department of Fine Arts in the king's house, on his visit to Latour Allard where he examined the Mexican collection. He concluded:

> Most of this curious collection, which, because of the very nature of its objects, can shed a bright light on the history of religious ceremonies in Mexico, does not belong in the Royal Museum, and can only be housed in a library. It is

made of: 1st a written work in the Spanish language, richly illustrated by original drawings by Mr. Dupaix: the naivety of these drawings is a sure warrant of their authenticity; 2nd a book written on magais [sic] paper with notes by Botterini [sic], an Italian author who wrote on Mexico; 4th [sic] a rather large quantity of idols in clay and other materials, a few fragments of architecture and various utensils for every day use. This last part *only* could fit within the collection of the museum, as it would be useful indeed to compare the art objects from different peoples and to follow their progress according to their degrees of civilization. But Latour Allard has firmly asserted that he did not wish to split anything from his collection, for which he avowed he wanted the sum of *Two hundred thousand francs*. I have not entered into any negotiation on that price, which seems rather steep, and I think that Mr. Latour Allard could lower his pretension, if one was to seriously deal with his collection. (ibid.; original emphasis)

On August 31, 1826, Théodore (1782–1859), count of Turpin de Crissé, inspector general of the Department of Fine Arts in the House of the King, wrote a letter to Forbin in which he could not hide his horror regarding these Mexican pieces: "In terms of art, nothing can be more wretched, more barbarous than these Idols or these simulacra of deities; it seems they are the fruit of the darkest and most extravagant imagination; the monsters invented by the Indians and the horrible Gaul figures are yet more bearable than the ones gathered in this collection" (ibid.).

Théodore nevertheless conceded a certain interest in the architecture reproduced in Castañeda's drawings for sale at the same time as the collection of objects: "Some of the monuments of such a particular architecture present however a great interest because of the singular aspects of the temples, the sacrifice altars, and the tombs they represent" (ibid.). He concluded:

I can, Mr. Viscount, only repeat what has been told to you about the lack of relevance of this collection for the Museum of Antiquities. It is thus on the subject of the possible interest it could have for the archaeological science that you have deigned consult me, as well as on the advantage to be derived from making such an acquisition for the royal library or for the private library of the King. (ibid.)

He did not give his opinion on the price, which by then had been reduced to 60,000 francs. The sum was still deemed too high, however, and the king denied the acquisition.

On December 2, 1826, a commission had been convened, among whose members were Abel Rémusat (1788–1832) and Jean-François Champollion (1790–1832), as well as a certain Dubois, a student of David, the draughtsman of Egyptian antiquities of the Charles X Museum who knew the resale value of the objects. The commission was entrusted with the task of "reporting on the state and the historical interest of a collection of Mexican monuments trans-

THE REAL EXPEDICIÓN ANTICUARIA COLLECTION

 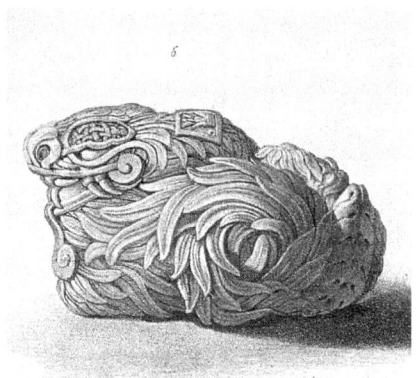

19.4A. *Feathered serpent. Pinkish volcanic stone; 30 × 54 × 54 cm. Photo by Hughes Dubois.*

19.4B. *Drawing by Aglio 1831. Latour Allard collection (MQB 71.1887.155.1).*

ported to Paris by Mr. Latour-Allard."[10] In its report the committee "recognizes unanimously that this collection, though not extensive and made up of small sized pieces, nevertheless presents a real interest for historical studies, in that, with the exception of a few pieces which have been dispersed among the various cabinets, it is the only one of its nature in Europe to date" (ANP O/3/1417).

The commission added that

> viewed as art objects, these monuments are only of a mediocre interest, as they are the product of a civilization in its infancy, or of a civilization that became stationary after its first tries at Art . . . In a historical perspective, one cannot doubt that most of the objects of Mr. Latour Allard's collection are related to [a] religious cult and to the Mythology of the Mexicans from before the Spanish Conquest; but as we are today almost completely deprived of written or traditional documents that could explain these extraordinary representations and allow one to associate each monument to the mythological Idea it is supposed to express, Science can only draw [little] proven information from these figures, information such as this Science requires nowadays. (ibid.)

Then an argument of a different nature was put forward:

> However, the reason itself that has caused these monuments to lose their historical interest in the present state of our knowledge also contributes to give them a real attractiveness, though quite different in nature: one knows that the Spaniards, conquerors of the Mexican Empire, strove with a fatal perseverance to completely destroy all traces of the ancient Aztec institutions. In particular, sculpture monuments were the object of this interdiction. Those who, quite by chance, escaped that almost total destruction have thus acquired a certain importance. This pleads in favor of Mr. Latour-Allard's collection, and it is undoubtedly due to these reasons that he places the price at sixty thousand francs for the set of the monuments he owns. (ibid.)

Champollion submitted the commission's report to the king on January 31, 1827. On February 9 the king thanked the commission but still did not believe he should acquire the collection. The ministery then wrote to Latour Allard:

> I placed under the King's eyes the report of the commission gathered to examine the Mexican antiquities that you have proposed to sell to the crown. I regret quite sincerely to have to tell you that H.R.H cannot acquire this collection, on which the commission has reported quite favorably, but the purchase of the same order done recently with public funds do [sic] not allow H.R.H. to add this new expense to the many costs that weigh at the time on the Crown's treasury. (ANP O/3/1427)

On June 24, 1827, Latour Allard wrote a letter to the new minister of the King's House in which, while apologizing for perhaps being overbearing, as he was "totally ignorant of the customs of France," explained that he had been "for over a year in Paris with a rather precious collection of Mexican antiquities, which has been seen and appreciated by several distinguished scientists, among whom [is] the famed Baron von Humboldt" (ibid.). He added, "If you would be so kind, Sir, to name a commission for the examination of this collection, and to enter in some agreement with me, my conditions would be most reasonable as, having to go back to attend to my own affairs in America, I am ready to [make] some concessions" (ibid.).

As confident as ever, Latour Allard even listed people he would have liked to see on the commission, "who are not likely to get influenced by the little faction that formed against me," proposing: "I would want it to be made up of Mr. Jomard and Mr. Warden, both members of the Royal Institute of France and having consecrated their lives to the study of the monuments from Egypt and the Americas, Mr. Rathiel, sculptor of her royal highness Madame the Duchess of Berry, and Mr. Espercieux, sculptor of statues" (ibid.).

The answer came quickly: there was no need for a new commission, all the more so since no funds were left.[11] Latour Allard then tried to sell his archaeological collection to the English (CMR s/n) and also in Berlin, but he met with refusals as he kept asking for a price others deemed too steep. That same year, though, Agostino Aglio (1777–1857) bought the complete set of the documents from him on behalf of Edward King (1795–1837), Lord Kingsborough (Latour Allard 1828: 277; Warden 1829: 45; Farcy 1834: viii). During one of his stays in Paris, Aglio drew sixteen of the archaeological pieces, which would be published over eleven lithographic plates in *Antiquities of Mexico* together with the texts and the drawings of the *Real Expedición Anticuaria* (Aglio 1831; Dupaix 1831).

On June 10, 1828, Latour Allard, apparently in desperate straits, made a new offer to the minister of the royal house: "In the dire situation in which I find myself, I cannot pretend to impose any condition anymore, I cannot hope for any profit, and let you fix a price, and will find myself happy if it can cover two thirds of the sum I have paid for the collection" (ANP O/3/1427). But the answer he received on June 17 was still negative. At last, on April 9, 1830, the count of Forbin again wrote to the viscount of La Rochefoucauld:

> Mr. Latour Allard's situation is becoming every day more difficult and his resources dwindle ever more. He has reached such a state of need and he is so closely pursued by his creditors that it would be possible, according to the report I received from Mr. Dubois, the draughtsman of Egyptian antiquities in the Musée Charles X and himself a connoisseur of art objects, to acquire the aforementioned collection for the price of six thousand francs . . . I believe that it would be useful, as well as educational and interesting to put these objects next to those of a similar nature which already belong to the museum of the Dauphin. (ibid.)

But this proposal also failed.[12]

MELNOTTE, OR "MR. X": SUCCESS AT LAST

Finally, in 1830 Latour Allard sold his collection to a private individual. The man was named Melnotte, an obscure individual about whom nothing else is known, not even his first name. He represented himself as "an ancient patented servant of his Majesty" (AMN A5). For a time, Melnotte was Latour Allard's neighbor when the latter was living in Paris. As early as 1834 Melnotte tried to sell the collection to the French court and later, as Latour Allard had before him, renewed his offer. On May, 15, 1846, he wrote: "For the past sixteen years, I have had in my possession a collection of Mexican antiquities, gathered on order of his Highness, the late King Charles IV of Spain, and having been the property of Mr. Latour Allard. I have not shown it to anyone" (ibid.).

Dubois came to see the collection, which by then consisted of 180 pieces, and gave Cailleux, the general director of the museums, a very favorable report on September 16, 1846:

> Mr. Melnotte's collection, which is much larger than any collection of this type brought to Europe, has a real value, due [to] the excellent choice of the pieces that compose it. None of those hideous fetishes, none of those rough clay drafts hand made by some savage people, but, on the contrary, this is the work of a nation that had already become familiarized with art processes, thus being able to give shape to granite, porphyry, and even to jasper, whose many varieties can only be carved with the use of a drill . . . The sum of six thousand francs, that Mr. Melnotte is asking, corresponds to the one I would have set myself for such a precious collection. (ibid.)

However, the purchase fell through. The proposal was renewed again in January, March, and May 1847 and yet again in March 1848.

> Finally, it is in December of 1849, after a last attempt by Melnotte on October 31, and on the proposal of Adrien de Longpérier (1816–1882), the curator of

sculptures and antiquities, that the Count Alfred Emilien de Nieuwerkerke (1811–1892), the director of the national museums, decides to purchase the collection for the sum of six thousand francs. One hundred and sixty-two objects are mentioned in the decree, but only one hundred and fifty-seven of them are taken and inventoried by the Louvre. In fact, in the registry of admissions to the museum collections, as compared with the catalogue of the collection established by Melnotte, which comprises one hundred and eighty pieces, twenty-two fragments of obsidian and stone from Palenque and Mitla are lacking. (Guimarâes 1996: 72–73)

DUELING INVENTORIES

Inventories of the Latour Allard collection began making the rounds in 1826, as soon as he started to promote the sale of his collection. The Murphy Inventory (appendix 3), with 182 numbers, was attached to the Tomás Murphy document. This inventory probably represents the original list and, in addition to the description of the pieces, provides their dimensions as well as the price for the entire collection. The other inventories, the one of the Center for Maya Research (1826) and that of the Louvre (1840), underline the importance of the publication of the Dupaix-Castañeda drawings because both refer to the illustrations of Lord Kingsborough's work, *Antiquities of Mexico*, published in 1831; such illustrated pieces initiated the beginnings of both lists.

The Center for Maya Research Inventory is fairly complete, incorporating not only descriptions and dimensions of the 183 objects but also data on the rest of the collection, such as "a few natural history specimens, among which [are] three large urns containing flowers from the tree of the hands (árbol de las manitas) preserved in alcohol" (CMR 1826). The Louvre Inventory dates back to 1840 and is very close to the preceding one. However, it does not give the dimensions of the objects and only has 157 numbers, as it does not contain the obsidian fragments or the stones from Palenque or Mitla. In addition, there is no mention of two mirrors (96 and 98).

In the Louvre there is also an inventory that corresponds to the state of the collection at the time it was sold to Melnotte in 1849. It lists 157 numbers, with a few variations when compared to the 1840 inventory: for instance, the writing table with low-reliefs on all four sides (no. 56) has become "a writing table supposed to have belonged to Montezuma" (Archives Centrales des Musées Nationaux 1840–1850: 3). On the Museum of the Quai Branly website one can find the ancient inventories from the Ethnography Museum of the Trocadero (a collection spread between numbers 20.001 and 20.652), the Museum of Man (coll. 87.155), and the Museum of the Quai Branly (MQB 71.1887.155).[13]

Today, 138 objects are attributed to the Latour Allard collection in the Museum of Man (and in the Museum of the Quai Branly). One certainly should look for

THE REAL EXPEDICIÓN ANTICUARIA COLLECTION

19.5A. *Flea with human face. Brownish-red volcanic stone; 30 × 22.4 × 45.5 cm. Photo by Daniel Ponsard.*

19.5B. *Drawing by Aglio 1831. Latour Allard Collection (MQB 71.1887.155.18).*

the remaining pieces within the objects [that] arrived in the Louvre without any mention of a donor's name (collection 87.50), but, for a number of objects, the confusion with the Franck collection (87.159) renders this task almost impossible. How indeed can one tell two house deities apart when no other description exists? (Guimarâes 1996: 73)

CONCLUSION: THE COLLECTION GOES PUBLIC

The purchase of the ancient Dupaix/Castañeda–Latour Allard–Melnotte collection in 1849 vastly enlarged the Precolumbian collections already in the Louvre Museum. Apparently thanks to this purchase, as early as 1850 Longpérier was able to open a small Mexican museum in a wing of the Louvre Palace. In 1851 this museum took the name Museum of American Antiquities, and this is where the best pieces of what was known at the time as the Latour Allard collection were exhibited (Anonymous 1852; Guimarâes 1994, 1996).

Unfortunately, despite public interest this American museum fell into neglect and had to be closed in 1870. The museum's Precolumbian collections were transferred to the Trocadero Palace, to the new Ethnographic Museum created on the occasion of the 1878 Universal Exhibition. There, they were to be added to other Precolumbian and ethnographic collections (López Luján and Fauvet-Berthelot 2005: 29–31). In the American gallery one could then see pieces from the Latour Allard collection, one of which was published by Ernest-Théodore Hamy (1842–1908), the museum's director.[14] In 1937 this institution was replaced by the Museum of Man, set up in a new building erected on the same site for the 1937 Universal Exposition under the aegis of Dr. Paul Rivet (1876–1958). The Aztec statuary of the Latour Allard collection remained in a choice position, in the window cases of the American gallery; their presentation evolved as the building was renovated, first in 1976 and again in 1992.

In 2000 the famous Quetzalcoatl feathered serpent from that collection returned to the Louvre in the Sessions Pavilion, which had been set up to present a set of "extra-European" pieces.[15] Finally in 2006, as was the case with all the collections of the ethnology laboratory of the Museum of Man, the Latour Allard collection was transferred to the new Museum of the Quai Branly. In the permanent exhibition, one can see today in the "Aztec room" eighteen pieces from that collection, as well as a stone statue, kept in the case dedicated to Teotihuacan.

Thus, from the *Real Expedición Anticuaria* to the Museum of the Quai Branly, the vagaries of Mexican history have allowed a collection initially gathered by order of the Spanish Crown to end up in its present resting place, in France. What is most important is the fact that this exceptional ensemble, a true part of the world patrimony, is now in a collection that is open to the public and has never been dispersed among private collectors. So today anyone can enjoy these wonderful works of art.

NOTES

1. When examining the list of the goods contained in the will, one clearly sees that Dupaix did not in fact claim ownership of the pieces collected during the three expeditions, either for the benefit of the Spanish government or for his own.

2. That is where William Bullock (1824) saw those pieces.

3. Today, several copies of the manuscripts and drawings of the *Real Expedición Anticuaria* are preserved, commissioned by the Colonial government as well as, later, by the Mexican government. They are kept in the Laboratorio de Antropología de la Universidad de Sevilla (Dupaix 1969), in the Museo Naval and the Biblioteca Nacional in Madrid (Palop Martínez and Cerdá Esteve 1997), in the American Philosophical Society in Philadelphia (Freeman 1962: 537), in the Biblioteca Nacional de Antropología e Historia of Mexico City (Dupaix 1969), and in the Library of Congress in Washington, DC. A copy dating back to 1821 has recently been seen on the private market.

4. However, a great number of the objects mentioned by Dupaix are not on that list, either because they were too heavy to be moved, because they were part of larger monuments, or possibly because they did not strike Elhuyar's fancy.

5. In Elhuyar's list, one easily recognizes several pieces on exhibit today in the Museum of the Quai Branly: a frog with a human face, a fish, a human skull, and a date 4 Acatl (MQB 71.1887.155.6, 17, 47, and 122; López Luján and Fauvet-Berthelot 2005: cat. 45, 56, 73, and 76).

6. The sculptures referred to as MQB 71.1887.155.16, 17, and 123 present a flat reverse side, exhibiting modern tool marks that smoothed out the surface after the original anchor tenon had been chopped off to reduce weight (ibid.: cat. 69, 73, and 86).

7. If the draft of a letter from Ignacio Cubas is correct, the Mexican National Museum was created in 1825 from the university collections and private gifts. But, for reasons that remain unclear, artifacts in the Seminario de Minas were not deposited in the museum at this time (AGN, Historia, vol. 116). Some of the pieces inventoried by the *Real Expedición Anticuaria* and that later arrived in the Seminario de Minas are today

THE *REAL EXPEDICIÓN ANTICUARIA* COLLECTION

in the Museo Nacional de Antropología, specifically a stone ring from Tlahuac, Distrito Federal (inv. 10–46484), an anthropomorphic wooden drum from Tepoyango, Tlaxcala (inv. 10–81663; Dupaix 1831: 2nd exp., figures 23, 121), and a Zapotec anthropomorphic stone sculpture from Zaachila, Oaxaca (cat. 6–6067; Sellen 2006).

8. At the time, Castañeda's economic situation was rather shaky. From time to time he received commissions from the Mexican government. In 1824 he was commissioned to make a complete set of copies of the drawings from the *Real Expedición Anticuaria* to be presented as a gift for the king of England (AHSRE 5–16–8651, 1824); this set is now part of the Kislak Collection of the Library of Congress in Washington, DC. In 1825 the government sent Castañeda to Huexotla, State of Mexico, to draw a complete set of the recently discovered monuments. That same year Castañeda advised the government to collect the antiques kept in Ciudad Real de Chiapas to further enrich the collections of the Museo Nacional (AGN, Historia, vol. 116). Castañeda died around 1834, while he was "Draughtsman with Door Keeper responsibilities" at the Museo Nacional (AHMNA, vol. 1, 1831).

9. On March 2, 1814, Latour Allard was raised to the rank of second lieutenant in the 44th Regiment of Infantry of the State of Louisiana (US Senate 1814, II: 496, 502). On March 23, 1832, from New Orleans, Latour Allard sent a letter to David Baillie Warden, a member of the Geographical Society in Paris. He mentioned the construction of a new canal in Louisiana that would link the suburb of Sainte-Marie to Lake Pontchartrain: "This canal, which passes in the back of our house, and gives it a greatly added value, is sixty feet wide, and will be able to accommodate very large cargo ships" (Latour Allard 1832).

10. Throughout the documents one finds two spellings: "Latour Allard" and "Latour-Allard." There is in fact some ambiguity regarding that name, as Latour could be a first name.

11. The famous Marquis Marie Joseph Paul Yves Roch Gilbert de Motier Lafayette (1757–1834) wrote a letter to Latour Allard from Paris on August 26, 1827. The latter was living at 54 bis rue Saint-Lazare, chaussée d'Antin at the time. In the letter Lafayette promised Latour Allard that he would get in touch with the French banker Laffitte: "I am sending Mr. Laffitte your letter as well as a copy of Mr. de Humboldt's, telling him the deep impressions they left on me, reminding him of my relationship with the Duplantier family, offering to intervene to get more information from Mrs. Brown and Mrs. Warden. I hope this will give rise to an opportunity for a meeting, and then your proposal would be made directly" (UNNC, Manuscript Collection n. 36; Series 2, Manuscripts 1785–1824, SCF1: 36). This letter is best understood in relation to attempts to sell the collection.

12. In 1831 Edmé-François Jomard (1777–1862) was still hoping to acquire the Latour Allard collection and combine it with other collections, thus creating an ethnographic museum in Paris (Hamy 1890: 180–184).

13. Museum of the Quai Branly website: http://www.quaibranly.fr/en/documentation/the-museum-documentation-and-archives-catalogue.html.

14. Drum MQB 71.1887.155.21 (López Luján and Fauvet-Berthelot 2005: cat. 80).

15. MQB 71.1887.155.1 (ibid.: cat. 60).

Marie-France Fauvet-Berthelot, Leonardo López Luján, and Susana Guimarães

APPENDIX 1

Objects of Latour Allard's collection formerly in the *Real Expedición Anticuaria* collection. MQB 71.1887.155.13 Chicomecóatl of stone (López Luján and Fauvet-Berthelot 2005: cat. 3). 14 Chicomecóatl of stone (cat. 9). 42 Chalchiuhtlicue—Chicomecóatl of stone (cat. 15). 3 Chalchiuhtlicue—Chicomecóatl of stone (cat. 16). 20 Chalchiuhtlicue—Chicomecóatl of stone (cat. 17). 47 Human skull of stone (cat. 45). 19 Quetzalcoatl—serpent of stone (cat. 50). 9 Xochipilli—turtle of stone (cat. 51). 6 Frog with human face of stone (cat. 56). 5 Flea with human face of stone (cat. 57). 60 Serpent—Quetzalcoatl of stone (cat. 60). 8 Dog of stone (cat. 62). 16 Lizard of stone (cat. 69). 17 Fish of stone (cat. 73). 7 Dahlia of stone (cat. 75). 122 Date 4 *Ácatl* of stone (cat. 76). 15 *Tepetlacalli* of stone (cat. 78). 10 Ritual ring of stone (cat. 84). MQB 71.1887.155.35 Ax of copper. 40 Mirror of pyrite. 83 Ax of green basalt. 94 Adornment of agate.

APPENDIX 2

Objects of Latour Allard's collection formerly in Guillermo Dupaix's collection. MQB 71.1887.155.88 Polisher of basalt. 131 Nucleus of obsidian. 133 Fragment of an obsidian nucleus, and probably 89 and 90 Bark paper beater. 91 Medallion of jasper. 92 Idem, dark green. 93 Medallion of agate. 94 Pendant. 97 Medallion of basalt. 108 and 109 Pendants of basalt. 135 and 136 Fragments of quartz. 137 Plaque of jasper.

APPENDIX 3

Inventory of Latour Allard's collection. AHSRE: Archivo Histórico "Genaro Estrada," Secretaría de Relaciones Exteriores, Mexico City, February 1, 1827. Catalog of the Collection d'antiquités Mexicaines de Mr. Latour Allard: 1st Lot. 1. Quadruped of granite, 16 inches long by 22 inches in diameter. 2. Head of a dead man in volcanic rock, 8 inches high by 10 inches long (neck included). 3. Rolled feathered rattlesnake. This piece of red granite is 12 inches high, 4 feet 4 inches in diameter, and weighs around 200 pounds. 4. Female statue of basalt, 2 feet high, 14 inches wide, and 6 inches deep. 5. Female statue of red granite, 15 inches high by 20 inches in diameter. 6. Statue of an Aztec priestess, very well decorated, of dark granite, 17 inches high, 9 inches wide, and 5 inches deep. 7. Rolled rattlesnake of dark granite; a female head emerges from its mouth, 18 inches high and 2 feet 3 inches in diameter. 8. Statue of an old man, 12 inches high, 7 inches wide, and 6 inches deep. 9. Statue of a crouching man with the hands on the knees, red granite, 18 inches high, 10 inches wide, and 8 inches deep. 10. Statue of an old man, granite, 12 inches high, 8 inches wide, and 5 inches deep. 11. Statue measuring 14 inches high, 10 inches wide, and 6 inches deep. 12. Statue of a woman, granite, 12 inches high, 8 inches wide, and

5 inches deep. 13. Statue of a woman of red volcanic granite, 10 inches high, 6 inches wide, and 4 inches deep. 14. Statue of a woman of gray granite, 8 inches high, 6 inches wide, and 3 inches deep. 15. Ornament of red granite depicting a personage in bas-relief, 12 inches high, 10 inches wide, and 4 inches deep. 16. Statue depicting a crouching woman with the head broken, 8 inches high. 17. Idem, 12 inches high, 8 inches wide, and 7 inches deep. 18. Statue of a woman of volcanic rock, 11 inches high, 7 inches wide, and 4 inches deep. 19. Man's head of volcanic rock, 12 inches high by 12 inches wide. 20. Torso, 12 inches high, 6 inches wide, and 4 inches deep. 21. Greenstone statue, wooden and sonorous, 2 inches high, 5 inches wide, and 3 inches deep. 22. Circular ornament of granite with the symbol of the month of June in relief, 11 inches in diameter and 18 lines wide. 23. Chapiter of granite, decorated with reliefs, 11 inches high and 8 inches in diameter. 24. Block of granite, decorated with reliefs on three of its sides, 11 inches high, 8 inches wide, and 7 inches deep. 25. Circular stone, 12 inches in diameter. On its upper surface is a bundle of arrows in relief. 26. Idem. 27. Idem. 28. Idem. 29. Box of granite, decorated with reliefs on the four sides, 11 inches high, 8 inches wide, and 7 inches deep. 30. Small statue of granite inside the granite box. 31. Squarish stone with several reliefs, 15 inches high, 15 inches wide, and 3 inches deep. 32. Turtle with a woman's head of volcanic granite, 10 inches high, 16 inches wide, and 10 inches deep. 33. Coiled rattlesnake of granite, 18 inches high and 2 feet 10 inches in diameter. 34. Lion of volcanic stone, 14 inches long and 20 inches in diameter. 35. Armadillo with a man's head of red granite, 18 inches long, 12 inches high, and 8 inches deep. 36. Frog of granite, 15 inches long, 11 inches high, and 9 inches deep. 37. Coiled rattlesnake of granite, 9 inches high and 2 feet 6 inches in diameter. 38. Crocodile of granite, 2 feet 2 inches long, 8 inches wide, and 6 inches deep. 39. Fish of granite, 31 inches long, 9 inches wide, and 3 inches deep. 40. Recumbent quadruped of granite, 12 inches long by 8 inches high. 41. Idem. 42. Idem. 43. Téponaclé [*sic* for *teponaztli*], or Aztec drum of ironwood, 1 foot 7 inches long and 6 inches in diameter. 44. Small rattlesnake of red granite. 45. Small animal of volcanic stone. 46. Idem. 47. Idem. 48. Idem. 49. Idem. 50. Idem. 51. Torso of jasper. 52. Hand of stone. 53. Small statuette of serpentine. 54. Idem. 55. Small mask (unknown stone). 56. Spatula of stone. 57. Idem. 58. Ax of basalt. 59. Idem. 60. Idem. 61. Chisel of basalt. 62. Idem. 63. Idem. 64. Idem. 65. Idem. 66. Idem. 67. Idem. 68. Idem. 69. Idem. 70. Idem. 71. Cutting implement of copper used for sacrifices. 72. Stone implement for grinding. 73. Idem. 74. Idem. 75. Ribbed implement of basalt (unknown function). 76. Idem. 77. Adornment of serpentine for the neck. 78. Idem. 79. Idem. 80. Idem. 81. Idem. 82. Idem. 83. Idem. 84. Idem. 85. Idem. 86. Adornment of agate for the neck. 87. Idem. 88. Idem. 89. Idem. 90. Idem of cornelian. 91. Idem of aventurine. 92. Idem of turquoise. 93. Idem of basalt. 94. Idem. 95. Idem. 96. Idem. 97. Idem. 98. Mirror of metal. 99. Idem. 100. Idem. 101. Idem. 102. Kind of flageolet of ceramics. 103. Idem. 104. Idem.

105. Idem, broken. 106. Idem, broken. 107. Idem, broken. 108. Ceramic stamp, so-called seal of Montezuma. 109. Idem. 110. Ceramic spindle-whorl. 111. Idem. 112. Idem. 113. Idem. 114. Idem. 115. Idem. 116. Idem. 117. Ceramic mold. 118. Idem. 119. Idem. 120. Small ceramic implement (unknown function). 121. Idem. 122. Foot of a ceramic vase. 123. Idem. 124. Idem. 125. Fragment of a small ceramic statue. 126. Another fragment. 127. Statuette of red ceramics depicting an Aztec woman with a baby on her hip, 6 inches high. 128. Small statuette of black ceramics, 5 inches high, depicting a woman nursing a crocodile. 129. Infant in a cradle of ceramics. 130. Ceramic statuette, 6 inches high, depicting a crouching woman with an infant on her knees. 131. Idem, smaller. 132. Ceramic statuette, 6 inches high, depicting a kneeling woman. 133. Idem. 134. Idem. 135. Idem. 136. Idem. 137. Ceramic statuette depicting a man with wolf's head. 138. Idem. 139. Ceramic statuette, 8 inches high, depicting an Aztec soldier with his armor. 140. Idem. 141. Idem. 142. Ceramic statuette, 8 inches high, depicting an Aztec priest. 143. Idem. 144. Ceramic statuette, 9 inches high, depicting a prince on his throne. 145. Small ceramic head. 146. Idem. 147. Idem. 148. Idem. 149. Idem. 150. Idem. 151. Idem. 152. Idem. 153. Idem. 154. Oval ceramic vase with 9 supports, 9 inches long. 155. Idem, rounded. 156. Idem, smaller, without supports. 157. Idem. 158. Idem. 159. Arrow head of obsidian. 160. Idem. 161. Idem. 162. Idem. 163. Blade of obsidian for clubs. 164. Idem. 165. Idem. 166. Idem. 167. Idem. 168. Idem. 169. Idem. 170. Idem. 171. Idem. 172. Idem. 173. Idem. 174. Idem. 175. Idem. 176. Idem. 177. Small stone covered with stucco from a building of Mitla. 178. Idem, collected in Palenque. 179. Idem, collected in Palenque. 180. Stucco, collected in Tezcuco. 181. Wooden coin used by the Spaniards in Mexico during the Conquest. 182. Idem.

2nd Lot. 1°. A box containing 120 plates in-folio outlined with Indian ink, representing all the Precolumbian monuments still preserved in Mexico. 2°. Three notebooks with manuscripts containing a travel account and descriptions of the monuments listed above. 3°. A notebook in-folio with fourteen pages made of agave paper containing several themes painted by the ancient Mexicans. It has notes written by the celebrated Boturini. 4°. A box containing thirty-eight color plates representing modern Mexican costumes and some popular scenes.

Price of the first lot: seventy thousand francs. Price of the second lot: seventy-five thousand francs.

Note. A discount will be applied to the person who buys all lots. There are also some objects of natural history, which will be given to the person who buys everything.

ARCHIVAL SOURCES

México

AGN: Archivo General de la Nación, México, DF.

AHMNA: Archivo Histórico del Museo Nacional de Antropología, México, DF.

AHSRE: Archivo Histórico "Genaro Estrada," Secretaría de Relaciones Exteriores, México, DF.

United States

CMR: Sir Thomas Phillipps Collection, Center for Maya Research, Barnardsvile, SC

NL: Edward E. Ayer Collection, Newberry Library, Chicago. IL

UNNC: Harry L. Dalton Collection, J. Murrey Atkins Library, University of North Carolina, Charlotte

UTBLAC: Nettie Lee Benson Latin American Collection, University of Texas, Austin

France

AMN: Archives Centrales des Musées Nationaux, Paris

ANP: Archives Nationales, Fonds de la Maison du Roi, Paris

REFERENCES CITED

Aglio, Agostino
    1831   Specimens of Mexican Sculpture in the Possession of M. Latour Allard in Paris. In *Antiquities of Mexico*, ed. Lord Kingsborough, vol. 4, pp. w/n. James Moyes, London.

Anonymous
    1826a   Antiquités mexicaines de M. Latour-Allard. *Revue encyclopédique* 31: 848–851.
    1826b   Mexican Antiquities. *Literary Chronicle and Weekly Review* 388 (October 21): 670. London.
    1852   Musée des Antiquités Américaines, au Louvre. Premier article. *Le Magasin Pittoresque* Vingtième année: 195–199.

Archives Centrales de Musées Nationaux
    1840–1850   Collection d'Antiquités Mexicaines formant le cabinet de M. Latour-Allard, mentionnées et gravées dans l'ouvrage de lord Kingsborough, publiée par M. Aglio. Paris, Série A3.

Bullock, William
    1824   *Six Months Residence and Travels in Mexico*. J. Murray, London.

Dupaix, Guillermo
    1831   Viages de Guillelmo Dupaix sobre las antigüedades mejicanas. In *Antiquities of Mexico*, ed. Lord Kingsborough, vol. 4, pp. w/n, and vol. 5, pp. 207–343. James Moyes, London.
    1834   *Antiquités mexicaines. Relation des trois expéditions du capitaine Dupaix, ordonnées en 1805, 1806, et 1807, pour la recherche des antiquités du pays*, 2 vols. Edited by Henri Baradère. J. Didot l'aîné, Paris.

1969 *Expediciones acerca de los antiguos monumentos de la Nueva España, 1805–1808*. Edited by José Alcina Franch. José Porrúa Turanzas, Madrid.

Estrada de Gerlero, Elena
    1994 La labor anticuaria novohispana en la época de Carlos IV: Guillermo Dupaix, precursor de la historia del arte prehispánico. In *XVII Coloquio Internacional de Historia del Arte. Arte, historia e identidad en América: Visiones comparativas*, vol. 1, ed. Gonzalo Curiel, Renato González Mello, and Juana Gutiérrez Haces, pp. 191–205. UNAM, México, DF.

Farcy, Charles
    1834 Discours Préliminaire. Historique des découvertes, et considérations sur leur importance. In *Antiquités mexicaines. Relation des trois expéditions du capitaine Dupaix, ordonnées en 1805, 1806, et 1807, pour la recherche des antiquités du pays*, vol. 1, ed. Henri Baradère, pp. i–xiii. J. Didot l'aîné, Paris.

Freeman, John Finley
    1962 Manuscript Sources on Latin American Indians in the Library of the American Philosophical Society. *Proceedings of the American Philosophical Society* 106 (6): 530–540.

Frieberg, Edna B.
    1980 *Bayou St. John in Colonial Louisiana, 1699–1803*. Harvey Press, New Orleans, LA.

Guimarâes, Susana
    1994 *Les anciennes collections précolombiennes au Louvre: Le musée des antiquités américaines de A. de Longpérier*. École du Louvre, Paris.
    1996 *Le musée des antiquités américaines du Louvre (1850–1887). Une vision du collectionnisme américain au XIXème siècle*. Microfiche 96 0564. Institut d'Ethnologie, Paris.

Hamy, Ernest-Théodore
    1890 *Les origines du Musée d'ethnographie. Histoire et documents*. Ernest Leroux, Paris.

Latour Allard
    1828 Extrait d'une lettre adressé à M. Warden par M. Latour-Allard, de la Nouvelle Orléans. Paris, le 23 avril 1828. *Bulletin de la Société de Géographie* 9: 276–277.
    1832 Nouveau canal dans la Louisiane. Extrait d'une lettre de M. Latour-Allard à M. Warden. Nouvelle-Orléans 23 mars 1832. *Bulletin de la Société de Géographie* 17: 304–305.

López Luján, Leonardo, and Marie-France Fauvet-Berthelot
    2005 *Aztèques. La collection de sculptures du Musée du Quai Branly*. Musée du Quai Branly, Paris.

Palop Martínez, Josefina, and Alejandro Cerdá Esteve
    1997 Nuevos documentos sobre las expediciones arqueológicas de Guillermo Dupaix por México, 1805–1808. *Revista Española de Antropología Americana* 27: 129–152.

Sellen, Adam T.
   2006   Procedencia perdida. La historia de una estatua zapoteca única. *Estudios Mesoamericanos* 7: 5–13.

US Senate
   1814   *Journal of the Executive Proceedings of the Senate of the United States of America.* Government Printing Office, Washington, DC.

Warden, David Baillie
   1829   Rapport de la commission de la Société royale des Antiquaires de France. *Bulletin de la Société de Géographie* 12: 43–48.

PART VI
ETHNOGRAPHY

20

YUCATEC MAYA AGRICULTURAL RITUAL SURVIVALS

Ruth Gubler

Modern religious practices among Yucatec Maya peoples are deeply rooted in the Prehistoric past. Agricultural ceremonies comprise a textured blend of Catholic liturgy grafted onto Precolumbian tradition. The supernatural beings the modern Yucatec Maya propitiate, express their gratitude to, and pray to for adequate rainfall and a bountiful harvest exist far beyond the walls of the Spanish churches, monasteries, and nunneries found in the towns and villages of the Yucatán Peninsula.

The *Dresden Codex* provides the earliest textual evidence about the nature of agricultural ceremonies among the ancient Maya; here, *chacs* are depicted as providers of rain. Moreover, there are glyphs that may refer to agricultural ceremonies, such as the *uahil col* (offering of first fruits) and the *chha chac* (rain ceremony) described later in this chapter. Postconquest sixteenth-century Yucatec sources, unlike those from the Mexica area, overlook such rituals. Apparently, the chroniclers of Colonial Yucatán were far more occupied with their missionary effort and expressing their dismay at the persistence of "idolatrous" practices than they were with describing such indigenous cultural practices in detail.

To link the glyphic evidence from the *Dresden Codex* to present-day ceremonial practices, we must consult historical sources, including the early–nineteenth-century report of José Granado Baeza (1946) describing a rain ceremony in Yaxcabá, an article by Thomas Gann (1918) about a chha chac performed in

Belize, and, most important, the first explicit description of such agricultural practices by Robert Redfield and Alfonso Villa Rojas (1934). Combined, these sources enable us to make inferences regarding the persistence of these agricultural practices among modern Yucatec Maya.

As we face the contamination of our atmosphere and water resources, denuded hills and forests, disappearing plants and wildlife—all caused by careless or destructive human agency—our current predicament seems a far cry from the respect and veneration with which more traditional peoples related to their surroundings. Perhaps in a way this has fueled our fascination with traditional cultures such as the Yucatec Maya. Among their surviving traditions are agricultural ceremonies performed to honor and propitiate the gods, assuage or influence them, plead for their protection and benevolence, and express thanks for the benefits they have bestowed.[1]

This chapter examines ritual traditions still performed in the Yucatán Peninsula.[2] Yucatec Maya agricultural ceremonies survive primarily because they do not pose a direct threat to Catholic doctrine,[3] because they are related to subsistence and survival, and because of a characteristic common to both native and Catholic belief systems: that supernatural powers can be influenced by petitioning and that divine intervention will produce favorable outcomes. However, after Hurricane Isidoro in September 2002, modernization made its presence increasingly felt, bringing massive changes and negatively impacting the traditions described (Gubler 2005).

In an earlier, animistic world, man was cognizant that for virtually every aspect of his existence he was utterly dependent on the supernatural beings that inhabited and owned the sacred space surrounding him. These extraordinary forces wielded enormous power over him and—alternately manifesting their beneficent as well as their malignant aspects—generated good or bad luck, misfortune in various guises, health or illness, and finally death.

It was an interdependent relationship in which, in reciprocation for their munificence, these sacred and all-powerful beings demanded in return that man revere, honor, and propitiate them with prayers and offerings, an obligatory reciprocity that is well expressed in a passage in the *Popul Vuh* from the Quiché Maya of the Guatemalan Highlands: "Speak, then, our names, praise us, your mother, your father. Invoke then, Huracán, Chipi Caculhá, Raxa-Caculhá, the Heart of Heaven, the Heart of Earth, the Creator, the Maker, the Forefathers; speak, invoke us, adore us, they were told" (Recinos, Goetz, and Morley 1950: 85).

As this Highland Maya myth has it, none of the beings created prior to man were capable of meeting these obligations. The gods' first creation, the four-footed animals and birds, could not utter words or speak like man; "they only hissed and screamed and cackled" (ibid.), unable to venerate their creators. The gods then made two more attempts to create "obedient, respectful beings who will nourish and sustain us" (ibid.: 86), but neither the creatures made of mud nor those of wood gave any thought to their creators and were thus destroyed. Only the last creation was successful: man, made from white and yellow corn, praised and gave thanks to his creators: "We really give you thanks, two and three times. We have been created, we have been given a mouth and a face, we speak, we hear, we think, and walk: we feel perfectly, and we know what is far and what is near . . . We give you thanks, then, for having created us, oh, Creator and Maker! for having given us being"[4] (ibid.: 168).

YUCATEC MAYA AGRICULTURAL SUPERNATURALS

For the Maya, nature was not—and neither is it today—an imprecise, impersonal, or passive force; rather, it is something alive, active, and omnipresent, a world inhabited by spirits that move freely within it. While imbued with a sacred character, this world can be dangerous, for it is inhabited by supernatural beings too. In Yucatán these supernaturals are the *balams*,[5] *chacs*,[6] *aluxes*,[7] and *yumtziloob*,[8] as well as the winds, which play an important role in the life and health of living beings.

These spirits are the owners of the natural environment—the earth, the untamed forest, the plants and animals that live within it, the caves and *cenotes*,[9] and other sources of water are all under their protection.[9] Therefore, when a *milpero*[10] cuts down the forest or kills a deer or collects honey, he is taking something that belongs to the spirits; obligated by that sense of reciprocity, he has to return a little of what he has taken from nature. As a sign of his subjection and to demonstrate his gratitude and devotion to the ancestral deities, man has to offer up prayers and make offerings, whether of animals, birds, or precious things, and, in ancient times, of human blood through sacrifice.

No matter how benevolent these gods can be, they can easily become angry over any infraction—even involuntary—committed by man. They punish him with illness or death in his family or with misfortunes such as unsuccessful harvests or the loss of livestock. That is why the *campesino*[11] considers it so essential to placate and honor them, for if he neglects to do so or otherwise fails to show his gratitude by performing these ceremonies, with the characteristic contradictory aspects of all Prehispanic deities, they can manifest their antagonistic nature.

For example, the Sun God in his positive aspect contributes to growth in nature, but his burning rays can also be the agents of destruction by causing drought and burning crops. Similarly, the rain created by the chacs is a blessing for the campesino as long as it is maintained within limits, but when these boundaries are overstepped, it causes destructive floods. In like manner the balams, located in the four corners of the village, share this dual nature. It is still believed, although less than in the past, that they wander around the outskirts of the pueblo watching over and protecting it by keeping out the evil winds, illnesses, and other dangers. Yet they, too, can be dangerous forces to be reckoned with if one fails to take them into account. For although the balams are said to protect children who are lost in the bush or the forest, these supernatural beings may on occasion carry them off. Such an experience can profoundly impact a child who, upon its return, may manifest signs of illness or be disoriented and even mute, although if treated by a *h-men* (shaman, or native priest) it will generally recover.

The chacs are identified with wells, caves, cenotes, and other sources of water, and it is they who bring the beneficent rain, transporting it in large calabashes. Yucatec myth describes them as four old men who, mounted on horses, ride throughout the land, although some of my contemporary informants tend to consider them as incorporeal beings or spirits. In their beneficent aspect the chacs are indispensable to man and beast alike because they bring the rain, the vivifying water.

The aluxes are mischievous beings who, although generally benign, may turn malignant if offended or if men contravene social rules. They are said to live in and around ancient ruins and are believed to be associated with, and even materialized in, the archaeological artifacts scattered throughout the area. In accord with their mischievous nature the aluxes play tricks on the milpero, but the general belief is that if they are kept well-disposed, they will also help him by protecting his *milpa*. They do this by keeping strangers from trespassing by throwing stones or making whistling sounds to frighten them away. If the intruders have taken maize or other produce from the milpa without permission, the aluxes are believed to punish the perpetrators with fevers, disorientation, illness, or personal misfortune.

Finally, there are the winds, which are indispensable to man and beast alike because they blow the clouds that bring the rain. Yet the winds are also dangerous because it is believed that when they blow from the cenotes, caves, and caverns, they can cause illness and even the death of passersby, especially women and children who are considered to be weaker than men and therefore more liable to be affected. Also, if, in violation of the taboo, someone comes too close to or enters a cave without obtaining permission (usually effected by a h-men) or fails to make a small offering, serious consequences can result.

The yumtziloob, deities associated with the natural environment, protect it and the animals that live in it, but again, if offended, they will manifest their malevolent nature. Man is supposed to be measured in all his actions, so if he fails to obey or respect nature by killing too many animals or cutting down too many trees, he will be punished.

In Yucatán, agricultural ceremonies continue to be performed today, although not with the same frequency as before. Of these, the uahil col, the *hetz luum,* and the chha chac have received the most attention in academic literature.¹² These ceremonies are performed for the specific purpose of influencing the supernatural beings and asking for their protection and blessing: the fertility of the milpa and the livestock of the rancho, and the security and health of their owner and his family.

YUCATECAN AGRICULTURAL RITUAL ORIGINS

We have few Colonial Period documents on the Yucatecan agricultural ritual origins. Fray Diego de Landa (1938 [1565]), Diego Lopez Cogolludo (1954 [1656]), Pedro Sánchez de Aguilar (1987 [1639]), and Fray Bernardo de Lizana (1893 [1633]) say nothing about them; nor is the *Relaciones Histórico-Geográficas de la Gobernación de Yucatán* (Garza 1983) of any help. Yet going back further in time, glyphic and visual elements that throw some light on the subject can be found in the *Dresden Codex*, which J. Eric Thompson believed was produced between AD 1200 and 1250 and was undoubtedly at least copied in part from earlier codices (Thompson 1972; Morley, Brainerd, and Sharer 1983: 517).

The *Dresden Codex* (1975), an indigenous manuscript written on gesso-coated *amate* paper, has a long chapter dealing with matters pertaining to the land and its productivity called the *Farmer's Almanac*, of which numbers 53–62 (29a–30a), 58a (30b–31b), 64 (29c–30c), and 68 (42c–45c) are particularly pertinent. They indicate the specific time for planting, sowing, and harvesting crops and predict periods of rain/dearth, fertility/infertility, life/death. An important aspect of these almanacs is the notable presence of the chacs, the rain gods, who play an important part in agriculture-dependent societies and who are shown with their distinct attributes and carrying out diverse activities. While other gods appear as well—for example, in Dresden Almanac 57 (42a–44) the old goddess of weaving (O), an aged merchant god, and a youthful deity, considered by Günter Zimmermann (1956) to be God H—they are much less frequent.

The almanacs reflect the various attributes of the rain gods and show them in different attitudes and activities. In Almanac 55 (31a–39a) a chac lying on the roof of a temple holds a maize sign, and Thompson (1972: 95) raises the possibility (though not the probability) that he may be receiving a prophecy, such as we find in the *Codex Pérez* and the *Book of Chilam Balam of Maní*: "Nacom Balam was lying down and motionless when he spoke to the priests, giving them advice and explanations, the sense of which they did not understand" (Craine and Reindorp 1979: 65–66).

Dresden Almanac 53 (29a–30a) shows the chacs seated on the cosmic trees in the four world-directions: red in the East, white in the North, black in the West, and yellow in the South, as well as in the center of the earth, *tan yol cab*, indicating their cosmographic position (Thompson 1972: 94).¹³ In Almanac 57 (42a–44a) the first four *thols*¹⁴ of the chant are addressed to the red, the black, and the yellow chac and in the East to the old goddess of weaving, here associated with the North (white). In every thol, offerings of food are followed by the glyph for eating or food (ibid.: 97–98).

According to Thompson, several of these thols are chants to the rain gods, although some are also divinatory in nature. He suggests that this type of song could have been used in a chha chac ceremony, or petition for rain (ibid.: 98). Almanac 58a (30b–31b) has another chant with food offerings to the chacs, each with his pertinent color and world direction. Both examples provide an interesting link to the agricultural rituals still carried out today.

Other scenes depict a chac beating a drum (Almanac 64: 29c–30c; Thompson 1972: 102), which is of interest in this context because sometimes in rain ceremonies performed today, four men are positioned, one in each corner of the milpa, and one of them taps an inverted calabash in a pail of water to replicate the sound of thunder. Other scenes show a chac paddling a canoe, sitting on clouds, sitting on a tree (Almanac 56: 40a–41a), holding a torch in both hands (ibid.: 31–39a), seated on a jaguar skin–covered stool and holding a maize sign, walking with an ax and pouch, sowing with a planting stick amid rain, walking over the milpa glyphs, falling from a celestial band (Almanac 61: 38b–41b), sitting astride a deer he appears to have killed (Almanac 64: 29c–30c), and menacing with an ax a seated figure identified as the maize god (Almanac 68: 42c–45c). These positive/negative aspects are a clear reference to the unpredictable nature of Prehispanic deities.

Based on a tentative meaning of *dza* as "to give," Thompson (1972: 102) suggests that the concept could signify (1) an offering, (2) North, (3) the white god, (4) Chac, (5) turkey meat, and (6) a jar of fermenting *balche*,[15] which is consistent with what is offered to agricultural deities today. Several almanac scenes show offerings of food identical to those of contemporary ceremonies. The maize glyph appears in three cases, and other offerings may include venison and, conceivably, agouti and fish (ibid.: 98). Today, venison is considered to be an offering particularly prized by the gods because deer are associated with untamed nature, are the largest animals in the forest, and are valued in Maya communities as a rare delicacy.

In addition to registering the activities of the chacs, numerous almanacs are divinatory in nature, prognosticating the weather and its effect on crops. Both the positive and negative nature of the chacs is shown. For example, Almanac 61 (38b–41b; Thompson 1972: 101) describes:

> T1 The sun amidst the black and white clouds, the moon amidst the black and white clouds. The black vulture amid the rain.
>
> T2 The white Chac sows.? Abundance of maize in the milpas.
>
> T3 The yellow Chac is set up? in the milpa. Very good tidings.
>
> T4 The (old) goddess of weaving is the affliction of the crops. Malignant fierce suns. Dull days.

YUCATEC MAYA AGRICULTURAL RITUAL SURVIVALS

T5 The red Chac in? the milpa.? Abundance of maize.

T6 Rain storage jars? in the Chac's abode? Heavy rains for many days. Woe to the maize seed.

T7 In the heart of the sky (on high) are Chac [and] the maize god. Abundance of maize.

T8 The flaming fire on high of Kinich Kakmo. Drought.

In addition, we find a good description of the offerings, as given in Almanac 58a (30b–31b):

T1 Set up to the east the red god. Offerings of maize and venison and *elotes* are Chac's food.

T2 Set up to the north the white god Chac. Turkey, *elotes*, and boiled? are his food.

T3 Set up in the west the black god Chac. Iguanas and maize and *elotes* are the impetuous black sprinkler's food.

T4 Set up in the south the yellow god Chac. Fish, *elotes*, fresh *elotes* are his food. (Thompson 1972: 98)

This tradition of prognostication is continued in the *Book of Chilam Balam*, for example, in the Kaua, Mani, Tizimin, Na, and Chan Cah. Although these sources were written down during the Colonial Period, they are obviously in much the same vein as the much earlier texts. Numerous passages in the Tizimin, Kaua, and Na and the *Codex Pérez* have calendars that foretell the good and bad days for every month of the year: rains or drought, health or illness, life or death, calamities or good fortune.

April 1: Nine Ahau A good day. Gods are manufactured.

April 3. Eleven Ik. Strong winds blow during the day.

April 10: Five Muluc. A bad day. Rainy day.

April 18: Thirteen Caban. A good day. The ear of corn sprouts.

April 29. Eleven Lamat. A bad day. The demons gather. One must keep a vigil three days and fast. (Craine and Reindorp 1979: 26)[16]

Finally, very important to this chapter's main subject is Thompson's (1972: 99) contention that these texts contain clear references to agricultural ceremonies such as the uahil col and the fact that some almanacs illustrate offerings being made to the chacs. For example, in Almanac 58a (29b–30b) the gods are seated in the four world directions receiving offerings of animals that have been hunted, plates of maize, balche, and similar items (Thompson 1972: 98), and in Almanac 58a (30b–31b) and also 64 (29c–30c), the song to the chacs is accompanied by offerings of food.

Although the glyphic texts in the *Dresden Codex* are formulated in esoteric terms that are characteristically ambivalent, it is very evident that the ancient deities had both benevolent and malignant aspects—particularly the chacs and balams, both of which are intimately associated with the field and bush and fertility.

In his commentary on Almanac 59 (31b–35b) Thompson (1972: 99) maintains that, although imperfect, the world directional and color glyphs suggest a chant and that there are also augural glyphs referring to drought, destructive storms, and abundance. Moreover, Thompson (ibid.) feels "little doubt that the chacs are depicted stationed by their heavenly reservoirs of water."

Propitiatory rituals continue to be performed throughout Indian Mesoamerica, for engaging in and fostering relationships with the agricultural deities maintains the obligatory reciprocity with the supernatural world. In modern Yucatán such rituals are the uahil col, the hetz luum for the protection of a field and its owner and his family, and the chha chac. All have the common purpose of honoring the gods and thanking them for their munificence.

PERSISTENCE AND CHANGE

The persistence of these agricultural rituals to the present suggests that they were performed during the entire Colonial Period. Nonetheless, as indicated, sixteenth-century sources for the Yucatán Peninsula are mute on this score: the *Relaciones* (1580s) provides no information in this regard; Landa (1938 [1565]), Cogolludo (1954 [1656]), and Lizana (1893 [1633]) are more concerned with conversion, extolling the friars' missionary activities; while Sánchez de Aguilar (1987 [1639]) is obsessed with the resurgence of "idolatry." To obtain a picture of agricultural ceremonies performed during the Colonial Period we must turn to an early–nineteenth-century source, a short *Informe* written by the parish priest of Yaxcabá, Granado Baeza, in 1813 (1946).

In formulating his reply to a questionnaire sent by the Spanish Overseas Ministry requesting information regarding the life and customs of the Indians of Yucatán, Granado Baeza indicates that while formerly the Indians had venerated figures made of clay or stone, it was unusual to find vestiges of "idolatry" in his bishopric. However, he does state that a ceremony persisted that the Indians called *tich* (meaning obligation[17] or sacrifice) and vulgarly called the *misa milpera*, or "cornfield mass," because it was an imitation of the real mass (ibid.: 17–18).

Although it is a short report, Granado Baeza's description is of interest because it shows that essentially the rite performed in 1813, most clearly resembling a chha chac, differs very little from the one still performed today. That is, there are common elements such as the building of an altar-table, the preparation of ceremonial *masa*, the sacrifice of a turkey, the invocation of the *pahuatuns* and of certain saints, the ritual offering to the world directions, and finally the ritual feasting of the participants.

Granado Baeza reports that the Indians prepared a *barbacoa*[18] or *tapezco*[19] of sticks, which served as a table, and on top they placed a turkey into whose beak the ritual specialist poured balche. This is an intoxicating drink made by the Maya with the bark of the tree of the same name, steeped for days in water and honey until it ferments. Then the turkey was killed and taken to be seasoned, while in an underground pit "some large maize cakes called *canlahuantaz*" (ibid.: 18) were baked. These cakes were made up of fourteen tortillas mixed with beans, about which I was unable to obtain more information. Once everything was ready, the tortillas were placed on the table, together with several small bowls of balche, and the ritual specialist incensed everything with copal.

After the ritual specialist had sprinkled the liquid toward the four winds and simultaneously invoked the four pauahtuns, one of the bowls was raised; while those present kneeled, it was applied to their mouths. The ceremony concluded with everyone eating and drinking to their satisfaction, and the one who made the offering was given the most, taking home a good portion of the feast (ibid.: 19).

Granado Baeza explains that he was told that the Holy Trinity was invoked and the Credo was recited and that sprinkling balche toward the four winds invoked the four pauahtuns, "lords or custodians of rain."[20] According to Granado Baeza, these gods were identified with four Catholic saints to whom God entrusted the rain: the red pauahtun with Santo Domingo, the white with San Gabriel, the black with San Diego, and the yellow with a goddess, Xkanleox or Saint Mary Magdalene (ibid.: 19–20).

While the ceremony in itself appears to have retained its autochthonous character, Granado Baeza's account represents a persistence of ancient beliefs as well as a strong Christian influence in the recitation of the Credo and the association of certain saints with the pauahtuns. Even balche was given a Christian meaning, as the "first water" or the first liquor God created and with which God the Father said the first mass.

For a more recent account of such ceremonies we turn to Redfield and Villa Rojas's *Chan Kom: A Maya Village* (1934), wherein an analysis is made of the ceremonies still performed in that Yucatec pueblo: *u hanli col*, *u hanli cab*, *hol-che*, and *ch'a chaac*.[21] Specific aspects of the ceremonies have changed over the seventy-five-plus intervening years, but only in minor detail. The ceremonies continue to be performed by a ritual specialist along the same general lines; offerings of *zaca*,[22] balche, *kol*,[23] *yachh*,[24] chickens, at least one turkey, and the ceremonial masa tamales known as *pibes* are still made; and the gods of the milpa, the balams, the chacs, and the aluxes, as well as God in Three Persons, the Virgin Mary, and the saints, continue to be invoked. Moreover, even taking into account regional and individual variations, basically the same model prevails.

We also have a description by Gann (1918) of a rain ceremony performed in Belize that in general terms reads very much like a contemporary report. As then, it continues to be considered the most important ceremony; as Gann notes (ibid.: 42), "it embraces the offerings and ritual of all the other ceremonies." He describes the preparation of the earth oven in which the masa tamales were cooked, as well as the clearing of a space in the midst of a grove of large trees where two rude huts thatched with guano leaf were erected and a rough altar was made of sticks bound together with vines. His description of the manner in which the pibes were made, how the calabashes were filled with balche, the ritual killing of the turkey and chickens, the offerings placed on the altar, the recitation of prayers, and the final distribution of food sounds remarkably contemporary.

TWENTY-FIRST–CENTURY RITUALS FROM A REMOTE PAST

Today, ceremonies very similar to those described by Thompson, Granado Baeza, and Redfield and Villa Rojas continue to be performed in Yucatán. Although each has a particular focus, all are an expression of gratitude to nature for blessing man with its bounty. The uahil col or *primicia* is a ceremony in which the campesino shows his gratitude by offering the first fruits of his milpa. As Dón Felipe expresses it (personal communication), "we give thanks that we have been given a good harvest." The hetz luum, however, is performed for various reasons. One is because the land is considered to be "ill," subject to evil influences that have impaired its productivity, which is reason enough to ask the gods to intervene and protect it. In another context, it is a request for permission to work a new piece of land. When a hetz luum is performed for a water well, it is to ensure a sufficient supply of water; when done for a corral, it is because animals have become sick or have died inside it, and the campesino wants to put an end to his bad luck. As for the chha chac, the most important and lavish of the ceremonies, while primarily a petition for rain, limiting it to this sole function fails to account for the sense of reciprocity-obligation lying at the heart of all these ceremonies and the perennial need to give thanks.

It is said that the land asks for (*pide*) such offerings, and the campesino considers it his obligation to return something to nature in the guise of supernatural beings, which have favored him.[25] This he does by promising to perform a ceremony every so often, for example, every one, two, three, four, or more years, a reflection of the continued importance of reciprocity that, as we have seen in the *Popul Vuh*, was an important aspect of the Maya worldview in the past.

The campesino firmly believes that such a promise is binding and that if he forgets or otherwise neglects to abide by it, things will begin to go wrong. Snakes and other vermin will invade his milpa, his animals will begin to die or his crops will not prosper, he will hear strange noises or see unexplainable things, and he and his family may fall ill or even die. These are all sure signs that it is time to perform a ceremony. Nonetheless, with the passing of time and the increasing expense, today such ceremonies are performed with much less frequency. As

YUCATEC MAYA AGRICULTURAL RITUAL SURVIVALS

20.1. *A modest offering, all the family could afford. Photo by Ruth Gubler, 1996.*

Dón Felipe says (personal communication): "Milpa is now only rarely made, there is a lack of faith, and many no longer are familiar with this tradition and make fun of it" (translation by the author).

If at a particular moment the necessary money is not available, there is illness in the family, or any other valid reason exists why the campesino cannot perform a proper ceremony, a small offering can be made to placate the land. This is done by placing a little zaca on the altar-table, offering a prayer (an Our Father and a Credo), and promising to have a proper ceremony as soon as possible (figure 20.1). A sumptuous offering for a uahil col stands in stark contrast, with its flowers, sprigs of rue, large picture of Christ, and table replete with fowl, ceremonial pibe tamales, and clay bowls filled with kol and yachh (figure 20.2).

When a decision has been made to have such a ceremony, the owner of a milpa or a rancho or the members of a cooperative call on a h-men (a ritual specialist or native priest) and ask him to perform it. The date is set, the fee is agreed on, and the different components necessary for the ceremony are determined: one or more turkeys, chickens, masa (maize dough), zaca, balche, honey, candles, copal, flowers, and other items. The h-men generally brings his own gourds; if the milpa owner does not have a cross, he will bring his own. The traditional or "correct" way to carry out such ceremonies used to take three days.

The first day a group of men, accompanied by a h-men, goes to a nearby cenote or cave to collect *zuhuy ha*, literally "virgin water." This is not a simple matter because first the h-men has to perform a small ceremony at the entrance

20.2. *Lavish offering for a uahil col. Photo by Ruth Gubler, 1994.*

of the cave in which he offers the spirits a bit of zaca and asks their permission to collect the water. The pools from which it is taken are generally deep within the cave and frequently difficult to reach. The second day a hunt is organized. For it to be successful, the h-men must have spent the previous night in vigil and prayer, asking the yumtziloob (spirits of the field and bush) for permission to kill one of their animals: generally a deer, although a peccary or another animal may be hunted or birds such as the *chachalaca*.[26] The third day culminates in the performance of all the activities directly related to the ceremony itself. Everyone—friends, relatives, even visitors—flocks to the site, and at the end of the ceremony a portion of the food from the altar is distributed among all present. Today, because of the cost, time, and effort involved, such ceremonies are generally performed in a single day, although the evening before may be spent in vigil, prayer, and ritual drinking.[27]

The h-men has to be there very early, if he has not spent the previous night(s) at the location in prayer and vigil and making preliminary preparations, assisted by those who have commissioned the ceremony. Although in principle at least some of the preparations should have been made ahead of time, very often this is not the case.[28] Those who have contracted the services of the h-men and are involved directly arrive early; so do those who have promised to contribute their labor: the men who dig the earth oven, the women who make the tortillas, and all those involved in the preparation of the foodstuffs. Because many of the pueblos now have a scarcity of men, women are increasingly taking over activities that were formerly men's responsibilities.

A *pib* (earth oven) is prepared by the men, who dig a large hole at a location chosen for that purpose. Large stones are brought in to line the pit. Leafy branches of trees such as *habin*[29] or *bob*,[30] *xaan*,[31] *chacah*,[32] or banana leaves, depending on the individual h-men or what is available in the area, will be used to cover the pib, and the bob leaves will also serve to wrap the pibes (sacred maize tamales).

After the stones have been placed on the firewood, the fuel is lit. Great care is taken that the fire does not go out, not only because that would delay the baking of the pibes but also because it could be interpreted as a sign that the gods of the milpa are angry. When the stones are hot enough the men bring out the pibes, place them on the cooking stones (figure 20.6), and cover them with leafy branches, fronds, or large leaves.[33] Then a thin layer of earth is shoveled on top, and everything is covered with sacks or a metal sheet. It takes approximately 1–1.5 hours for the pibes to be ready. The secret to ensure that the ceremonial pibes turn out well, according to Dón Felipe, is to throw a handful of salt, thirteen dry red chiles, and thirteen maize cobs on the pib; Dón Tono uses nine dry chiles and some salt.[34]

Generally, each person contributes something: chickens or perhaps a turkey (a highly prized sacrificial bird), some masa, honey, candles, or cash. One of the men, chosen by those commissioning the ceremony, is put in charge of making a list to register all the donations as they come in. This will be taken into account when it is time to distribute the food, and those who have contributed the most receive more generous portions. Everyone is busy, individuals or groups occupied with their own specific task. Some of the men watch over the pib, others prepare the henequen string for wrapping the sacred pibes, while the women prepare the masa for the tortillas. Everyone is cheerful; this is a celebration and a time for socializing and sharing (figure 20.3).

The h-men has been actively involved in the process the entire time, making sure everything is done correctly and setting up his *kanche*, the traditional high, square wooden altar. This has been prepared more or less elaborately; in any case, a cross or the image of a saint,[35] candles and *veladoras*,[36] flowers, and a clay pot with copal are indispensable. The degree of adornment depends on the individual h-men, although I have been told that in this regard the owner's wishes are respected.

When it is time to make the first offering, the h-men kneels in front of the kanche, calls upon the winds, and offers them a turkey (male or female) or in its stead a boiled turkey egg. He blesses the bird ritually by pouring a bit of balche into its beak (as Granado Baeza described in 1813) and then sacrifices it by cutting its tongue or neck and leaving it hanging on a branch to bleed to death. Then the chickens are killed and plucked; they are either kept whole or cut into pieces, then thrown into a large cauldron of boiling water to which previously chopped onions, tomatoes, and a bit of mint are added, as is *recado rojo*, which

20.3. *Preparing the ceremonial masa. Photo by Ruth Gubler, 1992.*

consists of achiote, Tabasco pepper, cumin, and cloves.[37] After the birds are taken out, half of the broth is set aside for the kol and half for the yachh; the masa is also divided in half for the same purpose. To make kol, some pibes are crumbled into the chicken broth; yachh consists of watered-down kol to which chopped chicken innards, fried with mint, scallions, and spices, are added.

Meanwhile, the women have gathered, generally under a *palapa* (palm-thatched roof or sun shade) or sometimes inside the house. They moisten the masa with salt and water and form it into small balls that are then patted into small, thick "tortillas," the basis of the ceremonial tamales. To prepare them, five to six leaves are laid out on the table and the fat masa "tortillas" are patted out on them; then the leaves are folded over the masa and wrapped with henequen strands (figure 20.5).

Two kinds of pibes are prepared; one or more large ones, called *hol che* or *noh uah*, are intended specifically for the supernatural beings, and an indeterminate number of small ones, called *noox* or *chicas*, are also prepared. Other large tamales are made to be distributed among the participants at the end of the ceremony. Dón Felipe generally prepares two hol che (as does Dón Tono) by placing thirteen tortillas one on top of the other and sprinkling moistened ground pumpkin seeds between each layer. Dón Casiano generally prepares four large pibes,[38] which consist of nine layers of tortillas: three with ground pumpkin seeds, three with black beans,[39] and three with chicken innards. Finally, he smears achiote on the last tortilla. He says that in the hetz luum, the noh uah are for the aluxes who protect the milpa.

20.4. *Noh uah with seven indentations. Photo by Ruth Gubler, 2003.*

20.5. *Table with wrapped pibes. Photo by Ruth Gubler, 1997.*

Finally, a number of indentations, or *ojitos* (little eyes), are made on top of the hol che. Dón Felipe makes four forming a cross, as does Dón Victor; but Dón Casiano makes nine, a file of seven indentations made lengthwise and one

20.6. *Placing the ceremonial pibes in the earth oven. Photo by Ruth Gubler, 1997.*

on each side (figure 20.4). The h-men sprinkles ground pumpkin seeds on top, generally but not always pours a bit of balche into the indentations, then covers them with a little masa.

The noox, or little ones, are made with twelve of the fat masa tortillas with a little dry ground pumpkin seed sprinkled on each layer; in a second arrangement the seeds may be alternated with beans. Dón Felipe calls them *piedritas* (pebbles) and they are rolled either into little balls or into a longish shape, like tamales. In ceremonies presided over by Dón Felipe, thirteen chicas were made. Dón Victor prepared four chicas, each made with nine layers of tortillas, but he says some h-men prepare up to thirteen. For their part, both Dón Casiano and Dón Tono say that no fixed number is required and that it depends on the amount of maize dough that is available.

All the ceremonies that have been described are divided into several stages. First, the h-men offers the previously blessed turkey to the winds, at which time he utters the first prayer. In a uahil col or chha chac (but not a hetz luum) the masa (ground maize from which the ceremonial tortillas are made) is blessed as well. Placing it in the middle of the mesa (table that serves as an altar), the h-men impresses a cross on top of the masa and blesses it with balche.

The h-men offers zaca (usually prepared early that day or brought fully prepared with the rest of the ingredients) and balche. During the entire time the h-men is presenting the offerings to the gods, he makes petitions for the well-being and prosperity of the milpa, rancho, or water well and for its owner. Then zaca is distributed to everyone, although balche is not passed around until the ceremonial tamales have been placed in the pib.

Finally, when the pibes have been taken out and everything is ready, the h-men places all the offerings on the kanche. Now comes the principal prayer in which he invites the spirits to come and feast on the meal that has been placed before them. It is also the moment when he repeats entreaties for the protection, health, and well-being of the owner(s) of the milpa and his family and begs the deities of the field and bush to ensure that the earth produces and the animals multiply. The turkey is placed atop bowls of the noh uah, the chickens, the sacred pibes, and five bowls of kol and five of yachh. The kol and yachh are arranged one in each corner of the table and one in the center. Some time elapses, allowing the gods to descend and feast on the offerings.

Then the h-men returns to the altar and once more addresses a long prayer to the gods, thanking them and asking for their continued protection and blessings. Kneeling in each corner and then in front of the altar, he symbolically offers the gods of the four world directions their portion. Starting in the East, then the North, West, and South, he first uses a small leaf to sprinkle the liquid and then, using the leg of a fowl (*mochh*), he throws some of the kol and yachh to the four world directions and the center. This is done for all of the ceremonies, although in the hetz luum for the milpa, as described later, the small packets are buried, and in that for a water well a portion is also cast into the well itself.

Having thus honored the supernatural beings, it is time to dismiss the winds. The h-men tells them that in the morning he had invited them to the feast but that now it is time for them to return to their place of origin. Taking the fifth bowl of yachh in his hand, he kneels in front of the altar and offers various prayers of thanksgiving: first a Credo, then an Our Father, followed by a song to the Holy Spirit, and finally thanks to God that all went well that day. He gives the bowl to the owner and has him pronounce God's blessing. Now it is time to distribute the food, and everyone lines up to receive his or her portion.

To formally end the ceremony, the pib is also given its portion. The h-men takes the remaining bowl of zaca from the table and throws the liquid into the pib, along with some of the ritual meal as well as the feathers and intestines of the fowls, and so on. This ends the milpero's obligation, but he has to keep in mind that he must offer another ceremony when it is due, according to the promise he made.

UAHIL COL, HETZ LUUM, AND CHHA CHAC

The procedure followed in each of the above-mentioned ceremonies and the elements that accompany them are basically very similar or, as some of my informants have told me, *siempre es lo mismo* (it is always the same). Although anthropologists categorize the ceremonies as intrinsically different according to the criteria discussed later, the Yucatec Maya seem to view them more in terms of similarity than of difference.

While individual differences exist regarding the specific purpose and particular details of each ceremony, there are indeed common denominators. In the first place, all rituals revolve around the milpa and its well-being. All require the services of a h-men, or ritual specialist, who generally has an assistant chosen from the community where the ceremony is being performed. This assistant helps the h-men in a number of ways, including fetching or placing items on the table, handing him objects, lighting candles, and incensing the altar with copal. While formerly the assistant had to be male, recently I saw a woman function as a helper at a hetz luum. While this might have occurred because she was a relative of the owner of the ranch and an *x-men* in her own right, when I asked the h-men he told me that today there is such a lack of men (as a result of migration) that more and more it falls to women to take over this and other tasks. In any case, the strict sex distinction that was formerly observed no longer applies.

All ceremonies follow a similar sequential pattern of activities (e.g., digging the pib, preparing the pibes, setting up the table-altar), use the same artifacts (e.g., a cross, an image of a saint or saints, calabashes, clay bowls, copal), have the same offerings (e.g., fowl, ceremonial tamales, zaca, balche), and use similar invocations. However, the similarities between the uahil col and the hetz luum are greater than those between either of those ceremonies and the chha chac.

The major common trait is that all ceremonies are petitionary, revolving around the invocation of the supernatural beings that rule the natural world and asking for their protection and blessing.[40] These invocations are of both Prehispanic and Christian origin: the yumtziloob, balams, aluxes, and, alternately, God in Three Persons, the Virgin Mary, and a plethora of Catholic saints. Petitions will vary depending on the type of ceremony and the prayers of each individual h-men, but they all express the campesino's deep gratitude for the plenitude of blessings received.

The uahil col, or thanksgiving, offers the first fruits of the milpa, while the hetz luum, or protection for the milpa, buries four small packets of *contras*[41] in each of the four corners and the center of the field to cleanse it and ward off evil spirits and winds.[42] When the ceremony is performed for a well or a corral, it is intended to give the rancho life, ensure sufficient water for the well, and placate the winds so no harm comes to the owner, the people who live and work there, or the animals.

The uahil col and the hetz luum may be held either by a single individual (the milpero) and his family and relatives or by a group of campesinos from a cooperative (such as orange growers or cattle breeders) who may decide to join together to hold these ceremonies. Because such ceremonies represent an extraordinary expense and are a burden on the campesino's already precarious existence, they cannot be held often. However, if at any point he cannot fulfill his obligations, a small ceremony will be sufficient to placate the gods until such time as it can be performed properly. Because of the sheer effort and great

20.7. *Contras and offerings for a hetz luum. Photo by Ruth Gubler, 1994.*

expense of a chha chac, however, it must of necessity be a communal affair, requiring the cooperation of a greater number of people—either members of a cooperative or an entire community or village.[43]

All of these ceremonies take place in a clearing in the bush, in an open field of a large cooperative, or in or near the milpa. A hetz luum for a rancho, however, will be performed in the corral, and one for a well will be held at its mouth. If for some reason a hetz luum for the milpa cannot be performed there (this does not apply to the other ceremonies), it can be held in the home of the owner or that of the officiating h-men. While in a hetz luum only the name of the milpa and its owner are usually mentioned, in that particular case its specific location, the number of mecates of which it is comprised, and other details must be mentioned.

The offerings are placed in holes dug in the four corners and center of the milpa. The h-men begins by dropping holy water into each hole, then the small packets, and finally small portions of the offerings presented on the table—zaca, balche, yachh, kol, a chicken or turkey leg, and others (figure 20.7). These are for the protection of the field, the domestic animals (in particular chickens and turkeys), and members of the family.

The composition of the contras varies according to the individual h-men. For example, Dón Felipe uses thirteen each of cacao beans, dry red chiles, cloves of garlic, grains of salt, and pieces of *yax halalche*,[44] a *Euphobiacea*. Dón Tono uses eighteen cacao beans, eighteen dry red chiles, a handful of rosemary, zaca, and balche; in the center he buries the head of the chicken, along with its beak and claws.

Aluxes, in the form of wax figures, may also be used to provide the required protection. Dón Casiano tells me that on occasion he prepares four such figures the night before, conjures and brings them to life at midnight, and buries them the next day in each of the four corners. Each is given a name, such as Juan, Pedro, or Mateo, and receives a piece of *pabilo* (string) in his right hand to serve as a whip with which to chase away intruders or unwanted spirits: *como chicote le va a servir* (Dón Casiano, personal communication, 2003). Doña Ana, whom I have known for over twenty-five years, tells me that occasionally she would prepare such figures, giving them a military rank such as sergeant, captain, or lieutenant and arming each with a small rifle. As an x-men (female ritual specialist) she once performed such ceremonies, but she is now too ill to do so.

There were never many x-men to begin with, and now there are even fewer. I know of only two: Doña Ana and Doña Fide, both widows of practicing *hmenoob*. However, the performance of agricultural ceremonies by female ritual specialists is generally said to be limited to the hetz luum, although Doña Ana told me (personal communication) that as a young girl she accompanied an x-men who performed a uahil col. A strict taboo applies to the performance of the chha chac, and it is not permissible for a woman to perform it, for it is believed that the ceremony would not turn out well and that it would entail danger for the x-men.

As for the hetz luum for the corral, what differentiates this ceremony and is its special earmark is the sacrifice of a two-year-old bull. A large hole is dug in the center of the corral where the animal is to be buried, and a pail of water is poured into it. After the animal is sacrificed, its various parts are reassembled: the head, neck, two feet, hide, and belly are laid out in such a way that they replicate and appear to be a living animal lying there. An altar-table is also erected on one side of the corral, and the usual offerings are placed upon it. Another hole is dug to one side of the small bull, and a cock is buried there. San Juan, the patron of livestock, has a particularly close association with the milpa and the corral. San Antonio Abad is another Saint whose blessing is solicited. For San Miguel a special ceremonial bread called cruz noh is prepared.

Chha chacs are in a category by themselves because they are much larger, more elaborate, and more expensive affairs and have unique characteristics. First, because of the ceremony's specific focus (the petition for rain), it is only logical that the chacs (rain gods) and the winds play the central role. As Dón Felipe (personal communication) expresses it: "With great confidence we ask God to send us rain that day. With all one's faith one asks the holy chacs to send it. The wind from *kaknab* [ocean or large body of water] is the one that brings the rain, and one also calls upon the *tsayal ik'*,[45] the winds from the cave, and from the ruins [*muul*] to send rain" (translation by the author). Here we find in these ceremonies a prime example of an easy accommodation of indigenous as well as Christian beliefs.

20.8. *Children impersonating frogs in a chha chac. Photo by Ruth Gubler, 1998.*

Typically, a type of bower is prepared with branches that cross over to form it, and calabashes will be hung from it containing zaca and balche. As Dón Victor put it, "It is like a church and the calabashes are like doors." While the branches of any kind of tree can be used for the bowers, Dón Victor considers *xul*[46] and *zipche*[47] to be the best; he also uses a creeper, *x tacanil*,[48] as "medicine" or protection against the winds, so no one will be harmed during the ceremony. Leaves of habin are placed on the kanche to serve as a tablecloth. Only these branches are used by my informants for the chha chac, although others may use the branches of zipche or another type of tree.

Another distinctive feature of the chha chac is the presence of four small boys who represent *sapitos* (small toads or frogs) and who are tied to the legs of the altar-table and utter onomatopoetic sounds. Because these animals are associated with rain, the children must imitate their croaking so that, by a kind of sympathetic magic, they attract the rain and cause it to fall. In addition, four more children accompany them (one on each side), and an older man is in charge, instructing them and offering them zaca, balche, and yachh (figure 20.8). Four old men playing the role of balams are also stationed at the corners of the terrain; the one to the north whistles, the one to the east throws small stones, the one to the west sings like a chachalaca, and the one to the south sings like another bird. One man has a pail of water in which a calabash floats upside down and which he beats with a small stick to replicate the noise made by thunder to attract the rain.

Not all of these elements need be present, however, and there are individual differences in the way h-men perform a chha chac. Dón Felipe has performed big affairs (for example, for an orange-growing cooperative) held in large clearings with a large attendance and all of the above-mentioned elements. Alternatively, some ceremonies performed by Dón Victor, at which I was present, were more intimate in nature. These were held in the bush with only a few milperos present. A distinctive feature of one of these ceremonies was that he had prepared a kind of ceremonial avenue a short distance behind the kanche, leading to what he called the *hol ha* (*cabeza de agua*) and at whose end he had made a stone altar upon which he had placed candles and a cross. Dón Victor explained that this served as a kind of marker so the gods would know where to go. A small gourd was placed in each corner of the altar, one in the middle of the avenue, and a sixth at the head of the hol ha. Another distinctive feature was that he had hung wooden crosses above the bower. However, there were no children taking the role of frogs, and no balams were present.

While, as we have seen, there are differences as well as similarities in the performance of these ceremonies, time has established a distinction of another sort in that formerly an entire village might have participated, a sort of collective effort destined to benefit everyone in the village. Dón Felipe described a very complex chha chac performed more than twenty years ago, for which no fewer than twelve arches were erected. The entire village cooperated in making the pib, and each villager brought an offering. An adoratory was prepared on which a statue of San Antonio, taken out of the church specifically for this occasion, was placed. After the distribution of food, a procession carried the image of the saint around the adoratory from right to left, with each person carrying a candle. Those assisting kissed the saint and made an offering of money. Dón Felipe made it clear that today such massive participation is the exception rather than the rule and that it occurs very rarely.

Recently, another h-men, Dón Casiano, told me that the whole town had turned out for a chha chac he performed in Citilcum. He said he was surprised and impressed by the large number of participants and the devotion with which they carried out their duties, something he had not seen in a very long time. In fact, he expressed renewed hope for the resurgence of such traditions.

THE IMPORTANCE OF CABALISTIC NUMBERS

Another constant element in all these rituals is the importance of certain cabalistic numbers, especially numbers 4, 5, 9, and 13. It is said that in the case of the number 4 the referents are the four world directions: *los cuatro puntos, las cuatro esquinas*. This perpetuates the description in the *Book of Chilam Balam of Chumayel* of how the red, white, black, and yellow stones, with their associated trees, plants, and birds, were set up: "The red flint stone is the stone of the red

20.9. *Preparing to offer the spirits their portion. Photo by Ruth Gubler, 2007.*

Mucencab. The red ceiba tree of abundance is his arbor which is set in the east. The red bullet-tree is their tree. The red zapote . . . The red vine . . . Reddish are their yellow turkeys. Red toasted [corn] is their corn" (Roys 1967: 64).

Later, it is recorded in the Ritual of the Four World-Quarters (Roys 1965:65) that, after Mizcit Ahau had swept the roads clean and the leagues were measured by Ah Ppizte, the land surveyor, a spokesman was placed at the head of the mat, followed by the red, white, black, and yellow wild bees with their associated flowers. Roys (ibid.) interprets this section as a legend of the supernatural occupation of the country in ancient times. This fourfold pattern is also present in the kanche and the way the offerings are placed in its four corners. Moreover, many deities, including the chacs, pauahtuns, and balams, are in fourfold form.

Five is an extension of the number 4, to which the very important center, the *quincunx*, has been added. Its significance is reflected in the setting up of the kanche, the altar-table that serves as a kind of world tree where the gods are invoked, descend, commune with man by partaking of his offerings, and then, after the h-men has dismissed them, return to their place of origin. It is also present in the utilization of five calabashes for the kol and yachh and five gourds for zaca and balche.

Numbers 9 and 13 have also been explained to me in terms that relate to 4 and 5: in the former, twice 4 and the center (9) and in the latter 3 times 4 plus the center. While an association with the *Bolon ti ku* (gods of the number 9) or the *Oxlahun ti ku* (gods of the number 13) cannot be established, Dón Felipe explained the importance of the number 13 in that originally there were thirteen winds; on another occasion he attributed its significance to the *"batan ik'"* (the greatest of the winds). In any case, when he performs a chha chac the number 13 plays an important role. He uses 13 gourds of zaca and 13 of balche, as well as 13 bowls of kol and 13 of yacch. The offerings hung on the arches also revolve around this number; there are 6 gourds of balche and 7 of zaca, 6 of kol and 7 of yachh.

PRAYERS AND INVOCATIONS

We now turn to a particularly important element around which every ceremony revolves: the prayers and invocations to the supernatural beings, either those of Prehispanic origin such as the yumtziloob, balams, and aluxes or, alternately, God in Three Persons, the Virgin Mary, and a plethora of Catholic saints whose help is invoked. Although many of the same spirits are called upon, petitions will vary depending on the type of ceremony and the particular prayers of each individual h-men. Their specific purpose is to propitiate and honor the gods, who have power over all living things. In submitting to them and showing respect and gratitude, man placates them and keeps them well-disposed.

While prayers vary from h-men to h-men, there are also similarities. First, they all show how easily Precolumbian and Christian elements have merged yet remained distinct within each specific tradition, alternating yet appearing to work in tandem. In his prayers the ritual specialist invokes the names of the chacs and the balams but curiously not those of the *bacabs*; Landa (1938) relates that the latter were four brothers whom God placed at the four world-quarters to hold up the sky. The ritual specialist also calls upon the winds of the four world directions and the yumtziloob on which the milpa, and therefore also the life of its owner, depends.

This survival can be traced back to at least the early Colonial Period and, by extension, perhaps to the Precolumbian past. However, at the same time there is a break with that past. The ancient gods are no longer present except for the few named earlier, and the balance is now tipped toward the Christian elements: God, the Virgin Mary, and those Catholic saints who, after the Conquest, were substituted for or assimilated with several of the ancient deities.

Syncretism appears in a prayer Dón Felipe recited at a chha chac, which I recorded. First, the h-men invoked God the Father, Son, and Holy Ghost and "my lord Jesus Christ, god-man, true creator and redeemer." This was followed by an apologetic confession of sins, pleading for forgiveness, promising to sin no more, and persevering in this intent until the end of one's days. Only then did the h-men address the yumtziloob, the balams, the aluxes, and the winds. From that point on the invocation of the ancient deities alternated with that of God in Three Persons, the Virgin, and a large number of Catholic saints:

I call upon God the Father, God the Son, God the Holy Spirit, I kneel before the greatness of the guardians of prosperity, I call upon the gods of the winds, my God, we are making the *primicia*, a holy prayer to the gods, a prayer for rain. I implore with devotion before the altar of the gods who are guardians of prosperity, the winds of the East, winds of the North, winds of the West, and winds of the South. My father, [I ask] this blessing on this day of holy days and with faith I ask for this holy rain. My God, send your blessing, Lord, I entreat you this sacred Thursday [the same winds are invoked again] . . . before the Holy Virgin, Holy Mary, I kneel to ask for this blessing.[49]

At the moment of offering zaca he said: "I offer this holy zaca, my God; give us this blessing. Lord, I call upon the Sacred Goddess of Water. I kneel and invoke with devotion and call on the name of the minor winds, the strong winds."

Once again God the Father, Son, and Holy Ghost were invoked, followed by a number of virgins: the Virgin of Mamita, the Virgin of Assumption, the Virgin of the Star, and saints like Saint Bernard, Saint Vicent Caballero, Saint Martin Caballero, and Saint Eustaquius. Next the h-men, offering a candle, again made a petition for the holy rain: "I kneel to call the rainy days, the four cardinal points of the sky, the winds that invigorate [literally 'make green'], the winds of the rain . . . St. Francis, St. Isidore, St. Anthony, all the wind gods." After repeated invocations of the Virgin and numerous saints, he once again turned to the wind gods: "the new winds and guardians of the caves, winds of the hills, guardian winds of the roads, guardians of the fields, of the corrals, winds of the houses, roaming winds . . . principal winds, hot winds [because the earth is hot], the clouds which cause the Holy Rain to fall on the gracia [maize], sprinkler guardians, Great God, Guardian of Prosperity, wind god of the plots of land, rain gods."

In this way the Yucatec Maya campesino interacts with the supernaturals. Propitiating and honoring the gods, he hopes to bend them to his will and therefore ensure his own well-being.

CONCLUSION

The question that remains is what the future holds for these ritual activities; will they survive against all odds, or will they ultimately disappear? While there is no way to foretell what the future will bring, we can extrapolate from existing trends. First, the raison d´être of agricultural ceremonies such as those described in this chapter is anchored in their relationship with the milpa, which makes their survival dependent on the continuation of that practice. Admittedly, making milpa is a secular activity destined to ensure a supply of food, but it also has deep religious undertones in the campesino's close relationship with the bush and the spirit world that inhabits it. Any deleterious impact on the one will automatically reverberate on the other. Once milpa is no longer made, there will be no reason to perform such ceremonies. Agriculture in Yucatán, and milpa in particular, is very precarious, and campesinos consistently appear to be the lowest on the totem pole in receiving government assistance. If help is given, it is often too little, or it is diverted by the officials in charge of dispensing it.

Thompson (1970: 283) has called attention to the quasi-religious, symbiotic relationship between the campesino and his milpa. While this may be true for older milperos, today it is not true for the younger generation, which, with increasing educational opportunities, has disassociated itself from farming as a way of life. Henequen, once another major source of work for the campesino, has also fallen on hard times, as evidenced by the large number of abandoned fields where it was once grown. Neither the family milpa nor the henequen industry can survive without the manpower to sustain them.

The continued performance of Yucatec Maya agricultural rituals obviously depends on whether the campesino continues to believe in animated nature and, consequently, in the necessity of placating the spirit world. Traditions are being lost, and today only the old milperos and rancheros still have such ceremonies performed. The young, with their parents' hard lot fresh in their minds, have no intention of following in their footsteps and in general have little use for these traditions (Gubler 2006a, 2006b). In addition, for those not engaged in getting an education, the lure of a golden opportunity in the United States is too great to resist. So job seekers continue to out-migrate, either to the States or to the resorts of Quintana Roo, leaving many Maya villages bereft of their young male population.

Finally, with the demise of many of the ritual specialists, it is alarming that many Yucatec Maya villages no longer have their own h-men. It is often necessary to seek one in a neighboring pueblo. If one is not found, it is impossible to perform the ceremony, leading to a continuing cycle of loss of such practices. In addition, there is no younger generation of h-men to take the place of the older, dying generation, for the young have no interest in this non-lucrative profession. This notwithstanding, many young Yucatec Maya continue to fear the influence of the supernaturals. But when asked if they will continue to practice the old ceremonies, most shake their heads, alleging that they are afraid to do so. More and more, the young have lost respect for their own traditions, and now they consider them merely superstitions. Therefore, one must conclude that the future of a tradition that has withstood the test of time over many, many centuries is very much at risk.

Acknowledgments. Throughout more than a quarter-century of fieldwork among the Yucatec Maya, I have been aided and supported by several *h'meno'ob*. These individuals constantly stress the reciprocity between man and the gods, and their rituals express gratitude for benefits received from the supernaturals. I am grateful, too, particularly to Dón Felipe and Dón Casiano, and want to thank all of these elders for the knowledge and kindness they have shared with me over the years.

NOTES

1. Powerful supernatural forces appear either in anthropomorphic form or as spirits, like the wind. I refer to them interchangeably as supernatural beings, gods, deities, and spirits.

2. My field research of around twenty-five years has been confined mainly to the State of Yucatán.

3. Protestantism is the modern battering ram employed against native traditions. It is a divisive force, pitting its converts against both traditionalists and Catholics (Gubler 2005: 39).

4. Having heard this, the *Popul Vuh* gods decided to limit man's knowledge and make him mortal.

5. Supernatural beings who protect and guard.

6. Rain gods.

7. Small forest spirits. Said to be the size of small children, they are sometimes described as wearing traditional clothing and a large hat. Redfield and Villa Rojas (1934: 120, figure 11) offer a pencil drawing of an alux made by two men of Chan Kom. Like other supernatural beings they can be malignant, but they are also the milpero's best ally in protecting his field and keeping intruders away.

8. Gods of the field and bush. Written as *yuntzilob* by other ethnographers.

9. Large, natural wells, sinkholes where the limestone has collapsed. From the Yucatec Maya word *d'zonot*.

10. *Milpa* means cornfield, not farm, just as in Yucatán a *rancho* is not a ranch but simply a place where domestic animals are raised. While dedicated mainly to the cultivation of maize, milperos also raise other crops such as beans and chile on their milpas and engage in hunting-and-gathering activities. Similarly, most rancheros are also milperos.

11. The nearest translation is "farmer." Since *campo* means the "country" or in English vernacular "the sticks," many urban dwellers consider campesinos to be rural bumpkins.

12. I am indebted to David Bolles for his help with the orthography of Maya terms.

13. There is a diagram of the Maya cosmos on pages 75 and 76 of the *Madrid Codex*.

14. This term is used by Thompson (1972: 19), according to the definition in the *Vienna Dictionary* as *columna de libro*.

15. Balche is a traditional, mildly alcoholic drink made of fermented maize flavored with the pulverized bark of *Lonchocarpus longistylus* Pittier (Mendieta and del Amo R. 1981: 201).

16. In addition, the *Codex Pérez* records the activities of the *Ah Toc*, or "burners," who start, run with, put out, and take the fire.

17. An offering or gift, equivalent to an *ofrenda* in archaeological Spanish.

18. The modern term *barbecue* had its genesis as the description of the lattice frame for either roasting or sun-drying meat, not, as commonly assumed, of the meat on that frame.

19. In Central America and Mexico, palm splints woven for use as a bed.

20. This reference seems contradictory because the pauahtuns are generally identified as wind gods, while the chacs are rain gods. But deity functions were not always clear-cut, and as winds the pauahtuns were, in effect, bringing the rain.

21. Here I follow the orthography of the authors.

22. A drink made of ground maize, water, and a little honey. If allowed to ferment, it becomes mildly alcoholic maize beer.

23. To make kol some pibes are crumbled into chicken broth, forming a thick gruel.

24. Yachh is kol thinned with water and broth, to which chopped livers and gizzards fried with mint, scallions, and spices have been added.

25. Actually, it is more in the nature of a demand.

26. A wild, ground-dwelling, chicken-sized, very noisy bird with brown back and wings, white belly, long tail with yellowish feathers, and red eyes.

27. Dón Victor recently told me that traditionally the ceremony took four days because of the four world directions.

28. This prolongs the h-men's presence to his detriment because he would otherwise be attending to his patients.

29. *Piscidia communis* (Blake) I. M. Johnston; *P. piscipula* (L.) Sarg. and *P. spp.* (Mendieta and del Amo R. 1981: 262).

30. *Coccoloba aff. barbadensis* Jacq. (ibid.: 107); *C. schiedeana* Lindau (ibid.: 108); *C. spicata* Lundell (ibid.).

31. *Inodes japa* (Wright) Standl. (ibid.: 181).

32. *Bursera simaruba* (L.) Sarg. (ibid.: 65).

33. Extra cooking stones are placed along the pit's edges because there is a tendency for the outmost pibes to be insufficiently cooked.

34. This, he says, is against *ziz kab* (a "cold hand"), which nowadays is considered a negative trait. Many things tend to turn out badly for a person with a "cold hand." This is particularly true in the case of agriculture. The harvest will not be good, for whatever was planted by a farmer with a "cold hand" may turn out to be sickly or die; the "cold hand" can be considered the opposite of a "green thumb." Yet, it is most curious that the 16th century Calepino de Motul (f.102v) defines ziz kab as "el que tiene buena mano para poner árboles" (Ciudad Read and Arzápalo Marín 1995); i.e. someone who obtains positive results when planting. It would be interesting to know how, when, and why the meaning of this concept changed from positive to negative.

35. Although it is said that any male saint will do, San Antonio and San Isidro Labrador seem to be favored.

36. Votive candle; shorter and much thicker than secular candles for lighting.

37. These cooking vessels can be enormous and easily require two men to carry them.

38. Dón Victor makes two piles of two noh uah (four in all), one pile for the aluxes, the other for the chacs. Like Dón Felipe (but unlike Dón Casiano), his noh uah consist of thirteen layers of tortillas.

39. As in the ceremony described by Granado Baeza (1946).

40. The purpose of each ceremony is nonetheless specific.

41. *Contras* is best translated as "countermeasures."

42. It can also be a formal request for permission to work a new piece of land.
43. Today such community efforts are infrequent, unusual, and rare.
44. *Pedilanthus nodiflorus* Millsp. (Mendieta and del Amo R. 1981: 244).
45. Wind that strikes a person, causing illness (David Bolles, personal communication).
46. *Harpalyce arborescens* A. Gray (Arellano Rodríguez et al. 2003: 349, no. 1285).
47. *Bunchosia glandulosa* Cav. (Mendieta and del Amo R. 1981: 63).
48. *Cissus rhombifolia* Vahl (ibid.: 100).
49. English translation after the Maya into Spanish translation by María Mercedes Cruz Bohórquez.

REFERENCES CITED

Arellano Rodríguez, José Alberto, José Salvador Flores Guido, J. Tun Garrido, and María Mercedes Cruz Bojórquez, eds.
    2003   *Nomenclatura, forma de vida, uso, manejo y distribución de las especies vegetales de la Península de Yucatán*. Etnoflora Yucatanense 20. Universidad Autónoma de Yucatán, Mérida.

Ciudad Real, Antonio de, and Ramón Arzápalo Marín, eds.
    1995   *Calepino de Motul: Diccionario Maya-Español*, 3 vol., Dirección General de Asuntos del Personal Académico [y] Instituto de Investigaciones Antropológicas, UNAM, México, DF.

Cogolludo, Diego Lopez
    1954 [1656]   *Historia de Yucatán*, 4th ed. Talleres Gráficos del Gobierno, Campeche, México, DF.

Craine, Eugene R., and Reginald C. Reindorp, trans. and eds.
    1979   *The Codex Pérez and Book of Chilam Balam of Maní*. University of Oklahoma Press, Norman.
    1980   Ediciones Cordemex, Mérida, Yucatán.

Dresden Codex
    1975   *Codex Dresdensis*. Commentary in German by Helmet Deckert and Ferdinand Anders. Akademische Druck und Verlagsanstalt, Graz, Austria.

Gann, Thomas W.F.
    1918   *The Maya Indians of Southern Yucatan and Northern British Honduras*. Bureau of American Ethnology Bulletin 64. Smithsonian Institution, Washington, DC.

Garza, Mercedes de la
    1983   *Relaciones Histórico-Geográficas de la Gobernación de Yucatán*, 2 vols. Fuentes para el Estudio de la Cultura Maya 1. UNAM, México, DF.

Granado Baeza, José
    1946   *Informe del cura de Yaxcabá, Yucatán, 1813*. Edited by Vargas Rea. Biblioteca Aportación Histórica, México, DF.

Gubler, Ruth
    2005   Continuity vs. Change in Traditional Yucatec Curing Practices: A Tradition in Crisis. *Acta Americana* 13 (1–2): 34–54.
    2006a   El papel de los curanderos y *h-meno'ob* en la época contemporánea en Yucatán. In *Los mayas de ayer y hoy*, vol. 2, ed. Alfredo Barrera Rubio and Ruth Gubler, pp. 1121–1144. Solar, Ediciones Editoriales, S.A. de C.V., México, DF.
    2006b   El papel del ritual y de la religión en la terapéutica de los curanderosy *h-meno'ob* yucatecos actuales. *Anales de Antropología* 40 (1): 133–165.

Landa, Fray Diego de
    1938 [1565]   *Relación de las cosas de Yucatán.* Edición Yucateca, Mérida.

Lizana, Fray Bernardo de
    1893   *Historía de Yucatán. Devocionario de Nuestra Señora de Izamal y conquista espiritual*, 2nd ed. Impresa en 1633. Museo Nacional de México, México, DF.

Mendieta, Rosa María, and Silvia del Amo R.
    1981   *Plantas medicinales del Estado de Yucatán.* Instituto Nacional de Investigaciones sobre Recursos Bióticos, Xalapa, Veracruz. Compañía Editorial Continental, S.A. de C.V., México, DF.

Morley, Sylvanus G., George W. Brainerd, and Robert J. Sharer
    1983   *The Ancient Maya*, 4th, revised ed. Stanford University Press, Stanford, CA.

Recinos, Adrian, Delia Goetz, and Sylvanus G. Morley, eds.
    1950   *Popol Vuh: The Sacred Book of the Ancient Quiche Maya.* University of Oklahoma Press, Norman.

Redfield, Robert, and Alfonso Villa Rojas
    1934   *Chan Kom: A Maya Village.* Carnegie Institution of Washington, Washington, DC.

Roys, Ralph L.
    1967   *The Book of Chilam Balam of Chumayel.* University of Oklahoma Press, Norman.

Sánchez de Aguilar, Pedro
    1987 [1639]   Informe contra idolorum cultures del Obispado de Yucatán. In *El Alma Encantada*, ed. Fernado Benítez, pp. 23–122. Anales del Museo Nacional de México, Instituto Nacional Indigenista, and Fondo de Cultura Económica, México, DF.

Thompson, J. Eric S.
    1970   *Maya History and Religion.* University of Oklahoma Press, Norman.
    1972   *A Commentary to the Dresden Codex.* American Philosophical Society, Philadelphia, PA.

Zimmermann, Günter
    1956   *Die Hieroglyphen der Maya Handschriften.* Cram, de Gruter, Hamburg, Germany.

21

MESOAMERICAN INDIAN CLOTHING: SURVIVALS, ACCULTURATION, AND BEYOND

Patricia R. Anawalt

H. B. Nicholson's passing from our midst gives occasion for pause and not a little introspection. Nick was justly famous for his detailed knowledge of the Pre- and Postconquest Aztec world as well as all matters Mesoamerican. He effortlessly navigated back and forth between archaeological and historical evidence, voyages that seemed daunting at best to most others. Looking back over the many years I have spent doing research with Mexican codices and Mesoamerican Indian clothing, I am struck by how important to me was Nick's constant encouragement and enthusiasm.

Style and technology, while linked, evolve independently of each other according to the differing demands of the culture or cultures within which they are found. In this chapter I return to two subjects that have fascinated me in the past and which continue to fascinate me: survivals (Anawalt 1984) and acculturation (Anawalt and Berdan 1994). As we shall see, just because new technologies are introduced, traditional styles need not change when adapted to them, and, given enough time, "new" or introduced styles become traditional themselves. In his studies of iconography and art history, H. B. Nicholson clearly understood the separation of style from technology in archaeological and ethnographic contexts, a concept not always easily grasped by his peers or his students. This thinking was a direct legacy of Nick's student years at Berkeley, where he was profoundly influenced by John H. Rowe who, in the late 1940s, was busy applying

Patricia R. Anawalt

21.1. *Mexico, with the Sierra Norte de Puebla and adjacent areas enlarged. From Sayer 1985: 11; redrawn by Rusty van Rossmann.*

Alfred Louis Kroeber's (1944) ideas about "style as culture" to his own Andean research. Nicholson's (1960, 1961, 1982) definition of the Mixteca-Puebla Style came to be one of his most famous contributions to Mesoamerican studies, one all of his students, myself included, certainly took to heart.

Nicholson was a recognized authority on how elements of dress or even hairstyle depicted in sculpture could be used for the identification of Aztec deities depicted in the Preconquest and Contact Period codices (Nicholson 1971, 1977a, 1977b). I shared his passion for the codices and discovered within them an almost inexhaustible source of information on ancient Mexican dress, elements of which still survive today in traditional Indian areas. I was honored to have Nick write the foreword for one of my first major books (Anawalt 1981) on the subject that has consumed my professional life for more than three decades. Over the many years of our acquaintance, Nick was a supportive and insightful mentor and friend. He taught me much, and I shall miss him.

THE SIERRA NORTE DE PUEBLA

One of the best areas for the study of both survivals and acculturation in Indian dress lies in a mountainous area of eastern Central Mexico, a unique and fascinating region known as the Sierra Norte de Puebla (figure 21.1) (Sodi 1968). Here, a portion of the State of Puebla abuts the State of Hidalgo to the west, while to the east it borders on the State of Veracruz, which stretches down to the Gulf Coast. The Sierra Norte de Puebla is a rugged region of *barrancas*, or impressively deep gullies, a location whose remoteness spared the area not only the full impact of the Spanish Conquest but also the arrival of "modern ways" well into the twenty-first century. The Sierra is unusual in several respects, including the juxtaposition of four different indigenous peoples living in artificially close proximity within a small radius. In its retention of traditional Indian culture and polyglot nature, the region is similar to the much more extensively studied Oaxacan and Chiapas Highlands and to Highland Guatemala.

The demographic situation in the Sierra Norte de Puebla came about as the result of the catastrophic population decline and forced resettlement that occurred almost half a millennium ago. Within less than a hundred years after the Spanish Conquest, the impact of European diseases on the Mexican Indians brought about the most devastating population drop in recorded history. In 1521 there were an estimated 10 to 15 million inhabitants in Central Mexico; by 1600 only about 1 million were left (Cook and Borah 1960; Borah and Cook 1963). Faced with this rapidly collapsing native population, the Spanish instigated a new settlement policy, *congregación*: relocating surviving ethnic groups in new towns, essentially "within the sound of a church bell," the better for missionary conversion and political control. The effects of this resettlement were still evident centuries later. Frederick Starr (1901), the pioneering American anthropologist who worked in the Sierra during the late nineteenth century, noted "strange interminglings" among the region's diverse peoples.

This was still true a century later when I worked in the Sierra from the early 1980s to the early 1990s. In fact, I deliberately chose the Sierra Norte de Puebla for research into clothing acculturation precisely because it was home to four distinct language groups: Highland Totonac, Tepehua, Otomí, and Nahuatl, the latter the tongue of the Aztec Empire still spoken by almost a million people in Central Mexico. Members of all four of these peoples live very near one another in the Sierra Norte de Puebla yet maintain autonomy in language and dress; all are still producing and wearing clothing styles reflecting varying aspects of their 500-year acculturation process. Despite the present incursion of roads, the Sierra often still resembles a landscape out of the past, a land where time does not always move logically into succeeding years and decades. The Sierra Norte de Puebla truly is a *Land of the Old Ways* where Prehispanic foods are prepared in Prehispanic ways, using Prehispanic condiments to produce Prehispanic treats. The Sierra has also retained old textile practices: not only are women still weaving on Prehispanic-style backstrap looms, they are also still producing Prehispanic-style garments almost identical to those that repeatedly appear on Aztec sculptures (figure 21.2) and in Aztec codices (figure 21.3).

21.2. *The Aztec fertility goddess Chalchiuhtlicue wearing a* quechquemitl. *Stone sculpture, Völkerkundliche Sammlungen Reiss-Engelhorn Museum, Mannheim, Germany. Photo by Jean Christen.*

21.3. *The Aztec* maguey/pulque *goddess Mayahual wearing a quechquemitl.* Codex Magliabechiano, *ca. 1566: folio 58. Photo by Don Cole.*

SURVIVALS: THE OLD CONTINUES

Beginning more than a century ago, anthropological interest in traditional Mesoamerican Indian clothing took two paths. The first was as an aside to standard ethnographic research on material culture (cf. Starr 1901; Blom and La Farge 1926), while the second (Lumholtz 1904; Nuttall 1909) was specifically concerned with clothing and clothing technology as a supposed Preconquest "survival," sometimes without much contextual reference to the cultural tradition of which it formed a part. Some of this attention to survivals was an early form of ethnoarchaeology or what, in Oliver La Farge's (1940) "Recent Indian" cultural-chronological category, some scholars call "archaeology on the hoof." But perhaps the earliest modern study (Nuttall 1888) pioneered the kind of research I would embark upon not quite a century later (Anawalt 1981), that of the identification of specific elements of dress and adornment in the native codices.

Research on indigenous clothing in Mesoamerica has greatly increased over the past three-quarters of a century until it now exists as a recognized subdivision of cultural anthropology and ethnohistory. Unfortunately, traditional dress, originally widespread, has diminished to the point where it survives only in pockets surrounded by the mainstream of modern culture and its cheap, mass-produced clothing. Today we face the conundrum of more and more people studying what fewer and fewer people do, or wear, as it were.

Most anthropologists consider traditional Indian clothing to be an external symbol of cultural identity and ethnic pride. It stands as a kind of "shorthand" for other, less tangible internal aspects of Indian culture, such as language, religion, belief, kinship, and so forth. But many do not recognize that most "traditional" Indian garb is today, and has been for the past 500 years, a combination of both ancient Indian and introduced Medieval to modern European styles and technologies. It has long been recognized that those who abandon traditional garb may still be culturally "Indian" but are now essentially incognito and can pass for *mestizos* or ladinos, at least until they open their mouths. Or, as the popular Guatemalan folk saying goes, if you want to "stop being an Indian," you simply put on shoes and move to the city.

Perhaps not coincidentally, the anthropological study of Mesoamerican Indian clothing has largely been the preserve of female scholars, such as Zelia Nuttall (1888), Lilly de Jongh Osborne (1935), Lila O'Neale (1945), Irmgard Weitlaner Johnson (1953), Joy Mahler (1965), Carmen Pettersen (1976), Ruth Lechuga (1982), Linda Asturias de Barrios (1985), Chloe Sayer (1985), Julia Hendon (2006), and myself (Anawalt 1976a, 1976b, 1981, 1984, 1996, 2003, 2007). But some male ethnographers and visual anthropologists, notably George Foster (1940) and Donald Cordry (1942), have also studied traditional clothing as part and parcel of their general interest in Indian culture and later came back to this subject in greatly expanded fashion. It may be no accident that both men did much of their best work as only half of husband-and-wife research teams—George and Mary Foster in their multigenerational studies of the Tarascan area of West Mexico, and Donald and Dorothy Cordry (1968) in their remarkable encyclopedic work *Mexican Indian Costumes*.

Perhaps the most traditional Preconquest Central Mexican article of clothing is the woman's quechquemitl. Many archaeological representations in both stone sculpture (figure 21.2) and ceramics establish without question the antiquity of this native dress form, which was also the diagnostic apparel of Aztec female deities. So far as my colleagues and I have been able to discover, this simply constructed garment is unique to Mesoamerica. The quechquemitl also appears on female deities in the Prehispanic codices. Mayahuel (figure 21.3), the goddess of pulque—the intoxicating drink made from the maguey plant—appears in *Codex Magliabechiano* wearing a quechquemitl. In *Codex Borbonicus* the corn deity Chicomecoatl is beautifully dressed in a quechquemitl and a magnificent, towering, amacalli paper headdress. Today in the Sierra native women still wear quechquemitl; one example is a Nahuatl speaker (figure 21.4) who displays both a quechquemitl and a Prehispanic-style headdress, topped by a second quechquemitl.

MESOAMERICAN INDIAN CLOTHING

21.4. *A Nahuatl-speaking Sierran woman wearing a quechquemitl. Her Prehispanic hairstyle is topped by a second quechquemitl. Photo by Patricia Anawalt.*

Despite the greater conservatism of female versus male dress, Prehispanic-style male garments are also still produced in the Sierra. One of the best examples is the sleeveless jacket, a descendant of the *xicolli*, the Prehispanic sacred jacket worn by the Aztec god Xiuhtecuhtli as represented in sculpture (Anawalt 1976a, 1976b). This ancient garment lives on, but the postmodern version can now have zippers, faux-fur collars, faux-ivory buttons, and a macrame hem.

For some time I have been intrigued by how one might establish how far back specific textile traits or elements might be found in Mesoamerica, especially in light of the poor preservation prospects in this culture area (Anawalt 1981, 1984, 1996; Anawalt and Berdan 1994; Anawalt and Davis 2001). Most Mesoamerican scholars consider textiles to be "archaeologically invisible," and in most cases they are—especially when one compares Mexico and Central America with Peru, where textiles are an expected category of archaeological evidence along the xeric coastal strip.

Conditions for preservation in Mesoamerican tombs and burials (dessication, for example, on the Chichimec desert frontier) or for wet preservation (in the tropical Maya lowlands) are iffy at best, and very few examples of preserved textiles are known from the archaeological record (but see Johnson 1954; Coggins and Shane 1984). This notwithstanding, very detailed textile representations in sculptural art are abundant among the Classic Period Maya (cf. Orellana, this volume) 1,000 years before the Aztec (Matos Moctezuma and Solis Olguin 2002). When coupled with many other representations on polychrome pottery (cf. Smith 1955) and ceramic figurines (cf. Corson 1973, 1976, 1977), we can not

525

only identify specific clothing forms and designs and sometimes even the colors, but we can also precisely date the time of their use.

Establishing the ancient presence of traits in a perishable medium is therefore difficult but possible. In earlier papers (Anawalt 1996; Anawalt and Davis 2001) I have explored how old the tradition of tie-dyeing is in Mesoamerica, using every possible kind of evidence from archaeological, iconographic, linguistic, and ethnoarchaeological sources. There is little doubt now that tie-dyeing was indeed a Preconquest Mesoamerican textile tradition, as others (cf. Pettersen 1976) have previously hinted. Similar research on when embroidery first appeared in Mesoamerica is also under way. Our earliest direct evidence comes from the Maya area, from both Chiapas (Johnson 1954) and Yucatán (Coggins and Shane 1984). There is also further evidence for Prehispanic embroidery, this time in Central Mexico, in the work of Fray Bernardino de Sahagún, the foremost sixteenth-century chronicler of the Aztecs. In Sahagún's great work, the *Florentine Codex*, he mentions embroidery—*tlamachtli*—seven times (1954, 8: 24, 25, 25; 1964, 10: 180, 180, 180, 188). In a passage from Book 10, *The People*, he repeatedly lauds the skill the women displayed in their intricate needlework.

ACCULTURATION: THE NEW BECOMES OLD

Prior to the Conquest, all Mesoamerican Indians wore traditional garments because they were the only clothing to be worn. With the Spanish Conquest came new items and ideas from selected sources and only a few Spanish regions (Foster 1960) rather than the full array of what was available throughout Europe at the time. After the Conquest, new raw materials, weaving technology, and design elements from Europe appeared in Mesoamerican Indian communities. Some of these introductions were selected for addition to the preexisting clothing repertoire, and some were actually forced upon the Indians. At the same time many Preconquest elements disappeared entirely (Anawalt 1984; Sayer 1985; Anawalt and Berdan 1994).

Technological influences from late Medieval or Renaissance European sources (e.g., wool, new dyes, metal sewing needles) merged with Precolumbian stylistic traditions to crystallize into a new cultural expression within only a few generations after the Conquest. The result was a syncretic form of Indian dress that, despite the introductions, still identified the wearer as a traditional Indian. More than a quarter-century ago I explored the differing traditions, both Indian and European, that combined to produce the distinctive native dress of the Maya Highlands of Guatemala (Anawalt 1984). I believed then, as now, that the Indians created a new and different culture, a synthesis of remnants of the Preconquest world and European elements from their Spanish conquerors. Precisely this kind of amalgamation, repeated over centuries, is recorded in many modern aspects of Indian dress (Anawalt 1984: 13).

MESOAMERICAN INDIAN CLOTHING

21.5. *A modern-day Sierran weaver working on an unusually long Prehispanic-style backstrap loom. Photo by Cristina Taccone.*

This observation applies no less to the Mexican Sierra Norte de Puebla. One might assume that the backstrap weaving of such ancient clothing styles would be the textile focus of the Sierra, but another emphasis receives far more attention today. The region's most ubiquitous and widely discussed clothing item, at least by the women, is a blouse descended from the European chemise. An Early Historic European example of this kind of chemise is visible on a fifteenth-century depiction of Queen Isabella of Portugal (figure 21.6). All traditional Sierran females wear this same Colonial-style blouse (figure 21.7), regardless of ethnic group: Highland Totonac, Tepehua, Otomí, and the Nauha, direct descendants of the Aztecs. The most unusual aspects of these Colonial-style blouses are the time, effort, and consideration that go into decorating the colorful panels that adorn the neck and sleeves. When these embroidered panels are completed, they are taken to be stitched up into a Sierran-style blouse by one of the few local women who own a sewing machine.

In an earlier paper Frances Berdan and I evaluated clothing as an external symbol of acculturation, considering five different acculturative processes: *replacement, adaptation, introduction, innovation,* and *persistence* (Anawalt and Berdan 1994). An example of functional *replacement* is the Preconquest man's abbreviated loincloth by the European white cotton *calzones*, or pants (figures 21.8, 21.9). I have noted how the Preconquest xicolli, a "godly jacket" (Anawalt 1976a, 1976b) with specific religious connotations, has been *adapted* over the centuries into the *cotorina*, a modern secular version. I have also called attention

527

Patricia R. Anawalt

21.6. *Ceramic sculpture of fifteenth-century Queen Isabella of Portugal. Her chemise, the prototype of the Colonial Period Mexican Indian blouse, is clearly visible. Kunstgewerbemuseum, Berlin. Photo by Edward Maeder.*

21.7. *Nahuatl-speaking Sierran woman wearing an embroidered chemise displays her handiwork: an embroidered blouse panel. Photo by Cristina Taccone.*

to the *introduction* of the European Colonial-style blouse or chemise (figures 21.6, 21.7) and to *innovation*: primarily in decorative style but sometimes through new or different technological applications, such as the machine embroidery of the Chachahuantla blouses of the Sierra. Finally, the *persistence* of the old quechquemitl, or "neck cape," design, uniquely Mesoamerican, is one of the best examples of an ancient "survival" into modern times.

For centuries indigenous dress has served as an immediately visible outward manifestation of local Indian identity and cultural pride. Native dress unmistakably identifies its wearer as Indian and often as a speaker of a specific language or even a resident of a specific Indian town. The traditional Indian *huipil* or *traje* serves as a badge of ethnic identity and racial pride from the Central Mexican Highlands (Cordry and Cordry 1968) to the Guatemalan Highlands (Pettersen 1976). And in recent decades native dress has also come to be accepted as a symbol of national pride and even national identity in both Mexico and Guatemala, even for non-Indians.

THE OLD BECOMES NEW AGAIN: INDIAN DRESS IN MODERN POPULAR CULTURE

In Mexico, traditional Indian communities are isolated from each other and are few and far between, except for a few remaining areas such as Highland

MESOAMERICAN INDIAN CLOTHING

21.8. *Postconquest Aztecs, dressed in Colonial white shirts and pants under their Prehispanic capes, pay homage to their Spanish conquerors. From Chávez-Orozco 1947: plate 7. Photo by Don Cole.*

21.9. *An older Sierran man wearing the white cotton shirt and pants first introduced by the conquering Spaniards in the sixteenth century and now unmistakably Indian. Photo by Cristina Taccone.*

Chiapas, Oaxaca, Yucatán, and, as we have seen in this chapter, the Sierra Norte de Puebla. For decades the Mexican government tried to integrate such communities into the national culture, to make them "less Indian" and "more Mexican," mainly through educational policy in public schools. But with the focus of the world on Mexico as a result of the 1968 Olympics and the realization that Mexican Indian culture was a national treasure profoundly appreciated by visitors from all other countries, the policy of forced acculturation began to change. Substantial portions of the world-class Anthropology Museum (cf. Ramírez Vázquez 1968) were devoted to Mexican Indian culture and dress. The institution is a focal point of Mexican national pride, and every person who visits it cannot

529

Patricia R. Anawalt

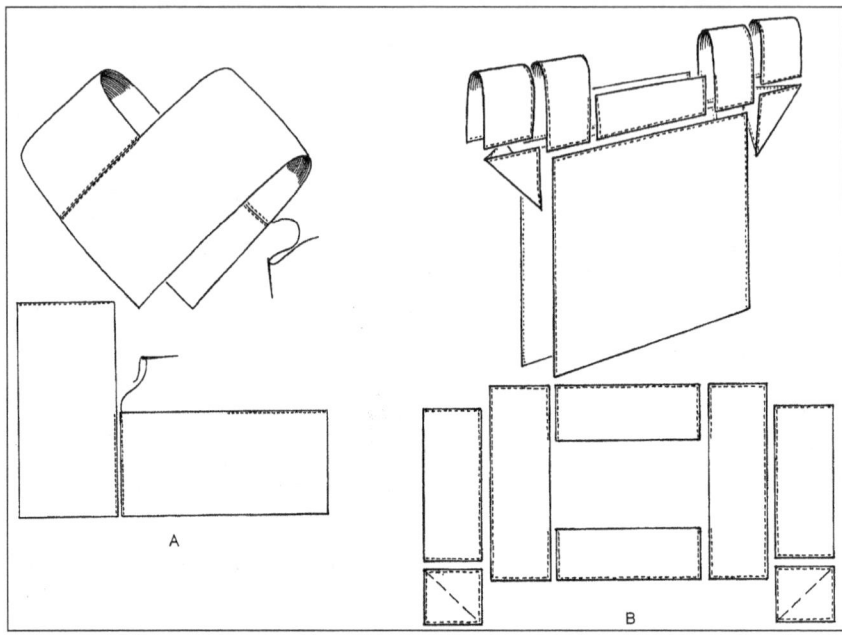

21.10. *Diagrammatic comparison of the (A) Prehispanic quechquemitl with the (B) European-introduced chemise. Drawings by Rusty van Rossmann, after Lechuga 1982.*

help but appreciate, at least vicariously, how wonderful the Mexican indigenous clothing tradition remains.

Moving south, Highland Guatemala remains justifiably famous as a stronghold of traditional Indian dress, and the benefits for national tourism have led the Guatemalan government for at least the past forty years to encourage local Indian communities to retain their lothing. Since 1969 the Festival Folklórico Nacional has been held annually the final week of July at Cobán, Alta Verapaz. Its high point is the Maya beauty contest, where contestants must be Maya speakers and wear their own village dress (Schackt 2005). National pride expressed in native Maya dress is also showcased on the international stage by the "Miss Guatemala" entries, albeit typically ladinas who dress up as Indians in various competitions. In 1975 the Guatemalan entry in the Miss Universe Pageant, Emy Elivia Abascal, took the Best National Costume prize for appearing in a spectacular long Ixil huipil from Nebaj; the same year Guatemala's entry in the Miss World Pageant, Diana Anker Chacón, was a no-show in London but posed for publicity stills in what looks very much like the same Nebaj Ixil huipil. There are two textile museums in Guatemala City, and the Guatemalan twenty-five-centavo piece depicts a Tzutujil woman resplendent in her traje, complete with textile headdress.

Manning Nash (1958) studied a traditional Quiché Maya community that, for over three-quarters of a century, supplied the workers for the largest textile factory in Central America. Cantel is just a dozen kilometers from Guatemala's second-largest city, Quetzaltenango, and one would assume that involvement with mechanization and the national, even the world economy would quickly erode traditional Indian values and lead to rapid acculturation. But what is not generally appreciated outside of Guatemala is that Quetzaltenango is essentially an Indian town, still known to one and all by its old name Xela (short for Xelajú) rather than by the name the Mexican Indian auxiliaries of the Spanish conquistadors gave it.

To the north of Xela lies Momostenango, the principal wool-producing center for Guatemala if not for all of Central America. Momostenango is another Indian town where wool, a Spanish-introduced material, is used to make traditional Indian clothing and blankets featuring Indian designs but using Spanish-introduced treadle looms. To the south lies the mainly ladino town of Salcajá, a center of tie-dyed weaving on Spanish-introduced foot looms by both Indians and non-Indians. The *cortes jaspiados*, or tie-dyed skirts, made there form the lower half of the majority of the traditional costume worn by Indian females throughout the Guatemalan Highlands. This high-quality fabric is a favorite of many Highland Maya groups and has had the effect of perpetuating traditional Indian dress throughout the Highlands by making it easily obtainable and affordable. This fabric is sold in every Indian market throughout the country to both Indians and tourists, right next to the huipils made on backstrap looms. So what do the Machine Age Maya factory workers of Cantel, too busy now to make their own clothing on backstrap looms, buy with their wages? Cotton cloth tie-dyed in traditional Indian style and wool blankets with traditional Indian designs. Modern technology, at least in Highland Guatemala, has not submerged the old, traditional Indian clothing styles but instead has led to their perpetuation and even expansion.

Moving back north, Indian dress has also come to be appreciated far beyond its contexts of origin, largely through its popularization by artists—be they avant-garde, popular, or even of the comic strip variety—on both sides of the US-Mexican border. Frida Kahlo (1907–1954), beginning in the late 1930s and increasingly so through the 1940s and into the early 1950s, portrayed herself in Mexican Indian costumes and frequently attended art events dressed in full Tehuana regalia. She recognized what was obvious to most Mesoamericanists by entitling one of her best-known works *Self-Portrait as a Tehuana* (1943). Overlooking Kahlo's many personal peculiarities and narcissisms, one is nevertheless struck by how much she popularized her selections from the traditional Mexican Indian clothing repertoire and made them familiar to art sophisticates all over the world.

Miguel Covarrubias (1904–1957) was a self-taught ethnographer and art historian and perhaps the most talented Mexican writer/artist of all time

Patricia R. Anawalt

21.11. *Mexican Indian clothing was made familiar to North Americans through the* Gordo *comic strip beginning in 1941. Gordo López plows his bean field (left) while his best friend, the Poet (center), cuts cane; both are wearing white cotton trajes (1947). (Right): Tehuana Mama, Gordo's eventual wife, cooks over a wood fire in traditional Tehuantepec garb (1960s). Courtesy, Ramona Arriola McNamara and the Bancroft Library, University of California, Berkeley.*

(Williams 1994). One of his most interesting publications was a *Vogue Magazine* article (Covarrubias 1942) that called attention to the modern "high fashion" aspect of Mexican Indian dress. The article had been inspired by a 1936 trip to Tehuantepec and by his wife's lifelong friend Frida Kahlo's propensity for wearing Tehuana trajes. Rosa Covarrubias had been born Rosemonde Cowan in Los Angeles, California, to a Scots father and a Mexican mother; she took dance classes at UC Berkeley and then moved to New York. After meeting and marrying Miguel Covarrubias, she began her own process of "mexicanization" but always maintained close contacts with the US art scene and North American artists. Five years after the publication of his *Vogue* article, Covarrubias (1947) put the Isthmus of Tehuantepec "on the map," so to speak, with his bestseller *Mexico South*. The book was illustrated with his own color renderings of Indian clothing, accompanied by Donald Cordry's black-and-white photos of local Indian dress and weaving.

Across the border, the brilliant and talented Gus Arriola (1917–2008) became the first and most famous Mexican American cartoonist and popular artist in California. Born in Arizona, he grew up in Los Angeles and attended Manual Arts High School two decades after Rosemonde Cowan/Rosa Covarrubias had gone there. Through his comic strip *Gordo* (1941–1985), Arriola brought Mexican Indian culture to a broad, non-anthropological North American audience that might otherwise have never been aware of it. At the peak of its popularity, *Gordo* appeared in more than 270 US newspapers and introduced millions of gringos to now-familiar Mexican Indian cultural elements, including traditional dress (Arriola 1950). Over time, Arriola's work grew from simple clichés to a quasi-ethnographic visual tour of Mexico, in black and white on weekdays but in technicolor on weekends. For his part, Gordo began his two-dimensional life in the 1940s as an Oaxacan Indian milpero, but by the late 1950s he had morphed into a tour guide. Gordo was immensely proud of Indian Mexico, and he and his friends wore the white cotton Indian traje (figure 21.11) while the female lead, Tehuana Mama, wore a full-blown Tehuana costume (Harvey and Arriola 2000). By the late 1960s *Gordo* was no longer recognized as simply a comic strip but was considered fine art with an ethnographic bent. UC Berkeley's Bancroft Library now holds the collected works of Gus Arriola.

If, as lamented earlier in this chapter, fewer and fewer older weavers and embroiderers are now making traditional Indian clothing, this unfortunate situation is at least partially offset by the much greater appreciation for the Mesoamerican Indian clothing tradition that continues to permeate throughout non-Indian culture in the Americas. The old ideas and traditions live on in new forms, changed perhaps, but still identifiable as distinctly Indian and distinctly Mesoamerican. They now belong to all of us, and all the world now treasures them.

REFERENCES CITED

Anawalt, Patricia R
- 1976a   The Xicolli: An Analysis of a Ritual Garment. *Actas del 41 Congreso Internacional de Americanistas* 2: 223–235. México, DF.
- 1976b   The Xicolli: "Godly Jackets" of the Aztecs. *Archaeology* 29 (4): 258–265.
- 1981   *Indian Clothing before Cortés*. Civilization of the American Indian Series 156. University of Oklahoma Press, Norman.
- 1984   Prehispanic Survivals in Guatemalan Dress. *El Palacio* 90: 13–19.
- 1996   Aztec Knotted and Netted Capes: Colonial Interpretations vs. Indigenous Primary Data. *Ancient Mesoamerica* 7: 187–206.
- 2003   Out of the Past: Ancient Clothing in Contemporary Indian Villages. *ARARA*, University of Essex, England. http://www.essex.ac.uk/arthistory/arara/99-04.archive/issue_six/paper4.html. Accessed April 19, 2012.
- 2007   *The Worldwide History of Dress: The Origin of Fashion from the Paleolithic to the Present*. Thames and Hudson, London.

Anawalt, Patricia R., and Frances Berdan
- 1994   Textiles as History: Clothing Clues to 500 Years of Mexican Acculturation. *Research and Exploration: A Scholarly Journal of the National Geographic Society* 10: 342–353.

Anawalt, Patricia R., and Virginia Davis
- 2001   Perished But Not beyond Recall: Aztec Textile Reconstruction via Word, Image, and Replica. In *Fleeting Identities: Perishable Material Culture in Archaeological Research*, ed. P. B. Drooker, pp. 187–209. Center for Archaeological Investigations, Southern Illinois University, Carbondale.

Patricia R. Anawalt

Arriola, Gus
    1950   *Gordo*. Doubleday, Garden City, NY.

Asturias de Barrios, Linda
    1985   *Comalapa: Native Dress and Its Significance*. Ixchel Museum of Indian Dress, Guatemala.

Blom, Franz, and Oliver La Farge
    1926   *Tribes and Temples*. Middle American Research Series 1. Tulane University, New Orleans, LA.

Borah, Woodrow, and Sherburne F. Cook
    1963   *The Aboriginal Population of Central Mexico on the Eve of the Spanish Conquest*. Ibero-Americana 45, Berkeley, CA.

Chávez-Orozco, Luis, ed.
    1947   *Códice Osuna*. Instituto Indigenista Interamericano, México, DF.

Codex Borbonicus
    1974   *Codex Borbonicus: Bibliothèque de l'Assemblè Nationale-Paris (Y 120) Vollstandige Faksimile-Ausgabe des Codex im Original-format*. Commentary by Karl Anton Nowotny and Jacqueline de Durand-Forest. Akademische Druck- u. Verlagsanstalt, Graz, Austria.

Codex Magliabechiano
    1970   *Codex Magliabechiana, CLXIII.3 (B.R. 232): Biblioteca Nazionale Centrale di Firenze*. In *Codices selecti photo-typices impressi*, vol. 23, facsimile ed. Commentary by Ferdinand Anders. Akademische Druck- u.Verlagsanstalt, Graz, Austria.

Coggins, Clemency Chase, and Orrin C. Shane III
    1984   *Cenote of Sacrifice: Maya Treasures from the Sacred Well at Chichén Itzá*. University of Texas Press, Austin.

Cook, Sherburne F., and Woodrow Borah
    1960   *The Indian Population of Central Mexico*. Ibero-Americana 44, Berkeley, CA.

Cordry, Donald
    1942   *Zoque Notes*. Pasadena Museum, Pasadena, CA.

Cordry, Donald, and Dorothy Cordry
    1968   *Mexican Indian Costumes*. University of Texas Press, Austin.

Corson, Christopher
    1973   Iconographic Survey of Some Principal Figurine Subjects from the Mortuary Complex of Jaina, Campeche, Mexico. *Contributions of the University of California Archaeological Research Facility* 18: 51–75. Berkeley, CA.
    1976   *Anthropomorphic Maya Figurines from Jaina Island, Campeche*. Ballena Press Studies in Mesoamerican Art, Archaeology, and Ethnohistory 1. Socorro, NM.
    1977   Stylistic Evolution of Jaina Figurines. In *Pre-Columbian Art History*, ed. Alana Cordy-Collins and Jean Stern, pp. 63–69. Peek Publications, Palo Alto, CA.

Covarrubias, Miguel
    1942   Women of Fashion of Tehuantepec, Mexico. *Vogue Magazine* 99 (2): 52–53, 86–87. New York.
    1947   *Mexico South: The Isthmus of Tehuantepec.* Alfred A. Knopf, New York.

Foster, George
    1940   *Notes on the Popoluca of Vera Cruz.* Instituto Panamericano de Geografía e Historia, México, DF.
    1960   *Culture and Conquest: America's Spanish Heritage.* Viking Fund Publications in Anthropology 27. Wenner-Gren Foundation for Anthropological Research, New York.

Harvey, Robert C., and Gus Arriola
    2000   *Accidental Ambassador Gordo: The Comic Strip Art of Gus Arriola.* University Press of Mississippi, Jackson.

Hendon, Julia A.
    2006   Textile Production as Craft in Mesoamerica: Time, Labor and Knowledge. *Journal of Social Archaeology* 6 (3): 354–378.

Johnson, Irmgard Weitlaner
    1953   El quechquemitl y el huipil. *Revista Mexicana de Estudios Antropológicos* 13: 241–257. México, DF.
    1954   Chiptic Cave Textiles from Chiapas, Mexico. *Journal de la Société des Américanistes,* n.s. 43: 137–147. Musee de l'Homme, Paris.

Kroeber, Alfred Louis
    1944   *Peruvian Archaeology in 1942.* Publications in Anthropology 4. Viking Fund, New York.

La Farge, Oliver
    1940   Maya Ethnology: The Sequence of Cultures. In *The Maya and Their Neighbors: Essays on Middle American Anthropology and Archaeology,* ed. Clarence L. Hay, Ralph L. Linton, Samuel K. Lothrop, Harry L. Shapiro, and George C. Vaillant, pp. 281–291. Appleton-Century, New York.

Lechuga, Ruth D.
    1982   *El traje indigena de Mexico.* Panorama Editorial, México, DF.

Lumholtz, Carl
    1904   Decorative Art of the Huichol Indians. *Memoirs of the American Museum of Natural History, Anthropology* 2 (3): 279–327. New York.

Mahler, Joy
    1965   Garments and Textiles of the Maya Lowlands. In *The Archaeology of Southern Mesoamerica,* ed. Gordon R. Willey, pp. 581–593. Handbook of Middle American Indians, vol. 3, Robert Wauchope, gen. ed. University of Texas Press, Austin.

Matos Moctezuma, Eduardo, and Felipe Solis Olguin
    2002   *Aztecs.* Royal Academy of Arts, London.

Nash, Manning
    1958   *Machine Age Maya: The Industrialization of a Guatemalan Community*. Memoir 87. American Anthropological Association, Washington, DC.

Nicholson, H. B.
    1960   The Mixteca-Puebla Concept in Mesoamerican Archaeology: A Re-Examination. In *Men and Cultures: Selected Papers from the Fifth International Congress of Anthropological and Ethnological Sciences*, ed. Anthony F. Wallace, pp. 612–617. University of Pennsylvania Press, Philadelphia.
    1961   The Use of the Term "Mixtec" in Mesoamerican Archaeology. *American Antiquity* 26 (3): 431–433.
    1971   Major Sculpture in Pre-Hispanic Central Mexico. In *Archaeology of Northern Mesoamerica*, Part 2, ed. Gordon F. Ekholm and Ignacio Bernal, pp. 92–134. Handbook of Middle American Indians, vol. 10, Robert Wauchope, gen. ed. University of Texas Press, Austin.
    1977a   Addenda: An Aztec Stone Image of a Fertility Goddess. In *Pre-Columbian Art History*, ed. Alana Cordy-Collins and Jean Stern, pp. 163–165. Peek Publications, Palo Alto, CA.
    1977b   An Aztec Stone Image of a Fertility Goddess. In *Pre-Columbian Art History*, ed. Alana Cordy-Collins and Jean Stern, pp. 145–162. Peek Publications, Palo Alto, CA.
    1982   The Mixteca-Puebla Concept Revisited. In *Art and Iconography of Late Post-Classic Central Mexico*, ed. Elizabeth H. Boone, pp. 227–254. Dumbarton Oaks, Washington, DC.

Nuttall, Zelia
    1888   *Standard or Head-Dress? An Historical Essay on a Relic of Ancient Mexico*. Papers of the Peabody Museum of Archaeology and Ethnology 1 (10). Harvard University, Cambridge, MA.
    1909   A Curious Survival in Mexico of the Use of the Purpura Shell-Fish for Dyeing. In *Anthropological Essays Presented to Frederick Ward Putnam, in Honor of His Seventieth Birthday, April 16, 1909*, ed. Franz Boas and Frederick W. Hodge, pp. 368–384. G. E. Stechert, New York.

O'Neale, Lila M.
    1945   *Textiles of Highland Guatemala*. Publication 567. Carnegie Institution of Washington, Washington, DC.

Osborne, Lilly de Jongh
    1935   *Guatemala Textiles*. Middle American Research Series Publication 6. Tulane University, New Orleans, LA.

Pettersen, Carmen L.
    1976   *The Maya of Guatemala: Their Life and Dress*. Museo Ixchel, University of Washington Press, Seattle.

Ramírez Vázquez, Pedro, ed.
    1968   *Mexico: The National Museum of Anthropology, Art, Architecture, Archaeology, Anthropology*. Harry N. Abrams, New York.

Sahagún, Fray Bernardino de
    1954   *Florentine Codex*, Book 8: *Kings and Lords*. Translated by Charles E. Dibble and Arthur J.O. Anderson. School of American Research and University of Utah Press, Santa Fe, NM.
    1961   *Florentine Codex*, Book 10: *The People*. Translated by Charles E. Dibble and Arthur J.O. Anderson. School of American Research and University of Utah Press, Santa Fe, NM.

Sayer, Chloe
    1985   *Costumes of Mexico*. University of Texas Press, Austin.

Schackt, Jon
    2005   Mayahood through Beauty: Indian Beauty Pageants in Guatemala. *Bulletin of Latin American Research* 24 (3): 269–287.

Smith, Robert E.
    1955   *Ceramic Sequence at Uaxactún, Guatemala*, 2 vols. Middle American Research Institute Publication 20. Tulane University, New Orleans, LA.

Sodi, Demetrio
    1968   Ethnography of the Sierra de Puebla. In *Mexico: The National Museum of Anthropology, Art, Architecture, Archaeology, Anthropology*, ed. Pedro Ramírez Vázquez, pp. 207–214. Harry N. Abrams, New York.

Starr, Frederick
    1901   Notes upon the Ethnography of Southern Mexico. *Proceedings of the Davenport Academy of Sciences* 8: 102–108.

Williams, Adriana
    1994   *Covarrubias*. University of Texas Press, Austin.

CONTRIBUTORS

PATRICIA R. ANAWALT, Center for the Study of Regional Dress, Fowler Museum, University of California, Los Angeles

ANTHONY F. AVENI, Department of Physics and Astronomy, Department of Sociology and Anthropology, Colgate University, Hamilton, New York

CARLOS A. BATRES, Department of Anthropology, Southern Illinois University, Carbondale and the Departamento de Antropología, Universidad de San Carlos de Guatemala

EMILIE CARREÓN BLAINE, Instituto de Investigaciones Estéticas y Facultad de Filosofía y Letras de la Universidad Nacional Autónoma de México

FREDERICK J. BOVE, Institute for Social, Behavioral and Economic Research (ISBER), University of California, Santa Barbara

MATTHEW A. BOXT, Department of Anthropology, California State University, Northridge

JAMES E. BRADY, Department of Anthropology, California State University, Los Angeles

ROBERT M. CARMACK, Department of Anthropology and the Institute for Mesoamerican Studies, State University of New York, Albany

BRIAN DERVIN DILLON, Independent Researcher, Sepulveda, California

MARIE-FRANCE FAUVET-BERTHELOT, Musée de l'Homme, Paris, France

Contributors

LAWRENCE H. FELDMAN, Independent Researcher, Owings Mills, Maryland

JOSÉ VICENTE GENOVEZ, Departamento de Historia, Área de Antropología, Universidad de San Carlos de Guatemala

PABLO ESCALANTE GONZALBO, Instituto de Investigaciones Estéticas y Facultad de Filosofía y Letras de la Universidad Nacional Autónoma de México

CARLOS JAVIER GONZÁLEZ GONZÁLEZ, Museo del Templo Mayor, Instituto Nacional de Antropología e Historia, México, DF

REBECCA B. GONZÁLEZ LAUCK, Instituto Nacional de Antropología e Historia, Tabasco, México

DAVID C. GROVE, Department of Anthropology, University of Illinois, Urbana-Champaign, and Department of Anthropology, University of Florida, Gainesville

RUTH GUBLER, Independent Researcher, Mérida, Yucatán, México

SUSANA GUIMARÂES, Musée Edgar Clerc, Guadeloupe

RICHARD D. HANSEN, Department of Anthropology, Idaho State University, Pocatello, and the Foundation for Anthropological Research & Environmental Studies (FARES)

ALFREDO LÓPEZ AUSTIN, Instituto de Investigaciones Antropológicas, Universidad Nacional Autónoma de México

LEONARDO LÓPEZ LUJÁN, Museo Templo Mayor, Instituto Nacional de Antropología e Historia, México, DF

ALEJANDRO MARTÍNEZ MURIEL (1946–2009), Coordinación de Arqueología, Instituto Nacional de Antropología e Historia, México, DF

GEOFFREY G. McCAFFERTY, Department of Archaeology, University of Calgary, Calgary, Alberta, Canada

SANDRA L. ORELLANA, Department of Anthropology, California State University, Dominguez Hills

ELOISE QUIÑONES KEBER, Department of Fine and Performing Arts, Baruch College, City University of New York

L. MARK RAAB, Department of Geosciences, University of Missouri, Kansas City

EDWARD B. SISSON, Department of Sociology and Anthropology, University of Mississippi, University

KEVIN TERRACIANO, Department of History, University of California, Los Angeles

INDEX

Page numbers in italics indicate illustrations

Abaj Takalik. *See* Takalik Abaj
Acatlán, 312
Acatzingo Viejo, artificial caves at, 282–83, *284*
Accession, Maya royal, 183, 185, 191–92, 201(n7), 204(n24)
Acculturation, 6, 123, 519, 521; and textile production, 526–28
Achiutla, 395
AGCA. *See* Archivo General de Central America
Aglio, Agostino, 474
Agriculture, 37, 62, 347, 516(n34); Colonial period ritual, 493–96; in Guatemala Piedmont, 96–97; in Mirador Basin, 145, 151, 155; rain ceremonies and, 496–97; Yucatec Maya rituals, 489–91, 496–514; Yucatec Maya supernaturals, 491–93
Agüera, Francisco, illustration of Tizoc Stone, 448
Ahuítzotl, 336
Aj K'ahk O-Chahk ("Fiery One of O-Chahk"), 186, 187
Aj Wäktun (Wäxtun) Yaxun B'ahläm ("Six-Stone Bird Jaguar"), 173, 178, 181, 185

Alamán, Lucas, 451, 466
Alcina Franch, José, 462
Alcoholism, 432, 433
Alfaro de Santa Cruz, Melchor, 76, 78
Alliances, 312; Mixteca-Puebla, 390–91
Alor González family, 57
Altars, 152; at Takalik Abaj, 96, 104, 106, 107
Altar-thrones, tabletop, 38, 49
Alta Verapaz, 277, 279, 530
Altepetl, 274, 398, 405
Aluxes, 492
Alvarado, Francisco de, *Vocabulario en lengua mixteca,* 396
Alvarado, Jorge de la Cruz, 404
Alvarado, Pedro de, in Pipil region, 232–33, 248
Alvarado Tezozómoc, Fernando (Hernando), 272, 341, 445; on Motecuhzoma II as Xipe Tótec, 346–47
Amapa, 303
Amate Phase, at Chalcatzingo, 35, 43–44, 46–48
Amoltepec (Yucunama), *397*, 402
Anahuac Basin, 338
Anahuac Xicalango, Province of, 63. *See also* Tabasco

541

Index

Anales de Cuauhtitlan: on Quetzalcoatl myth, 327–28; on tlacaxipehualiztli, 339–40
Anciennes villes du Nouveau Monde, Les (Charnay), 456
Anderson, Arthur, 22
Angostura Hydroelectric Dam Project, 213–14
Aniñes, 411(n3); Doña Catalina de Peralta's, 402–4; as social entities, 407–9; in Teozacualco, 401–2, 405
Anker Chacón, Diana, 530
Annals of the Kaqchikels, 356, 358–59; land claims, 371–72
"Anthropological Theory and Archaeological Fact" (Strong), 3
Antiguo Cuscatlan, 256
Antiquités mexicaines, 462
Antiquities collections, 461; *Real Expedición Anticuaria,* 463–78, 480–82
Antiquities of Mexico, 462, 474
Apodaca, Juan Ruíz de, 465
Aquiahuac Phase, 300
Architecture, ethnic identity and, 252–53
Archivo General de Central America (AGCA), 234, 235–36
Archivo General de la Nación (AGN), 402
Archivo General de los Indias, Contaduria, 420–21
Archbishops Stone, 442, *443,* 444
Arriola, Gus, *Gordo* comic strip, 532–33
Art, 3, 159; Mesoamerican, 19–20; Mixteca-Puebla tradition, 297–99; Nicholson on, 24–25
Arte en lengua mixteca (los Reyes), 399
Art of Aztec Mexico: Treasures of Tenochtitlan (exhibit), 25
Art styles: Early Maya, 107, 113–14, 119(table); Olmec, 34–35, 94, *95,* 102, 104, *106,* 107; Guatemala Pacific Piedmont, 111–15; Mixteca-Puebla, 59, 72, 293, 294–304, 309–10, 363, 389–91, 425; at Takalik Abaj monuments, 109–11
Asphaltum. *See* Chapapote
Astronomy: and Mexica calendar, 328–29, 334; and Quetzalcoatl myth, 327–28; rulership and, 156, 157, 178
Asunción Mita, 254
Atitlán, Lake, 362
Austria, Felipe de, 402
Authority: cacicazgo, 400–401; Maya, 149, 159; petates as symbols of, 396, 402–3. *See also* Rulership
Avilés, María B., 44

Axayácatl, 336
Axis mundi, 141, 323
Ayusi, 398
Aztec Empire, 64, 81, 312
Aztecs, xi, 8, 14, 20, 63, 77, 223; deities, 22, 322; religion, 23–24. *See also* Mexica; Nahua; Nathuatl
Aztecs of Mexico (Valliant), 14

Backstrap weaving, *527*
Badianus Manuscript, 81
B'ahläm Dynasty: founder of, 188–90; maintaining, 199–200; refounding ritual and iconography of, 177–98; at Yaxchilán, 173, 175, 176
Bajareque, 75–76
Bajos, in Mirador Basin, 142, 151
Ballcourts, 147, 245; distribution of, 211, 214; at Santa Rosa, 213, *215,* 215–23; skulls associated with, 223–24
Ballgame, 4, 224–25(n3); and human sacrifice, 211–12
Baradère, Jean-Henri, 462
Barlow, Robert, 14, 20
Barranca Phase, 35, 43
Bat Palace (Dos Pilas), cave under, 274–75
Beaufoy, Mark, 452
Belize, 302; chha chac ceremony in, 489–90; 497–98; Maya social organization in, 108, 139
Bernal, Ignacio, 20, 108
Bilbao, 101, 106, 108, 110, 114, 123, 125(n4)
Blackman Eddy, 139
Blom, Frans, 61, 64
Bloodletting, 181, 182–83, 186, 203–4(n22), 205(n36)
Blouses (chemise), Colonial-style, 527–28, *528,* 530
Bolón, la, 78–79
Bonampak, 173
Book of Chilam Balam of Chumayel, 510–11
Books of Chilam Balam, 495
Botanical remains, 73, 126(n5)
Bowditch, Charles P., 22
Brainerd, George, 17
Brujos, 125(n1). *See also* Chimánes; Shamans
Bullock, William, and Tizoc Stone, 449, 451, *453, 454*
Burford, John and Robert, 449
Burials, 106; at Coxcatlán Viejo, *314, 315;* royal Maya, 158–59, 160
Butterflies, 425, 434

Cabildos, 407–8, 409, 411(n13)
Cabrera, Estrada, 363
Cacao production, 96–97
Cacaxtla site, 300, 301
Caches, 315; ballcourt, 223–24; at Carolina site, 240–41
Cacicazgos, 312, 400–401, 406
Caciques, 372, 405
Cahyup, 239
Cakchiquel Maya. *See* Kakchiquel Maya
Calakmul, 160, 185, 200(n4)
Calderón de la Barca, Madame, 453
Calendar Round, 178
Calendars, 368; K'iche, 362–63, 364; on Tizoc Stone, 448, 449; and Xipe Tótec, 340–41
Calendrics: astronomy and, 328–29; K'iche, 363–65, 378(n30)
California Academy of Sciences, 19
California-Pacific International Exposition, 13–14
Calpolli, 391, 398, 405
Calpulcos, flayed skin in, 343, 344–45
Camacho, Sebastián, 468
Campeche, 143–44
Candelaria River system, 141
Cannibalism, 344
Cantel, 531
Cantera Phase, 35, 36, 37–43, 44, 49
CAP. *See* Chalcatzingo Archaeological Project
Captives: sacrifice of, 334, 342, 343–44, 345–46; women, 222–23
Caracol, caves at, 276–77
Cardinal directions, 516(n27); and colors, 156, 510–11
Carletti, Francesco, on Tizoc Stone, 445–46
Carnegie Institution, 14
Carolina-Gomera Complex: and Pipil Research Project, 236–39; survey and testing of, 239–49
Carolina site, 239; caches, 240–41; ceramics, 250, 251, 252
Carvings, Olmec-style, 34–35, 36–37. *See also* Monuments; Sculptures; Stelae
Casa Blanca, 123
Cascajal, 72
Caso, Alfonso, 14, 20, 336
Castañeda, José Luciano, 462, 463, 472; auction of Dupaix collection, 467, 469, 479(n9); and *Real Expedición Anticuaria*, 464–65
Castillo, Cristóbal del, Tizoc Stone, 446–47
Castillo, Juan, 462
Castro, Casimiro, illustration of Tizoc Stone, 452, *455*

Catholicism, and Maya agricultural ritual, 490, 497, 512–13
Caulote, 236, 241, *242*
Causeways: in Mirador Basin, *150*, 150–51, 154–55, 160; as umbilical cords, 155–56
Cave archaeology, 269, 276–77
Cave-architectural relationships, 279, 284; Maya, 269–71, *273*, 273–76, *280*, *281*, 281–83; at Teotihuacan, 271–72
Caves, 36; artificial, *280*, *281*, 281–83; at Dos Pilas, *273*, 273–76; and Maya architecture, 5, 269–71; symbolic importance of, 271–72, 277–79
Celestial bodies, 156, 157
Celís, Domingo de, 397
Cempohuallan, 330
Center for Maya Research, 476
Centla (Tabasco), 61
Central America, 231; Mixteca-Puebla style ceramics in, 302–3
Ceramics, 76, 144, 160, 161, 217; Colonial Period Cholula, 427–30; Epiclassic polychrome, 294, 296, 297–98, 302, *316*, 316–19; feathered serpent imagery on, 425, *426*, 434; Isla Alor, 66, 68–72, *76*; Ixtacapa Phase, 239, 240, 241, *242*–43, 244, 246, 247, 248–49, 250–52, 254; La Venta, 59, 83(n3); Mixteca-Puebla Style, 296, 297–98, 300, 301, 302–3, 389, 425; Pipil, 257–58; with Xipe Tótec images, *336*, *337*, *338*
Ceremonial dramas, K'iche, 367–68, 378–79(nn34, 35, 36, 37)
Cerro Chalcatzingo, 34, 36–37
Cerro de las Mesas, 59, 110, 117, 123
Cerro del Encanto mound group, 59, 83(n3)
Cerro Portezuelo, 17, 19
Chacs, 408, 492, 516(n20); in *Dresden Codex*, 493–94
Chajoma Kaqchikel, 356
Chalcatzingo, 3, 33, 102, 104, 105, 107; Amate Phase platform at, 43–44; processional arrangement of monuments, 50–52; stelae at, 37–43, 44–49, *49*; stone monuments at, 34–37; Terrace 6, 49–50, *50*
Chalcatzingo Archaeological Project (CAP), 35, 41, 42–43
Chalchuapa, 123
Champollion, Jean-François, 461, 472, 474
Chan Bahlum II, 157
Chan Kom: Maya Village (Redfield and Villa Rojas), 497
Chants, Yucatec Maya agricultural, 493–94

Index

Chapopote: from Isla Alor, 75, 76; historical use of, 77–81
Chapatengo-Chejel region, 214
Chapultepec Hill rock art, 336
Charles IV, King, 462
Charnay, Désiré, *Les anciennes villes du Nouveau Monde,* 456
Chemises, Colonial-style 527–28, *528, 530*
Chha chac ceremonies, 489–90, 493, 496–98; elements of, 508–10
Chiapas, 111, 463, 526, 529; Angostura Hydroelectric Dam Project, 213–14
Chichén Itzá, 123, 204(n25), 205(n36), 269, 270, 222
Chichicastenango, jade calendars from, 363, 377(n25)
Chichimecs, 312, 322
Chicomóztoc, 283, *285,* 338
Chimalhuacán (Mexico), 19
Chimalpopoca, and Xipe Tótec, 338–39
Chimánes (Maya priests), 93, 124
Chinampas, Mirador Basin, 151, 155
Chinautla, 360
Chipilapa, 235, 236, 244
Chitak Tzak, 252, 253
Chocho, 312, 409
Chocho-Mixtec areas, 398
Chocolá, 105, 110, 123, 125(n4)
Cholollan, 410
Cholula, 296, 304(n4), 391, 399, 425; Colonial Period ceramics in, 427–30; drinking establishment in, 432–33, 435; Mixteca-Puebla tradition, 297, 300, 301, 303, 390; as pilgrimage center, 6, 63, 303; pyramid at, 272–73; R-106 archaeology in, 426–27, 430–32; Xipe Tótec cult in, 345, 347
Chontal Maya, 61; and la Bolón, 78–79
Christianity, in documents, 373–74
Chronology, 361; Mirador Basin, 144–45; Takalik Abaj, 98–99
Chuitinamit/Chiya, 120, 363
Chuj Ka'jaus (Quiché Maya priests/shamans), 124
Cihuatán, 233, 256
Cihuatéotl, 322
Cimatan/Cimatlan, 63, 64, 78
Cintla complexes, 72
Cities, 59, 272; Early Mesoamerican, 108–9; Olmec, 111–13
City-states, Maya, 109, 120–21
Ciudad Real de Chiapas, 463, 466
Cival, 139, 159

Civales, 145, 151
Civilization, 4, 5; birth of Mesoamerican, 108–9
Classic Maya, 114, 122, 126(n9), 200–201(n5)
Classic Period, 58, 81, 250, 257, 301, 426–27
Cline, Howard F., 21
Clothing: as acculturation symbol, 527–28, *529;* Guatemala traditional, 530–31; Indian-style, 531–33; in Sierra Norte de Puebla, 521, *522, 523,* 523–26
Coatzacoalcos, 61, 62, 63, 64
Cobán, 530
Cobo, Bernabé, 402
Codex Borbonicus, 341, 348(n7)
Codex Borgia Group, 23, 319, 323, 334, 348(n7), 389
Codex Fejérváry-Mayer, 38
Codex Laud, 156
Codex Mendoza, 81
Codex Nuttall, 221
Codex Pérez, 495
Codex Telleriano-Remensis, 321, 320
Codex Vaticanus A, 283, 321
Codex Vaticanus B, 323
Codex Vindobonensis Mexicanus, 156
Codices: Colonial Nahua, 295; purpose of K'iche, 369–71. *See also by name*
Coe, Michael D., 58
Cogolludo, Diego López, 493, 496
Coixtlahuaca Valley, 312, 398, 409
Collected Works in North- and South-American Linguistics and Archaeology (Seler), 21–22
Colojate Phase, 233
Colonial Period, 6, 59, 120, 295, 364; Cholula, 426, *427,* 430–32; clothing styles, 527–28, *528;* Mixtecas, 395–407, 410(n1); Pipil in, 235–36; resistance, 432–33; Spanish government, 407–8; Yucatec Maya agricultural ritual, 493–96
Colored clays and sands, in Olmec sites, 103–4
Colors, and cardinal directions, 510–11
Comales, 247, 431; ethnicity and, 251–52; Prado Black, 250–51, 258
Community houses, triadic, 157
Comparato, Frank E., 22
Congregaciones, 521; Mixteca, 399–400
Conquest of Mexico (Prescott), 14
Conquest period, 6; on Guatemala Pacific Slope, 120, 234–35; in Tabasco, 59–62
Contuta, Juan Bautista, 400
Copán, 125(n4), 183, 187, 190, 224(n1), 277
Copilco, Province of, 62, 63

544

Corporate groups, Mixteca, 407–9
Cortés, Hernán, 59, 61, 420, 433
Cosmic Monster. *See* War Serpent
Cosmic Roads, causeways as, 156
Cosmology, 160, 279; caves and, 282–83, 284–85; Maya, 151–52, 177–98; Tamoanchan, 322–23
Costa Rica–Miahuatlán, 236, 237
Costa Rica site, 251, 247–48, 303
Costumbre, Modern Maya, 93, 124–25(n1)
Cotzumalguapa (Cotzumalhuapa), 249, 251–52, 253, 256
Cotzumalguapa (Cotzumalhuapa) Style sculpture, 244
Cotzumalhuapa (Cotzumalguapa) civilization, 101
Cotzumalhuapa (Cotzumalguapa) Sculptural Style, 106, 111, 114–15
Covarrubias, Miguel, 531–32
Coxcateca, 312
Coxcatlán, history of, 310–12
Coxcatlán Viejo, 312; Group H Plaza, 313–16
Coyoacan, 406
Cozumel Island, 63, 270
Cranial deformation, 219–20, *220*
Creation, 180, 278, 340, 357; accession and, 183, 185; cave as symbol of, 278, 282–83; and religious obligation, 490–91; three stones of, 158, 176, 182
Cremations, at Coxcatlán Viejo, *314*, 315
Crónica mexicana (Alvarado Tezozómoc), 445
Cross Group (Palenque), 157, 182–83, 192, 197
Cuauhtémoc, 78
Cuauhtinchan, 392
Cuernavaca, 408
Cuilapan, 399
Culhuacan, 406
Cults, Xipe Tótec, 334–35, 336–47
Cuscatlan, 256
Cuyamel, 277
Cylinders, stone, 441. *See also* Tizoc Stone

Dahlin, Bruce, 142
Dallas Altar, 181
Dampier, William, 59, 78
Dance dramas, 368
Decapitation, 4, 107, 195, 225(n5); and ballcourts, 212, 217, 224–25(n3); of Santa Rosa ballcourt skull, 219, 221
Dedicatory architecture, at Yaxchilán, 175–77
Deities, 22, 279; ceramic depictions of, 316–23; flaying and, *333*, 334, 336; Maya, 151, 182, 186, 201(n8), 492–93; Mixteca, 394, 409. *See also by name*
Díaz, Porfirio, 456
Díaz del Castillo, Bernal, 59, 60–61, 62, 63
Dibble, Charles, 22
Disinuu (Tlaxiaco), 395
Divination, 375; in agricultural almanacs, 494–95; and 260-day calendar, 366–67
Documents: Christian influence in, 373–74; control of, 369–70, 379(n40); evaluation and critique of, 355–56; historical roles of, 374–75; Mixteca, 392–95. *See also* Codices
Dos Pilas, 185, 277; caves and architecture at, *273*, 273–76, 284
Dramas, ceremonial, 367–68
Dresden Almanac, 493–95
Dresden Codex, 328; agricultural almanac in, 493–95; agricultural ritual, 489, 495–96
Drinking establishment, Cholula, 6, 431–33, 435
Duendes, Chontal Maya, 78–79
Dumbarton Oaks Summer Research Seminar on Codices of the Borgia Group, 310
Dupaix, Guillermo, 462, 448; collections made by, 463–65, 467, 478(n4)
Duponceau, Peter S., 470
Dúran, Diego, 341, 433
Dynasties: B'ahläm, 173, 175, 177–88, 189–98; refounding rituals and imagery of, 176, 188–89
Dzahui, 394, 409, 410(n1)
Dzahuico, 404
Dzini, 397, 398

Early Colonial period, 6, 23, 410(n1); Pipil, 234–35
Early Formative Period, 44, 66
Early Maya Horizon style, 119(table); on Takalik Abaj monuments, 104, 107, 109–11, 113
Early Middle Preclassic Period, Mirador Basin, 145–46
Early Postclassic Period, 123; Pacific Coast Guatemala, 233, 257; Mixteca-Puebla tradition, 300, 301; Pipil migrations, 233, 256; Takalik Abaj, 101, 120; Xipe Tótec images, 336–38, *339*
E-Group architecture, 147, *149*
Ehécatl-Quetzalcóatl, 340
El Bajío, 79, 114
El Baúl, 101, 110, 123, 125(n4)
El Castillo, 101

545

Index

El Chayal obsidian source, 253
El Chiquero, Stela 1, 154, *155*
El Convento site, 249
El Duende Complex (Dos Pilas), 273–74, 279
Elhuyar, Fausto de, 466; as Dupaix's executor, 463–65
Elites, 253, 312, 392; Carolina-Gomera Complex, 239–41, 243–44, 247; Maya, 140–41, 150, 151, 152; Mixtec, 396, 400–401; Mixteca-Puebla tradition, 297, 301, 303–4; tribute to, 408–9
El Jute, 237, 246–47, 251, 252
El Manatí, 79
El Mirador, 142, 145, 155, *158*, 159; monuments, 152, 154, 157
El Pesquero, 147, 159
El Salvador, 114, 125(n4); Pipil migrations to, 233, 256
El Transito, *427, 428*
El Ujuxte, 106
El Vergel, 214
Embroidery, 526
Epiclassic Period, 233, 294
Epi-Olmec writing, 116, 117
Escuintla region (Guatemala), 4–5, 232–33, 235
Esperanza, 236, 243–44, 251, 252
Esquipulas, 281
Essays in Anthropology, 8
Ethnicity, 5, 231; determining Pipil, 236, 249–54
Ethnohistory, 6, 7, 234, 279; Nicholson on use of, 20–22; Tabasco, 59–64
Exchange networks: Mixteca-Puebla alliance and, 390–91; obsidian, 253–54
Exotics: at Carolina site, 240, 241; Maya imports of, 145–46
Expediciones acerca de los antiguos monumentos de la Nueva España: 1805–1808, 462

Feathered Serpent, 187, 432; depictions and iconography of, *425, 426, 427, 428,* 429–30, *430, 433, 434*
Festival Folklórico Nacional (Guatemala), 530
Festivals, tlacaxipehualiztli, 333–34, 337–38, 342–46, 347
52-year cycles, 365, 378(n30)
Finca Acapulco, 214
Finca San Jerónimo, 245
Finca Teguantepeque, 245
Fire, iconography of, 158, 177, 187
Fish, Barbara, xii
Flaying: symbolic purpose of, 334, 335–36; tlahuahuaniztli, 342–44

Florentine Codex, 21, 22, 396, 433, 526; chapopote depicted in, 77–78, 81; Tizoc Stone in, 445, *447*
Forbin, count of (Louis Nicolas Philippe Auguste), 471–72, 475
Formative Period, 81; at Chalcatzingo, 35, 36, 37; at Isla Alor, 69, 73, 80
Foundation rituals, caves and, 277–78, 284–84
Founder Houses: and Tlaloc-Venus war cult, 183–84, 189; at Yaxchilán, 176, 199, 204(n27)
France, *Real Expedición Anticuaria* collection in, 471–73, 475–78
Fuentes y Guzmán, Antonio, 356
Fuentes y Guzmán, Francisco, 360–61, 362, 377(n17)

Gann, Thomas, on chha chac ceremony, 489–90, 497–98
Gender, identification of, 44, 44–46
Gibson, Charles, 21
Glass, John B., 21
Gods of Mexico, The (Spence), 14
Gold, Tenochtitlan, 419, 420, 421–22
Gomera, 244–45, 250, 252
Gomera-Chipilapa, 236, 244
Gómez, José, 449
Gómez Dávila, Rodrigo, 442
González Carvajal, Ciriaco, 462
González Lauck, Rebecca B., fieldwork, 57–58, 66
Gordo (comic strip), *532,* 532–33
Graham, Ian, 142
Graham, John A., at Takalik Abaj, *94*
Granado Baeza, José, 489, 496–97
Greenstone, 421–22, 464
Grijalva, Juan de, 59–61
Grijalva River, settlements at, 212–13
Group H Plaza (Coxcatlán), public architecture in, 313–16
Grube, Nikolai, 143
Guacasualco. *See* Coatzacoalcos
Gualdi, Pedro, painting by, *450,* 452
Guatemala, 7, 96, 120, 377(n23); cave sites in, 281–82; Escuintla region of, 4–5; Mirador Basin in, 143–44; traditional Indian dress in, 530–31; writing systems, 118–19. *See also various regions; sites*
Guatemalan Highlands, 120, 367; cave sites in, 281–82; document control in, 369–70; religious obligation in, 490–91
Guaxaca. *See* Oaxaca
Guazacapa, 235

546

INDEX

Guerrero, 335
Guerrero, Francisco, 442
Guinda tradition, 428
Guixquíl (chayote), 97
Gulf Coast, 77, 78, 81, 302
Gulf Coast Olmec: at Isla Alor, 56, 64–82; at La Venta, 55–56, 58–59; surveys of, 57–58
Gumarcaaj. *See* Q'umarkaaj; Utatlán
Guzmán, Antonio, *101*
Guzmán, Eulalia, on Chalcatzingo, 34–35
Guzmán, Gabriel de, 406, 407
Guzmán, Juan Manuel de, 402
Guzmán, Lázara de, 404
Guzmán, María de, 395–96

Hamy, Ernest-Théodore, 477
Handbook of Middle American Indians, 20–21
Harvard University, Nicholson's doctoral work at, 16, *18*
Hatch, Marion, 104
Headdresses, 196, 197; Tlaloc-Venus cult, *179*, 181, 188, 189; Water Jaguar, *193*, *194*, 194–95
Hearthstones, triadic, 157–58
Heizer, Robert F., *94*, 125(n2), 126(n8)
Henderson, Keith, 14
Hetz luum, 506–7; offerings and ritual, 498–505, 506–8
Heyden, Doris, "An Interpretation of the Cave underneath the Pyramid of the Sun in Teotihuacan, Mexico," 270–72
Hicks, Frederick, 19
Hieroglyphic texts, 177, 202–3(n18). *See also* Codices; Stelae
Hieroglyphs, Isthmian Script, 116–18
Highland Maya, 6; religious obligation, 490–91
High Priest's Grave (Chichén Itzá), 269, *270*
Hill-Caves of Yucatan, The (Mercer), 270
Historia General de las cosas de Nueva España (Sahagún), 21
Historians, K'iche, 365–67
Historia Tolteca-Chichimeca, 311–12
Histories: functions of, 369–71; K'iche, 357–58, 359–61, 376(n10), 379(n39); land claims, 371–72; oral transmission of, 367–68; pictorial, 361–62; Posthispanic K'iche, 372–74, 375
Historiography: Annals of the Kaqchikel, 358–59; K'iche Maya, 360–61, 369–71; *Popol Wuj*, 357–58, 378(n30)
H-men, and agricultural ritual, 492, 499–505, 510, 512–13
Households, and Mixteca land tenure, 404–7

House of Ix K'ab' al-Xok (Structure 23, Yaxchilán), 200(n4), 201(nn6, 9); accession and refounding rite iconography in, 177–98
Houses, 37; bajareque and chapopote construction, 75–79; Isla Alor, 64–65, 68, 82(n2)
Huauhquechula, 466
Huehuetéotl-Xiuhtecuhtli (Fire God), 336, 346
Huexotzingo (Huejotzingo), 297, 300, 345, 347, 391, 392
Huitzilopochtli, 223, 410
Human remains: in ballcourts, 217–24; at Coxcatlán Viejo, *314*
Human skins, and Xipe Tótec cult, 343–46
Human skull effigy, *315*; description of, *316*, 316–19; iconography of, 319–21, 322–23
Humboldt, Alexander von, 449, 461; on *Real Expedición* collection, 470–71

Iconography, 3, 4, 5, 118, 159, 336; Chalcatzingo monuments, 38, 41–42; feathered serpent, 425, *426*, 427, *428*, 429–30; human skull polychrome effigy, 319–21, 323–24; Mixteca-Puebla, 297–300, 425; Nicholson on, 23–25; Olmec-style monuments, 36–37; on Yaxchilán Structure 23 lintels, 176, 177–98
Identity, 5, 7; clothing and, 524, 530
Ideology, 20; Nicholson on, 23–25, 160
Ignacio Allende, 78
Ihuitlán, 312
Indian communities, in Mexico, 528–30
Inheritance, Mixtec, 395–96, 404
Interdisciplinary research, 7–8
"International Style," 391
"Interpretation of the Cave underneath the Pyramid of the Sun in Teotihuacan, Mexico, An" (Heyden), 270–71
Invocations, in Maya agricultural ritual, 512–13
Iscuintepeque, 233, 248
Isla Alor, 3, 63, 82(nn1, 2); archaeology of, 64–69; bajareque and chapopote, 75–79; ceramics, 68–72; description of, 56–57; occupation sequence at, 79–80; Postclassic Period, 81–82; subsistence, 73–74
Isthmian Script, 116–18
Iturrigaray, José de, 462
Itzamnah B'ahläm ("Shield Jaguar"): accession of, 201(n7), 202(n17), 204(n24); construction projects of, 173, 175–77; depictions of, *179*, 180–81, 182, *185*, 186, 188–89, 190, 192–94, *194*, 195–96, 197, 198; dynasty of, 199, 200; inscriptions about, 178, 183

547

Index

Itzpapalotl, 322; iconography of, 319–21, 323–24
Iximché, 120, 252, 281, 363
Ix K'ab'al Xok (Lady Xoc; Lady? Shark), 4; depictions of, *179*, 180, 181–83, *184*, 190–91, *193*, 196–97, 204(n28); lineage of, 185–86; role of, 176, 192, 199–200, 204(n27); and Yaxchilán Structure 23, 175–77, 198
Ix Päkal Xok, 185, 186
Ixtacapa Phase ceramics, 239, 242, 244, 245, 247, 248–49, 250–52
Ixtepeque, 234; obsidian from, 253–54
Izapa, 41, 110, 114, 123
Izapan Sculptural Style, 100, 111, 114, 118

Jade, 146, 363, 377(n25)
Jaguar platform/throne, 197
Jaguars, 194–95, 297
Jaguar War God, 190, 197, 204–5(n32)
Janab' Päkal ("Flower/Shield"), 185–86, 197
Jilotepeque Viejo, 239
Jiménez Moreno, Wigoberto, 14, 20; on Mixteca-Puebla Concept, 294–95

Kahlo, Frida, 531
Kakchiquel cultures, 234
Kakchiquel (Kaqchikel) Maya, 120, 248, 249, 252, 253, 368; calendrical systems, 364, 365; documents by, 355, 356, 358–59, 371–72
Kaminaljuyú, 105, 106, 110, 113, 122, 125(n4), 126(n6)
Kan, Michael, 19
Kanil K'iche, 356
K'än Joy Chitam II, 191, 197
Kan kingdom, 160
Kaqchikel. *See* Kakchiquel Maya
K'awil, 182, 183, 186, 188, 203(n22)
Kekchi, 279
K'iche Maya, 120, 157, 234, 257, 282, 376–77(nn10, 16), 377(n24), 379–80(nn38, 39, 45), 531; calendrics, 362–65, 378(n30); ceremonial dramas, 367–68, 378–79(nn34–37); documents, 355, 356; historical scribes, 365–67; historiography, 355, 357–58, 359, 360–61, 369–71, 378(n31); lineages, 253, 380(n46); pictorial histories, 361–62; Posthispanic histories, 371–74; at Takalik Abaj, 94, 96, 101, 122
King, Edward (Lord Kingsborough), 462, 474
Kingdoms, 120; Maya, 139–40, 160
Kingship, Maya, 4, 139, 144–51, 152, 154–59
K'iq'ab, 359, 373

Klor de Alva, J. Jorge, 22
Knowledge, control of, 369–70
Kroeber, Alfred L., 8, 520

Labor, 150; household and corporate, 407–9
Lacandón Maya, triadic community houses, 157
Lady 11 Serpent, decapitation of, 221
Lady Xoc. *See* Ix K'ab'al Xok
La Farge, Oliver, 61, 64
Lafayette, Marquis de (Marie-Joseph Paul Yves Roch Gilbert du Motier), 461, 479(n11)
La Florida, 147
Laguna de los Cerros, 107
La Isla, 248–49; Stela 1, 152, *153*
Lakes, subterranean, 275–76, *276*
La Lagunita, cave at, 281, *282*
La Mojarra, 116–17, 118
Land, Lewis K., collection of, 19–20
Landa, Diego de, 77, 493, 496
Land, 236, 370, 411(n11); Mixteca, 404–7; rituals for, 498–99
Land claims, K'iche histories, 371–72
Landscapes, 5, 278; constructed, 102–4
Languages: cosmopolitanism of, 123–24; in Sierra Norte de Puebla, 521; in Tabasco, 63–64
La Rochefoucaul, viscount of (Louis-Françoise-Sosthène), 471–72, 475
Las Casas, Bartolomé de, 356; on K'iche history, 360, 361–62, 369; on K'iche scribes, 365–66
Las Marías (El Salvador), 233, 256
Las Playas, 245–46, *246*, 250–51, 253
Las Playas-Teguantepeque, 236, 237
Late Classic Period, 101, 160, 294, 300
Late Colonial Period, Tizoc Stone in, 448–49
Late Middle Preclassic Period, Maya kingships, 146–51, 159
Late Postclassic Period, 6, 66, 120, 239; Miahuatlán region, 247–48; Pacific Coast sites, 245, 249; Pipil migrations, 234, 255, 256; Xipe Tótec cult, 338–47. *See also* Ixtacapa Phase
Late Preclassic Period, 139; Maya kingships, 141, 154–59; Takalik Abaj, 99, 101, 102, 105, *110*, 113
La Toronja, Stela 1, 154
Latour Allard, 474, 479(nn9, 11); as antiquities collector, 466–67; collection of, 461–62, 468–75, 480–82
La Venta, 3–4, 36, 55–56, 61, 83(n3), 102, 103, 104, 105, 106, 107, 111, 123, 126(n6), 278;

548

chapopote and, 79, 80; as city, 108, 109; Classic and Postclassic occupation of, 58–59; and Isla Alor, 65, 81; Nahuatl-speakers at, 63–64; survey around, 57–58
León, Juan de, 363
León y Gama, Antonio de, 448
Lind, Michael, 296
Lineages, 156; K'iche, 234, 253, 361, 367, 370, 372–73, 380(n46); of K'iche scribes, 365–66; Maya royal, 185–86; Nahua, 391–92; triadic architectures and, 157–58
Lintels, in Yaxchilán Structure 23, 177–98
Lithic technology, 74; Mirador Basin, 144–45
Lizana, Bernardo de, 493, 496
Llano Largo, 282
Loma Linda Complex, 236, 241
Long-count calendars, Maya, 364–65
Longpérier, Adrien de, 475–76
López Mateos, Adolfo, 457
Los Angeles County Museum of Art, 19
Los Cimientos–Tulamajillo, 239
Louvre Museum, 476, 477–78, 479
Lumholtz, Carl, vessel purchased by, 425, *426*
Lyon, George, 452

Macuspana district, 78
Maize, 126(n5), 201(n6), 347
Mam Maya, 93, 356; at Takalik Abaj, 101–2, 120, 122
Manantial, 237, 257
Maps, 362, 377(n23); Mixteca, 401, 402
Marriages, 312; Mixteca, 395–96, 399
Masagua Reddish-Brown comales, 251–52, 258
Masks, Maya, 159, 201(n8)
Matheny, Ray, 142
Matos Moctezuma, Eduardo, xii
Maximillian, Emperor, 453
Maya, 4–5, 6, 7, 14, 63, 151, 200–201(n5); calendrics, 363–65; caves and architecture, 269–71, *273*, 273–76, *280*, *281*, 281–83, *283*; city-states, 120–21; dedicatory structures, 175–77; diversity of, 121–22; dynastic iconography, 177–98; elite status, 140–41; kingships, 145–47; and la Bolón, 78–79; in Mirador Basin, 143–51; modern religious practices, 93, 124–25(n1), 489–513; Protoclassic, 100–101; ritual architecture, *147*, 147, *148*, *149*, 149–50, *150*; state-level societies, 139–40; stone monuments, 151–54; and Takalik Abaj, 113–14, 122; triadic architecture, 157–58; writing systems, 116, 118–19

Maya and Their Neighbors, The, 8
Maya Mountains, cave survey in, 277
Mayer, Brantz, 452–53
Mazacuat, 93
Meighan, Clement W., 17, 19
Melnotte, Mr., 475
Memorials, Maya buildings as, 177
Mendoza, Diego de, 400–401, 402–3
Mercer, Henry, *The Hill-Caves of Yucatan,* 270
Meseta Central, 294, 301
Mexica, 410; alliances, 312, 391, 392; and astronomy, 328–29; creation myths, 340–41; festivals, 335–36; Xipe Tótec festivals, 333–34
Mexican Manuscript Painting of the Early Colonial Period (Robertson), 295
Mexican National Museum, 466, 478–79(n7); Tizoc Stone in, 440, 451–52, 453, *455*, *456*
Mexico, 5–6; Indian dress in, 531–32; cultural identity and, 528–29; cultural patrimony, 7, 466, 468
Mexico, Basin/Valley of, 392, 463; Xipe Totéc images, 336–38
Mexico, Central, influence of, 122–23
Mexico City, 14, 466; Colonial period, 432, *446*; temalácatl stones, 343, 344, 441, 442; Tizoc Stone in, 443–57
Miahuatlán, 235, 236, 247–48
Mictlan, 323
Mictlantecuhtli, iconography of, 320, 323
Mictlantecuhtli Complex, 323
Middle Classic Period, 233, 234, 241
Middle Formative Period, 37, 66
Middle Preclassic Period: Maya kingdoms, 139, 141, 152–53; Takalik Abaj, 99, 101, 102, 103
Middle Preclassic Sculptural Horizon Style, 111
Migrations, 120, 311; Pipil, 231, 233–34, 247–48, 254–57
Miles, Susanna, 94
Military, 333; and Xipe Tótec cult, 336, 342–46
Milky Way, 156, 322
Milpas, in Maya agricultural ritual, 492, 502, 513–14, 515(n10)
Minatitlán, 78
Mirador Basin, 4, 109, 139, 140, 159; archaeological investigation of, 142–44, 160–61; causeways, 154–56; chronology, 144–45; geography of, 141–42; Late Middle Preclassic, 146–51; shell importation into, 145–46; stone monuments in, 151–52
Mirador Basin Project, 143–44
Miraflores Style, 113
Missionaries, and historical documents, 373–74

Index

Mitla, 463
Mixcóatl, 322
Mixco Viejo, 120, 281
Mixe, 63
Mixteca, Mixtecs, 6, 63, 294, 295, 296, 312, 410; archival sources, 392–95; hereditary elites, 400–401; land tenure and households, 404–7; Mixteca-Puebla Concept, 297, 302, 389, 390; multilingualism, 398–99; royal residences, 401–4, 407–9, 411(n4); sociopolitical organization, 395–400
Mixteca Alta, 297, 301, 390, 405, 410; archival sources for, 393–94; place terms in, 396, 397
Mixteca Baja, 295, 297, 301, 390, 404; archival sources for, 393, 394; place terms in, 396, 397–98, 411(n2)
Mixteca-Puebla: Discoveries and Research in Mesoamerican Art and Archaeology (Nicholson and Quiñones Keber), 293, 296
Mixteca-Puebla Concept, 293, 304, 389; Cholula and, 390–91; origins of, 294–97
Mixteca-Puebla Style, 363, 389, 425; ceramics in, 59, 72
Mixteca-Puebla tradition, 6, 309–10; elites and, 303–4; iconography of, 297–300; origin and diffusion, 300–303
Moloacán, oil seeps in, 78
Momostenango, 356, 362, 367, 377(n20), 379(n40), 531
Monte Albán, 59, 463; Xipe Tótec images at, 336, 337, 338
Monumental architecture, in Mirador Basin, 146–47
Monument museums, at Takalik Abaj, 104–105, 106
Monuments, 157, 177; at Chalcatzingo, 36, 39–46, 50, 51; collection of, 465–66; early records of, 462–63; Olmec-style, 34–37, 95, 106; paired, 38, 41; and Maya social status, 140–41, 151–54; at Takalik Abaj, 94, 95, 96, 101, 104–5, 107
Montezuma. *See* Motecuzoma II
Morelos, 33, 463
Motecuzoma I (Motecuhzoma Ilhuicamina), 312, 338, 442
Motecuzoma (Motecuhzoma) II, 2, 336, 343, 346–47, 419, 420
Mother Goddess, 336
Motolinía, Toribio Benavente, 328–29
Mountains, 278; and caves, 273–74
Moyotlán, 339
Müller, Florencia, 296

Municipal councils, Mixteca elites, 407–8, 409
Murals, 294, 363, 377–78(n26); Mixteca-Puebla tradition and, 297, 298, 300, 302
Murphy, Tomás, 467, 468–70, 476
Murphy Inventory, 476
Museo Nacional de las Culturas, 14
Museum of American Antiquities, 477
Museum of Man (San Diego), 13
Museum of the Quai Branly, 461, 476–77, 479
Myths, 178, 155, 223, 272, 322, 357; caves of origin, 281–82; of la Bolón, 78–79; Olmec carved depictions of, 36–37; Quetzalcoatl, 327–28; Xipe Tótec and, 338, 339–41
Myths of Mexico and Peru (Spence), 14

NAA. *See* Neutron activation analysis
Nahua-Mixteca style, 391
Nahua, Nahuatl, 5, 6, 7, 236, 258, 274, 395, 396, 408, 409, 411(nn3, 4), 521; cultural organization, 391–92; household organization, 404–5; land tenure, 406, 411(n11); at La Venta, 63–64; migrations, 231, 233–34, 255; Pacific Coast Guatemala, 241, 244, 247; sociopolitical organization, 392, 398
Nahui Ollin (Fifth Sun), 340
Nakbé, 142, 159, 161; causeways, 150, 155; early occupation of, 144, 145; monumental architecture, 146–47, 147, 148, 157; monuments at, 141, 152
Nanahuatzin, 340
Naranjo, 185
National Museum of Anthropology (Chapultepec), 529–30; Tizoc Stone in, 6, 456–57
Nebel, Carlos, *Viaje pintoresco y arqueológico sobre la parte más interesante de la República Mexicana*, 452
Nebula M42, 157–58
Neutron activation analysis (NAA), 69–70, 72, 251
New World Archaeological Foundation (NWAF), 212–13
Nicholson, Henry B. (Nick), x–xiii, 1–2, 3, 5, 33, 159–60, 223, 269, 310, 423, 519, 520; career of, 11–13; childhood influences on, 13–14; on ethnohistory, 20–22; on ideology and iconography, 23–25; and interdisciplinary research, 7–8; as Mesoamerican art expert, 19–20; and Mixteca-Puebla Concept/Style, 293–94, 295–97, 309, 389–90; university education of, 14–16; at UCLA, 17, 19–20; on Xipe Tótec, 334–35

550

Nicholson Award for Excellence in Mesoamerican Studies, H. B., xii
Nicoya region, 303
Nijaib K'iche, 356
9 Wind, 410
Nobility, 361; Mixteca, 395–96, 400–401, 405–6; at Yaxchilán, 185–86
Nochixtlán, 402; tripod vessel from, *298*
Noguera, Eduardo, 296
Nonoalca-Pipil, 234, 255
Nonohualca Chichimeca, 312
Ñudzahui, 394–95, 410(n1). *See also* Mixteca
Nuevo Mundo village, 237, 245, 246, 251, 252
Numbers, cabalistic, 510–12
Ñundecu (Achiutla), 395
Ñuu, 395, 396–97, 398–99, 405, 411(n2)
Ñuuñañu, 404
NWAF. *See* New World Archaeological Foundation

Oaxaca, 294, 395, 463, 529; Mixteca-Puebla tradition, 300, 301; Xipe Tótec's origins in, 335, 336
Oaxaca Valley, 406, 409; archival sources, 393, 394; exchange networks, 390–91; place terms in, 396, 398–99
Obsidian, 74, 146; at Carolina site, 240, 241; ethnic identity and, 253–54
Obsidian butterfly, polychrome effigy, 319–21
Occupation surfaces, at Isla Alor, 66–68
O-Chahk (Chahk), 186, *187*, 203–4(n22)
Ochpaniztli, 336
Ocotelulco, 297
Offerings: Maya agricultural, 498–508; modern Maya, 93, 124–25(n1); Pipil, 240–41
Oil seeps, and asphaltum, 78, 79
Ollas, at R-106 site, 431–32
Olmeca, 63
Olmeca-Xuixtotin peoples, 82
Olmec civilization, 3–4, 106, 107, 122; chapopote use, 76–79; cities, 111–12; colored clays and sands in, 103–4; as cosmopolitan, 123–24; development of, 108, *109*; at Isla Alor, 66, 68–76; at La Venta, 55–56, 58–59; monument museums, 104–5; as non-literate, 115–16; at Pipil sites, 253–54; Protohistoric Period, 63–64. *See also* Takalik Abaj
Olmec style, 102; stone monuments, 34–35, 94, *95*, 104, *106*, 107, 109–11
Oral histories, 375; K'iche, 367–68
Ordáz, Diego de, 61
Orrego Corzo, Miguel, 96, 102, 104

Osorio, Pedro, 402
Osteological analysis, of Santa Rosa skull, 218–20
Otomí-speakers, 7, 521
Otumba (Estado de México), 74
Oxkintok, 277

Pacal the Great, 157
Pacbitun, 139
Pachuca, obsidian form, 74, 253, 254
Pacific Slope/Coast (Guatemala), 96, 108, 110, 256; art styles, 111–15; Pipil migrations to, 231, 233–34, 254–57; Pipil on, 232–33; Pipil sites, 239–49; writing systems, 118–19
Pajuil site groups, 236, 241–43
Palaces, 419; Dos Pilas, 274–75; Mixteca, 401–4, 407–9
Palenque, 191, 463; Jaguar War God, 190, 197–98; Cross Group at, 157, 182–83, 192; and Yaxchilán, 173, 186
Palma River, Olmec populations on, 57–58
Palo Gordo, 101, 126(n6)
PALV. *See* Proyecto Arqueológico La Venta
PAPTC. *See* Proyecto la Arqueología del Preclásico Temprano en Chalcatzingo
Paredes, María de, 404
Paso y Troncoso, Francisco, 21
Pedernal, 154
Peralta, Catalina de, 400–401; aniñe of, 402–3
Petates, as symbols of authority, 396, 402–3
Petén, 100–101, 108, 139. *See also various sites*
Pictorials, 361–63, 377(nn20, 23)
Piedmont, Guatemala, 120; agriculture, 96–97; art styles, 111–15
Piedras Negras, 173
Pilgrimages, 6, 63, 160, 303, 338, 410
Pimentel y Guzmán, Agustín Carlos, 404, 408
Pipil, 5; archaeological sites, 239–49; conquest-era populations, 234–35; determining ethnicity of, 249–54; historic documentation of, 235–36; migrations of, 233–34, 254–57; in Pacific Coast Guatemela, 232–33, 234–35; research on, 236–39; trade relations, 257–58
Pipil Research Project, 231–32; goals and methods of, 236–39
Place, caves as symbolism of, 277–79
Place names: Mixtec, 395–99; Nahua, 274, 398
Platforms, at Chalcatzingo, 37, 38, 43–44, 46–48, 49
Plazas, 104; at Coxcatlán Viejo, 313–16
Pohl, John, 390–91
Poinsett, Joel R., 470

Index

Point Barrow, excavations at, 16, *17*
Pokomam (Poqomam) Maya, 120, 356, 360
Politics, in Kaqchikel histories, 358–59
Polol, 270
Pomar, Juan Bautista, on tlahuahuanaliztli, 343, 344, 346
Popoluca, 63
Popol Vuh (*Popol Wuj*), 156, 279, 356, 365, 369, 375, 376(n9), 377(n19), 378(n30), 379(n39), 378(n31); as K'iche history, 357–58, 359, 361; land claims and, 371–72; on religious obligation, 490–91; sociopolitical order in, 370–71; triadic symbols, 157–58
Possession, acts of, 402–3
Postclassic Period, 6, 8, 122, 425, 428; Isla Alor, 64, 66–68, 72, 73, 74, 79–80, 81–82; Olmec, 58–59
Potbellies, 99, 125–26(n4)
Potonchan, 61
Prado Black comales, 250–51, 252, 258
Prayers, in Maya agricultural ritual, 512–13
Precolumbian Art from the Land Collection, 19–20
Pre-proto-Sokean language, 116–17
Prescott, William, *Conquest of Mexico*, 14
Priests, Maya, 93, 124
Primeros Memoriales (Sahagún), 21, 22, 396
Primeros Memoriales by Fray Bernardino de Sahagún, 22
Primeros Memoriales: Paleography of Nahuatl Text and English Translation, 22
Processional arrangement, of Chalcatzingo monuments, 37, 50–52
Proskouriakoff, Tania, 16
Protoclassic Period, Takalik Abaj, 100–101, 115
Protohistoric Period, 63, 72
Proto-Maya style, 113
Proyecto Arqueológico La Venta (PALV), 57–58
Proyecto la Arqueología del Preclásico Temprano en Chalcatzingo (PAPTC), 37; discoveries of, 38–43
Puebla, 399, 463, 466; Black on red pottery, 428–29; and Mixteca-Puebla Concept, 294, 297, 389
Puebla-Tlaxcala Zone, 301
Pulquerías, archaeological evidence for, 431–32, 435
Pusilha, 270
Pyramid of the Sun (Teotihuacan), *271*, *272*; cave under, 277, 282, 284
Pyramids, 103, 278; and caves, 272–74; Maya, 146–47, *150*

Quauhtochco, 72
Quatrefoil-knot design, 180, 181
Quechquemitl, *522*, *523*, 524, *525*, *530*
Quetzalcoatl, x, xi, xii, *2*, 14, 20, 340, 359, 425, 429, 410, *431*, *433*, *434*, 478; and Venus, 327–28, 329
Quetzaltenango, 531, 356
Quiché. *See* K'iche Maya
Quiché Vinac, 368
Quiñones Keber, Eloise, 22, 296, 390
Q'ukumatz, 359, 370, 373
Q'umarkaaj (Gumarcaaj), 234, 281, 372, 376(n10). *See also* Utatlán

Rab'inal (Rabinal), 234, 257, 360
Rabinal Achi ("Dance of the Tun"), 356, 368, 379(n35)
Radiocarbon dates, 66, 98(table), 144, 241, 250, 251(table)
Rain ceremonies, Yucatec Maya, 489, 496–98, 508–9
RAINPEG. *See* Regional Archaeological Investigation of the North Petén, Guatemala
Ralda family, *117*, 124, 125(n3)
Ramsey, James, 296
Razonamientos de mi viaje alrededor del mundo (Carletti), 445–46
Real Expedición Anticuaria, 462; collection from, 463–79
Real Seminario de Minas, Dupaix's collections at, 463–64, 466
Redfield, Robert, 490, 497
Red Tezcatlipoca, Xipe Tótec as, 340, 341, *342*, 347, 348(n7)
Reducciones, Pipil, 236
Regional Archaeological Investigation of the North Petén, Guatemala (RAINPEG), 143
Relaciones geográficas (Mixteca), 401, 402
Relaciones Histórico-Geográficas de la Gobernación de Yucatán, 493
Relación Geográfica de Acolman, 345
Relación Geográfica de Atitlán, 362
Religion, x, 3, 5, 278, 279; Aztec, 22, 23; Mesoamerican, 409–10; modern Maya, 7, 78–79, 124–25(n1), 489–513; native Maya, 366–67; rain, humidity, and agricultural fertility in, 334–35
Remanso Ceramic Group, 247, 249
Remesal, Antonio de, 59
Rémusat, Abel, 472
Residences: Mixteca royal, 401–4; Nakbé, 145

INDEX

Resistance, Colonial period, 432–33
Retalhuleu, 109, 120, 126(n7), 356
Revitalization movement, 433–34
Rey, El (Monument 1, Chalcatzingo), 36
Reyes, Antonio de los, *Arte en lengua mixteca*, 399
Río Azul, 159
Ritual of the Four World-Quarters, 511
Rituals, rites, 333; cabalistic numbers in, 510–12; caves and, 277–78; dynastic refounding, 176, 178, 185; Maya, 366–67, 492–514. *See also* Sacrifices
Rivet, Paul, 477
Robertson, Donald: *Mexican Manuscript Painting of the Early Colonial Period*, 295; Mixteca-Puebla Concept, 296–97
R-106 project, 426–27, 430–32
Rowe, John H., 15, 20, 519–20
Royal Expedition in Search of Antiquities, 462
Royalty, 361; Mixteca, 395–96
Roys, Ralph, 59
Rulership, 37, 140, 178, 336; accession rights, 189–90; K'iche, 361, 370, 372–73; iconography of Maya, 177–98; Maya, 145–46, 151–52; Mixteca, 400–401, 407–9; Yaxchilán, 185–86

Saavedra, Felipe de, 395
Sacapulas map, 362
Sac Balam, 157
Sacbeob. *See* Causeways
Sacred places, 34, 279
Sacrifices, 4, 6, 124–25(n1), 188, 299, 347, 508; ballgame and, 211–12, 223–24; bloodletting, 181, 182–83, 186, 203–4(n22), 205(n36); decapitation, 195, 217; gladiatorial, 333, 335, 342–44, 441, 455; last human sacrifice in Maya area, 124–125(n1); tlahuahuanaliztli, 334, 345; of turkeys, 496, 497
Sagas, heroic, 357
Sahagún, Bernardino de, 21, 59, 340, 433, 445, 526; on chapopote, 77, 79; on Tabasco, 62–63
Sajcabajá area, 363, 377(n24)
Sak Nikté, 185
San Andrés Sajcabajá, 363
San Antón Muñón Chimalpahin Quauhtlehuanitzin, Domingo, 398
San Bartoló, 158, 159
Sánchez de Aguilar, Pedro, 493, 496
San Cristóbal de las Casas, 463
San Cristóbal Verapaz, 360
San Diego Museum, 13

San Isidro Piedra Parada. *See* Takalik Abaj
San Jerónimo Phase, 233
San Juan Perdido, 249
San Lorenzo, 78, 79, 102, 103, 104, 106, 107, 108, 126(n6)
San Luis Potosí, 302
San Mateo (Chiapas), 214
San Martín Jilotepeque (Guatemala), 239; obsidian form, 74, 146, 253
San Miguel Teguantepeque, 245
San Pedro Mártir Yucunama, 397, 402
San Pedro y San Pablo Yucundaa (Teposcolula), 397, 404
Sansuantzi. *See* Coxcatlán Viejo
Santa Clara la Laguna, 356
Santa Cruz del Quiche, 356, 376(n8)
Santa Lucia Cotzumalguapa, 245
Santa Margarita. *See* Takalik Abaj
Santa María Volcano, 124–25(nn1, 2); and Takalik Abaj, 93, 97, 102, 107
Santa Rita Ceramic Group, 252
Santa Rita Corozal (Belize), Mixteca-Puebla tradition, 302, 303
Santa Rosa (Chiapas), 212; ballcourt at, 215, 215–17; ballcourt skull, 217–23, 225(n4); layout of, 213, 214–15, 215
Santiago Atitlán, 361
Santiago Yodzonduhua, 397
Santiago Yolomecatl, 400, 404
Schieber de Lavarreda, Christa, 104
Scholes, France, 59
Scribes (escribanos): K'iche historical, 365–67; Mixteca, 392, 394
Sculpture dumps, Olmec, 106
Sculpture of Ancient West Mexico: Nayarit, Jalisco, Colima, 19
Sculptures, 4, 14, 61, 93, 125–26(n4), 177, 244, 294; defacing and burial of, 101, 107; on Guatemalan Pacific Slope, 111–15; with Isthmian script, 116–17; monumental stone, 24–25, 34–37, 94; in monument museums, 104–5; movement of, 105–6; and social status, 140–41; at Takalik Abaj, 99, 100, 108, 109–11, 119–20, 126(n6)
Sedano, Francisco, 448
Seler, Eduard Georg, 16, 334; *Collected Works*, 21–22
Self-Portrait as a Tehuana (Kahlo), 31
Settlement patterns, Pipil region, 252–53
Shamans, 157, 514; and agricultural ritual, 492, 499–505, 510, 512–13; invocation and prayers, 112–13. *See also* Chimánes

553

Index

Shell, marine, in Mirador Basin, 145–46
Shields, 197, 205(n35)
Shook, Edwin, at Takalik Abaj, *94*
Sibun Valley, 277
Sierra Norte de Puebla, 7, 520, 529; clothing styles, 521, *522, 523,* 524–26
Siete Orejas volcano, 102
Simaj, Miguel, *117*
Sin Cabezas, 107
Siñi, 397, 398
Sinto, Beto, 93–94, *94,* 124
Siqui, 397, 398
Skulls: in ballcourts, 223–24, 224–25(n3); at Santa Rosa Ballcourt, 217–23
Snake platform/throne, 182
Social hierarchy: Maya, 140–41, 145, 150–51; stone monuments and, 151–54
Sociopolitical organization: Mixteca, 395–400, 407–8; Nahua, 392, 398
Soconusco region, 231, 245
Spanish, 236, 421; colonial authority, 400–401, 432; on K'iche histories, 360–62; and Mixtec social organization, 399–400, 407–8; and native documents, 373–75, 394
Spanish Conquest, 1, 368; of Pacific Coast Guatemala, 232–33; in Tabasco, 59–62; in Tenochtitlan, 419–20, 441–42; tribute records, 421–22
Spence, Lewis, 14
Spindle whorls, asphaltum-painted, 79
Spraje, Ivan, 143
Spring equinox, and Xipe Tótec festival, 334
Springs, 272; and Maya architecture, 273–74
Squier, Robert, 59
Stafford, Proctor, 19
Stars, triadic symbolism and, 157–58
State-level societies, Maya, 139–40
Stelae, 37, 108, 190; at Chalcatzingo, 37–43, 44–49, *49;* Isthmian script on, 116–17, 118; Mirador Basin, 152, *153,* 154; at Takalik Abaj, 96, 99–100, 101, 104, 107, 108, *113*
Stirling, Matthew, 58; at La Venta, 63–64
Stone monuments, 439; at Chalcatzingo, 34–37; Maya kingships and, 140–41, 151–54, 157; at Takalik Abaj, 93, *94, 95;* Tizoc, 6, *440,* 440–56
Strombus shells, in Mirador Basin, 145, *146*
Strong, William Duncan, 3
Structure 23 (Yaxchilán), 175–77, 200(n4), 201(nn6, 9); Itzamnah B'ahläm depictions in, 178, *179,* 179–81; Ix K'ab'al Xok depictions in, 181–83; lintels in, 177–98

Structures N4-19, 20 (Dos Pilas), cave under, 275–76
Suárez Cruz, Sergio, 426
Subsistence, Isla Alor, 73–74, 80, 81
Sullivan, Thelma, 22
Sun, creation of Fifth, 338, 340–41
Sun God, Yucatec Maya, 491–92
Supernaturals: Maya depictions of, 141, 151–52; Olmec stone depictions of, 36–37; Yucatec Maya agricultural, 491–93
Survivals, 519; textile, 523–26
Symbolism, 272, 379(n38); Maya rulership, 145–46, 180; sacbeob/causeway, 155–56; triadic, 157–58, 182

Tabasco, 72; bajareque and chapopote in, 75–79; ethnohistory of, 59–64; Olmec culture in, *57,* 58; Postclassic occupation, 81–82
Tabletop altar-throne, at Chalcatzingo, 38, 49
Takalik Abaj, 4, 122, *123,* 124–25(nn1–4); cacao production, 96–97; construction of, 102–3; early writing at, 116, 118–19; location of, 96–98; Maya informants, 93–94, *94;* monument museums at, 104–5; occupational sequence at, 98–102; Olmec and Maya sculptures at, 109–11; as Olmec city, 112–13; rebuilding and sculpture repositioning at, 105–6; sculpture sources at, 106–7; stone monuments and sculptures at, 93–94, *94, 95,* 114, *117,* 119–20, 126(n6)
Taltique, 360
Tamasulapa, 397, 398
Tamoanchan, 321, 322, 323–24
Tamoanchan Xochitlicacan, 322
Tamub K'iche, 356
Tanduaa, 404
Taro, New World, 97
Taxcal, 103
Taylor, Edward T., 452
Teccalli, 391–92, 405
Tecpan, 392
Tecpantlalli, 406
Tecuciztecatl, 340
Tecuhilhuitontli (Small Festival of the Lords), 336
Tecuhtli, 345–46, 347
Teguantepeque, 235, 236, 245
Tehuacán, history of, 310–12
Tehuacán Valley, 6, Mixteca-Puebla traits, 297, 300
Tekum (Umam), 359, 373, 380(n50)

554

INDEX

Temalácatl, 343, 344, 441, 455. See also Tizoc Stone
Temple of the Cross (Palenque), 192
Temple of the Feathered Serpent (Teotihuacan), 187–88
Temple of the Foliated Cross (Palenque), 182–83
Temple of Huitzilopochtli (Tenochtitlan), flaying sacrifices on, 343–44
Temple of Quetzalcoatl (Cholula), 303
Temple of the Sun (Palenque), 197–98
Temple of the Warriors (Chichén Itzá), 222
Temple of Xipe Tótec (Tenochtitlan), 347
Temple of Yopico, 441
Templo Mayor, 272, 409–10; excavations of, xi, 23
Tenochca Hueitlatoani, 336
Tenochtitlan, 6, 223, 239, 272; dismantling of, 441–42; Spanish taking of, 419–20, 421–23; Templo Mayor, 409–10; Xipe Tótec in, 333, 339, 342–47
Tenosique, 63
Tenpatzacapan, 312
Teotihuacan, 59, 126(n9), 225(n4), 233, 234, 257, 294, 340; cave under Pyramid of the Sun, 271, 272, 277, 282, 284; imagery related to, 181, 183, 204(n28); Temple of the Feathered Serpent at, 187–88; and Tikal, 122–23; Xipe Tótec images, 336, 339
Teotitlán del Camino, 312
Teozacualco, Map of, 401–2
Tepehua-speakers, 7, 521
Tepeílhuitl (Hill Festival), 336
Tepepulco, 21
Teposcolula (Yucundaa), 394, 397, 399, 406, 408; anñe at, 402–4; Spanish colonial authority and, 400–401
Tequiha, attaining rank of, 346, 348(n5)
Terminal Classic Period, 66, 101
Terrace 6 (Chalcatzingo): construction of, 49–50, 50; platforms and stelae on, 40–49; processional arrangement on, 50–52. See also Terraces
Terraces (Chalcatzingo), 37; platforms and stelae on, 40–43, 44, 46; at Takalik Abaj, 102–3. See also Terrace 6
Teualco (Tenochtitlan), 419
Texas-Montana Complex, 234, 241, 250, 254, 257
Texcalapan, 340
Textiles: Guatemalan traditional, 530–31; Sierra Norte de Puebla, 521, 523–28

Texupa (Tejupan), 395, 402
Thols, in *Dresden Codex*, 493–94
Thompson, J. Eric, 16, 59; on cave-architecture relationships, 269–70
Thrones, reed-mat, 403; tabletop altar-, 38, 49
Tikal, 59, 125(n4), 149, 151, 157, 158, 159, 183, 187, 197, 204(n23); and Teotihuacan, 122–23
Tilantongo, 399
Time, mythic and calendrical, 329–30
Tintal, 155, 157, 159
Tiquisate Zone, 234
Titulo de Ixhuatán, El, 235
Titulo K'oyoi, 362, 377(n21)
Titulo de Sacapulas, 234
Titulos, 366, 371, 376(nn4, 5), 379–80(nn45, 52)
Tizatlán, 297
Tizoc Stone, 6, 42; conquest scenes on, 440, 440–41; post-Conquest locations and descriptions of, 445–57; recovery of, 443–45
Tlacaxipehualiztli, 333–34, 337–38, 341, 347; human skin used in, 344–46; on origin of, 339–40
Tlacocomoco, 338–39
Tlahuahuanaliztli, 333, 335; victims of, 342–45; warriors and, 345–46
Tlahuizcalpantecuhtli, 321, 323
Tlaloc, 409–10; imagery of, 181, 186, 188, 189, 190
Tlaloc-Venus war cult, 183, 200–201(n5), 202(n16); dynastic founders and, 189–90; imagery of, 176, 197; at Yaxchilán, 176, 181, 191, 199
Tlatelolco, 77, 223
Tlatlauhqui Tezcatlipoca, 340
Tlatoani, 346, 347, 396
Tlaxcala, 398; Mixteca-Puebla tradition and, 297, 300, 301, 391; Xipe Tótec cult in, 345, 347
Tlaxiaco, 397, 399
Tlazeoltétl (Toci), 335–36
Tniño, 407–9
Tochtepec, Province of, 64
Toci (Tlazeoltétl), 335–36
Toj lineage, 234
Tollan, 311, 330, 410
Tollan Ceramic Complex, 251
Tolq'om, 368, 379(n36)
Tolteca-Chichimeca, 312
Toltecs, 123, 359, 389; Pipil migrations, 233–34, 255, 256
Tombs, 177; Monte Albán, 336, 338, 339; royal, 158–59

555

Index

Tonacacíhuatl, 322
Tonacatecuhtli, 322
Tonalá (Tumalo), 62
Tonalá River, 57, 60, 62
Tonalpohualli, 294, 328
Toniná, 173
Topiltzin-Quetzalcoatl, xi, 16, 20, 26, 329, 433
Topiltzin Quetzalcoatl: The Once and Future Lord of the Toltecs (Nicholson), 26
Torres site, 59
Totocalco, 420
Totonacs, 302, 521
Tozzer, Alfred Marston, 8
Trade, 173, 225(n4), 390; Pipil region, 249, 253–54, 257–58
Treasure houses, at Tenochtitlan, 419–20
Tres Zapotes, 110, 123
Triadic Architectural Style, 157–58, 182
Tribute, 372; Mixteca payment of, 392, 408–9; Spanish records of, 421–23
Trocadero Palace, 477
Tukurub, 360
Tula, 233, 234, 389, 390
Tulum, 270, 302, 303
Tunnels, as artificial caves, 282–83
Tupilco, Laguna, 63
Tuquchee revolt, 364
Turibinella angulata, in Mirador Basin, 145
Turkeys, rain ceremony sacrifice of, 496, 497
Turpin de Crissé, count of (Théodore), 472
Tuxtla statuette, 117
260-day calendar, 329, 362–63; and divination, 366–67
Tzutujil Maya, 120, 247, 257, 356, 361, 362
Tzompantli, female skulls on, 222–23

Uaxactún, 147, 157, 159
Ucareo, obsidian from, 74
Uixtoti, 63
Umbilical cord, symbology of, 155–56
Underworld, iconography of, 197, 204–5(n32)
Universal Exhibitions, 477
University of California, Berkeley, 14, 15–16, 96
University of California, Los Angeles (UCLA), 143; H. B. Nicholson at, 17, 19–20
Upper Tres Zapotes Polychrome wares, 59
Urbanism, 4, 108, 123
Usumacinta region, 173
Utatlán, 120, 377–78(n26); Cave 1 at, *280, 281, 282, 283*. See also Q'umarkaaj
Utazingo, 235, 236

Vaca Plateau, 277
Valenzuela, Nicolas de, 157
Valliant, George, 20; *Aztecs of Mexico*, 14; on Mixteca-Puebla culture, 294, 310, 389
Variedades, 249
Venus, 204(n24), 330, 378(n30); imagery of, 182, 204(n23); and Quetzalcoatl, 327–28, 329
Veracruz, 72, 78, 463, 466
Viaje pintoresco y arqueológico sobre la parte más interesante de la República Mexicana (Nebel), 452
View of Mexico City exhibition, 449
Villa Rojas, Alfonso, 490, 497
Villa-Señor y Sánchez, José Antonio de, 59
Villa Vicente Guerrero, 78
Vocabularies, Mixteca, 394–95
Vocabulario en lengua mixta (Alvarado), 396, 411(n2)
Volcán Chicabal, 97, 102, 124–25(n1)
Volcanic eruptions, 93, 102, 125(n2)

Wakna, 147, *149*, 157, 158–59
Waldeck, Jean-Frédéric, 470
Warfare, 6, 61, 122–23, 173, 200–201(n5), 299, 361; iconography of, 182, 187, 197
Warriors, 441; iconography of, 188–89, 197, 205(n36); tecuhtli/tequiha rank, 345–46, 348(n5); and tlahuahuanaliztli, 343, 344–45; women, 221–22, 223
War Serpent, 201(n6), 204(nn23, 25); at Teotihuacan, 187–88; at Yaxchilán, 176, 190, 191, 199, 202(n12), 203(n21)
Water, symbolic importance of, 180, 182, 197, 497, 492
Water Jaguar, *193, 194,* 194–95
Water platform/throne, 191–92
Wealth, Maya elite, 140–41
Western Belize Regional Cave Project, 276–77
Wetlands, Mirador Basin, 145, 151
Willey, Gordon R., 16
Wills, Mixtec, 395–96, 404
Wind gods (pauhtuns), 492, 516(n20)
Women, 4, 336, 400, 408; and ballcourt sacrifice, 217–23; buildings owned by, 175, 177; depicted in Chalcatzingo monuments, 38, 40, 44–46, *46*; ritual domains of, 182, 185; as warriors, 221–22
Work of Bernardino de Sahagún, The, 22
Writings, Mixteca, 393–95
Writing systems, 3; Isthmian Script, 116–18; K'iche, 360, 361–63; origins of, 115, 118–19
Wuqamaq', 370–71

INDEX

Xanthasoma. *See* Taro, New World
Xibalba, 279
Xicalango, 63
Xicolli, 525
Ximénez, Francisco, 59, 356, 361
Xinca region, 252, 253
Xipe Tótec, *348,* 441; cult of, *334,* 334–35, 338–47; festivals, 333–34; origins of, 336–38
Xiuhtecuhtli iconography, 320–21, 525
Xochicalco, 282, *430*
Xochipala, 221
Xochipilli (God of Song and Dance), 336
Xochiquétzal, 336
Xochitlicacan, 321
Xoconusco, 239
Xócotl Huetzi, 336
Xpantzay Kaqchikel, 356
Xulnal, 144, 147, 157

Yanhuitlan (Yodzocahi), 394, 398, 402, 406, 407, 410(n1)
Yaxcabá, agricultural ceremonies in, 489, 496–97
Yaxchilán, 4, 173, *174;* B'ahläm dynasty history at, 177–98; dedicatory structures at, 175–77; royalty of, 185–86

Yi'chaak K'ak, 159
Yodzocahi, 402
Yolanda site, 248, 251, 252
Yolanda-Utazingo, 236
Yolomecatl, 400, 404
Yopico, 338–39, 347
Yucunama, *397,* 402
Yucundaa (Teposcolula), 402, 403
Yucatán, 526, 529
Yucatec Maya, 277, 381(n58); agricultural ritual, 489, 492–514; agricultural supernaturals, 491–92, *493*
Yuhuitayu, 395–97, 411(n2); hereditary rulers and, 400–401; land tenure, 405–6; multilingual, 398–99; residences, 401–4
Yumtziloob, 492

Zaachila, 463
Zaculeu, 120, 281
Zapotecs, 6, 312, 399, 409
Zapotitlán, 356
Zaqi K'axol ("Dance of the Conquest"), 368
Zaragosa, obsidian from, 74
Závala, Silvio, 20
Zumárraga, Juan de, 442

www.ingramcontent.com/pod-product-compliance
Lightning Source LLC
Chambersburg PA
CBHW071327080526
44587CB00017B/2756